TWENTIETH-CENTURY CENTURY AMERICA:
Recent Interpretations

SECOND EDITION

TWENTIETH-CENTURY AMERICA:
Recent Interpretations

SECOND EDITION

edited by

BARTON J. BERNSTEIN
Stanford University

and

ALLEN J. MATUSOW
Rice University

Under the General Editorship of
JOHN MORTON BLUM, Yale University

 HARCOURT BRACE JOVANOVICH, INC.
New York   Chicago   San Francisco   Atlanta

TO THE MEMORY OF DAVID M. POTTER

ISBN: 0-15-592391-9

Library of Congress Catalog Card Number: 79-190749

Printed in the United States of America

Preface

Historians are not, nor should they be, unaffected by the times in which they live and write. The tumultuous decade just past had a particularly profound impact on historical scholarship. The sudden emergence of ghetto rebellion, antiwar protest, and radical criticism forced historians to reexamine the past in their search for the origins of present problems and analogues to present events. In selecting themes for this collection, we have frankly been guided by contemporary concerns. Specifically, we have tried to provide historical illumination for the problems of business-government relations, race relations, poverty, cultural antagonism, and war. Most of the essays reprinted here were written in the 1960's.

Business-government relations have troubled Americans sporadically during this century. Sometimes the economic and political consequences of corporate concentration alarm reformers, who then undertake to end the subservience of government to big business, usually with disappointing or ironic result. Race relations did not become a major concern of the American people until after the Second World War, but the manner in which previous generations treated the problem tells much about the present crisis and the limits of earlier social understanding. As for the enduring problem of poverty, Americans have sometimes ignored, sometimes acknowledged, its reality, the response of each generation revealing in large measure its perception of the whole social order. Cultural antagonism occurs when social groups challenge prevailing norms and mores. Such antagonism has been most acute in the 1920's and 1960's, and the essays on this theme deal mainly with these two decades. The last theme, the sources and consequences of war, has only recently been regarded as of crucial relevance for American domestic society. Until the rise of fascism in the 1930's, American participation in international wars seemed to be the exception. Since the Second World War, war and preparation for war have become a permanent condition of American life. Scholars have accordingly begun to investigate the consequences of America's past wars on domestic dissent, distribution of power, and relations among social groups. The essays we have selected are not confined to these five themes; they do not reflect a single point of view nor do they necessarily agree with our own analyses of the American past. Wherever possible and desirable, we have established a historical dialogue by presenting differing interpretations of important events or movements.

Each of the four parts of the book is introduced by a brief discussion of the period covered and the problems of historical interpretation it presents. In addition, we have introduced each essay with background information and some critical reflections. Following the introduction to each part and each essay we have appended an annotated bibliography to assist students in their reading and research. The scholarly literature on the period since 1945 will, we hope, be of service to those professors and students interested in the postwar years as a subject for historical inquiry.

The titles in the bibliographies available in paperback are marked by an asterisk. We have generally not included in the bibliography for an essay a title that had previously been mentioned in the bibliography for the part, in the introduction, or in the essay itself.

We gratefully acknowledge the wise counsel of John M. Blum, Otis L. Graham, Jr., and Otis A. Pease who assisted us in shaping the first edition. John Blum has also aided us in defining this edition, and we are also grateful to Berenice Carroll, Dan T. Carter, Fred Cohen, Blanche Weisen Cook, Theodore Friedlander, Nancy and Richard Gillam, David M. Kennedy, Warren Kimball, Kenneth Kusmer, Meredith Marsh, Bryan Strong, Athan Theoharis, Sharon Traweek, William M. Tuttle, Jr., Nancy J. Weiss, and Allen Yarnell for their generous assistance.

Susan Felder and Laurie Finkelstein typed the manuscript with unfailing good humor. To Oscar Handlin, director of the Charles Warren Center at Harvard University, where each of us has been a fellow, we owe a debt of gratitude for providing the personnel and facilities that aided our work.

BARTON J. BERNSTEIN and ALLEN J. MATUSOW

Contents

IV. THE ERA OF THE COLD WAR   338

I

The Progressive Era

At the turn of the century, a vague disquiet had begun to pervade America. The preceding generation had witnessed the stunning triumphs of industrialism, the near-transformation of America into an urban society, and periodic eruptions of bitter class warfare. As the twentieth century began, the Jeffersonian self-image so long cherished by Americans seemed suddenly obsolete, and the individualistic ethic shaped in the rural past seemed obviously untenable. Historians call the complex, confused, and often contradictory responses to this crisis the Progressive movement.

The Progressive movement has been most often regarded as a popular revolt against the consequences of the new organization of American life. Traditional accounts emphasize that progressivism was a rebellion against the unfettered power of large corporations and against the political machines that corrupted public institutions and negated democracy. It was also an expression of concern for the innocent victims of the new order: the workers and immigrants confined to slums and exploited by corporations and politicians. Historians customarily note that before 1900, Populists, labor leaders, and fringe intellectuals had failed in their attempt to convince the

1

middle-class American of the need for reform. But after 1900, the urban middle classes, especially small businessmen and independent professionals, joined the reform army and gave progressivism its distinctive character.

Particularly since the Second World War, many historians (most notably Richard Hofstadter in his influential *The Age of Reform* [1955]) have pointed out that the Progressive movement, despite its passionate rhetoric and energetic activity, actually achieved relatively little in the way of reforms. Economically secure and essentially optimistic in their social views, middle-class progressives enacted only mild measures that never really threatened existing power relationships. When rural progressives like Wisconsin's great Senator Robert M. La Follette attempted to enact programs to smash corporate power, they found few who would follow them. To democratize the political order, the progressives designed mechanical reforms like the direct primary, which achieved only indifferent success in countering boss rule. In the realm of social justice, the movement on the state level did cause child labor to be outlawed, some protection of women workers to be extended, and programs of workmen's compensation to be initiated, but the United States remained far behind Europe in the field of social welfare. At the end of the Progressive Era, unskilled workers were still unorganized, poverty was still the lot of large numbers of Americans, and, in spite of the income tax amendment, inequalities in the distribution of the national wealth remained essentially uncorrected. Recognizing how limited the progressive accomplishments were, many historians in the last twenty years have judged the movement as essentially conservative.

Some recent writers, such as Robert Wiebe, Gabriel Kolko, Samuel Hays, and James Weinstein, find the Progressive movement conservative not because it seemed to offer only mild opposition to big businessmen, but because big business itself played a major role in shaping the so-called progressive legislation. This new research successfully challenges the old notion of progressive politics as a simple dualistic struggle between middle-class reforms and major business interests. Thus in the great battle to regulate railroads, shippers fought for governmental authority to lower rates, and in time the railroads themselves saw in federal regulation a way to curb harmful competition within the industry. Because they desired efficiency, businessmen participated in other areas of reform such as conservation of natural resources and municipal reform movements. Gabriel Kolko has even argued that progressivism was dominated by big businessmen who sought escape from competition and instability through federal regulation of their industries. In Kolko's view, progressivism was not conservative because it did so little to curb business; rather, it was conservative because it did so much to assist the corporate order in achieving its present dominance. Kolko and Weinstein have been criticized for not adequately explaining the complexity of social forces operating in the progressive period, but their work has gained recognition for casting discredit on the traditional interpretation of the movement. As a result, at this stage of historical inquiry, scholars of progressivism are faced with the task of devising a new synthesis.

The foreign policy of the progressive years was marked by continued commercial expansion abroad and repeated intervention in Latin America. Adhering to his Big Stick policy, President Theodore Roosevelt "liberated" the Panamanian isthmus and intervened elsewhere in the Caribbean with Marines. In many ways the conduct of foreign policy in these years supports those historians who now argue that government in the Progressive Era actually best served the interests of big business. Although Roosevelt usually emphasized the nation's duty while embarking on his imperialist ventures, President Taft proudly labeled his own policy "Dollar Diplomacy" and openly linked his efforts to the needs and desires of financiers and industrialists who wanted markets and stability. Though most Americans, including many progressives, were not deeply interested in foreign policy during the years before the First World War, a few, like Senators Robert La Follette and William Borah, opposed Taft's policies because they objected to American imperialism. The State Department, the Wisconsin progressive charged, was becoming "a trading post for Wall Street interests" (*La Follette's Weekly*, June 29, 1912). Repudiating "Dollar Diplomacy" and explicitly denying that "a gunboat goes with each bond," Woodrow Wilson believed that the United States would be more successful in expanding trade if it did not seek special favors or resort to coercion. Nevertheless, to establish the stability essential for an expanding trade and to protect American security in the hemisphere, the Wilson administration in practice continued to intervene in Latin America. In time, Wilson entered the First World War to protect and further a world order conducive to American political and economic objectives. And at the Paris Peace Conference in 1919 he became the most eloquent spokesman for the democratic-capitalist ideology that America ever produced. Though Wilson was not primarily seeking to advance the prosperity of American business corporations in his efforts at war and peace, the international system he envisioned was the one in which such corporations could best flourish. Whether Wilson's role during and following the First World War should be viewed as an expression of the progressive spirit depends on the still undetermined answer to the question, what is progressivism?

SUGGESTED READING

Richard Hofstadter's *The Age of Reform* * (1955) is a sensitive, speculative and important interpretation of progressivism. His concept of the "status revolution," based in part on George Mowry's "The California Progressive and His Rationale; A Study in Middle-Class Politics," *Mississippi Valley Historical Review*, XXXVI (Sept. 1949), has been criticized by many historians, including Norman Wilensky in *Conservatives in the Progressive Era: The Taft Republicans of 1912* (1965). Hofstadter, in *The American Political Tradition* * (1948), also provides critical interpretations of the two progressive Presidents.

Eric Goldman, in *Rendezvous with Destiny* * (1952), understands progressivism as part of the healthy liberal reform movement. Samuel Hays's *The Response to Industrialism* * (1957) and Robert Wiebe's *The*

Search for Order * (1967) are ambitious efforts to place the reform movement in a broader context of responses to instability. Wiebe seeks also to explain progressivism in terms of the rise of an upwardly mobile "new middle class." Louis Galambos, in "The Emerging Organizational Synthesis in Modern American History," Business History Review, XLIV (Autumn 1970), noting the emphasis on the rise of national organizations, the bureaucratic order, scientific management, professionalization, and shifts in values, summarizes the new synthesis. Otis L. Graham, Jr.'s The Great Campaigns * (1971) also analyzes the period and the literature.

John M. Blum's The Republican Roosevelt * (1954) is a perceptive analysis of Roosevelt's conservatism and an outgrowth of his work with Elting Morison et al., eds., The Letters of Theodore Roosevelt, 8 vols. (1951–58), an indispensable source for understanding Roosevelt. George Mowry's The Era of Theodore Roosevelt, 1900–1912 * (1958) remains the best volume on Roosevelt's presidency and can be supplemented for the later years by Mowry's Theodore Roosevelt and the Progressive Movement * (1946), which reveals more of an agrarian bias. Carleton Putnam is writing a multi-volume study of the Roosevelt administration; the first volume, Theodore Roosevelt: The Formative Years (1958), a detailed study, is available.

Arthur Link's Woodrow Wilson and the Progressive Era, 1910–1917 * (1954) is the best single volume on Wilson's early presidency and more critical than Link's authoritative series, Wilson, 5 vols. (1947–65). John M. Blum's Woodrow Wilson and the Politics of Morality * (1956) is a brief, critical interpretation.

The Progressive Era * edited by Arthur Mann, (1963) is a dated collection on the period, and has been replaced by Progressivism * edited by David Kennedy (1971). Midwestern politics are surveyed in Russell B. Nye's Midwestern Progressive Politics * (1959), which traces the reform movement back to the agrarian unrest of the 1890's. James Holt, in Congressional Insurgents and the Party System, 1909–1916 (1967), perceptively analyzes the insurgents in the Senate, and concludes that most were not involved in the protests of the 1890's.

The best general interpretations of Southern progressivism are C. Vann Woodward's The Origins of the New South (1951), a splendid study, and George B. Tindall's The Emergence of the New South (1967), a fine synthesis of the period from 1913 to 1945.

Attitudes toward poverty are ably described by Robert Bremner in From the Depths * (1956), and social workers are studied by Allen F. Davis in Spearheads for Reform (1967). David Shannon's The Socialist Party * (1950); Ira Kipnis' The American Socialist Movement, 1897–1912 (1952); Daniel Bell's "The Background and Development of Marxian Socialism in the United States," in Donald Egbert and Stow Persons, eds., Socialism and American Life (1952); and Bell's "Socialism: The Dream and the Reality," Antioch Review, XII (Mar. 1952), are criticized severely by James Weinstein, who argues in "The American Socialist Party, Its Roots and Strength," Studies on the Left, I (Fall 1960), and in Decline of Socialism in America, 1912–1925 (1967) that socialism was strong even during the war and was weakened not by official suppression but the split over bolshevism. John Laslett, in *Labor and the Left: A Study of Socialist and Radical Influences in the American Labor Movement, 1881–1924* (1970), analyzes the successes and failures of the left in six unions. Kenneth McNaught, in "American Progressives and the Great Society," *Journal of American History*, LIII (Dec. 1966), contends that socialism failed because the American liberal tradition lacks a tolerance for political deviations.

The intellectual history of these years has been interpreted by many writers. Morton White's *Social Thought in America: The Revolt Against Formalism* * (1949) is a bold and pioneering volume that concentrates on five men. Henry May, in *The End of American Innocence* * (1959), locates in the years before Versailles many of the ideas attributed to intellectuals in the 1920's, an interpretation first sketched by May in "Rebellion of the Intellectuals, 1912–1917," *American Quarterly*, VIII (Summer 1956). Charles Forcey's *The Crossroads of Liberalism: Croly, Weyl, Lippmann, and the Progressive Era* * (1961) focuses on the intellectuals of the *New Republic*. David Noble's *The Paradox of Progressive Thought* (1958) is an often convoluted analysis of reform thought partly summarized in his essay by the same title in *American Quarterly*, V (Fall 1953). Daniel Levine, in *The Varieties of Reform Thought* (1964), emphasizes the diversity among such reformers as Jane Addams and Samuel Gompers and concludes by questioning the concept of progressivism. Christopher Lasch, in *The New Radicalism in America: The Intellectual as a Social Type* * (1965), argues that "modern radicalism or liberalism can best be understood as a phase of the social history of the intellectuals," and examines, among others, Jane Addams, Randolph Bourne, Mabel Dodge Luhan, and Lincoln Steffens. Nathan Hale's *Freud and the Americans: The Beginnings of Psychoanalysis in the United States, 1876–1917* (1971) is an important volume.

Howard K. Beale's *Theodore Roosevelt and the Rise of America to World Power* * (1956) remains the best volume on Roosevelt's foreign policy, but it should be supplemented by Charles Neu's *An Uncertain Friendship; Theodore Roosevelt and Japan, 1906–1909* (1967). William E. Leuchtenburg, in "Progressivism and Imperialism: The Progressive Movement and American Foreign Policy, 1898–1916," *Mississippi Valley Historical Review* (Dec. 1952), argues that the progressives were usually imperialists. He is supported in part by William Appleman Williams, who in *The Tragedy of American Diplomacy,* * rev. ed. (1962) places the expansionist foreign policy in a larger framework of political capitalism, and by Jerold Israel, in *Progressivism and the Open Door: America and China, 1905–1921* (1971). Leuchtenburg's analysis is criticized by, among others, Barton J. Bernstein and Franklin A. Leib in "Progressive Republican Senators and American Imperialism, 1898–1916: A Reappraisal," *Mid-America*, L (July 1968), who find that an important part of the progressive community moved to oppose Caribbean adventurism, and by John M. Cooper, in "Progressivism and American Foreign Policy: A Reappraisal," *Mid-America*, LI (Oct. 1969), who seeks to relate positions on foreign policy to attitudes toward power.

J. JOSEPH HUTHMACHER

Urban Liberalism and the Age of Reform

INTRODUCTION

Though one segment of the Progressive movement was located in the agrarian West and sent to the Congress such men as William Borah of Idaho and George Norris of Nebraska, another segment was rooted largely in the cities east of the Mississippi. By 1910, cities and towns already contained almost half of America's population and were beginning to dominate American culture. Confronted with social problems different from rural America, cities developed their own brands of progressivism and produced reformers like Jane Addams of Chicago's Hull House, Robert Wagner of New York, and Louis Brandeis of Boston—men and women sympathetic to the plight of industrial workers.

It is the issue of urban reform and its sources of support that concerns J. Joseph Huthmacher, professor of history at the University of Delaware and the author of the following essay. Fo-

FROM J. Joseph Huthmacher, "Urban Liberalism and the Age of Reform," *Mississippi Valley Historical Review*, XLIX (September, 1962), pp. 231–41. Reprinted by permission.

cusing on political activities and legislative efforts, he differs with the analyses of Richard Hofstadter and George Mowry and concludes that the Progressive Era cannot be understood "exclusively" as a manifestation of the middle-class Yankee ethos. Lower-class workers, he contends, contributed much of the support for reform legislation, and without their endorsement some important liberal reforms would have failed. Unlike some middle-class reformers, workers were unconcerned about maintaining individualism and laissez-faire, but they would join with reformers to support bread-and-butter issues beneficial to themselves.

Huthmacher's interpretation can be questioned on both empirical and conceptual grounds. His case rests on scanty evidence from two states—New York and Massachusetts. But Richard Abrams in *Conservatism in the Progressive Era* (1964) disputes Huthmacher's findings for Massachusetts, and notes, to cite just one point, that insurgents in that state generally feared non-Yankee wage-earning classes. In his analysis, Huthmacher does not carefully distinguish between the actions of legislators and the wishes of their constituents, but rather interprets the actions of legislators as the automatic reflections of their constituents' demands. On this basis he proceeds to offer some hypotheses about the nature of lower-class liberalism and the aspirations and political consciousness of immigrants and their children. Moreover, his generalizations lump together Italians, Irishmen, and Jews, assuming without proof that they held similar views and that generational distinctions were unimportant. Finally, he does not measure the comparative importance of workers and their representatives in the reform movement. While Huthmacher is probably correct in stating that workers *sometimes* provided important support for reform, one can still logically accept the view that many workers often were an obstacle to some types of reform and that other workers constituted the majority of the socialist movement in the East. Nevertheless, Huthmacher's conception of urban workers as supporters of certain liberal reforms is a useful corrective to earlier interpretations that denied to this group any place in the progressive coalition. His analysis also compels historians to move beyond the consideration of needs and hopes expressed by political leaders and to examine the political and social beliefs, as well as the voting patterns, of citizens of different classes and ethnic backgrounds.

Most historians of twentieth-century America would agree that the effective beginnings of the present-day "people's capitalism"—the present-day liberalism—can be traced back to the Progressive Era. And most of them would agree that the essential ingredient which made possible the practical achievement of reforms at that time was the support given by city dwellers who, at the turn of the century, swung behind reform movements in large numbers for the first time since America's rush into industrialism following the Civil War. True, the Populists and other agrarian radicals had done spadework on behalf of various proposals in the late nineteenth century, such as trust regulation, the income tax, and direct election of senators. But their efforts had gone unrewarded, or had been frustrated by enactment of half-way measures. Not until the reform spirit had seized large numbers of urbanites could there be hope of achieving meaningful political, economic, and social adjustments to the demands of the new industrial civilization.

Between 1900 and 1920 American statute books became studded with the results of urban-oriented reform drives. The direct primary, the initiative, the Seventeenth Amendment; the Clayton Act, a revived Interstate Commerce Commission, and the Federal Trade Commission; workmen's compensation, child labor laws, and Prohibition—these and many other achievements testified to the intensity of Progressivism. It is admitted, of course, that not everything done in the name of reform was desirable. Some measures, notably Prohibition, are counted today as being wrong-headed, while some political panaceas like the direct primary elicited an undue degree of optimism on the part of their exponents. Nevertheless, the Progressive Era did witness America's first modern reform upsurge, and much of substantial worth was accomplished. Moreover, it established patterns and precedents for the further evolution of American liberalism, an evolution whose later milestones would bear the markings "New Deal" and "New Frontier."

In accounting for the genesis and success of urban liberalism in the Progressive Era, however, the historians who have dominated its study thus far have concentrated on one population element, the urban middle class, and its Yankee-Protestant system of values. "The great majority of the reformers came from the 'solid middle class,'" Professor George E. Mowry tells us. "If names mean anything, an overwhelming proportion of this reform group came from old American stock with British origins consistently indicated." Professor Richard Hofstadter adds that "the key words of Progressivism were terms like *patriotism, citizen, democracy, law, character, conscience* . . . terms redolent of the sturdy Protestant Anglo-Saxon moral and intellectual roots of the Progressive uprising." [1] The component parts of this amorphous middle class, and the reasons for their new interest in reform at the turn of the century, have been described by various scholars.[2] We have

---

[1] George E. Mowry, *The Era of Theodore Roosevelt, 1900–1912* (New York, 1958), 86; Richard Hofstadter, *The Age of Reform* (New York, 1955), 318.

[2] Mowry, *Era of Theodore Roosevelt;* Hofstadter, *Age of Reform;* C. Wright Mills, *White Collar* (New York, 1951); Eric Goldman, *Rendezvous with Destiny* (New York, 1952); Samuel P. Hays, *The Response to Industrialism, 1885–1914* (Chicago, 1957).

been told about the "white collar" group which saw, in the increasing bu-
reaucratization of big business, the blotting out of its traditional belief in the
American "rags to riches" legend. Some writers have dwelt upon the middle-
class intellectuals—writers, publicists, ministers, college women, professors
—who, in response to changing patterns of social thought represented by the
rise of "realism" in literature, religion, and the social sciences, determined to
uplift the living conditions of their less fortunate brothers. Others have examined the "Old Aristocracy" threatened by a "status revolution," and fighting
to maintain the degree of deference that had been theirs before the rise of the
newly rich moguls of business and finance.

Imbued with this mixture of selfish and altruistic motives, reinforced by
the pocketbook-pinching price inflation that got under way in 1897, the urban middle-class reformers set out to right the wrongs of their society. They
introduced a variety of new democratic techniques into our political mechanics, in an attempt to break the grip of the corrupt bosses who manipulated
irresponsible immigrant voters and unscrupulous businessmen in ways that
subverted good government. They augmented the government's role as
watchdog over the economy, either to maintain the traditional "small business" regime of competitive free enterprise, or at least to make sure that
oligopolists passed on to consumers the benefits of large-scale operation.
Through the activities of their philanthropic organizations, coupled with
support of paternalistic labor and social welfare legislation, the middle-class
reformers also sought to uplift the standards of the alien, slum-dwelling, urban working class to something more closely approximating the Yankee-
Protestant ideal. So runs the "middle-class" interpretation of Progressivism,
an interpretation which has set the fashion, by and large, for scholarly work
on the subject.

There is no doubt, of course, that discontented elements among the urban middle class contributed much to Progressivism, or that the historians
who have explored their contributions and their motives deserve the plaudits
of the profession. Nevertheless, it may be pertinent to ask whether these historians have not overstressed the role of middle-class reformers, to the neglect or exclusion of other elements—such as organized labor—who have
had something to do with the course of modern American liberalism.[3] More
particularly, a number of circumstances call into question the assertion that
"In politics . . . the immigrant was usually at odds with the reform aspirations of the American Progressive." [4] If such were the case, how does one

---

[3] The suggestions made in this and the following paragraphs stem primarily from the author's research for *Massachusetts People and Politics, 1919–1933* (Cambridge, Mass.,
1959), and for a projected biography of Senator Robert F. Wagner of New York. Senator
Wagner's papers are deposited at Georgetown University, Washington, D.C.

[4] Hofstadter, *Age of Reform*, 180–81. It is clear, of course, that Professor Hofstadter is
referring not only to the first-generation immigrants themselves, but to the whole society
which they, their offspring, and their culture were creating within our industrial, urban
maze.

explain the drive and success of Progressive Era reform movements in places like New York and Massachusetts—states that were heavily populated with non-Protestant, non-Anglo-Saxon immigrants and sons of immigrants? How could reformers succeed at the polls or in the legislatures in such states if, "Together with the native conservative and the politically indifferent, the immigrants formed a potent mass that limited the range and the achievements of Progressivism"?[5] Moreover, how does one explain the support which individuals like Al Smith, Robert F. Wagner, James A. Foley, James Michael Curley, and David I. Walsh gave to a large variety of so-called Progressive measures in their respective office-holding capacities?[6] Surely these men do not conform to the middle-class, Yankee-Protestant "Progressive Profile" as etched by Professor Mowry.[7]

If the Progressive Era is to be considered a manifestation of the Yankee-Protestant ethos almost exclusively, how does one explain the fact that in the legislatures of New York and Massachusetts many reform bills received more uniform and consistent support from respresentatives of the urban lower class than they received from the urban middle-class or rural representatives? Some of the most effective middle-class reformers, such as social worker Frances Perkins, realized this fact at the time and charted their legislative strategy accordingly.[8] It may be pointed out also that, even when submitted to popular referendums, typically Progressive measures sometimes received more overwhelming support in the melting-pot wards than they received in the middle-class or rural constituencies. This was the case, for example, in Massachusetts when, in 1918, the voters passed upon a proposed initiative and referendum amendment to the state constitution. Such circumstances become especially compelling when we remember that reform measures, no matter how well formulated and publicized by intellectuals, cannot become effective in a democracy without skillful political generalship and—even more important—votes.

---

[5] *Ibid.*, 181.

[6] Oscar Handlin, *Al Smith and His America* (Boston, 1958); Joseph F. Dinneen, *The Purple Shamrock: The Honorable James Michael Curley of Boston* (New York, 1949); Dorothy G. Wayman, *David I. Walsh: Citizen Patriot* (Milwaukee, 1952). See also Arthur Mann, *La Guardia: A Fighter against His Times* (Philadelphia, 1959). Among the measures which Robert F. Wagner introduced as a New York state senator between 1909 and 1918 were the following: a bill to provide for direct election of United States senators; a bill to authorize a twenty million dollar bond issue for conservation and public development of state water power; a direct primary bill; a short-ballot bill; a resolution to ratify the federal income tax amendment; a bill establishing the Factory Investigating Commission; a civil rights bill; a woman suffrage amendment to the state constitution; numerous bills for child labor regulation; a bill to extend home rule to municipalities; a bill to establish a minimum wage commission for women; a bill limiting the issuance of labor injunctions; a bill to authorize municipal ownership of power plants; and a corrupt practices bill.

[7] Mowry, *Era of Theodore Roosevelt*, chap. 5.

[8] Frances Perkins, *The Roosevelt I Knew* (New York, 1946), 12–26.

Marshaled together, then, the foregoing evidence suggests that the triumphs of modern liberalism in the Progressive Era, and in subsequent reform eras, were owed to something more than a strictly middle-class dynamism. It indicates that the urban lower class provided an active, numerically strong, and politically necessary force for reform—and that this class was perhaps as important in determining the course of American liberalism as the urban middle class, about which so much has been written.

Today's liberals look to the "northern" Democrats and the "eastern" Republicans—those whose elections are due largely to the votes of the urban working class—for support of their proposals. If, as is contended, this phenomenon of urban lower-class liberalism can be traced back beyond the election of 1960, beyond the New Deal, and to the Progressive Era, then the probing of its chronological origins and the operational details of its emergence present wide fields for fruitful research. In the process of such studies, many other questions will present themselves to the investigator. What were the sources of lower-class interest in reform? How did its sources affect its nature, specific content, and practical effects? How, if at all, did urban lower-class liberalism differ in these respects from urban middle-class liberalism? At the risk of premature generalization, tentative suggestions, indicated by research thus far conducted, may be set forth regarding these matters.

The great source of urban working-class liberalism was experience. Unlike the middle-class reformers, who generally relied on muckrakers, Social Gospelers, and social scientists to delineate the ills of society, the urban working class knew at first hand the conditions of life on "the other side of the tracks." Its members and spokesmen grew to manhood "in the midst of alternately shivering and sweltering humanity in ancient rat-infested rookeries in the swarming, anonymous, polyglot East Side, an international center before the U.N. was dreamed of," where "souls and bodies were saved by the parish priest, the family doctor, and the local political saloonkeeper and boss who knew everyone and was the link between the exploited immigrant and the incomprehensible, distant law." [9] Such people were less imbued than the middle class with the "old American creed" which expounded individualism, competition, and laissez-faire free enterprise as the means of advance from "rags to riches." Their felt needs, largely of the bread and butter type, were of the here and now, and not of the middle-class variety which fastened upon further advancement to a higher station from one already fairly comfortable. Moreover, their constant immersion in the depths of human misery and frailty, and the semi-pessimistic nature of their religious psychology, limited their hopes for environmental improvement within the bounds of reasonable expectation. Their outlook tended to be more practical and "possibilistic" than that of some middle-class Progressives who allowed their reform aspira-

[9] Robert Moses, "Salute to an East Side Boy Named Smith," *New York Times Magazine* (October 8, 1961), 113.

tions to soar to Utopian heights, envisaging a "Kingdom of God on Earth" or a perfect society to be achieved by means of sociological test tubes. Finally, the previous political experience of the immigrant workers, centering about their security-oriented relations with a paternalistic ward boss, conditioned them to transfer the same functional conception to the city, state, and national governments as they became progressively aware of their ability, through their voting power, to make those governing bodies serve their needs. Consequently, their view of government was much less permeated with fears of paternalism and centralization than that of traditionally individualistic middle-class reformers, many of whom abated their attachment to the laissez-faire principle with only the greatest trepidation.[10]

The influence of these conditioning factors seems clearly discernible in the specific types of reform programs to which the urban lower class and its spokesmen lent greatest support. It is commonplace to say, for example, that the immigrants were not interested in political machinery reforms simply as reforms. Unlike the remaining middle-class "genteel reformers," they did not look upon political tinkering as the be-all and end-all of reform. Yet it is an injustice to imply that the immigrants' attitude on this matter was due to an inherent inability to comprehend the Yankee-Protestant concept of political behavior, and that they were therefore immune to all proposals for political reform. These lower-class voters seemed willing enough to support specific proposals which would enable them to secure the voice necessary to satisfy their economic and social needs, recognizing, quite properly, that the latter were the real sources of society's maladjustment. Since the rural areas of Massachusetts generally controlled the Bay State legislature, the urban working class supported the initiative and referendum amendment which might enable them to by-pass tight-fisted rural solons. Since the same situation prevailed in the New York legislature, the New York City delegation was glad to secure popular election of United States senators. In brief, it would seem that the line-up on such questions depended more upon local conditions of practical politics than upon the workings of a Yankee-Protestant ethos.

In the realm of economic reform, pertaining particularly to the problem of "big business," indications are that the urban lower class tended—unwittingly, of course—to favor the "New Nationalism" approach of Herbert Croly and Theodore Roosevelt over the "New Freedom" of Wilson and the trust-busters. Its members had seldom experienced the white collar group's "office boy to bank president" phenomenon themselves. They had never been part of the "Old Aristocracy," and hence had not suffered a downward revision in status at the hands of big business moguls. They shared few of the aspirations of the industrial "small businessman" and, indeed, recognized that the latter was all too frequently identified with sweatshop conditions.

---

[10] See Hofstadter, *Age of Reform*, chap. 6.

Consequently, the urban lower class was little stirred by Wilsonian cries to give the "pygmies" a chance. To workers the relative size of the employer's establishment was quite immaterial so long as he provided job security and adequate wages and working conditions, and passed some of the benefits of large-scale production on to consumers in the form of lower prices. Governmental stabilization of the economy and regulation of big business might well prove more successful in guaranteeing these conditions than would government antitrust drives. As a result, we find urban lower-class representatives introducing a large variety of business regulatory measures on the local and state levels during the Progressive Era. And it is symbolic, perhaps, to find Senator Robert F. Wagner introducing the National Industrial Recovery Act in 1933, while Senator David I. Walsh of Massachusetts had sponsored somewhat similar, forerunner, measures in Congress during the 1920's.

What has been said above indicates the basis for urban lower-class interest in the many types of social welfare and labor measures which became novelties, and then commonplace enactments, during the Progressive Era. If the middle class faced the fear of insecurity of status, then the working class faced an equally compelling fear of insecurity of livelihood and living conditions. The precarious condition of the lower class had now become known even to those on the better side of the tracks and, partly for humanitarian reasons and partly to defend their own civilization against a "revolution from below," middle-class reformers had become interested in social justice movements—which involved "doing things for others." But the recipients of this benevolence might surely be expected to show at least an equal interest in such movements—which involved doing something for themselves. That such was the case is clearly indicated by study of the legislative history of measures like workmen's compensation, widows' pensions, wages and hours legislation, factory safety legislation, and tenement laws in the legislatures of New York and Massachusetts during the Progressive years. The representatives of lower-class constituencies were the most active legislative sponsors and backers of such bills and, in collaboration with middle-class propagandists and lobbyists, they achieved a record of enactments which embraced much of the best and most enduring part of the Progressive Era's heritage.

The operations of the New York State Factory Investigating Commission are a case in point. Established by the legislature following the tragic Triangle Shirtwaist Company fire in 1911, the Commission recommended and secured passage of over fifty labor laws during the next four years, providing a model factory code that was widely copied in other states. The Commission's most active legislative members were State Senator Robert F. Wagner and Assemblyman Alfred E. Smith, two products of the East Side, while its most effective investigator and lobbyist was Miss Frances Perkins, a middle-class, college trained social worker. (It should be noted also that the Commission received notable assistance from Samuel Gompers and other leaders of organized labor.) Again it is rather striking to observe that the Social Security Act of 1935, which began the transfer of industrial security matters from the state to the national level, was introduced by Senator Wagner, to be administered by a federal Department of Labor headed by Miss Perkins.

Effective social reform during the Progressive Era, and in later periods, seems thus to have depended upon constructive collaboration, on specific issues, between reformers from both the urban lower class and the urban middle class (with the further co-operation, at times, of organized labor). Of course, such co-operation could not be attained on all proposals that went under the name of social "reform." When, during the Progressive Era, certain old-stock, Protestant, middle-class reformers decided that the cure for social evils lay not only in environmental reforms, but necessitated also a forcible "uplifting" of the lower-class immigrants' cultural and behavior standards to "100 per cent American" levels, the parting of the ways came. Lower-class reform spokesmen had no use for compulsory "Americanization" through Prohibition, the closing of parochial schools, or the enforcement of puritanical "blue laws." Nor had they any use for immigration restriction laws which were based upon invidious, quasi-racist distinctions between allegedly "superior" and "inferior" nationality stocks.[11] To them reform, in so far as the use of government compulsion was concerned, was a matter of environment. The fundamentals of a man's cultural luggage—his religion, his emotional attachment to his "old country" and its customs, his habits and personal behavior—were of concern to himself and his God, and to them alone. The lower-class reformers were products of the melting pot, and most of them took seriously the inscription on the base of the famous statue in New York harbor. True, there were many religious and ethnic differences among the component elements of the lower class, which often resulted in prejudice and violence. But each of these elements resented the Old Stock's contention that all of them were equally inferior to the "real Americans" of Yankee-Protestant heritage, and they resisted the attempts, which grew as the Progressive Era wore on, to enforce conformity to a single cultural norm.

In so far as conformity-seeking "cultural" reforms were enacted in the Progressive years, then, the responsibility must be assigned to urban middle-class reformers, joined in this instance by their rural "bible belt" brethren. The lower class can share no part of the "credit" for reforms like Prohibition. But in resisting such movements, were they not waging an early fight on behalf of what we today call "cultural pluralism"—acceptance of which has

---

[11] "If the literacy test was not applied to the Irish and the German, why should it now be applied to the Jew, the Italian or the Slav of the new immigration? Like our ancestors, they are now flying from persecution, from ignorance, from inequality; like our ancestors they expect to find here freedom and equal opportunity. Are we going to deny them an equal opportunity? Are we going to withhold from them the equality and opportunities which our fathers enjoyed?" (Excerpt from a speech by Robert F. Wagner in the New York State Senate, on a resolution which he introduced in 1917 petitioning Congress not to pass the literacy test bill. Wagner Papers).

become a cardinal tenet in the standard definition of "liberalism" in the modern world? Indeed, it may not be too much to say that in all three fields of reform—the political and economic, as well as the social—indications are that the urban lower-class approach was more uniformly "advanced" than that of the middle class, in the sense of being more in line with what has become the predominant liberal faith in modern America. After all, does not the lower-class reform impulse, as outlined above, resemble the "hard-headed," realistic, and pluralistic liberalism for which spokesmen like Reinhold Niebuhr and Arthur Schlesinger, Jr., plead today, so that the "Children of Light" might not fall easy prey to the "Children of Darkness"? [12]

It is not contended, of course, that all members of the urban working class became interested in reform during the Progressive Era, any more than it can be contended that all members of the urban middle class did so. The same "sidewalks of New York" that produced Al Smith and Robert Wagner continued to produce their share of "unreconstructed" machine politicians, whose vision never rose above their own pockets. Nor is it argued that the nature and zeal of lower-class attachment to liberalism remained constant throughout the twentieth century, or that the degree of co-operation attained with other reform minded elements remained unchanging. In the 1920's, for example, mutual suspicion and distrust, based largely on ethnic or "cultural" differences, seem to have displaced the former mood of limited collaboration between lower- and middle-class spokesmen, and in these changed circumstances Progressive-type measures found little chance of enactment. It is also possible that the high level of general prosperity prevailing since 1941 has vitiated urban working-class devotion to economic reform, and that the increasing degree of acceptance enjoyed by ethnic elements formerly discriminated against is causing their members to forget the lessons of cultural pluralism. All of these matters deserve further study.

The last-mentioned problems, dealing with the contemporary scene, may lie more properly within the realm of the political scientist and sociologist. But surely the evolution of America's twentieth-century liberal society, from the Progressive Era through the New Deal, is a province for historical inquiry. It is suggested that the historians who enter it might do better if they modify the "middle-class" emphasis which has come to dominate the field and devote more attention to exploring hitherto neglected elements of the American social structure. Such exploration necessitates tedious research, focusing at first on the local and state levels, in unalluring source materials such as local and foreign-language newspapers, out-of-the-way manuscript collections, and the correlations between the make-up and voting records of small-scale election districts. In the course of this research, however, our conception of the Progressive Era, and of recent American history as a whole,

---

[12] See, for example, Reinhold Niebuhr, *The Children of Light and the Children of Darkness* (New York, 1945); Arthur M. Schlesinger, Jr., *The Vital Center* (Boston, 1949).

may undergo change. In fact, it may even begin to appear that "old fashioned" political historians, if they inform their work with up-to-date statistical and social science skills, still have as much to contribute to our knowledge of ourselves as do the intellectual and social historians, who are, perhaps, sometimes prone to over-generalize on the basis of historical psychoanalysis.

SUGGESTED READING

For support for Huthmacher's analysis, see his "Charles Evans Hughes and Charles F. Murphy: The Metamorphosis of Progressivism," *New York History*, XLVI (Jan. 1965), and his *Senator Robert F. Wagner and the Rise of Urban Liberalism* (1968); see also Robert Wesser's "Charles Evans Hughes and the Urban Sources of Political Progressivism," *New York History*, L (Oct. 1966), and his *Charles Evans Hughes: Politics and Reform in New York* (1967); and Nancy J. Weiss's *Charles Francis Murphy, 1858–1924: Respectability and Responsibility in Tammany Politics* (1968). For evidence that bosses and urban politicians supported reform legislation in Massachusetts, see Richard B. Sherman, "Foss of Massachusetts, Demagogue v. Progressive," *Mid-America*, XLIII (Apr. 1961), and John D. Buenker, "The Mahatma and Progressive Reform: Martin Lomasney as Lawmaker, 1911–1917," *New England Quarterly*, XLIV (Sept. 1971). For other evidence, see Philip Gleason, "An Immigrant Group's Interest in Progressive Reform: The Case of the German-American Catholics," *American Historical Review*, LXXIII (Dec. 1967); and Buenker, "Edward F. Dunne: The Urban New Stock Democrat as Progressive," *Mid-America*, L (Jan. 1968), and "The Urban Political Machine and the Seventeenth Amendment," *Journal of American History*, LVI (Sept. 1969). In the last-mentioned essay, Buenker also suggested that historians should "concentrate their attention less on the concept of a [Progressive] movement" and more on the sources of support for legislation passed.

None of these studies adequately assesses the comparative importance of the urban workers in the reform coalitions, but Michael Rogin, in "Progressives and the California Electorate," *Journal of American History*, LV (Sept. 1968), relying heavily on an analysis of voting statistics, finds that the progressive Hiram Johnson lost much of his earlier support among the rural voters after 1910 and came to depend on the votes of working-class immigrants. In *The Intellectuals and McCarthy: The Radical Specter* (1967), Rogin, however, notes, again on the basis of an analysis of voting statistics, that progressivism was not based in the cities of Wisconsin and the Dakotas.

GABRIEL KOLKO

The Triumph of Conservatism

INTRODUCTION

As he has made clear in two books (*Railroads and Regulation, 1877–1916* [1965] and *The Triumph of Conservatism* [1963], Gabriel Kolko, professor of history at York University in Canada, believes that federal regulation in the Progressive Era was inspired by big businessmen primarily to escape the harsh consequences of competition, and also to avoid the more cumbersome, less controllable, state regulation and the "nascent radicalism" in the states. Primarily to restrict competition, for example, railroad leaders in need of binding pooling agreements and noncompetitive freight rates sought rescue through establishment of the Inter-

FROM Gabriel Kolko, *The Triumph of Conservatism*, pp. 1–10, 279–87. © by The Free Press of Glencoe, a Division of The Macmillan Company, 1963. Reprinted with permission of The Macmillan Company. Part [I] represents the "Introduction" and part [II] "Conclusion: The Lost Democracy."

state Commerce Commission (ICC) and passage of such legislation as the Hepburn and Elkins acts. Big meat-packers, interested
in expanding export markets and bringing their unregulated
small competitors under tough inspection laws, inspired and
supported most of the provisions of the Meat Inspection Act of
1906.

Unlike Robert Wiebe in *Businessmen and Reform* (1962),
who stresses the disunity of the American business community
(eastern versus western businessmen, shippers versus railroads,
big versus small), Kolko contends that the big businesses were
united by common goals and values and wielded sufficient power
to realize their aims. Kolko argues not merely that progressivism
was the tool of big business, but also that progressivism set the
pattern for later business-government relations and in large measure shaped the modern corporate order. Using progressivism as
a test case of twentieth-century liberalism, he has found that liberal political leaders were recruited from the same social class
as big businessmen and shared the same values. Liberals were,
in fact, the handmaidens of corporate enterprise.

However arresting Kolko's thesis is, it has been subject to
certain criticisms. By concentrating exclusively on business-government relations, he has neglected other aspects of the Progressive movement, such as social-justice legislation, which may
not in fact be the triumph of conservatism. He has also ignored
the powerful agitation on the national level and the efforts of progressive senators like Robert La Follette and William Borah for
regulatory legislation. In looking briefly at the state level and the
movement of corporations for federal regulation partly to escape
state controls and the "nascent radicalism" in the states, he is
very sketchy on the nature of, and the sources of support for,
this radical impulse.

Given his assumptions about business domination of politics and the presumed understanding by big businessmen of the
need for federal regulation, he does not adequately explain why
the desired legislation was not passed earlier and why it was
often opposed. The evidence presented in *The Triumph of Conservatism* fails to prove either that most big businessmen had a
clear conception of "political capitalism," or that they succeeded
in passing legislation equal to their conception. In the Roosevelt
years, for example, the legislative establishment of the Bureau of
Corporations did not directly assist in reducing competition. That
agency, as well as the détente agreements between the House of
Morgan and the administration, protected corporations from arbitrary executive interference, and possibly from Congressional
and popular antagonisms, not from the perils of laissez faire. The
executive was promising not to act in unfriendly or unpredictable
ways and thereby created an environment for businessmen to
continue some of their efforts to limit competition (business con-
solidations and agreements) that many businessmen, according

to Kolko, knew did not work. In general, the industrial sector during the progressive years was not seriously affected by such legislation as the Federal Trade Commission, though it may still be argued that railroad legislation and the Federal Reserve System rationalized the transportation and financial sectors of the economy.

Scholars have also questioned Kolko's analysis of particular episodes. In *Change and Continuity in Twentieth-Century America: The 1920's* (1968), John Braeman disputes Kolko on the forces behind the Meat Inspection Act of 1906 and the role played in it by the big meat-packers, finding that they in reality opposed any regulation not controlled by themselves. Robert U. Harbeson, reviewing Kolko's book in a long essay, "Railroads and Regulation, 1877–1916, Conspiracy or Public Interest?" (*Journal of Economic History*, XXVII [June 1967]), argues that the ICC did not favor the railroads at the expense of shippers and consumers. Albro Martin, in *Enterprise Denied: Origins of the Decline of American Railroads, 1897–1917* (1971), also challenges Kolko's contentions about the sources and achievements of the progressive reform legislation for railroads. Edwin A. Purcell, Jr., in "Ideas and Interests: Businessmen and the Interstate Commerce Act" (*Journal of American History*, LIV (Dec. 1967), finds "widespread and vocal opposition . . . [by] many railroad executives" to the Interstate Commerce Act, but he concludes that there was also widespread support among businessmen for regulation because they sought "federal intervention as a means of protecting their own individual interests."

Despite these criticisms, Kolko's important work has compelled historians to reconsider the nature of liberal reform, has focused attention on the analysis of the role of the state and of power in the political economic system, has promoted a reconsideration of the nature and ideology of big business, and has emphasized the need for reinvestigating the sources and effects of progressive legislation. Probably no other American historian has so broadened the scope of the analysis of twentieth-century American history and raised such basic questions about ideology, social structure, class domination, power, and consensus. His studies of the Progressive Era, as well as his earlier examination of *Wealth and Power in America* (1962) and his later important volumes on the Cold War, have marked him as an intellectual leader among the radical or New Left historians.

[I]

*T*his [study] is motivated by a concern with the seemingly non-academic question of "what might have been." All men speculate or dream as they choose, but the value of the speculation depends on the questions asked and on the way they are answered. Speculation of the type prompting this [study] has its value only if it leads to the reexamination of what happened— what *really* happened—in the past.

The political or economic history of a single nation, especially during a specific, critical period which has a determining influence on the decades that follow, should be examined with provocative questions in mind. And there is no more provocative question than: Could the American political experience in the twentieth century, and the nature of our economic institutions, have been radically different? Every society has its Pangloss who will reply in the negative. But to suggest that such a reply is mere apologetics would be a fruitless, inaccurate oversimplification. Predominantly, the great political and sociological theorists of this century have pessimistically described and predicted an inexorable trend toward centralization, conformity, bureaucracy—toward a variety of totalitarianism—and yet they have frequently been personally repelled by such a future.

Unless one believes in an invisible, transcendent destiny in American history, the study of men and institutions becomes the prerequisite for discovering how one's question should be answered. The nature of the questions in this study demands that history be more than a reinterpretation of what is already known, in large part because what is known is insufficient, but also because histories of America from the turn of the century onwards have all too frequently been obsessed by effects rather than causes. Theories and generalizations based on such an approach have ignored concrete actions and intentions, and for this reason the study of consequences and effects has also been deficient.

Assuming that the burden of proof is ultimately on the writer, I contend that the period from approximately 1900 until the United States' intervention in the war, labeled the "progressive" era by virtually all historians, was really an era of conservatism. Moreover, the triumph of conservatism . . . was the result not of any impersonal, mechanistic necessity but of the conscious needs and decisions of specific men and institutions.

There were any number of options involving government and economics abstractly available to national political leaders during the period 1900–1916, and in virtually every case they chose those solutions to problems advocated by the representatives of concerned business and financial interests. Such proposals were usually motivated by the needs of the interested businesses, and political intervention into the economy was frequently merely a response to the demands of particular businessmen. In brief, conservative solutions to the emerging problems of an industrial society were almost uniformly applied. The result was a conservative triumph in the sense that there was an effort to preserve the basic social and economic relations essential to a capitalist society, an effort that was frequently consciously as well as functionally conservative.

I use the attempt to preserve existing power and social relationships as

the criterion for conservatism because none other has any practical meaning. Only if we mechanistically assume that government intervention in the
economy, and a departure from orthodox laissez faire, automatically benefits
the general welfare can we say that government economic regulation by its
very nature is also progressive in the common meaning of that term. Each
measure must be investigated for its intentions and consequences in altering
the existing power arrangements, a task historians have largely neglected.

I shall state my basic proposition as baldly as possible so that my essential theme can be kept in mind. . . . For the sake of communication I will
use the terms *progressive* and *progressivism*, but not, as have most historians,
in their commonsense meanings.

Progressivism was initially a movement for the political rationalization
of business and industrial conditions, a movement that operated on the assumption that the general welfare of the community could be best served by
satisfying the concrete needs of business. But the regulation itself was invariably controlled by leaders of the regulated industry, and directed toward
ends they deemed acceptable or desirable. In part this came about because
the regulatory movements were usually initiated by the dominant businesses
to be regulated, but it also resulted from the nearly universal belief among
political leaders in the basic justice of private property relations as they essentially existed, a belief that set the ultimate limits on the leaders' possible
actions.

It is business control over politics (and by "business" I mean the major
economic interests) rather than political regulation of the economy that is the
significant phenomenon of the Progressive Era. Such domination was direct
and indirect, but significant only insofar as it provided means for achieving a
greater end—political capitalism. *Political capitalism* is the utilization of
political outlets to attain conditions of stability, predictability, and security
—to attain rationalization—in the economy. *Stability* is the elimination of
internecine competition and erratic fluctuations in the economy. *Predictability* is the ability, on the basis of politically stabilized and secured means, to
plan future economic action on the basis of fairly calculable expectations. By
security I mean protection from the political attacks latent in any formally
democratic political structure. I do not give to *rationalization* its frequent
definition as the improvement of efficiency, output, or internal organization
of a company; I mean by the term, rather, the organization of the economy
and the larger political and social spheres in a manner that will allow corporations to function in a predictable and secure environment permitting reasonable profits over the long run. My contention . . . is not that all of these
objectives were attained by World War I, but that important and significant
legislative steps in these directions were taken, and that these steps include
most of the distinctive legislative measures of what has commonly been
called the Progressive Period.

Political capitalism, as I have defined it, was a term unheard of in the

Progressive Period. Big business did not always have a coherent theory of economic goals and their relationship to immediate actions, although certain individuals did think through explicit ideas in this connection. The advocacy of specific measures was frequently opportunistic, but many individuals with similar interests tended to prescribe roughly the same solution to each concrete problem, and to operationally construct an economic program. It was never a question of regulation or no regulation, of state control or laissez faire; there were, rather, the questions of what kind of regulation and by whom. The fundamental proposition that political solutions were to be applied freely, if not for some other industry's problems then at least for one's own, was never seriously questioned in practice. My focus is on the dominant trends, and on the assumptions behind these trends as to the desirable distribution of power and the type of social relations one wished to create or preserve. And I am concerned with the implementation and administration of a political capitalism, and with the political and economic context in which it flourished.

Why did economic interests require and demand political intervention by the *federal* government and a reincarnation of the Hamiltonian unity of politics and economics?

In part the answer is that the federal government was *always* involved in the economy in various crucial ways, and that laissez faire never existed in an economy where local and federal governments financed the construction of a significant part of the railroad system, and provided lucrative means of obtaining fortunes. This has been known to historians for decades, and need not be belabored. But the significant reason for many businessmen welcoming and working to increase federal intervention into their affairs has been virtually ignored by historians and economists. This oversight was due to the illusion that American industry was centralized and monopolized to such an extent that it could rationalize the activity in its various branches voluntarily. Quite the opposite was true.

Despite the large number of mergers, and the growth in the absolute size of many corporations, the dominant tendency in the American economy at the beginning of this century was toward growing competition. Competition was unacceptable to many key business and financial interests, and the merger movement was to a large extent a reflection of voluntary, unsuccessful business efforts to bring irresistible competitive trends under control. Although profit was always a consideration, rationalization of the market was frequently a necessary prerequisite for maintaining long-term profits. As new competitors sprang up, and as economic power was diffused throughout an expanding nation, it became apparent to many important businessmen that only the national government could rationalize the economy. Although specific conditions varied from industry to industry, internal problems that could be solved only by political means were the common denominator in those industries whose leaders advocated greater federal regulation. Ironically, contrary to the consensus of historians, it was not the existence of monopoly that caused the federal government to intervene in the economy, but the lack of it.

There are really two methods, both valid, of examining the political control of the economy during the period 1900–1916. One way would be to examine the effects of legislation insofar as it aided or hurt industries irrespective of those industries' attitude toward a measure when it was first proposed. The other approach is to examine the extent to which business advocated some measure before it was enacted, and the nature of the final law. Both procedures will be used in this study. The second is the more significant, however, since it points up the needs and nature of the economy, and focuses more clearly on the disparity between the conventional interpretation of progressivism and the informal realities. Moreover, it illustrates the fact that many key businessmen articulated a conscious policy favoring the intervention of the national government into the economy. Because of such a policy there was a consensus on key legislation regulating business that has been overlooked by historians. Important businessmen did not, on the whole, regard politics as a necessary evil, but as an important part of their larger position in society. Because of their positive theory of the state, key business elements managed to define the basic form and content of the major federal legislation that was enacted. They provided direction to existing opinion for regulation, but in a number of crucial cases they were the first to initiate that sentiment. They were able to define such sentiment because, in the last analysis, the major political leaders of the Progressive Era—Roosevelt, Taft, and Wilson—were sufficiently conservative to respond to their initiatives.

Although the main view in the business community was for a rationalization of the conditions of the economy through political means, advocates of such intervention, the J. P. Morgan interests being the most notable, were occasionally prepared to exploit the government in an irregular manner that was advantageous as well. The desire for a larger industrial stability did not exclude an occasional foray into government property, or the utilization of the government to sanction a business arrangement of questionable legality. Such side actions, however, did not alter the basic pattern. In addition, business advocacy of *federal* regulation was motivated by more than a desire to stabilize industries that had moved beyond state boundaries. The needs of the economy were such, of course, as to demand federal as opposed to random state economic regulation. But a crucial factor was the bulwark which essentially conservative national regulation provided against state regulations that were either haphazard or, what is more important, far more responsible to more radical, genuinely progressive local communities. National progressivism, then, becomes the defense of business against the democratic ferment that was nascent in the states.

Federal economic regulation took two crucial forms. The first was a series of informal détentes and agreements between various businesses and the federal government, a means especially favored by Theodore Roosevelt. The second and more significant approach was outright regulation and the creation of administrative commissions intended to maintain continuous supervision over phases of the economy. We shall examine both forms from the viewpoint of their origins, intent, and consequences; we shall examine, too, a number of movements for regulation that failed to find legislative fulfilment of any sort but that provide insight into the problems and needs of the economy in the Progressive Era.

If business did not always obtain its legislative ends in the precise shape it wanted them, its goals and means were nevertheless clear. In the long run, key business leaders realized, they had no vested interest in a chaotic industry and economy in which not only their profits but their very existence might be challenged.

The questions of whether industrialism imposes narrow limits on the economic and political organization of a society, or on the freedom of men to alter the status quo in some decisive way, have been relatively settled ones for the large majority of social scientists. Max Weber, perhaps more than any social theorist of the past century, articulated a comprehensive framework which has profoundly influenced Western social science to answer such questions in the positive. The bureaucratic nature of the modern state and of modern industry, to Weber, restricted all possibilities for changing the basic structure of modern society. The tendency toward centralization in politics and industry, toward a mechanical impersonality designed to maximize efficiency, seemed to Weber to be the dominant theme in Western society, and the Weberian analysis has sunk deep roots into academic discussions of the problem. The systematic economics of Karl Marx—as opposed to that of "Marxists"—also sustained the argument that the basic trend in capitalist development was toward the centralization of industry. Indeed, such centralization was an indispensable aspect of Western industrialism, and could not be circumvented. Both Marx and Weber, one an opponent of capitalism and the other indifferent to it, suggested that industrialism and capitalism, as they saw both develop, were part of the unalterable march of history.

The relevance of the American experience to the systematic theories of both Weber and Marx will be explored in greater detail in the conclusion, my argument being that neither of the two men, for all their sensitivity and insight, offered much that is of value to understanding the development of capitalism and industrialism in the United States. Indeed, the American experience, I shall try to contend, offers much to disprove the formal theories of probably the two greatest social theorists of the past century. It is perhaps unfair to Marx, who based his case on the conditions existing in England and Western Europe in the mid-nineteenth century, to burden him with American history at the beginning of the twentieth, but he was not terribly modest about its applicability, and any respectable theory should have the predictive value its author ascribes to it. Weber, on the other hand, frequently stated that the United States was the prime example of modern capitalism in the twentieth century, if not the best proof of his theory.

American historians, with some notable exceptions, have tended, without relying on comprehensive theoretical systems of the Weberian or Marxist variety, also to regard the development of the economy as largely an impersonal, inevitable phenomenon. All too frequently they have assumed that concentration and the elimination of competition—business giantism or monopoly—was the dominant tendency in the economy. The relationship between the growth of new competition and new centers of economic power and the legislative enactments of the Progressive Era has been virtually ignored. On the contrary, federal legislation to most historians has appeared to be a reaction against the power of the giant monopoly, or a negative response to the very process of industrialism itself by a threatened middle-class being uprooted from its secure world by corporate capitalism. A centralized economy, historians have asserted, required a centralized federal power to prevent it from damaging the public interest, and the conventional political image of the Progressive Era is of the federal government as a neutral, if not humane, shield between the public and the Morgans, Rockefellers, and Harrimans. Progressivism has been portrayed as essentially a middle-class defense against the status pretensions of the new industrialists, a defense of human values against acquisitive habits, a reassertion of the older tradition of rural individualism.

Recent historians have, for the most part, assumed monopoly was an economic reality concomitant with maximum efficiency even where . . . it was little more than a political slogan. For it is one thing to say that there was a growth of vast accumulations of corporate power, quite another to claim that there existed a largely monopolistic control over the various economic sectors. Power may be concentrated, as it was, but the extent of that concentration is crucial. Historians of the period have too often confused the power of corporate concentration with total monopoly. The distinction is not merely important to American economic history, it is vital for the understanding of the political history of the period. And to the extent that historians have accepted the consensus among contemporaries as to the inevitable growth of monopoly at the turn of the century, they have failed to appreciate the dynamic interrelationship between politics and economics in the Progressive Era.

I shall be accused of oversimplifying what historians have written about the Progressive Era, and with some justice. But I believe it can be stated that although there are important and significant monographic works or histories of specific phases of progressivism which provide evidence to disprove aspects of such a comprehensive interpretation, no other theory of the nature of the Progressive Era has, in fact, yet been offered. And even most of the critical historians have accepted the traditional view of progressivism as a whole. No synthesis of the specific studies disproving what is, for better or worse, the conventionally accepted interpretation among historians of the Progressive Period, has been attempted. Nor has there really been a serious effort to re-examine the structural conditions and problems of the economy during the period and to relate them to the political and especially the detailed legislative history of the era. And it is here, more than any other place, that a new synthesis and a new interpretation is required.

Yet the exceptional historical works that have raised doubts about specific phases of the larger image of progressivism are suggestive in that they indicate that the time for reinterpreting the Progressive Era and the nature, character, and purpose of progressivism, is opportune. The work of the Handlins, Louis Hartz, and Carter Goodrich, to name only a few, in showing the *dependence* of business on politics for government aid and support until the Civil War, suggests that the unity of business and politics was still a relatively fresh memory by the end of the nineteenth century. Sidney Fine has pointed out how many businessmen treated laissez faire and Social Darwinian doctrine gingerly when it was to their interest to have the government aid them. William Miller has shown that the background and origins, and hence the status, of the triumphant industrialists was respectable and at least well-to-do, implicitly raising questions about the status conflict between the allegedly old elite and the new. John Morton Blum has expressed doubts as to the radicalism of Theodore Roosevelt, whom he has portrayed as a progressive conservative, but ultimately a conservative. And, perhaps more than anyone else, Arthur S. Link has critically dissected the history of the Wilson Administration in a manner that forces the historian to doubt whether the conventional usage of the term "progressive" really describes the New Freedom.

Although other monographs and studies can be cited, there are still too many loose ends in the traditional view of the Progressive Period, and no synthesis. More important, there has been no effort to study the entire period as an integrated whole. The very best work, such as Link's, deals with presidential periods, but the movements for legislative enactments ran through nearly all the administrations, and can only be really understood in that context. For without such a comprehensive view, the origins and motives behind the legislative components of the Progressive Period cannot be fully comprehended, assuming that there is some correlation between intentions or purposes and results. And although historians have increasingly been puzzled by the growing incompatibility of the specific studies with the larger interpretation, they have not been able to reconcile or explain the disparities. The Progressive Era has been treated as a series of episodes, unrelated to one another in some integrated manner, with growing enigmas as the quantity of new research into the period increases. The Progressive Party was one incident, the Food and Drug Act another, the conservation movement yet one more event.

In this study I shall attempt to treat the Progressive Era as an interrelated and, I hope, explicable whole, set in the context of the nature and tendencies of the economy. Ultimately, the analysis that follows is of interest only if it throws light on the broader theoretical issues concerning the extent to which a larger industrial necessity imposed limits on the political structure, and the manner in which politics shaped the economic system.

[II]

The American political experience during the Progressive Era was conservative, and this conservatism profoundly influenced American society's response to the problems of industrialism. The nature of the economic process in the United States, and the peculiar cast within which industrialism was molded, can only be understood by examining the political structure. Progressive politics is complex when studied in all of its aspects, but its dominant tendency on the federal level was to functionally create, in a piecemeal and haphazard way that was later made more comprehensive, the synthesis of politics and economics I have labeled "political capitalism."

The varieties of rhetoric associated with progressivism were as diverse as its followers, and one form of this rhetoric involved attacks on businessmen —attacks that were often framed in a fashion that has been misunderstood by historians as being radical. But at no point did any major political tendency dealing with the problem of big business in modern society ever try to go beyond the level of high generalization and translate theory into concrete economic programs that would conflict in a fundamental way with business supremacy over the control of wealth. It was not a coincidence that the results of progressivism were precisely what many major business interests desired.

Ultimately businessmen defined the limits of political intervention, and specified its major form and thrust. They were able to do so not merely because they were among the major initiators of federal intervention in the economy, but primarily because no politically significant group during the Progressive Era really challenged their conception of political intervention. The basic fact of the Progressive Era was the large area of consensus and unity among key business leaders and most political factions on the role of the federal government in the economy. There were disagreements, of course, but not on fundamentals. The overwhelming majorities on votes for basic progressive legislation is testimony to the near unanimity in Congress on basic issues.

Indeed, an evaluation of the Progressive Era must concede a much larger importance to the role of Congress than has hitherto been granted by historians who have focused primarily on the more dramatic Presidents. Congress was the pivot of agitation for banking reform while Roosevelt tried to evade the issue, and it was considering trade commissions well before Wilson was elected. Meat and pure food agitation concentrated on Congress, and most of the various reform proposals originated there. More often than not, the various Presidents evaded a serious consideration of issues until Congressional initiatives forced them to articulate a position. And businessmen seeking reforms often found a sympathetic response among the members of the House and Senate long before Presidents would listen to them. This was particularly true of Roosevelt, who would have done much less than he did were it not for the prodding of Congress. Presidents are preoccupied with patronage to an extent unappreciated by anyone who has not read their letters.

The Presidents, considered—as they must be—as actors rather than ideologists, hardly threatened to undermine the existing controllers of economic power. With the possible exception of Taft's Wickersham, none of the major appointees to key executive posts dealing with economic affairs were men likely to frustrate business in its desire to use the federal government to strengthen its economic position. Garfield, Root, Knox, Straus—these men were important and sympathetic pipelines to the President, and gave additional security to businessmen who did not misread what Roosevelt was trying to say in his public utterances. Taft, of course, broke the continuity between the Roosevelt and Wilson Administrations because of political decisions that had nothing to do with his acceptance of the same economic theory that Roosevelt believed in. The elaborate relationship between business and the Executive created under Roosevelt was unintentionally destroyed because of Taft's desire to control the Republican Party. Wilson's appointees were quite as satisfactory as Roosevelt's, so far as big business was concerned, and in his concrete implementation of the fruits of their political agitation—the Federal Reserve Act and the Federal Trade Commission Act—Wilson proved himself to be perhaps the most responsive and desirable to business of the three Presidents. Certainly it must be concluded that historians have overemphasized the basic differences between the Presidents of the Progressive Era, and ignored their much more important similarities. In 1912 the specific utterances and programs of all three were identical on fundamentals, and party platforms reflected this common agreement.

This essential unanimity extended to the area of ideologies and values, where differences between the Presidents were largely of the sort contrived by politicians in search of votes, or seeking to create useful images. None of the Presidents had a distinct consciousness of any fundamental conflict between their political goals and those of business. Roosevelt and Wilson especially appreciated the significant support business gave to their reforms, but it was left to Wilson to culminate the decade or more of agitation by providing precise direction to the administration of political capitalism's most important consequences in the Progressive Era. Wilson had a small but articulate band of followers who seriously desired to reverse the process of industrial centralization—Bryan and the Midwestern agrarians reflected this

tradition more than any other group. Yet ultimately he relegated such dissi-
dents to a secondary position—indeed, Wilson himself represented the
triumph of Eastern Democracy over Bryanism—and they were able to influence only a clause or amendment, here and there, in the basic legislative
structure of political capitalism.

But even had they been more powerful, it is debatable how different
Bryanism would have been. Bryan saw the incompatibility between giant
corporate capitalism and political democracy, but he sought to save democracy by saving, or restoring, a sort of idealized competitive capitalist economy which was by this time incapable of realization or restoration, and was
in any event not advocated by capitalists or political leaders with more
power than the agrarians could marshal. Brandeis, for his part, was bound by
enigmas in this period. Big business, to him, was something to be ultimately
rejected or justified on the basis of efficiency rather than power accumulation. He tried to apply such technical criteria where none was really relevant,
and he overlooked the fact that even where efficient or competitive, business
could still pose irreconcilable challenges to the political and social fabric of a
democratic community. Indeed, he failed to appreciate the extent to which it
was competition that was leading to business agitation for federal regulation,
and finally he was unable to do much more than sanction Wilson's actions as
they were defined and directed by others.

There was no conspiracy during the Progressive Era. It is, of course, a
fact that people and agencies acted out of public sight, and that official statements frequently had little to do with operational realities. But the imputa-
tion of a conspiracy would sidetrack a serious consideration of progressivism.
There was a basic consensus among political and business leaders as to what
was the public good, and no one had to be cajoled in a sinister manner. If
détentes, private understandings, and the like were not publicly proclaimed
it was merely because such agreements were exceptional and, generally
known, could not have been denied to other business interests also desiring
the security they provided. Such activities required a delicate sense of public
relations, since there was always a public ready to oppose preferential treatment for special businesses, if not the basic assumptions behind such arrangements.

Certainly there was nothing surreptitious about the desire of certain
businessmen for reforms, a desire that was frequently and publicly proclaimed, although the motives behind it were not appreciated by historians
and although most contemporaries were unaware of how reforms were implemented after they were enacted. The fact that federal regulation of the
economy was conservative in its effect in preserving existing power and economic relations in society should not obscure the fact that federal intervention in the economy was conservative in purpose as well. This ambition was
publicly proclaimed by the interested business forces, and was hardly conspiratorial.

It is the intent of crucial business groups, and the structural circumstances within the economy that motivated them, that were the truly significant and unique aspects of the Progressive Era. The effects of the legislation were only the logical conclusion of the intentions behind it. The ideological consensus among key business and political leaders fed into a stream of common action, action that was sometimes stimulated by different specific goals but which nevertheless achieved the same results. Political leaders, such as Roosevelt, Wilson, and their key appointees, held that it was proper for an industry to have a decisive voice or veto over the regulatory process within its sphere of interest, and such assumptions filled many key businessmen with confidence in the essential reliability of the federal political mechanism, especially when it was contrasted to the unpredictability of state legislatures.

Business opposition to various federal legislative proposals and measures did exist, of course, especially if one focuses on opposition to particular clauses in specific bills. Such opposition, as in the case of the Federal Reserve Bill, was frequently designed to obtain special concessions. It should not be allowed to obscure the more important fact that the essential purpose and goal of any measure of importance in the Progressive Era was not merely endorsed by key representatives of businesses involved; rather such bills were first proposed by them.

One can always find some businessman, of course, who opposed federal regulation at any point, including within his own industry. Historians have relished in detailing such opposition, and, indeed, their larger analysis of the period has encouraged such revelations. But the finding of division in the ranks of business can be significant only if one makes the false assumption of a monolithic common interest among all capitalists, but, worse yet, assumes that there is no power center among capitalists, and that small-town bankers or hardware dealers can be equated with the leaders of the top industrial, financial, and railroad corporations. They can be equated, of course, if all one studies is the bulk of printed words. But in the political as well as in the economic competition between small and big business, the larger interests always managed to prevail in any specific contest. The rise of National Association of Manufacturers in the Progressive Era is due to its antilabor position, and not to its opposition to federal regulation, which it voiced only after the First World War. In fact, crucial big business support could be found for every major federal regulatory movement, and frequent small business support could be found for any variety of proposals to their benefit, such as price-fixing and legalized trade associations. Progressivism was not the triumph of small business over the trusts, as has often been suggested but the victory of big businesses in achieving the rationalization of the economy that only the federal government could provide.

Still, the rise of the N.A.M. among businessmen in both pro- and antiregulation camps only reinforces the fact that the relationship of capitalists to the remainder of society was essentially unaltered by their divisions on federal intervention in the economy. In terms of the basic class structure, and the conditions of interclass relationships, big and small business alike were hostile to a labor movement interested in something more than paternalism and inequality. In this respect, and in their opposition or indifference to the very minimal social welfare reforms of the Progressive Era (nearly all of which were enacted in the states), American capitalism in the Progressive Era acted in the conservative fashion traditionally ascribed to it. The result was federal regulation in the context of a class society. Indeed, because the national political leadership of the Progressive Period shared this *noblesse oblige* and conservatism toward workers and farmers, it can be really said that there was federal regulation because there *was* a class society, and political leaders identified with the values and supremacy of business.

This identification of political and key business leaders with the same set of social values—ultimately class values—was hardly accidental, for had such a consensus not existed the creation of political capitalism would have been most unlikely. Political capitalism was based on the functional unity of major political and business leaders. The business and political elites knew each other, went to the same schools, belonged to the same clubs, married into the same families, shared the same values—in reality, formed that phenomenon which has lately been dubbed The Establishment. Garfield and Stetson met at Williams alumni functions, Rockefeller, Jr. married Aldrich's daughter, the Harvard clubmen always found the White House door open to them when Roosevelt was there, and so on. Indeed, no one who reads Jonathan Daniels' remarkable autobiography, *The End of Innocence,* can fail to realize the significance of an interlocking social, economic, and political elite in American history in this century.

The existence of an Establishment during the Progressive Era was convenient, even essential, to the functional attainment of political capitalism, but it certainly was not altogether new in American history, and certainly had antecedents in the 1890's. The basic causal factor behind national progressivism was the needs of business and financial elements. To some extent, however, the more benign character of many leading business leaders, especially those with safe fortunes, was due to the more secure, mellowed characteristics and paternalism frequently associated with the social elite. Any number of successful capitalists had long family traditions of social graces and refinement which they privately doubted were fully compatible with their role as capitalists. The desire for a stabilized, rationalized political capitalism was fed by this current in big business ideology, and gave many businessmen that air of responsibility and conservatism so admired by Roosevelt and Wilson. And, from a practical viewpoint, the cruder economic conditions could also lead to substantial losses. Men who were making fortunes with existing shares of the market preferred holding on to what they had rather than establishing control over an industry, or risking much of what they already possessed. Political stabilization seemed proper for this reason as well.

It allowed men to relax, to hope that crises might be avoided, to enjoy the bountiful fortunes they had already made.

Not only were economic losses possible in an unregulated capitalism, but political destruction also appeared quite possible. There were disturbing gropings ever since the end of the Civil War: agrarian discontent, violence and strikes, a Populist movement, the rise of a Socialist Party that seemed, for a time, to have an unlimited growth potential. Above all, there was a labor movement seriously divided as to its proper course, and threatening to follow in the seemingly radical footsteps of European labor. The political capitalism of the Progressive Era was designed to meet these potential threats, as well as the immediate expressions of democratic discontent in the states. National progressivism was able to short-circuit state progressivism, to hold nascent radicalism in check by feeding the illusions of its leaders—leaders who could not tell the difference between federal regulation *of* business and federal regulation *for* business.

Political capitalism in America redirected the radical potential of mass grievances and aspirations—of genuine progressivism—and to a limited extent colored much of the intellectual ferment of the period, even though the amorphous nature of mass aspirations frequently made the goals of business and the rest of the public nearly synonymous. Many well-intentioned writers and academicians worked for the same legislative goals as businessmen, but their innocence did not alter the fact that such measures were frequently designed by businessmen to serve business ends, and that business ultimately reaped the harvest of positive results. Such innocence was possible because of a naive, axiomatic view that government economic regulation, per se, was desirable, and also because many ignored crucial business support for such measures by focusing on the less important business opposition that existed. The fetish of government regulation of the economy as a positive social good was one that sidetracked a substantial portion of European socialism as well, and was not unique to the American experience. Such axiomatic and simplistic assumptions of what federal regulation would bring did not take into account problems of democratic control and participation, and in effect assumed that the power of government was neutral and socially beneficent. Yet many of the leading muckrakers and academics of the period were more than naive but ultimately conservative in their intentions as well. They sought the paternalism and stability which they expected political capitalism to bring, since only in this way could the basic virtues of capitalism be maintained. The betrayal of liberalism that has preoccupied some intellectual historians did not result from irrelevant utopianism or philosophical pragmatism, but from the lack of a truly radical, articulated alternative economic and political program capable of synthesizing political democracy with industrial reality. Such a program was never formulated in this period either in America or Europe.

Historians have continually tried to explain the seemingly sudden collapse of progressivism after the First World War, and have offered reasons that varied from moral exhaustion to the repression of nonconformity. On the whole, all explanations suffer because they really fail to examine progressivism beyond the favorable conventional interpretation. Progressive goals, on the concrete, legislative level, were articulated by various business interests. These goals were, for the most part, achieved, and no one formulated others that big business was also interested in attaining. Yet a synthesis of business and politics on the federal level was created during the war, in various administrative and emergency agencies, that continued throughout the following decade. Indeed, the war period represents the triumph of business in the most emphatic manner possible. With the exception of a brief interlude in the history of the Federal Trade Commission, big business gained total support from the various regulatory agencies and the Executive. It was during the war that effective, working oligopoly and price and market agreements became operational in the dominant sectors of the American economy. The rapid diffusion of power in the economy and relatively easy entry virtually ceased. Despite the cessation of important new legislative enactments, the unity of business and the federal government continued throughout the 1920's and thereafter, using the foundations laid in the Progressive Era to stabilize and consolidate conditions within various industries. And, on the same progressive foundations and exploiting the experience with the war agencies, Herbert Hoover and Franklin Roosevelt later formulated programs for saving American capitalism. The principle of utilizing the federal government to stabilize the economy, established in the context of modern industrialism during the Progressive Era, became the basis of political capitalism in its many later ramifications.

In this sense progressivism did not die in the 1920's, but became a part of the basic fabric of American society. The different shapes political capitalism has taken since 1916 deserve a separate treatment, but suffice it to say that even Calvin Coolidge did not mind evoking the heritage of Theodore Roosevelt, and Hoover was, if anything, deeply devoted to the Wilsonian tradition in which Franklin Roosevelt gained his first political experience.

SUGGESTED READING

Kolko's *The Triumph of Conservatism* ° (1963) was the subject for a session at the American Historical Association annual meeting (1966), and edited versions of the criticisms by Gerald Nash, J. Joseph Huthmacher, and Richard Abrams appear in Otis L. Graham, Jr., ed., *From Roosevelt to Roosevelt* ° (1971). John Braeman, in a review-essay "Seven Progressives," *Business History Review*, XXXV (Winter 1961), follows the usual analysis of progressivism, breaking the political reformers into two groups—"moderns" (Perkins, Stimson, Croly, and Roosevelt) who championed regulation of corporations and meeting the nation's internation responsibilities abroad, and "traditionalists" (LaFollette and Borah), who hoped to recapture rural America and became isolationists.

G. Cullom Davis, in "The Transformation of the Federal Trade Commission, 1914–1929," *Mississippi Historical Review*, LIV (Dec. 1962), disagrees with Kolko's interpretation of the FTC. Support of Kolko's, thesis is found in James Weinstein's *The Corporate Ideal in the Liberal State, 1900–1918* ° (1968), which includes his "Big Business and the Origins of Workmen's Compensation," which originally appeared in *Labor History*, VIII (Spring 1967); and in Martin Sklar's "Woodrow Wilson and the Political Economy of United States Liberalism," *Studies on the Left*, I (Fall 1960). Weinstein argues that some of the social-justice legislation was part of the conservative movement and views these reforms as part of corporate liberalism.

Melvin Urofsky's *Big Steel and the Wilson Administration* (1969) and Paul A. C. Koistinen's "The Industrial-Military Complex in Historical Perspective: World War I" and Robert Cuff's "A Dollar-a-Year Man in Government: George N. Peek and the War Industries Board," both in *Business History Review*, XLI (Winter 1967), are important for a study of business-government relations during the war. They disagree with Robert Himmelberg ("The War Industries Board and the Antitrust Question," *Journal of American History*, LII [June 1965] and Daniel Beaver (*Newton D. Baker and the American War Effort, 1917–1919* [1966]), who minimize or neglect the efforts of big businessmen serving in the government to use their influence to assist major corporations and to protect the corporate order they dominated.

Kolko's analysis of railroad regulations has been challenged in varying degrees by Stanley Caine in *The Myth of a Progressive Reform: Railroad Regulation in Wisconsin, 1903–1910* (1970); Mansel G. Blackford in "Businessmen and the Regulation of Railroads and Public Utilities in California During the Progressive Era," *Business History Review*, XLIV (Autumn 1970); and K. Austin Kerr in *American Railroad Politics, 1914–1920: Rates, Wages, and Efficiency* (1968).

PETER G. FILENE

An Obituary
for "The Progressive Movement"

INTRODUCTION

In the essay reprinted below, Peter Filene, an American historian
at the University of North Carolina, examines the literature on the
Progressive movement and concludes that no such "movement"
ever really existed. A movement, he argues, must have a program, identifiable values, coherent membership, and homogeneous supporters. Since historians cannot agree on the geographical and class location of the Progressive movement or on
its program and values, Filene concludes that the scholarly belief

FROM Peter G. Filene, "An Obituary for 'The Progressive Movement,' " *American Quarterly*, XXII (Spring 1970), pp. 20–34. Copyright © 1970, by the Trustees of the University of Pennsylvania. Reprinted by permission of the University of Pennsylvania and
Peter G. Filene.

The author is indebted to Frederick A. Bode and Donald G. Matthews, at the University of North Carolina at Chapel Hill, for their valuable suggestions.

in its existence had best be abandoned. His argument summarizes the emerging conviction of many practicing historians.

Though Filene effectively disposes of the notion of a Progressive movement, he seems briefly to suggest in the concluding section of his article that there may have been a Progressive Era. Regrettably, he does not explore this possibility. If indeed a Progressive Era existed, then it might still be possible to rescue the concept of progressivism from historical oblivion. To argue the existence of a Progressive Era, historians must search not for men with consistent programs but for patterns of social development that distinguish the years 1900–17 from other historical periods. Filene's excellent review of the literature suggests that these patterns of development may be as elusive as the "movement" he fails to find. And there is no doubt that generalizations once popular about the Progressive Era are no longer tenable. But it is probably too soon to abandon the conventional identification of this period or the effort to find beneath the diversity of programs and values a distinctive character in these years.

Recent scholarship, especially that of Samuel P. Hays, Robert Wiebe, and Gabriel Kolko, has begun to suggest a tentative framework for making sense of a Progressive Era. After a generation of rapid industrialization and attendant social chaos, the American people in the first decades of this century attempted to restore order. The desire for efficiency and stability—for rationalization of the new industrial system—was not universal, but it encompassed a variety of separate and often contradictory interests. The impulse toward rationalization was largely used by the dominant business corporations for their own ends. Businesses employed the enlarged powers of the national government to help curb competition. They cooperated in the conservation movement to assure that exploitation of natural resources would be intelligent and scientific. Many businessmen encouraged company unions and social-welfare measures to ease the discontent that could threaten their control of the new industrial system. And they began to apply the techniques of rational management to their own corporations. Beneath the surface confusions of this period, it might be argued, the urge to order was at work and indeed realized its objectives.

If this interpretation proves viable, does it rescue the concept of progressivism? It might not perhaps violate language to label progressive an epoch in which social forms achieved a higher level of rationality. If, however, the word *progressive* is taken to denote historical situations in which the dispossessed redress the social balance, then the years 1900–17 were not progressive, and some other label would be more appropriate.

*W*hat was the progressive movement?" This deceptively simple question, posed in different ways, holds prominent rank among the many controversies which have consumed historians' patient energies, spawned a flurry of monographs and articles, and confused several generations of students. Progressivism has become surrounded with an abundant variety of scholarly debates: did it derive from agrarian or urban sources? was it a liberal renaissance or a liberal failure? was it liberal at all? was it nostalgic or forward-looking? when did it end, and why? Into this already busy academic arena Richard Hofstadter introduced his theory of a "status revolution" in 1955, generating even more intensive argument and extensive publication. Yet one wonders whether all this sound and fury does indeed signify something. If sustained research has produced less rather than more conclusiveness, one may suspect that the issue is enormously complex. Or one may suspect that it is a false problem because historians are asking a false question. This essay seeks to prove the latter suspicion— more precisely, seeks to prove that "the progressive movement" never existed.

Before entering such an overgrown and treacherous field of historical controversy, one should take a definition as guideline—a definition of "movement." Significantly, historians have neglected the second half of their concept. They have been so busy trying to define "progressive" that they have overlooked the possibility that the word "movement" has equal importance and ambiguity. According to most sociologists, a social movement is a collectivity acting with some continuity to promote or resist a change in the society. On the one hand, it has more organization, more sustained activity and more defined purpose than a fad, panic, riot or other kind of mass behavior. On the other hand, it has a more diffuse following, more spontaneity and broader purpose than a cult, pressure group, political party or other voluntary association. Like such associations, however, it consists of persons who share a knowing relationship to one another. The members of a social movement combine and act together in a deliberate, self-conscious way, as contrasted to a noncollective or "aggregative" group (such as blondes or lower-income families) which has a common identity in the minds of social scientists or other observers rather than in the minds of members themselves.[1]

Having distinguished a social movement from other forms of collec-

---

[1] Ralph M. Turner and Lewis M. Killian, *Collective Behavior* (Englewood Cliffs, N.J., 1957), pp. 308–9; Kurt Lang and Gladys Engel Lang, *Collective Dynamics* (New York, 1961), pp. 493, 496–97; Robert F. Berkhofer Jr., *A Behavioral Approach to Historical Analysis* (New York, 1969), pp. 76–79.

tive behavior, one can then analyze its internal characteristics along four dimensions: program, the values which underlie this program, membership and supporters. Of these four, the program or purpose is indispensable, for otherwise there would be no reason for persons to combine and to undertake action. Amid their many disagreements, historians of the progressive movement seem to disagree least on its goals. In fact, they maintain substantially the same definition as Benjamin De Witt offered in 1915: the exclusion of privileged interests from political and economic control, the expansion of democracy and the use of government to benefit the weak and oppressed members of American society.[2] More specifically, the standard list of progressive objectives includes: constraints on monopolies, trusts and big banking interests; regulation of railroad rates; lower tariffs; the direct primary; initiative, referendum and recall; direct election of U.S. Senators; women's suffrage; child- and female-labor laws; pure food and drug laws and conservation.

But as soon as some of these issues are examined in detail, the progressive profile begins to blur. For either the historians or their historical subjects have differed sharply as to whether a "real" progressive subscribed to one or another part of the program. The most familiar debate focused on federal policy toward trusts and has been immortalized in the slogans of "New Nationalism" versus "New Freedom." In 1911 Theodore Roosevelt bitterly rebuked those of his alleged fellow-progressives who wanted to split industrial giants into small competitive units. This kind of thinking, he claimed, represents "rural toryism," a nostalgic and impossible desire for an economic past. Roosevelt preferred to recognize big business as inevitable and to create a countervailing big government. But alas, he lamented, "real progressives are hampered by being obliged continually to pay lip loyalty to their colleagues, who, at bottom, are not progressive at all, but retrogressive."[3] Whether Roosevelt or the rural tories were the more "real" progressives depends, presumably, on which side of the argument one stands. In any case, subsequent historians have echoed the Bull Moose by typically describing the big-business issue as "one of the more basic fault lines" and as "uneasiness and inconsistency" in "the progressive mind"—

[2] Benjamin Parke De Witt, *The Progressive Movement: A Non-partisan Comprehensive Discussion of Current Tendencies in American Politics* (New York, 1915), pp. 4–5; Arthur S. Link, *Woodrow Wilson and the Progressive Era, 1910–1917* (New York, 1954), pp. 1–2, 59; George E. Mowry, *The Era of Theodore Roosevelt and the Birth of Modern America, 1900–1912* (New York, 1958), pp. 41–42, 81, 82; Richard Hofstadter, *The Age of Reform: From Bryan to F.D.R.* (New York, 1955), pp. 5–6, 168, 227, 238, 240, 254, 257; Russel B. Nye, *Midwestern Progressive Politics: A Historical Study of Its Origins and Development, 1870–1958* (East Lansing, Mich., 1959), pp. 183–88; Irwin Yellowitz, *Labor and the Progressive Movement in New York State, 1897–1916* (Ithaca, N.Y., 1965), p. 83.

[3] Roosevelt to Alfred W. Cooley, Aug. 29, 1911, quoted in Mowry, *Era of Theodore Roosevelt*, p. 55.

although this singular split mentality suggests at least schizophrenia, if not two minds.[4]

If this were the only divisive issue within the progressive program, it would not raise serious doubts about the movement's identity. But it is just one of many. The Federal Reserve Act of 1913 created, according to Arthur Link, a conflict between "uncompromising" and "middle-of-the-road" progressives.[5] In another sector of the economy, legislation on behalf of workers split the movement into two factions, whom one historian distinguishes as the more conservative "political Progressives" and the more liberal "social Progressives." But even the latter group disagreed occasionally on the extent and the tactics of their general commitment to social welfare on behalf of labor.[6] A final example of progressive disunity concerns the struggle to achieve women's suffrage, a cause that has generally been attributed to the progressive movement. Yet progressive Presidents Roosevelt and Wilson entered late and grudgingly into the feminists' ranks; William Borah preached states rights in opposition to enfranchisement by federal action and Hiram Johnson never reconciled himself to the idea under any circumstances.[7] More general evidence emerges from a study of two Congressional votes in 1914 and 1915, both of which temporarily defeated the future 19th Amendment. Using a recent historian's list of 400 "progressives," one finds progressive Congressmen almost evenly split for and against women's suffrage.[8]

Thus, several central items in the progressive program divided rather than collected the members of that movement. This fact alone should raise questions and eyebrows, given the definition of a social movement as a "collectivity." Two other issues also deserve attention because their role in the progressive movement, significantly, has divided historians as much as

---

[4] *Ibid.*, p. 55; Hofstadter, *Age of Reform*, p. 245. Recently some historians have claimed that Wilson actually shared Roosevelt's basic economic views, at least before 1913, and that the New Freedom–New Nationalism dichotomy is illusory. So far, however, this revisionist view has not been widely adopted. See James Weinstein, *The Corporate Ideal in the Liberal State: 1900–1918* (Boston, 1968), pp. 162–66; and Gabriel Kolko, *The Triumph of American Conservatism: A Reinterpretation of American History, 1900–1916* (New York, 1963), pp. 205–11.

[5] *Woodrow Wilson and the Progressive Era*, p. 55.

[6] Yellowitz, *Labor and the Progressive Movement in New York State*, pp. 2, 78, 112, and chaps. v–vi, *passim*.

[7] Eleanor Flexner, *Century of Struggle: The Woman's Rights Movement in the United States* (Cambridge, Mass., 1959), pp. 276–79, 307–10; Alan P. Grimes, *The Puritan Ethic and Woman Suffrage* (New York, 1967), pp. 101–3, 129–30; Claudius O. Johnson, *Borah of Idaho*, rev. ed. (Seattle, 1967), pp. 180–83.

[8] Counting votes paired, 19 of 46 progressives voted against the Amendment. Otis L. Graham Jr., *An Encore for Reform: The Old Progressives and the New Deal* (New York, 1967), pp. 213–17; *Congressional Record*, vol. 91, pt. 5, 63rd Cong., 2nd Sess., p. 5108, and vol. 52, pt. 2, 63rd Cong., 3rd Sess., pp. 1483–84.

the progressives themselves. Nativism offers a prime instance. Hofstadter, George Mowry, Oscar Handlin and William Leuchtenburg stress the progressives' more or less vehement repugnance toward the immigrants crowding into urban slums; Mowry even perceives a distinct strain of racism. But Eric Goldman and John Higham dispute this portrait. Although conceding that many progressives were troubled by the influx of foreigners and that a few favored restrictive laws, these two historians claim that progressive sentiment tended to look favorably upon the newcomers. Higham does find a swerve toward nativism among many progressives after 1910; yet Handlin uses the same date to mark increasing progressive cooperation with the immigrants. Still another scholar has at different times taken somewhat different positions. In 1954 Link claimed that immigration restriction was advocated by "many" reform leaders, while in 1959 he attributed it to the entire movement.[9]

The prohibition issue has fostered an equally bewildering disagreement. A few historians refer to prohibition of liquor simply as a progressive measure.[10] Most others, however, discern division within the movement, but they do not draw their dividing lines in the same ways. James H. Timberlake, for example, argues that the liquor question cut the progressive movement into two fairly homogeneous groups: the old-stock middle classes, who favored prohibition; and those identified with the lower classes, who opposed it. When the Senate overrode President Taft's veto of the Webb-Kenyon bill, for instance, nearly all of the midwestern progressives voted dry, whereas half of the wet votes came from the urban-industrial northeast. Studies of progressivism in California, Ohio and Washington confirm this class differentiation.[11] But Andrew Sinclair describes

---

[9] Mowry, *Era of Theodore Roosevelt*, pp. 92–94; Hofstadter, *Age of Reform*, pp. 179–81; Oscar Handlin, *The Uprooted: The Epic Story of the Great Migrations That Made the American People*, pp. 217–20, 224–25; William E. Leuchtenburg, *The Perils of Prosperity, 1914–1932* (Chicago, 1958), pp. 126–27; Eric Goldman, *Rendezvous with Destiny: A History of Modern American Reform* (New York, Vintage ed., 1958), p. 60; John Higham, *Strangers in the Land: Patterns of American Nativism, 1860–1925* (New Brunswick, N.J., 1955), pp. 116–23, 176–77; Link, *Woodrow Wilson and the Progressive Era*, p. 60; Link, "What Happened to the Progressive Movement in the 1920's?" *American Historical Review*, LXIV (July 1959), 847. An analyst of Iowa progressives infers from the larger percentage of foreign-born in his progressive than in his non-progressive sample that the progressive movement was not anti-immigrant: E. Daniel Potts, "The Progressive Profile in Iowa," *Mid-America*, XLVII (Oct. 1965), 261, note 19.

[10] Link, "What Happened to the Progressive Movement in the 1920's?" pp. 847–48; Leuchtenburg, *Perils of Prosperity*, pp. 126–27; George B. Tindall, "Business Progressivism: Southern Politics in the Twenties," *South Atlantic Quarterly*, XLII (Winter 1963), 93–94.

[11] James H. Timberlake, *Prohibition and the Progressive Movement, 1900–1920* (Cambridge, Mass., 1963), pp. 2–5, 163; Spencer C. Olin Jr., *California's Prodigal Sons: Hiram Johnson and the Progressives, 1911–1917* (Berkeley and Los Angeles, 1968), p. 54; Hoyt Landon Warner, *Progressivism in Ohio, 1897–1917* (Columbus, Ohio, 1964), pp. 153, 191, 473; Norman Clark. "The 'Hell-Soaked Institution' and the Washington Prohibition Initiative of 1914," *Pacific Northwest Quarterly*, LVI (Jan. 1965), 10–15.

instead a rural (dry)–urban (wet) split within the progressive movement.[12] Recent investigations by a political scientist and a sociologist propose a third typology, namely that prohibition was supported by those who were rural *and* old middle class.[13] Meanwhile, Hofstadter offers the most ambiguous analysis. On the one hand, he exculpates progressives from the taint of dryness, stating that "men of an urbane cast of mind, whether conservatives or Progressives in their politics, had been generally antagonistic, or at the very least suspicious, of the pre-war drive toward Prohibition." On the other hand, he acknowledges that most progressive Senators voted for the Webb-Kenyon bill in 1913 and that prohibition typified the moral absolutism of the progressive movement.[14]

In the flickering light of these myriad disagreements about progressive goals, both among progressives and their historians, the concept of a "movement" seems very much like a mirage. Not so, replies Hofstadter. "Historians have rightly refused to allow such complications to prevent them from speaking of the Progressive movement and the Progressive era," he contends.

> For all its internal differences and counter-currents, there were in Progressivism certain general tendencies, certain widespread commitments of belief, which outweigh the particulars. It is these commitments and beliefs which make it possible to use the term "Progressive" in the hope that the unity it conveys will not be misconstrued.

Thus Hofstadter finds an integral movement by turning to the values underlying the specific goals. Optimism and activism—these, he says, are the ideological or temperamental traits distinguishing progressives.[15]

Discrepancies emerge quickly, however. As Hofstadter himself notes, threads of anxiety cut across the generally optimistic pattern of the progressive mind. Mowry describes the ambivalence even more emphatically: "the progressive was at once nostalgic, envious, fearful, and yet confident about the future," he writes. "Fear and confidence together" inspired progressives with a sense of defensive class-consciousness.[16] Of course, human attitudes are rarely all of a piece, and certainly not the attitudes of a large

---

[12] *Prohibition: The Era of Excess* (Boston, 1962), pp. 95–96.

[13] Grimes, *Puritan Ethic*, pp. 132–34; Joseph R. Gusfield, *Symbolic Crusade: Status Politics and the American Temperance Movement* (Urbana, Ill., 1963), pp. 7–8, 98–105, 108–9.

[14] Hofstadter, *Age of Reform*, pp. 287 and note, pp. 290, 16.

[15] Hofstadter, ed., *The Progressive Movement, 1900–1915* (Englewood Cliffs, N.J., 1963), pp. 4–5; similarly, Goldman, *Rendezvous with Destiny*, pp. 64–65; Graham, *Encore for Reform*, pp. 10–14; Henry F. May, *The End of American Innocence: A Study of the First Years of Our Own Time, 1912–1917* (New York, 1959), pp. 20–25.

[16] *Era of Theodore Roosevelt*, p. 103.

group of persons. Moreover, this mixture of ideological mood—this ambivalence—fits well into Mowry's and Hofstadter's description of progressives as status-threatened members of the middle class.

Nevertheless, even this more precise generalization about progressive values encounters difficulties, primarily because it is not precise enough. It generalizes to the point of excluding few Americans in the prewar era. As Henry F. May has remarked, the intellectual atmosphere before World War I consisted of a faith in moralism and progress—and almost everyone breathed this compound eagerly. In order to distinguish progressives from others, then, one must specify their values more strictly. Activism, Hofstadter's second progressive trait, at first seems to serve well. Unlike conservatives of their time, progressives believed that social progress could and should come at a faster rate via human intervention, particularly governmental intervention.[17] Yet this ideological criterion works paradoxes rather than wonders. It excludes not simply conservatives, but Woodrow Wilson and all those who subscribed in 1913 to his "New Freedom" philosophy of laissez faire and states rights. In order to salvage Wilson as a progressive, one must expand the definition of progressivism beyond optimism and activism to include a belief in popular democracy and opposition to economic privilege. Wilson's adherence to three of these four values in 1913 qualified him as a progressive, according to Arthur Link, but not as an "advanced progressive." In the latter faction of progressives, who demanded a more active federal government, Link includes socialists, New Nationalists, social workers and others.[18]

This expanded definition of progressive values performs the job required of any definition: distinguishing something from something else. But at the same time it recreates the very subdivisions within the "progressive movement" concept which Hofstadter had sought to overcome. Indeed, this internal fragmentation of the concept does not stop with "advanced" and unadvanced progressives. Robert H. Wiebe and other historians, for example, have discovered numerous businessmen who qualify as progressive by their support for federal economic regulation and civic improvement. But these same individuals diverged sharply in ideology. They doubted man's virtuousness, believed that progress comes slowly, trusted in leaders rather than the masses as agents of progress, and generally preferred to purify rather than extend democracy. In short, their progressive activism blended with a nonprogressive skepticism and elitism. Do these reform-minded businessmen—"corporate liberals," as James Weinstein calls them—deserve membership in the progressive movement? Wiebe claims that they do, despite the ideological exceptions. Weinstein and Gabriel Kolko go further, arguing that these businessmen formed a sa-

---

[17] May, *End of American Innocence*, pp. 9–21.

[18] *Wilson: The New Freedom* (Princeton, N.J., 1956), pp. 241–42.

lient, if not dominant, thrust of influence and ideas within progressivism; they were not merely supporting actors but stars, even directors.[19] Regardless of their exact role in the cast of progressives, their presence introduces still more disconcerting variety into the already variegated historical concept.

The ideological identity of the progressive movement provokes confusion in one final way. "To the extent that they [the Wilsonian Democrats] championed popular democracy and rebelled against a *status quo* that favored the wealthy," Link has asserted, "they were progressives."[20] Yet many progressives, self-styled or so-called or both, spoke in less than wholeheartedly democratic tones. Louis D. Brandeis, for instance, called upon his fellow lawyers to take "a position of interdependence between the wealthy and the people, prepared to curb the excesses of either." Henry L. Stimson nominated for the same mediating role his colleagues in the Republican Party, whom he described as "the richer and more intelligent citizens of the country." Numerous other progressives, drawing upon Mugwump ancestry or teachings, tinged their democratic creed with similar paternalism. As defenders of the middle class, they shared none of the essentially populist fervor expressed by William Jennings Bryan or Samuel (Golden Rule) Jones.[21] They flinched from such unreserved democrats as Robert La Follette, who once declared: "The people have never failed in any great crisis in history."[22] Their misgivings toward immigrants, labor unions and women's suffrage accentuate the boundaries within which many progressives hedged their democratic faith.

Considering this mixed set of values which can be ascribed to the progressive movement, it is hardly surprising that old progressives later diverged drastically in their evaluation of the New Deal. Otis Graham has studied 168 individuals who survived into the 1930s and whom contemporaries or historians have considered "progressive." (He confesses, incidentally, that "we cannot define what the word 'progressive' means with preci-

---

[19] Robert H. Wiebe, *Businessmen and Reform: A Study of the Progressive Movement* (Cambridge, Mass., 1962), pp. 210–12; Weinstein, *The Corporate Ideal in the Liberal State*, esp. pp. ix–xv; Kolko, *Triumph of American Conservatism*. The enigmatic status of these businessmen also holds true for certain politicians. Massachusetts before 1900 instituted many of the democratizing and regulatory laws which progressives would later struggle to achieve elsewhere. In terms of practice, then, Bay State leaders like Henry Cabot Lodge belonged in the progressive movement; but in terms of political philosophy they did not qualify. See Richard M. Abrams, "A Paradox of Progressivism: Massachusetts on the Eve of Insurgency," *Political Science Quarterly*, LXXV (Sept. 1960), 379–99.

[20] *Wilson: The New Freedom*, p. 241.

[21] Quoted in Hofstadter, *Age of Reform*, p. 264. See also Mowry, *Era of Theodore Roosevelt*, chap. v, esp. pp. 89, 103–04.

[22] Quoted in Nye, *Midwestern Progressive Politics*, p. 186.

sion. . . .") Of his sample, he finds five who were more radical than the
New Deal, 40 who supported it, and 60 who opposed it. The remainder either retreated from political concern or left insufficient evidence for evaluation.[23] This scattered, almost random distribution reiterates indirectly the
fact that progressives espoused, at best, a heterogeneous ideology.

Analysis of a social movement begins with its goals and its values because without them there would be no movement. Progressivism lacked
unanimity of purpose either on a programmatic or on a philosophical
level. Nevertheless, these pervasive disagreements need not automatically
preclude the use of a single concept, "the progressive movement," to embrace them all. If the differences of opinion correlate with different socio-
economic groupings among the membership, then the incoherence would
be explained and rendered more coherent. If progressive opponents of
women's suffrage, for example, derived entirely from the South (which, by
the way, they did not), one could deny that "the progressive movement"
vacillated on the issue. One could instead argue that their "southernness"
caused some members of the movement to deviate from progressivism on
this particular question. The exception would prove the rule. Multivariate
analysis would thus find a collective pattern in a seemingly incoherent
group of men and ideas.

Historians have indeed sought to extract such correlations. Russel B.
Nye suggests a geographical criterion: "The reason for the Midwest's failure to produce a national leader," he writes,

> lay in the fact that the movement itself was a distinctively Midwestern
> thing that developed regional politicians who were chiefly concerned with
> regional problems. Progressivism in its Eastern phase—as represented by
> Theodore Roosevelt and Woodrow Wilson—attained national power and
> dealt with national issues, but it was not the same thing.[24]

Unfortunately, this regional dichotomy solves only the problem of leadership; by joining the ideologically incompatible Roosevelt and Wilson, it
does nothing to explain how they belong in the same movement.

Mowry offers a more complex geographical categorization when he
suggests that the Wilsonian "New Freedom" type of progressive came from
regions of farms and small towns in the South and West. Men like Bryan,
La Follette and Governor Albert Cummins of Iowa differed from Roosevelt
by fearing strong federal government and preferring to destroy rather than
regulate trusts.[25] Yet this analysis also collides with the facts. A biographical profile of several hundred Progressive Party leaders and their Republi-

---

[23] *Encore for Reform,* pp. 187, 191–93.

[24] *Midwestern Progressive Politics,* p. 184.

[25] *Era of Theodore Roosevelt,* pp. 54–55.

can opponents in Iowa in 1912 indicates no clear-cut geographical pattern. On the one hand, 70 per cent of the Cummins progressives came from rural or small-town areas. On the other hand, 54 per cent of the Roosevelt progressives came from the same types of places. The difference does tip slightly in favor of Mowry's thesis, but too slightly to sustain his argument.[26]

Attempts to establish a coherent pattern of multiple correlations between progressive factions and progressive ideas apparently lead to a dead end. In fact, even the less ambitious research simply to generalize about the movement's membership has produced baffling inconsistencies. The more that historians learn, the farther they move from consensus. In the 1950s Mowry and Alfred D. Chandler drew the first systematic profiles of progressive leaders in California and the Progressive Party respectively. Their studies produced similar results: progressive leaders were overwhelmingly urban, middle-class, native-born, Protestant, young (often under 40 years of age), college-educated, self-employed in professions or modest-sized businesses, and rather new to politics. Almost none were farmers or laborers.[27] Subsequent composite biographies of progressives in Massachusetts, Washington, Iowa and Baltimore have found virtually identical traits.[28] On the basis of such data, Mowry and Hofstadter have devised their famous theory of "the status revolution": the progressive movement, they say, resulted from the attempts by the old urban middle class, whose status was threatened by the plutocrats above them and the workers and immigrants below, to restore their social position and to cure the injustices in American society.[29]

---

[26] Potts, "The Progressive Profile in Iowa," p. 262. The complete table, in absolute numbers rather than percentages, is as follows:

PROGRESSIVES			
ROOSEVELT	CUMMINS	STANDPATS	
13	23	23	Rural
56	57	56	Towns 500 to 10,000
36	23	27	Cities over 10,000
12	2	15	Cities 30,000 to 50,000
11	10	5	Des Moines

[27] Alfred D. Chandler Jr., "The Origins of Progressive Leadership," in Elting Morison, ed., *The Letters of Theodore Roosevelt* (Cambridge, Mass., 1954), Vol. VIII, Appendix III, pp. 1462–65; Mowry, *The California Progressives* (Berkeley, 1951), pp. 87–89.

[28] Richard B. Sherman, "The Status Revolution and Massachusetts Progressive Leadership," *Political Science Quarterly*, LXXVIII (Mar. 1965), 59–65; William T. Kerr Jr., "The Progressives of Washington, 1910–1912," *Pacific Northwest Quarterly*, LV (Jan. 1964), 16–27; Potts, "The Progressive Profile in Iowa," pp. 257–68; James B. Crooks, *Politics & Progress: The Rise of Urban Progressivism in Baltimore, 1895 to 1911* (Baton Rouge, La., 1968), chap. viii.

[29] Hofstadter, *Age of Reform*, pp. 135–66; Mowry, *Era of Theodore Roosevelt*, chap. v.

Recent research, however, has raised questions both about the reliability of these biographical data and about the validity of the "status revolution" theory. Samuel P. Hays, for example, has found that the municipal-reform movements in Des Moines and Pittsburgh were led by upper-class groups and opposed by both the lower and middle classes.[30] Progressive leaders in Ohio also deviated somewhat from the accepted profile. For one thing, more than 10 per cent of them were laborers; furthermore, the two outstanding figures, Samuel M. Jones of Toledo and Tom L. Johnson of Cleveland, were *nouveaux riches* businessmen who lacked a college education.[31] On a more impressionistic basis Joseph Huthmacher has claimed that members of the urban masses played a larger role in the progressive movement than has hitherto been recognized.[32]

Most challenging, however, is Otis Graham's statistical survey of 140 progressives surviving into the 1930s. Contrary to the urban character described by Chandler and Mowry, 50 per cent of these men and women were raised in small towns and 20 per cent on farms. Even more noteworthy is their diversity of class origins. Fewer than three out of five progressives were born into the middle or upper-middle classes. Almost 20 per cent had "wealthy" parents, while 27 were born in lower or lower-middle economic ranks. By the time of adulthood almost all of them had climbed into or above the middle class, but the fact is that a significant proportion had not begun there.[33]

These various studies refine rather than refute the conventional portrait of the progressive movement. They relieve its uniformly middle-class WASP appearance. But other research has created greater reverberations, threatening to overturn the entire theory of a "status revolution." Composite biographies of progressive leaders in Massachusetts, Iowa, Washington, Wisconsin, and Toledo, Ohio, have generally confirmed the Chandler-Mowry-Hofstadter profile; but they have found almost identical traits in nonprogressives. That is, the progressives resembled their opponents in terms of class, occupation, education, age, religion, political experience and geographical origin. The sociological characteristics which had been presumed to be peculiarly "progressive" turn out to be common to all political leaders of the era. Hence one can no longer explain the progressive movement as the middle-class response to an upheaval in status because nonpro-

---

[30] "The Politics of Reform in Municipal Government in the Progressive Era," *Pacific Northwest Quarterly*, LV (Oct. 1964), 159–61.

[31] Warner, *Progressivism in Ohio*, pp. 22–23, 46 note 2.

[32] "Urban Liberalism and the Age of Reform," *Mississippi Valley Historical Review*, XLIX (Sept. 1962), 231–41. See also the analysis of North Dakota progressives in Michael Paul Rogin, *The Intellectuals and McCarthy: The Radical Specter* (Cambridge, Mass., 1967), pp. 116–20.

[33] *Encore for Reform*, pp. 198, 201–3.

gressives also shared that status.[34] Conversely, many businessmen in the towns and smaller cities of the South and Midwest suffered the anxieties of status decline, but they generally opposed change more often than they sponsored it. Prospering businessmen, not languishing ones, furnished both the ideas and the impetus for reform.[35] In short, any attempt to interpret the progressive movement in terms of status must confront the disconcerting fact that progressive leaders were indistinguishable from their nonprogressive contemporaries.[36]

If efforts to identify a coherent progressive program, ideology and membership shatter against the evidence of incoherence, there is still less hope for success in identifying a homogeneous progressive electorate. Historians working in the ante-computer era had to be content with impressionistic data. In general they claimed that progressivism drew political support from urban middle-class voters as well as farmers and organized labor.[37] So far only a few scholars have investigated this topic with the sophisticated tools of behavioral social science. According to research in the state of Washington, for example, the progressive electorate tended to comprise the more prosperous and educated population, both in agricultural and in urban-industrial areas.[38] In South Dakota, prewar progressives also found support among the rich, but not especially the urban, native-born or Protestant rich.[39] In Wisconsin, on the other hand, Michael Rogin has found that the poorer the county, the higher the progressive vote.[40] His analysis of progressivism in California, South Dakota and North Dakota uncovers still another electoral pattern: namely, a shift from middle-class

---

[34] Sherman, "The Status Revolution and Massachusetts Progressive Leadership"; Potts, "The Progressive Profile in Iowa"; Kerr, "The Progressives of Washington, 1910–1912"; David P. Thelen, "Social Tensions and the Origins of Progressivism," *Journal of American History*, LVI (Sept. 1969), 330–33; Jack Tager, "Progressives, Conservatives, and the Theory of the Status Revolution," *Mid-America*, XLVIII (July 1966), 162–75.

[35] Wiebe, *Businessmen and Reform*, p. 210; Sheldon Hackney, *Populism to Progressivism in Alabama* (Princeton, N.J., 1969), pp. 330–31.

[36] The significance of status anxiety, or status inconsistency—not only in the progressive case, but in general—is very uncertain. Social scientists are earnestly debating whether it bears a reliable relationship to political attitudes. See, e.g., K. Dennis Kelley and William J. Chambliss, "Status Consistency and Political Attitudes," *American Sociological Review*, XXXI (June 1966), 375–82; David R. Segal, "Status Inconsistency, Cross Pressures, and American Political Behavior," *ibid.*, XXXIV (June 1969), 352–59; Gerard Brandmeyer, "Status Consistency and Political Behavior: A Replication and Extension of Research," *Sociological Quarterly*, VI (Summer 1965), 241–56; and Gerhard E. Lenski, *Power and Privilege: A Theory of Social Stratification* (New York, 1966), pp. 86–88.

[37] E.g., Link, "What Happened to the Progressive Movement in the 1920's?" pp. 838–39.

[38] Kerr, "The Progressives of Washington, 1910–1912," pp. 21–27.

[39] Rogin, *Intellectuals and McCarthy*, pp. 144–46.

[40] *Ibid.*, p. 70.

to lower-class support, and in California a shift as well from rural to urban. Theodore Roosevelt's campaign as Progressive Party candidate in 1912, however, did not conform to this latter pattern. According to Rogin, "the electoral evidence questions whether the Progressive Party was typically progressive."[41]

This intriguing, if not bewildering distinction between the legitimacies of big-P and little-p progressivism neatly capsulates the problem. At least since the time that Roosevelt claimed to represent the "real" progressives, the identity of the progressive movement has been in doubt. The more that historians have analyzed it, the more doubtful that identity. In each of its aspects—goals, values, membership and supporters—the movement displays a puzzling and irreducible incoherence. Definition thus becomes a labored process. Arthur Link's effort deserves attention because, in its very concern for precision, it dissolves "the progressive movement."

". . . the progressive movement," he writes,

> never really existed as a recognizable organization with common goals and a political machinery geared to achieve them. [In short, it was not a group, or collectivity.] Generally speaking . . . , progressivism might be defined as the popular effort, which began convulsively in the 1890's and waxed and waned afterward to our own time, to insure the survival of democracy in the United States by the enlargement of governmental power to control and offset the power of private economic groups over the nation's institutions and life. [That is, the movement endured through the New Deal and at least into the Eisenhower years, when Link was writing.] Actually, of course, from the 1890's on there were many "progressive" movements on many levels seeking sometimes contradictory objectives. [The single movement was really multiple and sought not merely various, but inconsistent goals. Yet] the progressive movement before 1918 . . . , despite its actual diversity and internal tensions . . . , did seem to have unity; that is, it seemed to share common ideals and objectives. This was true in part because much of the motivation even of the special-interest groups was altruistic (at least they succeeded in convincing themselves that they sought the welfare of society rather than their own interests primarily). . . .[42]

Link's definition, climaxing in a statement which hovers between paradox and meaninglessness, suggests that historians of the progressive movement are struggling desperately to fit their concept onto data that stubbornly spill over the edges of that concept. Their plight derives largely from the fact that they are dealing with an aggregative group as if it were a collective group. That is, they move from the observation that many

---

[41] *Ibid.*, pp. 120, 148; and Michael Rogin, "Progressivism and the California Electorate," *Journal of American History*, LV (Sept. 1968), 301–3, 305, 308–10.

[42] "What Happened to the Progressive Movement in the 1920's?" pp. 836–37.

Americans in the early 20th century were "reformers" to the assertion that these Americans joined together in a "reform movement." But this logic is elliptical, slurring over the intermediate question of whether the reformers themselves felt a common identity and acted as a collective body. Certainly one would not assume that mystics or conservatives or conscientious objectors constitute "movements" in behalf of their beliefs. Yet students of the progressive movement have made precisely this assumption, only to find that the facts do not form a bridge leading from a progressive aggregate to a genuine progressive collectivity.

When historical evidence resists the historian so resolutely, one must question the categories being used. For those categories are constructs, artifices by which one tries to make sense of the inert and profuse evidence. When they create less rather than more sense, they should be abandoned. As Lee Benson has remarked about "Jacksonian Democracy": "If at this late date the concept remains unclarified, it seems reasonable to doubt that it is solidly based in reality." [43]

Benson rejected the category of "Jacksonian Democracy" and confronted the historical evidence without the distorting preconceptions which it entailed. He began inductively to make a new and better order out of the same data over which historians had quarreled for so long with increasingly contradictory conclusions. "The progressive movement" deserves the same treatment. Because it does not serve to organize the phenomena in coherent ways, it should be discarded. Modifications and qualifications are not sufficient, as Link's effort demonstrates, because they modify and qualify a "movement" that did not exist in historical reality, only in historians' minds.

Nor is a shift of terminology sufficient. George Tindall has tried, for example, to escape Link's dilemma by defining progressivism as "the spirit of the age rather than an organized movement. . . ." [44] The notion of a *Zeitgeist* performs the useful function of periodization, setting these decades apart from the "eras" before and after. But its usefulness stops at the general level of analysis. To speak of a "progressivism" or "the progressive era" is to wrap the entire peiod within an undifferentiated ideological embrace without saying anything about the diversity within the period. One thereby overwhelms the very distinctions which are crucial to an understanding of the conflicts and changes that took place.

Salvage efforts should be resolutely resisted. A diffuse progressive "era" may have occurred, but a progressive "movement" did not. "Progressives" there were, but of many types—intellectuals, businessmen, farmers, labor unionists, white-collar professionals, politicians; lower, middle and

---

[43] *The Concept of Jacksonian Democracy: New York as a Test Case* (Princeton, N.J., 1961), p. 330.

[44] Tindall, "Business Progressivism: Southern Politics in the Twenties," p. 93.

upper class; southerners, easterners, westerners; urban and rural. In explaining American responses to urbanization and industrialization, these socio-economic differences are more important than any collective identity as "progressives." A cotton manufacturer and "unmistakably Progressive" governor like Braxton Comer of Alabama, for example, favored railroad regulation but opposed child-labor laws.[45] Urban machine politicians like Martin Lomasney of Boston and Edwin Vare of Philadelphia, who have usually been ranked as enemies of progressivism, supported the constitutional amendment for direct election of United States senators because this reform would reduce the power of rural state legislators. Significantly, Vare's rival, Boies Penrose, whose machine controlled politics on the state level, opposed the amendment.[46] Thus the conventional label of "progressive" not only oversimplifies the facts, but handicaps effective analysis of them. One might just as well combine Jane Addams, Frances Willard and Edward Bellamy as "reformers," or Andrew Carnegie and Samuel Gompers as "advocates of capitalism."

At this point in historical research, the evidence points away from convenient synthesis and toward multiplicity. The progressive era seems to be characterized by shifting coalitions around different issues, with the specific nature of these coalitions varying on federal, state and local levels, from region to region, and from the first to the second decades of the century.[47] It may be helpful to think of this period in the way that Bernard Bailyn has characterized the first half of the 18th century. The traditional patterns of social values and political interaction gave way under the force of American circumstances, but did not become transformed into a new pattern. Instead, political factionalism and ideological improvisation— what one might call opportunism—became more and more prevalent. Only in the face of British pressure did this fragmentation coalesce sufficiently to form something like a coherent social movement—namely, the Revolution.[48] In contrast to the 18th century, the diverse factions of the early 20th century never experienced the unifying crucible of a crisis. World War I, despite President Wilson's earnest "progressive" rhetoric, was too remote from the domestic concerns of so-called progressives. The war did not create a progressive movement; on the contrary, it served as yet another issue around which the factions formed new coalitions.

---

[45] Hackney, *Populism to Progressivism in Alabama*, pp. 122, 243, 276–77.

[46] John D. Buenker, "The Urban Political Machine and the Seventeenth Amendment," *Journal of American History*, LVI (Sept. 1969), 305–22.

[47] See, e.g., Hackney, *Populism to Progressivism*, esp. chaps. xii–xiii; Richard M. Abrams, *Conservatism in a Progressive Era: Massachusetts Politics, 1900–1912* (Cambridge, Mass., 1964), pp. 235–38; Robert H. Wiebe, *The Search for Order, 1877–1920* (New York, 1967), chaps. vii–viii; John D. Buenker, "The Progressive Era: A Search for a Synthesis," *Mid-America*, LI (July 1969), 175–94.

[48] *The Origins of American Politics* (New York, 1968).

The present state of historical understanding seems to deny the likelihood of a synthesis as convenient and neat as "the progressive movement." In their commitment to making sense of the past, however, historians will continue to search for conceptual order. Perhaps, after further studies of specific occupations, geographical areas and issues, a new synthesis will appear. But if that is to occur, the "progressive" frame of reference, carrying with it so many confusing and erroneous connotations, must be put aside. It is time to tear off the familiar label and, thus liberated from its prejudice, see the history between 1890 and 1920 for what it was—ambiguous, inconsistent, moved by agents and forces more complex than a progressive movement.

SUGGESTED READING

David P. Thelen, in "Social Tensions and the Origins of Progressivism," *Journal of American History,* LVI (Sept. 1969), contends that historians should abandon the effort to define a normative progressive type and instead focus on why different types came together in the Progressive movement. He suggests that for various sectors—rural and urban; lower, middle, and upper class; farmers, workers, and businessmen—the answer may lie in the searing experience of the depression of the 1890's. The result, at least for a season, was cooperation by reformers. In contrast, John Buenker, in "The Progressive Era: A Search for a Synthesis," *Mid-America,* LI (July 1969), abandons the effort to define a normative progressive type or a progressive movement, stresses the divisions along cultural, economic, and geographical lines, finds that there were shifting coalitions based on temporary agreements and without concurrence on philosophies, and concludes that these coalitions were part of the attempt "to cope with the circumstances of the new environment."

An important, often neglected, analysis of progressivism is Samuel P. Hays's "The Politics of Reform in Municipal Government in the Progressive Era," *Pacific Northwest Quarterly,* LV (Oct. 1964). Unfortunately, historians have generally neglected Hays' very important article on municipal reform, though his earlier volume on conservation has influenced Samuel Haber in *Efficiency and Uplift: Scientific Management in the Progressive Era, 1890–1920* (1964) and Roy Lubove in *The Progressives and the Slums* (1963). Hays has more fully developed his ideas in "The Social Analysis of American Political History, 1880–1920," *Political Science Quarterly,* LXXX (Sept. 1965), and in "Political Parties and the Community-Society Continuum," in William N. Chambers and Dean Burnham, eds., *The American Party Systems* ° (1967).

NANCY J. WEISS

From Black Separatism to Interracial Cooperation: The Origins of Organized Efforts for Racial Advancement, 1890–1920

INTRODUCTION

Why, in the years between 1890 and 1920, asks Nancy Weiss of Princeton University, were interracial organizations for racial advancement moderately successful while exclusively black groups failed to maintain themselves or to improve conditions for their race? This striking difference in results, she concludes, can be explained in "large measure" by how these reform groups drew the color line. The racially integrated Urban League and the National Association for the Advancement of Colored People were able to "do something practical" (to quote Gunnar Myrdal) for blacks, but such purely black organizations as the Afro-American

This essay was written especially for this volume. The author wishes to thank Professor James M. McPherson of Princeton University for invaluable assistance in its preparation.

League and the Niagara Movement, as well as the black-led National Equal Rights League, were "disappointments."

All-black groups, Dr. Weiss maintains, could not escape the formidable liabilities of their strategy: black separatism to achieve racial integration. This strategy cut them off from the indispensable financial resources, political power, and legal talent that only whites could supply. Without white support and leadership, these groups could not influence (white) public opinion or even initiate many legal suits to push back the swelling tides of discrimination and segregation.

Even if all-black groups had been prepared to use violent tactics or had sought to organize black communities for protest and self-help, these efforts would have been unsuccessful in opposing discrimination and segregation in an often-hostile white society. Though Dr. Weiss does not deal in depth with these radical approaches, her analysis suggests why they would have failed. Violence by blacks, of course, would have provoked even more violence from whites and would have cost many blacks their lives. Organization of the black community, while perhaps increasing racial pride, could not have effectively provided access to political power, which whites controlled. Nor, given the customary low incomes of blacks, did the community generally have the economic power to use such tactics as boycotts in order to pry concessions from white society. August Meier and Elliot Rudwick have uncovered evidence of approximately thirty boycotts against Jim Crow transportation in southern cities between 1900 and 1906, but only three were even temporarily successful without court intervention.

All-black organizations, Weiss contends, were also disadvantaged by the lack of organizational experience among blacks, by the elitism of the reformers, and by the fierce rivalry for leadership. Because blacks did not have many opportunities for advancement, leadership of a major race organization, she explains, was one of the few avenues to prestige and prominence. Disputes, therefore, were more likely. This intriguing insight will undoubtedly trouble some scholars who may contend that it was neither rivalry for office nor lack of organizational experience but simply the frustrations of blacks struggling to change white society that led to bitter differences.

Some may also question her final judgment that the tactics of the NAACP and Urban League allowed them "to win small but essential victories and to build up a constituency that would eventually support more substantial change." The moderate successes of interracial cooperation might in fact have encouraged blacks to depend on white beneficence and to deny their color and heritage. The great black support for the Garvey movement in the 1920's might suggest that separatism, rather than integration, met the needs of black people by promoting pride in race. If so, then all-black organizations of earlier years were closer (than the NAACP or Urban League) to the appropriate strategy by endorsing black separatism as a tactic—even though these all-black groups aimed for a racially-integrated society. Ultimately, these criticisms, as well as Weiss's conclusions, compel a reexamination of assumptions, but this controversy, like many on racial strategies and goals, is not susceptible to resolution on the basis of empirical evidence and objective standards.

*I*n his classic study of race relations in the United States, the Swedish social economist Gunnar Myrdal wrote, "When we look over the field of Negro protest and betterment organizations, we find that *only when Negroes have collaborated with whites have organizations been built up which have had any strength and which have been able to do something practical.* . . . all purely Negro organizations have been disappointments." [1] Myrdal's observation, published in 1944, is a particularly apt commentary on the experience of the last decade of the nineteenth century and the first two decades of the twentieth—the seminal period for the development of modern racial reform movements. Of the organizations dedicated to racial advancement founded during those years, those that were all black in leadership and membership—especially the Afro-American League (later the Afro-American Council) and the Niagara Movement—soon succumbed to external pressures and internal tensions, making scarcely a dent in the shape of American race relations. Those that were interracial in composition, however—most notably the National Association for the Advancement of Colored People and the National Urban League—began during the 1910's to accomplish some of their objectives and to build durable organizational structures that allowed them to carry the struggle for equality into our own time.

A leading black newspaper of the time, the Washington *Bee*, put the case rather baldly in a scathing summary of the career of W. E. B. Du Bois, founder of both Niagara and the NAACP:

> Dr. Du Bois, without the aid of white people tried to organize the Niagara Movement and keep it going, it soon died. . . . Everything he has attempted without the aid of white people has died, and if . . . liberal and generous-hearted white people . . . were to cease to aid him tomorrow and cease paying his salary, both he and his venture [the NAACP] would drop out of sight. [2]

---

[1] Gunnar Myrdal, *An American Dilemma: The Negro Problem and Modern Democracy* (New York, 1944), p. 853.

[2] Editorial, Washington *Bee*, May 18, 1912.

As the personal animosity between Du Bois and the *Bee*'s editor, W. Calvin Chase, should suggest, the newspaper's account of Du Bois' fortunes, though accurate on its face, does not tell the whole story. Whether they were all-black or interracial is an important, but not a sufficient explanation for the fate of the racial reform efforts of Du Bois and his contemporaries. This article will attempt to evaluate the various factors that determined the fortunes of organizations for racial advancement over the period 1890–1920.

[I]

The comparative fluidity of race relations in the era of Reconstruction deteriorated by the end of the nineteenth century into increasingly rigid segregation and discrimination, so that the 1890's and early 1900's marked what Rayford W. Logan has called "the nadir of the Negro's status in American society." [3] Cities and states enacted Jim Crow legislation disfranchising blacks and prohibiting racial mixing in transportation facilities, public institutions, places of public accommodation, employment, housing, and most other spheres of daily life. The new laws often simply confirmed long-honored customs, and the proscriptions on paper frequently represented only a part of the segregation and discrimination actually practiced.[4]

"The Negro problem" became increasingly national during these years as northward migrations built the foundations of the urban racial ghetto. In 1900, although 90 percent of the nation's 8.8 million blacks still lived in the South, both New York and Philadelphia had black populations exceeding 60,000, while Chicago's was just over 30,000.[5] The Great Migration of the First World War, which brought perhaps 300,000 to 400,000 blacks northward in the space of three years (we have no exact figure), set the future demographic pattern of the black population. The percentage of blacks who lived in urban centers (cities with a population of 2,500 or more) increased from 27.4 in 1910 to 34 in 1920; while the dozen southern cities with more than 25,000 black inhabitants in 1920 witnessed a black

[3] Rayford W. Logan, *The Betrayal of the Negro: From Rutherford B. Hayes to Woodrow Wilson* (New York, 1965), p. 62.

[4] C. Vann Woodward, *The Strange Career of Jim Crow*, 2nd ed., rev. (New York, 1966), Chapter 3; C. Vann Woodward, *Origins of the New South, 1877–1913* (Baton Rouge, La., 1951), Chapters 12–14; David W. Southern, *The Malignant Heritage: Yankee Progressives and the Negro Question, 1901–1914* (Chicago, 1968), Chapter 1; Logan, *The Betrayal of the Negro*, especially Chapter 9.

[5] Bureau of the Census, *Negro Population: 1790–1915* (Washington, 1918), pp. 24, 33; National Urban League, "The Social Adjustment of Negroes in the United States: A Special Memorandum submitted to the President, Franklin D. Roosevelt . . ." April 15, 1933, p. 5, National Urban League Library, New York.

population increase of 20.1 percent over the decade 1910–20, the rate of increase in their twelve northern counterparts was over three times as high, or 62.8 percent.[6]

Statistics underscore the plight of blacks in the early twentieth century. Four-fifths of all those who were employed in 1910 earned their livings in agriculture or domestic and personal service; in a throwback to slavery, three-quarters of all black farmers were tenants or sharecroppers. Black children in 1910 were only three-quarters as likely as whites to be in school, and the rate of illiteracy in the black population, though cut almost in half between 1890 and 1910, was still six times that of whites. Lynching, though on the decline in absolute terms after 1892, became an increasingly brutal and sadistic crime perpetrated more and more exclusively against blacks. The average annual number of lynchings fell from 188 in the 1890's to 93 in the 1900's and 62 in the 1910's, but whereas whites had accounted for 32 percent of the lynch victims in the 1890's, they were only 9 percent of those killed in the 1910's. The intensification of mob violence, marked by riots between 1898 and 1908 in Wilmington, North Carolina, New York, New Orleans, Atlanta, and Springfield, Illinois, culminated in outbreaks of serious racial violence in East St. Louis, Illinois, Chicago, and more than two dozen other cities during the First World War and the "Red Summer" of 1919.[7]

The deterioration of race relations in this period went on with the acquiescence if not encouragement of the federal government. Even the most reform-minded progressives had a negative record on the issue of race. President Theodore Roosevelt was a Social Darwinist who believed "that as a race, and in the mass, the [blacks] are altogether inferior to the whites."[8] Although Roosevelt appointed some qualified blacks to federal offices, relied on the advice of Booker T. Washington, and spoke out against lynching, some of his actions—especially his summary discharge of

---

[6] Bureau of the Census, *Negro Population: 1790–1915*, pp. 24, 73–74, 88; V. D. Johnston, "The Migration and the Census of 1920," *Opportunity*, I (Aug. 1923), 237; William S. Rossiter, *Increase of Population in the United States, 1910–1920*, Census Monographs I (Washington, 1922), p. 124.

[7] Bureau of the Census, *Negro Population: 1790–1915*, pp. 377, 404, 526, 571; James M. McPherson, "The Antislavery Legacy: From Reconstruction to the NAACP," in Barton J. Bernstein, ed., *Towards a New Past: Dissenting Essays in American History* (New York, 1968), pp. 145–46; Walter White, *Rope and Faggot: A Biography of Judge Lynch* (New York, 1929), appendix; Elliott M. Rudwick, *Race Riot at East St. Louis, July 2, 1917* (New York, 1966); Arthur I. Waskow, *From Race Riot to Sit-In, 1919 and the 1960s: A Study in the Connections Between Conflict and Violence* (Garden City, N.Y., 1967), pp. 12–174.

[8] Theodore Roosevelt to Owen Wister, Apr. 27, 1906, in Elting E. Morison, ed., *The Letters of Theodore Roosevelt*, Vol. V (Cambridge, Mass., 1952), p. 226, which is quoted in George Sinkler, *The Racial Attitudes of American Presidents: From Abraham Lincoln to Theodore Roosevelt* (Garden City, N.Y., 1971), p. 318.

three companies of black infantry who refused to inform on their fellows who had allegedly shot up the town of Brownsville, Texas—dismayed and alienated his black supporters.[9] During Woodrow Wilson's administration, already meager black patronage reached new lows, and segregation became the official policy in the federal departments in Washington. President Wilson, who believed in the social separation of the races and who was fond of telling darky stories at cabinet meetings, maintained in the face of strong protests that the Jim Crow arrangements were "to their [the blacks'] advantage." [10]

[II]

In response to these conditions blacks embarked on organized efforts for racial reform. Given the widespread white disaffection from the black cause in the years after Reconstruction, it is not surprising that the notion that blacks could ameliorate their lot by banding together and helping themselves became the dominant faith in the last decades of the nineteenth century. In the transition from the outspoken protest of Frederick Douglass to the accommodationist leadership of Booker T. Washington, blacks turned inward, as if wincing from repeated slaps from white America. With a new emphasis on education and economic self-sufficiency, self-help and racial solidarity became watchwords that applied to the whole spectrum of black activity. All-black business enterprises, schools, churches, social clubs, mutual benefit societies, and fraternal organizations reflected the widespread determination of the race to look to its own for avenues of advancement.[11]

In this atmosphere it made sense that the initial efforts to protest the denial of black rights should also be couched in terms of racial separatism. T. Thomas Fortune, the founder of the Afro-American League, aptly explained the logic of not relying on the good offices of whites: "We think it has been thoroughly demonstrated," he wrote in 1887, "that the white people of this country have determined to leave the colored man alone to fight his battles. . . ." Given the seeming desertion of whites from the cause of black rights, the path was clear: "There is no dodging the issue; we have got to take hold of this problem ourselves, and make so much noise that all

[9] On Roosevelt's racial policies see also Seth M. Scheiner, "President Theodore Roosevelt and the Negro, 1901–1908," *Journal of Negro History*, XLVII (July 1962), 169–82.

[10] Woodrow Wilson to H. A. Bridgman, Sept. 8, 1913, in Ray Stannard Baker, *Woodrow Wilson, Life and Letters*, Vol. IV (Garden City, N.Y., 1931), p. 223. On Wilson's racial policies see also Nancy J. Weiss, "The Negro and the New Freedom: Fighting Wilsonian Segregation," *Political Science Quarterly*, LXXXIV (Mar. 1969), 61–79.

[11] On the development of the ideology of self-help and racial solidarity, see August Meier, *Negro Thought in America, 1880–1915: Racial Ideologies in the Age of Booker T. Washington* (Ann Arbor, Mich., 1963), Part II.

the world shall know the wrongs we suffer and our determination to right those wrongs." [12]

There was already a precedent for this type of organized protest in the Negro convention movement. Negro conventions met irregularly from 1830 to 1890 to protest slavery, segregation, and discrimination, to consider proposals for emigration, and to encourage racial progress through racial solidarity, education, vocational training, economic advancement, and moral uplift. But the conventions never jelled into a sustained national effort: they were sporadic, lacking in continuity, plagued by divided leadership and disagreement over strategy (emigration was one of the most divisive issues), and relatively ineffectual. [13] The first serious attempt to create a permanent, on-going national organization for black protest was the formation of the Afro-American League, the prototype of modern racial reform movements. [14]

The Afro-American League was the brainchild of T. Thomas Fortune, the prominent editor of the New York *Age*, one of the most influential race papers of its day. Fortune called on black leaders to band together in a national organization that could effectively protest disfranchisement, "the universal and lamentable reign of lynch and mob law," discrimination in the distribution of funds for public education, the "odious and demoralizing" southern prison system, and segregation in transportation facilities and places of public accommodation. [15]

The League was designed to help blacks to "take hold of" and attack their problems. It was tacitly understood, although unstated in its constitution, that it would be an organization for blacks only. Of the 141 delegates from twenty-three states who attended the founding convention at Chicago in January 1890, not one was white. No whites had been invited, and mes-

---

[12] New York *Freeman*, May 28, 1887.

[13] Howard Holman Bell, *A Survey of the Negro Convention Movement, 1830–1861* (New York, 1969), *passim;* William H. Pease and Jane H. Pease, "The Negro Convention Movement," in Nathan I. Huggins, Martin Kilson, and Daniel M. Fox, eds., *Key Issues in the Afro-American Experience*, Vol. I (New York, 1971), pp. 191–205; August Meier and Elliott Rudwick, *From Plantation to Ghetto*, rev. ed. (New York, 1970), pp. 107–11, 130–34, 148–49; Meier, *Negro Thought in America*, pp. 4–10, 44, 69–71, 128.

[14] On the connections between the convention movement and the League, see Leslie H. Fishel, Jr., and Benjamin Quarles, *The Black American: A Documentary History* (Glenview, Ill., 1970), p. 325; Meier, *Negro Thought in America*, p. 129, who says that the League was "clearly a continuation of the Convention Movement"; and Robert L. Factor, *The Black Response to America: Men, Ideals, and Organization from Frederick Douglass to the NAACP* (Reading, Mass., 1970), p. 120, who speaks of Fortune's recognition of the weakness of the convention movement and his intention to create an organization to remedy its deficiencies.

[15] New York *Freeman*, June 4, 1887; New York *Age*, Jan. 25, 1890; Factor, *The Black Response to America*, p. 120; Emma Lou Thornbrough, "The National Afro-American League, 1887–1908," *Journal of Southern History*, XXVII (Nov. 1961), 495–96.

sages of interest and advice received from sympathetic whites generated controversy among delegates who mistrusted their intentions.[16]

There were some dissenting voices; for example, a black newspaper in New Orleans, the *Crusader,* greeted the call for the League with editorials deploring the formation of "a distinct Negro organization"; convinced that there were still "white men, loyal and true men" who would be glad to join in a movement for black rights, the *Crusader* warned that "any separate organization, or any drawing of the race or color line in matters of public concern by either side is injurious to both." [17] But Fortune anticipated these criticisms and had a ready answer for those who shrank from a separatist effort: "Whenever colored men talk of forming anything in which they are to be the prime movers and their grievances are to be the subjects to be agitated," he said, "a vast array of men . . . cry aloud that 'colored men should be the last persons to draw the color line.'" What the critics forgot, Fortune noted, was that whites had drawn the color line first—and it was that that necessitated and justified black separatist action. He urged the Chicago convention, "Let us stand up like men in our own organizations where color will not be a brand of odium." [18]

If racial solidarity was to provide the underpinnings for the new organization, agitation and protest were to be its approach. In his address to the founding convention, Fortune defended agitation, even revolution, as necessary and legitimate tools to achieve black rights. It was "time to begin to fight fire with fire. . . . It is time to face the enemy and fight inch by inch for every right he denies us." [19] The League's principal methods—influencing public opinion and seeking court action in cases of denial of black rights—laid the pattern for later, more sophisticated protest organizations; its stated goals—"to break down color bars, . . . [to obtain] for the Afro-American an equal chance with others in the avocations of life, and to . . . [secure] the full privileges of citizenship"—would be repeated almost verbatim throughout the history of protest movements, from the Ni-

---

[16] Thornbrough, "The National Afro-American League," 498; Meier, *Negro Thought in America,* p. 129; Factor, *The Black Response to America,* pp. 120–22.

[17] Excerpted in New York *Age,* Nov. 9, 1889; Feb. 1, 1890. See also Springfield (Ill.) *State Capital,* excerpted in New York *Freeman,* June 25, 1887. In 1889 the Detroit *Plaindealer* conducted an opinion poll on the proposed League and found that several newspaper editors and other individuals opposed the idea of an all-black organization, preferring to draw on people of all races who favored equal rights. See Audrey A. Walker, "An Experiment in Non-Partisanship by the Negro, 1884–1903," unpublished master's thesis, Howard University, 1958, pp. 17, 20. When the League was revived as the Afro-American Council in 1898, similar arguments for a biracial effort were again voiced, most notably by W. Calvin Chase, the editor of the Washington *Bee.* See Walker, "An Experiment in Non-Partisanship," p. 60.

[18] New York *Age,* Jan. 25, 1890.

[19] *Ibid.*

agara Movement of the 1900's to the civil rights movement of the 1950's and 1960's.[20]

Nevertheless, the Afro-American League itself failed to prosper. The reluctance of some leading blacks to lend their active endorsement (for example, Frederick Douglass, P. B. S. Pinchback, and John R. Lynch shied away from the League, along with other professional politicians and most of the black clergy), and the opposition of others to a racially exclusive organization, undoubtedly helped to diminish the group's effectiveness.[21] It was defunct by 1893, and though revived in 1898 under the name of the Afro-American Council,[22] its remaining decade was little more effective than its initial three years. The Council adopted numerous resolutions reiterating Fortune's early statements on black rights and grievances,[23] but with the exception of unsuccessful participation in a couple of test cases of state constitutional provisions disfranchising blacks, it did very little to implement the program it espoused. Lack of adequate financial resources and lack of mass support handicapped the Council as they had crippled the League. The Council's chief problem, however, was that it became a pawn in the battle between Booker T. Washington and his more militant foes. It fell victim to intense internal dissension as supporters of Washington fought successfully to wean it away from its initial militance and to bring it within the sphere of influence of the prominent spokesmen of accommodation. The Council continued to protest, albeit politely, even when it took on a more conciliatory and conservative cast after the turn of the century, but its protests to the outside world were really overshadowed by the debates and struggles within the organization itself.[24]

[III]

The controversy between advocates of accommodation and advocates of protest helped to kill the Afro-American Council, but it also gave birth to

---

[20] Constitution and Address to the Nation of the Afro-American National League, New York, Jan. 25, 1890, in Fishel and Quarles, *The Black American*, p. 326; New York *Freeman*, Sept. 10, 1887; New York *Age*, Jan. 25, 1890.

[21] Walker, "An Experiment in Non-Partisanship," pp. 37–39; Factor, *The Black Response to America*, pp. 126–27.

[22] *Colored American*, Sept. 24, 1898. The new Council had the same objectives as the League; see Mrs. N. F. Mossell, "The National Afro-American Council," *Colored American Magazine*, III (Aug. 1901), 291–305.

[23] For one example, see Address of the Afro-American Council, 1903, in Herbert Aptheker, ed., *A Documentary History of the Negro People in the United States* (New York, 1951), p. 888.

[24] Thornbrough, "The National Afro-American League," *passim*; Stephen R. Fox, *The Guardian of Boston: William Monroe Trotter* (New York, 1970), pp. 46–49; Factor, *The*

the Niagara Movement. The Movement, so named because it originated at a meeting of twenty-nine black leaders near Niagara Falls, Canada, in July 1905, was founded in much the same spirit that had motivated the Afro-American League. Its objective was equal rights for blacks; its method, agitation and protest; its ideology, self-help and racial solidarity. But unlike the Afro-American Council, which moderated its protest as it came under the control of accommodationists, the Niagara Movement remained a radical organization throughout its brief life.

The immediate cause of its founding was the failure to effect a working rapproachement between the warring forces of Booker T. Washington and W. E. B. Du Bois. Du Bois was dismayed at Washington's faith in conciliation and accommodation at a time when any objective measurement showed that segregation and discrimination were growing more intense instead of abating. He felt that the Tuskegeean's emphasis on economic and moral uplift was a case of misplaced priorities; for Du Bois, full civil and political rights were the immediate objective, an objective that could be realized only through outspoken agitation and protest. Washington's ideas were all the more objectionable to Du Bois and his allies because of Washington's near-total influence over the opinions and activities of blacks and the philanthropy and political patronage of whites.[25] The Niagara Movement was both a philosophical declaration of independence from the Tuskegee standard and a vehicle for vigorous action in behalf of black rights. So, at least, the Movement read on paper; in fact, its faltering progress during its brief existence belied the initial promise of its rhetoric.

The objectives of Niagara closely followed those of the original Afro-American League. While neither of them made systematic distinctions between segregation and discrimination, their rhetoric and programs indicate that they saw the two as twin facets of the same problem. The Movement called upon blacks to protest "the curtailment of their political . . . [and] civil rights," "the denial of equal opportunities . . . in economic life," and, in short, "any discrimination based simply on race or color." The men of Niagara sought full manhood suffrage, equal access to public accommodations and to schooling through the college level, equitable treatment before the law, and legislation to enforce the Thirteenth, Fourteenth, and Fifteenth Amendments. Along with these goals went an outspoken espousal of protest; in a clear slap at the accommodationism of Booker T. Washington, the members of the Niagara Movement flatly denied "that the Negro-American assents to inferiority, is submissive under oppression and

---

Black Response to America, pp. 129–30; Meier, *Negro Thought in America*, pp. 130, 172–74, 176, 180–81; Walker, "An Experiment in Non-Partisanship," Chapter 3 and pp. 133–34.

[25] On the Washington–Du Bois controversy, see Meier, *Negro Thought in America*, especially Chapters 7 and 11.

apologetic before insults," and they insisted on "persistent manly agitation," "plain, blunt complaint," and "unfailing exposure to dishonesty and
wrong" as "the ancient, unerring way to liberty." [26]

The program of Niagara echoed the abolitionist tradition and foreshadowed the modern movement for civil rights. As a newspaper reported
of one of its meetings, "it seemed like a revival of the old spirit of
abolitionism—with the white man left out." [27] The white man had been left
out for the same reasons that he had been excluded from the Afro-American League. As J. Max Barber, editor of *The Voice of the Negro* and a par-
ticipant in the Niagara Falls conference, explained, whites had once taken
an active role in pleading and promoting the cause of blacks. Recently,
however, "white men are not so easily found who would take up the cause
of the black man and state it in unmincing words as in the past." And, as a
result, "black men have now come forward to plead their own cause." [28]

The Niagara Movement was more than just a black organization; in
Du Bois' words, it was representative of "the very best class of Negro
Americans." [29] Following Du Bois' theory that leadership and progress
come through the example and exertions of a small elite, the Movement
drew its membership almost exclusively from among the "thoughtful" and
"dignified" blacks who made up the Talented Tenth—doctors, lawyers,
journalists, ministers, educators, and businessmen.[30] In order to protect the
Movement against infiltration by henchmen of Booker T. Washington, prospective members were carefully screened (the Tuskegee machine's success
in planting men to spy on Niagara demonstrated the imperfections in that
procedure). The result of this elitist selectivity, a contemporary wrote, was
to make Niagara into "a cult instead of a crusade." [31]

---

[26] Niagara's Declaration of Principles, 1905, in Aptheker, ed., *Documentary History*, pp.
901–04; Niagara Address of 1906, in Aptheker, ed., *Documentary History*, pp. 907–10;
W. E. B. Du Bois, "The Niagara Movement," *Voice of the Negro*, II (Sept. 1905),
620–21.

[27] Quoted in Ray Stannard Baker, *Following the Color Line: American Negro Citizenship in the Progressive Era* (New York, 1908), p. 224.

[28] "What is the Niagara Movement?" *Voice of the Negro*, II (Sept. 1905), 647.

[29] Quoted in Elliott M. Rudwick, *W. E. B. Du Bois: Propagandist of the Negro Protest*
(New York, 1968), p. 95.

[30] Fox, *The Guardian of Boston*, p. 113; W. E. B. Du Bois, "The Growth of the Niagara
Movement," *Voice of the Negro*, III (Jan. 1906), 43; Du Bois, "The Niagara Movement," 619.

[31] William H. Ferris, *The African Abroad: or His Evolution in Western Civilization;
Tracing His Development Under Caucasian Milieux*, Vol. II (New Haven, Conn., 1913),
p. 912, quoted in Fox, *The Guardian of Boston*, p. 114. On Washington's infiltration of
Niagara, see Elliott M. Rudwick, "The Niagara Movement," *Journal of Negro History*,
XLII (July 1957), 182 (this article is incorporated with minor modifications as Chapter
5 of Rudwick's book *W. E. B. Du Bois*), and Fox, *The Guardian of Boston*, especially
pp. 94, 101.

The narrow base of Niagara's membership foreshadowed the difficulties that would beset its work. Branches of the Movement called public meetings and distributed literature to protest discrimination, and they cooperated with other local protest groups, especially the predominantly white Constitution League. They pressed with a couple of successes for the appointment of blacks to municipal positions, and they brought test cases of Jim Crow laws, with one notable victory involving segregated railroad cars in interstate transportation. And through their lobbying they helped to secure the defeat of an amendment to the Hepburn railroad rate bill that would have sanctioned Jim Crow passenger cars.[32] But their victories were few. Obstructed at every turn by the powerful Tuskegee Machine, the Movement was cut off from important sources of funding and political influence and from powerful organs of the black press. Internally the Movement suffered from factionalism and disorganization; one Massachusetts black was so disgusted by the wrangling at a meeting he attended that he refused to join the organization. "I could not see how . . . [it] could do any effective work," he wrote Du Bois, "where 'good fellowship' seemed to be lacking." [33] Lack of funds made it impossible to institute necessary court suits or to carry out ambitious programs of publicity and education; lack of organization and continuity made it difficult for the various departments and committees of the Movement to do much more than issue annual exhortations to action.[34]

[IV]

It is an oversimplification to say flatly that the failure of the Afro-American Council and the Niagara Movement can be attributed to the single fact that they were all-black organizations. Yet the forces that laid them low are all traceable, at least indirectly, to the problems inherent in the way they chose to draw the color line. In a period when different theories of racial advancement were so hotly debated, an all-black organization could scarcely help but become an ideological battleground. Ray Stannard Baker, the white journalist who made a careful study of race relations during the Progressive Era, made a point of remarking on the fact that blacks

---

[32] J. Max Barber, "The Niagara Movement at Harper's Ferry," *Voice of the Negro,* III (Oct. 1906), 406, 408; Niagara Activities, 1907–08, in Aptheker, ed., *Documentary History,* pp. 914–15; Fox, *The Guardian of Boston,* p. 101; Rudwick, "The Niagara Movement," 190.

[33] Thomas D. Brown to W. E. B. Du Bois, May 24, 1909, W. E. B. Du Bois Papers in custody of Herbert Aptheker, New York.

[34] Francis L. Broderick, *W. E. B. Du Bois: Negro Leader in a Time of Crisis* (Stanford, Calif., 1959), pp. 77–78; Fox, *The Guardian of Boston,* p. 101; Rudwick, "The Niagara Movement," *passim.*

were "so torn by cliques and divided by such wide differences of opinion" over how to handle "their own problem." [35] For Oswald Garrison Villard, grandson of the famed abolitionist William Lloyd Garrison and himself a principal founder of the NAACP, "the way the colored people fight among themselves" was "the thing that discourages me more than anything else about the colored situation." [36] Blacks, too, lamented the apparent inability of the leaders of the race "to work together harmoniously"; "We must learn," Booker T. Washington wrote, "to lay aside . . . personal differences and subordinate . . . personal opinions to the general welfare. . . . In this respect white people excel us so very much." [37]

The fierce personal and philosophical struggle for race leadership in the late 1890's and early 1900's made all the institutions of the black community especially vulnerable as spoils of the battle. This was true of the pulpit and the press, but it was especially true of organizations specifically dedicated to racial advancement. For Irish Catholics, the routes to power in America were so well established at this time that Charles Francis Murphy, an untutored product of New York's Lower East Side, could take control of Tammany Hall and the New York Democratic organization in 1902 without the slightest factional struggle.[38] But no such pattern for the acquisition of authority had yet been set in black America. Since leadership of a successful organization for racial advancement could very well mean recognition as the national spokesman for the race, the competion for influence and control was especially keen.

Intraracial friction resulted not only from ideological disputes between Washingtonians and Du Boisians, but also from clashes of personality and ambition between aspiring leaders of similar ideological persuasions. In the most notable example, Du Bois described Boston *Guardian* editor William Monroe Trotter, once his ally in the anti-Washingtonian ranks, as a splendid person in many respects, but one who was impossible to work with unless Trotter was in command.[39] Their inability to cooperate seemed to one contemporary observer to be "chiefly responsible for the dissolution of the Niagara Movement." [40] Part of the problem was that their

---

[35] Baker, *Following the Color Line*, pp. 216–17.

[36] To Francis Jackson Garrison, Oct. 23, 1906, Oswald Garrison Villard Papers, Houghton Library, Harvard University.

[37] To Daniel Murray, Mar. 6, 1904, Booker T. Washington Papers, Box 4, Manuscript Division, Library of Congress.

[38] See Nancy Joan Weiss, *Charles Francis Murphy, 1858–1924: Respectability and Responsibility in Tammany Politics* (Northampton, Mass., 1968).

[39] To Alexander Walters, April 7, 1908, Du Bois Papers.

[40] Reverdy C. Ransom, *The Pilgrimage of Harriet Ransom's Son* (Nashville, Tenn., n.d.), p. 164, quoted in Fox, *The Guardian of Boston*, p. 114. See also Logan, *The Betrayal of the Negro*, p. 342, and Rudwick, "The Niagara Movement," 200.

difficult personalities made it hard to subordinate temperamental differences. But each of them was also personally ambitious and thus unwilling to yield to the other's direction. It was little wonder that the Detroit *Plaindealer* felt that "as a race, we have produced more 'leaders' and fewer followers than any people under the sun." [41]

The pressures of internal dissension and external sabotage spawned by the tension between aspiring leaders and between theories of accommodation and protest were simply too much for a fledgling black organization to survive. But even without such handicaps, lack of money, organizational experience, and a secure popular base made it difficult for any protest organization to succeed. Blacks in the decades after Reconstruction had little money to give to such an effort; moreover, many of the wealthiest blacks who had successfully made their way in the white world and who might have made significant contributions eschewed protest activities, emulated upper- and middle-class whites, and deliberately avoided all possible identification with the plight of the black race as a whole. Given the prevalence of accommodationist theories, whatever philanthropy they engaged in was more likely to be directed toward black education or local mutual benefit and social service ventures.[42]

The black community of the late nineteenth and early twentieth century was also short on practical organizational experience. In the words of Booker T. Washington,

> Another element of weakness which shows itself in the present stage of the civilisation of the Negro is his lack of ability to form a purpose and stick to it through a series of years, if need be,—years that involve discouragement as well as encouragement,—till the end shall be reached.

"The same," Washington correctly observed, "would be true of any race with the Negro's history." [43] Given their background of enslavement and exploitation, blacks could not have been expected immediately to succeed at getting together and pursuing goals that would benefit the race. The years around the turn of the century were the seminal period for black self-help. There had to be some opportunity for trial and error, some opportunity to gain solid, practical knowledge of how to go about creating and sustaining a working national protest organization. Because of their place in time, the Afro-American Council and the Niagara Movement could not help but be affected by these burdens.

---

[41] May 6 and June 3, 1892, quoted in Otto H. Olsen, *Carpetbagger's Crusade: The Life of Albion Winegar Tourgee* (Baltimore, 1965), p. 318.

[42] Arnold M. Rose, *The Negro's Morale: Group Identification and Protest* (Minneapolis, 1949), pp. 67–68, 71–72, offers a useful analysis of the reluctance of upper- and upper-middle-class blacks to support black protest activities.

[43] Booker T. Washington, *The Future of the American Negro* (Boston, 1899), pp. 167–68.

The elitist cast of the membership of these organizations further handicapped their efforts. Deliberately separated from white America, these men and women were equally distant from the black masses. Many of the leaders of the Niagara Movement and the Afro-American Council scorned and mistrusted the great mass of poorly educated, lower-class blacks. For the majority of blacks, the principles for which the race leaders fought often seemed to have little practical relevance to the immediate, daily struggle for survival. In the case of the Afro-American League, its domination by editors and the absence from its ranks of politicians and preachers automatically handicapped its communication with a heavily illiterate, or at least nonreading, black population. Most blacks, even many among the Talented Tenth, were not yet ready to embrace the vigorous protest that Niagara in particular espoused.[44] This inability to gain mass support was certainly not peculiar to all-black organizations (it was later a liability of the National Urban League and the NAACP), but its impact on them was especially acute, for it left them in a kind of limbo, lacking the clout that came either from alliance with influential whites, or from the actively massed support of thousands of blacks.[45]

All of the foregoing disabilities were in some respect functions of the racial exclusiveness of the Afro-American Council and the Niagara Movement. Yet the reason for their failure lies not only—not even primarily—within the organizations themselves. The fortunes of any organization working for racial advancement depended directly on the mood of white America. And in the era of the Afro-American Council and the Niagara Movement, the years of the national apotheosis of Jim Crow, the political and economic power centers of the country simply were not paying very much attention to the plight of blacks.

It is this last point—the crucial role of whites in the progress of black men—that explains the ultimate, indeed the necessary ineffectiveness of all-black efforts for racial advancement in the early twentieth century. Given the objectives they posited and the field they set out to cover, black self-help was an appropriate, viable approach for the work of any limited, local organizations, such as fraternal organizations, mutual benefit societies, women's clubs, and church groups.[46] But the larger, different objec-

---

[44] Rudwick, "The Niagara Movement," 198–99; Rose, *The Negro's Morale*, p. 32; Factor, *The Black Response to America*, p. 126; Logan, *The Betrayal of the Negro*, p. 342; Fox, *The Guardian of Boston*, p. 113.

[45] Nor was the lack of close contact with the masses peculiar to this period; see Ralph J. Bunche, "The Programs of Organizations Devoted to the Improvement of the Status of the American Negro," *Journal of Negro Education*, VIII (July 1939), 547; Myrdal, *An American Dilemma*, p. 835.

[46] Booker T. Washington, *The Story of the Negro: The Rise of the Race from Slavery*, Vol. II (New York, 1909), Chapters 6 and 12; W. E. Burghardt Du Bois, ed., *Efforts for Social Betterment among Negro Americans* (Atlanta, 1909), *passim;* Meier, *Negro Thought in America*, Chapter 8.

tives of national racial reform movements hinged inextricably on white action. Voting rights, jobs, access to places of public accommodation—the
whole list of black grievances—depended for their resolution on white cooperation. The anomaly of separatist efforts to secure integration was more
than a matter of semantics; it made little practical sense not to enlist sympathetic whites in the struggle at hand.

Interracial cooperation found sanction in the leading black thinking
of the day. Both Booker T. Washington and W. E. B. Du Bois subscribed
to an ideology of self-help and racial solidarity, but they also recognized
the essential role of whites in racial progress. "While it is a great truth to
say that the Negro must strive and strive mightily to help himself," Du
Bois wrote in his famous *Souls of Black Folk*, "it is equally true that unless
his striving be not simply seconded, but rather aroused and encouraged,
by the initiative of the richer and wiser environing group, he cannot hope
for success." His message throughout that book was that blacks, like "all
backward peoples," needed "cooperation," "leadership," and "training"
from whites in order to realize "effectual progress." [47]

While Washington urged blacks to pull themselves up by their own
bootstraps, he also reminded them time and again that the common destiny
of the two races made interracial cooperation essential to black advancement. "Any movement for the elevation of the Southern Negro" needed
"the cooperation," "the sympathy and support of the best white people" in
order to succeed. For whites, after all, "control government and own the
property. . . ." [48] This lesson applied equally in the North and in the
South. It was fundamental to the progress of any minority group: where
the desired changes in minority status depended on some exercise of power
by the majority, it was essential to enlist sympathetic and influential members of the majority in the minority's cause.

[V]

The shift from self-help to organized interracial cooperation manifested itself in the foundation at the close of the first decade of the twentieth century of what were to become the two major interracial organizations in
the field of racial advancement—the National Association for the
Advancement of Colored People (founded 1909–10) and the National
Urban League (founded 1910–11). Although these organizations shared
only a few of the same personnel, their supporters as a group were ex-

---

[47] W. E. Burghardt Du Bois, *The Souls of Black Folk* (New York, 1903), pp. 53, 79, 126,
128–29, 132.

[48] E. Davidson Washington, ed., *Selected Speeches of Booker T. Washington* (Garden
City, N.Y., 1932), pp. 2, 75–77; Booker T. Washington, *My Larger Education* (Garden
City, N.Y., 1911), pp. 23–24.

tremely similar.[49] They drew upon the same kinds of black leaders that had been active in the Afro-American Council and the Niagara Movement. Born primarily in the South during the Civil War and Reconstruction, the blacks who sat on the boards of the NAACP and the Urban League in the 1910's had become pillars of the black professional and business communities in New York and other major cities, North and South. They were the success stories of black America: doctors, lawyers, ministers, educators, businessmen, and publicists, four-fifths of whom had gone to college, more than half of whom held graduate degrees. They were not always wealthy, but their exceptional educational backgrounds and their occupations marked them as leading members of the tiny black upper-middle and upper classes—a group that typically scorned lower-class lifestyles (even though it generally depended on the black masses for its livelihood), imitated the values and culture of white middle-class America, and exhibited a "conservative outlook" on life.[50]

The most crucial difference between the NAACP and the Urban League and their predecessors lay in their reliance on whites. Like the progressive movements, the NAACP and the League in the 1910's drew heavily on the nation's white Anglo-Saxon Protestant, upper-middle-class, urban elite. Their white board members were extremely well-educated; nearly three-fourths had attended college, with the large majority of these earning degrees and going on to graduate study.[51] They were predominantly pro-

---

[49] The names of the board members of the NAACP and the Urban League during the 1910's were compiled from notices of annual elections to the boards in *Crisis* and in the minutes of the League's annual meetings, National Urban League Papers, Manuscript Division, Library of Congress. Charles Flint Kellogg, *NAACP: A History of the National Association for the Advancement of Colored People*, Vol. I: 1909–1920 (Baltimore, 1967), pp. 304, 306, lists the NAACP's boards for 1910 and 1912. The biographical information on which the collective biographical portraits in the text are based comes principally from the various editions of *Who's Who in America* and *Who's Who in Colored America*, and from obituaries in the New York *Times*, as well as from other biographical dictionaries. In all, forty-nine men and women (eleven blacks, thirty-six whites, two race unknown) are known to have been members of the Urban League's board during the 1910's and fifty-two (twenty-two blacks, twenty-nine whites, one race unknown) served on the NAACP's board. The generalizations in the text are based on information about the forty-seven Urban Leaguers and fifty-one NAACP board members who have been positively identified.

[50] This is E. Franklin Frazier's description in *Black Bourgeoisie: The Rise of a New Middle Class in the United States* (New York, 1957), p. 91. Other useful analyses of the black upper-middle and upper classes are St. Clair Drake and Horace R. Cayton, *Black Metropolis: A Study of Negro Life in a Northern City* (New York, 1945), Chapters 16–19, 22, and Myrdal, *An American Dilemma*, Chapters 14 and 32.

[51] Most of the NAACP and Urban League board members would have been in college sometime between the late 1870's and early 1890's. To give some idea of how unusually well-educated they were, the percentage of all eighteen- to twenty-one-year-olds in the United States who were attending college was 2.72 in 1880 and 3.04 in 1890. Those who actually graduated were considerably fewer—roughly 1 percent of the twenty-two-year-olds in each of those years received bachelor's degrees. (*Historical Statistics of the United States: Colonial Times to 1957* [Washington, 1960], pp. 211–12.)

fessionals; two-thirds of the Urban Leaguers and four-fifths of the NAACP board members were lawyers, educators, social workers, publicists, or ministers,[52] while the rest (with one or two exceptions) were businessmen or philanthropist-reformers. Their average age on joining the board was forty-one for the League and forty-six for the NAACP—old enough to have carved out secure positions in their professions and in their communities. Four-fifths of them lived in New York,[53] the financial, professional, and communications center of the nation. Strongly influenced by the social justice currents of the Progressive Era, they were articulate, respected spokesmen, both nationally as well as locally, for a wide range of progressive reforms.

The NAACP and the Urban League by tacit understanding divided between themselves the great tasks in the work of racial advancement.[54] Cast in the mold of neoabolitionism, the NAACP fought to secure for black citizens the political and civil rights guaranteed them under the constitution of the United States. Its founding came as a response to the rigidification of Jim Crow and the increasing racial repression of the 1890's and early 1900's. In seeking integration and equal rights for blacks, the organization worked chiefly through political and legal channels and advocated public protest and agitation as legitimate, indeed essential, tools for influencing policy. During its first decade, the NAACP used private lobbying and public protest in an unsuccessful effort to overturn the Wilson administration's policy of segregation in government agencies and discrimination in federal appointments. It began a long series of court tests to secure the enforcement of the Fourteenth and Fifteenth Amendments, and it won some victories: a Supreme Court decision in 1915 outlawed grandfather clauses in state voting requirements and another in 1917 prohibited residential segregation by city ordinance. It launched a decades-long campaign against lynching and provided legal assistance for victims of racial violence and Jim Crow justice. The organization initiated efforts to stop discrimination in education and professional activities. Sometimes it was necessary to retreat to an endorsement of separate-but-equal tactics, as in its successful efforts to open military officers' ranks to blacks, which resulted in separate training camps.[55]

---

[52] In 1910, 1.3 percent of the employed blacks over ten years of age and 4.9 percent of the employed whites earned their livings as professionals; see Bureau of the Census, *Negro Population: 1790–1915*, pp. 503, 510.

[53] In 1910, 5.2 percent of the United States population came from New York City; see Bureau of the Census, *Thirteenth Census of the United States Taken in the Year 1910*, Vol. I: *Population, 1910: General Report and Analysis* (Washington, 1913), pp. 26, 86.

[54] For an account of the division of work between the NAACP and the Urban League, see Nancy Joan Weiss, " 'Not Alms, But Opportunity': A History of the National Urban League, 1910–1940," unpublished doctoral dissertation, Harvard University, 1969, Chapter 2.

[55] Kellogg, *NAACP, passim.*

The Urban League was dominant in the areas of economic opportunity and social welfare. The League came into existence in response to the plight of blacks in northern cities in the early part of the twentieth century. The NAACP, although it added its "first distinctively southern member" (a black man) to its board only in 1919,[56] dealt mainly with southern problems, while the Urban League in the 1910's worked chiefly in the North. Its efforts during its corresponding first decade were much quieter and much less controversial than those of the NAACP. It sought jobs and decent housing for migrants and offered them counseling on behavior, dress, sanitation, health, and homemaking. It trained black social workers and placed them in such community service positions as family caseworkers, probation officers, settlement house workers, supervisors of day nurseries and boys' and girls' clubs, and travelers' aid workers. The League unsuccessfully petitioned the American Federation of Labor to end lily-white union policies. And it conducted scientific investigations of conditions among urban blacks as a basis for practical reform.[57] While the NAACP used the tactics of protest and agitation, the Urban League's tools were primarily those of negotiation, persuasion, education, and investigation. It emphasized economic opportunity and social adjustment rather than political and civil rights, and it stressed private, friendly conciliation rather than overt protest or lobbying in its relations with white employers.[58]

Both the NAACP and the National Urban League were concerned that blacks be accorded the full responsibilities and opportunities of first-class citizenship. Both conceptualized segregation and discrimination as interrelated aspects of the same problem, even though occasionally their short-run efforts dealt more with inequality of treatment than with the fact of racial separation. The NAACP, like its most important black founder W. E. B. Du Bois, believed that ensuring recognition and free exercise of the legal rights of blacks was the most important task at hand. The Urban League, on the other hand, more in the spirit of Booker T. Washington, wanted to make certain that blacks would be prepared, through a stake in the nation's economy and a mastery of the perils of city life, to assume the burdens and rewards of being a citizen.[59]

---

[56] *Crisis*, XVII (Jan. 1919), 122.

[57] Weiss, " 'Not Alms, But Opportunity,' " especially Chapters 3–5.

[58] On the differing types of protest strategies, see James H. Laue, "The Changing Character of Negro Protest," American Academy of Political and Social Science, *The Negro Protest* (Philadelphia, 1965 [originally a special issue of *Annals*, CCCLVII, Jan. 1965]), pp. 121–22.

[59] For an exposition of these approaches, see, for example, Whitney M. Young, Jr., "Civil Rights Action and the Urban League," in Arnold M. Rose, ed., *Assuring Freedom to the Free: A Century of Emancipation in the USA* (Detroit, 1964), pp. 210, 213; Willis D. Weatherford and Charles S. Johnson, *Race Relations: Adjustment of Whites*

Just as the NAACP and the Urban League shared the same ultimate goals but differed in their tactical approaches and programmatic emphases, so they shared the common guiding principle of interracial cooperation but differed in their experience with its practical application. The founders of both organizations were extremely conscious of interracial cooperation as a fragile experiment; they believed that whites and blacks could make distinctive, mutually reinforcing contributions to the cause of racial advancement, but they recognized that bringing the two races together on an equal footing would be a delicate task.

Du Bois had written in 1903 that "Human advancement is not a mere question of almsgiving, but rather of sympathy and cooperation among classes who would scorn charity"; he came away from the organizational meetings for the NAACP with a "vision of future co-operation," not the old kind "between giver and beggar," but rather "a new alliance between experienced social workers and reformers," whites and blacks "in touch on the one hand with scientific philanthropy and on the other with the great struggling mass of laborers of all kinds, whose condition and needs knew no color line." [60] In the same spirit, the founders of the Urban League took particular pains to point out that interracial cooperation meant just what it said, and not the antagonism and paternalism so often characteristic of black-white relationships; whites were "to be asked to work WITH Negroes for their mutual advantage and advancement rather than working *for* them as a problem." [61]

In espousing cooperation, both the Urban League and the NAACP paid conscious heed to Booker T. Washington's insistence on the interdependence and common destiny of the black and white races. Ruth Standish Baldwin, widow of the president of the Long Island Railroad and cofounder of the League with the black sociologist George Edmund Haynes, expressed this ideal of interracial cooperation most succinctly in a statement that would become the League's informal credo: "Let us work, not as colored people nor as white people for the narrow benefit of any group alone, but *together* as American citizens, for the common good of our com-

---

and Negroes in the United States (Boston, 1934), p. 541; Francis L. Broderick and August Meier, eds., *Negro Protest Thought in the Twentieth Century* (Indianapolis, 1965), p. xxv; "The Answer to the 'Negro Problem,'" *Coronet*, XXV (Apr. 1949), 132.

[60] Du Bois, *The Souls of Black Folk*, p. 138; W. E. Burghardt Du Bois, "National Committee on the Negro," *Survey*, XXII (June 1909), 409.

[61] George Edmund Haynes, "The Birth and Childhood of the National Urban League," Apr. 20, 1960, pp. 8–9, Urban League Folder, Moorland Foundation, Howard University. See also George Edmund Haynes, "Interracial Social Work Begins," National Urban League, *40th Anniversary Year Book, 1950* (New York, 1951), p. 7; Chicago *Defender*, May 4, 1935; and George Edmund Haynes, "The American Interracial Problem and Techniques of Interracial Cooperation," undated mimeographed notes for address to Dayton Public Forums, in George Edmund Haynes scrapbooks in possession of Mrs. George Edmund Haynes, Mt. Vernon, New York.

mon city, our common country." [62] Urban League literature made so much
of interracial cooperation that it sometimes sounded as though the organization believed it had invented the concept. This was obviously an exaggeration, but it is probably true that no group institutionalized or publicized interracial cooperation quite so strongly as the Urban League, which
congratulated itself on its "greatest achievement"—transforming "this idea
from mere academic formula into vigorous reality." [63]

On a practical level, interracial cooperation very often meant white
domination in terms both of numbers and influence. Only about one-sixth
of the members of the Urban League's first executive board were black,
and the proportion of black members fluctuated between one-quarter and
one-third during the remaining years of the 1910's. The League's officers
(with the exception of most of the vice presidents) were white, but the operating staff, including the executive secretary, was always entirely black.
The NAACP came closer to a real racial balance in its early boards of
directors (in 1910 and 1912, for example, about two-fifths of the members
were black), but during the organization's first decade, its entire executive
leadership was white, with the exception of W. E. B. Du Bois, director of
publications and research and editor of *Crisis*. The president, the chairman
of the board, and the chairman of the legal committee continued to be
white for many years, but James Weldon Johnson became the Association's
first black executive secretary in 1920, and from that point on, the practical
"day by day work" of the organization remained in the hands of blacks.[64]

Although there was never any debate at the time of their founding
over whether the NAACP and the Urban League should be interracial organizations, there was considerable soul-searching during the 1910's over
whether interracial leadership would work. The cause of the questioning
was the flare-up of intraorganizational disputes, which seemed to some of
those involved to be the outgrowth of racial friction. At the Urban League,

---

[62] To L. Hollingsworth Wood, June 1, 1915, in Executive Board Minutes, National
Urban League Papers. Also quoted in New York *Age*, June 17, 1915. For many years,
every sheet of Urban League stationery carried this quotation printed on its reverse
side. Robert L. Jack, *History of the National Association for the Advancement of Colored People* (Boston, 1943), p. 98, quotes the NAACP's *Fourteenth Annual Report*
(1923), p. 39, to the effect that one of the basic principles of the NAACP was "that the
destinies of the Negro and white races of the American continent are inseparable; that
the races must, therefore, in the fullest sense work together for the realization of the
principles on which the American nation was founded."

[63] "Editorials: The Urban League—Twenty-Five Years," *Opportunity*, XIII (Nov. 1935),
327. See also National Urban League, *The Urban League—Its Story* (New York, 1938),
p. 3, pamphlet in Arthur A. Schomburg Collection, New York Public Library; *Opportunity*, VIII (Mar. 1930), 71; and E. Franklin Frazier, who credits the League with "first
[projecting] a plan of inter-racial cooperation in attacking the race problem. . . ." in
"Social Work in Race Relations," *Crisis*, XXVII (Apr. 1924), 254.

[64] Rudwick, *W. E. B. Du Bois*, p. 130; Broderick, *W. E. B. Du Bois*, p. 91; Mary
White Ovington, *The Walls Came Tumbling Down* (New York, 1947), pp. 111, 176; Kellogg, *NAACP*, p. 291.

as might be expected both from its more conservative bent and from the fact that blacks from the first dominated its working staff, such interracial tensions were, at least on the surface, minimal. There were minor indications that George Haynes was not always treated by whites in a manner befitting the organization's chief executive officer. L. Hollingsworth Wood —secretary of the League, Mrs. Baldwin's successor as president, and from the beginning one of its most influential white members—apparently did not know his executive secretary well enough to avoid addressing him as "Haines." At one point in 1915 Haynes was forced into a protracted correspondence with Wood and assistant treasurer Victor H. McCutcheon (also white) over permission to buy a $21 file cabinet with a lock for his office.[65] Yet these incidents were, at most, probably no more than indications of an unconscious paternalism on the part of the whites involved.

The major conflict within the League developed as a power struggle between Haynes, who was based in Nashville to organize and teach in a department of sociology at Fisk University and to develop a pioneering program for training black social workers, and his black assistant executive secretary, Eugene Kinckle Jones, who was in daily charge of the main office in New York. In part a dispute over priorities in the development of the League's work, it ended with the appointment in 1918 of Jones as full-time executive secretary, and, eventually, Haynes' resignation from the organization.[66] Such jockeying for position and influence was hardly surprising in view of the mere handful of leadership positions open to blacks in any organization at that time. That it did not seriously weaken the Urban League, as such internal disputes had in the case of the Afro-American Council and the Niagara Movement, is at least partly attributable to the stabilizing influence of the League's white officers.

Unlike the experience of the Urban League, interracial friction within the NAACP became so strong during the 1910's that its leaders began to question the validity of the interracial premises on which the organization was based. The trouble centered around W. E. B. Du Bois, and while the principal root of the problem was his difficult personality that made it hard for him to work harmoniously with anyone, white or black, the fact that he was the Association's sole black executive at that point caused the tensions to appear to be a function of race. In addition to temperamental clashes, the substantive issue at stake involved the degree of independence Du Bois would have in the editing and management of *Crisis*.[67]

There were continuing tensions between Du Bois and the NAACP's

---

[65] Haynes to Wood, Oct. 4, 7, 19, and 25, 1915; Wood to Haynes, Oct. 5 and 9, 1915; Haynes to McCutcheon, Oct. 8, 1915; McCutcheon to Haynes, Oct. 13 and 22, 1915; all in George Edmund Haynes Papers, Erastus Milo Cravath Library, Fisk University.

[66] Weiss, " 'Not Alms, But Opportunity,' " Chapter 6.

[67] For a full account of the friction, see Kellogg, *NAACP*, Chapter 5; Fox, *The Guardian of Boston*, pp. 141–44; Rudwick, *W. E. B. Du Bois*, pp. 165–78.

white executive secretaries, first Frances Blascoer and then May Childs Nerney, largely because of personal friction and the ill-defined line of demarcation between the duties of the secretary and the director of publications and research.[68] The major conflict of jurisdiction, however, came between Du Bois and the chairman of the board, Oswald Garrison Villard. Villard understood his position as chairman—"*the* executive of the association"—to give him "certain authority over the paid staff." [69] But Du Bois balked at Villard's direction concerning *Crisis:* "I count myself not as your subordinate but as a fellow officer," he told Villard, and he expected to exercise "reasonable initiative and independence in carrying out my part of the work," subject to orders from no one but the full board.[70] The upshot of the controversy was that Villard resigned as chairman of the board.

Although his resignation stemmed from an honest jurisdictional dispute, compounded by personality conflicts (Du Bois himself admitted that his temperament was "a difficult one to endure"), Villard's apparent attempts to yoke Du Bois smacked of racial tensions. His resignation dismayed one of the NAACP's key white board members, Mary White Ovington, who called it "a confession to the world that we cannot work with colored people unless they are our subordinates." The rift, she felt, would have ramifications well beyond the NAACP:

> everyone who believes in segregation will become a little more firmly convinced that he is right. And when we demand that some colored man be put in office and be given a place in which he will be the equal of a white man, we shall be told, "You can't give a nigger a big job. Haven't you found it out yourselves." It puts us back five years.[71]

Du Bois, too, felt that his problems with his white colleagues were motivated by a more fundamental problem; unconscious prejudice, he said, was the "*real* rift in the lute." [72]

There was probably some basis for Du Bois' attribution of the difficulties within the NAACP to racial tensions. Even the most dedicated of

---

[68] Oswald Garrison Villard to Francis Jackson Garrison, Feb. 7 and 11, 1913, Villard Papers; May Childs Nerney to Archibald Grimke, Nov. 2, 1913, Archibald Grimke Papers, Moorland Foundation, Howard University; Kellogg, *NAACP*, pp. 93–94, 101, 103.

[69] Oswald Garrison Villard to Joel Spingarn, Mar. 20, 1913, Joel E. Spingarn Papers, Moorland Foundation, Howard University. See also Oswald Garrison Villard to Board of Directors, NAACP, Nov. 19, 1913, Villard Papers.

[70] Memorandum from W. E. B. Du Bois to Oswald Garrison Villard, Mar. 18, 1913, Villard Papers.

[71] W. E. B. Du Bois to Joel E. Spingarn, Oct. 28, 1914, James Weldon Johnson Collection, Beinecke Library, Yale University; Mary White Ovington to Oswald Garrison Villard, Nov. 23, 1913, Villard Papers.

[72] W. E. B. Du Bois to Joel E. Spingarn, Oct. 28, 1914, Johnson Collection.

the Association's white leaders had been guilty of lapses of outright pater- nalism. The comments of white participants after the founding conference of the National Negro Committee in 1909 (it became the NAACP in 1910) revealed that they had not yet become accustomed to accepting blacks as equal partners. "I find myself still occasionally forgetting that the Negroes aren't poor people for whom I must kindly do something," Mary White Ovington wrote, "and then comes a gathering such as that last evening, and I learn they are men with most forceful opinions of their own." [73] Or, as Oswald Garrison Villard, the presiding chairman of the conference, de- scribed it, "All of the speeches from the floor were by colored people—how they do love to talk!—and hardly one was relevant, while not one contrib- uted anything of value." [74]

It is easy to understand why such attitudes, even if unconsciously held and infrequently expressed, should have combined with Du Bois' su- persensitivity and natural suspicion of white intentions to make tensions that could have occurred in any organization regardless of racial complex- ion seem in this situation to be a function of race. It was probably inevita- ble in such circumstances, with Du Bois' opponents generally all white, that in discussions of the distribution of power within the Association "the old race issue would be played to the nth degree." [75] Whites found them- selves defenseless against "the attempt, always fatal, to put all our difficul- ties on the ground of race prejudice"; the charge that prejudice, conscious or not, underlay disputes within the NAACP was virtually impossible to refute but equally difficult to avoid,[76] so that some of the organization's white officers came to the conclusion that the only way to eliminate persis- tent racial tensions would be for them to resign and be replaced by blacks.[77]

Du Bois took the conflict within the NAACP as a symptom of the dis- ease that had stricken previous interracial efforts for racial advancement: "No organization like ours ever succeeded in America," he wrote his friend Joel Spingarn, who had followed Villard as chairman of the board; "either it became a group of white philanthropists 'helping' the Negro like the Anti-Slavery societies; or it became a group of colored folk freezing out their white co-workers by insolence and distrust. Everything tends to this

---

[73] Mary White Ovington to Oswald Garrison Villard, June 2, 1909, Villard Papers.

[74] Oswald Garrison Villard to Francis Jackson Garrison, June 4, 1909, Villard Papers. See also Fox, *The Guardian of Boston*, pp. 142–43, for more evidence of the ambivalent racial attitudes of whites in the NAACP.

[75] May Childs Nerney to Archibald Grimke, Oct. 15, 1914, Grimke Papers.

[76] May Childs Nerney to Archibald Grimke, undated letter, 1913 file, Grimke Papers.

[77] May Childs Nerney to Archibald Grimke, Oct. 15, 1914; Joel E. Spingarn to Archi- bald Grimke, Dec. 16, 1915; both in Grimke Papers.

break along the color line." [78] It was all too easy, as Du Bois later explained in his autobiography, for whites, by virtue of "superior training or
. . . influence or . . . wealth," to take charge and use "the colored membership as their helpers and executive workers. . . ." If blacks should attempt
to take control, "the whites become dissatisfied and gradually withdraw."
The way to save the NAACP—"the experiment"—he told Spingarn, was
"by trusting black men with power." [79]

And the way for blacks to exercise real power in an interracial organization, Du Bois had come to believe, was to recognize the inevitability of
"the color line" and divide the work of the NAACP into two co-equal
branches, one headed by a black official, the other by a white. He hoped
that Spingarn, whom he felt was free of the prejudice that had affected Villard, would see things his way; but within a year of his quarrel with Villard, he found himself in the same kind of jurisdictional dispute with Spingarn. Du Bois demanded complete control over the affairs of *Crisis*,
including its financing, but Spingarn balked, and the board backed him up.
It seemed to Du Bois that he was being relegated to a position as Spingarn's assistant. The NAACP, he told one of his black friends on the board,
was falling into the old trap: it was becoming an organization of whites
working for blacks but refusing to give blacks real power.[80]

Du Bois' difficulties with the white leadership of the NAACP reem-
phasized his essential ambivalence on the question of tactics in the struggle for racial advancement. For while he supported the interracialism of
the NAACP and looked toward integration as the ultimate goal; he also
advocated self-help and self-sufficiency in racial institutions as a short-run
vehicle for progress. The separatist side of Du Bois came out in a 1915 editorial in *Crisis* exhorting blacks to "not only support but control this [the
NAACP] and similar organizations and hold them unwaveringly to our objects, our aims and our ideals." [81] Although he distrusted whites, Du Bois
compromised enough to continue as editor of *Crisis* until 1934. And despite
his distress over the rifts the color line caused within the Association, he
felt, at least in retrospect, that the NAACP had managed "to an unusual
degree . . . to achieve an equality of racial influence without stressing race
and without allowing undue predominance to either group." [82]

------

[78] W. E. B. Du Bois to Joel E. Spingarn, Oct. 28, 1914, Johnson Collection.

[79] Ibid.; W. E. Burghardt Du Bois, *Dusk of Dawn: An Essay Toward an Autobiography
of a Race Concept* (New York, 1940), p. 227.

[80] W. E. B. Du Bois to Joel E. Spingarn, Oct. 28, 1914, Johnson Collection; Du Bois to
George W. Crawford, Nov. 23, 1914, Du Bois Papers; Kellogg, *NAACP*, pp. 101–04.

[81] Quoted in Rudwick, *W. E. B. Du Bois*, p. 171. See also Broderick, *W. E. B. Du
Bois*, pp. 100–04.

[82] Du Bois, *Dusk of Dawn*, p. 227.

[VI]

Wary of the tensions inherent in interracial efforts, not all blacks chose to follow Du Bois' path of compromising and working with whites in order to gain the benefits their influence and support might bring to the cause of racial advancement. The most notable holdout was Boston *Guardian* editor William Monroe Trotter, first and most outspoken of the anti-Washingtonian radicals. Trotter shied away from the NAACP because he believed that it would be dominated by whites.[83] As early as 1903 he had founded his own protest group, the Boston Suffrage League (which quickly became the New England Suffrage League and then the National Negro Suffrage League), as an alternative to an Afro-American Council dominated by Washington. That League never amounted to anything, and in April, 1908, Trotter and a handful of other black radicals founded the Negro-American Political League. The immediate impulse for the new organization was the desire to defeat the Republicans in the upcoming presidential election. The League went through various reincarnations as the National Independent Political League, the National Independent Political Rights League, the National Independent Equal Rights League, and finally the National Equal Rights League.[84]

The NERL's purpose was "to organize Americans of African extraction or descent for concerted, collective action locally and nationally against every denial of justice, of liberty, of political and of civil rights . . . and to inculcate racial self-respect which calls for assertion of equal rights and privileges."[85] Like the NAACP, it was a protest organization dedicated to seeking integration and equal rights; in addition, it encouraged blacks to form an independent voting bloc in order to have some political leverage, and it actively supported or opposed candidates for political office on the basis of their stand on the race issue.[86]

Trotter chose to go his own way for several reasons. He saw an "urgent, fundamental need" for both "racially autonomous organizations" and "friend-helping cooperative organizations" in the struggle for racial advancement. He believed that the central role of whites in the NAACP would have a moderating influence on what he considered to be essential

---

[83] Rudwick, *W. E. B. Du Bois*, p. 125; Fox, *The Guardian of Boston*, p. 130.

[84] Fox, *The Guardian of Boston*, pp. 76–77, 82, 110–12, 162, 179, 186; Charles W. Puttkammer and Ruth Worthy, "William Monroe Trotter, 1872–1934," *Journal of Negro History*, XLIII (Oct. 1958), 305.

[85] NERL constitution in Boston *Guardian*, July 14, 1923, p. 4, quoted in Fox, *The Guardian of Boston*, p. 240.

[86] See Fox, *The Guardian of Boston*, Chapter 5, on its political activities.

radical tactics and objectives. Although his group always included a few whites, he thought that a black-run organization was the proper vehicle for the fight for black rights, and he was proud of the fact that the NERL was "an organization of the colored people and for the colored people and led by the colored people." As an egotist and a difficult personality in his own right, he preferred the independence and absolute control available to him in the NERL to the compromises and shared spotlight that would come with the NAACP. And finally, as a foe of Du Bois, he could hardly work comfortably within the same organization.[87]

The NERL may have succeeded in satisfying Trotter's psychic needs, in providing a vehicle for his personal militance, and in answering the need he saw for at least one black-led protest group on a national level. But attractive as it may have been in principle, it was a practical failure. Relations between the NAACP and the NERL were strained to the point that Trotter complained that the NAACP ought to "be free from the spirit of decrying or slighting equal rights organizations whose members and officers are colored, free from even the appearance or suspicion of wishing to destroy or weaken or tacitly disdain such."[88] The two organizations constantly clashed; their objectives and methods were the same, and their efforts along parallel lines inevitably overlapped and caused trouble. In the case of the fight against Wilsonian segregation policies, the NAACP and the National Independent Political League (an earlier version of the NERL), each jealous and suspicious of the other, scrambled to be the first to reveal the administration's continuing misdeeds and thus win points as the leader of the protest. More than once the NAACP, having laid careful plans for a protest effort, found Trotter's group ready to jump the gun with independent action likely to upset the favorable atmosphere the NAACP had labored to create.[89]

"There are individual sharpshooters fighting their own effective guerilla warfare," Du Bois conceded in *Crisis*. "We greet them and give them all credit. There are a few organizations here and there with some activity. We would not detract a moment from the value of their work." But the concession was guarded at best; despite the efforts of others, Du Bois asserted, the fact remained that the NAACP was "the battle line"—the only protest group in the country "with permanent headquarters, paid officials, active nation-wide membership, live local branches, a national organ, law officers and traveling organizers, all organized and prepared to make a front forward fight on racial prejudice in this land."[90] Although Du Bois

---

[87] Quoted in Fox, *The Guardian of Boston*, pp. 140, 202. See also pp. 141, 280, and Puttkammer and Worthy, "William Monroe Trotter," 304–06.

[88] William Monroe Trotter to Joel Spingarn, Jan. 2, 1913, Spingarn Papers.

[89] Fox, *The Guardian of Boston*, pp. 141, 161, 173–75, 244–45, 280.

[90] *Crisis*, VII (1913–14), 133–34, quoted in Fox, *The Guardian of Boston*, p. 176.

was obviously boasting, he also put his finger on the distribution of power in the fight for black rights; the NAACP survived to win victories for racial advancement, while the NERL was little more than a paper organization by the 1920's and is now all but forgotten.

[VII]

Certainly Trotter's lack of organizational talent, his inability to get along with others, and the internal schisms that split his League [91] accounted for a large part of the NERL's failure. But the basic reason it died while the NAACP flourished was that the NAACP, like the National Urban League, enjoyed the obvious advantages of interracial leadership. Not the least of these was financial. The black community alone could never have funded the organizations, whether because of poverty, apathy, or conservatism, and the simple realities of race relations in the early decades of this century meant that it took white spokesmen to secure substantial white money. Close to nine-tenths of NAACP members were black by 1919, but blacks (largely through membership dues) accounted for only half of the organization's annual income. The Urban League, which was not a mass-membership organization, did not even have this reservoir of dollar and two-dollar contributions. In the years for which records are available by race, blacks contributed only about 10 percent of the funds received by the League, and figuring out methods of increasing black support was a matter of recurring concern to the executive board, since "white friends" would be more likely to increase their contributions if "the colored people who have met with prosperity" demonstrated their willingness "to share it with their less fortunate brothers." [92]

The officers of the Urban League were predominantly white, a former president of the organization has explained, "on the premise that we were dependent on white money." [93] The bulk of the League's funds came from a handful of white contributors, many of whom had personal or professional ties to its officers or board members. For example, John D. Rockefeller, Jr., who through personal gifts and the Laura Spelman Rockefeller Memorial became the League's single largest donor, had developed a close association with William H. Baldwin, Jr., through the General Education Board, and the friendship carried over to Ruth Standish Baldwin after her husband's death. Another of Baldwin's friends, Andrew Carnegie, made

---

[91] On the splits within the League, see Fox, *The Guardian of Boston*, pp. 164–65.

[92] National Association for the Advancement of Colored People, *Tenth Annual Report, 1919* (New York, 1920), pp. 84–86; Eugene Kinckle Jones to "My dear M . . . ," Mar. 24, 1920, Robert Russa Moton Papers, General Correspondence, Box 17, Tuskegee Institute. For other evidence of the continuing efforts to increase black contributions, see Weiss, " 'Not Alms, But Opportunity,' " pp. 418–22 and n. 60, p. 422.

[93] William H. Baldwin to Nancy J. Weiss, Apr. 30, 1969.

small personal contributions to the League, with much larger sums coming from the Carnegie Corporation of New York. Chicago philanthropist and department store–mail order house magnate Julius Rosenwald's ties to the League were cemented through his friend and cousin Paul J. Sachs, who was a member of the executive board.[94]

The irony is that it took millionaires to fund such modest operations. The Urban League's budget for its first year was only $8,800, and the NAACP subsisted on an annual income of between $11,000 and $15,000 from 1912 to 1917.[95] That the organizations had to resort to men like Rockefeller and Rosenwald to come up with such pitifully small sums testifies to just how hard it was to summon support for racial advancement in the 1910's.

Besides providing financial assistance, the interracial leadership of the NAACP and the Urban League gave the fight for racial advancement prestige, powerful contacts, professional skills, and a broader, potentially more receptive audience.[96] When the NAACP, anxious to head off the formation of a rival organization to its Washington branch, pointed out that "no other organization or committee can possibly have the influence back of it that ours has through such representatives as Mr. [Oswald Garrison] Villard with his powerful paper, Mr. [Moorfield] Storey, one of the greatest lawyers in this country, Mr. Jacob H. Schiff and many others that we might name," it was no idle boast.[97] The time and professional talents of white leaders—lawyers like Storey, Clarence Darrow, Paul D. Cravath; bankers like Paul J. Sachs or Algernon S. Frissell; social workers like Jane Addams, Lillian Wald, Mary White Ovington—were essential to the efforts of both the NAACP and the Urban League. Few blacks had the education, training, financial resources, and leisure to enable them to devote themselves to the low-paid or voluntary work of these organizations.[98]

---

[94] National Urban League Executive Board Minutes, Mar. 6, 1912, pp. 6–7, in L. Hollingsworth Wood Papers, in custody of Mrs. L. Hollingsworth Wood and Mr. and Mrs. James Wood, Mount Kisco, New York; William H. Baldwin to Nancy J. Weiss, Feb. 28, 1969; Paul J. Sachs to Julius Rosenwald, June 27, 1914; Rosenwald to Sachs, June 30, 1914, both in Julius Rosenwald Papers, Box 18, University of Chicago Library; Edwin R. Embree and Julia Waxman, *Investment in People: The Story of the Julius Rosenwald Fund* (New York, 1949), pp. 25, 179–80. For additional information on the financial relationship to the League of these and other major donors, see Weiss, " 'Not Alms, But Opportunity,' " pp. 405–15.

[95] National Urban League, Budget—1911–1912, Wood Papers; Kellogg, *NAACP*, pp. 106–07.

[96] Meier, *Negro Thought in America*, p. 182; Rose, *The Negro's Morale*, p. 33; Kellogg, *NAACP*, p. 118.

[97] May Childs Nerney to the Manager of the Afro-American Company, July 20, 1915, National Association for the Advancement of Colored People Papers, Manuscript Division, Library of Congress.

[98] August Meier and Elliott Rudwick, "Radicals and Conservatives: Black Protest in Twentieth-Century America," in Peter I. Rose, ed., *Americans from Africa*, Vol. II: *Old*

The NAACP's legal work is a case in point. A dearth of trained, competent black lawyers made it essential that volunteer white attorneys handle the bulk of the work for a number of years. But the reliance on white lawyers was a matter of advantage as well as necessity. When Harvard-trained Boston Brahmin Moorfield Storey, a former president of the American Bar Association, argued the grandfather clause case before the Supreme Court, he brought to bear personal connections, experience, and influence that Butler R. Wilson, a leading black Boston lawyer who had to struggle to win admission to the ABA because of his race, could simply never have mustered.[99] Similarly, Oswald Garrison Villard, editor of the widely read New York *Evening Post,* could reach—and thus possibly educate and influence—a much larger, more powerful audience than Fred R. Moore, editor of the black New York *Age,* could ever have hoped to command. Urban League board members like Felix Adler, Roger N. Baldwin, and Sophonisba P. Breckinridge brought the League training in social work and practical experience in social service and reform that were invaluable in the development of its work. Comparable professional guidance and support could not have come from blacks, since there was no body of professional black social workers to draw from at the time the League was founded.

White leadership and support gave the NAACP easy access to the ears of public officials and the pages of influential newspapers and journals; it enabled the Urban League to gain a hearing from major employers, union leaders, community chests, and local, state, and federal government officials and agencies. Moreover, important white endorsement gave the organizations' work (which was, in the context of the times, both controversial and, in the case of the NAACP, radical) a stamp of respectability and credibility and a chance for success that it would not otherwise have had.

Given the distribution of power in the United States and the nature of the objectives of the NAACP and the Urban League, they could not have functioned in the early part of the twentieth century without white support. As Gunnar Myrdal wrote,

> the power situation is such in America that Negroes can never hope to break down the caste wall except with the assistance of white people. Indeed, the actual power situation makes it *an obvious Negro interest and,*

Memories, New Moods (New York, 1970), p. 125; Kellogg, *NAACP,* p. 293; Ovington, *The Walls Came Tumbling Down,* p. 111; Wilson Record, "Negro Intellectual Leadership in the National Association for the Advancement of Colored People: 1910–1940," *Phylon,* XVII (Fourth Quarter 1956), 381–82; Weiss, " 'Not Alms, But Opportunity,' " Chapter 11.

[99] In fact, in 1903, when the Afro-American Council was preparing a test case of an Alabama voter registration law, there was only one black lawyer in the country who had ever won a case before the Supreme Court. See Thornbrough, "The National Afro-American League," 508–09.

>*consequently, a general American interest to engage as many white groups as possible as allies in the struggle against caste.*[100]

White leadership and support gave the organizations access to and some influence with the white political, economic, and social establishment that held the power to change significantly the way in which American blacks were being forced to live.

But despite these advantages, the actual accomplishments of the NAACP and the Urban League were quite limited. White support provided an important opening wedge for change, but the resistance of white power centers made any progress painfully hard to achieve. For example, the NAACP's fight against the imposition of segregation in the federal departments failed largely because it came up against the personal prejudices of the President and members of his cabinet, the personal preferences of white civil service employees, and the hard facts of national politics. The NAACP could persuade, petition, or hold protest meetings, but even its ultimate weapon—the threat of active political opposition in the next election—carried little weight at a time when most blacks were barred by legal devices or white pressure from going to the polls. It was politically more advantageous to the President to cultivate the support of southern congressional powers for important pieces of progressive legislation than it was to risk alienating them by pressing for the appointment of black officials or for the establishment of a National Race Commission to investigate the problems of blacks.[101] Comparable political considerations were to play a large part in the frustration of the NAACP in its efforts to secure federal antilynching legislation. The Urban League's attempts to open jobs to blacks encountered the hostility of organized labor, the refusal of whites to work side by side with (or under the authority of) blacks, and the convictions of employers concerning the untrustworthiness and limited abilities of black workers. None of these attitudes could be quickly overcome.[102] Both the NAACP and the Urban League succeeded admirably in finding friends in high places, in enlisting white allies in their struggle, and in pursuing paths to reform traditionally sanctioned by the dominant white majority.[103] But white America was just not ready to redress the centuries-old heritage of discrimination and denied opportunities for its black minority.

---

[100] Myrdal, *An American Dilemma*, p. 853.

[101] Weiss, "The Negro and the New Freedom."

[102] Weiss, " 'Not Alms, But Opportunity,' " Chapters 4 and 9.

[103] Robert L. Zangrando, "The 'Organized Negro': The National Association for the Advancement of Colored People and Civil Rights," in James C. Curtis and Lewis L. Gould, eds., *The Black Experience in America* (Austin, Tex., 1970), pp. 153–58.

These organizations can hardly be faulted for playing by the rules of American reform. The slow, laborious process of investigation, publicity, protest, education, legislation, and court action duplicated the methods of the progressives and their predecessors in their campaigns for social justice and economic and political reform.[104] Though these tactics may have been inadequate to bring on the virtual revolution in race relations that justice demanded, they were the only realistic way at that time to chip away at the edifice of segregation and discrimination. To be sure, other groups in the early part of the century—particularly radical labor organizations—tried more drastic tactics;[105] but given the nature of their leadership, the NAACP and the Urban League could hardly have been expected to embrace the I.W.W.'s program of picketing, sit-down strikes, and sabotage. Besides, the entire top leadership and many of the rank and file of the I.W.W. landed in jail by the late 1910's; though the efforts of the NAACP and the Urban League fell far short of their ultimate goals, their tactics at least enabled them to win small but essential victories and to build up a constituency that would eventually support more substantial change.

Ralph Bunche was no doubt right in pointing out the drawbacks to the route of interracial cooperation and progressive-style reform; it seems self-evident that white influence and the need "to create a sympathetic response . . . among influential elements in the controlling [white] population" necessarily muted the militance of organizations working for racial advancement.[106] Yet in the political and intellectual climate that prevailed, and in light of the passivity of the black masses, there was no real constitu-

---

[104] *Ibid.*, pp. 153–54.

[105] Some blacks in this period also tried what would today be construed as more "radical" tactics. There were black boycotts of newly-segregated streetcars in the South and schools in the North, but these were in fact essentially conservative efforts designed to recapture an unsegregated status quo. See August Meier and Elliott Rudwick, "The Boycott Movement Against Jim Crow Streetcars in the South, 1900–1906," *Journal of American History*, LV (Mar. 1969), 756–75, and, by the same authors, "Negro Boycotts of Jim Crow Schools in the North, 1897–1925," *Integrated Education*, V (Aug.-Sept. 1967), 57–68. In the heat of passions provoked by the Atlanta riot of 1906, Oswald Garrison Villard and some of his abolitionist relatives raised the possibility of boycotts or even a black general strike to underscore demands for black rights. But Villard continued to believe that the "best" methods of racial protest were "argument . . . and reason," and he and the others steadfastly rejected violence. These more sober views prevailed later in the ideology and program of the NAACP. See Villard's speech to the Afro-American Council, Oct. 10, 1906, copy in Villard scrapbook; Francis Jackson Garrison to Villard, Oct. 24, 1906; and Villard to Robert E. Jones (editor of the *Southwestern Christian Advocate*), in an undated letter in reply to Jones to Villard, Dec. 1, 1906, all in the Villard Papers; as well as William Lloyd Garrison, Jr., to Francis J. Grimke, Oct. 30, 1906, and Francis Jackson Garrison to Grimke, Nov. 6, 1906, both in Carter G. Woodson, ed., *The Works of Francis J. Grimke*, Vol. IV (Washington, 1942), pp. 101–02.

[106] Ralph J. Bunche, "A Critical Analysis of the Tactics and Programs of Minority Groups," *Journal of Negro Education*, IV (July 1935), 316.

ency and no real prospect of success for greater militancy in the first decades of the century.

Progress depended on convincing whites of the essential fairness and indeed expediency of equal justice and opportunity for blacks; it depended also on the politicization, urbanization, and education of the black masses. The circumstances that made possible the effectiveness of nonviolent direct action in the 1950's and 1960's did not exist, either in the receptivity of the white population or in the condition of blacks. During the years 1890–1920, hardly more than a generation removed from the demise of Reconstruction, blacks were still in considerable part an ex-slave population, concentrated primarily in the rural South (and thus geographically as well as culturally distant from the base of operations of the NAACP and the Urban League). Their educational level, political consciousness, and sense of group identity were still barely above a minimum. Within such a population it would have been difficult to forge an effective instrument of protest. For the NAACP and the Urban League, the difficulty of the task was compounded by the nature of their leadership. Well-educated, middle- and upper-middle-class, relatively prosperous, and securely established in business and the professions, these men and women, black or white, had the experience, talent, connections, and wherewithal to make each organization a going concern. What they lacked, however, was an inherent personal understanding of the problems and experiences of the black masses. Bridging this class gap was an enormous task that the organizations' leaders were generally unable to accomplish.[107]

The efforts of interracial cooperation suffered, then, first from an inability to dissipate the deep-rooted, firmly held prejudices of white America. They were hampered, too, by their elitist orientation that precluded effective mobilization of the black masses. Finally, they suffered from the inability of blacks to present a united front. An account of tensions confronting the NAACP in the 1920's by James Weldon Johnson, the organization's first black executive secretary, serves equally well to describe the situation in earlier decades; he had to struggle, Johnson said, "to rouse Negroes themselves from apathy, to win over hostile factions and bring about joint action within the race." The problems of the NAACP stemmed not only from "outside forces antagonistic to the Negro race," but from the "envies, bickerings, rancors, . . . pure maliciousness . . . [and] honest opposition" of blacks themselves.[108]

Common to many organizations, such strains were especially pronounced in the fledgling protest organizations because of the newness of

---

[107] Zangrando, "The 'Organized Negro,'" 153–58; and Weiss, "'Not Alms, But Opportunity,'" pp. 374–403, describe the leadership of the two organizations.

[108] James Weldon Johnson, *Along This Way: The Autobiography of James Weldon Johnson* (New York, 1933), p. 408.

their effort and the scarcity of choice leadership positions for blacks; they could not help but hamper the organizations' effectiveness. Moreover, ideological and personal conflicts such as those between the Washingtonians and the Du Boisians and between Du Bois and Trotter helped to sustain white resistance to change insofar as they demonstrated that blacks themselves could not agree on the direction change should take. "Wouldn't it be a glorious thing," the Chicago *Defender* mused, "if the Booker T. Washington faction, the Du Bois faction, and the Monroe Trotter faction would get together on a common ground and fight unitedly for the things that they are now fighting singly for?" [109]

But the *Defender's* hope remained only a dream at the close of the second decade of the century, and despite a unity conference of important black leaders at Amenia, New York, in the summer of 1916 (which Trotter failed to attend), little significant progress was made toward harmony among the different viewpoints and organizations (indeed, yet another element of divisiveness would emerge with the rise of Marcus Garvey).[110] The proliferation of organizations—both loose factions and formal groups—in the same fight without meaningful coordination of their efforts was inefficient and destructive to their ultimate goal. As the NAACP warned a potential rival organization in the nation's capital, "we fear that this idea of organizing another Vigilance Committee is simply the old story of division and disagreement which has been the history of the colored people for the last sixty years. . . . To start another organization will not help colored people but in the end will hurt them as it will be regarded everywhere by thinking people as another evidence of disorganization.[111]

Given these obstacles, the beginning of organized interracial protest could hardly have been expected to have brought racism and discrimination to a definitive end. That these organizations accomplished what they did testifies to the benefits of interracial cooperation; that they accomplished so little in face of the tremendous need is proof of the depths of American racism.

SUGGESTED READING

August Meier's *Negro Thought in America, 1880–1915: Racial Ideologies in the Age of Booker T. Washington* ° (1963), a study by a white liberal active in the civil rights movement, is a sensitive,

---

[109] Chicago *Defender*, Jan. 9, 1915, quoted in Fox, *The Guardian of Boston*, p. 187.

[110] On Amenia, see Rudwick, *W. E. B. Du Bois*, pp. 185–90, and Fox, *The Guardian of Boston*, pp. 202–04.

[111] May Childs Nerney to the Manager of the Afro-American Company, July 20, 1915, NAACP Papers.

thoughtful volume that notes, among other themes, that Booker T. Washington privately sought to undermine racial segregation, which his accommodationist public expressions countenanced and justified in the short run. W. E. B. DuBois, Washington's chief ideological adversary among black reform leaders, is the subject of Elliott M. Rudwick's *W. E. B. DuBois: Propagandist of the Negro Protest,*° 2nd ed. (1968) and Francis L. Broderick's *W. E. B. DuBois: Negro Leader in a Time of Crisis* ° (1959). Stephen R. Fox's *The Guardian of Boston: William Monroe Trotter* ° (1970), an expanded honors thesis written originally at Williams College, is the only substantial study of Trotter. Emma Lou Thornbrough's "The National Afro-American League, 1887–1908," *Journal of Southern History,* XXVII (Nov. 1961), and Elliott Rudwick's "The Niagara Movement," *Journal of Negro History,* XLII (July 1957), which is quite similar to a chapter in his book on DuBois, are the best studies of these two organizations. Charles Flint Kellogg's *NAACP: A History of the National Association of Colored People, 1909–1920* (1967) is a useful survey of the organization's early history. James McPherson, in "The Antislavery Legacy: From Reconstruction to the NAACP," in Barton J. Bernstein, ed., *Towards A New Past: Dissenting Essays in American History* ° (1968), examines the post–Civil War attitudes of abolitionists and their heirs up to the founding of the NAACP.

The conditions of life in the North for blacks are dealt with by Gilbert Osofsky in *Harlem: The Making of A Ghetto, 1890–1930* ° (1966); Seith Scheiner in *Negro Mecca: A History of the Negro in New York City* (1965); and Allan Spear in *Black Chicago: The Making of a Negro Ghetto, 1890–1920* ° (1967), the most successful of the three. The relations of blacks and the labor movement are explored in Bernard Mandel's "Samuel Gompers and the Negro Workers, 1886–1914," *Journal of Negro History,* XL (Jan. 1955), which traces the AFL leader's shift from blaming white workers for racial discrimination to his endorsing the exclusion of blacks from the labor movement and then blaming them for failing to establish working-class solidarity; Herbert Gutman's "The Negro and the United Mine Workers of America," in Julius Jacobson, ed., *The Negro and the American Labor Movement* ° (1968), which stresses that the United Mine Workers was an interracial organization; and Paul Worthman and James Green's "Black Workers in the New South, 1865–1915," in Nathan I. Huggins *et al.,* eds., *Key Issues in the Afro-American Experience,* Vol. II (1971) which emphasizes the failure by the 1910's of industrial unionism in the South and the efforts of black and white workers to overcome racial hostility and instill class consciousness. For early examples of black militance against Jim Crow, see August Meier and Elliott Rudwick's articles "The Boycott Movement Against Jim Crow Streetcars in the South, 1900–1906," *Journal of American History,* LV (Mar. 1969); "Negro Boycotts of Jim Crow Streetcars in Tennessee," *American Quarterly,* XXI (Winter 1969); "Negro Boycotts of Jim Crow Schools in the North, 1897–1925," *Integrated Edu-*

cation, V (Aug.–Sept. 1967); and "Early Boycotts of Segregated Schools: The East Orange, New Jersey, Experience, 1899–1906" *History of Education Quarterly,* VII (Spring 1967).

For studies of violence against blacks, see Arthur Waskow's *From Race Riot to Sit-In* [*] (1966); Elliott Rudwick's *Race Riot at East St. Louis* (1966); William Tuttle's *Race Riot: Chicago in the Red Summer of 1919* (1971); Charles Crowe's "Radical Massacre in Atlanta, September 22, 1906," *Journal of Negro History,* LIV (Apr. 1969); and James Crouthemal's "The Springfield Race Riot of 1908," *Journal of Negro History,* XLV (July 1960).

Dewey W. Grantham's "The Progressive Movement and the Negro," *South Atlantic Quarterly,* LIV (Oct. 1955); David Southern's *The Malignant Heritage: Yankee Progressives and the Negro Question, 1901–1914* (1968); Allen Davis' *Spearheads of Reform: The Social Settlements and the Progressive Movement, 1890–1914* (1967), which contains a chapter on social workers and blacks; and Gilbert Osofsky's "Progressivism and the Negro: New York, 1900–1915," *American Quarterly,* XVI (Summer 1964) are useful for exploring the relationship between progressivism and attitudes toward blacks. George Fredrickson's *The Black Image in the White Mind: The Debate on Afro-American Character and Destiny, 1817–1914* (1971) is a penetrating volume.

For analyses of Roosevelt's and Wilson's handling of the black problem, see Seth Scheiner's "President Roosevelt and the Negro, 1901–1908," *Journal of Negro History,* XLVII (July 1962); Willard Gatewood's *Theodore Roosevelt and the Art of Controversy* (1970); James Tinsley's "Roosevelt, Foraker, and the Brownsville Affair," *Journal of Negro History,* LXI (Jan. 1956); Kathleen Wogelmuth's "Woodrow Wilson's Appointment Policy and the Negro," *Journal of Southern History,* XXIV (Feb. 1958), and "Woodrow Wilson and Federal Segregation," *Journal of Negro History,* XLIV (Apr. 1959); Henry Blumenthal's "Woodrow Wilson and the Race Question," *Journal of Negro History,* XLVIII (Jan. 1963); Nancy J. Weiss's "The Negro and the New Freedom: Fighting Wilsonian Segregation," *Political Science Quarterly,* LXXXIV (Mar. 1969); and Jane L. Scheiber and Harry N. Scheiber's "The Wilson Administration and the Wartime Mobilization of Black Americans," *Labor History,* X (Summer 1969).

ARTHUR S. LINK

Wilson the Diplomatist: The Problems of Neutrality and the Decisions for War

INTRODUCTION

Aside from a few individuals like the diplomat Lewis Einstein, who argued from the beginning of the First World War that the American national interest was at stake, Walter Lippmann, who soon reached a similar conclusion, and Theodore Roosevelt, who added to this belief a lust for combat, American citizens and politicians hoped during the early years of the war that their nation could remain uninvolved in the conflict. Woodrow Wilson, despite his own Anglophilia, exhorted the nation to act and speak in "the spirit of neutrality and friendship," and in 1916 the Democratic party reelected Wilson on the slogan "He kept us out of war." Yet in the spring of 1917, a reluctant America found herself en-

FROM Arthur S. Link, *Wilson the Diplomatist: A Look at His Major Foreign Policies* (Baltimore: The Johns Hopkins Press, 1957), pp. 31–33, 35–50, 73–90. Reprinted by permission of The Johns Hopkins Press.

meshed in the tragedy of the war in Europe. Scholars have since engaged in often fierce controversies as to why Wilson decided to intervene and whether that decision was correct and in America's interest.

As the First World War recedes more deeply into history, much of the passion has ebbed from these controversies. Certain contentions popular with the revisionists of the 1920's and 1930's who wrote amid the great disillusionment with the peace settlement, have dropped out of the scholarly dialogue. No longer do historians assert that the bankers and munitions-makers drove the United States into war in order to save their loans and to create wider markets for war supplies. Other revisionist contentions are still subjects for debate: Did Wilson's pro-British sympathies ultimately lead America to war? Did Wilson practice an unneutral diplomacy that acquiesced in British violations of international law but condemned lesser or equally severe German violations? Was the need for trade with the Allies at the heart of decisions that ultimately led to war? Did the President exploit the issue of unrestricted submarine warfare to justify larger aims? In other words, why could not the administration have accepted submarine warfare and thereby avoided war? Or could other administration policies have made Germany's unrestricted submarine warfare unnecessary in 1917? For the revisionists—Harry Elmer Barnes, Edwin Borchard, C. Harley Grattan, Charles C. Tansill, and others—American entry into the First World War was avoidable and a great mistake. They charged that Wilson's idealism cloaked darker purposes and led to entry into a war that was detrimental to America's welfare.

In the 1940's and 1950's, as America confronted Nazi Germany on the battlefields and the Soviet Union in a tense, armed truce, another group of scholars, the realists, focused on different issues and made very different assumptions about the conditions necessary to America's welfare. Indicting much of American foreign policy for innocence, excessive moralism, and legalism, these scholars—especially Hans Morgenthau, Robert Osgood, Walter Lippmann, and George Kennan—concluded that America had a stake in the First World War soon after Sarajevo. They contended that intervention was not a mistake but in the national interest: America's entry was essential to preserving the European balance of power (with a strong Britain) on which American security rested. Most lamented that Wilson had delayed before committing America to combat and contended that Wilson had not understood the need to intervene in order to maintain the balance of power. They criticized him for not understanding power politics, for not recognizing America's real interest, and for basing American foreign policy on idealism, rather than on national self-interest. Unlike the revisionists, the realists affirmed the sincerity of Wilson's idealism, but usually judged his adherence to it as regrettable. The realists believed that the war should have been fought on behalf of American security, not to "make the world safe for democracy"—a utopian aim in their opinion. Wilson's idealism, according to them, had often been utopian, had lost sight of the need to limit national goals to national capabilities, and had inspired great hopes in Americans that could not be fulfilled, thereby insuring later disillusionment and reaction.

Responding partly to the issues raised by the revisionists, and to a few of those raised by the realists, Arthur S. Link, professor of history at Princeton University and author of the definitive study of *Wilson,* 5 vols. (1947–65), presents in the following excerpt from *Wilson: The Diplomatist* (1957) a sympathetic defense of the President's policies. He stresses the narrowing channels in which Wilson had to maneuver because of the desire of most Americans to maintain neutrality, the need for continued trade, especially with the Allies, the increasing restrictions of British maritime policy, and the challenges created by Germany's submarine warfare. All these factors inexorably restricted Wilson's options and are the reasons for the fatalism that Link periodically expresses as he examines the course of the President he so much admires. Link concludes that Wilson struggled to maintain neutrality despite his pro-British sentiments, and that it was ultimately Germany's unrestricted submarine warfare that compelled him to move from armed neutrality to war.

Link seeks to rebut the contention, best expressed by Paul Birdsall in 1939, that the administration's ban on foreign loans was (1) relaxed in 1915 in order to finance the foreign trade that the economy needed, and (2) that this reversal of policy ultimately led to the unrestricted submarine warfare that provoked American intervention. In examining the first part of this argument, Link admits that the need for trade contributed to this reversal. But he also adds that another reason for this decision was that Wilson had come to recognize that the ban was unneutral. In Link's later volume *Wilson: The Struggle for Neutrality, 1914–1915* (1960), he admits that the reasons for this reversal in loan policy remain a matter of speculation, for there is only direct evidence of what Wilson's associates thought, not of why he acted.

But one can go on to ask a more basic question: If the American economy had not depended on foreign trade, would a President have been free to follow policies—including restrictions on trade and loans to belligerents—that would have kept America out of war? Some historians answer, yes. They conclude that the Allies without American aid and shipments would have collapsed before 1917, or that there would have been no need (contrary to Ernest May, *The World War and American Isolation* [1959]) for Germany's unrestricted warfare. Either way American shipping and lives would not have been lost and the United States would therefore not have gone to war.

Critics of Wilson have also suggested that he had more alternatives than he realized and chose wrongly, or at least unwisely, in guiding the nation during the period of neutrality. Why did he not ban the trade in munitions and the travel of American passengers? In December of 1914, he failed to support the Hitchcock bill to end the trade in munitions, which enjoyed both legal precedents and political support. In 1913, the United States had imposed an embargo on arms to Mexico, and Denmark, Sweden, Italy, Norway, the Netherlands, and Spain were barring the munitions trade in 1914. The administration was simply incorrect in concluding that an embargo would violate neutrality. And in the late winter of 1916, after the sinking of the *Persia* and the resultant anger of Congressmen that American passengers had been the target of U-boats, the President probably could have secured a restriction on travel abroad. Had he obtained an arms embargo, the result would probably have been a German victory, and America would not have entered the First World War. To accept a restriction on travel, Wilson would have had to give up freedom of the seas, the struggle to preserve the rights of neutrals, and defense of American honor. But these were values on which he was unprepared to yield. He was not, then, a prisoner of history, as some historians contend, but a prisoner of his own values.

Germany, according to Link, had by its policy of unrestricted warfare so flagrantly assaulted American lives and property that Wilson had to go to war in 1917. He saw no other way to protect American rights as a neutral. Beneath these *immediate* circumstances, Link suspects, there were deeper considerations subtly influencing Wilson. "It was Wilson's apparent fear," Link wrote in 1957, "that the threat of a German victory imperiled the balance of power and all his hopes for the future reconstruction of the world community." After additional research, however, Link altered his judgment in 1963. He no longer believed that the President knew, or was influenced by the fear, that the Central Powers in 1917 were about to win. Nor was Wilson concerned about national security in his decision to go to war. Link stressed "Wilson's conviction that the war was in its final stages, American belligerency would have the effect of shortening, not prolonging the war, and belligerency had the one advantage of guaranteeing him an important role in peacemaking." Link's analysis, then, agrees in some important points with the interpretations offered by the realists, but he differs from them on the value of Wilson's idealism.

N. Gordon Levin, a historian of the left, in *Woodrow Wilson and World Politics: America's Response to War and Revolution* (1968) has advanced an alternative, and challenging, conception of Wilson and his decision to go to war. Modifying Link's analysis, Levin acknowledges Wilson's efforts to maintain neutrality but places his thought within the larger framework of liberal capitalism. "The submarine warfare used by Germany," Levin argues, "could not help but be threatening to Wilson, whose vision both of America's expansionist mission and of a liberal world order, was so deeply related to a concern for freedom of the seas and the maintenance of international law" (p. 33). Wilson, throughout much of the early war, according to Levin, hoped to reshape the world order through a negotiated peace ("western liberal capitalist unity under American guidance"); but by early 1917, when confronted by Germany's unrestricted submarine warfare, the President came to define the war as a conflict between an aggressive German autocracy and a defensive Allied democracy, and concluded that a peaceful Imperial Germany could not be integrated into a liberal capitalist community. Guided by this new definition of the issues, Wilson considered American intervention justifiable and necessary. Levin views Wilson as having considerable freedom to maneuver and as acting primarily to advance the values of a liberal capitalist system. Wilson, rather than being a prisoner of history, was a vigorous proponent of a particular conception of world order.

For Woodrow Wilson and the American people, who had a positive disinclination to play the game of power politics, events on the international stage intruded in an ironic if fateful way from 1914 to 1917. By the spring of 1915 the United States was the only great power not directly involved in the war then raging from western Europe to the Far East. Desiring only to deal fairly with both sides and to avoid military involvement, the President soon found that neutrality, as well as war, has its perplexities and perils.

The way in which Wilson met the challenges to America's peace and security raised by the death grapple between the opposing alliances has never been fully explained, notwithstanding scores of books and articles. Too often, historians, in company with public men, have looked for culprits instead of facts. Too often they have misunderstood the facts even when they found them. Too often they have written as if Wilson and his advisers made policy in a vacuum independent of the interplay of conflicting pressures. If we can see the President's policies of neutrality in the light of his convictions and objectives, the pressures and events (both domestic and foreign) that bore constantly upon him, and the alternatives between which he was often forced to choose—if we can do this, then perhaps we will see that his task in foreign policy at this juncture was not as simple as it has sometimes been described.

Among the most pervasive pressures controlling Wilson's decisions throughout the period 1914–1917 were the attitudes and opinions of the American people concerning the war and America's proper relation to it. Few presidents in American history have been more keenly aware of risks that the leader runs when he ceases to speak for the preponderant majority. "The ear of the leader must ring with the voices of the people. He cannot be of the school of the prophets; he must be of the number of those who studiously serve the slow-paced daily need." Thus Wilson had written in 1890; [1] thus he believed and practiced while formulating his policies toward the belligerents in the First World War.

The dominant American sentiment throughout the period of nonintervention can be summarily characterized by the single adjective "neutral." This is not to say that Americans had no opinions on the merits of the war and the claims of the opposing alliances, or that there were no differences among the popular reactions. It is simply to state the fairly obvious fact that the preponderant majority, whose opinions played a decisive role in shaping Wilson's policies, did not believe that their interests and security were vitally involved in the outcome of the war and desired to avoid participation if that were possible without sacrificing rights that should not be yielded. The prevalence and astounding vitality of neutralism, in spite of the severest provocations and all the efforts of propagandists on both sides, formed at once the unifying principle of American politics and the compelling reality with which Wilson had to deal from 1914 to 1917.

On the other hand, it would be a large error to imply that Wilson was a prisoner of the public opinion of the majority, and that his will to adopt sterner policies toward one group of belligerents or the other was paralyzed by the stronger counterforce of neutralism. Actually, the evidence points overwhelmingly to the conclusion that Wilson personally shared the opinions of the majority, in brief, that he was substantially neutral in attitude, and that his policies were controlled as much by his own convictions as by the obvious wishes of the people.

.   .   .   .   .

. . . it would be a difficult task to prove that Wilson's pro-British sympathies were ever controlling or indeed even very strong. At no time did he act like a man willing to take measures merely to help his supposed friends. On the contrary, all his policies were aimed either at averting American participation on Britain's side or at ending the war on terms that would have denied the spoils of victory to Britain and her allies. If this is too big an assertion to be taken on faith, then perhaps the reasons for making it will become apparent as we see the way in which Wilson executed policies toward the two leading antagonists.

---

[1] T. H. Vail Motter (ed.), *Leaders of Men* (Princeton, N.J., 1952), p. 43.

All authorities, whether friendly or hostile to Wilson, would agree that the acid tests of his neutrality were the policies that he worked out and applied vis-à-vis the British from 1914 to 1917. He has been most condemned by that group of historians highly censorious of his policies, generally known as revisionists, on this score—for becoming the captive of pro-Allied influences within his administration, for condoning such sweeping British control of neutral commerce that the Germans were forced to resort to drastic countermeasures, for permitting American prosperity to become dependent upon loans and exports to the Allies, in short, for permitting a situation to develop that made it inevitable that the United States would go to war if the success of Allied arms was ever seriously threatened.

Like most fallacious arguments, this one contains a certain element of plausibility. Wilson did condone a far-reaching British maritime system. American neutrality did work greatly to the benefit of the Allies. The error arises in saying that these things occurred because Wilson and his advisers necessarily wanted them to occur.

Perhaps the best way to gain a clear understanding of why Anglo-American relations developed as they did from 1914 to 1917 is to see how the policies that decisively shaped those relations emerged in several stages in response to certain pressures, events, and forces. The first stage, lasting from August, 1914, to about August, 1915, was in many ways the most critical, because the basic American response to the war and to the British maritime system was formulated then. That response was governed in the first instance by two domestic realities: the overwhelming, virtually unanimous, American desire to be neutral, and the pressures in the United States for a large measure of free trade with Britain's enemies.

In view of the prevailing American sentiment at the outbreak of the war, a policy of strict official neutrality was the only possible course for the United States government. This fact prompted the President's official proclamations of neutrality, supplemented by his appeal to the American people for impartiality in thought; the subsequent working out by the State Department of the elaborate technical rules to preserve American neutrality; and the establishment of a Joint State and Navy Neutrality Board to advise the various departments upon the correct interpretation of international law.

One cannot read the records revealing how these policies were formulated without being convinced that their authors were high-minded in their determination to be fair to both sides. Indeed, Wilson and the man who chiefly influenced him in the formulation of the rules of neutrality, Secretary of State Bryan, were so intent upon being fair to the Germans that they adopted policies during the first months of the war that were highly disadvantageous to the British, if not unneutral. One was to prevent the sale of submarine parts, and hence parts for any naval craft, by a private American firm to the British government, on the ground that such a

sale would be "contrary to . . . strict neutrality." Wilson persisted in supporting Bryan in this matter, in spite of advice from Counselor Lansing
and the Joint Neutrality Board to the effect that their position was contrary to international law.

Infinitely more damaging to the Allies was the administration's second effort to lean over backward in being "strictly" neutral—the ban of
loans by American bankers to the belligerent governments that the President permitted Bryan to impose in August, 1914. From a technical viewpoint, the ban was not unneutral, but it was highly prejudicial to the Allies because its effect was potentially to deny them their otherwise legal
right to purchase supplies in the American market. These two incidents are
not to be understood as revealing any anti-British bias on the part of Wilson and Bryan, although British officials at the time were convinced that
they did. I mention them only to show what an important role the administration's desire to be impartial played in the formation of policies vis-à-vis
the British during the early period of American neutrality.

The other pressure shaping American policies at this time was the
force of combined demands at home for the virtually free transit of American ships and goods to the European neutrals and the belligerent Central
Powers. So powerful were these demands, especially from cotton growers
and exporters and their spokesmen in Congress, that Wilson personally
sponsored two measures highly disadvantageous to the British and unneutral in fact as well as in spirit. One was a change in the ship registry law,
put into effect by an act approved August 18, 1914, which made it easy for
German or other foreign shipping firms to take out American registry for
their vessels. The other was a plan to establish a federal corporation to
purchase German ships in American ports and to use them to carry supplies to the belligerents, particularly to Germany. Wilson applied heavy
pressure to obtain congressional approval of this, the so-called ship-
purchase bill, during the short term from December, 1914, to March, 1915;
he failed only because of a stout senatorial filibuster.

In negotiations with the British government during the early months
of the war, Wilson fought hard in response to domestic pressures to keep
the channels of international commerce open to American ships and goods.
He did not go as far in defense of neutral rights as some of his predecessors, but he did suggest a code so sweeping that an enforcement of it
would have meant almost total destruction of the British system of maritime controls. Specifically, the President first proposed on August 6, 1914,
that the belligerents adopt the rules of naval warfare laid down in the Declaration of London of 1909, a convention never ratified by Great Britain or
the United States, which permitted the free transit of all goods except
those obviously contraband. When the British rejected this suggestion, the
President came back on October 16, proposing a compromise that would
have still seriously impaired the effectiveness of British sea power. When

this effort also failed, Wilson then announced that his government would assert and defend all its rights under international law and treaties.

I have described these policies and proposals because they so clearly reveal Wilson's neutral intentions and what he would have done in matters of trade had he been able to make the rules himself. But he obviously could not follow his personal preferences alone or respond only to domestic pressures. In seeking to assert and defend American neutral rights he ran head-on into a reality as important as the reality of the pressures at home. It was the British determination to use sea power to prevent American ships and goods from going to the sustenance of the German economy and military forces.

British assumption of a nearly absolute control of the seas washing western Europe began with relatively mild measures in August, 1914, and culminated in the suppression of virtually all commerce to the Central Powers in March, 1915. For the British, this was not a question of adhering to the laws of blockade or of violating them, or of doings things merely to be nice to American friends. It was a question of achieving their supreme objective, to deprive their enemies of vital raw materials and goods, without risking the alienation of the United States. The controlling fact for the British was the necessity of preserving American friendship, in order to assure the uninterrupted rhythm of the North Atlantic trade. . . .

The crucial question all along, therefore, was whether the United States, the only neutral power strong enough successfully to challenge the British measures, would acquiesce or resist to the point of threatening or using force. The American response during the formative period of neutrality was, in brief, to accept the British system and to limit action against it to a vigorous assertion of American legal rights for future adjudication. All this is too well known to require any further exposition. What is not so well understood are the reasons why Wilson and his advisers acquiesced in a solution that denied the objectives that they and a large segment of the American public demanded. These reasons may be briefly summarized, as follows:

First, the British maritime system, in spite of American allegations to the contrary, enjoyed the advantage of being legitimate and usually legal, or nearly so, by traditional criteria. It was legitimate rather than fraudulent, and legal rather than capricious or terroristic, in its major aspects because the British did in fact hold undisputed sea supremacy and were therefore able to execute their controls in an orderly fashion. In asserting their own rights, the Americans could not well deny the advantages that accrued to the British by virtue of their sea power. The British, for example, had an undoubted right to establish a blockade of the Central Powers, and the American attempt to persuade the London government to use techniques effective only in the days of the sailing ship did not have much cogency in the twentieth century.

Second, much of the success of the British in establishing their control depended upon the way in which they went about it. Had they instituted their total blockade at the outset of the war, the American reaction would undoubtedly have been violent. Instead, the British applied their controls gradually, with a careful eye upon American opinion, using the opportunities provided by recurrent crises in German-American relations to institute their severest measures.

Third, the British were careful never to offend so many American interests at one time that retaliation would have been inevitable, or any single interest powerful enough by itself to compel retaliation. . . .

Fourth, there was great significance in the language and symbolism that the British Foreign Office used in defending the measures of the Admiralty and Ministry of Blockade. By justifying their maritime system in terms of international law and the right of retaliation, and (at least before the summer of 1916) by making an honest effort to meet American objections half way when possible, the British made it almost inevitable that the Washington authorities would have to reply in the same language, thus giving a purely *legal* character to the issues involved and for the most part avoiding raising the issues of sovereignty and inherent national rights. The significance of this achievement can be seen in the conviction of Wilson and the majority of Americans that the Anglo-American disputes did involve only property rights, which should be vindicated only by an appeal to much-controverted international law. Moreover, by appealing to the American government and people in the name of friendship and by always professing their devotion to the cause of humanity, the British succeeded in evoking strong feelings of sympathy and understanding on the other side of the water.

Finally, the British were able partially to justify their own blockade measures as legitimate adaptations to a changing technology by pointing to precedents established by the Washington government itself during the American Civil War. To be sure, the British drew some incorrect analogies (as Lansing pointed out) between American and British practice; even so, their main contention—that the American government had also stretched the rules of blockade to allow for technological changes—was essentially correct.

Wilson's refusal to challenge the British maritime system, in short, to break the British blockade, was almost inevitable in view of the facts we have just reviewed, *if the President's objective was simply to maintain as best he could the neutral position of the United States.* An absolute neutrality was in any event impossible because of the total character of the war and America's importance in the world economy. It often happened that any action by the United States inevitably conferred a benefit on one side and thereby injured the other, at least indirectly. In these circumstances, neutrality often consisted of doing the things that would give the least unwarranted or undeserved advantages.

By this standard, it would have been more unneutral than neutral for

Wilson to have broken the British maritime system by enforcing highly doubtful technical rights under international law. Judged by practical standards rather than by the often conflicting criteria of neutrality, Wilson's acceptance of the British system seems realistic and wise—indeed, the only choice that he could have made in the circumstances. This is true because the results of destroying the British blockade would have been the wrecking of American friendship with the two great European democracies and the probable victory of the Central Powers, without a single compensating gain for the interests and security of the United States. Only the sure achievement of some great political objective like a secure peace settlement, certainly not the winning of a commercial advantage or the defense of doubtful neutral rights, would have justified Wilson in undertaking a determined challenge to British sea power.

The second stage in Anglo-American relations, lasting from the summer of 1915 to the late spring of 1916, saw the development of the natural economic consequence of the American adjustment to tightening British control of the seas. That consequence was the burgeoning of an enormous war trade between the United States and the Allies. The United States became the storehouse and armory of the Allies neither because there was any conspiracy on the part of certain pro-Allied leaders in Washington to make American prosperity dependent upon an Allied victory, nor because American businessmen and bankers were willing to incur the risks of war in order to increase their profits. The United States became the storehouse of the Allies for the simple reason that Great Britain and not Germany controlled the seas.

The war trade itself was entirely neutral. Indeed, any action by the United States government to impede it, unless undertaken for overriding political motives, would have been grossly prejudicial and unneutral. If it had been permitted to develop in a normal way, this commerce would have raised no important problems in the relations of the United States with the Allies. A problem of the first magnitude did arise, however, because the President, in the summer of 1914, had permitted Secretary Bryan to enforce his own private moral views by imposing a ban on loans by American bankers to the belligerents.

· · · · ·

Bryan's ban could not survive the development of the war trade on a large scale because, in the first place, it (like the Embargo of 1808) was potentially nearly as disastrous to the United States as to the Allies. American material well-being was in large measure dependent upon foreign trade, and particularly upon trade with the Allied world. Such trade was possible during wartime only if American businessmen were willing to do for the Allies what they always did for solvent customers in temporary straits, namely, sell them goods on credit.

The most important reason that Bryan's embargo could not survive, however, was that it was an essentially unneutral policy that impeded the growth of the chief economic consequence of American neutrality, the legitimate war trade. The credit embargo and the war trade could not both survive. The former gave way because Wilson finally realized that it would be as unneutral to interfere with the extension of credit as it would be to stop the flow of goods. Bryan's ban was in a sense, therefore, a casualty chiefly of American neutrality.

. . . .

The second stage in Anglo-American relations also witnessed the apparent convergence of the diplomatic policies of the two countries on the high level. During the summer and autumn of 1915 Colonel Edward M. House, Wilson's confidant and principal adviser on foreign policy, conceived a plan by which the American and British leaders would join hands to press for an end to the war through Wilson's mediation. The British Foreign Secretary, Sir Edward Grey, replied that his government would co-operate only if the Washington administration were willing to go beyond simple mediation and would agree to join a postwar international organization established for the purpose of effecting disarmament, maintaining freedom of the seas, and preserving peace. Wilson hopefully consented, and House went to Berlin, Paris, and London in January, 1916, to lay the diplomatic basis of mediation.

In London, House worked out in documentary form with Grey and the other members of the British Cabinet the specific terms of Anglo-American co-operation. Initialed by House and Grey on February 22, 1916, and known as the House-Grey Memorandum or Agreement, this document declared that President Wilson was ready, upon hearing from England and France that the time was ripe, to propose that a conference be called to end the war. Should the Allies accept and Germany refuse the invitation, the United States would "probably" enter the war against Germany. Should the conference meet and Germany refuse to accept a reasonable settlement, then the United States would also "probably" enter the war on the Allied side.

To the so-called revisionists the conclusion of the House-Grey Agreement is irrefutable proof that Wilson had abandoned neutrality and meant to take the country into war at the first opportunity. . . .

. . . .

The revisionists are correct in asserting that the conclusion of the House-Grey Agreement marked the beginning of a new and epochal phase in Wilson's policies toward the belligerents. Otherwise they have missed the entire meaning of the affair, for the House-Grey Agreement was in Wilson's purpose *not an instrument of intervention, but a means of averting American involvement.* The truth of this important generalization will perhaps become evident when we recall the realities of the American diplomatic situation during late 1915 and early 1916, and when we understand Wilson's motives and intentions in devising a solution.

The overshadowing reality confronting the makers of American foreign policy at this time was the grave possibility of war with Germany over the submarine issue. It caused Wilson and Lansing, for example, to abandon ambitious plans for further intervention in Mexico. It speeded the American acquiescence in the British maritime system. Most important, it prompted the President and his advisers to search for ways to avert the rupture that might draw the United States into the maelstrom.

One way out of the predicament was to come to a full understanding with the German government over the issues involved in the submarine controversy. This is what Lansing attempted to do and almost succeeded in accomplishing during his negotiations over the *Lusitania* affair. Another way out and a surer means of averting the peril of American involvement in the future was to bring the war itself to an end through Wilson's mediation. It seemed at the time that the best hope of peace lay in Anglo-American co-operation for a peace of compromise, specifically in the kind of co-operation detailed in the House-Grey Agreement.

Thus Wilson approved this plan of mediation, but with a full realization that certain obligations and risks were involved. There was the necessity of giving positive assurances to the Allies, for they would have been at a fatal disadvantage in a peace conference without American support, in view of the strategic advantages that the Germans then enjoyed on the Continent of Europe. There was, moreover, the risk of war if the Germans refused to approve an armistice or proved to be unreasonable at a peace conference after agreeing to end the fighting. However, Wilson gave the necessary assurances in the belief that the risk of war involved was insignificant as compared to the greater danger of hostilities with Germany if he could not somehow bring the war to an end. This, then, was his dominant motive in sending House to Europe in January, 1916, and in approving the House-Grey Agreement at the cost of Lansing's proposed compromise for submarine warfare.

In the final analysis, our judgment of Wilson's mediation plans must depend upon the kind of settlement that he had in mind and for which he was willing to run the risk of war in order to achieve peace. It is clear that Wilson envisaged a "reasonable" settlement based upon recognition that the war was a stalemate and upon a return for the most part of the *status quo ante bellum.* It meant, Wilson also hoped, the kind of settlement in which all the belligerents would forego annexations and indemnities, put aside past differences, and join hands with the United States to create a new international order. In his final discussions with the British Cabinet, Colonel House made it clear that this, and this only, was the kind of settlement that Wilson was prepared to use the House-Grey Agreement to achieve. In other words, as House told the British leaders, the President would "throw the weight of the United States on the side of those wanting a just settlement—a settlement which would make another such war impossible." [2]

. . . .

In the circumstances prevailing during the late autumn and early winter of 1916–1917, the Germans had three possible choices of policy. These were, first, to join hands with Wilson in a drive for peace generally on the President's terms; second, to make a limited bid for victory by intensifying the submarine war at the risk of alienating the United States; and, third, to make a supreme bid for victory by instituting a total blockade of all commerce to the British Isles. The situation from the German point of view was such that this choice would not depend upon anything that Wilson did or said, unless, of course, the President could be used as a German pawn or was willing openly to support Germany's war objectives. The German decision would depend entirely upon a realistic evaluation of the possibilities of the military situation, that is, upon whether the Imperial army and navy were capable of imposing terms upon the enemies of the Reich.

Discussions of these possibilities had begun in Germany in earnest in mid-August, 1916, as a consequence of the urgent demand of the Admiralty for permission to resume unrestricted submarine attacks in the near future. The civilian and military leaders rejected the demand at a conference at Pless Castle on August 31, 1916, on the ground that the navy did not have enough submarines to enforce a blockade and that it would obviously be foolhardy to risk American retaliation at this time. Actually, it was the new commanders of the army, Generals Paul von Hindenburg and Erich von Ludendorff, who made this decision. The military situation, they said, was too menacing to justify assuming the risk of war with America. There was heavy Allied pressure on the western front; above all, there was the grave danger of an Allied invasion of the Balkans, which might cause the collapse of Austria-Hungary.

Events of the late summer and early autumn combined inexorably to create a new situation in which a different decision would be made. First, the great British offensive on the Somme, aimed at tearing a huge hole in the German lines and a thrust into Belgium, failed; as a result, the German position in the West was again secure. Second, after dawdling in the matter for nearly two years, the Admiralty had finally launched a large program of submarine construction and the training of crews; by the end of

---

[2] The Diary of Edward M. House, February 14, 1916, MS in the Yale University Library.

the year it would be possible to talk in terms of dealing England a death-blow underseas. Finally, the army's counteroffensive against the Russians and its smashing victory over Rumania removed all cause for concern about the security of Austria-Hungary and the Balkans.

. . . .

Almost formless at the outset of the war, German war objectives had grown in a direct ratio to the progress of the Imperial armies in the field. By the late autumn of 1916 the military situation was so favorable and the potentialities of an effective submarine blockade were so great that the German leaders inevitably abandoned thought of a compromise peace and began to plan for a settlement that would remove all threats to future German security. As drawn up by [Theobald von] Bethmann-Hollweg, amended by Hindenburg, and approved by the German and Austrian governments, the German peace terms were breathtaking in scope. They included, in the East, the establishment of a Polish kingdom under German control and German annexation of Lithuania and Courland on the Baltic; in the West, destruction of British naval supremacy, an idemnity from England and France, the annexation of strategic parts of France and Belgium, and the reconstruction of Belgium as a German vassal; and, overseas, the annexation of all or part of the Belgian Congo. To be sure, these were the maximum German objectives at the time; a realization of even part of them, however, would have secured German domination of Europe for years to come.

This was the kind of settlement that the German leaders were determined to obtain through peace negotiations. They knew that they could never obtain such terms, or even a large part of them, through Wilson's mediation. They knew that Wilson would demand, among other things, the restitution of a free and independent Belgium and perhaps the return of Alsace-Lorraine to France. Acceptance of Wilson's mediation and a compromise peace, even one based entirely upon the *status quo ante bellum*, would, in German eyes, be tantamount to defeat, for it would mean the frustration of everything for which so much German blood had been shed. As a consequence, no German leader, civilian or military, ever seriously considered accepting Wilson's *mediation*. During all the high-level discussions about peace plans, no German leader ever seriously mentioned such a possibility. On the contrary, all German diplomatic efforts were concentrated upon the goal of preventing Wilson's mediation, or "meddling," as the Germans called it.

This statement needs some clarification. The Germans were eager, almost desperately eager, to win the President's support for their peace plans. They wanted Wilson's help in forcing the Allies to the peace table at a time when all the odds favored the winning of a German peace. They were willing to give pledges of postwar disarmament and membership in a

League of Nations, if this were necessary to win the President's support. But they did not want, indeed, they would not permit, Wilson's mediation or even his presence at the peace conference.

Wilson did not know these facts during the first stages of the peace discussions, but the truth finally came out in January, 1917, when the President begged the Foreign Office in Berlin to come out frankly and fully in acceptance of his mediation. Then the German leaders had to say that they would welcome Wilson's co-operation only after the peace treaty had been signed, not at the conference of belligerents itself. Shrewdly perceiving the German intentions, Wilson refused to be a pawn in Berlin's game.

Wilson's refusal meant that the German leaders would now proceed to consider means of achieving through force what they had failed to win by their inept diplomacy. The High Command had already made the decision by late December; it was confirmed by a conference of all leaders at Pless Castle on January 9, 1917. That decision was, in brief, to begin unrestricted submarine warfare against all shipping, belligerent and neutral, in the approaches to the British Isles and the eastern Mediterranean after January 31.

It was easily the most fateful decision made by any government during the course of the war, and the German records fully reveal the reasons for its adoption. It now seemed beyond all doubt that the navy had sufficient power to establish an effective submarine blockade of the British Isles, for it could send between twenty-five and thirty submarines into western waters by February 1, 1917, and a growing number after that date. Moreover, other circumstances, particularly a short wheat crop in the New World, augured well for the success of the blockade. Indeed, on a basis of elaborate calculations the Admiralty spokesmen guaranteed absolutely to reduce the British to actual starvation within five months after the submarine blockade began. If this were possible, then Germany had it within her power to win a total victory and a settlement that would establish the Reich in an unassailable position. To the military leaders, who had despaired of winning the war in the trenches, it was an opportunity that could not be refused.°

Fear of American belligerency no longer had any effect on German policy in such an atmosphere of confident expectation. The German leaders all assumed that a wholesale attack on American maritime commerce would drive the United States into the war. These same leaders also concluded that American belligerency would not make any difference. On the contrary, American participation would have certain positive advantages, for

---

° *Editors' note.* "Additional work in German sources," Link later wrote, "has persuaded me that the decision was born not only of hope but of desperate despair occasioned by the Allied rebuff of the German peace offer and the conviction that Germany would inevitably lose the war if she could not obtain some decision by 1917" (*Wilson the Diplomatist*, 2nd ed. [1963], p. xiv).

it would mean the diversion of huge quantities of food and matériel to an American army in training during the very period when the U-boats would be winning the war on the seas. But in any event, American participation was in the circumstances necessary to the success of the German plans, because the submarine blockade could succeed only if it were total, that is, only if American as well as British ships were prevented from carrying life-giving supplies to the beleaguered British Isles. Of course, no German leader wanted recklessly to provoke an American declaration of war; all Germans, however, were prepared to incur American belligerency if they could win the war by so doing.

It was the only decision that seemed possible to the Imperial military commanders. No nation involved in a desperate war for survival will fail to use a weapon, whether it be the submarine or the atomic bomb, when that weapon promises to bring quick and overwhelming victory. But the submarine campaign brought catastrophic defeat to Germany and misfortunes unnumbered to the world because it destroyed all possibility of a peace of reconciliation. . . .

There remains only one further question, whether the Germans decided to go the whole length and to attack American shipping because they believed that the United States would enter the war in any case if they violated the *Sussex* pledge. In other words, did the Germans conclude that there was little point in confining unrestricted attacks to armed merchantmen or to *belligerent* shipping, armed and unarmed, because any deviations from the rules of cruiser warfare would provoke American intervention? This is an academic question, but an important one, because the answer to it sheds additional light upon Wilson's intentions and the German choice of alternatives.

There is much evidence that by the end of 1916 Wilson was prepared to effect a sharp diplomatic withdrawal if both belligerent groups refused to heed his peace appeal. He knew that if the war proceeded the belligerents would use every means at their command to end it, and that this would mean a severe intensification of the struggle on the seas, to the further detriment of neutral rights. It seems almost certain that he would have accepted unrestricted submarine attacks against *armed* merchantmen. On January 10, 1917, the German government informed the State Department that its submarines would hereafter attack armed merchant ships without warning, because these ships had all been offensively armed and instructed to attack submarines. . . .

We can go further and say that it seems also possible that Wilson would not have broken diplomatic relations over unrestricted submarine attacks against all *belligerent* merchantmen, exclusive, perhaps, of passenger liners. Much would have depended upon American public opinion, which then seemed overwhelmingly opposed to war for the vindication of the right of Americans to travel on belligerent vessels. Much would have

depended upon the President himself, but his determination to avoid participation had never been stronger than at this time. "There will be no
war," he told Colonel House on January 4, 1917.

> This country does not intend to become involved in this war. We are the
> only one of the great white nations that is free from war to-day, and it
> would be a crime against civilization for us to go in.

The Germans never seriously considered adopting these limited alternatives, not because they believed that any infraction of the *Sussex* pledge
would automatically provoke American intervention, but because they
thought that they could win only by enforcing a total blockade. But if it is
true that Wilson would not have gone to war if the Germans had confined
their attacks to belligerent merchantmen, then we are confronted with one
of the supreme ironies of history. By doing the thing that seemed the best
guarantee of victory, the Germans assured their own defeat. By failing to
adopt the limited policies, they threw away their one chance of success,
which might well have come after the collapse of Russia and a devastating
attack on Allied commerce.

President Wilson's response to the German blockade proclamation
lends additional evidence to my theory that the United States might not
have broken diplomatic relations if the Germans had exempted American
shipping from the wrath of their underseas campaign. The German Ambassador delivered copies of the German blockade announcement to Lansing
and House on January 31, 1917. Wilson did not act like a man who had a
predetermined course of action in mind. Even in the face of a German declaration of war against American commerce, he hesitated to take any step
that might lead to war. He was willing, he told Lansing, to go to almost
any lengths "rather than to have this nation actually involved in the conflict."

There was, however, only one decision that Wilson could now make.
No great power could continue to maintain diplomatic intercourse with a
government that promised to destroy its shipping and slaughter its citizens
in violation of national and treaty rights and solemn pledges. Small neutral
states like Holland and Norway had no choice but to suffer under protest,
but a great nation like the United States had responsibilities commensurate
with its power and influence. Continuing to maintain relations with Berlin
after the issuance of the blockade proclamation of January 31 would have
meant nothing less than Wilson's condoning of the German assault upon
American rights and lives. The remarkable thing is not that Wilson severed
diplomatic relations as he did on February 3, but that he hesitated at all.

To engage in a debate at this point over the reasons for Wilson's sev-
erance of diplomatic relations with Germany would obscure a development

that was vastly more important than the handing of passports to the German Ambassador. It was Wilson's announcement, made in an address to Congress on February 3, 1917, that the United States would accept the new submarine blockade and would not go to war, in spite of the break in relations, provided that the Germans did not carry out their threat to destroy American ships and lives. This is the clear meaning of the following paragraph in Wilson's address:

> Notwithstanding this unexpected action of the German Government, . . . I refuse to believe that it is the intention of the German authorities to do in fact what they have warned us they will feel at liberty to do. I cannot bring myself to believe that they will indeed pay no regard to the ancient friendship between their people and our own or to the solemn obligations which have been exchanged between them and destroy *American ships and take the lives of American citizens* in the wilful prosecution of the ruthless naval programme they have announced their intention to adopt. Only actual overt acts on their part can make me believe it even now.

Wilson then announced what he would do in the event that his confidence in the "sobriety and prudent foresight" of the German leaders proved unfounded:

> I shall take the liberty of coming again before the Congress, to ask that authority be given me to use any means that may be necessary for the protection of our seamen and our people in the prosecution of their peaceful and legitimate errands on the high seas.[3]

In short, Wilson was saying that he would follow a policy of watchful waiting and govern his future policies in response to what the Germans did. If they spared American ships and lives, presumably upon American ships of all categories and upon belligerent unarmed passenger vessels, then he would do nothing. If they attacked American ships, then he would defend them by an armed neutrality. This, obviously, was not the language of war, such as Lansing had urged the President to use. It was the language of a man determined to avoid such full-fledged commitment as a war declaration would imply, willing in the worst event only to protect "our seamen and our people in the prosecution of their peaceful and legitimate errands on the high seas."

Throughout the first weeks of February, 1917, the President waited patiently to see what the future would bring. At any moment the German government could have removed the possibility of war with the United States by declaring that it would respect American shipping and take all possible care to protect American lives on belligerent ships. But when the

---

[3] Ray S. Baker and William E. Dodd (eds.), *The Public Papers of Woodrow Wilson, The New Democracy* (2 vols.; New York, 1926), II, 425. Italics added.

Swiss Minister in Washington offered to serve as an intermediary in any discussions between Berlin and Washington, the German Foreign Office replied that not even the re-establishment of diplomatic relations with the United States would prompt the Imperial government to reconsider "its resolution to completely stop by submarines all importations from abroad by its enemies."

In spite of the obvious German determination to enforce a total blockade, Wilson refused to permit the defense departments to make any important preparations for war. He would not do anything to cause the Germans to think that he was contemplating hostilities. As the days passed, however, the pressures for an end to watchful waiting and for the adoption of at least an armed neutrality mounted almost irresistibly. Members of the Cabinet, shipowners, a large majority of the newspapers, and a growing body of public opinion combined in the demand that the President either convoy merchantmen or arm them with naval guns and crews. Still protesting that the people wanted him to avert any risk of war, Wilson gave in to their wishes on about February 25. Going to Congress the following day to request authority to arm merchantmen and to "employ any other instrumentalities or methods that may be necessary and adequate to protect our ships and our people in their legitimate and peaceful pursuits on the seas," he carefully explained that he was not contemplating war or any steps that might lead to war. "I merely request," he said,

> that you will accord me by your own vote and definite bestowal the means and the authority to safeguard in practice the right of a great people who are at peace and who are desirous of exercising none but the rights of peace to follow the pursuits of peace in quietness and good will—rights recognized time out of mind by all the civilized nations of the world. No course of my choosing or of theirs will lead to war. War can come only by the wilful acts and aggressions of others.[4]

Although a small group of senators prevented approval of a bill authorizing Wilson to arm merchantmen, the President took such action anyway on March 9, 1917. At the same time, he called Congress into special session for April 16, 1917, presumably in order to ask the legislative branch to sanction a more elaborate program of armed neutrality, which he set to work with his advisers in the Navy Department to devise.

By the middle of March, therefore, it seemed that Wilson had made his decision in favor of a limited defensive war on the seas. "We stand firm in armed neutrality," he declared, for example, in his second inaugural address on March 5, "since it seems that in no other way we can demonstrate what it is we insist upon and cannot forego." Yet on April 2 (he had meanwhile convened Congress for this earlier date), scarcely more than a month

[4] *Ibid.*, pp. 428–32.

after he had uttered these words, he stood before Congress and asked for a declaration of full-fledged war. What events occurred, what forces were at work, what pressures were applied during this brief interval to cause Wilson to make the decision that he had been trying so desperately to avoid? We should perhaps put the question in a less positive way, as follows: What caused the President to abandon armed neutrality and to *accept* the decision for war?

There was first the fact that from the end of February to the end of March the Germans gave full evidence of their determination to press a relentless, total attack against all ships passing through the war zones that enveloped western Europe. The sinking of the British liner *Laconia* without warning on February 25 and with loss of American life, the ruthless destruction of three American merchantmen (*City of Memphis, Illinois,* and *Vigilancia*) ° on March 18, and the relentless attacks against the vessels of other neutral nations, to say nothing of the slashing attacks against Allied merchant shipping, removed all doubt in Wilson's mind about the deadly seriousness of the German intention to conduct total warfare against all commerce and human life within the broad war zones.

The more the character of the submarine blockade became apparent, the stronger the conviction grew in the President's mind that armed neutrality was neither a sufficient response physically, nor a proper or legally possible one. He explained this conviction in his war message:

> It is a war against all nations. . . . The challenge is to all mankind. When I addressed the Congress on the 26th of February last, I thought that it would suffice to assert our neutral rights with arms, our right to use the seas against unlawful interference, our right to keep our people safe against unlawful violence. But armed neutrality, it now appears, is impracticable. Because submarines are in effect outlaws when used as the German submarines have been used against merchant shipping, it is impossible to defend ships against their attacks as the law of nations has assumed that merchantmen would defend themselves. . . . It is common prudence in such circumstances, grim necessity indeed, to endeavour to destroy them before they show their own intention. They must be dealt with upon sight, if dealt with at all. The German Government denies the right of neutrals to use arms at all within the areas of the sea which it has proscribed, even in the defense of rights which no modern publicist has ever before questioned their right to defend. The intimation is conveyed that the armed guards which we have placed on our merchant ships will be treated as beyond the pale of law and subject to be dealt with as pirates would be. Armed neutrality is ineffectual enough at best; in such circumstances and in the face of such pretensions it is worse than ineffectual; it is likely only to produce what it

---

° *Editors' note.* "Only the *Illinois* and the *Vigilancia*," Link later noted, "were sunk without warning; the *City of Memphis* was destroyed after warning and evacuation of crew" (*Wilson the Diplomatist,* 2nd ed. [1963], p. xv).

was meant to prevent; it is practically certain to draw us into the war without either the rights or the effectiveness of belligerents.[5]

This passage, in my opinion, reveals the *immediate* reason why Wilson made his decision for war. It was simply that the German assault upon American lives and property was so overwhelming and so flagrant that the only possible way to cope with it was to claim the status of a belligerent in order to strike at the sources of German power. "I would be inclined to adopt . . . [armed neutrality]," the President wrote only two days before he delivered his war message,

indeed, as you know, I had already adopted it, but this is the difficulty: . . . To make even the measures of defense legitimate we must obtain the status of belligerents.[6]

Certainly Wilson had convinced himself that this was true, but I have a strong suspicion that he would have stood doggedly by his first decision to limit American action to a defense of rights on the seas if this decision had not been overridden by convictions, events, pressures, and ambitions that were themselves decisive in Wilson's final shift from armed neutrality to war, in forcing him to the conclusion that the *immediate* circumstances left the United States with no choice but full-scale participation.

One of the most important of these factors was the subtlest and the one for which the least direct evidence can be adduced. It was Wilson's apparent fear that the threat of a German victory imperiled the balance of power and all his hopes for the future reconstruction of the world community. We must be careful here not to misinterpret his thoughts and motives. There is little evidence that he accepted the decision for war because he thought that a German victory would seriously endanger American security, because he wanted to preserve Anglo-American control of the North Atlantic sea lanes, or because he desired to maintain the traditional balance of European power because it served American interests. Nor is there any convincing evidence that Wilson's attitude toward the objectives of the rival alliances had changed by the time that he made his final decision.[°]

---

[5] *Papers Relating to the Foreign Relations of the United States, 1917, Supplement 1, The World War* (Washington, 1931), pp. 196–97.

[6] Wilson to Matthew Hale, March 31, 1917, Wilson Papers, Library of Congress.

[°] *Editors' note.* In 1963, Link modified these judgments. He doubted that the President knew, or was influenced by the fear, that the Central Powers were about to win the war. Nor is there any evidence "that Wilson was importantly motivated by considerations of national security in his own decision for war." Link "would have given greater emphasis . . . to Wilson's conviction that the war was in its final stages, American belligerency would have the effect of shortening, not prolonging the war, and belligerency had the advantage of guaranteeing him an important role in peacemaking" (*Wilson the Diplomatist*, 2nd ed. [1963], p. xv).

On the other hand, there was now a great and decisive difference in the relative position of the belligerents: The Allies seemed about to lose the war and the Central Powers about to win it. This, almost certainly, was a governing factor in Wilson's willingness to think in terms of war. Germany, he told Colonel House, was a madman who must be curbed. A German victory meant a peace of domination and conquest; it meant the end of all of Wilson's dreams of helping to build a secure future.

As the President pondered America's duty at this juncture in history, the answer must have seemed obvious to him—to accept belligerency, because now only through belligerency could the United States fulfill its mission to insure a just and lasting peace of reconciliation. This could be accomplished only by preventing a German victory and only by the assertion of such power and influence among the Allies as would come to the United States by virtue of its sacrifice of blood and treasure.

If the immediate events made a war resolution necessary, then the goal of a righteous peace was the objective that justified full-scale participation in Wilson's mind and raised that effort to a high and noble plane. It was, therefore, not war in anger that he advocated, not war sheerly in defense of national rights, but, as he put it in his war message,

> [war] for democracy, for the right of those who submit to authority to have a voice in their own governments, for the rights and liberties of small nations, for a universal dominion of right by such a concert of free peoples as shall bring peace and safety to all nations and make the world itself at last free.

The combined weight of official and public opinion was another pressure meanwhile driving Wilson toward acceptance of the decision for war. It was a fact of no little consequence that by the end of March every important member of the administration, including those members of the Cabinet who had heretofore opposed any bellicose measures, urged the President to admit that a state of war with Germany in fact existed. Public opinion had remained stubbornly pacific until near the end of February, 1917. Then the publication of the Zimmermann telegram, in which the German government proposed to Mexico a war alliance against the United States, the sinking of the *Laconia,* and above all, the destruction of American ships in the war zones after mid-March generated a demand for war that grew with mounting crescendo in all sections and among all classes, until it seemed beyond doubt to be a national and a majority demand. It was further stimulated by news of the downfall of the czarist regime and the establishment of a provisional republican government in Russia—news that convinced many wavering Americans that the Allies were indeed fighting for democracy and also changed overnight the large and influential American Jewish community from a position of strong hostility toward the Allies to one of friendship.

This was all a development of profound importance for a leader as keenly sensitive to public opinion as was Woodrow Wilson. He could have joined forces with the large antiwar minority to resist the demand for war; indeed, he probably would have done so had he been convinced that it was the wise and right thing to do. The point is not, therefore, that public opinion *forced* Wilson to accept the decision for war, but that it facilitated doing what Wilson for other reasons now thought was necessary and right to do.

All this is said without any intention of implying that Wilson ever *wanted* war. The agony of his soul was great as he moved through the dark valley of his doubts. He had no illusions about the merits of the conflict into which he and his people were being drawn. He saw the risks of intervention, both to his own nation and to the world, with remarkable clarity. But he could devise no alternative; and he set aside his doubts in the hope that acting now as a belligerent, with all the power and idealism of the American people sustaining him, he could achieve objectives to justify the misery of mankind.

SUGGESTED READING

Good surveys of the historiographical controversy on entry into the war include Richard Leopold's "The Problem of American Intervention, 1917: An Historical Retrospect," *World Politics*, II (Apr. 1950); Ernest May's *American Intervention: 1917 and 1941* ° (1960); and Daniel Smith's "National Interest and American Intervention, 1917: An Historiographical Appraisal," *Journal of American History*, LII (June 1965).

D. F. Fleming's "Our Entry in the World War in 1917: The Revised Version," *Journal of Politics*, II (Feb. 1940) is a hostile appraisal of revisionism. Among the major revisionist works are Harry Elmer Barnes's *Genesis of the World War* (1926); Edwin Borchard and William Lage's *Neutrality for the United States* (1937); Charles C. Tansill's *America Goes to War* (1938); and Paul Birdsall's "Neutrality and Economic Pressures, 1914–1917," *Science and Society*, III (Spring 1939). The early revisionists are analyzed by Warren Cohen in *The American Revisionists* (1967).

The best statements of the realist appraisal of Wilson are those of George Kennan in *American Diplomacy* ° (1950); Robert Osgood in *Ideals and Self-Interest in America's Foreign Relations* ° (1953); and Hans Morgenthau in *In Defense of the National Interest* (1951). Walter Lippmann, in *Shield of the Republic* ° (1943), and Edward Buehrig, in *Woodrow Wilson and the Balance of Power* (1955), contend that Wilson understood that American security depended on maintaining the balance of power.

The attitudes of the business community to neutrality and the war have never been systematically studied, but Harold Syrett's "The Business Press and American Neutrality, 1914–1917," *Mississippi Valley Historical Review*, XXXII (Sept. 1945), is useful.

The response of progressives to the war has been dealt with by Walter Trattner in "Progressivism and World War I: A Re-Appraisal," *Mid-America*, XLIV (July 1962); Trattner finds a mixed pattern, contrary to William E. Leuchtenburg's conclusion (in "Progressivism and Imperialism") that the progressives were generally strong supporters of imperialism. Howard W. Allen's "Republican Reformers and Foreign Policy, 1913–1917," *Mid-America*, XLIV (Oct. 1962), and Warren Sutton's "Progressive Republican Senators and the Submarine Crisis, 1915–1916," *Mid-America*, LVII (Apr. 1965), also dissent from Leuchtenburg's thesis.

N. Gordon Levin's *Woodrow Wilson and World Politics* ° (1968) places Wilson's thought within the larger framework of liberal capitalist ideology. Levin's book was favorably reviewed by Arthur Link in the *New York Times Book Review* (April 28, 1968). For theories similar to Levin's, see Arno J. Mayer's *The Political Origins of the New Diplomacy, 1917–1918* (1959) and *Politics and Diplomacy of Peacemaking* ° (1968).

The fight over the League is interpreted by D. F. Fleming in *The United States and the League of Nations, 1918–1920*, 2nd ed. (1968); and by Thomas A. Bailey in *Woodrow Wilson and the Lost Peace* (1944) and in *Woodrow Wilson and the Great Betrayal* (1945). Two essays on Wilson and collective security are D. F. Fleming's "Woodrow Wilson and Collective Security Today," *Journal of Politics*, XVIII (Nov. 1956), and Edward Buehrig's "Woodrow Wilson and Collective Security," in Buehrig, ed., *Wilson's Foreign Policy in Perspective* (1957).

Carl Parrini, in *Heir to Empire: United States Economic Diplomacy, 1916–1923* (1969) places American policy in the broader context of seeking economic expansion abroad.

II

The Twenties

The 1920's has seemed to many historians an aberrant decade, a kind of vacuum between the progressive period and the crisis of the Depression. Warren G. Harding contributed the most famous phrase of the era in his campaign for the presidency in 1920: He urged "not heroism but healing, not nostrums but normalcy"; and thereby delivered both an obituary and a manifesto.

In the 1920's, doubts about big business that prevailed in the first two decades of the century evaporated, and in their place occurred a near-universal celebration of America's business civilization. The heroes of this civilization were not crusading politicians or morally outraged journalists, but tycoons like Henry Ford, the high priest of mass production and inventor of the conveyor belt. When this unlettered mechanic pronounced an aphorism like "Machinery is the new Messiah," his views received reverent attention.

Many intellectuals once critical of business power came in the 1920's to proclaim its beneficence. Lincoln Steffens wrote, "Big business in America is producing what the Socialists held up as their goal: food, shelter, and clothing for all. You will see it during the Hoover administration." The greatest of the so-called progressive historians, Charles A. Beard, concluded his monumental book *The Rise of American Civilization* (1927) by observing that the period of the 1920's was "the dawn, not the dusk, of the gods." Only the literary intellectuals rejected the values of business culture, but they rejected politics and reform as well. Retreating into personal and esthetic experience, writers like Ernest Hemingway and Ezra Pound expressed their dissent by taking up residence abroad.

In the realm of politics the issues and coalitions of the 1920's bore scant resemblance to those of progressivism. The Republican party found that its open commitment to single-interest government did not bar it from national supremacy. Social conflict rather than concern with trusts or civic corruption now dominated politics. In 1916 Woodrow Wilson had assembled the classic progressive coalition: Southern and Western agrarians aligned with laborers, social workers, and the concerned middle classes of the cities. But in the 1920's rural America made its last stand against the values cultivated by the metropolis, and the unity of the old progressive coalition was shattered.

The small towns of the West and South provided millions of recruits for the crusade of the Ku Klux Klan against blacks, Catholics, Jews, and new immigrants who had crowded into the big cities. In 1921 and in 1924 congressmen from the South and West passed immigration acts that discriminated against Southern and Eastern Europeans. Those scientific concepts that were opposed to their religious beliefs and that threatened to spread from the city into the American village caused the rural fundamentalists to rally around the campaign of William Jennings Bryan to expel Darwinism from the public schools. Small-town Americans also provided a sympathetic public for the prosecution at the *Tennessee v. John Thomas Scopes* trial. And of course the Eighteenth Amendment, which outlawed the manufacture and sale of alcoholic beverages, tellingly revealed the diverging morality of dry Protestants in the American countryside and thirsty sophisticates and immigrants in the city.

The Democratic party was nearly destroyed by the conflict between its urban and rural wings. In 1924 at its national convention in Madison Square Garden, the party had to endure more than one hundred deadlocked ballots, with Governor Al Smith of New York City's Irish slums and William Gibbs McAdoo, a former Georgian, each refusing to defer to the other. As testimony to the party's impotence as a counter to business domination, the Democrats chose as their compromise nominee John W. Davis, a Wall Street lawyer with impeccable conservative credentials.

But it would be a mistake to stress only the differences between progressivism and the attitudes of the 1920's, for many historians have come to see the decade as continuous with the preceding years. For instance, Arthur S. Link's article, reprinted in this part, describes the persistence of progressivism among the Western and Southern congressmen, who passed farm-relief legislation and fought for public power, and among the labor leaders and social workers, who were somewhat successful at the state level. Robert M. La Follette, running in 1924 on a third-party progressive ticket without funds or organization, polled at least 16.6 percent of the vote, although some historians argue that much of his support came from groups who were grateful for his antiwar stand in 1917 rather than for his progressivism. Even the ugliest aspects of the 1920's—Prohibition, the racism of the movement for immigration restriction, and the perverted idealism of the Ku Klux Klan —have been ascribed to the progressive mood that had gone sour.

The continuity between the progressive years and the 1920's has seemed most obvious for those who have argued that progressivism sealed the alliance between big business and the government. Dedicated to laissez faire only in theory, Republican politicians lavished government favors on businessmen. With the antitrust laws suspended, the government smiled on a flourishing merger movement and actually encouraged the formation of trade associations in which firms of the same industry devised various forms of cooperation. Secretary of the Treasury Andrew Mellon promoted tax policies designed to favor wealthy individuals and business corporations. Against the best advice of professional economists, Republican administrations sponsored the highest tariffs in American history. And under Herbert Hoover, the Commerce Department sought ways to maximize business efficiency and assiduously cultivated foreign markets.

Beyond this cooperation between business and government, the 1920's shared still another characteristic with the progressive years: the refusal to come seriously to grips with widespread poverty and inequality of wealth. While labor productivity rose 32 percent and corporate profits soared 62 percent from 1923 to 1929, real wages increased only 8 percent. Farmers were mired in depression, and their share of the national income fell from 17 percent in the good year of 1919 to 8 percent in 1929. Sixteen million of America's twenty-seven million families in the 1920's lived on an income of less than $2,000, which was then regarded as the minimum for maintaining health and decency. In the end, the nation paid a penalty for the structural weaknesses in the economy, for they contributed to the Great Depression of 1929, which brought the 1920's to a sad conclusion.

SUGGESTED READING

William Leuchtenburg's *The Perils of Prosperity, 1914–1932* * (1958) remains the finest volume interpreting the 1920's. For a perceptive journalistic account, see Frederick Lewis Allen's *Only Yesterday* (1931). Eric Goldman, in *Rendezvous with Destiny* * (1952), analyzes the decade as "the shame of the Babbitts." Paul Carter's *The Twenties in America* * (1968) is a breezy survey of the culture.

John Hicks's *Republican Ascendancy, 1921–1933* * (1960) is seldom more than a superficial analysis. Arthur Schlesinger, Jr.'s *The Crisis of the Old Order* * (1957), the first volume of *The Age of Roosevelt,* is a better study, though it emphasizes Republican mistakes from a New Deal perspective. Otis L. Graham, Jr., in *The Great Campaign* * (1971), briefly interprets the decade. Karl Schriftgeisser's *This Was Normalcy* (1948) is deeply critical of Republican policies, but it is disappointing for it seldom penetrates below the surface. Malcolm Moos, in *The Republicans* (1956), treats Republican policies more favorably. Robert K. Murray's *The Harding Era: Warren G. Harding and His Administration* (1969) is the best study of the subject. Donald McCoy's *Calvin Coolidge* (1967) is a solid political study that demolishes old myths.

Frank Freidel's *Franklin D. Roosevelt,* Vol. II, *The Ordeal* (1954) is an excellent book on Democratic politics during the decade. It should be supplemented by J. Joseph Huthmacher's *Massachusetts People and Politics, 1919–1933* (1959); David Burner's *The Politics of Provincialism: The Democratic Party in Transition, 1918–1932* (1968); and Samuel Lubell's *The Future of American Politics* * (1952), all of which stress the shift of the city populations toward the Democratic Party. This thesis was first developed by Samuel Eldersveld in "The Influence of Metropolitan Party Pluralities in Presidential Elections Since 1920," *American Political Science Review,* XLIII (Dec. 1949), and has since been modified by Jerome Clubb and Howard Allen in "The Cities and the Election of 1928: Partisan Realignment?" *American Historical Review,* LXXIV (Apr. 1969).

Historians are still struggling to gain a clear focus on the 1920's, and much of the intellectual history is limited to particular individuals or narrow movements. Revealing studies include Henry May's "Shifting Perspectives on the 1920's," *Mississippi Valley Historical Review,* XLIII (Dec. 1956); Lucille Birnbaum's "Behaviorism in the 1920's," *American Quarterly,* VII (Spring 1955), a study first prepared in May's graduate seminar; Arthur Mizener's "The Novel in America: 1920–1940," *Perspectives USA,* XV (Spring 1956); Clarke A. Chambers' "The Belief in Progress in Twentieth-Century America," *Journal of the History of Ideas,* XIX (Apr. 1958); and Warren Susman's "The Useless Past: American Intellectuals and the Frontier Image, 1910–1930," *Bucknell Review,* XI (Mar. 1963). Loren Baritz's "The Culture of the Twenties," in Stanley Coben and Lorman Ratner, eds., *The Development of an American Culture* * (1970), is a fine analysis. Alfred Kazin, in *On Native Grounds* (1942), analyzes the literature of the decade.

John W. Ward, in "The Meaning of Lindberg's Flight," *American Quarterly,* X (Spring 1958), emphasizes the nostalgia for the past and for lost values. This theme is also examined in Charles Anderson's "The Metamorphosis of American Agrarian Idealism in the 1920's and 1930's," *Agricultural History,* XXXV (Oct. 1961). Lawrence W. Levine's *Defender of the Faith: William Jennings Bryan* * (1965) is an excellent examination of the later Bryan and the ideas he represented. Don S. Kirschner's *City and Country: Rural Responses to Urbanization in the 1920's* (1970) is a fine examination of the political-cultural conflict. Clarke Chambers, in *Seedtime of Reform: American Social Service and Social Action, 1918–1933* * (1963), finds a strong social welfare movement in the decade.

Arthur Link's article in this section; Burl Noggle's "The Twenties: A New Historiographical Frontier," *Journal of American History,* LIII (Sept. 1966); and Don S. Kirschner's "Conflicts and Politics in the 1920's: Historiography and Prospects," *Mid-America,* XLVIII (Oct. 1966), are fine introductions to the historical literature on the decade. *Change and Continuity in Twentieth-Century America: The 1920's,* edited by John Braeman *et al.* (1968) is a volume of useful essays. *The Twenties,* * edited by Joan H. Wilson (1972), is a collection of interpretations of the decade.

ARTHUR S. LINK

What Happened
to the Progressive Movement
in the 1920's?

INTRODUCTION

Arthur S. Link, who has devoted most of his scholarly life to a
multi-volume biography of Woodrow Wilson, attempts in the following essay to define progressivism, account for its deterioration after 1918, and demonstrate its partial survival in the 1920's.
Complex and subtle, Link's important article has done much to
discredit the old notion of fundamental discontinuity between
progressivism and the ideology of the 1920's. But however bold,
his efforts are not entirely convincing.

FROM Arthur S. Link, "What Happened to the Progressive Movement in the 1920's?,"
American Historical Review, LXIV (July, 1959), pp. 833–51. Reprinted by permission of
the author.

This paper was read in a slightly different form before a joint meeting of the American
Historical Association and the Mississippi Valley Historical Association in New York City
on December 28, 1957.

Link himself would concede that the prewar reform ethos did not survive into the 1920's and that democratic idealism was scarcely in evidence. Furthermore, he slides over the problem of the apparently contradictory character of progressivism by simply including all unresolved contradictions within his conception of it. Thus he asserts that prewar progressivism embraced both democratic idealists and special interest groups, both middle-class citizens disturbed by business power and businessmen committed to the "strengthening instead of the shackling of the business community." Link's overly inclusive conception of progressivism allows him to claim a strange assortment of activities in the 1920's as evidence of progressivism's survival: the fight for public power and government encouragement of private monopoly, special-interest legislation for farmers and racist immigration laws, prohibition, and tariff protectionism.

In short, working with an inadequate notion of progressivism, Link has necessarily presented a flawed case, for until historians form a convincing conception of what progressivism was before the war, they will find it nearly impossible to trace its course afterward.

*I*f the day has not yet arrived when we can make a definite synthesis of political developments between the Armistice and the Great Depression, it is surely high time for historians to begin to clear away the accumulated heap of mistaken and half-mistaken hypotheses about this important transitional period. Writing often without fear or much research (to paraphrase Carl Becker's remark), we recent American historians have gone on indefatigably to perpetuate hypotheses that either reflected the disillusionment and despair of contemporaries, or once served their purpose in exposing the alleged hiatus in the great continuum of twentieth-century reform.

Stated briefly, the following are what might be called the governing hypotheses of the period under discussion: The 1920's were a period made almost unique by an extraordinary reaction against idealism and reform. They were a time when the political representatives of big business and Wall Street executed a relentless and successful campaign in state and nation to subvert the regulatory structure that had been built at the cost of so much toil and sweat since the 1870's, and to restore a Hanna-like reign of special privilege to benefit business, industry, and finance. The surging tides of nationalism and mass hatreds generated by World War I continued to engulf the land and were manifested, among other things, in fear of communism, suppression of civil liberties, revival of nativism and anti-Semitism most crudely exemplified by the Ku Klux Klan, and in the triumph of racism and prejudice in immigration legislation. The 1920's were an era when great traditions and ideals were repudiated or forgotten, when the American people, propelled by a crass materialism in their scramble for wealth, uttered a curse on twenty-five years of reform endeavor. As a result, progressives were stunned and everywhere in retreat along the entire political front, their forces disorganized and leaderless, their movement shattered, their dreams of a new America turned into agonizing nightmares.

To be sure, the total picture that emerges from these generalizations is overdrawn. Yet it seems fair to say that leading historians have advanced each of these generalizations, that the total picture is the one that most of us younger historians saw during the years of our training, and that these hypotheses to a greater or lesser degree still control the way in which we write and teach about the 1920's, as a reading of textbooks and general works will quickly show.

This paper has not been written, however, to quarrel with anyone or to make an indictment. Its purposes are, first, to attempt to determine the degree to which the governing hypotheses, as stated, are adequate or inadequate to explain the political phenomena of the period, and, second, to discover whether any new and sounder hypotheses might be suggested. Such an effort, of course, must be tentative and above all imperfect in view of the absence of sufficient foundations for a synthesis.

Happily, however, we do not have to proceed entirely in the dark. Historians young and old, but mostly young, have already discovered that the period of the 1920's is the exciting new frontier of American historical research and that its opportunities are almost limitless in view of the mass of manuscript materials that are becoming available. Thus we have (the following examples are mentioned only at random) excellent recent studies of agrarian discontent and farm movements by Theodore Saloutos, John D. Hicks, Gilbert C. Fite, Robert L. Morlan, and James H. Shideler; of nativism and problems of immigration and assimilation by John Higham, Oscar Handlin, Robert A. Devine, and Edmund D. Cronon; of intellectual currents, the social gospel, and religious controversies by Henry F. May, Paul A. Carter, Robert M. Miller, and Norman F. Furniss; of left-wing politics and labor developments by Theodore Draper, David A. Shannon, David Bell, Paul M. Angle, and Matthew Josephson; of the campaign of 1928 by Edmund A. Moore; and of political and judicial leaders by Alpheus T. Mason, Frank Freidel, Arthur M. Schlesinger, Jr., Merlo J. Pusey, and Joel F. Paschal.[1]

---

[1] Theodore Saloutos and John D. Hicks, *Agrarian Discontent in the Middle West, 1900–1939* (Madison, Wis., 1951); Gilbert C. Fite, *Peter Norbeck: Prairie Statesman* (Columbia, Mo., 1948), and *George N. Peek and the Fight for Farm Parity* (Norman, Okla., 1954); Robert L. Morlan, *Political Prairie Fire: The Nonpartisan League, 1915–1922* (Minneapolis, Minn., 1955); James H. Shideler, *Farm Crisis, 1919–1923* (Berkeley, Calif., 1957); John Higham, *Strangers in the Land: Patterns of American Nativism, 1860–1925* (New

Moreover, we can look forward to the early publication of studies that will be equally illuminating for the period, like the biographies of George W. Norris, Thomas J. Walsh, and Albert B. Fall now being prepared by Richard Lowitt, Leonard Bates, and David Stratton, respectively, and the recently completed study of the campaign and election of 1920 by Wesley M. Bagby.[2]

Obviously, we are not only at a point in the progress of our research into the political history of the 1920's when we can begin to generalize, but we have reached the time when we should attempt to find some consensus, however tentative it must now be, concerning the larger political dimensions and meanings of the period.

In answering the question of what happened to the progressive movement in the 1920's, we should begin by looking briefly at some fundamental facts about the movement before 1918, facts that in large measure predetermined its fate in the 1920's, given the political climate and circumstances that prevailed.

The first of these was the elementary fact that the progressive movement never really existed as a recognizable organization with common goals and a political machinery geared to achieve them. Generally speaking (and for the purposes of this paper), progressivism might be defined as the popular effort, which began convulsively in the 1890's and waxed and waned afterward to our own time, to insure the survival of democracy in the United States by the enlargement of governmental power to control and offset the power of private economic groups over the nation's institutions and life.

Brunswick, N. J., 1955); Oscar Handlin, *The American People in the Twentieth Century* (Cambridge, Mass., 1954); Robert A. Devine, *American Immigration Policy, 1924–1952* (New Haven, Conn., 1957); Edmund D. Cronon, *Black Moses: The Story of Marcus Garvey and the Universal Negro Improvement Association* (Madison, Wis., 1955); Henry F. May, "Shifting Perspectives on the 1920's," *Mississippi Valley Historical Review*, XLIII (Dec., 1956), 405–27; Paul A. Carter, *The Decline and Revival of the Social Gospel* (Ithaca, N. Y., 1956); Robert M. Miller, "An Inquiry into the Social Attitudes of American Protestantism, 1919–1939," doctoral dissertation, Northwestern University, 1955; Norman F. Furniss, *The Fundamentalist Controversy, 1918–1931* (New Haven, Conn., 1954); Theodore Draper, *The Roots of American Communism* (New York, 1957); David A. Shannon, *The Socialist Party of America: A History* (New York, 1955); Daniel Bell, "The Background and Development of Marxian Socialism in the United States," *Socialism and American Life*, ed. Donald D. Egbert and Stow Persons (2 vols., Princeton, N. J., 1952), I, 215–405; Paul M. Angle, *Bloody Williamson* (New York, 1952); Matthew Josephson, *Sidney Hillman: Statesman of American Labor* (New York, 1952); Edmund A. Moore, *A Catholic Runs for President: The Campaign of 1928* (New York, 1956); Alpheus Thomas Mason, *Brandeis: A Free Man's Life* (New York, 1946), and *Harlan Fiske Stone: Pillar of the Law* (New York, 1956); Frank Freidel, *Franklin D. Roosevelt: The Ordeal* (Boston, 1954); Arthur M. Schlesinger, Jr., *The Age of Roosevelt: The Crisis of the Old Order* (Boston, 1957); Merlo J. Pusey, *Charles Evans Hughes* (2 vols., New York, 1951); Joel Francis Paschal, *Mr. Justice Sutherland: A Man against the State* (Princeton, N J., 1951).

[2] Wesley M. Bagby, "Woodrow Wilson and the Great Debacle of 1920," MS in the possession of Professor Bagby; see also his "The 'Smoked-Filled Room' and the Nomination of Warren G. Harding," *Mississippi Valley Historical Review*, XLI (Mar., 1955), 657–74, and "Woodrow Wilson, a Third Term, and the Solemn Referendum," *American Historical Review*, LX (Apr., 1955), 567–75.

Actually, of course, from the 1890's on there were many "progressive" movements on many levels seeking sometimes contradictory objectives. Not all, but most of these campaigns were the work of special interest groups or classes seeking greater political status and economic security. This was true from the beginning of the progressive movement in the 1890's; by 1913 it was that movement's most important characteristic.

The second fundamental fact—that the progressive movements were often largely middle class in constituency and orientation—is of course well known, but an important corollary has often been ignored. It was that several of the most important reform movements were inspired, staffed, and led by businessmen with very specific or special-interest objectives in view. Because they hated waste, mismanagement, and high taxes, they, together with their friends in the legal profession, often furnished the leadership of good government campaigns. Because they feared industrial monopoly, abuse of power by railroads, and the growth of financial oligarchy, they were the backbone of the movements that culminated in the adoption of the Hepburn and later acts for railroad regulation, the Federal Reserve Act, and the Federal Trade Commission Act. Among the many consequences of their participation in the progressive movement, two should be mentioned because of their significance for developments in the 1920's: First, the strong identification of businessmen with good government and economic reforms for which the general public also had a lively concern helped preserve the good reputation of the middle-class business community (as opposed to its alleged natural enemies, monopolists, malefactors of great wealth, and railroad barons) and helped to direct the energies of the progressive movement toward the strengthening instead of the shackling of the business community. Second, their activities and influence served to intensify the tensions within the broad reform movement, because they often opposed the demands of farm groups, labor unions, and advocates of social justice.

The third remark to be made about the progressive movement before 1918 is that despite its actual diversity and inner tensions it did seem to have unity; that is, it seemed to share common ideals and objectives. This was true in part because much of the motivation even of the special-interest groups was altruistic (at least they succeeded in convincing themselves that they sought the welfare of society rather than their own interests primarily); in part because political leadership generally succeeded in subordinating inner tensions. It was true, above all, because there were in fact important idealistic elements in the progressive ranks—social gospel leaders, social justice elements, and intellectuals and philosophers—who worked hard at the task of defining and elevating common principles and goals.

Fourth and finally, the substantial progressive achievements before 1918 had been gained, at least on the federal level, only because of the temporary dislocations of the national political structure caused by successive popular uprisings, not because progressives had found or created a viable organization for perpetuating their control. Or, to put the matter another way, before 1918 the various progressive elements had failed to destroy the existing party structure by organizing a national party of their own that could survive. They, or at least many of them, tried in 1912; and it seemed for a time in 1916 that Woodrow Wilson had succeeded in drawing the important progressive groups permanently into the Democratic party. But Wilson's accomplishment did not survive even to the end of the war, and by 1920 traditional partisan loyalties were reasserting themselves with extraordinary vigor.

With this introduction, we can now ask what happened to the progressive movement or movements in the 1920's. Surely no one would contend that after 1916 the political scene did not change significantly, both on the state and national levels. There was the seemingly obvious fact that the Wilsonian coalition had been wrecked by the election of 1920, and that the progressive elements were divided and afterward unable to agree upon a program or to control the national government. There was the even more "obvious" fact that conservative Republican presidents and their cabinets controlled the executive branch throughout the period. There was Congress, as Eric F. Goldman had said, allegedly whooping through procorporation legislation, and the Supreme Court interpreting the New Freedom laws in a way that harassed unions and encouraged trusts.[3] There were, to outraged idealists and intellectuals, the more disgusting spectacles of Red hunts, mass arrests and deportations, the survival deep into the 1920's of arrogant nationalism, crusades against the teaching of evolution, the attempted suppression of the right to drink, and myriad other manifestations of what would now be called a repressive reaction.[4]

Like the hypotheses suggested at the beginning, this picture is overdrawn in some particulars. But it is accurate in part, for progressivism was certainly on the downgrade if not in decay after 1918. This is an obvious fact that needs explanation and understanding rather than elaborate proof. We can go a long way toward answering our question if we can explain, at least partially, the extraordinary complex developments that converge to produce the "obvious" result.

For this explanation we must begin by looking at the several progressive elements and their relation to each other and to the two major parties after 1916. Since national progressivism was never an organized or independent movement (except imperfectly and then only temporarily in 1912), it could succeed only when its constituent elements formed a coalition strong

---

[3] Eric F. Goldman, *Rendezvous with Destiny* (New York, 1953), 284. The "allegedly" in this sentence is mine, not Professor Goldman's.

[4] H. C. Peterson and Gilbert C. Fite, *Opponents of War, 1917–1918* (Norman, Okla., 1957); Robert K. Murray, *Red Scare: A Study in National Hysteria, 1919–1920* (Minneapolis, Minn., 1955).

enough to control one of the major parties. This had happened in 1916, when southern and western farmers, organized labor, the social justice elements, and a large part of the independent radicals who had heretofore voted the Socialist ticket coalesced to continue the control of Wilson and the Democratic party.

The important fact about the progressive coalition of 1916, however, was not its strength but its weakness. It was not a new party but a temporary alliance, welded in the heat of the most extraordinary domestic and external events. To be sure, it functioned for the most part successfully during the war, in providing the necessary support for a program of heavy taxation, relatively stringent controls over business and industry, and extensive new benefits to labor. Surviving in a crippled way even in the months following the Armistice, it put across a program that constituted a sizable triumph for the progressive movement—continued heavy taxation, the Transportation Act of 1920, the culmination of the long fight for railroad regulation, a new child labor act, amendments for prohibition and woman suffrage, immigration restriction, and water power and conservation legislation.

Even so, the progressive coalition of 1916 was inherently unstable. Indeed, it was so wracked by inner tensions that it could not survive, and destruction came inexorably, it seemed systematically, from 1917 to 1920. Why was this true?

First, the independent radicals and antiwar agrarians were alienated by the war declaration and the government's suppression of dissent and civil liberties during the war and the Red scare. Organized labor was disaffected by the administration's coercion of the coal miners in 1919, its lukewarm if not hostile attitude during the great strikes of 1919 and 1920, and its failure to support the Plumb Plan for nationalization of the railroads. Isolationists and idealists were outraged by what they thought was the President's betrayal of American traditions or the liberal peace program at Paris. These tensions were strong enough to disrupt the coalition, but a final one would have been fatal even if the others had never existed. This was the alienation of farmers in the Plains and western states produced by the administration's refusal to impose price controls on cotton while it maintained ceilings on the prices of other agricultural commodities,[5] and especially by the administration's failure to do anything decisive to stem the downward plunge of farm prices that began in the summer of 1920.[6] Under the impact of all these stresses, the Wilsonian coalition gradually disintegrated from 1917 to 1920 and disappeared entirely during the campaign of 1920.

---

[5] On this point, see Seward W. Livermore, "The Sectional Issue in the 1918 Congressional Elections," *Mississippi Valley Historical Review*, XXXV (June, 1948), 29–60.

[6] Arthur S. Link, "The Federal Reserve Policy and the Agricultural Depression of 1920–1921," *Agricultural History*, XX (July, 1946), 166–75; and Herbert F. Margulies, "The Election of 1920 in Wisconsin: The Return to 'Normalcy' Reappraised," *Wisconsin Magazine of History*, XXXVIII (Autumn, 1954), 15–22.

The progressive coalition was thus destroyed, but the components of a potential movement remained. As we will see, these elements were neither inactive nor entirely unsuccessful in the 1920's. But they obviously failed to find common principles and a program, much less to unite effectively for political action on a national scale. I suggest that this was true, in part at least, for the following reasons:

First, the progressive elements could never create or gain control of a political organization capable of carrying them into national office. The Republican party was patently an impossible instrument because control of the GOP was too much in the hands of the eastern and midwestern industrial, oil, and financial interests, as it had been since about 1910. There was always the hope of a third party. Several progressive groups—insurgent midwestern Republicans, the railroad brotherhoods, a segment of the AF of L, and the moderate Socialists under Robert M. La Follette—tried to realize this goal in 1924, only to discover that third party movements in the United States are doomed to failure except in periods of enormous national turmoil, and that the 1920's were not such a time. Thus the Democratic party remained the only vehicle that conceivably could have been used by a new progressive coalition. But that party was simply not capable of such service in the 1920's. It was so torn by conflicts between its eastern, big city wing and its southern and western rural majority that it literally ceased to be a national party. It remained strong in its sectional and metropolitan components, but it was so divided that it barely succeeded in nominating a presidential candidate at all in 1924 and nominated one in 1928 only at the cost of temporary disruption.[7]

Progressivism declined in the 1920's, in the second place, because, as has been suggested, the tensions that had wrecked the coalition of 1916 not only persisted but actually grew in number and intensity. The two most numerous progressive elements, the southern and western farmers, strongly supported the Eighteenth Amendment, were heavily tinged with nativism and therefore supported immigration restriction, were either members of, friendly to, or politically afraid of the Ku Klux Klan, and demanded as the principal plank in their platform legislation to guarantee them a larger share of the national income. On all these points and issues the lower and lower middle classes in the large cities stood in direct and often violent opposition to their potential allies in the rural areas. Moreover, the liaison between the farm groups and organized labor, which had been productive of much significant legislation during the Wilson period, virtually ceased to exist in the 1920's. There were many reasons for this development, and I mention only

---

[7] For a highly partisan account of these events see Karl Schriftgiesser, *This Was Normalcy* (Boston, 1948). More balanced are the already cited Freidel, *Franklin D. Roosevelt: The Ordeal*, and Schlesinger, *The Age of Roosevelt: The Crisis of the Old Order*.

one—the fact that the preeminent spokesmen of farmers in the 1920's, the new Farm Bureau Federation, represented the larger commercial farmers who (in contrast to the members of the leading farm organization in Wilson's day, the National Farmers' Union) were often employers themselves and felt no identification with the rank and file of labor.

It was little wonder, therefore (and this is a third reason for the weakness of progressivism in the 1920's), that the tension-ridden progressive groups were never able to agree upon a program that, like the Democratic platform of 1916, could provide the basis for a revived coalition. So long as progressive groups fought one another more fiercely than they fought their natural opponents, such agreement was impossible; and so long as common goals were impossible to achieve, a national progressive movement could not take effective form. Nothing illustrates this better than the failure of the Democratic conventions of 1924 and 1928 to adopt platforms that could rally and unite the discontented elements. One result, among others, was that southern farmers voted as Democrats and western farmers as Republicans. And, as Professor Frank Freidel once commented to the author, much of the failure of progressivism in the 1920's can be explained by this elementary fact.

A deeper reason for the failure of progressives to unite ideologically in the 1920's was what might be called a substantial paralysis of the progressive mind. This was partly the result of the repudiation of progressive ideals by many intellectuals and the defection from the progressive movement of the urban middle classes and professional groups, as will be demonstrated. It was the result, even more importantly, of the fact that progressivism as an organized body of political thought found itself at a crossroads in the 1920's, like progressivism today, and did not know which way to turn. The major objectives of the progressive movement of the prewar years had in fact been largely achieved by 1920. In what direction should progressivism now move? Should it remain in the channels already deeply cut by its own traditions, and, while giving sincere allegiance to the ideal of democratic capitalism, work for more comprehensive programs of business regulation and assistance to disadvantaged classes like farmers and submerged industrial workers? Should it abandon these traditions and, like most similar European movements, take the road toward a moderate socialism with a predominantly labor orientation? Should it attempt merely to revive the goals of more democracy through changes in the political machinery? Or should it become mainly an agrarian movement with purely agrarian goals?

These were real dilemmas, not academic ones, and one can see numerous examples of how they confused and almost paralyzed progressives in the 1920's. The platform of La Follette's Progressive party of 1924 offers one revealing illustration. It embodied much that was old and meaningless by this time (the direct election of the president and a national referendum before the adoption of a war resolution, for example) and little that had any real significance for the future.[8] And yet it was the best that a vigorous and idealistic movement could offer. A second example was the plight of the agrarians and insurgents in Congress who fought so hard all through the 1920's against Andrew Mellon's proposals to abolish the inheritance tax and to make drastic reductions in the taxes on large incomes. In view of the rapid reduction of the federal debt, the progressives were hard pressed to justify the continuation of nearly confiscatory tax levels, simply because few of them realized the wide social and economic uses to which the income tax could be put. Lacking any programs for the redistribution of the national income (except to farmers), they were plagued and overwhelmed by the surpluses in the federal Treasury until, for want of any good arguments, they finally gave Secretary Andrew Mellon the legislation he had been demanding.[9] A third and final example of this virtual paralysis of the progressive mind was perhaps the most revealing of all. It was the attempt that Woodrow Wilson, Louis D. Brandeis, and other Democratic leaders made from 1921 to 1924 to draft a new charter for progressivism. Except for its inevitable proposals for an idealistic world leadership, the document that emerged from this interchange included little or nothing that would have sounded new to a western progressive in 1912.

A fourth reason for the disintegration and decline of the progressive movement in the 1920's was the lack of any effective leadership. Given the political temper and circumstances of the 1920's, it is possible that such leadership could not have operated successfully in any event. Perhaps the various progressive elements were so mutually hostile and so self-centered in interests and objectives that even a Theodore Roosevelt or a Woodrow Wilson, had they been at the zenith of their powers in the 1920's, could not have drawn them together in a common front. We will never know what a strong national leader might have done because by a trick of fate no such leader emerged before Franklin D. Roosevelt.

Four factors, then, contributed to the failure of the progressive components to unite successfully after 1918 and, as things turned out, before 1932: the lack of a suitable political vehicle, the severity of the tensions that kept progressives apart, the failure of progressives to agree upon a common program, and the absence of a national leadership, without which a united movement could never be created and sustained. These were all weaknesses that stemmed to a large degree from the instability and failures of the progressive movement itself.

---

[8] For a different picture see Belle C. La Follette and Fola La Follette, *Robert M. La Follette* (2 vols., New York, 1953); and Russel B. Nye, *Midwestern Progressive Politics, 1870–1950* (East Lansing, Mich., 1951). Both works contribute to an understanding of progressive politics in the 1920's.

[9] Here indebtedness is acknowledged to Sidney Ratner, *American Taxation: Its History as a Social Force in Democracy* (New York, 1942).

There were, besides, a number of what might be called external causes for the movement's decline. In considering them one must begin with what was seemingly the most important—the alleged fact that the 1920's were a very unpropitious time for any new progressive revolt because of the ever-increasing level of economic prosperity, the materialism, and the general contentment of the decade 1919 to 1929. Part of this generalization is valid when applied to specific elements in the population. For example, the rapid rise in the real wages of industrial workers, coupled with generally full employment and the spread of so-called welfare practices among management, certainly did much to weaken and avert the further spread of organized labor, and thus to debilitate one of the important progressive components. But to say that it was prosperity per se that created a climate unfriendly to progressive ideals would be inaccurate. There was little prosperity and much depression during the 1920's for the single largest economic group, the farmers, as well as for numerous other groups. Progressivism, moreover, can flourish as much during periods of prosperity as during periods of discontent, as the history of the development of the progressive movement from 1901 to 1917 and of its triumph from 1945 to 1956 prove.

Vastly more important among the external factors in the decline of progressivism was the widespread, almost wholesale, defection from its ranks of the middle classes—the middling businessmen, bankers, and manufacturers, and the professional people closely associated with them in ideals and habits—in American cities large and small. For an understanding of this phenomenon no simple explanations like "prosperity" or the "temper of the times" will suffice, although they give some insight. The important fact was that these groups found a new economic and social status as a consequence of the flowering of American enterprise under the impact of the technological, financial, and other revolutions of the 1920's. If, as Professor Richard Hofstadter had claimed,[10] the urban middle classes were progressive (that is, they demanded governmental relief from various anxieties) in the early 1900's because they resented their loss of social prestige to the *nouveaux riches* and feared being ground under by monopolists in industry, banking, and labor—if this is true, then the urban middle classes were not progressive in the 1920's for inverse reasons. Their temper was dynamic, expansive, and supremely confident. They knew that they were building a new America, a business civilization based not upon monopoly and restriction but upon a whole new set of business values—mass production and consumption, short hours and high wages, full employment, welfare capitalism. And what was more important, virtually the entire country (at least the journalists, writers in popular magazines, and many preachers and professors) acknowledged that the nation's destiny was in good hands. It was little wonder, therefore,

---

[10] Richard Hofstadter, *The Age of Reform: From Bryan to F.D.R.* (New York, 1955), 131 ff.

that the whole complex of groups constituting the urban middle classes, whether in New York, Zenith, or Middletown, had little interest in rebellion or even in mild reform proposals that seemed to imperil their leadership and control.

Other important factors, of course, contributed to the contentment of the urban middle classes. The professionalization of business and the full-blown emergence of a large managerial class had a profound impact upon social and political ideals. The acceleration of mass advertising played its role, as did also the beginning disintegration of the great cities with the spread of middle- and upper-middle-class suburbs, a factor that diffused the remaining reform energies among the urban leaders.

A second external factor in the decline of the progressive movement after 1918 was the desertion from its ranks of a good part of the intellectual leadership of the country. Indeed, more than simple desertion was involved here; it was often a matter of a cynical repudiation of the ideals from which progressivism derived its strength. I do not mean to imply too much by this generalization. I know that what has been called intellectual progressivism not only survived in the 1920's but actually flourished in many fields.[11] I know that the intellectual foundations of our present quasi-welfare state were either being laid or reinforced during the decade. Even so, one cannot evade the conclusion that the intellectual-political climate of the 1920's was vastly different from the one that had prevailed in the preceding two decades.

During the years of the great progressive revolt, intellectuals—novelists, journalists, political thinkers, social scientists, historians, and the like—had made a deeply personal commitment to the cause of democracy, first in domestic and then in foreign affairs. Their leadership in and impact on many phases of the progressive movement had been profound. By contrast, in the 1920's a large body of this intellectual phalanx turned against the very ideals they had once deified. One could cite, for example, the reaction of the idealists against the Versailles settlement; the disenchantment of the intellectuals with the extension of government authority when it could be used to justify the Eighteenth Amendment or the suppression of free speech; or the inevitable loss of faith in the "people" when en masse they hounded so-called radicals, joined Bryan's crusade against evolution, or regaled themselves as Knights of the Ku Klux Klan. Whatever the cause, many alienated intellectuals simply withdrew or repudiated any identification with the groups they had once helped to lead. The result was not fatal to progressivism, but it was serious. The spark plugs had been removed from the engine of reform.

The progressive movement, then, unquestionably declined, but was it

---

[11] *Ibid.*, 5, 131, 135 ff. For a recent excellent survey, previously cited, see Henry F. May, "Shifting Perspectives on the 1920's." Schlesinger's previously cited *Age of Roosevelt* sheds much new light on the economic thought of the 1920's.

defunct in the 1920's? Much, of course, depends upon the definition of terms. If we accept the usual definition for "defunct" as "dead" or "ceasing to have any life or strength," we must recognize that the progressive movement was certainly not defunct in the 1920's; that on the contrary at least important parts of it were very much alive; and that it is just as important to know how and why progressivism survived as it is to know how and why it declined.

To state the matter briefly, progressivism survived in the 1920's because several important elements of the movement remained either in full vigor or in only slightly diminished strength. These were the farmers, after 1918 better organized and more powerful than during the high tide of the progressive revolt; and politically conscious elements among organized labor, particularly the railroad brotherhoods, who wielded a power all out of proportion to their numbers; the Democratic organizations in the large cities, usually vitally concerned with the welfare of the so-called lower classes; a remnant of independent radicals, social workers, and social gospel writers and preachers; and finally, an emerging new vocal element, the champions of public power and regional developments.

Although they never united effectively enough to capture a major party and the national government before 1932, these progressive elements controlled Congress from 1921 to about 1927 and continued to exercise a near control during the period of their greatest weakness in the legislative branch, from 1927 to about 1930.

Indeed, the single most powerful and consistently successful group in Congress during the entire decade from 1919 to 1929 were the spokesmen of the farmers. Spurred by an unrest in the country areas more intense than at any time since the 1890's,[12] in 1920 and 1921 southern Democrats and midwestern and western insurgents, nominally Republican, joined forces in an alliance called the Farm Bloc. By maintaining a common front from 1921 to 1924 they succeeded in enacting the most advanced agricultural legislation to that date, legislation that completed the program begun under Wilsonian auspices. It included measures for high tariffs on agricultural products, thoroughgoing federal regulation of stockyards, packing houses, and grain exchanges, the exemption of agricultural cooperatives from the application of the antitrust laws, stimulation of the export of agricultural commodities, and the establishment of an entirely new federal system of intermediate rural credit.

When prosperity failed to return to the countryside, rural leaders in Congress espoused a new and bolder plan for relief—the proposal made by George N. Peek and Hugh S. Johnson in 1922 to use the federal power to obtain "fair exchange" or "parity" prices for farm products. Embodied in the

---

[12] It derived from the fact that farm prices plummeted in 1920 and 1921, and remained so low that farmers, generally speaking, operated at a net capital loss throughout the balance of the decade.

McNary-Haugen bill in 1924, this measure was approved by Congress in 1927 and 1928, only to encounter vetoes by President Calvin Coolidge.

In spite of its momentary failure, the McNary-Haugen bill had a momentous significance for the American progressive movement. Its wholesale espousal by the great mass of farm leaders and spokesmen meant that the politically most powerful class in the country had come full scale to the conviction that the taxing power should be used directly and specifically for the purpose of underwriting (some persons called it subsidizing) agriculture. It was a milestone in the development of a comprehensive political doctrine that it was government's duty to protect the economic security of all classes and particularly depressed ones. McNary-Haugenism can be seen in its proper perspective if it is remembered that it would have been considered almost absurd in the Wilson period, that it was regarded as radical by non-farm elements in the 1920's, and that it, or at any rate its fundamental objective, was incorporated almost as a matter of course into basic federal policy in the 1930's.

A second significant manifestation of the survival of progressivism in the 1920's came during the long controversy over public ownership or regulation of the burgeoning electric power industry. In this, as in most of the conflicts that eventually culminated on Capitol Hill, the agrarian element constituted the core of progressive strength. At the same time a sizable and well-organized independent movement developed that emanated from urban centers and was vigorous on the municipal and state levels. Throughout the decade this relatively new progressive group fought with mounting success to expose the propaganda of the private utilities, to strengthen state and federal regulatory agencies, and to win municipal ownership for distributive facilities. Like the advocates of railroad regulation in an earlier period, these proponents of regulation or ownership of a great new natural monopoly failed almost as much as they had succeeded in the 1920's. But their activities and exposures (the Federal Trade Commission's devastating investigation of the electric power industry in the late 1920's and early 1930's was the prime example) laid secure foundations for movements that in the 1930's would reach various culminations.

Even more significant for the future of American progressivism was the emergence in the 1920's of a new objective, that of committing the federal government to plans for large hydroelectric projects in the Tennessee Valley, the Columbia River watershed, the Southwest, and the St. Lawrence Valley for the purpose, some progressives said, of establishing "yardsticks" for rates, or for the further purpose, as other progressives declared, of beginning a movement for the eventual nationalization of the entire electric power industry. The development of this movement in its emerging stages affords a good case study in the natural history of American progressivism. It began when the Harding and Coolidge administrations attempted to dispose of the government's hydroelectric and nitrate facilities at Muscle Shoals, Alabama, to private interests. In the first stage of the controversy, the progressive objective was merely federal operation of these facilities for the production of cheap fertilizer—a reflection of its exclusive special-interest orientation. Then, as new groups joined the fight to save Muscle Shoals, the objective of public production of cheap electric power came to the fore. Finally, by the end of the 1920's, the objective of a muultipurpose regional development in the Tennessee Valley and in other areas as well had taken firm shape.

In addition, by 1928 the agrarians in Congress led by Senator George W. Norris had found enough allies in the two houses and enough support in the country at large to adopt a bill for limited federal development of the Tennessee Valley. Thwarted by President Coolidge's pocket veto, the progressives tried again in 1931, only to meet a second rebuff at the hands of President Herbert Hoover.

All this might be regarded as another milestone in the maturing of American progressivism. It signified a deviation from the older traditions of mere regulation, as President Hoover had said in his veto of the second Muscle Shoals bill, and the triumph of new concepts of direct federal leadership in large-scale development of resources. If progressives had not won their goal by the end of the 1920's, they had at least succeeded in writing what would become perhaps the most important plank in their program for the future.

The maturing of an advanced farm program and the formulation of plans for public power and regional developments may be termed the two most significant progressive achievements on the national level in the 1920's. Others merit only brief consideration. One was the final winning of the old progressive goal of immigration restriction through limited and selective admission. The fact that this movement was motivated in part by racism, nativism, and anti-Semitism (with which, incidentally, a great many if not a majority of progressives were imbued in the 1920's) should not blind us to the fact that it was also progressive. It sought to substitute a so-called scientific and a planned policy for a policy of laissez faire. Its purpose was admittedly to disturb the free operation of the international labor market. Organized labor and social workers had long supported it against the opposition of large employers. And there was prohibition, the most ambitious and revealing progressive experiment of the twentieth century. Even the contemned anti-evolution crusade of Bryan and the fundamentalists and the surging drives for conformity of thought and action in other fields should be mentioned. All these movements stemmed from the conviction that organized public power could and should be used purposefully to achieve fundamental social and so-called moral change. The fact that they were potentially or actively repressive does not mean that they were not progressive. On the contrary, they superbly illustrated the repressive tendencies that inhered in progressivism precisely because it was grounded so much upon majoritarian principles.

Three other developments on the national level that have often been cited as evidences of the failure of progressivism in the 1920's appear in a somewhat different light at second glance. The first was the reversal of the tariff-for-revenue-only tendencies of the Underwood Act with the enactment of the Emergency Tariff Act of 1921 and the Fordney-McCumber Act of 1922. Actually, the adoption of these measures signified, on the whole, not a repudiation but a revival of progressive principles in the realm of federal fiscal policy. A revenue tariff had never been an authentic progressive objective. Indeed, at least by 1913, many progressives, except for some southern agrarians, had concluded that it was retrogressive and had agreed that the tariff laws should be used deliberately to achieve certain national objectives—for example, the crippling of noncompetitive big business by the free admission of articles manufactured by so-called trusts, or benefits to farmers by the free entry of farm implements. Wilson himself had been at least partially converted to these principles by 1916, as his insistence upon the creation of the Federal Tariff Commission and his promise of protection to the domestic chemical industry revealed. As for the tariff legislation of the early 1920's, its only important changes were increased protection for aluminum, chemical products, and agricultural commodities. It left the Underwood rates on the great mass of raw materials and manufactured goods largely undisturbed. It may have been economically shortsighted and a bad example for the rest of the world, but for the most part it was progressive in principle and was the handiwork of the progressive coalition in Congress.

Another development that has often been misunderstood in its relation to the progressive movement was the policies of consistent support that the Harding and Coolidge administrations adopted for business enterprise, particularly the policy of the Federal Trade Commission in encouraging the formation of trade associations and the diminution of certain traditional competitive practices. The significance of all this can easily be overrated. Such policies as these two administrations executed had substantial justification in progressive theory and in precedents clearly established by the Wilson administration.

A third challenge to usual interpretations concerns implications to be drawn from the election of Harding and Coolidge in 1920 and 1924. These elections seem to indicate the triumph of reaction among the mass of American voters. Yet one could argue that both Harding and Coolidge were political accidents, the beneficiaries of grave defects in the American political and constitutional systems. The rank and file of Republican voters demonstrated during the preconvention campaign that they wanted vigorous leadership and a moderately progressive candidate in 1920. They got Harding instead, not because they wanted him, but because unusual circumstances permitted a small clique to thwart the will of the majority.[13] They took Coolidge as their

---

[13] Much that is new on the Republican preconvention campaign and convention of 1920 may be found in William T. Hutchinson, *Lowden of Illinois: The Life of Frank O. Lowden* (2 vols., Chicago, 1957).

candidate in 1924 simply because Harding died in the middle of his term and there seemed to be no alternative to nominating the man who had succeeded him in the White House. Further, an analysis of the election returns in 1920 and 1924 will show that the really decisive factor in the victories of Harding and Coolidge was the fragmentation of the progressive movement and the fact that an opposition strong enough to rally and unite the progressive majority simply did not exist.

There remains, finally, a vast area of progressive activity about which we yet know very little. One could mention the continuation of old reform movements and the development of new ones in the cities and states during the years following the Armistice: For example, the steady spread of the city manager form of government, the beginning of zoning and planning movements, and the efforts of the great cities to keep abreast of the transportation revolution then in full swing. Throughout the country the educational and welfare activities of the cities and states steadily increased. Factory legislation matured, while social insurance had its experimental beginnings. Whether such reform impulses were generally weak or strong, one cannot say; but what we do know about developments in cities like Cincinnati and states like New York, Wisconsin, and Louisiana[14] justifies a challenge to the assumption that municipal and state reform energies were dead after 1918 and, incidentally, a plea to young scholars to plow this unworked field of recent American history.

Let us, then, suggest a tentative synthesis as an explanation of what happened to the progressive movement after 1918:

First, the national progressive movement, which had found its most effective embodiment in the coalition of forces that reelected Woodrow Wilson in 1916, was shattered by certain policies that the administration pursued from 1917 to 1920, and by some developments over which the administration had no or only slight control. The collapse that occurred in 1920 was not inevitable and cannot be explained by merely saying that "the war killed the progressive movement."

Second, large and aggressive components of a potential new progressive coalition remained after 1920. These elements never succeeded in uniting effectively before the end of the decade, not because they did not exist, but because they were divided by conflicts among themselves. National leadership, which in any event did not emerge in the 1920's, perhaps could not have succeeded in subduing these tensions and in creating a new common front.

Third, as a result of the foregoing, progressivism as an organized national force suffered a serious decline in the 1920's. This decline was heightened by the defection of large elements among the urban middle classes and the intellectuals, a desertion induced by technological, economic, and demo-

---

[14] See e.g., Allan P. Sindler, *Huey Long's Louisiana: State Politics, 1920–1952* (Baltimore, Md., 1956).

graphic changes, and by the outcropping of certain repressive tendencies in progressivism after 1917.

Fourth, in spite of reversals and failures, important components of the national progressive movement survived in considerable vigor and succeeded to a varying degree, not merely in keeping the movement alive, but even in broadening its horizons. This was true particularly of the farm groups and of the coalition concerned with public regulation or ownership of electric power resources. These two groups laid the groundwork in the 1920's for significant new programs in the 1930's and beyond.

Fifth, various progressive coalitions controlled Congress for the greater part of the 1920's and were always a serious threat to the conservative administrations that controlled the executive branch. Because this was true, most of the legislation adopted by Congress during this period, including many measures that historians have inaccurately called reactionary, was progressive in character.

Sixth, the progressive movement in the cities and states was far from dead in the 1920's, although we do not have sufficient evidence to justify any generalizations about the degree of its vigor.

If this tentative and imperfect synthesis has any value, perhaps it is high time that we discard the sweeping generalizations, false hypotheses, and clichés that we have so often used in explaining and characterizing political developments from 1918 to 1929. Perhaps we should try to see these developments for what they were—the normal and ordinary political behavior of groups and classes caught up in a swirl of social and economic change. When we do this we will no longer ask whether the progressive movement was defunct in the 1920's. We will ask only what happened to it and why.

SUGGESTED READING

Historians have generally contended that Link overstated his case for the continuation of progressivism in the 1920's. Herbert Margulies, in "Recent Opinion on the Decline of the Progressive Movement," *Mid-America*, XL (Oct. 1963), summarizes the various positions. Among those who modify Link's analysis are Paul Glad, in "Progressives and the Business Culture of the 1920's," *Journal of American History*, LIII (June 1966), and George Tindall, "Business Progressivism: Southern Politics in the Twenties," *South Atlantic Quarterly*, LXII (Winter 1963). Jackson K. Putnam's "The Persistence of Progressivism in the 1920's? The Case of California," *Pacific Historical Review* (Nov. 1966), should also be consulted.

Louis Galambos' *Competition and Cooperation: The Emergence of a National Trade Association* (1966) and his earlier article "The Cotton-Textile Institute and the Government: A Case Study in Interacting Values Systems," *Business History Review*, XXXVIII (Summer

1964), are fine studies of one trade association and its efforts to restrain competition and seek federal assistance; in part they correct the analysis of James Prothro's *The Dollar Decade: Business Ideas in the 1920's* (1954), which focuses largely on the public statements of laissez-faire by the National Association of Manufacturers and the Chamber of Commerce. Morrell Heald, in "Business Thought in the Twenties: Social Responsibility," *American Quarterly*, XIII (Summer 1961), cites instances of social responsibility in the decade. Otis Pease, in *The Responsibilities of American Advertising: Private Control and Public Influence, 1920–1940* (1958) is an important and penetrating volume on the neglected subject of advertising in American history and is also informative on business and public values between the two world wars.

JOHN HIGHAM

The Tribal Twenties

INTRODUCTION

Politics was boring in the 1920's, and class antagonisms were muted, but bitter conflicts nonetheless divided the American people. These conflicts were social, and they were occasioned in the main by the efforts of small-town America to make a last stand against rum, popery, Darwinian biology, and foreigners. At their best, Americans have championed tolerance and cultural pluralism, but in the decade that began really with the First World War, these values were frequently repudiated.

During the war, the demand for total conformity—"100 percent Americanism" in the phrase of that day—knew no limits of region or class. Aroused patriots turned savagely on the 2.3 mil-

FROM John Higham, *Strangers in the Land* (New Brunswick, N.J.: Rutgers University Press, 1955), pp. 265–72, 274–76, 276–82, 285–99. Reprinted by permission of Rutgers University Press.

lion foreign-born German-Americans, who they assumed were bent on domestic sabotage. Local officials banned German publications, whole states forbade the teaching of German in high schools, German music fell from favor, and sauerkraut was transformed into "liberty cabbage." Empowered by the Sedition Act of 1918 to prosecute those expressing disloyal opinions, the Justice Department relied in part on private vigilante groups to locate sympathy for the Kaiser. One such organization, the American Protective League, had an estimated 250,000 members in 1,200 localities, and it used sometimes ruthless methods to promote the sale of war bonds, enforce the draft, and obtain compliance with wartime economic regulation.

The passion for ideological conformity, first whipped up during the war, continued to thrive in the anxious atmosphere of 1919. Prices were rising rapidly, four million workers were on strike, Bolshevism seemed ready to spread from Russia into central Europe, and in June, anarchists lent credence to rumors of revolution in America by trying to blow up prominent citizens. Many of the strikers were foreign born, as were most of the anarchists and the members of the newly founded American communist parties. Business spokesmen spread the notion that social unrest was the work of foreign radicals, and a gullible public readily agreed. The result was the famous Red Scare of 1919.

At first the Wilson administration resisted the hysterical demands for drastic action to save the Republic. But in October 1919, the Senate unanimously passed a resolution asking Attorney General A. Mitchell Palmer how he intended to meet the threat of radicalism. Palmer bears the ultimate responsibility for the excesses of the crackdown that followed, but as biographer Stanley Coben makes clear (*A. Mitchell Palmer: Politician* [1963]), the real mastermind of the Palmer raids was J. Edgar Hoover, the twenty-four-year-old head of the Justice Department's General Intelligence Division, whose job it was to collect information on radical activity. Hoover's target was foreign radicals. The Immigration Act of 1917, as amended, provided that aliens who were anarchists or who advocated violent overthrow of the government or belonged to groups espousing such beliefs could be deported on warrants signed by the Secretary of Labor. Armed with this statute, Hoover obtained warrants, rounded up some radicals in November 1919, and then on January 2, 1920, sent his agents into thirty-three cities to raid radical meeting places. These raids, the most massive violation of civil liberties in American history, led to the arrest of six thousand persons.

In the next months Hoover became convinced that May Day, 1920, would see the uprising of the Reds in America. Consequently, Palmer began issuing daily warnings, and the authorities readied themselves for revolution. When May Day passed without incident, Palmer became the object of general ridicule, and the hysteria that had sustained the Red Scare rapidly subsided. In the meantime, Assistant Secretary of Labor Louis Post canceled warrants of doubtful legality. When he had finished, only some six hundred aliens were still deportable.

As shown by the abridged chapter reprinted below from John Higham's *Strangers in the Land,* nativism persisted into the 1920's. Higham, who is professor of history at the University of Michigan, has written a brilliant history of American nativism, which he defines as an "intense opposition to an internal minority on the grounds of its foreign (that is, un-American) connections." Nativism, he says, usually took three distinct forms: anti-Catholicism, antiradicalism, and Anglo-Saxon racism. When the nation faces a crisis, nationalism tends to become nativism, and minorities suffer accordingly. The historical evidence is too unwieldy to always fit Higham's neat scheme. Other scholars, moreover, prefer to ascribe the success of immigration restriction in 1924 not to some cyclical change of the nation's mood, but to the culmination of sixty years of gradual animosity toward foreigners. Nevertheless, Higham has illuminated some of the darker recesses of the American experience.

*I*n its basic patterns, the new ferment of 1920–1924 was far from new. The nativisms that came to the fore in 1920 essentially continued prewar trends. They consisted largely of hatreds—toward Catholics, Jews, and southeastern Europeans—that had gathered strength in the late Progressive era, reaching a minor crescendo in 1914. The war had simply suspended these animosities while American nationalism vented itself in other directions. Once the war and immediate postwar period passed, the two leading nativist traditions of the early twentieth century, Anglo-Saxonism and anti-Catholicism, reoccupied the field. Anti-radicalism, their historic partner, had grown hugely under the conditions which temporarily blocked the other two, but its collapse cleared the way for their revival.

As they passed into the 1920's, the Anglo-Saxon and anti-Catholic traditions retained the distinctive character that the prewar decade had stamped upon them. Racial nativism remained fixed on the new immigration (together with the Japanese), rooted in primitive race-feelings, and rationalized by a scientific determinism. It owed to the early twentieth century its prophet, Madison Grant, its southern and western political leadership, and its nation-wide appeal. Anti-Catholic nativism similarly exhibited the characteristics it had developed just before the war. Whereas racism knew no limits of section or class and preserved an air of respectability, anti-Romanism throve outside of the big cities and the cultivated classes. Reborn after 1910 in the small towns of the South and West, religious nativism resumed its prewar pattern of growth, feeding on the continuing surge of rural fundamentalism and the deepening frustration of progressive hopes. Despite the incongruities between religious and racial xenophobias, they had begun to intersect before the World War in the demagoguery of Tom Watson and, less melodramatically, in the program of the Junior Order United American Mechanics. After the war, the two traditions flowed together in the comprehensive nativism of the Ku Klux Klan, an organization which itself dated from 1915.

Yet the tempestuous climate of the early twenties is not to be accounted for simply as a resumption of storms after a temporary lull. The very fact that the lull did prove temporary, that old hatreds came to life after the war instead of being consumed by it, needs explanation. In some degree the causes lay in the objective circumstances of 1920. That year, as part of a general adjustment to peacetime conditions, two factors which time and again in American history had encouraged anti-foreign outbreaks vividly reappeared. One was economic depression, the other a fresh wave of immigration. During the latter months of the year the war and postwar boom collapsed. For a year and a half businessmen, farmers, and workers felt the pinch of hard times, with all the consequences of unemployment, credit stringencies, and tobogganing prices. Unfortunately for the immigrants, the economic down-swing synchronized with a sudden revival of immigration. Virtually halted by the war, immigration had remained at low ebb through 1919 and into the early months of 1920. In the second half of 1919 so many aliens, flushed with wartime savings and embittered toward America, had returned home to Europe that immigration figures showed a net loss. But the tide turned decisively around the end of May 1920. By early September an average five thousand arrivals per day were pouring into Ellis Island. Before the year was out newspapers teemed with hostile comment on the relation between this torrential influx and the worsening unemployment problem. Some thought that immigration was undermining the whole economic system.[1]

A third well-known irritant to ethnic relations intruded into the postwar era, assuming somewhat more importance than it had hitherto displayed. Whereas the scale of immigration and the state of the economy had often contributed significantly to nativist movements, the association of foreigners with crime had not affected their reception to a comparable degree. Crime had helped to make anti-foreign stereotypes rather than anti-foreign hatreds. Prohibition, however, created a much more highly charged situation, for it precipitated a head-on collision between mounting lawlessness and a new drive for social conformity.

---

[1] "The New Tide of Immigration," *Current History*, XII (1920), 704–705; *Literary Digest*, LXII (July 26, 1919), 96, LXV (June 5, 1920), 32, LXVI (September 11, 1920), 18, LXVII (December 18, 1920), 9, and LXVII (December 25, 1920), 14.

On the one hand, the Eighteenth Amendment attempted an unprecedented regimentation of morality by law. Although a tradition of reform
originally sired the prohibition movement, its national triumph awaited the
strenuous spirit of conformity which the war unleashed. Riding the wave of
100 per cent Americanism, the Drys identified their crusade to regulate behavior with preservation of the American way of life. On the other hand,
constraint bred revolt. Prohibition aggravated the normal lawlessness of a
postwar era by opening a vast illicit traffic in alcohol. The immigrants,
whose own cultures imposed no alcoholic taboos, were Wets by habit and
conviction. The dazzling opportunities that prohibition created for organized gangsterism thrust immigrant children into a special notoriety, for
city gangs had long recruited a high proportion of their members in the
disorganizing environment of foreign slum quarters. Thus the ban on alcohol hit the immigrants two ways: it increased their conspicuousness as lawbreakers and brought down upon their heads the wrath of a 100 per cent
American morality.

By the end of 1919 the press was commenting on a rising "crime
wave" and speculating on its alien origins,[2] but it remained for the eruption at West Frankfort to demonstrate the intensity of the hatred of foreign
lawlessness. In the years ahead similar feelings would find a powerful outlet through the hooded legions of the Ku Klux Klan; in the Midwest the
Klan delivered more real assaults on the bootleggers than on any other target. At the same time, one state after another tackled the specter of the foreign criminal with legislation to disarm all aliens. Wyoming took particular care to forbid the possession by aliens of "any dirk, pistol, shot gun,
rifle, or other fire arm, bowie knife, dagger, or any other dangerous or
deadly weapon." [3]

The resumption of immigration, the onset of depression, a wave of
crime—each of these formed part of a social pattern shaped by a return to
peace, and all three had precedents in the circumstances of earlier peacetime eras in which nativism flourished. But if these events help to account
for the regeneration of historic xenophobias in 1920, in themselves they can
hardly explain the peculiar force and magnitude that the reawakened
hatreds now displayed. Indeed, the alien lawbreaker owed his new significance as an anti-foreign symbol more largely to a state of mind that had
crystallized during the war than to the objective circumstances of the postwar period. In many respects the level of hysteria in the early twenties was

---

[2] *Literary Digest*, LXIII (December 27, 1919), 14.

[3] Frank Bohn, "The Ku Klux Klan Interpreted," *American Journal of Sociology*, XXX
(1925), 399; Stanley Frost, "When the Klan Rules," *Outlook*, CXXXVI (1924), 262;
Pauli Murray, ed., *States' Laws on Race and Color* (n.p., 1950), 123, 259, 290, 378, 423,
504, 524. Without attempting a systematic coverage, this volume contains the Wyoming
statute and similar ones passed by six other states, all within the period 1921–1925.

a heritage of mind and spirit from the World War. Pre–1914 traditions supplied the massive roots of that hysteria; post–1919 conditions provided fertile soil for a new season of growth; but 100 per cent Americanism was the vital force that gave it abundant life.

On first thought one may wonder how the new nationalism survived so vigorously the transition from war to peace, when many other wartime ideals were shipwrecked. It is important to realize that during the years from 1915 to 1919, 100 per cent Americanism shared in the heady optimism that flourished during the war and collapsed soon after. If the guardians of an exclusive loyalty had nothing else in common with the cosmopolitan, democratic nationalists, at least they felt a common exaltation. Despite the obsessive fears that tortured the 100 per centers, they too looked forward to a brave new world once the nation had passed through its ordeal. To be sure, their assurance was a grimmer and narrower thing than that of their liberal opponents; real victory would require iron resolution and heroic measures. But a crusading idealism formed a fundamental part of the 100 per cent American outlook. The millennial expectations dominant in public opinion since 1898 had reached a culmination during the war period, deeply affecting almost the whole spectrum of American thought, and 100 per centers acquired much of their evangelical zeal from the gerneral hope that the war's turmoil would usher in a purified, regenerate society. So Americanizers set about with a will to transform the immigrants; patriotic clergymen testified to the spiritually ennobling results of warfare; prohibitionists carried the point that outlawing alcohol would accomplish a general moral improvement and call for little enforcement at that; few seriously challenged President Wilson's vision of a new reign of peace founded on a league of nations.

Perhaps this utopian spirit could not long have survived unsullied under any circumstances. Certainly the harsh facts of the postwar world produced, during 1919 and 1920, a general disillusion. The quarreling at Versailles and the class strife that broke out at home and abroad began the process of deflation and embitterment. It went forward under the influence of partisan wrangling in Congress, economic depression, the manifest failure of Americanization, and the scandalous consequences of prohibition. The letdown seriously undermined democratic, cosmopolitan values, for many who held them abandoned a crusading stance, repudiating their ideals as delusive, nationalism as nasty, and society as unsalvageable. One hundred per cent Americanism, on the other hand, had a built-in shock-absorber which not only saved it from disintegrating but converted every disappointment into rebounding aggressiveness. Believing implicitly that the great source of evil lay outside of their own society, super-nationalists could not hold their own principles at fault when failure mocked them. The trouble must come instead from the tenacity and secret cunning of alien influences, together with a lack of sufficient solidarity on the part of true Americans in resisting them. The nation must gird anew against protean forces working in ever grander and more mysterious ways. Thus, instead of crippling the force of 100 per cent Americanism, the discouragements of 1919–1920 broadened the fears which it expressed and turned it against enemies vaguer and more elusive than either the German or the Bolshevik.

The persistence, then, of the fundamental premises of wartime nationalism was crucial to the nativist climate of the early twenties, but equally important was the loss of the spirit of confidence characteristic of the war years. In their own fashion, 100 per centers reflected the general psychological letdown. They ceased on the whole to look forward to a total defeat of the forces of darkness. The evil was too great, the world too deeply infected. Americans must concentrate their efforts on holding their present ground. In short, 100 per cent Americanism passed entirely to the defensive. Its aggressions took the form not of conquest but of a holding operation to save "the last best hope of earth." The result was an intense isolationism that worked hand in hand with nativism. By mid–1920 a general revulsion against European enganglements was crystallizing. In the debate over the Versailles Treaty an afterglow of Wilsonian ideals had lingered through 1919, and the League of Nations commanded immense support in public opinion (though with increasing qualifications) until the early months of 1920. By autumn not 10 per cent of the daily press, and hardly a single national magazine, still backed the league.[4] America now seemed vulnerable to European influences of every kind. Policies of diplomatic withdrawal, higher tariffs, and more stringent immigration restriction were all in order.

Flowering of Racism

Logically, a nationalism so committed to isolation, so distrustful of entanglements with Europe, should find expression in a general revulsion against all foreigners. Indeed, an indiscriminate anti-foreignism did extend far and wide in the early twenties. It echoed through the debate on the League of Nations; it swayed the policies of the American Legion and rumbled in the "konklaves" of the Ku Klux Klan; it unloosed a new torrent of state legislation excluding aliens from a great many occupations.[5] Nevertheless the most intense and significant anti-foreign feelings still focused on symbols of

---

[4] Thomas A. Bailey, *Woodrow Wilson and the Great Betrayal* (New York, 1945), 47, 153, 201–204, 225–26, 266, 273–74, 289–90; John M. Blum, *Joe Tumulty and the Wilson Era* (Boston, 1951), 254.

[5] On anti-alien legislation see Chapter XI, note 1. Good examples of the connection between anti-League and anti-foreigner attitudes are in Ira E. Bennett, *Editorials from The Washington Post 1917–1920* (Washington, 1921), 420, 569–75; *Grizzly Bear*, XXV (September, 1919), 6, and XXVI (April, 1920), 5.

hatred more specific than the whole foreign population. One hundred per cent Americanism had greatest impact through interaction with older cultural traditions.

As the Red Scare subsided, the Anglo-Saxon tradition displayed more than ever the special magnetism it acquired in the prewar period. No other nativism spoke with equal authority or affected so much of American society. This was the flowering time of the semi-scientific racism that had burgeoned in the decade before the war. Although this ideology had the limitation (from a 100 per cent point of view) of not rejecting all Europeans, it was peculiarly well suited as a channel for the defensive nationalism of an age undergoing disillusion. In the nineteenth and early twentieth centuries racial nativism had developed in minds of a gloomy cast; it registered a failure of nerve on the part of an exhausted elite. Explicitly, racism denied the regnant optimism of the Progressive era; a pessimistic determinism imprisoned ideals within iron laws of heredity. Thus, when the utopian hopes of the war years dissolved, the harsh racial doctrines fitted a prevailing mood. Those doctrines not only explained the apparent imperviousness of the immigrant to Americanization. They also accounted for the failure of all efforts at universal uplift. And they showed that the United States could trust in no ideals save those that rested upon and served to protect the nation's racial foundations.

Intellectually the resurgent racism of the early twenties drew its central inspiration from Madison Grant's *The Passing of the Great Race*. The book had caused no considerable comment when first published in 1916, but now it enjoyed a substantial vogue. New editions appeared in 1921 and 1923, bringing total sales to about sixteen thousand copies.[6] Grant himself never became widely known in spite of sympathetic comments in the editorials of such influential publications as the New York *Times* and the *Saturday Evening Post*.[7] However, his emotionally charged formulation of a thoroughgoing racial philosophy stirred the imagination of many literate people. He inspired a bevy of popular writers and influenced a number of scholarly ones. More than anyone else he taught the American people to recognize within the white race a three-tiered hierarchy of Mediterraneans, Alpines, and Nordics, to identify themselves as Nordic, and to regard any mixture with the other two as a destructive process of "mongrelization."

Of all of the nativist ideologies, racism most directly contradicted the central democratic postulate of equal rights, and it is significant that Grant's ideas flourished at a time when the whole postwar reaction put democratic values at a discount. The Young Intellectuals were cheering H. L. Mencken's raucous denial of the possibility of a civilized life in a de-

---

[6] New York *Times*, May 31, 1937, p. 15.

[7] *Ibid.*, February 20, 1921, p. 2; *Saturday Evening Post*, CXCIII (May 7, 1920), 20.

mocracy; a chorus of lawyers and business spokesmen was proclaiming the United States a representative republic rather than a democracy;[8] the Harding administration was providing an uninspiring example of democracy in action. In this context race-thinkers tended generally to reflect the contemptuously anti-equalitarian outlook that had been one of the unusual qualities of Grant's book when it first appeared. For example, Prescott F. Hall, whose earlier racial diatribes had shown a certain caution and restraint, now characterized the "fatuous belief in universal suffrage" and "the lust for equality" as forms of paranoia.[9] Other nativist writers argued that science proves the "basic fact" of inequality or that democracy perpetuates mediocrity. Lothrop Stoddard, a lawyer in Brookline, Massachusetts, with a Ph.D. in history, wrote a whole book on the menace of the Under Man—the racially impoverished opponent of all elites.[10]

Stoddard was Grant's leading disciple. Unlike most of the new racist intellectuals, however, his main preoccupation concerned the rapid multiplication of the yellow and brown races and the danger—spectacularly stated in 1920 in *The Rising Tide of Color*—that they would soon overwhelm the whole white world. His disillusion with the outcome of the World War took the form of a belief that it was actually a civil war which had vitally impaired white solidarity. Consequently Stoddard was hardly a nationalist at all in any explicit sense. Nevertheless he agreed with Grant that the white man's salvation rested with the Nordics and that the immigration of inferior white races would mongrelize the Nordic into "a walking chaos, so consumed by his jarring heredities that he is quite worthless."[11] Grant, in fact, advised Stoddard during the writing of the book and contributed an introduction to it.

· · · ·

---

[8] *American Industries*, XX (October, 1919), 18; American Constitutional Association, *American Ideals* (Charleston, W. Va. [1924], 5; Albert Greene Duncan, *The Spirit of America* (University of Rochester Bulletin, Ser. XVI, No. 3, November, 1920), 15; James M. Beck, *The Constitution of the United States, Yesterday, Today—and Tomorrow?* (New York, 1924), 206–209, 288–309.

[9] "Aristocracy and Politics," *Journal of Heredity*, X (1919), 166. Hall was deeply impressed by Grant's book, though he had already come to roughly the same point of view through his own studies of European racist literature. Grant, in turn, thought well of Hall and was an active member of Hall's Immigration Restriction League as early as 1905. The relation between the two men may be traced in the Files of the Immigration Restriction League (Houghton Library, Harvard University).

[10] Harry Huntington Powers, *The American Era* (New York, 1920), 184; Frances Rumsey, "Racial Relations in America," *Century Magazine*, XCVII (1919), 786; Theodore Lothrop Stoddard, *The Revolt Against Civilization: The Menace of the Under Man* (New York, 1922).

[11] *The Rising Tide of Color Against White World Supremacy* (New York, 1920), 166 and *passim*.

Fundamentally, of course, the fusion of racism with eugenics meant that scientists who were not anthropologists were acquiescing in a disreputable anthropological theory. European anthropologists in the late nineteenth century had offered much evidence that the population of Europe might be classified into three general physical types; that these types carried with them hereditary cultural traits the scientists had never proved. Yet it was the cultural rather than the physical qualities of races that gave eugenicists and other nativists most concern. However much they might gloat over the external proportions of the "Old American" head, their main interest centered on what lay inside that head and how its contents differed from the moral, political, and intellectual characteristics of differently shaped crania. Grant's *The Passing of the Great Race* had simply assumed, on the basis of some scraps of historical data, a correlation between racial physique and racial culture. But loose historical assertions seemed hardly convincing to earnest eugenicists disciplined to the virtues of statistical analysis. Their willingness to accept the Nordic theory depended to no small degree on a timely stimulus and a fresh group of allies which eugenics received in the postwar era from the field of psychology.

Although eugenicists had exercised their hereditarian bias before the war in counting the number of great men produced by various racial and national groups, they had had no way of comparing the supposedly inborn mental endowments of those groups as a whole. On the eve of the war, however, psychologists forged a wonderful new instrument for measuring some of the psychic differences between races. This was the intelligence test. Allegedly IQ scores did not reflect education. Were they not, therefore, independent of all environmental influences? So leading American psychologists contended. Just then, the war, by calling forth a mass army, fortuitously provided an opportunity for applying group tests on a large scale. Robert M. Yerkes, president of the American Psychological Association, and the corps of distinguished psychologists who aided him in the United States Army's new psychological testing program, gathered a mass of data on the intellectual ability of Negro, native white, and foreign-born soldiers. Published after the war, their studies showed what other investigators were simultaneously learning in testing school children: that northern Europeans scored almost as well as native whites, whereas soldiers born in Latin and Slavic countries averaged significantly lower.[12] Eugenicists seized avidly on these findings as a clinching proof of the racial philosophy and of the inferiority of the new immigration.

Although Yerkes and other psychologists deplored the extravagant

---

[12] Robert M. Yerkes, ed., *Psychological Examining in the United States Army*, Memoirs of the National Academy of Sciences, XV (Washington, 1921), 693. Contemporaneous civilian studies are summarized in William McDougall, *Is America Safe for Democracy?* (New York, 1921), 56–68. For background see Gardner Murphy, *Historical Introduction to Modern Psychology* (New York, 1949), 351–62.

statements in which nativistic popularizers of their work indulged, they themselves fell increasingly under the Nordic spell. In 1921 William McDougall, perhaps the most eminent social psychologist of his generation, advanced a racial interpretation of history based on the data of the intelligence tests. McDougall had long been an ardent eugenicist in England, but only after coming to the United States in 1920 did he emerge as a champion of Nordic superiority. Meanwhile, Yerkes and one of his Army colleagues, Professor Carl C. Brigham, were recasting into racial categories the evidence which they had assembled during the war on the intelligence of immigrant nationalities. Inspired by reading the books of Madison Grant and Charles W. Gould, the psychologists realized how neatly their own studies might serve to substantiate the conception of a hierarchy of European races in America. Thus Brigham's book, *A Study of American Intelligence,* triumphantly concluded: "The intellectual superiority of our Nordic group over the Alpine, Mediterranean and negro groups has been demonstrated." [13] With such authority to sustain them, it is little wonder that not only many eugenicists but also a broad segment of literate opinion in America accepted the tenets of racial nativism as proved truths of science.

.   .   .   .

Public opinion echoed the perturbations of the nativist intelligentsia as never before. The general magazines teemed with race-thinking, phrased nearly always in terms of an attack on the new immigration. By no means all of the discussion displayed the sharp outlines of the Nordic theory. The more old-fashioned Anglo-Saxon concept sometimes served as well, while other writers spoke in behalf of "the American type" or "the old stock." [14] As scientific racism spread downward from patrician circles, it blended with the cruder Anglo-Saxon nativism that was pushing upward from the grass roots of the South and West. The two streams of racial nationalism reinforced one another: the national news magazine *Current Opinion* wrote about keeping America white with as much gusto as the Imperial Wizard

---

[13] Carl C. Brigham, *A Study of American Intelligence* (Princeton, 1923), vi, 192; Robert M. Yerkes, "Testing the Human Mind," *Atlantic Monthly,* CXXXI (1923), 364–65; McDougall, *Is America Safe?* On the popular discussion of the Army intelligence tests see Arthur Sweeney, "Mental Tests for Immigrants," *North American Review,* CCXV (1922), 600–12; *Literary Digest,* LXXVII (June 2, 1923), 27–28; William C. Bagley, "The Army Tests and the Pro-Nordic Propaganda," *Educational Review,* LXVII (1924), 179–87.

[14] See, for example, William S. Rossiter, "What Are Americans?" *Atlantic Monthly,* CXXVI (1920), 270–80; Ramsay Traquair, "The Caste System of North America," *Atlantic Monthly,* CXXXI (1923), 417–23; Charlotte Perkins Gilman, "Is America Too Hospitable?" *Forum,* LXX (1923), 1983–89; *World's Work,* XLVI (1923), 123; *Literary Digest,* LXVII (December 18, 1920), 9, and LXXXI (June 7, 1924), 15.

of the Ku Klux Klan discussed the lessons of eugenics.[15] No one any longer, except possibly some immigrant spokesmen, claimed that America's genius derived from racial mixture. In the former muckraking weekly, *Collier's,* George Creel, who had shown much sympathy toward the immigrants during the war, now denounced them as "so much slag in the melting pot. Opposed at every point to the American or Nordic stock. . . ." [16]

Like every fever in the public imagination, this one could not help but have its droll aspects. Perhaps the Sacramento Church Federation, in asserting that world evangelization depended on the Nordic race, excited mirth in only the most irreverent circles. Certainly the racial controversy over the discovery of America was sober enough, for Professor Osborn argued learnedly that Columbus derived from Nordic blood, whereas others pressed the claims of that indubitable blond, Leif Ericson.[17] By any standard, however, the case of Alzamon Ira Lucas, Psy.D., Ph.D., transgressed the common decencies. Dr. Lucas directed the American Super-Race Foundation, which proposed to awaken all Americans of Caucasian blood to the importance of their preservation. It was unfortunate that on the eve of a Congress of Superior Caucasians called by Dr. Lucas in New York, the world learned that he was a gentleman of African descent and a former minister in a Negro Baptist church.[18]

The International Jew

Of all the European groups that lay outside of the charmed Nordic circle none was subjected to quite so much hatred as the Jews. They had always played a special role in the American imagination, but until the postwar period anti-Jewish sentiment, though unique in kind, probably did not exceed in degree the general level of feeling against other European nationalities. The fear of a Jewish money-power during the 1890's and Georgia's emotional debauch at the height of the Frank Case in 1914 were merely preludes to the much more widespread and tenacious anti-Semitism that developed after the World War. No pogrom has ever stained American soil, nor did any single anti-Jewish incident in the 1920's match the violence of the anti-Italian riot in southern Illinois. Nevertheless the Jews faced a sustained agitation that singled them out from the other new immi-

---

[15] *Current Opinion,* LXXIV (1923), 399; Hiram W. Evans, *The Menace of Modern Immigration* (Dallas, 1923), 5, 12–15.

[16] George Creel, "Close the Gates," *Collier's,* LXIX (May 6, 1922), 9.

[17] Francis W. Coker, *Recent Political Thought* (New York, 1934), 322; New York *Times,* July 30, 1922, sec. 7, p. 8; *American Standard,* I (April 15, 1924), 18–19. On the Sacramento Church Federation see *New Republic,* XXXVIII (1924), 217.

[18] New York *World,* January 13, 1924, p. 3.

grant groups blanketed by racial nativism—an agitation that reckoned them the most dangerous force undermining the nation.

During a period of a general weakening in democratic values social discrimination against Jews would undoubtedly have spread even if no new ideological attack on them had occurred. After the war a flood of Jewish students into private eastern colleges resulted in restrictions on admission similar to those earlier adopted by preparatory schools and college fraternities. Beginning in 1919, New York University instituted stringent restrictions. Columbia soon cut the number of Jews in her incoming classes from 40 to 22 per cent. At Harvard, where Brahmin students feared that the university was becoming a new Jerusalem, President Lowell in 1922 moved, with unseemly frankness, to raise the bars.[19] At the same time job opportunities were continuing to shrink. By the end of the twenties one informed estimate indicated that Jews were excluded from 90 per cent of the jobs available in New York City in general office work.[20]

What was startling, however, was not so much the steady growth of discrimination as the rise of a new anti-Semitic nationalism. On the whole the wartime spirit of fraternity had repressed and inhibited anti-Semitic ideas. Nevertheless, the seeds of a new movement against Jews were to be found in the 100 per cent Americanism of the war years. The more wealthy and prominent Jews in the United States were of German background. Certain 100 per centers, therefore, applied to the Jews the suspicion of all things German. Among some of the bitter, overwrought men who believed that the Wilson administration was dealing laxly, perhaps treasonably, with traitors within and enemies without, dark rumors circulated concerning German-Jewish influence in high places. Henry Cabot Lodge and others whispered about secret ties between Wilson and Germany through Paul Warburg, a recent Jewish immigrant who sat on the Federal Reserve Board. "The government," a Texas businessman exploded, "seems to be permeated with the atmosphere of different kinds of Jews." [21]

The growth of anti-radical nativism during the war opened another channel for anti-Semitic feelings—one that broadened enormously after the armistice. Morris Hillquit's remarkably strong showing as the Socialist, anti-war candidate for mayor of New York City in 1917 gave a good many

---

[19] *Nation*, CXIV (1922), 708; Harry Starr, "The Affair at Harvard," *Menorah Journal*, VIII (1922), 263–76; Harris Berlock, "Curtain on the Harvard Question," *Zeta Beta Tau Quarterly*, VII (May, 1923), 3–5.

[20] Heywood Broun and George Britt, *Christians Only: A Study in Prejudice* (New York, 1931), 231–32.

[21] Letter to Thomas W. Gregory, June 26, 1918, in Gregory Papers (Division of Manuscripts, Library of Congress); Henry Cabot Lodge to Theodore Roosevelt, January 15, 1915, in Roosevelt Papers, Box 286 (Division of Manuscripts, Library of Congress); Elting E. Morison, ed., *The Letters of Theodore Roosevelt* (Cambridge, 1951–1954), VIII, 1304.

people a glimpse of the radical ferment at work in Lower East Side tene-
ments. Leon Trotsky's departure for Russia in 1917, after a brief stay in
New York, and the sympathy with which other Russian Jews in the United
States greeted the Bolshevik revolution sharpened an emerging image of
the Jew as a subversive radical. In September 1918, Brooklyn witnessed the
debut of a periodical "Devoted to the Defense of American Institutions
Against the Jewish Bolshevist Doctrines of Morris Hillquit and Leon
Trotsky." [22]

The Big Red Scare turned these surreptitious by-products of the war
into a thriving anti-Jewish agitation. Most commonly, of course, the nativists of 1919 identified radicalism with foreigners generally, so that anti-
Semitism remained a subordinate aspect of an attack upon the larger immigrant community. Nevertheless, the Jew offered the most concrete symbol
of foreign radicalism, and his significance as such increased very greatly
when 100 per cent Americanism burst through the confining dikes of wartime unity. Stories circulated about the streets of New York to the effect
that every Jewish immigrant would become a soldier in the revolutionary
army assembling in America. A Methodist clergyman testified before a Senate committee that Bolshevism in Russia was drawing much of its inspiration and support from the Yiddish sections of New York. The same doctrine that Bolshevism was a Jewish movement echoed from public meetings
and from the pulpits of many churches. A powerful propaganda organization of conservative businessmen in the Midwest, the Greater Iowa
Association, spread word throughout the state that Russian Jewish ped-
dlers were disseminating Bolshevik literature.[23]

This was the atmosphere in which the most important anti-Semitic
document of the early twentieth century came to America, and gained a
certain credence. After Lenin seized power in Russia, Czarist sympathizers
introduced into western Europe and the United States a spurious concoc-
tion, usually known as "The Protocols of the Elders of Zion," produced by
the Russian secret police at the beginning of the century. The "Protocols"
revealed a conspiratorial plan for establishing a Jewish world dictatorship.

---

[22] *The Anti-Bolshevist,* I (September, 1918), 1. The whole pattern of the new anti-Semitic ideology appears here in embryo: the linking of German-Jewish bankers with Rus-
sian-Jewish Bolshevists, the charge that the Jews hastened American entry into the war
and then treacherously prolonged it, the fear of international influences such as the
League of Nations. On the identification of Jewry with Bolshevism see also New York
Times, November 19, 1917, p. 2, and Jacob Schiff to Louis Marshall, August 19, 1918,
in Archives of the American Jewish Committee, Box 72 (New York).

[23] Benjamin Antin, *The Gentleman from the 22nd* (New York, 1927), 82; *Hearings:
Brewing and Liquor Interests and German and Bolshevik Propaganda* (Senate Subcommittee on the Judiciary, 66 Cong., 1 Sess., Washington, 1919), III, 112 ff.; *Literary Digest,* LXI (April 19, 1919), 32, and LXV (May 8, 1920), 52; *Nation,* CXI (1920), 493;
Harry Schneiderman to Cyrus Adler, December 29, 1919, and Herbert Hirsch to American Jewish Committee, January 9, 1920, in A.J.C. Archives, Box 132.

Purportedly drawn up by the leaders of world Jewry, the plan involved financial monopoly, chaos, war, and revolution.[24] Everywhere the intrigues of the Elders were advanced as an explanation for the downfall of Russia and the spread of Bolshevism. The "Protocols" reached America in 1918 through Czarist army officers who had come to this country on a military mission, notably through Lieutenant Boris Brasol. Brasol foisted upon the Military Intelligence Division of the United States Army an English translation of the "Protocols" and started typewritten copies circulating in other influential circles in Washington, D. C. A renegade associate, one Casimir Pilenas, tried to extort $50,000 for the manuscript from the American Jewish Committee.[25]

Although Brasol failed to influence governmental policy, he did get the "Protocols" before a larger public through the aid of two organizations engaged in 100 per cent American propaganda. One of these, the National Civic Federation, had adopted a nationalist line (in place of its original program of collaboration between capital and labor) too recently to give Brasol more than a little, covert support; the director, Ralph Easley, was forced to edit all anti-Semitism from Brasol's contributions to N.C.F. propaganda.[26] But the American Defense Society, the very quintessence of 100 per cent Americanism, took the White Russian and the "Protocols" under its wing. (Brasol had been in close contact with the chairman of the society even before the war ended.) Apparently under its subsidy, a small publishing house issued an American edition of the "Protocols" in August 1920. The American Defense Society then distributed copies among its members. Other copies of the book, which included much supplementary data on the responsibility of the Jews for Bolshevism, were sent to many Congressmen.[27] Shortly thereafter one of the society's most active members, the well-known publisher, George Haven Putnam, put out an American edition

---

[24] John S. Curtiss, *An Appraisal of the Protocols of Zion* (New York, 1942).

[25] Statement by Dr. Harris A. Houghton, February 9, 1919, and Cyrus Adler to Louis Marshall, April 25, 1921, in A.J.C. Archives, Box 132; Stephen S. Wise to Thomas W. Gregory, December 3, 1928, and Gregory to Wise, December 10, 1928, in Gregory Papers. Correspondence with and about Pilenas is in A.J.C. Archives, Box 75.

[26] Ralph Easley to J. P. Morgan, July 8, 1920, in Files of the National Civic Federation (Manuscript Division, New York Public Library); Norman Hapgood, "The Inside Story of Henry Ford's Jew-Mania," *Hearst's International*, XLII (September, 1922), 133–34.

[27] Hapgood, "Inside Story," *Hearst's International*, XLII (August, 1922), 45, 119; Cyrus Adler to Louis Marshall, September 15, 1920, and Adolph Kraus to Henry B. Joy, October 20, 1920, in A.J.C. Archives, Box 132; *The Protocols and World Revolution* (Boston, 1920). See also Brasol to Theodore Roosevelt, September 13, 1918, in Roosevelt Papers, Box 188. Meanwhile this enterprising officer was writing an anti-Semitic work of his own, *The World at the Cross Roads* (Boston, 1921), and a theoretical critique of Marxism, *Socialism vs. Civilization* (New York, 1920). Later Brasol became an authority on criminology.

of *The Cause of World Unrest,* a British polemic based upon the "Protocols." [28]

Up to this point the anti-Semitic movement had fed largely on the Red Scare, reflecting the conditions of 1917–1919 rather than the newer anxieties emerging in 1920. At the very time, however, when anti-Semitism was coming into the open and the "Protocols" were beginning to play a small part in molding public opinion, anti-radical nativism was subsiding. Instead of collapsing with it, the anti-Jewish strain in 100 per cent Americanism outlived that early phase and passed on from a time of war and revolution to one of depression and disillusion. The importance of anti-Semitism actually increased in the course of this transition, because in 1920 it came out from under the shadow of the Red Scare; it became in its own right one of the major nativisms of the early twenties.

Far from interfering with this shift, the "Protocols" presented revolution merely as one instrument by which the Jew sought mastery of the world; they could be read in other lights aside from the glare of Bolshevism. Although fear of Jewish radicalism remained an important element in the anti-Semitic complex, the character of the assault broadened significantly. The Bolshevik theme fused with an onslaught on Jewish capitalism and a supplementary attack on Jewish morality; and over all of these clashing charges hovered an image of the Jew as a peculiarly and supremely international force.

Though the "Protocols" served to substantiate the menace of the "International Jew," his entry into the stream of American nativism was largely independent of such exotic documents. Twice before 1920 this world-wide power, conspiring against all nations, had invaded American imaginations: once during the "battle of the standards" in the 1890's, again (on a more limited scale) during the Frank Case on the eve of the World War. At both times factors that reappeared in 1920 had contributed to the concept. Both the nineties and 1914 were periods of depression, in which the countryside suffered at least as much as the city from impersonal economic forces of international proportions. When hard times struck again in 1920, they bore down especially heavily on the agricultural areas. Townsfolk and rural people who had followed Bryan and Watson in the nineties now saw their wartime gains wiped out and the subjugation of their agrarian society confirmed. Also, the twenties repeated a second characteristic of the 1890's, namely, a strong, diffuse nationalism not confined to a single foreign adversary but rather distrustful of a whole outside world. The isolationist reaction evident in 1920 pressed home the danger of world entanglements in a more conscious and articulate way than ever before. Whereas imperi-

---

[28] *The Cause of World Unrest* (New York, 1920). The depth of Putnam's own anti-Semitism is fully revealed in Putnam to Lee Weiss, March 13, 1922, and Schneiderman to Marshall, March 14, 1922, in A.J.C. Archives, Box 132.

alism had swallowed up the free-floating jingoism of the nineties, and hy-
phenism had absorbed the assorted anti-foreign movements of 1914, the
disillusion that followed the war left nationalists with no alternative to a
thoroughgoing revulsion from all global crusades or encounters. Thus,
while economic distress aroused old resentments at an alien money-power,
isolation seemed a last defense against a threatening world.

It may be significant too that the very disillusion responsible for the
recoil from international engagements closed in upon democratic reform as
well. Though convinced that things had gone terribly wrong at home and
abroad, men lacked the confidence to renew the progressive spirit of the
prewar years. Their sense of social malaise, unallayed by substantial institutional reconstruction, found more shadowy and less rational objects. All
of the xenophobias rampant in postwar America benefited from this failure
of democratic morale, for it meant that the chief ideological check on the
nativist traditions in the Progressive era was now relaxed. As far as anti-
Semitism is concerned, the decline of progressivism helps to explain why
the kind of sentiment that Tom Watson had incited during the Frank Case
became much more widespread in the early twenties. Watson had appealed to rural or small-town progressives whose faith in concrete reform
was already foundering and whose hatred of the trusts could be partially
deflected to world conspiracies, Catholic and Jewish. Under the impact of
the far greater disillusion of the postwar period, many more of the same
kind of people found a substitute for reform in tilting at an international
enemy, half banker and half Bolshevik.

.   .   .   .   .

Another index of the locus and relative importance of the anti-Semitic theme may be found in the chief organization that fostered it, the Ku
Klux Klan. Since all of the xenophobias of the 1920's flowed into this central apotheosis of a tribal spirit, the Klan furnishes a kind of litmus-paper
test of rural nativism. Significantly, the Klan's home was not in the great
cities. Its strength came chiefly from the towns, from the villages, and from
the ordinarily tranquil countryside. Through the theory and practice of a
"noble Klannishness," anti-Semitism achieved, for the first time in American history, substantial organizational expression.

Klan propaganda echoed . . . [Henry Ford's] attack on the Jewish
banker-Bolshevik, adding a special emphasis on vice that reflected the
powerful strain of evangelical morality in the organization. To the Klan the
Jew stood for an international plot to control America and also for the
whole spectrum of urban sin—for pollution of the Sabbath, bootlegging,
gambling, and carnal indulgence. Thus Klan publications described the
Jew as a subversive radical, a Shylock seeking power through money, and
a "Christ-killing" monster of moral corruption. All of these destructive
forces radiated from the centers of population, and Klansmen had the

assurance—in the words of one Oregon spellbinder—that in some cities "the Kikes are so thick that a white man can hardly find room to walk on the sidewalk." [29]

Still, later generations of Americans, remembering the Hitlerite groups of the 1930's, can easily exaggerate the part that anti-Semitism played in the organized nativism of the postwar decade. The Jew occupied, on the whole, a distinctly secondary rank in the Klan's demonology. On the level of ideas, other passions outweighed, other hatreds outreached the attack on the Jew. As for direct action, he suffered largely from sporadic economic proscriptions. In southern as well as western towns boycotts harassed long-established Jewish merchants; sometimes enterprising Klansmen launched their own proudly labeled "100 per cent American" clothing stores.[30] But personal violence was quite rare. Klan energies found larger outlet in the older, more massive traditions of American nativism. It is time to turn to the whole range of the Klan's operations, and to its central meaning.

The Klan Rides

In Atlanta on October 16, 1915, exactly two months after the Leo Frank lynching and at a time when excitement over the case still ran high in Georgia, William J. Simmons conjured into being the Invisible Empire of the Knights of the Ku Klux Klan and anointed himself its Imperial Wizard. For a number of years Simmons had made a living in the rural South as a salesman and organizer of national fraternal orders. He had promoted, or at least belonged to, more than a dozen of them, including Masonry, the Knights Templar, and the Woodmen of the World; in the latter he held the rank of colonel. As befitted a southern "colonel," he had cultivated a majestic presence and a grand manner that belied his village origin. Now Colonel Simmons was launching a secret order of his own.

The idea was not wholly spontaneous. The Frank lynchers had called themselves the "Knights of Mary Phagan," and Tom Watson was currently writing about the need for a new Ku Klux Klan.[31] In the same year a tremendously successful historical film (*The Birth of a Nation*) glorified the long-defunct Klan which ex-Confederates had organized in the Reconstruction era to intimidate Carpetbaggers and Negroes. Simmons was just the

---

[29] "Memorandum on the Activities of the Ku Klux Klan in the State of Oregon," in General Records of the Department of Justice, File 198589 (National Archives); *The Imperial Night-Hawk*, June 27, 1923, p. 6; Bohn, "Klan Interpreted," 387–88.

[30] See correspondence of October 25, 1921, May 16, 1922, and June 24, 1924, in Justice File 198589; Samuel Taylor Moore, "Consequences of the Klan," *Independent*, CXIII (1924), 534–35.

[31] Woodward, *Tom Watson*, 443; New York *Times*, June 26, 1915, p. 4.

man to revive a vanished sectional institution as an instrument of modern American nationalism. His cloudy wits spun with the myths and history of the South; his heart exuded southern sentiment as a plum does juice. From his father, a small-town doctor and an ex-officer in the original Klan, Simmons heard bewitching tales of how it saved white civilization. Undoubtedly he knew also about the subsequent tradition of night-riding, by which rural bands often masked in white caps meted out informal justice upon their neighbors. He liked to trace his original inspiration to a vision that came upon him at the turn of the century not long after he returned from serving in the Spanish-American War—a vision that turned the clouds one day into white-robed horsemen galloping across the sky.

Simmons supplemented these romantic traits with an evangelical piety, a fine dramatic sense and, above all, the gift of the word. Converted by "the old-time religion" at a camp meeting, he had tried his hand at preaching before turning to the more lucrative field of fraternal work, and he remained a mellifluous orator. His first acts as Imperial Wizard were to draw up the high-sounding ritual of the Kloran, create a galaxy of Kleagles, Kligrapps, Cyclops, Geniis, and Goblins, and summon his little band of followers to Stone Mountain, where they dedicated themselves before a flaming cross and a flag-draped altar to uphold Americanism, advance Protestant Christianity, and eternally maintain white supremacy.

In modeling his little society fairly closely on the Klan of yore, Simmons had in mind the same social objective of controlling the Negroes, who were (he believed) getting "uppity" again. Even at the outset, however, there were important differences between the two organizations, and they grew more sharp as the new Klan evolved. The latter, unlike its predecessor, was formed partly as a money-making scheme; Simmons, who was half visionary and half promoter, designed his own Klan as a fraternal order in the hope of enriching himself by selling insurance benefits to the membership.[32] Although the Klan failed to develop along such lines, it always remained something of a racket.

More importantly, it differed from the first Klan in being an avowedly *patriotic* fraternal order. Apparently the Colonel did not begin with an overtly nativist program, but his venture reflected a strong nationalist impulse. It embodied the twentieth century fusion of primitive race-feelings with Anglo-Saxon nationalism. The nineteenth century Klan, a product of sectional strife, had championed white supremacy (and white supremacy only) at a time when southern race-feelings clashed directly with nationalism. The new Klan reflected the coalescence of racial and na-

---

[32] The best accounts of Simmons and of the Klan's early years are in Robert L. Duffus, "Salesmen of Hate: The Ku Klux Klan," *World's Work*, XLVI (1923), 31–33; *Hearings: The Ku Klux Klan* (House Committee on Rules, 67 Cong., 1 Sess., Washington, 1921), 67–69; Winfield Jones, *Knights of the Ku Klux Klan* (New York, 1941), 72–82; William G. Shepherd, "How I Put Over the Klan," *Collier's*, LXXXII (July 14, 1928), 5–7, 32–35.

tional loyalties. Simmons' organization dramatized what the more diffuse movements of the early twentieth century had already revealed: the South was pushing into the forefront of American nativism. Thus in contrast to the first Klan, which admitted white men of every type and background, the second Klan accepted, only native-born Protestant whites and combined an anti-Negro with an increasingly anti-foreign outlook. Always Anglo-Saxon nationalism remained one of the main pillars of its strength.

For five years after its founding, the Invisible Empire was far more invisible than imperial. It recruited during that time a maximum of five thousand members and attracted practically no public attention. Part of its weakness came from Simmons' impracticality. He wasted money, kept careless accounts, and generally showed no business sense. A greater impediment, however, was the temporary subsidence of racial nationalism just at the time when the Klan was forming. The war period offered very little occasion for and indeed inhibited the Klan's *raison d'être*. Significantly, the order seems to have made what little progress it did by adapting itself to the typical pattern of wartime 100 per cent Americanism. Simmons joined an auxiliary of the American Protective League, turned his followers to spy-hunting, and began to envisage the Klan not as a benevolent order but as a vast secret service agency. One of the early, if not the first, public appearances of the Klan occurred late in the war in Montgomery, Alabama, when a hundred hooded Klansmen paraded through the main streets warning slackers and spies to get out of town and demanding that all others aid the Red Cross and buy their share of Liberty bonds.[33] Thereafter, wherever the Klan went and whatever it did, it persistently worked to enforce the 100 per cent American ethic of coercive conformity. The success of the Klan awaited, however, the return of a climate of opinion congenial to its own distinctive background.

The period of expansion began in the summer of 1920. Simmons joined forces with a pair of hard-boiled publicity agents, dour-faced Edward Y. Clarke and his plump partner, Mrs. Elizabeth Tyler. Both had long experience in fund-raising drives. They took over the actual management of the Klan, entering a contract with Simmons that guaranteed them $8 out of every $10 initiation fee collected by their organizers. Clarke and Tyler then launched an impressive membership campaign, operating partly through newspaper publicity, more largely through agents who usually started in a community by soliciting at the Masonic lodges.[34] In the next sixteen months they brought in about ninety thousand members. For this accomplishment Clarke and Tyler have generally received the whole credit. The secret of their success, however, lay essentially in the mood and

---

[33] William G. Shepherd, "Ku Klux Koin," *Collier's*, LXXXII (July 21, 1928), 8–9; New Orleans *Times-Democrat*, September 23, 1918.

[34] C. Anderson Wright to Warren G. Harding, September 22, 1921, and "Memo on the Klan in Oregon," in Justice File 198589.

circumstances of 1920. The whole complex of factors—depression, prohibition, and immigration; disillusion, isolationism, and reaction—that shunted
100 per cent Americanism into the older nativistic channels contributed to
the Klan's growth. Never before had a single society gathered up so many
hatreds or given vent to an inwardness so thoroughgoing.

Among the special circumstances stimulating the Klan's initial surge,
not least was the agricultural depression that began in 1920. As cotton
prices plunged catastrophically, desperate farmers in half a dozen states re-
sorted to the old practice of night-riding in order to check the sale of cotton. All through the fall and winter of 1920–21 masked bands roamed the
countryside warning ginneries and warehouses to close until prices advanced. Sometimes they set fire to establishments that defied their edict.
Occasionally there was shooting.[35] Klan officials disavowed and apparently
disapproved of this wave of economic terrorism, which indeed was soon
suppressed by law enforcement officials. Like previous nativist organizations, the Klan had no economic program and rarely functioned in economic
terms except to enforce a pattern of discrimination. Nevertheless the gin-
burners frequently wore Ku Klux garb,[36] and their nocturnal exploits drew
attention to the potentialities of the hooded order. Night-riding of a different kind flourished within the Klan, and it seems hardly doubtful that the
organization diverted farmers' economic frustrations into more socially acceptable types of aggression.

The first acknowledged public appearances of the Klan in the postwar period reflected its underlying racial spirit. On the eve of the election
of 1920, Klansmen paraded in many southern towns as a silent warning
against Negro voting.[37] A large number of anti-Negro outrages were committed in the next few months under Klan auspices, provoked partly by
fear that a "New Negro" had emerged from the war. (In point of fact,
Negro veterans returning from France in 1919 and 1920 were often determined to stand militant and upright.) The men in white bludgeoned employers into downgrading or discharging Negro employees, intimidated
Negro cotton-pickers into working for wages they would not otherwise accept, forced Negro residents out of a part of South Jacksonville coveted by
whites, and branded the letters "KKK" on the forehead of a Negro bell-
boy.[38] In these early months of expansion the organization presented itself
very largely as a means for keeping "the nigger in his place."

---

[35] New York *Times*, 1920: October 7, p. 1, October 11, p. 1, October 28, p. 17, and November 1, p. 1; 1921: January 24, p. 1, and March 7, p. 15.

[36] *Ibid.*, October 20, 1920, p. 12, and November 1, 1920, p. 27.

[37] Walter F. White, "Election by Terror in Florida," *New Republic*, XXV (1921), 195;
New York *Times*, October 31, 1920, p. 12.

[38] Samuel D. Miller to Chief of Bureau of Investigation, September 25, 1921, Lena M.
Clarke to Bureau of Investigation, October 17, 1921, and J. H. Williams to Department

White supremacy remained an important theme even when the Klan spread into the North, but it would be a mistake to regard the Negro issue as the mainspring of its career. Fear of the "New Negro" rapidly declined as he either accepted his old place or moved to northern cities. By mid–1921 the Klan was specializing in attacking white people, and thereafter the great bulk of its disciplinary activities in all parts of the country had to do with whites.[39] This shift of emphasis by no means indicated a slackening of the racial imperative. To a considerable degree, however, it suggested that race-thinking was more and more taking a nativistic and nationalistic direction. The Klan's snowballing advance in the early twenties paralleled the upthrust of racial nativism in public opinion generally. And within the order an insistence on preserving the superiority of the old Anglo-Saxon stock over foreigners of every description became pronounced. Edward Y. Clarke exemplified this trend in 1922 by defining the Klan's mission as one of creating national solidarity by protecting "the interest of those whose forefathers established the nation." [40] Other Klan leaders, in particularizing on the old stock's interest, called immigration restriction the most momentous legislative issue of the day, asserted that only Anglo-Saxons or nordics had an inherent capacity for American citizenship, damned "the cross-breeding hordes" of the new immigration, and trembled lest the "real whites" fail to keep the nation "free from all mongrelizing taints." [41] This emphatic Anglo-Saxonism did not, of course, prevent the same men from ranting loudly at foreigners as such, on the plea that America must be made safe for Americans.

If the Ku Klux Klan had mobilized only this much of the emotional ferment of the period, if it had functioned only through an Anglo-Saxon version of 100 per cent Americanism and through related fears of Jews and of foreigners generally, it would have incarnated a very large part of the current tribal spirit. Yet the Klan had another big side. By embracing the anti-Catholic tradition along with the racial tradition and the new anti-Semitism, it comprehended the whole range of post–1919 nativism. Anti-Catholicism did not prevail as widely in American public opinion as did the Anglo-Saxon ideas reflected in the organization; an urban, materialistic

---

of Justice, September 8, 1921, in Justice File 198589; Charles P. Sweeney, "The Great Bigotry Merger," *Nation*, XCV (1922), 8; New York *Times*, April 3, 1921, p. 13.

[39] *Literary Digest*, LXX (August 27, 1921), 12; Robert L. Duffus, "How the Ku Klux Klan Sells Hate," *World's Work*, XLVI (1923), 179.

[40] *Literary Digest*, LXXIV (August 5, 1922), 52. Although Clarke's whole statement was somewhat more loosely phrased than I have suggested, this was his essential meaning.

[41] Ku Klux Klan, *Papers Read at the Meeting of Grand Dragons . . .* (Asheville, 1923), 132–33; Hiram W. Evans, *The Menance of Modern Immigration* [Dallas, 1923], 20; *Imperial Night-Hawk* (Atlanta), May 25, 1923, p. 5, July 12, 1923, p. 2, August 15, 1923, p. 6, and January 23, 1924, p. 2; Chicago *Dawn*, June 2, 1923, p. 12.

culture had stifled in too many Americans the religious feelings on which Protestant xenophobia fed. Due, however, to the semirural base of the Klan, within its ranks anti-Catholicism actually grew to surpass every other nativistic attitude. In fact, a religious impulse, perverted but not devoid of idealistic implications, accounts for much of the Klan's distinctive energy, both as a nativist organization and as an agent of other kinds of repressions too.

Although the Klan was Protestant from the day its first cross burned on Stone Mountain, an anti-Catholic emphasis came into the order only in the course of its expansion in 1920 and 1921. Simmons, Clarke, and Tyler had not at first expected to sell the organization as a bulwark against Rome. The Klan's stress on religious nativism, even more than the parallel expansion of its Anglo-Saxon agitation, reflected the passions of the people who joined it.[42] By 1920 the anti-Catholic crusade that had appeared in the South and West after 1910 was reasserting itself more powerfully than ever. Under a prohibitionist governor, Alabama pointed the way as early as 1919. While laying plans for inspecting convents, the state also challenged Catholic (and secular) sentiment by requiring daily Bible reading in the public schools, thus reviving a trend begun in Pennsylvania in 1913.[43] The following year the tide came in strongly. Tom Watson's Senatorial campaign spread about Georgia an impression that President Wilson had become a tool of the Pope; Governor Sidney J. Catts stomped up and down Florida warning that the Pope planned to invade the state and transfer the Vatican there; an able journalist reported that anti-Catholicism had become "second only to the hatred of the Negro as the moving passion of entire Southern communities"; Michigan and Nebraska debated constitutional amendments banning parochial schools; and in Missouri the once-mighty anti-Catholic weekly, *The Menace*, revived under a new name, *The Torch*.

Sentiment of this kind amounted to a standing invitation to secret societies. The first to respond prominently was not the Klan but rather the True Americans, a local southern organization. The T.A.'s acquired such influence in Birmingham in 1920 that they dominated the city administration and secured a purge of Catholic municipal employees.[44] Before long Ku Kluxers eclipsed and very likely absorbed the True Americans. Klan propaganda, reviving all of the old stories about arms stored in Catholic

[42] Sweeney, "Great Bigotry Merger," 9.

[43] Alvin W. Johnson and Frank H. Yost, *Separation of Church and State in the United States* (Minneapolis, 1949), 33.

[44] Sweeney, "Bigotry in the South," 585–86. It is significant that in this 1920 article Sweeney, who later took part in the New York *World's* investigation of the Klan, does not mention the hooded order. On the movement against parochial schools in Michigan and Nebraska see *Foreign-Born*, December 1920, p. 42.

church basements, began to lay special stress on the menace of Rome to the nation. Instead of relying entirely on professional organizers, the Klan engaged itinerant preachers as heralds of its message. Increasingly its arrival in a new area was signaled by public lectures on popish conspiracies to destroy *"the only truly Christian nation . . .* where prophecy is being fulfilled." [45] As if to demonstrate that the hatred transcended rhetoric, in the summer of 1921 a Methodist minister who belonged to the Klan shot to death a Catholic priest on his own doorstep, and incendiaries destroyed a Catholic church in Illinois two hours after a monster Klan initiation. [46]

The storm of anti-Catholic feeling, for which the Klan proved a wonderfully sensitive barometer, was closely related to the growth of fundamentalism. This militant repudiation of a liberalized gospel and a secularized culture was making itself felt in the closing years of the Progressive era, but only after the World War did it become a major force in American Protestantism. In truth, fundamentalism owed so much to the emotional aftermath of the war that one may almost define it as the characteristic response of rural Protestantism to the disillusion following America's international crusade. The wartime hope for a new and beatific world had produced nothing but crime, moral chaos, and organized selfishness on a grander scale than before. Surely here was proof that the nation had misplaced its faith, that the only true salvation for a sinful society lay in blotting out the whole spirit of innovation and returning to the theological and moral absolutism of an earlier day. Insistence on a Biblical Christianity naturally sharpened the historic lines of Protestant-Catholic cleavage, but the vigor of anti-Catholicism in the twenties could only result from the affiliations between fundamentalism and 100 per cent Americanism. The fundamentalist determination to fix and purify a Protestant orthodoxy followed the same channels and obeyed the same laws that governed the course of 100 per cent Americanism. Both epitomized a kind of crusading conformity, reacted to a common disillusion, and represented an urge for isolation from an evil world. Who can wonder that the two movements intermingled in rural areas, or that fundamentalism energized a religious version of postwar nationalism? [47]

Simmons' religiously tinged imagination had given the Klan an ap-

---

[45] Duffus, "Klan Sells Hate," 180. Quotation is from *The Foreign Language Press: America's Greatest Menace* [n.p., 1924]. For other illustrations see S. L. Baugher to Attorney General, October 15, 1921, in Justice File 198589; and Stanley Frost, *The Challenge of the Klan* (Indianapolis, 1924), 128–42.

[46] Charles P. Sweeney, "Bigotry Turns to Murder," *Nation*, CXIII (1921), 232–33, and "Great Bigotry Merger," 8.

[47] Norman F. Furniss, *The Fundamentalist Controversy, 1918–1931* (New Haven, 1954), 37–38, suggests caution in assuming a direct connection between the Klan and fundamentalism as organized movements. On the other hand, his careful study provides abundant evidence that they drew upon common attitudes.

propriate structure for the anti-Catholic spirit that it absorbed and magnified. The flaming crosses burning on hillsides, the altars erected at meetings, and the kneeling posture of suppliants at initiation ceremonies were central in the Klan's symbolism. Every klavern, or local unit, had a kludd, its chaplain, who opened each meeting with a prayer; the closing ritual consisted of a "kloxology." As the Klan grew, it emphasized increasingly its militant Protestantism. Well-known hymns were modified and adopted as Klan songs. It became common practice for Klansmen to march in a silent body into a Protestant church in the middle of a Sunday service and hand the minister a donation.[48] The organization took a close interest in compulsory Bible reading in the public schools, and in several states it lent strong support to Bible-reading bills.[49] "Patriotism and Christianity," said one Exalted Cyclops, "are preeminently the moving principles of the Knights of the Ku Klux Klan." Another boasted: "The Klan stood for the same things as the Church, but we did the things the Church wouldn't do." [50]

The things that the church would not do included general boycotts of Catholic businessmen, bringing pressure against Catholic public officials, and intimidation of many Catholic individuals. It would be futile, however, to try to estimate how much of this strong-arm activity applied to Catholics as opposed to foreigners, Jews, Negroes, and plain old-stock Americans. Contemporary accounts seldom identified the background of the Klan's victims, a circumstance which in itself suggests how manifold the proscriptions were. The significant fact was that the crusading, evangelical spirit behind the Klan turned it into a general instrument for moral regulation. Quite possibly (since it centered in areas where its foreign and Catholic enemies constituted only a small minority), most of the Klan's coercions affected other native white Protestants. Certainly it differed from prewar nativist societies not only in embracing a variety of xenophobias but also in ranging far beyond nativistic limits. Somewhat like the wartime American Protective League, the Klan watched everybody.

In its function as censor and policeman of local morality, the Klan brought to a head the 100 per cent American heritage as it survived into the twenties. Impatient of legally constituted authority yet dedicated to the maintenance of law and order, local Klans saw themselves as agents for accomplishing what government was failing to do: they would work a moral regeneration by compelling all deviants or backsliders to adhere to the ancient standards of the community. Hardly any infraction of the village code seemed too petty for intervention. An undertaker refused the use of his

---

[48] Emerson H. Loucks, *The Ku Klux Klan in Pennsylvania* (Harrisburg, 1936), 118–24.

[49] *American Standard,* I (May 20, 1924), 12–17; *Illinois Fiery Cross,* February 22, 1924, p. 5, and March 28, 1924, p. 1.

[50] K.K.K., *Papers,* 124; Loucks, *Klan in Pennsylvania,* 39.

hearse to a bereaved family unable to pay cash in advance; Klansmen drove him out of town. A businessman failed to pay a debt or practiced petty extortions; Klansmen tarred and feathered him. A husband deserted his family, or failed to support it, or maintained illicit relations with women, or gambled too much; Klansmen paid him a minatory call. A widow of doubtful virtue scandalized the neighbors; Klansmen flogged her and cut off her hair.[51] Prohibition especially drew the order's vigilance. Its most spectacular clean-up campaign occurred in Herrin, Illinois, where lax law enforcement permitted wide-open saloons and flagrant vice, and where the large Italian Catholic population was held chiefly at fault. There the Klan carried out mass raids on homes and roadhouses, engaged in pitched battles with the bootlegging faction, and temporarily seized the city government by force. The chaos extended over a two-year period, brought twenty deaths, and subsided finally in a great religious revival.[52]

Throughout this regulatory activity runs the war-born urge for conformity that had passed from anti-hyphenism, Americanization, and Palmer raids into fundamentalism and prohibition. No less important here is the other side of the 100 per cent American spirit, its crusading idealism. Ku Kluxers repeatedly justified their programs of action in terms of reform, though the reform consisted essentially of stabilizing the old order of things; and when first organized in a community, the Klan usually had the support of some of the "best people," intent partly on improving the local situation.[53] In the generation before the war this evangelical zeal for reform had poured into progressivism. The war directed it partly toward an international crusade, partly toward the maintenance of homogeneity. When the disillusion that followed the war choked off any large international or progressive outlet for moral idealism, about all that remained of it in small-town America turned inward, in a final effort to preserve the values of the community against change and against every external influence. Professor Frank Tannenbaum has summed up a good part of the Klan spirit as "an attempt to destroy the 'evil' that stands in the way of the millennial hope—a hope made vivid to many souls who actually believed that the war would usher in a 'world fit for heroes to live in.' " [54] Perhaps, in the

---

[51] Many such instances are in Loucks, *Klan in Pennsylvania*, 40–43. See also Frost, "Klan Rules," 262; Max Bentley, "A Texan Challenges the Klan," *Collier's*, LXXII (November 3, 1923), 11, 22; C. M. Hughes to Attorney General, June 26, 1921, in Justice File 198589.

[52] Angle, *Bloody Williamson*, 134–205.

[53] Duffus, "Klan Sells Hate," 179; Henry Zweifel to Attorney General, July 22, 1921, in Justice File 198589; Edward T. Devine, "The Klan in Texas," *Survey*, XLVIII (1922), 10–11; Robert S. Lynd and Helen Merrell Lynd, *Middletown: A Study in Contemporary American Culture* (New York, 1929), 481.

[54] Frank Tannenbaum, *Darker Phases of the South* (New York, 1924), 16–17. There are also perceptive comments in Loucks, *Klan in Pennsylvania*, 38–39; and Frederic C.

pageant of American history, the white-robed Klansman should stand in the place of Santayana's genteel New Englander as the Last Puritan.

It was ironical but inevitable that the Klan crusade to purify and stabilize spread contamination and strife everywhere it went. The secrecy with which the order operated served to cloak many an act of private vengeance. With poetic justice it was held responsible for crimes and cruelties that others committed in its name. Still worse, the Klan rent families, communities, and states, turning husband against wife, neighbor against neighbor, and man against man, until it compacted an opposition as lawless as itself. And while hatred bred hatred outside its ranks, the poison of corruption worked within.

In 1921 the Klan crossed the Mason and Dixon Line and began to attract nation-wide attention. By the end of the year it claimed to be operating in forty-five states and enrolling a thousand members a day.[55] Nineteen twenty-two saw a tremendous expansion, demonstrated by great public ceremonies at which a thousand or more initiates would be sworn in at once.[56] At the same time, like its nineteenth century predecessors, the organization entered politics, not with any positive program but simply to show its strength by winning elections. In Georgia the Klan was instrumental in putting a very friendly governor in the state capitol. In Texas it spent lavishly in money and effort to send Earl Mayfield to the United States Senate. In Oregon Klan sentiment wrought a virtual political revolution, defeating a governor who had tried to suppress its activities and installing a legislature that proceeded to enact several anti-Catholic measures.[57] Hundreds of candidates for local offices in many states were indebted to the Klan vote.

Political power greatly increased the divisive effects of the organization, partly because the Klan itself became an issue in elections, partly because law enforcement officials often dared not curb its terrorism. Thus in the latter part of 1922 local authorities in Morehouse Parish, Louisiana, proved helpless in the face of a near-civil war between the Klan-infested parish seat of Bastrop and the more leisurely and aristocratic town of Mer Rouge. Bastrop was Dry and Baptist; Mer Rouge held the Klan and all its

---

Howe, *The Confessions of a Reformer* (New York, 1925), 17. One of the New York *World* investigators of the Klan reported in 1921 that in every case of violence which he had studied the victim was told that his punishment resulted from some violation of moral or statutory law; *Hearings: Ku Klux Klan* (House Committee on Rules, 67 Cong., 1 Sess.), 15.

[55] Jones, *Klan*, 111–12. The chronology of the Klan's growth may be followed in the New York *Times Index*.

[56] *Literary Digest*, LXXIV (August 5, 1922), 44–46.

[57] *Ibid.*, LXXIII (June 10, 1922), 15, and LXXIV (August 5, 1922), 14; Waldo Roberts, "The Ku-Kluxing of Oregon," *Outlook*, CXXXIII (1923), 490–91; John W. Owens, "Does the Senate Fear the K.K.K.?" *New Republic*, XXXVII (1923), 113–14. On Georgia see New York *Times*, November 18, 1923, sec. 2, p. 1.

ways in contempt. A series of whippings culminated in the abduction and murder of a well-known Mer Rouge planter's son and his companion. For months thereafter troops sent by the governor kept order while the pro-Klan sheriff and district attorney stood idle. Twice the Morehouse grand jury refused to admit that a crime had been committed.[58]

Meanwhile internecine strife rocked the Invisible Empire. While its national officials exercised very little control over the local klaverns, an authoritarian constitution gave the members practically no control over their national leaders. For many of the latter the organization had an attraction quite different from that which drew its followers. It was immensely lucrative, and the profits to be extracted from membership fees and political corruption incited constant turmoil at the top. Clarke levied upon the Klan royally; Simmons, who was drunk or sick much of the time, was putty in his hands. When news got around in the fall of 1921 that Clarke was living with his confederate, Mrs. Tyler, this affront to Klan morality strengthened a group endeavoring to unseat him, but Simmons clung to Clarke and banished his principal enemies. Clarke held on against mounting opposition until November 1922, when a coalition of state leaders got rid of him by intimidating Simmons into retiring to an honorary position. Simmons retained a following and later tried to regain control, but the national headquarters had passed definitely into the hands of a moon-faced Texas dentist, Hiram Wesley Evans. Ultimately Simmons sold out his interest in the Klan to the Evans group for a sum which they announced as $90,000 but which he said should have been $146,000.[59] Evans regularized financial practices somewhat, but still the money flowed richly into many pockets.[60]

The Klan torrent rolled onward through 1923, reaching a high point late in the year. By that time the organization had enrolled an aggregate membership probably close to three million. Arkansas and Oklahoma fell vassal to it, and a spectacular expansion in the Midwest made Indiana and Ohio the leading Klan states in the nation. Except for Colorado, the order touched the Rocky Mountain states only negligibly; it left no considerable impression on the Atlantic seaboard outside of Pennsylvania and upstate New York.[61] In Indiana and Texas, however, it could organize vast public gatherings attended by seventy-five thousand people.

[58] *Literary Digest*, LXXVI (January 13, 1923), 10–12, and (March 31, 1923), 10–11; Leonard Lanson Cline, "In Darkest Louisiana," *Nation*, CXVI (1923), 292–93; Duffus, "Klan Sells Hate," 174–77.

[59] This story is best followed in the New York *Times*, September, 1921–February, 1924, supplemented by Loucks, *Klan in Pennsylvania*, 45–48, and Francis Ralston Welsh to Calvin Coolidge, December 28, 1923, in Justice File 198589.

[60] Frost, *Challenge of the Klan*, 21–27; Jones, *Klan*, 143; Edgar Allen Booth, *The Mad Mullah of America* (Columbus, 1927), 133–36.

[61] The most careful breakdown, presenting an estimate of cumulative membership through May 1923, is in Robert L. Duffus, "The Ku Klux Klan in the Middle West,"

The tremendous midwestern expansion in 1923 threw a new demagogue into the limelight and opened another chapter in the struggle within the Klan. D. C. Stephenson emerged as the dominant figure in the northern Klans. He could corrupt a legislator as effectively as he could organize a membership drive, and with equal ease he could convince the rural masses that the President of the United States was leaning on him for advice. He lived in bacchanalian style on an estate in Indianapolis; his political ambitions were boundless. As his power grew, he strove to wrest the national headquarters from Evans. All through 1923 the fight for control went on behind the scenes, with Stephenson perhaps partly in alliance with the disinherited Simmons faction. In November an Evans henchman murdered Simmons' attorney, supposedly to prevent an impending exposé. Somehow, that may have turned the tables against Stephenson. He surrendered his position in the national hierarchy of the Klan, but he rather than Evans retained paramount influence in Indiana.[62]

While this internal struggle raged, opposition was mounting on all sides. All along, the urban press and urban liberals had denounced the Klan with singular unanimity. Now it was also rousing a more formidable popular resistance. Old-stock conservatives, horrified at the chaos that the Klan bred, rallied against it. So did the miscellaneous corruptionists and enraged minorities it attacked. In the winter of 1922–23 the conservative governor of Kansas opened a drive against the organization by bringing suit to restrain it from all public appearances or activities. New York, under its Catholic governor, Al Smith, took a series of legal steps that inhibited Klan operations there. Minnesota, Iowa, and Michigan passed laws forbidding the wearing of masks in public.[63]

Oklahoma's flamboyant governor, John Walton, cast legality to the winds in trying to crush the hooded order. Although elected by a farmer-labor coalition in 1922, he soon showed greater friendliness toward grafters and big oil interests. The Klan supposedly controlled the state legislature and the Tulsa local government. Walton, in August 1923, took advantage of a series of floggings to put Tulsa County under marital law (later extended to the whole state). He imposed censorship on the leading Tulsa

---

World's Work, XLVI (1923), 363–64. I add a half million to Duffus' total because of the remarkable continuing growth in subsequent months in Indiana, Ohio, and probably elsewhere. See New York *Times,* November 1, 1923, p. 1, and November 8, 1923, p. 3; *Literary Digest,* LXXIX (November 24, 1923), 13–14.

[62] Booth, *Mad Mullah,* 34–35, 90, 131–32, 300; John Bartlow Martin, *Indiana: An Interpretation* (New York, 1947), 189–94; New York *Times,* November 6, 1923, p. 1, and November 18, 1923, sec. 2, p. 2.

[63] Duffus, "Klan in Middle West," 365–66; *Literary Digest,* LXXVII (June 9, 1923), 12–13; New York *Times,* 1923; April 10, p. 26, June 28, p. 2, July 26, p. 1, August 31, p. 10, and September 11, p. 19. On newspaper opposition to the Klan see *Literary Digest,* LXXIII (June 10, 1922), 15, and LXXIV (August 5, 1922), 49.

newspaper, forbade Klan meetings, established military courts to try Klan vigilantes, and used the National Guard to prevent the legislature from convening. When the legislature did succeed in assembling in November, it promptly impeached the governor.[64]

At the same time, anti-Klan mobs were beginning to lash back at the organization in areas where the immigrants were strongly entrenched. A bomb wrecked the offices of the Klan newspaper in Chicago. In a suburb of Pittsburgh an angry throng pelted a white-robed parade with stones and bottles, killing one Klansman and injuring many others. In the small industrial city of Steubenville, Ohio, a mob of three thousand attacked a meeting of one hundred Klansmen. In Perth Amboy, New Jersey, a mob six-thousand-strong, led by Jews and Catholics, closed in on a Klan meeting place, overwhelmed the entire police and fire departments, and fell upon some five hundred Ku Kluxers, kicking, stoning, and beating them as they fled.[65]

Such, from the West Frankfort riots of 1920 to the collapse of civil government in Oklahoma three years later, from the triumphant demonstrations of racist scholarship to the nightmares of Henry Ford, were some of the fruits of nativism in a postwar world neither brave nor new.

SUGGESTED READING

Higham's volume, when it first appeared, received critical reviews from Oscar Handlin in *Political Science Quarterly*, LXXI (Sept. 1956), and from Nathan Glazer in *Commentary*, XXI (June 1956). Each questioned Higham's effort to relate waves of nativism to crises in national confidence, which he related primarily to the business cycle. Handlin especially challenged Higham's theory that there was a stream of nativism that burst into the open in times of crisis, and contended that the movement for immigration restriction stood apart from the nativism of the pre–1890's. Both critics contended that America was actually shifting away from egalitarianism and toward a set of values in which racism and conservatism held a major place. In "Another Look at Nativism," *Catholic Historical Review*, XLIV (July 1958), Higham reconsidered his own analysis and stressed that nativism, rather than being viewed simply as a sour, unpleasant intolerance, must be interpreted also in terms of the rivalries for power,

---

[64] See the running account in the *Literary Digest*, September 22, 1923–December 8, 1923, and in *Outlook*, September 26, 1923–November 28, 1923; also Bruce Bliven, "From the Oklahoma Front," *New Republic*, XXXVI (1923), 202–205.

[65] New York *Times*, 1923: April 7, p. 15, August 17, p. 1, August 26, p. 1, and August 31, p. 1.

deference, and wealth in which men compete—the rivalries arising from "objective conditions."

Stanley Coben, in "A Study in Nativism: The American Red Scare of 1919–1920," *Political Science Quarterly*, LXXIX (Mar. 1964), seeks to explain the period in terms of social psychology and cultural anthropology, but only loosely connects the events and the theories. Paul L. Murphy's "Sources and Nature of Intolerance in the 1920's," *Journal of American History*, LI (June 1964), is unsuccessful in explaining the origins of prejudice—a continuing problem for historians. Oscar Handlin, in *The American People in the Twentieth Century* ° (1954), investigates nativism in the 1920's. William Preston's *Aliens and Dissenters: Federal Suppression of Radicals, 1903–1933* ° (1963) offers a useful perspective. A theoretical perspective on nativism and responses to immigration is provided by Milton Gordon in *Assimilation in American Life* ° (1965), who is critical of Handlin's assumptions on nativism.

David Chalmers's *Hooded Americanism* ° (1965) and Kenneth Jackson's *The Ku Klux Klan in the City, 1915–1930* ° (1968) replace John Mecklin's *The Ku Klux Klan: A Study of the American Mind* (1924). An essay on the Klan by Robert Moats Miller, "The Ku Klux Klan," as well as a frankly revisionist study of fundamentalism by Paul A. Carter, "The Fundamentalist Defense of the Faith," in *Change and Continuity in Twentieth-Century America: The 1920's*, edited by John Braeman *et al.* (1968), should also be consulted.

IRVING BERNSTEIN

The Worker in an
Unbalanced Society

INTRODUCTION

The American labor movement, after a burst of growth in the
First World War, suffered an unexpected decline in the 1920's.
Membership dropped from 5 million in 1920 to 3.6 million in 1923
and hovered near that level for the rest of the decade. Effective
unionization was concentrated in a few industries—coal, railroads, construction, and clothing. Labor organizations were
largely or totally absent from such newer and bitterly antiunion
industries as rubber, electrical equipment, and automobiles and

FROM Irving Bernstein, *The Lean Years: Workers in an Unbalanced Society,* pp. 47–51,
53–67, 69–72, 75–76, 80–82. Copyright © 1960 by Irving Bernstein. Reprinted by
permission of the publisher, Houghton Mifflin Company. Song excerpt on page 170 from
American Ballads and Folk Songs, collected, adapted, and arranged by John A. and Alan
Lomax, copyright 1934 by John A. and Alan Lomax. Reprinted by permission of Alan
Lomax. Song excerpt on pages 174–75 from *Negro Songs of Protest,* by Lawrence Gellert and Elie Siegmeister, published by the American Music League, 1936. Reprinted by
permission of Lawrence Gellert and Elie Siegmeister.

were ineffectual in such older industries as steel and oil. Strike-
breaking, crusades against the union shop, and welfare unionism
all helped cut membership rolls. Divisions within the working
class, the hostility of the courts to unions, improved techology,
and unemployment also explain what once seemed to economists
a paradox—the decline of unionism during a period of apparently general prosperity.

But as Irving Bernstein, historian of the twentieth-century
American worker and professor at U.C.L.A., makes clear in the
essay reprinted below, the history of American labor is actually
far broader than the history of the labor movement. Only recently, after freeing themselves from the long domination of
John R. Commons and his associates, who concentrated on
the labor movement, have American historians come to analyze
the life, institutions, and conditions of the workingman.

The data are often fragmentary and the difficulties of ana-
lyis and historical reconstruction formidable in this undertaking.
Ordinary workers leave little documentation; they are often simply names on tax lists and in census records. Despite the historical research of the past three decades on the life of the immigrant and the recent studies in urban history, scholars still know
very little about the life—much less the aspirations and
expectations—of workers at the broad base of American city
populations. In spite of these difficulties, Bernstein is able to
sketch the facts of poverty and unemployment among workers in
the 1920's and to reach certain conclusions about the absence of
working-class consciousness.

*T*he symbol of the twenties is gold. This was the age of the gold
standard, a time when people with money slept with confidence: their bank-
notes were redeemable in the precious metal. Small boys received gold
watches on ceremonial occasions, and little girls were given gold pieces as
birthday gifts. The noted Philadelphia banking family, the Stotesburys,
equipped their bathroom with gold fixtures ("You don't have to polish them
you know"). Writing in gloomy 1932, the economist Frederick C. Mills spoke
of the economy of the twenties as having "the aspects of a golden age." The
historians Charles and Mary Beard titled the introductory chapter on the
twenties of *America in Midpassage* "The Golden Glow." To a contemporary
reader the title seemed just right.

Yet hindsight finds the image unfitting. The twenties were, indeed,
golden, but only for a privileged segment of the American population. For
the great mass of people whose welfare is the concern of this study—workers
and their families—the appropriate metallic symbol may be nickel or copper
or perhaps even tin, but certainly not gold. Although on the surface Ameri-

can workers appeared to share in the material advantages of the time, the serious maladjustments within the economic system fell upon them with disproportionate weight. This interplay between illusion and reality is a key to the period. In fact, this was a society in imbalance and workers enjoyed few of its benefits.

In the twenties two population changes occurred that were to prove profoundly significant to labor: the shift from farm to city speeded up and immigration from abroad slowed down. The American farmer's venerable propensity to move to town reached a climax. During the ten years from 1920 to 1929, according to the Department of Agriculture, 19,436,000 people made the trek; in every year except 1920 and 1921 over 2 million left the land, though many returned. The farm population, despite a higher fertility rate, declined by 3.7 per cent between 1920 and 1930 (31.6 to 30.4 million), while the nonfarm population rose by 24.6 per cent (74.1 to 92.3 million). Not only did these displaced husbandmen go to town; they appear to have gone to the big towns. Communities with over 100,000 grew by 32.4 per cent from 1920 to 1930, while those with 2500 to 5000 increased by only 7.6 per cent. Never before had the United States experienced such an immense flow from farm to city.

·   ·   ·   ·   ·

The impact of this movement upon labor can hardly be exaggerated. Employers, despite the drop in immigration from abroad, had at their disposal a great pool of workmen, particularly the unskilled and semiskilled. This large labor supply, inured to the low level of farm income, relieved an upward pressure on wage rates that might have occurred. Workers drawn from a rural background were accustomed to intermittency and so did not insist on regularity of employment. Although they adapted readily to machinery, they were without skills in the industrial sense. The fact that the price of skilled labor was high and of unskilled low induced management to substitute machines for craftsmen. The displaced farmers carried into industry the agricultural tradition of mobility, especially geographic and to a lesser extent occupational. They brought with them, as well, the conservative outlook and individualistic accent of the rural mind. Since they were predominantly of older stocks, their entry into the urban labor force had an Americanizing influence, reversing the tendency to ethnic diversity produced by the wave of immigration that preceded World War I. There was, however, one divisive element in this trend to homogeneity: the Negro's emergence on a large scale in the urban working class.

The unskilled rural Negro of the South won his foothold in northern industry during the war, particularly in the metalworking, auto, and meat industries. By 1923, for example, Ford had 5000 colored employees. In the early twenties the demand for this class of labor was brisk, but slacked off after 1924, when industry in the North achieved a labor supply equilibrium.

Some 1,200,000 Negroes migrated from South to North between 1915 and 1928. At this time the Negro took a long stride in the direction of integration with the dominant urban industrial society in America. Folklorists at the end of the twenties, for example, found a Negro cook in Houston singing:

> Niggers gittin' mo' like white folks,
> Mo' like white folks every day.
> Niggers learnin' Greek and Latin,
> Niggers wearin' silk and satin—
> Niggers gittin' mo' like white folks every day.

To the employer the agricultural influx was a blessing. The resulting surplus of labor gave him little cause to fear turnover; money wage rates were stable; and unionism was in the doldrums. To the labor movement the migration was a short-term disaster. In the economic and political context of the twenties this accretion to the urban labor force was unorganizable. For the economy as a whole the movement was, of course, both inevitable and desirable, but it carried a danger. With a larger number of people now wholly dependent upon wages and salaries, President Hoover's Committee on Social Trends noted, "any considerable and sustained interruption in their money income exposes them to hardships which they were in a better position to mitigate when they were members of an agricultural or rural community." [1]

．　．　．　．

During the twenties declining immigration joined a falling birth rate to slow population growth, with the obvious implication for the labor force. As significant as the gross change was its selective character; the entry of unskilled labor from abroad was virtually halted, while the inflow of skilled workmen, for whom there was a considerable demand, was little impaired. The old American custom of employing the most recent immigrants to do the heaviest and dirtiest work had produced constant upward occupational mobility. Now it would be harder for the worker to rise and, by the same token, easier for him to develop class consciousness. Further, as Sumner H. Slichter pointed out, restriction required management to reverse its policy "to adapt jobs to men rather than men to jobs." Hence employers sought to use labor

---

[1] The basic data appear in *Historical Statistics*, 29, 31; National Resources Committee, *The Problems of a Changing Population* (Washington: 1938), 88; Harry Jerome, *Mechanization in Industry* (New York: National Bureau of Economic Research, 1934), 122–25; Edward E. Lewis, *The Mobility of the Negro* (New York: Columbia University Press, 1931), 131–32; National Urban League, *Negro Membership in American Labor Unions* (New York: National Urban League, 1930), 8; John A. and Alan Lomax, comps., *American Ballads and Folk Songs* (New York: Macmillan, 1934), xxx, *Recent Social Trends*, vol. 2, p. 806.

more efficiently. A key solution, of course, was mechanization, helping to explain the high rate of technological advance during the decade.[2]

·   ·   ·   ·

The conditions for mechanization were almost ideal: wages were high in relation to the price of machinery, immigration was limited, and the capital market was abundant and easy. These factors created—as the current phrase had it—the Machine Age. Eugene O'Neill wrote a play about it, *Dynamo*, as did Elmer Rice with *The Adding Machine*. The term "robot," exported from Czechoslovakia, became part of the American language.[3]

The march of machinery in the twenties affected almost every segment of the economy, and a few dramatic illustrations suggest its impact. In 1927 the introduction of continuous strip-sheet rolling opened a new era in sheet-steel and tin-plate production; a continuous mill had the capacity of forty to fifty hand mills. The Danner machine for glass tubing, first offered in 1917, completely replaced the hand process by 1925. The Ross carrier for handling lumber came into general use. The first successful machine to produce a complete cigar was patented in 1917; by 1930, 47 per cent of the 6.5 billion cigars turned out were made by machine. Mechanical coal-loading devices were widely accepted, while mine locomotives displaced the horse and the mule for haulage. Heavy construction was revolutionized by the power shovel, the belt and bucket conveyor, pneumatic tools, the concrete mixer, the dump truck, and the highway finishing machine. The street-railway industry converted to the one-man trolley. Several communication devices won general acceptance: the automatic switchboard and dial telephone, the teletype, and the market-quotation ticker. The motion picture industry entered a new phase with production of the first "talkie" in 1926. More important in the aggregate than these spectacular innovations, however, were the countless small changes which produced, for example, extraordinary increases in output in blast furnaces, in pulp and paper manufacture, in the automobile and rubber tire industries, and in beet sugar mills. Between 1919 and 1929, horsepower per wage earner in manufacturing shot up 50 per cent, in mines and quarries 60 per cent, and in steam railroads 74 per cent.[4]

---

[2] Preston William Slosson, *The Great Crusade and After, 1914–1928* (New York: Macmillan, 1930), 299–301; *Historical Statistics*, 33; "The U.S. Steel Corporation: III," *Fortune*, 13 (May 1936), 136; H. B. Butler, *Industrial Relations in the United States* (Geneva: International Labor Office, 1927), 14; Sumner H. Slichter, "The Current Labor Policies of American Industries," *QJE*, 43 (May 1929), 393.

[3] *The Daily Mail Trade Union Mission to the United States* (London: Daily Mail, [1927]), 81, 84. See also Parliament of the Commonwealth of Australia, *Report of the Industrial Delegation . . .* (Canberra: 1927), 16–17, and André Siegfried, *America Comes of Age* (New York: Harcourt, Brace, 1927), 149; Edward Bliss Reed, ed., *The Commonwealth Fund Fellows and Their Impressions of America* (New York: Commonwealth Fund, 1932), 90. The American employer is quoted in D. D. Lescohier, *What Is the Effect and Extent of Technical Changes on Employment Security?* (American Management Association, Personnel Series No. 1, 1930), 12.

[4] Jerome, *Mechanization, passim*.

Advancing technology was the principal cause of the extraordinary increase in productivity that occurred during the twenties. Between 1919 and 1929, output per man-hour rose 72 per cent in manufacturing, 33 per cent in railroads, and 41 per cent in mining. Put somewhat differently by David Weintraub, unit labor requirements (the number of man-hours required per unit of output) declined between 1920 and 1929 by 30 per cent in manufacturing, 20 per cent in railroads, 21 per cent in mining, and 14 per cent in telephone communications. Mills estimated that the physical volume of production for agriculture, raw materials, manufacturing, and construction climbed 34 per cent from 1922 to 1929, an average annual increment of 4.1 per cent. It was his impression that services, if they had been measurable, would have shown an even faster rate of growth. In fact, Americans generally were inclined to explain their economic society largely in terms of its mounting fruitfulness. When W. Wareing, an official of the British Amalgamated Engineering Union, asked John W. Lieb, vice-president of the Edison Company of New York, the secret of high wages, the reply came back promptly: "Productivity."

Rising output was the central force in the steady growth of national income during the twenties. Measured in current prices, which fluctuated narrowly, Simon Kuznets found that national income moved from $60.7 billion in 1922 to $87.2 billion in 1929, a gain of 43.7 per cent, or an average increment of 6.2 per cent per year. The share going to wages and salaries mounted from $36.4 billion to $51.5 billion, an increase of 41.5 per cent. The wage and salary proportion remained unusually constant at about 59 per cent of national income. The share of dividends rose more sharply from $3 billion in 1922 to $6.3 billion in 1929, up 110 per cent. This resulted in a relative increase in dividends from 5 per cent to 7.2 per cent of national income. Wage earners, in other words, did not enjoy as great a rise in income as did those in the higher brackets. A noted study by the Brookings Institution confirms this with respect to the wage and salary share, concluding that "since the war salaries have expanded much more rapidly than wages." [5]

The labor force that shared this national income entered a new phase in the twenties, a slowing rate of growth accompanied by a shift from manual to nonmanual employment. Immigration restriction joined with a falling birth rate to retard population advance. In contrast to a gain of 24 per cent in the first decade of the century, between 1920 and 1930 the number of people ten years old and over rose only 19 per cent.

---

[5] *Historical Statistics*, 71–72; David Weintraub, "Unemployment and Increasing Productivity," in National Resources Committee, *Technological Trends and National Policy* (Washington: 1937), 77; Frederick C. Mills, *Economic Tendencies in the United States* (New York: National Bureau of Economic Research, 1932), 243–51; *Daily Mail*, 21; Simon Kuznets, *National Income and Its Composition, 1919–1938* (New York: National Bureau of Economic Research, 1941), vol. 1, pp. 216–17; Maurice Leven, Harold G. Moulton, and Clark Warburton, *America's Capacity to Consume* (Washington: Brookings, 1934), 28.

More dramatic than slowing over-all growth was the marked movement from blue-collar to white-collar work, from physically productive to overhead employment. The total number of gainful workers advanced from 41.6 to 48.8 million between 1920 and 1930, a gain of 17.4 per cent. Despite this, the extractive industries—agriculture, forestry and fisheries, and mining—suffered a loss of 3.4 per cent, from 12.2 to 11.9 million persons. Similarly, the manufacturing labor force remained almost stationary, rising only 0.9 per cent from 10,890,000 in 1920 to 10,990,000 in 1930. By contrast, the predominantly white-collar and service industries rose sharply. Trade, finance and real estate, education, the other professions, domestic and personal service, and government employment climbed 45.7 per cent from 11.5 to 16.7 million.

The same pattern emerges when the analysis is transferred from industry to occupation. Between 1920 and 1930, the number of manual workers in the labor force (farmers, farm laborers, skilled workers and foremen, semiskilled workers, and laborers) rose only 7.9 per cent from 28.5 to 30.7 million. Nonmanual workers (professionals, wholesale and retail dealers, other proprietors, and clerks and kindred workers) advanced 38.1 per cent from 10.5 to 14.5 million. During the twenties, that is, the American worker on an increasing scale took off his overalls and put on a white shirt and necktie.

Or, put on an elegant frock, silk stockings, and high-heeled shoes, for women entered the labor force at an accelerated pace at this time. The number of females fifteen and over gainfully occupied rose 27.4 per cent between 1920 and 1930, from 8.3 to 10.6 million. By the latter date, in fact, almost one of every four persons in the labor force was a woman. In Middletown the Lynds found that 89 per cent of the high school girls expected to work after graduation, only 3 per cent indicating they definitely would not. This female employment came as a jolt to foreigners, especially the British.

> It was a remarkable sight to see rows of bobbed, gum-chewing, spruce females seated on each side of a rapidly moving conveyor and so busily engaged with their work that not one of them had time to cast a passing glance upon the group of stalwart Britishers, who had considerable difficulty in following the movements of their nimble fingers.

Even more impressive was the 28.9 per cent increase between 1920 and 1930 in the number of employed married women, a rise from 1.9 to 3.1 million. In Middletown the old rule that a girl quit her job with marriage broke down under economic necessity in the twenties. A jobless husband or a need to support a child's education forced working-class mothers into the factories, shops, and offices. The female influx was another bar to organization. Even women who intended to work permanently carried over a vestigial attitude of impermanency that made them hesitant to take out union cards.

The decade of the twenties by contrast witnessed a decline in the employment of children. While in 1910 about one fourth of the boys aged ten to fifteen and one eighth of the girls of the same ages were employed, by 1930 the proportion of boys dropped to 6 per cent and of girls to 3 per cent. The Lynds found an almost total absence of child labor in Middletown. This great social advance was accompanied by a sharp rise in school attendance. The total increase at all levels of education exceeded 6 million between 1919 and 1928. The percentage of those between 14 and 17 enrolled in high school rose from 32 per cent in 1920 to 51 per cent in 1930. "If education is oftentimes taken for granted by the business class," wrote the Lynds, ". . . it evokes the fervor of a religion, a means of salvation, among a large section of the working class." There were many reasons for the decline in child labor: laws in most states fixing a minimum age for employment and compelling school attendance, the pressure of reform groups and organized labor, advancing mechanization, an adequate adult labor supply, and rising personnel standards in industry.

.   .   .   .

The worker was seldom afforded the opportunity to rise in the social scale. He lacked the qualifications for the professions and the capital for business. His main hope for upward mobility was within the hierarchy of the firm that employed him. Even here, however, the opportunities were limited. In twenty-one months in 1923–24, plants employing 4240 workers in Middletown had only ten vacancies for foremen—one chance in 424. A businessman, the Lynds found, looked forward to the steady improvement of his lot. But, "once established in a particular job, the limitations fixing the possible range of advancement seem to be narrower for an industrial worker." His position, of course, was more dismal if he happened to be a member of a minority group. In greater or lesser degree, the Irish, the Italians, the Jews, the Mexicans, and the Negroes suffered in the labor market. To dwell only upon the last, the ones who probably enjoyed the doubtful distinction of sustaining the most severe discrimination: Negroes were the last to be hired and the first to be fired, were seldom allowed to do skilled work and almost never given supervisory jobs, were assigned the older, dirtier, and less pleasant work places, were paid less for the same work, and were often denied membership in labor unions. A Negro song of protest went this way:

Trouble, trouble, had it all mah day.
.   .   .   .
Cain't pawn no diamonds,
Can't pawn no clo'
An' boss man told me,
Can't use me no mo'.

Rather get me a job, like white folks do.
Rather get me a job, like white folks do.

Trampin' 'round all day,
Say, "Nigger, nothin' fo' you." [6]

This complaint could have been voiced as well by white members of the labor force, since the prosperity of the twenties was accompanied by heavy unemployment. Foreign observers reported more men than jobs in each locality they visited. The absence of government statistics, disgraceful in itself, makes it impossible to report the actual volume of joblessness. Evidence that severe unemployment existed, however, is beyond dispute. The noted Brookings Institution study, *America's Capacity to Produce,* estimated that the economy in 1929 operated at only 80 per cent of its practical capacity. Weintraub calculated that the jobless constituted 13 per cent of the labor force in 1924 and 1925, 11 per cent in 1926, 12 per cent in 1927, 13 per cent in 1928, and 10 per cent in 1929. Woodlief Thomas made minimum unemployment estimates for nonagricultural industries of 7.7 per cent in 1924, 5.7 per cent in 1925, 5.2 per cent in 1926, and 6.3 per cent in 1927.

.   .   .   .

So severe, in fact, was unemployment during the decade that social workers, burdened with the misery that followed in its wake, became alarmed. The International Conference of Settlements, meeting at Amsterdam in 1928, heard the Belgian economist Henri de Man claim that industrialism produced both more goods and more permanently unemployed. The National Federation of Settlements, convening in Boston that same year, found that unemployment was the prime enemy of the American family. Nor were all employers as callous as those in Middletown. It was on December 17, 1928, that President Daniel Willard of the Baltimore & Ohio made his famous statement before the Couzens Committee:

> It is a dangerous thing to have a large number of unemployed men and women—dangerous to society as a whole—dangerous to the individuals who constitute society. When men who are willing and able to work and want to work are unable to obtain work, we need not be surprised if they steal before they starve. Certainly I do not approve of stealing, but if I had to make a choice between stealing and starving, I would surely not choose to starve—and in that respect I do not think I am unlike the average individual.

The least onerous form of unemployment—seasonal—worsened during the twenties. Mild government pressure to regularize production in those trades noted for intermittency—construction, garments, maritime, and entertainment—had no noticeable effect. In addition, the great new automo-

---

[6] Lynds, *Middletown,* 48, 68; Herman Feldman, *Racial Factors in American Industry* (New York: Harper, 1931), ch. 2; John Greenway, *American Folksongs of Protest* (Philadelphia: University of Pennsylvania Press, 1953), 113.

tive industry and its suppliers contributed heavily to seasonality. "Because of the ease with which labour can be obtained and discarded," an Australian observed, "there is little necessity for the employer to stabilize his rate of production over the year."

Far more serious was technological unemployment, the price paid for progress. A paradox of the American economy in the twenties was that its glittering technical achievement gave birth to a dismal social failure. At the top of the boom in 1929 Wesley Mitchell wrote that technological unemployment "is a matter of the gravest concern in view of the millions of families affected or threatened . . . and in view of their slender resources." Weintraub estimated that between 1920 and 1929 in manufacturing, railways, and coal mining, machines displaced 3,272,000 men, of whom 2,269,000 were reabsorbed and 1,003,000 remained unemployed. There were, naturally, sharp variations in employment impact among industries. This is evident from Jerome's figure on labor time saved by particular machines: talkies saved 50 per cent, cigar machines 50 to 60 per cent, the Banbury mixer 50 per cent, the highway finishing machine 40 to 60 per cent, and various coal loaders 25 to 50 per cent.

. . . Jerome found that mechanization had a differential impact in various segments of the industrial process: in material handling it displaced the unskilled; in systematizing the flow of production it reduced the skilled; in displacing manual by machine processing it usually diluted skills; in improving already mechanized operations it cut down on the semiskilled; in stimulating machine construction and repair it increased the demand for the skilled. A workman taking a job in the twenties had little way of knowing whether his skills would improve or decline; he could be reasonably certain, however, that a machine would soon change the content of his job.

. . . . .

Labor's burden in this period of prosperity was not limited to unemployment; workers faced as well an unequal distribution of income. There were in 1929, the Brookings Institution found, 27,474,000 families of two or more persons. Nearly 6 million families, over 21 per cent, received less than $1000 per year; about 12 million, more than 42 per cent (including those below $1000), had incomes under $1500; nearly 20 million, 71 per cent (including those under $1500), took in less than $2500. The combined incomes of 0.1 per cent of the families at the top of the scale were as great as those of the 42 per cent at the bottom. The number who received over $1 million per year rose from 65 in 1919 to 513 in 1929. The distorted distribution of savings was even more striking. The 21,546,000 families at the low end, 78.4 per cent, had no aggregate savings at all, while the 24,000 families at the high end, 0.9 per cent, provided 34 per cent of total savings. The authors of *America's Capacity to Consume* went further:

It appears . . . that . . . income was being distributed with increasing in-equality, particularly in the later years of the period. While the proportion of high incomes was increasing . . . there is evidence that the income of those at the very top was increasing still more rapidly. That is to say, in the late twenties a larger percentage of the total income was received by the portion of the population having very high incomes than had been the case a decade earlier.

Inequality in distribution exerted a constant pressure upon those at the bottom of the scale to supplement the head of family's job earnings. A study of federal workers in five cities in 1928 with salaries not in excess of $2500 showed that 15 to 33 per cent of the husbands took outside work, 15 to 32 per cent of the wives got jobs, and many children contributed to family income. Only 2 to 10 per cent of the families lived within the husband's government salary.

Even in the relatively prosperous year 1929 a majority of workers' fami-lies failed to enjoy an "American standard of living." This conclusion cannot be substantiated precisely, because the government made no survey of work-ers' budgets between 1919 and the mid-thirties, another illustration of the sorry state of labor statistics. The most careful contemporary student of the problem, Paul Douglas, made estimates for larger cities that can be keyed in roughly with the family income distribution published in *America's Capac-ity to Consume*. Though Douglas' work, *Wages and the Family*, appeared in 1925 it is not inapplicable to 1929, because retail prices fluctuated fairly nar-rowly.

Douglas set out four standards of living: poverty, minimum subsis-tence, minimum health and decency, and minimum comfort ("the American standard"). At the poverty level the family would have an inadequate diet, overcrowding, and no resources for unexpected expenses. This would cost a family of five $1000 to $1100. In 1929 there were 5,899,000 families of two or more with incomes of less than $1000. The minimum subsistence level was sufficient to meet physical needs with nothing left over for emergencies or pleasures. To reach it a family of five needed $1100 to $1400. There were 11,653,000 families of two or more who received less than $1500. The mini-mum health and decency level supplied adequate food, housing, and cloth-ing as well as a modest balance for recreation. It cost $1500 to $1800. There were 16,354,000 families with incomes under $2000. Since "the American standard" required an income of $2000 to $2400, it seems safe to conclude that the majority of wage earners' families failed to reach this level.

Income inequality and the relatively low standard of living of Ameri-can workers, however, did not arouse social protest. There were two princi-pal reasons for this silence. The first, doubtless the more important, was that the material well-being of the employed sector of the labor force was improv-ing. Lincoln Steffens wrote in 1929: "Big business in America is producing what the Socialists held up as their goal: food, shelter and clothing for all."

Douglas estimated that the average annual earnings of employed workers in all industries, including agriculture, advanced from $1288 in 1923 to $1405 in 1928, a gain of 9.1 per cent. Their real annual earnings improved slightly more, 10.9 per cent. The movement of wages, money and real, actually understates the impact of the rising standard of life because it fails to account for either the diversity of items on which income was spent or the benefits available free. In the twenties consumption broadened markedly to encompass goods and services that made life easier and more diverting—automobiles, telephones, radios, movies, washing machines, vacuum cleaners, and electric iceboxes, as well as improved medicine, hospitalization, and life insurance. The growth of installment buying made the consumer durables available to many with small cash resources. To a limited extent workers were able to share in this advance; ownership of a Model T, even if shared with the finance company, was more than entertaining: it inclined one to accept things as they were. In addition, all segments of the population benefited from the sharp improvement in free social services, most notably education, but including also public libraries, playgrounds and parks, and public health facilities.

The other reason for the failure of social protest to emerge was that the standard of living of American workmen, regardless of its deficiencies, was among the highest in the world, a consideration of no mean importance to urban masses who were largely immigrants themselves or the children of immigrants. Foreign observers visiting this country were, on the whole, impressed with the differential in living standards between the United States and their own nations. "Taken all in all," André Siegfried remarked, "the American worker is in a unique position." [7]

The uniqueness of the American worker's position in the late twenties with respect to wages, hours, and conditions of employment deserves examination. In so far as wages are concerned, it is necessary to note again the

---

[7] Leven, et al., America's Capacity, 54–56, 93, 103–4; "Cost of Living of Federal Employees in Five Cities," MLR, 29 (Aug. 1929), 315; Paul H. Douglas, Wages and the Family (Chicago: University of Chicago Press, 1925), 5–6; Steffens to Jo Davidson, Feb. 18, 1929, in Letters of Lincoln Steffens, Ella Winter and Granville Hicks, eds. (New York: Harcourt, Brace, 1938), vol. 2, p. 830; Paul H. Douglas, Real Wages in the United States, 1890–1926 (Boston: Houghton Mifflin, 1930), 391; Paul H. Douglas and Florence Tye Jennison, The Movement of Money and Real Earnings in the United States, 1926–28 (Chicago: University of Chicago Press, 1930), 27. Wages in 1929 differed little from 1928 figures. Annual earnings in manufacturing rose to $1341 in 1929 from $1325 in 1928. Since the cost of living also advanced, by one point, real wages rose by a fraction of 1 per cent. Paul H. Douglas and Charles J. Coe, "Earnings," American Journal of Sociology, 35 (May, 1930), 935–39; Recent Economic Changes, vol. 1, pp. 60–67, 325; Recent Social Trends, vol. 2, pp. 827, 858–89, 915–26; Siegfried, America Comes of Age, 159. See also Daily Mail, 23. Some of the British made the admission more cautiously, while an Australian stated flatly that real wages were higher in his country. Report of the Delegation Appointed to Study Industrial Conditions in . . . the United States, Cmd. 2833 (Mar. 1927), 33; Adam, An Australian, 46.

inadequacy of the statistics. Though they are superior to those for employment, the data leave much to be desired. Those who doubt this statement are referred to the preface of Douglas' *Real Wages in the United States, 1890– 1926* for an account of the extraordinary expenditure of energy demanded of the serious student of wages at that time. To this must be added some reluctance by employers, the prime source, to reveal how much they paid their workers.

During the prosperity of the twenties wages, money and real, moved gently upward. Unlike the two preceding periods of good times, the turn of the century and the first war, there was no sharp rise. In fact, wages in the era 1923–29 were characteristically stable, reflecting the surplus of labor and weak unions.

Average hourly earnings in all industries, according to Douglas, advanced from 66.2¢ in 1923 to 71¢ in 1928. A survey of 1500 manufacturing plants by the National Industrial Conference Board revealed that their average hourly earnings moved from 54¢ in 1923 to 58.1¢ in 1929. Hourly earnings in bituminous coal fell from 84.5¢ in 1923 to 68.1¢ in 1929. Railroad earnings moved from 56.5¢ in 1923 to 62.5¢ in 1929. The average hourly earnings of common laborers in the basic steel industry were 41.7¢ in 1923 and 41.4¢ in 1929. The average daily wages without board of farm laborers were $2.25 in both years.

Weekly earnings, according to the same sources, were cut from a similar pattern. The Douglas figures for all industries were $30.39 in 1923 and $33.32 in 1928. The NICB series for manufacturing advanced from $26.54 in 1923 to $28.24 in 1929. Weekly earnings in bituminous coal were virtually unchanged, $25.60 in 1923 and $25.72 in 1929. On the railroads there was a rise from $26.65 in 1923 to $28.49 in 1929. Farm wages without board per month were $48.25 in 1923 and $51.22 in 1929.

The movement in real wages was little different since the Bureau of Labor Statistics Cost of Living Index showed virtually no change in the terminal years. Real hourly earnings in all industries, Douglas found, rose 7.2 per cent between 1923 and 1928, while real weekly earnings, reflecting some drop in hours, advanced only 2.5 per cent. The NICB, covering real earnings in manufacturing at the end of the period, found that hourly rose 2.1 per cent and weekly 0.7 per cent between the opening quarter of 1928 and final quarter of 1929.

. . . .

[A] differential of note in the twenties was that between union and nonunion rates. Although it is not possible to measure this spread statistically, its existence is beyond question. Douglas, for example, calculated average hourly earnings in 1926 for the following predominantly organized industries: building trades $1.313, granite and stone $1.301, newspaper printing $1.150, book and job printing $1.037, planing mills $1.027, metal trades 96.1¢, baking 92.5¢, and bituminous coal 71.9¢. By contrast, earnings in the following mainly nonunion manufacturing industries in 1926 were: steel 63.7¢, shoes 52.8¢, meat packing 49.4¢, woolens 49.1¢, sawmills 36.1¢, and cotton 32.8¢. An Australian delegation which visited the United States in 1927 concluded that unions had a substantial effect in keeping nonunion rates from falling, since employers feared that wage cuts would lead to organization. This differential, like the others, widened during the twenties. That is, some unions, particularly in the building trades, pushed wages up more rapidly than did the employers of unorganized workers. A study by Frederick C. Mills of the annual rate of advance in nine wage series between 1922 and 1929 planned union wages in the lead. Trade unions, though on the defensive at this time, succeeded in maintaining and even improving wage differentials over unorganized workers, another illustration of the inequity of income distribution inasmuch as union membership was heavily weighted by the skilled.

· · · ·

The stickiness of money and real wages between 1923 and 1929, at a time when productivity was rising dramatically, had an unhealthy effect upon the economy as a whole. As Douglas observed, "This failure of real wages to advance was at least one cause of the rising profits during this period, and was consequently an appreciable factor in the extraordinary increase of stock market values which occurred." Between 1923 and 1929, according to Simon Kuznets, the dividend component of national income rose 64.1 per cent while wages and salaries advanced only 20.6 per cent. The cases of U.S. Steel and Toledo-Edison are instructive. While hourly earnings in Big Steel rose modestly and weekly earnings fell, profits almost doubled between 1923 and 1929. Toledo-Edison's net earnings advanced from $2.8 million in 1925 to $4.5 million in 1929; no general wage increase was granted during this period. Noting the sharp rise in profit margins, Mills commented, "An ultimate explanation of the economic collapse which was precipitated in 1929 must give full weight to this striking fact." [8]

· · · ·

Although there was a good deal of talk in the twenties about shortening the work week, almost no one did anything about it. The steel industry, in the face of public condemnation of the twelve-hour day during the 1919 strike, improved hours early in the decade. Yet in 1929 average full-time weekly hours were still 54.6, and 14 per cent of steel employees customarily worked in excess of sixty hours. The AFL endorsed the five-day week in 1926 but made no effort to achieve it. In January 1928 the Clothing Workers sought the forty-hour week in the Chicago and Rochester markets without success. The railway unions, disturbed over technological unemployment, came out

---

[8] NICB, *Wages . . . 1914–1929*, 201; Butler, *Industrial Relations*, 37; Douglas, *Real Wages*, 590; Kuznets, *National Income*, 332–33, 352–53; U.S. Steel Corp., *Annual Report, 1955*, 30–31; Charles P. Taft, 2d, to Martin Egan, June 7, 1934, Record Group No. 25, National Archives; Mills, *Economic Tendencies*, 404.

for the eight-hour day and the five-day week in April 1929, but accomplished nothing. The notable gains were made by the decade's most prominent anti-Semite, Henry Ford, and the Jewish Sabbath Alliance. Ford inaugurated the five-day week in his plants in 1926, and the Alliance persuaded a matzoth factory to institute this schedule shortly afterward. A survey in 1928 uncovered only 216,000 workers on five days, many of them working as many hours as they had on the six-day week. The only general improvement that occurred was the five-and-one-half-day week; the Lynds found that the Saturday half holiday prevailed in Middletown.

Unions, excepting the case of Ford, were mainly responsible for these modest gains. Further, organized workers enjoyed a marked superiority in hours of work. Douglas found that in 1926 average weekly hours in six primarily union manufacturing industries were 45.9 in contrast with 52.2 in the eight predominantly nonunion industries he studied.

The economic significance of stability of hours at a high level in the face of rising productivity is much the same as that for wages. Advancing technology permitted a sharp reduction in the work week; with spotty exceptions, no gains were made. Nor is there any evidence that American workers, as distinguished from unions, sought shorter hours. As an Australian observer remarked:

> I think that the most striking thing about labor in America is that it has become the slave of the paymaster. In Australia men value their hours of leisure too highly to sell them for any wages. In America men can be got to work . . . for almost any hours if it means extra pay.[9]

* * * *

The urban worker without effective means of voicing his grievances within the shop began to express them haltingly by indirection in his vote. The inadequacy of the statistics measuring the economic lot of labor in the twenties is compounded in an attempt to assess political behavior, for the election results afford no precise way of separating voters who were workers from those who were not. Nor did the 1928 presidential election, the basis of the present analysis of workers' political attitudes, provide evidence of a labor vote as such.

The presidential race in which Herbert Hoover decisively defeated Alfred Smith has been conventionally regarded as a triumph for the *status quo,*

---

[9] Douglas, *Real Wages,* 112–16, 208; Solomon Fabricant, *Employment in Manufacturing, 1899–1939* (New York: National Bureau of Economic Research, 1942), 234; Lazare Teper, *Hours of Labor* (Baltimore: Johns Hopkins University Press, 1932), 35; BLS, Bull. No. 513, *Wages and Hours,* 4; "Hours of Labor and the 7-Day Week in the Iron and Steel Industry," *MLR,* 30 (June 1930), 184–85; Marion Cotter Cahill, *Shorter Hours: A Study of the Movement Since the Civil War* (New York: Columbia University Press, 1932), *passim;* "Extent of the Five-Day Week in Manufacturing," *MLR,* 30 (Feb. 1930), 368; Lynds, *Middletown,* 54; Adam, *An Australian,* 117–18.

an election in which the voters of the nation reaffirmed their approval of the happy marriage between the Republican Party and Coolidge prosperity. As a Hoover campaign card put it:

HARD TIMES
Always come when Democrats try to run the nation.
ASK DAD—HE KNOWS!
Take No Chances!
Vote a Straight Republican Ticket!!

To be sure, domestic bliss was ruffled by two seemingly extraneous issues: prohibition and Al Smith's Catholicism. According to the usual view of the election, the "real" issues of the day—the fragility of prosperity, the sorry plight of coal and textiles, the farm depression, and the inequities in income distribution—were largely ignored.

Reassessment of the 1928 election against the backdrop of political developments in the thirties has placed it not at the close of an old era but rather at the onset of a new one. There can be no doubt of the soundness of this approach and its relevance to the present study.

The central emerging force in American political society at this time was what Samuel Lubell has called the revolt of the city. The 1920 census was the first to show that a majority of the people in the United States lived in urban areas. The immense movement of population to the cities came primarily from immigration and secondarily from agrarian regions, largely the Appalachian area and the South. Both streams flowed into the urban working class and contributed to its growth by a much higher birth rate than that characteristic of the older stocks that formed the backbone of the middle class and the Republican Party. Between 1920 and 1928 some 17 million potential voters reached the age of twenty-one, mainly the children of poor immigrants and migrants to the cities. To them, Lubell has observed, "the loyalties of Appomattox and the Homestead Act were details in history books"; nor did they owe allegiance to the individualistic tradition of the farm and the small town.

The 1928 presidential election was the first in which this emergent force became evident, but it was not as sharply defined as it was to become later, reflecting the crosscurrents of a transition phase. In part the conflict was between city and farm, in part between the ethnic strains of the "new" immigration pressing for status against the older Anglo-Saxon and northern European stocks, in part between Catholics and to a lesser extent Jews pushing into a dominantly Protestant society, and in part between the working and middle classes. Where the new forces joined, as in Boston, the Democrats made sweeping gains by virtue of the coincidence of urbanism, Irish Catholicism, and the working class. Where they were blurred, as in Los Angeles, the Democrats made only slight advances because urbanism was diluted by transplanted midwestern farmers who were mainly old stock Protestants and were without a working-class outlook.

. . . .

In conclusion, city workers and coal miners, their numbers growing prodigiously, began in the twenties that great movement into the Democratic Party that was to become so critical a feature of American politics in ` the following decade. In large part this voting shift spoke with the voice of protest. But the grievances of labor in 1928 were primarily related to status, ethnic and religious minorities yearning for equality. In lesser part the complaints were economic. With the crash and the Great Depression that followed, economic protest became the cutting edge of politics; at that time American labor was simply to reaffirm in larger measure the political choice it had already made.

By way of postscript for 1928 it is necessary to chart the dismal labor showing of the Marxist parties. Norman Thomas on the Socialist ticket polled only 268,000 votes, more than a third of them in New York. He ran far behind Debs's 902,000 in 1920. The Communists, led by William Z. Foster, did much worse, winning only 48,000 adherents. American labor, obviously, showed little inclination to choose either of these parties as the vehicle of protest.[10]

Although the 1928 election was a portent for the future, its contemporary significance for labor lay in the fact that Hoover and the Republican Party scored a signal victory. This could not have occurred unless many workers had voted for Hoover, and their willingness to do so is suggestive of their social outlook at the end of the twenties.

Observers were struck with the materialism that permeated all levels of American society, including labor; workers shared with their bosses a devout reverence for the almighty dollar. In Middletown workmen derived little satisfaction from their work. "There isn't twenty-five per cent of me paying attention to the job," a bench molder stated. Since this frustration was linked to a dim prospect for advancement as workers, the more energetic strove to enter the middle class. The acquisition of money was the main objective of life, and people were measured by the externals money bought—where they lived, how they lived, the make of car they drove. In the shops, workers were more concerned with maximizing income than with learning skills or gaining leisure by shorter hours.

Inasmuch as this materialism was joined to a vestigial rural tradition of individualism as well as a heterogeneous labor force, trade unionism found the social climate forbidding. As Lewis L. Lorwin pointed out, "The desire for steady employment and higher earnings became more dominant in the minds of the workers than the feeling for industrial freedom and independence."

---

[10] Peel and Donnelly, *1928 Campaign*, 171.

Among the workers who benefited economically the mood was conservative. "The American workman," a French visitor observed, "when he
realizes that society assures him a comfortable income, is ready to accept the
existing organization of industry. He has made an excellent place for himself
. . . so he has no wish to destroy it by stirring up a revolution." From the
standpoint of social outlook Douglas emphasized the direction rather than
the amount of change in real wages. The fact that the lot of the workers was
improving rather than deteriorating made them "more satisfied with the social and political system." "Arise ye wretched of the earth," the appeal of the
"Internationale," he found "curiously unreal to the better-paid American
workers who, with few exceptions, are not afflicted with starvation, and the
more skilled of whom own automobiles, radio sets, small homes, and bank
books, as well as chains." [11]

This comment by Douglas raises a question: Did a working "class"
emerge? Manipulations of census data are not significant because the problem
is in the realm of ideas rather than of statistics. The answer is two-headed
and, in a sense, internally contradictory. On the one hand, a growing proportion of the labor force found itself in an employee rather than a self-employed
status, a fact of immense importance in the daily lives of the people involved.
On the other hand, they failed to develop class consciousness—self-
realization as a proletariat—in the Marxist sense.

This dichotomy formed the central finding of *Middletown:*

> It is . . . this division into working class and business class that constitutes
> the outstanding cleavage in Middletown. The mere fact of being born upon
> one or the other side of the watershed roughly formed by these two groups is
> the most significant single cultural factor tending to influence what one does
> all day long throughout one's life; whom one marries; when one gets up in
> the morning; whether one belongs to the Holy Roller or Presbyterian church;
> or drives a Ford or a Buick; whether or not one's daughter makes the desirable
> high school Violet Club; or one's wife meets with the Sew We Do Club or
> with the Art Students' League; whether one belongs to the Odd Fellows or to
> the Masonic Shrine; whether one sits about evenings with one's necktie off;
> and so on indefinitely throughout the daily comings and goings of a Middle-
> town man, woman, or child.

Yet, search as they did, the Lynds failed to find evidence of working-class
consciousness. Radical movements had no influence; left-wing publications
were virtually unknown; and even the relatively conservative AFL struggled
merely to survive. Though the great majority of workers were destined to
remain workers for the duration of their productive lives, many were sus-

---

[11] Lynds, *Middletown,* 75; Lewis L. Lorwin, *The American Federation of Labor* (Washington: Brookings, 1933), 239; Siegfried, *America Comes of Age,* 165; Douglas, *Real
Wages,* 572–74.

tained by the hope of rising to a higher class. Large majorities of high school boys and girls, for example, could find nothing upsetting in the fact that some people were rich. If the collectivity of workers constituted a "class," it was an inert body with little dynamism or direction.[12] The labor movement reflected this inertia.

SUGGESTED READING

Aside from the reminiscences of workers, the records of scattered social organizations, and such studies as the Lynds' *Middletown* ° (1967), historians have little basis for conclusions about class consciousness and social aspirations of workers in the 1920's. Even reliance on content analysis of popular literature cannot definitively answer such questions as whether the Horatio Alger myth constituted part of the worker's system of beliefs or whether it was simply a symbolic source of escape. Leo Lowenthal's study "Biographies in Popular Magazines," reprinted without much change in his *Literature, Popular Culture, and Society* (1961), suggests the possibilities of content analysis.

The literature on the economy of the 1920's is ample. George Soule's *Prosperity Decade: From War to Depression: 1917–1929* (1947) is an adequate survey of the decade. Joseph Schumpeter's "The American Economy in the Interwar Period: The Decade of the Twenties," *American Economic Review*, XXXVI (May 1946), is also useful.

Philip Taft's *The A. F. of L. in the Time of Gompers* (1957) and *The A. F. of L. from the Death of Gompers to the Merger* (1959) are still the best organizational histories of the federation in this period. Ronald Radosh, in "The Corporate Ideology of Labor Leaders from Gompers to Hillman," *Studies on the Left*, VI (Nov.–Dec. 1966), places the labor movement within the framework of corporate liberalism. David Brody's *Labor in Crisis: The Steel Strike of 1919* ° (1962), though dealing with a slightly earlier period, is a better source on labor history and the workingman. Henry Pelling's *American Labor* (1960) has a brief chapter on organized labor entitled "Suffering from Prosperity." Robert H. Zieger's *Republicans and Labor, 1919–1929* is a useful study.

Valuable contemporary essays include Sumner Slichter's "The Current Labor Policies of American Industries," *Quarterly Journal of Economics*, XLIII (May 1929); David Saposs' "The American Labor Movement Since the War," *Quarterly Journal of Economics*, XLVI (Feb. 1935); and Lyle Cooper's "The American Labor Movement in Prosperity and Depression," *American Economic Review*, XXII (Dec. 1932).

---

[12] See Tillman M. Sogge, "Industrial Classes in the United States in 1930," *JASA*, 28 (June 1933), 199–203; Lynds, *Middletown*, 23–24.

WILLIAM L. O'NEILL

The End of Feminism

INTRODUCTION

Like black history, which attracted little attention before the civil rights movement of the 1960's, women's history was largely neglected until the rise of women's liberation. A few well-established historians, however, like David M. Potter and Carl Degler, and some younger scholars, including Aileen Kraditor, Christopher Lasch, Gerda Lerner, William L. O'Neill, and David M. Kennedy, began exploring the field before the events of the late 1960's made it popular.

While some of the work focused directly on such basic issues as sex roles and family structure, more of the scholarship was devoted to studies of notable women, suffragists, and other

FROM William L. O'Neill, *The Woman Movement: Feminism in the United States and England* (New York: Barnes & Noble, 1969). Reprinted by permission of George Allen & Unwin Ltd.

feminists—the woman's movement. O'Neill, professor of history at Rutgers University, who first published an important volume on *Divorce in the Progressive Era* (1967), moved on to examine the related issue of the rise and decline of American feminism. In *Everyone Was Brave: The Rise and Fall of Feminism in America* (1969), and in "Feminism as a Radical Ideology," in Alfred Young, ed., *Dissent: Explorations in Radical America* (1969), he has developed an analysis that he draws on in the following selection.

O'Neill, among others, has noted that many feminists often claimed superior moral virtues for women, a view that could be considered a variation of the Victorian mystique. The suffragists, he contends, persuaded

> organized middle-class women, . . . a potent force for reform in the Progressive era, that they needed the vote in order to secure the healthier and broader domestic life that was their main objective; feminists had not, however, convinced bourgeois women that they were greatly deprived and oppressed and that they had unrealized capabilities.

The movement for the vote, he concludes, was based on a "spurious unity" and pursued for the wrong reasons.

His analysis loosely depends on a troubling distinction between what he calls "social feminists" and "hard-core feminists"—a distinction that he believes became crucial and visible in the 1920's. The social feminists, according to his definition, placed particular social reforms ahead of women's rights, while the hard-core feminists placed women's rights first. The value of this distinction is limited because it obscures basic issues. What rights did feminists of either type believe women should have? Did they seek equality with men? How did they define such equality?

In the following selection, drawn from *The Woman Movement: Feminism in the United States and England* (1969) a book that examines the women's movement in the United States and England, O'Neill sketches the collapse of feminism in America and offers some contrasts with the British experience.

*N*ineteen-hundred-and-twenty was the moral pinnacle of American feminism. The hopes and dreams of three-quarters of a century had matured at virtually the same moment. Prohibition and woman suffrage, the two objects most passionately desired by middle class women, had been secured. Child labour, to social feminists the greatest scandal of the day, was on the verge of extinction thanks to a congressional Bill passed in 1918. The problems of working women had been eased by the establishment of maximum hour laws and the progress of minimum wage legislation. Even the cause of peace, so dear to the hearts of women and only recently in such disarray, had gained a new lease on life through the League of Nations. With women ensconced in a variety of new occupations because of the war, with female students pouring into the colleges at an even greater rate than before, the feminist thrust seemed more powerful than ever. In England, too, morale was high. Many of the same conditions obtained as in America. The promise of a brilliant postwar reconstruction had not yet faded. The Labour Party's quick rise to at least a semblance of power made it appear that the wartime slogan of 'homes fit for heroes' was to become a genuine programme.

It soon became evident, however, that in neither country were there to be sweeping social reforms, and that in America even the gains already made were vulnerable. As always, woman suffrage once enacted became a dead issue, but it was not so with Prohibition. Within a few years the prevalence of bootlegging demonstrated that Prohibition was unenforceable and, indeed, almost unbearable. The 'drys' retained sufficient political strength to block Repeal until 1933, but they could not keep Americans from drinking, nor prevent the whole notion of reform through constitutional amendment from being discredited. Hence, when in 1922 the Supreme Court pronounced the national child labour law to be unconstitutional, social feminists were unable to secure a constitutional amendment permitting congressional action on child labour. Such a Bill passed easily through the Congress, only to be voted down in state after state, partly for fear that it was a Communist trick to nationalize children, chiefly because of a wholesale reaction against the regulation of morals symbolized by the Volstead Act and the Eighteenth Amendment. Similarly, when the Court struck down a minimum wage Bill social feminists were powerless to stem the adverse tide. Not until the Second New Deal did the Court reverse its position on minimum wage laws for working women. The child labour amendment was never passed.

These defeats were but symptoms of a general malaise. Reforms of every type experienced heavy weather in the 1920s, and those women's organizations geared for reform foundered when they did not trim sail. The social settlements gave up their grander aspirations and were content to play small if useful roles as service stations in the city wilderness. The General Federation of Women's Clubs wobbled badly for several years and then recovered, but it never regained its old prestige and momentum. Hardest hit were the élite units in the women's army of reform. The National Consumers' League was devastated by Progressivism's collapse, red-baited savagely by the super-patriotic organizations then becoming a permanent part of American life, and demoralized by its failure to secure the child labour amendment. Rebellious member leagues and a wounding struggle over who was to be its president—the incumbent, former Secretary of War Newton D. Baker who had protected the NCL in wartime but was now in disrepute for criticizing organized labour, or John R. Commons, a distinguished liberal economist at the University of Wisconsin—almost finished off the League. It made something of a comeback in the 1930s and survives today, but with little of its original drive and élan.

The National Women's Trade Union League suffered also, especially from an abortive venture in international co-operation. Social feminists were always interested in kindred foreign organizations. The rise of a powerful, world-wide labour movement gave the NWTUL a further reason for developing its international contacts. In 1919 when the International Labor Conference met in Washington the League arranged for a congress of working women to meet in connection with it. Out of this congress developed the International Federation of Working Women established in 1921 with Mrs. Robins as president. Trouble developed almost immediately. The European delegates (including England's National Federation of Working Women) were both too radical and too sectarian for the American delegates. Economic difficulties in their home countries made the European women unusually militant. They were also tied more closely to union movements of a social democratic complexion. On the other hand, they were far more suspicious of Catholics and Communists than the ideologically unsophisticated Americans. By 1923 when the IFWW met for a second time most delegates wanted to merge with the International Federation of Trade Unions. The Americans resisted this, ostensibly because the AFL with which they were affiliated did not belong to the IFTU, really because they felt that as a section of the IFTU women would be merely appendages of a masculine structure. The American delegates put their roles as feminists ahead of their interests as trade unionists. Undeterred, the majority went ahead and became a department of the IFTU, while the NWTUL resigned from the movement it had brought into being. The Americans, thoroughly disconcerted by their European adventures, congratulated themselves on a lucky escape. Yet the NWTUL dwindled away until after World War II it was disbanded. Women never achieved an important position in the American trade union movement, while in England they became union heads and cabinet officers.

The relationship between feminism and the masses of employed women was, however, more complicated than this. In addition to the Anglo-American division on feminist priorities, there developed in both countries a dispute over the wisdom of protective legislation as such. In England, and especially in America, the multitude of laws regulating female employment were virtually the only benefits working women had derived from feminism, which was otherwise of, by, and for the middle classes. The value of these benefits was questioned even before the war ended. In America extreme feminists began turning up at legislative hearings to testify that protective laws handicapped women in the competition for jobs. In 1919 Mrs. Sidney Webb, a late convert to woman suffrage but a steady friend of working women, filed a minority report of the War Cabinet Committee on Women in Industry which protested that special treatment for women workers only perpetuated their inferior status. Labour Party women, including Margaret Bondfield, the leading female trade unionist, did not generally agree with her. However, the three major feminist organizations—the Women's Freedom League, the National Union of Societies for Equal Citizenship (which succeeded the NUWSS) and the new Six Point Group—endorsed Mrs. Webb's position. Broadly speaking, the division in England was between extreme feminists and the social feminists in the NUSEC, on the one hand, and the female Labourites who were not really feminists at all, on the other.

The American alignment was rather different. Only the militant Woman's Party opposed special protective legislation. Against it during most of the 1920s were ranged every important social feminist body, except for the American Association of University Women (formerly the ACA) which was neutral. Trade Union women and their allies in the NWTUL and the NCL, who did not constitute a separate force as in England, were included in the social feminist consensus. Because the American Federation of Labor supported them, social feminists found it easy to accuse the Woman's Party of being anti-labour. There was a grain of truth to this charge. It was also true that the Woman's Party's employed members were mainly business and professional women not covered by protective laws. But the WP was quick to point out that while the AFL favoured special legislation for working women, it considered independent trade union action to be the best protection for working men. It was liable to the charge, therefore, that it favoured the regulation of women precisely because such laws made them less competitive. Militant feminists believed the AFL was working both sides of the street. It evaded its obligation to organize working women by asserting their need for protective laws, knowing that these laws did not so much protect women as keep them from desirable employments.

For its part, the WP was accused of being more concerned with its proposed constitutional amendment than with the plight of working women. Even after 1920 women continued to be discriminated against by law in hundreds of different ways. The WP had attempted to redress each grievance by sponsoring specific pieces of legislation in state legislatures. But while it framed hundreds of Bills, few of them were enacted. The Party resolved, therefore, to solve the problem at one stroke by securing an amendment to the Constitution declaring that 'men and women shall have equal rights throughout the United States'. This equal rights, or blanket amendment would surely have nullified most industrial legislation that applied only to women. The WP had to defend itself against the charge that it cared nothing for the problems of working women, and did so by taking an offensive position against the whole concept of special protective legislation. The ensuing struggle sharply divided organized women who were forced to choose between their interests as women and their interests as reformers. Most of them chose the latter. In the process, however, the woman movement was destroyed. It had rested on the false assumption that women possessed a special unity independent of class and occupation, and untainted by self-interest. As much as anything else, the fight over the equal rights amendment made this position impossible to sustain.

The 1920s were subversive of the woman movement in other ways. Women were thought to be especially pacific thanks to their mother instinct, the lack of which made men destructive by nature. Yet, as Jane Addams sorrowfully observed, when women finally became members of Congress they were united only by their common enthusiasm for a larger army and navy. When women gained the ballot it was to be used for constructive social purposes, but the Nineteenth Amendment proved only that there was no women's vote. Women voted much as men did, except on a handful of issues concerning personal morality. Henceforth politicians had to be more careful of their drinking and wenching, but otherwise the enfranchisement of women meant little to them. In fact, once the women's vote was shown to be a paper tiger, female organizations often carried less weight with professional politicians than before.

Nor were women's concrete gains so durable as had been supposed. Women moved into the colleges in greater numbers, but their share of the total enrolment declined. In 1920 they constituted 47.3 per cent of all college students; by 1950 their percentage had fallen to 30.2. In 1956 only a third of all master's degrees were awarded to women, as against 40 per cent in 1930. In 1920 women earned one out of every six doctorates compared with one out of ten in 1956. Their role in the work force has been equally unimpressive. More and more women obtained jobs, but they continued to be at the bottom levels of business and industry. New occupations were opened up, but old ones were lost so that in recent years the degree of occupational sex segregation has been about the same as it was in 1900.[1] The income of employed women increased, but the earnings of men rose even faster.

Conditions in England were somewhat less depressing. Women did not gain equal suffrage until 1928, and so the unifying effects of suffragism persisted longer than in America. There was no great surge of reform after the war, but this was offset to a degree by the Labour Party's growth. For reasons that are far from clear, Englishwomen did better in politics and

---

[1] This fact has been established by Edward Gross, 'Plus ca Change . . . The Sexual Structure of Occupations Over Time,' an unpublished paper delivered at the 1967 meeting of the American Sociological Society.

the professions than their American sisters. A larger percentage of working women were organized in trade unions. Broadly speaking, however, women continued to play a subordinate role in England as in America. In neither country did the expectations of feminists come anywhere near realization.

Satisfactory explanations for the collapse of feminism are not easily come by. For nearly a hundred years the advancement of women had been a salient feature of Anglo-American life. Votes for women was the most dramatic accomplishment of this movement, but while it was thought a harbinger of things to come, it really constituted the last significant demand that organized women were able to make. Partly this was, as I have suggested, because the struggle for suffrage imposed a spurious unity. Once gained, there was nothing to take the vote's place as a rallying point. Even more, by the time women secured the vote they had sufficient experience as students, workers and professionals to appreciate the disadvantages of these public roles. To succeed in the world they had to abandon their sexual functions altogether. Or, they could attempt to combine their public and private lives to the disadvantage of both. Much had changed in the last several generations, but the old conflict between home and work had not. Women could be mothers, and they could be workers. They could not, however, perform with equal facility in both categories at once. Things might have been different if society had lightened their burden with extensive nursery facilities, paid maternity leaves, and the like. In the event, it did not. Again, if marriage had been redefined so as to give husbands and wives equal responsibilities women might not have found it more difficult to balance the demands of home and work than men did. This also failed to happen. Under the circumstances women could hardly be blamed for declining public roles that brought them few rewards and many hardships. By the 1920s it was becoming evident that their emancipation had been largely negative. The formal barriers to equal opportunity were down, yet the social changes which would enable them to take advantage of this fact had not been made. Thus, like racial minorities, they were free in theory but not in practice.

Added to this were social and ideological changes that made domesticity seem more attractive. Ambitious women had traditionally escaped the domestic trap by declining to marry, a decision made all the easier by the low esteem in which sexual relations were held. Victorians did not view celibacy as a particularly deprived state. One was denied children, of course; still, one was also spared the coarse and painful means by which they came into being—processes especially repugnant to women of taste and sensibility. By the 1920s this was no longer true. Sexual fulfillment was not yet regarded as an inalienable human right, but neither was it seen as a hopeless, if not actually unspeakable, dream. What is usually called the revolution in morals was, if not quite a revolution, real enough. For a variety of reasons women's sexual practices do seem to have changed after the war. Everyone felt this at the time, and the few sexual studies made then were confirmed later by the Kinsey report on women. The incidence of pre-marital intercourse among middle class women rose sharply in the twenties. Prostitution declined. The Victorians had resolved to destroy the double standard of morals by compelling men to be as chaste as women. This proved to be unfeasible. Women got what they wanted all the same. If men and women could not be equally chaste, they could, at least, be equally promiscuous. Of course, this is to overstate the change. Women continue to be somewhat less active sexually than men, and the double standard of morals was modified rather than abolished. But the convergence of masculine and feminine sexual practices that became manifest in the 1920s is still going on, which suggests that in time a rough parity will finally be reached. The flappers and jazz babies we associate with the Roaring Twenties may not have been typical, but they did reflect, however garishly, a fundamental and enduring alteration in the sexual lives of women.

These changes in sexual behaviour were accompanied by new, or apparently new, ideas. Radical feminists in the nineteenth century had gingerly explored the possibilities of free love in hopes of breaking out of the domestic trap. Orthodox feminists rejected this view, not only for its obvious dangers, but especially because they felt women's subjugation was based on those very sexual characteristics that radical women hoped to exploit. To theorists like Charlotte Perkins Gilman the exaggerated emphasis on women's sexual role was precisely the means by which they were chained to home and family. Women needed to be freed from sex, and not encouraged actively to pursue what could only lead to earlier marriages and larger families. Time was to prove her right. The increased awareness of feminine sexuality that developed in the 1920s resulted in the teenage marriages and the baby boom of the 1940s and 50s.

This was not only because early intercourse produces unexpected babies and promotes early marriage, but also because shifts in the climate of opinion encouraged women to develop both their erotic and maternal capacities. For functional reasons orthodox feminists had stressed the ways in which women resembled men. Women were urged to compete with men, to acquire the same training and fill the same jobs. In the 1920s, however, the tide turned. Now women were again asked to discover what was unique about themselves, to cease their vain and sterile competitions with men, to develop their special capabilities. Closer examination revealed, to no one's great surprise, that what was unique about women was their wombs. Betty Friedan, in her spirited polemic, calls this new orientation *The Feminine Mystique*. Andrew Sinclair, perhaps more accurately, terms it the New Victorianism.[2] To the old saw that 'woman's place is in the home' was added a

---

[2] Betty Friedan, *The Feminine Mystique* (New York 1963); Andrew Sinclair, *The Better Half* (New York 1965).

codicil—'and in the bed'. Thus, the traditional domestic system was reconciled with the newer ideas about sex. Women were to enjoy more sexual opportunities before marriage, and, presumably, deeper gratifications within it, while discharging the same responsibilities as before.

The pioneer sexual ideologists, whom I elsewhere have described as New Moralists, seem not to have anticipated this development.[3] In the 1890s people like Edward Carpenter and Havelock Ellis began advocating sexual freedom and expertise for moral and aesthetic reasons. They wanted to clear away the layers of Victorian hypocrisy and obfuscation so that everyone could live full and beautiful sex lives. Because they were feminists they felt women would profit especially from the erotic revolution they hoped to launch. Most of them thought that sexual freedom would inevitably force other desirable changes in the relations between men and women. Few of them realized that their new wine would pour so easily from the old bottles. Nor did they anticipate the effects of psychoanalysis. When Freud first became popular in the 1920s he was thought to favour promiscuous sexuality. His teachings did help to sexualize the climate of opinion, but as Freud himself entertained conventional Victorian views on women his work in the long run lent strength to the anti-feminist reaction. Women who competed with men were now seen as victims of penis envy. They suffered from a castration complex. They were immature, fixated at an early state of development. Well-balanced adult women understood that fulfillment came from bearing and raising children. Their talent was for nurture, its proper setting was the home.[4] If this summary seems to caricature psychoanalysis, that is because the popular dissemination of complex intellectual systems depends on their being reduced to convenient formulae. Darwinism becomes Social Darwinism; Marxism becomes Maoism. Psychoanalysis became variously, a dogmatic religion, a parlour game of searching for 'Freudian slips', and a bag of labels marked 'penis envy' and the like.

Other factors were responsible too. Women grasped at psychoanalytic straws, after all, because the body of feminist thought was simply inadequate to their needs. Emancipation had not made women happier or more satisfied, and feminists were unable to explain why. American feminists conducted a rather elaborate post-mortem during the 1920s without coming to any reliable conclusions. . . . Clearly the woman question had not been successfully answered, perhaps it had not even been asked—at least in the proper way. Feminists had been unable to erect a suitable ideol-

---

[3] See the chapters 'Origins of the New Morality', in my *Divorce in the Progressive Era* (New Haven 1967).

[4] A valuable counterweight to the classical Freudian view is Karen Horney, *Feminine Psychology* (New York 1967). Ronald V. Sampson's *The Psychology of Power* contains an illuminating critique of Freud's attitude toward women.

ogy during their glory years; who then could expect them to when the dimensions of their failure were just becoming evident? It would be rash indeed of me to offer here a solution to the feminist dilemma. What Elizabeth Cady Stanton and Charlotte Perkins Gilman could not do is surely beyond my powers. Yet, I think it possible now, because we have evidence that they lacked, to point out the direction that feminists ought to have taken. The success of Sweden, and the failure of Anglo-American society, have to be the key items in this respect. Women may not be entirely equal with men in Sweden, but Sweden is closer to that goal than any other country. Its combination of an advanced welfare state, and a willingness to re-examine traditional ideas about sex, maternity and male-female relationships would seem to be responsible. The decline of feminism in England, and especially in America, was then, rooted in a failure of intellectual nerve.

Still, who can blame these splendid women for failing to accomplish what the whole of Anglo-American civilization, with its vast physical and intellectual resources, could not do? They dreamed of freedom, they dreamed of justice, most of all, they dreamed of equality, of a society in which every individual could reach the limit of his own possibilities. In America especially, where poverty and prejudice put such strains on the fabric of society, we can ill-afford to patronize any group, however mistaken, that laboured to make good the promise of our national life. Generations of valiant women struggled, not just for their own sakes, but for us all. If they had been wiser and more daring they would have come closer to building the good society of their dreams. Yet, of what reformers can this not be said? The Reverend Samuel J. May, who was both a feminist and an abolitionist, put it very well when, writing to a friend, he summed up his colleagues in the anti-slavery movement in terms descriptive of feminists too:

> You must not expect those who have left to take up this great cause that they will plead it in all that seemliness of phrase which the scholars . . . might use. But the scholars, and the clergy and the statesmen had done nothing. We abolitionists are what we are—babes, sucklings, obscure men, silly women, . . . sinners, and we shall manage the matter we have taken in hand just as might be expected of such persons as we are. It is unbecoming in abler men who stood by, and would do nothing, to complain of us because we manage the matter no better.

SUGGESTED READING

Eleanor Flexner, in *Century of Struggle: The Woman's Rights Movement in the United States* ° (1959), surveys the movement for women's suffrage, and Aileen Kraditor's *The Ideas of the Woman's Suffrage Movement, 1890–1920* (1965) is a discriminating analysis. *Up*

From the Pedestal: Selected Writings in the History of American Feminism,° edited by Aileen Kraditor (1970), has a perceptive introduction and reprints materials largely from the nineteenth century and only occasionally from after the progressive years. Two briefer collections are *The American Woman: Who Was She?* ° edited by Anne F. Scott (1971), *The New Feminism in Twentieth-Century America,*° edited by June Sochen (1971).

Carl Degler, in "Revolution without Ideology: The Changing Place of Women in America," in Robert Lifton, ed., *The Woman in America* ° (1965) argues that feminism failed because it lacked an ideology in "pragmatic America." David M. Kennedy's *Birth Control in America: The Career of Margaret Sanger* ° (1970) deals with the efforts to achieve birth control, provides a biography of Mrs. Sanger, and examines the responses to her efforts. James McGovern, in "The American Woman's Pre–World War I Freedom in Manners and Morals," *Journal of American History,* LV (Sept. 1968), sketches conditions before the war, and Kenneth Yellis, in "Prosperity's Child: Some Thoughts on the Flapper," *American Quarterly,* XXI (Spring 1969), relates the "flapper" to American culture. Mari Jo Buhle *et al.,* in "Women in American Society: An Historical Contribution," *Radical America,* V (July–Aug. 1971), offer an exploratory study of women's history.

CARL N. DEGLER

The Ordeal of Herbert Hoover

INTRODUCTION

Though the nation would later repudiate him and turn elsewhere for leadership, few men in American political life during the 1920's seemed by training and experience better prepared than Herbert Hoover to deal with the Great Depression. His successful directorship of European relief won the admiration of businessmen and the nation's respect, and his achievements as Secretary of Commerce seemed to confirm their judgment. In that position he sought to continue the wartime cooperation among businessmen, and he sponsored trade associations so that industries might escape from some of the perils of competition.

Opposed to laissez faire, Hoover was not an uncritical observer of American society in the 1920's. In 1922, in his book *American Individualism,* he acknowledged "the faulty results of our system":

> the spirit of lawlessness; the uncertainty of employment in some callings; the deadening effect of certain repetitive processes of manufacture; the 12-hour day in a few industries; unequal voice in bargaining

FROM Carl N. Degler, "The Ordeal of Herbert Hoover," *The Yale Review,* LII (Summer, 1963), pp. 563–83. Copyright © 1963 by Yale University. Reprinted by permission.

for wage in some employment; arrogant domination by some employers and some labor leaders; child labor in some states; inadequate instruction in some areas; unfair competition in some industries; some fortunes excessive far beyond the needs of stimulation to initiative; survivals of religious intolerance.

Hoover's suggestions' for correcting these faults were sometimes obscure and often ambiguous; the book evidences a tension between affirming the spirit of voluntarism and relying on the government to maintain equality of opportunity. Although Hoover's preference for cooperation rather than economic conflict led him to favor unions for workers, trade associations for industry, marketing cooperatives for farmers, and even collective bargaining to avoid strife between classes, he sought to keep government above these interests and out of the control of any particular one. "It is where dominant private property is assembled in the hands of the groups who control the state that the individual begins to feel capital as an oppressor," he warned.

Historians, including Carl Degler, the author of the following essay and professor of history at Stanford University, have found in *American Individualism* clues to explain Hoover's responses to the Depression. Degler sees continuities with progressivism in Hoover's bold efforts to deal with the Depression, but he notes also the restrictions imposed by Hoover's ideology that barred truly effective action: his fears of public relief eroding the human spirit, his often dogged reliance on voluntarism and local initiative, his opposition to the idea of allowing the government to compete with private enterprise, his concern for budget balancing.

Yet Degler believes, as did Walter Lippmann during the early years of Roosevelt's Administration, that Hoover was not the last of the old Presidents. But whereas Lippmann found Hoover the first of the new Presidents, Degler concludes that he was a "transitional figure in the development of government as an active force in the economy in times of depression." This view, curiously, is at odds with Degler's interpretation in 1959 of the New Deal as "The Third American Revolution," for that view stressed the discontinuity between Hoover and Franklin D. Roosevelt and attributed to the Roosevelt years some important changes that the author later located during Hoover's tenure.

*I*n 1958 Herbert Hoover published a book about his old chief entitled *The Ordeal of Woodrow Wilson*. Wilson's struggle for the League was short and his part in it has gained lustre with passing years. Not so with the ordeal of Herbert Hoover. The Great Depression was considerably longer and his reputation has never been free from the memory of that ordeal. Today, in fact, there are two Hoovers. The first is the living man, the former President who has unstintingly and very capably served Democratic and Republican Administrations alike. He is the Hoover of nation-wide birthday celebrations, of rhapsodic editorials, of admiring Republican national conventions. That conception bears almost no relation to the second, the historical Hoover. In the history books his Administration is usually depicted as cold-hearted, when not pictured as totally devoid of heart, inept, or actionless in the face of the Great Depression. Simply because of the wide gulf between the two Hoovers it is time to try to answer the question William Allen White posed over thirty years ago. Writing an evaluation of Hoover's Administration in the *Saturday Evening Post* of March 4, 1933, White closed his piece with the following words: "So history stands hesitant waiting for time to tell whether Herbert Hoover . . . by pointing the way to social recovery . . . is the first of the new Presidents . . . or whether . . . he is the last of the old."

The notion of two Hoovers should never have grown up; his life and views were too consistent for that. During Hoover's tenure of office, Theodore Joslin, his press secretary, undertook to examine closely all the President's utterances and writings of the preceding ten or eleven years. "In all of those million-odd words, dealing with every important subject," Joslin reported in 1934, "the number of times he reversed himself or modified an important position could be counted on the fingers of one hand." And so it has remained even after March 4, 1933.

Nor were those principles, to which Hoover held so consistently, simply conservative ones, as has so often been assumed. In 1920, for example, when Hoover's political career began, he was the darling of the progressives who still clustered about the figure of the fallen Wilson. College and university faculties were calling upon Hoover to run for president that year—on either ticket. Indeed, his silence as to which party he belonged to, for a time caused his name to figure as prominently in Democratic primaries as in Republican. For example, he received the most votes by far in the Michigan Democratic primary that year. That year, too, Franklin Roosevelt, who was also a member of Woodrow Wilson's Administration, wrote Josephus Daniels that Herbert Hoover "is certainly a wonder, and I wish we could make him President of the United States. There could not be a better one." (Nor did Roosevelt's enthusiasm cool until much later. In 1928 he refused to write an article against Hoover's candidacy because Hoover was "an old personal friend.")

Hoover's principles were distinctly and publicly progressive. In 1920, for example, he defended the principle of collective bargaining and the right to strike—two very unpopular principles at that date—before a frosty Chamber of Commerce in Boston. As Secretary of Commerce in the Harding Administration he opposed the sweeping federal injunction against the railroad strikers and worked with Harding to have the steel industry abandon the twelve-hour day. In his book of guiding principles, *American Individualism,* which he published in 1922, he was careful to distinguish his views from laissez-faire capitalism. The American way, he insisted, "is not capitalism, or socialism, or syndicalism, nor a cross breed of them." It did include, though, government regulation in order to preserve equality of opportunity and individual rights. "This regulation is itself," he pointed out, "proof that we have gone a long way toward the abandonment of the 'capitalism' of Adam Smith. . . ." While Secretary of Commerce in the 1920's he instituted much needed regulations for the burgeoning radio and airplane industries. It was Herbert Hoover who said in 1922 at the first conference on radio that "the ether is a public medium and its use must be for the public benefit. The use of radio channels is justified only if there is public benefit. The dominant element of consideration in the radio field is, and always will be, the great body of the listening public, millions in number, country-wide in distribution." In the same address, he said, "It is inconceivable that we should allow so great a possibility for service to be drowned in advertising chatter." In 1928 he was recommending that a three billion dollar reserve of public works be built up to serve as an economic stabilizer in times of recession.

In short, though he served both Harding and Coolidge, Herbert Hoover was not of their stripe. As he himself said later in his memoirs, "Mr. Coolidge was a real conservative, probably the equal of Benjamin Harrison. . . . He was a fundamentalist in religion, in the economic and social order, and in fishing." (The last because Coolidge, the fishing tyro, used worms for bait.) Moreover, unlike Coolidge, Hoover did not publicly ignore the scandals that rocked the Harding Administration. In June 1931, while dedicating the Harding Memorial at Marion, Ohio, Hoover went out of his way to speak of the tragedy of Warren Harding and of the enormity of the betrayal of a public trust by Harding's friends.

Hoover's record as president contains a number of truly progressive achievements. Although he cannot take credit for initiating the Norris-La Guardia Act of 1932, the fact remains that one of the most important prolabor acts in the whole history of American labor was signed by Herbert Hoover. Like other progressives, he sponsored legislation for conservation like the giant Boulder Dam project and the St. Lawrence Seaway.

But perhaps the most striking example of Hoover's willingness to recognize the new role of government in dealing with the complexities of an industrial economy was his breaking precedent to grapple directly with the Depression. From the outset Hoover rejected the advice of his Secretary of the Treasury, Andrew Mellon, who, as Hoover himself said, was a country-banker of narrow social vision. Mellon believed the crash should be permitted to run its course unmolested. His simple formula in a depression, as he told Hoover, was "Liquidate labor, liquidate stocks, liquidate farms, liquidate real estate." A panic, he told the President, was not so bad. "It will purge the rottenness out of the system. High costs of living and high living will come down. People will work harder, live more moral lives. Values will be adjusted, and enterprising people will pick up the wrecks from less competent people."

In contrast, Hoover's anti-depression action was swift in coming. Within a matter of weeks after the great crash of the stock market at the end of October, Hoover called a meeting of prominent business, labor, and farm leaders to work out plans for preventing the market crash from adversely affecting the rest of the economy. A week later he met for the same purpose with railway presidents. The economic leaders agreed to his plan of holding the line on wages and encouraging industrial expansion. In his annual message to Congress in December 1929, Hoover proudly told of these and other efforts his Administration had made to stem the economic decline. These efforts, he said, "must be vigorously pursued until normal conditions are restored." In January he continued to expand public works on Boulder Dam and on highway construction. By the end of July 1930, the Administration had got underway $800 million in public works, and the President called upon the states and local units of government to follow the national government's example in order to provide as much employment as possible.

The President was well aware of the unprecedented character of his swift anti-depression action. He said as much in his message to Congress in December 1929; he made the same point more explicitly at the Gridiron dinner in April 1930. The country, he said, had avoided the dole and other unsatisfactory devices to meet unemployment by "voluntary cooperation of industry with the Government in maintaining wages against reductions, and the intensification of construction work. Thereby we have inaugurated one of the greatest economic experiments in history on a basis of nation-wide cooperation not charity."

At first Hoover was optimistic about the effects of his program. Several times during the first year he compared the economic decline with that of 1921–22, usually with the observation that the earlier one was the more difficult. As he told the Chamber of Commerce in May 1930, the amount of public works contracted for was already three times the amount in the corresponding period of the previous "great depression."

Yet his optimism did not keep him from action. One thing he emphasized was the necessity of learning from this Depression about the prevention of future ones. He advocated better statistical measures and reform of the banking structure to prevent the drain of credit from productive to speculative enterprise, such as had led to the stock market boom and crash. Moreover, although he emphasized from the beginning that the Depression was "worldwide" and that its "causes and its effects lie only partly in the United States," he did not use this as an excuse for inactivity. There was no need simply to wait for the rest of the world to recover, he said, "We can make a very large degree of recovery independently of what may happen elsewhere." In October 1930 he told the American Bankers Association that depressions were not simply to be borne uncomplainingly. "The economic fatalist believes that these crises are inevitable and bound to be recurrent. I would remind these pessimists that exactly the same thing was once said of typhoid, cholera, and smallpox." But instead of being pessimistic, medical science went to work and conquered those diseases. "That should be our attitude toward these economic pestilences. They are not dispensations of Providence. I am confident in the faith that their control, so far as the cause lies within our own boundaries, is within the genius of modern business."

Hoover also told the bankers that he could not condone the argument which had been reported from some of them that the people would have to accept a lower standard of living in order to get through the Depression. Such a suggestion, he said, could not be countenanced either on idealistic or on practical grounds. To accept it would mean a "retreat into perpetual unemployment and the acceptance of a cesspool of poverty for some large part of our people." Several times during the Depression Hoover made it clear that the government had a responsibility to employ as many as possible as its contribution to the mitigation of the unemployment which was growing alarmingly.

The failure of the economy to respond to treatment and the loss of many Republican seats in the elections of 1930 caused Hoover for a while to place new emphasis upon the foreign sources of the Depression. At the end of 1930 he told the Congress that the "major forces of the depression now lie outside of the United States." In fact, though, the real collapse of the European economy was still almost six months away. Hoover was most fearful that the growing Congressional demands for new expenditures would throw the budget out of balance. His concern about the budget and his hostility toward the Congress were both measured in his tactless remark at a press conference in May 1931 that "I know of nothing that would so disturb the healing process now undoubtedly going on in the economic situation" as a special session of Congress. "We cannot legislate ourselves out of a world economic depression; we can and will work ourselves out."

The last sentence, because it was obviously too sweeping to be accurate, was to plague him for years. More important, he quite clearly did not believe it himself, since he later advocated legislation for just the purposes he said it could not serve. In the very next month, for example, he explained at some length to a group of Republican editors just how much the Administration had been doing to extricate the country from the Depression. "For the first time in history the Federal Government has taken an extensive and positive part in mitigating the effects of depression and expediting recovery. I have conceived that if we would preserve our democracy this leadership must take the part not of attempted dictatorship but of organizing cooperation in the constructive forces of the community and of stimulating every element of initiative and self-reliance in the country. There is no sudden stroke

of either governmental or private action which can dissolve these world difficulties; patient, constructive action in a multitude of directions is the strategy of success. This battle is upon a thousand fronts." Unlike previous
administrations, he continued, his had expanded, instead of curtailing, public works during a depression. Public works expenditures, both by the federal
and state governments, he said, continued to increase. Some two billion dollars were being spent, and a million men were employed on these projects.
Aid was also being given to farmers in the drought areas of the South and the
Middle West.

    That Hoover truly favored action over patient waiting for the storm to
lift was further shown in his elaborate twelve-point program for recovery
presented in his annual message in December 1931. Among his recommendations was the Reconstruction Finance Corporation, which would become one
of the major agencies of his Administration and of the New Deal for stabilizing banks and aiding recovery. At a press conference the same month he
emphasized anew the desirability of domestic action. "The major steps we
must take are domestic. The action needed is in the home field and it is
urgent. While reestablishment of stability abroad is helpful to us and to the
world, and I am convinced that it is in progress, yet we must depend upon
ourselves. If we devote ourselves to these urgent domestic questions we can
make a very large measure of recovery irrespective of foreign influences." By
early February 1932 the Reconstruction Finance Corporation was in operation. That same month he persuaded the Congress to enact the Glass-Steagall
banking bill, which increased the bases for Federal Reserve bank reserves
and thus expanded credit and conserved gold. The purpose of the RFC was
to shore up failing banks and other financial institutions caught in runs upon
their deposits. With the permission of the Interstate Commerce Commission,
the RFC could also extend financial aid to railroads.

    Beyond these operations, though, the President would not let the lend-
ing agency go. Especially did he resist federal aid to the unemployed, although the demands for it were growing monthly. He even opposed Congressional appropriations to the Red Cross on the ground that they would
dry up private sources of relief funds. A dole, he said in 1931, must be avoided
at all costs because "the net results of governmental doles are to lower wages
toward the bare subsistence level and to endow the slackers." He did urge
the citizenry generously to support, as he did himself, private charities, like
the Red Cross, which were carrying so much of the burden of unemployment
relief. At no time, of course, did Hoover object to helping the unemployed; he
was no Social Darwinist arguing for the survival of only the fittest. Again and
again, using the most idealistic language, he called upon Americans to extend a hand to those fellow citizens in need. But as much as he publicly and
privately deplored the suffering which the economic crisis brought, he feared
and deplored even more the effects which would be sure to follow if the federal government provided relief to the unemployed. Nowhere was the rigid-

ity of Hoover's highly trained, agile, and well-stocked intellect more apparent than in this matter. Throughout his years as president, despite the cruelest of sarcastic barbs in the press and from the public platform, he held to his position.

Yet surprising as it may seem today, for a long time the country was with him. This was true even during 1931 and early 1932 when it was becoming increasingly evident that private charities, municipal relief funds, and even the resources of the states were inadequate to meet the costs of providing for ten or eleven million unemployed. Already in August 1931 Governor Franklin Roosevelt had told the New York legislature that unemployment relief "must be extended by government—not as a matter of charity but as a matter of social duty." Yet, as late as February 1932 the country was still following Hoover's view of relief and not Roosevelt's. This was shown by the fate of a bill sponsored by liberal Senators Robert M. La Follette, Jr. of Wisconsin and Edward F. Costigan of Colorado to provide federal money to the states for relief. The bill was defeated by a vote of 48 to 35. Democratic Senators made up some forty percent of the votes which killed the measure.

By May 1932, though, the pressure for some federal assistance in relief matters was building up fast. The National Conference of Social Workers, which in the previous year had refused to endorse the principle of federal relief, now switched to supporting it. More important from Hoover's standpoint was the announcement by Senator Joseph Robinson, the conservative Democratic leader in the Senate, that he was joining the liberals in favoring federal relief. Within two days the President announced, after consultation with Robinson, that the RFC would hereafter lend money to the states if their resources for relief were exhausted. The next day the President defended the extraordinary powers of the RFC as necessitated by the economic emergency. In words which sound in retrospect like those of his successor, he said, "We used such emergency powers to win the war; we can use them to fight the depression, the misery and suffering from which are equally great."

Soon thereafter, though, the President demonstrated that he would not take another step toward putting the federal government into the relief field. Two bills by Democrats which went beyond his limits were successfully vetoed. After Congress had adjourned in July 1932, he issued a nine-point program for economic recovery, but most of the items on it were old and the rest were only recommendations for exploratory conferences. By the summer of 1932, then, the Hoover program for recovery had been completed; his principles would permit him to go no further.

As one reviews the actions which Hoover took it is impossible to describe him as a do-nothing president. He was unquestionably one of the truly activist presidents of our history. But he was an activist within a very rigid framework of ideology. Of all American presidents, Herbert Hoover was probably the most singlemindedly committed to a system of beliefs. His pragmatism was well hidden and what there was of it emerged only after great prodding from events. To a remarkable degree, one can observe in his acts as president those principles of individualism which he set forth so simply in his book ten years before. The very same principle, for example, which prevented his sanctioning federal relief to the unemployed, dictated the tone and content of his veto of the bill to create a government corporation to operate Muscle Shoals. The government, he said, should not compete with private enterprise. Moreover, such a project, by being run by the federal government, abrogated the basic principle that all such enterprises should be "administrated by the people upon the ground, responsible to their own communities, directing them solely for the benefit of their communities and not for the purposes of social theories or national politics. Any other course deprives them of liberty." It was this same belief in individual freedom and cooperation which kept him from accepting a governmental system of old age and unemployment insurance. He advocated such measures only when undertaken voluntarily and through private insurance companies.

Even the Reconstruction Finance Corporation, perhaps his most enduring anti-depression agency, was created to assist private business, not to supplant it. True, it was a credit agency in competition with private enterprise, but it was designed to perform tasks which no private institution dared risk; the competition was therefore minimal if not nonexistent. Moreover, although it has been frequently alleged that the RFC lent money to corporations while the Administration denied relief to the unemployed, in Hoover's mind the distinction was crucial and real. The RFC was making loans which would be repaid—and most were—when the banks got back on their feet; it was not making grants. Even when Hoover did permit the RFC to lend money to the states for relief purposes he still insisted that no grants of federal funds be made.

But there was an even more important social justification for agencies like the RFC and the Federal Home Loan Board, which Congress created in July 1932 at the President's request. Hoover recognized as no president had before that the welfare of society was dependent upon business and that government, therefore, must step in. He did this, not because, as some critics said, he favored business over the common people, but because he recognized that if the banks failed the economy would collapse, savings would be lost, and jobs destroyed. The RFC and the Federal Home Loan Board, in effect, socialized the losses of financial institutions by using government to spread their obligations through society. Hoover was not prepared, though, to socialize the losses of the unemployed. That step in ameliorating the impact of the Depression was undertaken by the New Deal through the WPA and other relief agencies. In this respect Hoover was a transitional figure in the development of the government as an active force in the economy in times of depression. He was the first to smash the old shibboleth of government unconcern and impotence.

Perhaps his long-term role was even greater. In the face of great oppo-

sition and much outright hostility, he made a determined and even courageous effort to give the business community and voluntary private agencies a
chance to show whether they could bring the nation out of a depression.
Their failure to do so gave a moral as well as a political impetus to the New
Deal. Just as after Munich no one could say the West had not done its utmost
to meet Hitler halfway, so after Hoover's Administration no one could say
that government had rushed in before other social or economic agencies had
been given a try. That this was so goes a long way toward explaining the
remarkable consensus among Americans ever since the 1930's that government has the prime responsibility for averting or cushioning the effects of a
depression.

A second principle which stopped Hoover from permitting the federal
government to provide relief was his conviction that the budget must not be
unbalanced. As early as February 1930 he warned the Congress against extravagance and told of his own efforts to economize. Economy was essential,
he emphasized, in order to avoid increasing taxes. But as decreasing revenues began to fall behind expenditures, Hoover's concern to keep the budget
in balance overcame his reluctance to increase taxes. On July 1, 1931 the deficit was almost $500 million—an astronomical figure in those days when the
total federal budget was less than $4 billion. In December of that same year
Hoover recommended an increase in taxes. When Congress proved dilatory
he told a press conference in March 1932 that a balanced budget "is the very
keystone of recovery. It must be done." Anything less would undo all the
recovery measures. "The Government," he warned, "no more than individual families can continue to expend more than it receives without inviting
serious consequences."

Hoover recommended a manufacturers' sales tax as the chief new revenue device, in which suggestion he was joined by the new Democratic
Speaker of the House, John Nance Garner of Texas. Garner enjoyed a reputation for being hostile to business and something of a radical in the old Populist tradition, but in the matter of bringing the budget into balance he stood
foursquare with the President. Congress did not pass the sales tax, but it did
pass one of the largest peacetime tax increases in American history.

Today it seems incredible that in a time of economic slump when consumer purchasing power was the principal requirement for recovery, the nation should elect to take money out of the hands of consumers. Yet this was
precisely what the bill, recommended and signed by the Republican President and passed by the Democratic House, entailed. In fact, when in the
course of the debate the House seemed hesitant about increasing taxes, the
Democratic Speaker, John Garner, could not contain his anxiety. Conspicuously forsaking the Speaker's chair, Garner advanced to the well of the
House to make an earnest plea for more taxes. At the conclusion of his speech,
he asked "every man and every woman in this House who . . . is willing to
try to balance the budget to rise in their seats." Almost the whole House,

with its majority of Democrats, rose to its feet, to a growing round of applause. When he asked those who did not want to balance the budget to rise, no one did. The overwhelming majority of the newspapers of the country strongly commended the Congress in June 1932 for its efforts to balance the budget through increased taxes.

During the campaign of 1932 the Democrats continued to equal or even outdo Hoover in their slavish adherence to the ideal of a balanced budget. Franklin Roosevelt, for example, unmercifully attacked the Administration for its extravagance and its unbalanced budget, calling the fifty percent increase in expenditures since 1927 "the most reckless and extravagant past that I have been able to discover in the statistical record of any peacetime government anywhere, any time." He promised a cut of 25 percent in the budget if he were elected. Nor was this simply campaign oratory. As Frank Freidel has observed in his biography, Roosevelt was perfectly sincere in his dismay at the Hoover deficit and he would continue to be regretful about deficits until well after 1933.

From the record, then, it is evident that Democrats were in no better theoretical position to deal with the Depression than Hoover. Leaders of both parties thought of the government as a large household whose accounts must be balanced if national bankruptcy were to be avoided. Neither party could conceive of the central role which government must play in the economy in an industrial society in time of depression. It would take the whole decade of the New Deal and the continuance of the Depression before that fact would be learned by leaders and people alike.

Despite his fixation on the question of the budget, Hoover's conception of the Depression was sophisticated, rational, and coherent; the remedies he suggested were equally so, given his assumptions. In trying to find a way out, Hoover placed most reliance on what modern economists would call the "expectations" of businessmen. If businessmen feel that times are good or at least that they are getting better, they will invest in new plant and equipment, which in turn will employ men and create purchasing power. In substance, the remedies Hoover offered were designed to raise the expectations of businessmen and to maintain purchasing power until the economy picked up again. His first step was securing agreement among businessmen to hold the line on wages in order to keep purchasing power from falling. (And, by and large, as a result of his efforts, wage rates did not fall until the middle of 1931, but employment did, with, unfortunately, the same effect.) A second step in his program was to use government to help out with public work projects and, when private agencies proved inadequate, to provide credit through agencies like the RFC and the Home Loan Board. Finally, as a third arrow in his anti-depression quiver, Hoover sought, through the prestige of his office, to create that sense of confidence and approaching good times which would encourage businessmen to invest. As it turned out, though, he gambled and lost. For with each successive ineffectual statement, the value of his words dropped, until, like the worthless coins of a profligate monarch who debases his own coinage, they were hurled back at his head by a disenchanted press and people.

The Hoover recovery program failed, but probably no government program then thought permissible could have been any more successful. Certainly the New Deal with its more massive injection of government money into the economy succeeded little better. It ended the decade with 9.5 million still unemployed, and industrial production remained below the 1929 level throughout the 1930's except for a brief period in late 1936 and early 1937. On the other hand, most of the countries of Western and Central Europe regained the 1929 level of production by early 1935.

Part of Hoover's ordeal during the Great Depression undoubtedly derived from his personality, which, for a president, was unusual. Indeed, until he became President he had rarely been connected with government other than in an office which was nonpartisan or which he soon made so. Outwardly, at least, he was far removed from the stereotype of the politician; he could not slap a back or utter a guffaw. He appeared shy in public, though stolid was a more accurate description. A bulky man of over 200 pounds, standing almost six feet when he entered the White House, he gave a paradoxical impression of conservative solidity and beaming youth at the same time. His public speech, like his writing, was formal, often stiff, and sometimes bordered on the pedantic. Early in Hoover's Administration, soon after the stock market crash, William Allen White, a Hoover supporter, spotted the new President's weakness. "The President has great capacity to convince intellectuals," he wrote. "He has small capacity to stir people emotionally and through the emotions one gets to the will, not through the intellect." Even Hoover's press secretary recognized that he "experienced the greatest difficulty in interpreting himself and his acts to the public." Indeed, it was characteristic of Hoover that though he found speech writing one of the most laborious of his tasks, he insisted upon writing all his own speeches. The compulsion could be at least enervating, and at worst dangerous to his health. Often he traded sleep for time to work on his speeches and at least once, at St. Paul in the campaign of 1932, he was on the verge of collapse from fatigue. His method of writing was tedious and incredibly time-consuming, involving innumerable drafts, meticulously gone over by himself, only to have still further proofs run off for more rewriting. Yet, after all this effort, his final draft usually was dry, too long, and ponderous.

In view of his poor public image, it is not surprising that for most of his presidency, Hoover's relations with the press were strained when not downright painful. Although he continued the press conferences which Wilson had begun, they were formal affairs with written questions; many reporters were convinced that the President concealed more than he revealed in the meetings. But it was probably Hoover's sensitivity to criticism that worked the real damage. His annual addresses to newspapermen at the Gridiron

Club, which, as was customary, mercilessly lampooned his administration, often carried an edge, betraying his sensitivity to the press corps' jibes. Only occasionally did his private wit break through in public. At the Gridiron Club dinner in December 1932, after his defeat for reelection, he puckishly said, "You will expect me to discuss the late election. Well, as nearly as I can learn, we did not have enough votes on our side. During the campaign I remarked that this Administration had been fighting on a thousand fronts; I learned since the campaign that we were fighting on 21 million fronts." (The size of the Democratic vote.) This was one of the rare times that Hoover poked fun at himself in public.

Yet, despite his difficulties as a public figure, in private Hoover was neither phlegmatic nor shy. In fact he was extremely convivial, seeking constant company, whether at the White House or at his retreat on the Rapidan in the Blue Ridge Mountains. His wife told Joslin that the President could not be happy without numbers of people around him. His friends cherished his constant flow of stories and he delighted in his cigars and pipe. He was an outdoor type of man, reveling in fishing and hiking. Although he liked a joke, he rarely laughed out loud, though his friends knew well his soft chuckle. His own brand of humor could be heavy-handed. Thus in January 1931, when addressing the National Automobile Chamber of Commerce, he observed, with a smile, that 3.5 million cars had been sold in the first year of the depression and that consumption of gasoline was up five percent. "This certainly means," he twitted, "that we have been cheerful in the use of automobiles; I do not assume they are being used for transportation to the poorhouse. While I am aware that many people are using the old automobile a little longer it is obvious that they are still using it and it is being worn out. Altogether the future for the industry does not warrant any despondency." Will Rogers was not so sure. Some months later in a radio broadcast, he drawled, "We are the first nation in the history of the world to go to the poorhouse in an automobile."

Part of the reason Hoover resented the barbed comments of the press was that he worked so hard. It was as characteristic of Herbert Hoover that he was the first president to have a telephone on his desk as it was characteristic of Calvin Coolidge that he refused to have one. Hoover rose at 6 a.m. each morning, joined a group of his friends for a brisk half-hour session with a five pound medicine ball on an improvised court on the White House grounds, then went in to breakfast. He was at his desk by 8:30. He worked steadily all day, smoking incessantly, and usually well into the night. Often he would wake up in the middle of the night and pore over papers or write for an hour or two before going back to sleep. Nevertheless, he rose at the same early hour. Subordinates were not always able to keep up with his pace; some had to be dispatched to rest, but Hoover, miraculously, never succumbed to his self-imposed regimen. His secretary reports that he was not sick a single day of the four years he spent in the White House. A few days at the camp on the Rapidan or a short trip usually sufficed to restore his energies and his will to work. But toward the end of his tenure, even the optimism and strength of a Hoover faltered, at least once. He told his secretary, "All the money in the world could not induce me to live over the last nine months. The conditions we have experienced make this office a compound hell."

Aside from the circumstances in which he found himself as President, one of the reasons the office was "hell" was that Hoover was a poor politician. Often it is said that he did not like politics, or even that he was above politics. Both statements describe the image he held of himself, but many of Hoover's actions while in office are clearly partisan and political. If, for example, he could objectively recognize the weaknesses of the Harding Administration once he was elected president, he could also say during the campaign of 1928 that "the record of the seven and one years" of Coolidge and Harding "constitutes a period of rare courage in leadership and constructive action. Never has a political party been able to look back upon a similar period with more satisfaction." In December 1931, when some voices were calling for a coalition government to deal with the worsening depression, Hoover made it clear that he would have nothing to do with Democrats. "The day that we begin coalition government you may know that our democracy has broken down," he told newspapermen at a Gridiron Club dinner. On the other hand, he could appoint Democrats to office, as he did former Senator Atlee Pomerene to head the RFC when he wanted that office to win support from Democrats. Nor was he devoid of political dramatics. In September 1931 he made a quick descent upon the American Legion Convention in Detroit in a successful effort to stop the Legion from going on record in favor of a bonus for veterans. By going all the way to Detroit, speaking for eleven minutes, and then immediately leaving for Washington again, he demonstrated the importance of his message and the weight of the schedule of work he pursued in Washington. Moreover, as the account written by his Press Secretary Joslin makes clear, he was no more above benefiting from parliamentary trickery in Congress than the next politically-minded president. As Joslin wrote, "It was characteristic of the President to hit back when attacked." Hoover suffered deeply when attacked, and he did not turn the other cheek. As William Allen White, who supported and admired the President, wrote in 1933, "he was no plaster saint politically. He had, during his three years, rather consistently and with a nice instinct chosen to honor in public office men of a conservative type of mind." Moreover, the behind-the-scenes circumstances of his nomination in 1928 and his renomination in 1932, both of which were steam-roller operations, should remove any doubts about his willingness and ability to use devices and tactics quite customary in politics.

No, it was not that he was above politics or that he really despised the operations of politicians. His difficulty was that he was temperamentally incapable of doing what a politician has to do—namely, to admit he could be wrong and to compromise. In the whole volume of his memoirs devoted to the Depression there is not a single mention of a major error on his part, though his opponents are taxed with errors in every chapter. Over a hundred pages of the volume are devoted to the answering of every charge of Franklin Roosevelt in 1932. Nowhere, though, does he notice that in 1932, he himself in his speech at Detroit incorrectly quoted Roosevelt and then proceeded to criticize at length his opponent for something he never said. This inability to admit error, to compromise, William Allen White recognized in 1931 as Hoover's undoing. After all, White wrote, "Politics . . . is one of the minor branches of harlotry, and Hoover's frigid desire to live a virtuous life and not follow the Pauline maxim and be all things to all men, is one of the things that has reduced the oil in his machinery and shot a bearing. . . ." Hoover's inability to admit error and the seriousness with which he viewed himself are both illustrated in another incident during the campaign of 1932. One of the Democrats' favorite sports that year was recalling, with appropriate sounds of derision, Hoover's remarks in 1928 to the effect that the United States was well on the way to abolishing poverty. Hoover, instead of admitting he had been somewhat optimistic, once again donned his hair shirt and stolidly endorsed the earlier statement because, as he said, it expressed the ideals for which Americans stood. Yet this was in the middle of the Depression and he was running for reelection.

In good times, Herbert Hoover's humble birth might have been an asset, but in the Great Depression it was not. Left an almost penniless orphan at nine, Hoover became a world figure and a millionaire before he was forty-five. With such spectacular success behind him it was understandable that he should think, albeit mistakenly, that anyone could achieve at least half as much as he. Undoubtedly his own experience fostered his insistence, throughout his life, that individual initiative was the prime motive force in a good society. What to other men appear as obstacles or handicaps, to the self-made man appear, at least in retrospect, as goads or incentives. Like most such men, Hoover attributed his success to will. When Theodore Joslin once asked him what had been his boyhood ambition, he replied without hesitation, "to be able to earn my own living without the help of anybody, anywhere." To such a man individual effort seems capable of moving mountains unaided; he is loath to see it shunted aside by collective action even in times of economic dislocation. The self-made man can indeed be the wrong man at such times.

Nor was it an accident that the other prominent self-made politician of the time, Alfred E. Smith, was also doubtful about the virtues of government aid to the unemployed, that he should attack Franklin Roosevelt for accusing the Hoover Administration of aiding the corporations and ignoring the poor. "I will take off my coat and vest," Smith vowed in the spring of 1932, "and fight to the end against any candidate who persists in any demagogic appeal to the masses of the working people of this country to destroy themselves by setting class against class and rich against poor." In a short time, Smith's views, like Hoover's, would bring him to outright opposition to the New Deal. It is not without significance in this respect that Roosevelt, who came to represent government benevolence toward the unemployed, was no self-made man, but lived securely and unadventurously on inherited wealth.

The differences in social origins of Roosevelt and Hoover, of course, are only one facet of the divergence between the Hoover Administration and the New Deal. Indeed, since the 1930's it has become commonplace to see Hoover and Roosevelt as opposites. Certainly there are differences—and important ones—between the administrations of the two Presidents, but we are now far enough removed from both to recognize also the real continuity between them that William Allen White was prescient enough to foresee dimly. When the two administrations are seen against the backdrop of previous administrations and earlier social attitudes, the gulf between them shrinks appreciably. Both men, it is worth recalling, were protégés of Woodrow Wilson; both of them, therefore, accepted a role for government in the economy which added up to a sharp departure from laissez-faire. Both, in the course of their respective administrations, drew upon their experiences in the First World War, where they had seen government intervening in the economy. Hoover's RFC, for example, was frankly modeled, as he said, after the War Finance Corporation. Both saw big business standing in need of controls, and, for a while, both believed that cooperation between business and government was the best way to achieve that control. Hoover, for instance, cited the Federal Reserve System as the ideal kind of business and government cooperation for purposes of regulating the economy; Roosevelt in the NRA also placed his trust in controls worked out through business and government cooperation. Moreover, both Roosevelt and Hoover took the view that it was government's responsibility to do something about a depression; neither man was willing to subscribe to the view which prevailed before 1929—namely, that economic declines were simply natural phenomena through which the nation struggled as best it could and that government could not be expected to do much about them.

Finally, it is also worth noticing that the temperament of the two men, their conceptions of America and of its future are much closer than the conventional picture paints them. (It was Roosevelt, during the campaign of 1932, who created the erroneous image of Hoover as the man without faith or hope in the future.) All through the Depression, Hoover's unvarying theme was that all this would pass and the essential vigor of the American economy would reassert itself. Undoubtedly he counted too heavily on the influence of his words to overcome the lack of business confidence, but there is no question of his optimistic outlook. One measure of it was the shock he received when he read Roosevelt's address to the Commonwealth Club in San Francisco. That was the speech in which Roosevelt talked about the frontier being ended and opportunities for economic growth being limited. Hoover took up the challenge, denying "the whole idea that we have ended the advance of

America, that this country has reached the zenith of its power, the height of its development. That is the counsel of despair for the future of America. That is not the spirit by which we shall emerge from this depression." The important point is that such pessimism was really not expressive of Roosevelt's thought, either. Although historians have frequently referred to the Commonwealth Club address as the one clear indication during the campaign of 1932 of the philosophy behind the New Deal, we now know that the speech was neither written by Roosevelt, nor read by him before he appeared before his audience. As Rexford Tugwell has pointed out, the Commonwealth Club address, which Berle and he wrote, did not reflect Roosevelt's true attitude toward the American economic future. Indeed, its very singularity among Roosevelt's campaign speeches demonstrates how foreign it was to Roosevelt's feelings and convictions. The speech belied his abundant enthusiasm for the future, and his deep faith in the country and its capacities. Moreover, he soon contradicted its import in his Inaugural Address, when he electrified the country with the cry, "All we have to fear is fear itself."

How ironical that these words of Roosevelt should be so well known, when it was Herbert Hoover who all along had been saying the same thing— in less graphic and less credible language, to be sure—but saying it nonetheless. That fact, too, contributed to the ordeal of Herbert Hoover.

SUGGESTED READING

Richard Hofstadter, in *The American Political Tradition* ° (1948), on the basis of much of the same evidence that Degler uses, is harshly critical of Hoover, calling him a "Utopian Capitalist." In addition to emphasizing the limitations of his ideology, Hofstadter notes Hoover's charges that the Depression was foreign-born and the contradiction between Hoover's concern with expanding foreign trade and his failure to understand that the high tariff made it impossible for prospective buyers to sell in the American market. William Appleman Williams, in *The Contours of American History* ° (1961), argues that Hoover's responses to the Depression were limited by his ideological fear of placing the control of government in the major organized blocs (labor, business, and agriculture), a situation that Hoover described as "a syndicalist nation on a gigantic scale." In "A Vote for Herbert Hoover," *New York Review of Books* (Nov. 5, 1970), Williams sketches some of these ideas.

Hoover in his *Memoirs*, 3 vols. (1951–52), discusses his political experience in the Great Depression and offers a spirited defense of his policies. Favorable studies of the administration are provided by W. S. Myers and W. H. Newton in *The Hoover Administration: A Documented Narrative* (1936) and by Ray Lyman Wilbur and Arthur Hyde in *The Hoover Policies* (1937).

Albert Romasco's *The Poverty of Abundance: Hoover, the Nation, the Depression* ° (1965), published shortly before Hoover's presidential papers became available to scholars, describes the President's efforts to halt the economic downturn. Harris G. Warren's *Herbert Hoover and the Great Depression* ° (1959) is also worth consulting. Joan H. Wilson has a forthcoming study of Hoover (1972). Walter Lippmann, in "The Permanent New Deal," *Yale Review*, XXIV (June 1935), stresses the continuities between Hoover's efforts and the early New Deal. Jordan A. Schwarz's *The Interregnum of Despair: Hoover, Congress, and the Depression* (1970) is an important study focusing on the Congress and the Executive during the Depression years of Hoover's administration.

Gerald D. Nash, in "Herbert Hoover and the Origins of the Reconstruction Finance Corporation," *Mississippi Valley Historical Review*, XLVI (Dec. 1959), notes, unlike Degler, Hoover's reluctance to accept the legislation for the RFC. In "Herbert Hoover and the Federal Farm Board Project," *Mississippi Valley Historical Review*, XLII (Mar. 1956), James H. Shideler discusses a pre-Depression agency. William R. Johnson, in "Herbert Hoover and the Regulation of Grain Futures," *Mid-America*, LI (July 1969), examines Hoover's support for regulation.

Kent Schofield's "The Public Image of Herbert Hoover in the 1928 Campaign," *Mid-America*, LI (Oct. 1969) examines the "highly successful blend of modern and traditional themes" in Hoover's public image. The significance of Al Smith's Catholicism in Hoover's election is discounted by Richard Hofstadter in "Could a Protestant Have Beaten Hoover in 1928?" *Reporter*, XXII (Mar. 17, 1960), and by Paul A. Carter in "The Other Catholic Candidate: The 1928 Presidential Bid of Thomas J. Walsh," *Pacific Northwest Quarterly*, LV (Jan. 1964).

III

The New Deal and the Coming of War

As a problem for historical interpretation, the New Deal presents fewer difficulties than either progressivism, a movement that continues to defy definition, or the 1920's, whose complex contradictions still are unresolved. Unlike the preceding periods, the New Deal was dominated by a single political figure—Franklin D. Roosevelt; and from the beginning the New Deal had a clearly defined task: to repair the breakdown in the economic order. Historians have thus focused their attention on the New Deal's efforts to revive and reorder the economy and have asked the same questions about the period: To what extent was the New Deal a break with the American past? Did it effect significant changes in the social and economic structure of American society? Was it revolutionary or conservative?

Perhaps the debate can be clarified by phrasing the question at issue in such a way that the task of analysis can be made more precise: To what extent did the New Deal redistribute wealth and power in America? This formulation relegates to secondary importance inquiries into the progressive roots of the New Deal or the extent of Roosevelt's break with America's laissez-faire past. The major subject for investigation instead becomes the ways in which New

Deal measures in operation affected various interests and classes, and a new series of questions presents itself: Did the lower classes gain from the New Deal a significant measure of security from the excesses of the business cycle? Did labor increase its power in dealing with capital? Was the autonomy of large corporations diminished by the expansion of state power? Did New Deal tax measures correct the maldistribution of wealth in America?

The New Deal's social-welfare program for the lower classes, for example, illustrates the ambiguity of its accomplishment and the difficulty of passing simple judgment. In initiating social security, public housing, minimum wages, and unemployment insurance, New Dealers unquestionably made a contribution to many of the nation's economically vulnerable citizens. Yet scholars who argue that the New Deal was conservative have not been impressed. They point out that only in the United States are government pensions partially financed from the current earnings of workers, that the social-security tax on wages is regressive, and that the Social Security Act originally exempted millions who were most in need of coverage.

As for public housing, the Government built only 180,000 units during the New Deal, and, as is now well known, the concept of slum clearance too often meant removal rather than improvement of the poor. At a time when twelve million workers in interstate commerce were earning less than forty cents an hour, Congress set the minimum wage at twenty-five cents an hour and extended coverage to only half a million workers. As for unemployment insurance, it was administered by the states, lacked federal standards, and was marred by widely varying benefits. Emphasizing the limits of this legislation, critics of the New Deal find its welfare program designed to appease popular discontent with the least cost to the nation's wealthier classes.

Roosevelt's belated support of the labor movement in the 1930's was certainly his most important contribution to redistributing power in the economic order. In 1933 only 2.8 million workers, mostly in the AFL, were in unions; however, partly because of the administration's vigorous implementation of the Wagner Act (1935), which granted labor the legal right to bargain collectively, a period of unprecedented growth ensued. Led by John L. Lewis, a group of rebels bolted the AFL in 1935 and established the rival CIO, which organized workers by industry rather than craft and so at last offered unskilled workers a place in the American union movement. By the beginning of the Second World War the AFL had 4.5 million members, and the CIO claimed 5 million.

The dark age of the company union was over. But critics have argued that the positive effects of the union movement of the 1930's have been overrated. Unions have generally abandoned their earlier idealism for the pursuit of narrow self-interest and are conservative bulwarks of the existing order. Moreover, the growth of unions after 1935 has not increased labor's overall share of the national income, but has merely meant disproportionate wage gains for union workers at the expense of the nonunionized half of the labor force. Thus one of the major effects of unionization has been to increase inequalities within the working class.

As for the power of big business, the New Deal did expand the scope of government regulation, thereby diminishing in some measure the autonomy of businessmen. As a result of New Deal legislation, the Securities and Exchange Commission began policing the stock market, the Federal Reserve Board enjoyed wider powers, and the Federal Power Commission and Interstate Commerce Commission were granted greater authority to stabilize power and transportation rates. Congress created a Maritime Commission to subsidize the merchant marine and a Civil Aeronautics Authority (later, Board) to regulate the airlines. It passed the Robinson-Patman Act to prevent wholesalers and manufacturers from discriminating on behalf of chain stores to the disadvantage of small retailers, and it passed bills to permit the coal and oil industries to stabilize production. In one of their most controversial efforts, New Dealers in 1935 pushed through an act that loosened the grip of giant holding companies on the electric-power industry.

But those who argue the conservative meaning of the New Deal have pointed out that regulation may be on behalf of the interests to be regulated, and indeed New Deal legislation helped certain businesses by imposing order on chaotic industries (for example, coal) and by restraining competition harmful to industrial stability. Though forced to permit the government to participate in making crucial regulatory decisions, businessmen in the affected industries suffered neither declines in their profits nor real threats to the existing structure of the corporate order. Whether because of the New Deal or in spite of it, big business remained in command of the American economy.

The available evidence yields a more certain conclusion on the effect of tax measures on wealth distribution. Some redistribution of wealth occurred during the New Deal, but not much. Figures in Herman Miller's *Income Distribution in the United States* (1966) indicate that from 1935–36 through 1941 (that is, from the year of the New Deal tax reform until the beginning of the Second World War) the personal income share of the highest fifth fell from 52 to 49 percent. The result was a gain of 1 percent for each of the middle three income fifths but no change in the share (4 percent) received by the lowest fifth. The most significant innovation in government taxation in Roosevelt's administration occurred not during the Depression, but at the time of the Second World War when the need to pay for the war forced the government to reduce income-tax exemptions until the number of Americans paying income taxes rose from 4 million in 1939 to 42.4 million in 1944. For the first time middle- and lower-class Americans were ensnared in the income-tax system, where most remained thereafter.

This analysis of alterations in the structure of the economy and society admittedly has ignored changes in ideology and ethos. Certainly such changes during the New Deal were real. But the ultimate test of how significant new ideas are is their success or failure in affecting the social system —and the changes in ideology and ethos were not far reaching or greatly influential during the New Deal in changing the structure of American society or in redistributing power.

SUGGESTED READING

Though some of the larger questions about the New Deal still remain unexamined, the literature on the period and on its President is already voluminous. Frank Freidel is writing the authoritative multi-volume biography (*Franklin D. Roosevelt,* 3 vols. [1952–56]); the latest volume has reached the election of 1932. In *The New Deal in Historical Perspective* * (1965) he has offered an interpretation of the New Deal. Arthur Schlesinger, Jr. has completed three impressive volumes of his generally admiring study *The Age of Roosevelt;* the last two volumes, *The Coming of the New Deal* * (1958) and *The Politics of Upheaval* * (1960) are on the early New Deal years.

James MacGregor Burns's *Roosevelt: The Lion and the Fox* * (1956) is often critical of Roosevelt and his departures from reformism and Keynesianism. Rexford G. Tugwell, one of Roosevelt's early advisors, in *The Democratic Roosevelt* (1957), applauds the efforts of the so-called First New Deal but is disturbed by later policies, particularly by the shift to antitrust activities. His interpretation appeared earlier in a series of articles in *Western Political Quarterly* (June 1948), *Political Quarterly* (July–Sept. 1950), *Antioch Review* (Dec. 1953), and *Ethics* (1953–54). This volume should be supplemented by Tugwell's *The Brains Trust* (1968).

Mario Einaudi, in *The Roosevelt Revolution* (1959), and Carl Degler, in *Out of Our Past,* * 2nd ed. (1970), praise the New Deal and view it as a sharp break with the past. Eric Goldman's *Rendezvous with Destiny* * (1952) is an important study of the movement of the American polity away from laissez faire and toward the beneficent liberalism that he finds in the New Deal. Richard Hofstadter, in *The Age of Reform* * (1955), departing from his earlier more critical analysis of the New Deal in *The American Political Tradition* * (1948), emphasizes the "revolutionary" aspects of the New Deal, stresses its discontinuity with the moralism and cautious reforms of the progressive years, and finds much to praise in the response of the New Deal to the need for reform and to the challenge of the Depression. Broadus Mitchell's *Depression Decade, From New Era through New Deal* * (1947) is an economic history critical of the New Deal that affirms the conservatism of Roosevelt's policies. This view also receives support from Philip Selznick in *TVA and the Grass Roots, A Study in the Sociology of Formal Organization* (1949); from Rexford G. Tugwell and E. C. Banfield in "Grass Roots Democracy —Myth or Reality?," *Public Administration Review,* X (Winter 1950); and from William Appleman Williams in *The Contours of American History* * (1961). Irving Bernstein's *The Turbulent Years: A History of the American Worker, 1933–1941* (1970) is a useful volume. Walter Galenson, in *The CIO Challenge to the AFL* (1960), and David Brody, in "The Emergence of Mass Production Unionism," in John Braeman *et al.,* eds., *Change and Continuity in Twentieth-Century America* * (1964), offer slightly different analyses of the rise of the CIO.

Sidney Fine's *The Automobile Under the Blue Eagle* (1963) is a thorough study of the National Recovery Administration labor code in the automobile industry, and Irving Bernstein, in *The New Deal Collective Bargaining Policy* (1950), examines the legislative history of major labor bills during Roosevelt's first three years in office. There is still need for an analysis of the dynamics of the sit-down strikes, but Sidney Fine's

"The General Motors Sit-Down Strike: A Re-examination," *American Historical Review*, LXX (Apr. 1965), is the best study of the events. Jerold Auerbach's *Labor and Liberty: The La Follette Committee and the New Deal* (1967) is strong on civil liberties and the difficulties confronted by organized labor.

David E. Conrad, in *The Forgotten Farmer: The Story of Share Croppers and the New Deal* (1965); Jerold Auerbach, in "Southern Tenant Farmers: Socialist Critics of the New Deal," *Labor History*, VII (Winter 1966); and M. S. Venkartaramani, in "Norman Thomas, Arkansas Sharecroppers and the Roosevelt Agricultural Policies, 1933–1937," *Mississippi Valley Historical Review*, XLVII (Sept. 1960), all present evidence critical of New Deal agricultural policies. Grant McConnell, in *The Decline of Agrarian Democracy* (1959), examines the American Farm Bureau and its great power. Christiana M. Campbell's *The Farm Bureau and the New Deal* (1962) provides a detailed study of the Bureau. Richard S. Kirkendall's *Social Scientists and Farm Politics in the Age of Roosevelt* (1966) is a useful volume on a largely neglected topic. Sidney Baldwin's *Poverty and Politics: The Rise and Decline of the Farm Security Administration* (1967) and John Shover's *Cornbelt Rebellion: The Farmer's Holiday Association* (1965) are important for understanding farm discontent and the farm programs of the New Deal.

The best surveys of New Deal scholarship are Richard S. Kirkendall's article "The Great Depression: Another Watershed in American History?" in John Braeman *et al.,* eds., *Change and Continuity in Twentieth-Century America* * (1964), and Kirkendall's "The New Deal as Watershed: The Recent Literature," *Journal of American History*, LIV (Mar. 1968). Leuchtenburg's "The New Deal and the Analogue of War," in Braeman's book cited above, is an important essay. Daniel Aaron's *Writers on the Left* * (1961); James B. Gilbert's *Writers and Partisans* (1968); Otis L. Graham, Jr.'s *An Encore for Reform: The Old Progressives in the New Deal* * (1967); and Warren Susman's "The Thirties," in Stanley Coben and Lorman Ratner, eds., *The Development of an American Culture* * (1970), are valuable for understanding the intellectual history of these years.

James Patterson's *Congressional Conservatism and the New Deal* (1967) is a fine study of the actions of the conservative coalition, and should be supplemented by his "The Failure of Party Realignment in the South, 1937–1939," *Journal of Politics*, XXVII (Aug. 1965). Samuel Lubell's *The Future of American Politics* * (1951) remains the best general analysis of the New Deal coalition. James Patterson's *The New Deal and the States: Federalism in Transition* (1969) is useful for a study of federal-state relations.

The New Deal, * edited by Otis L. Graham, Jr. (1971), is the best collection of interpretations of the New Deal. *Franklin D. Roosevelt: A Profile,* * edited by William E. Leuchtenburg (1967) is also a fine collection of previously published materials on FDR, and includes Clarke Chambers' "FDR: Pragmatist-Idealist," *Pacific Northwest Quarterly*, LII (Apr. 1961); Richard Hofstadter's essay on Roosevelt from *The American*

Political Tradition * (1948); and Morton Frisch's "Roosevelt the Conservator: A Rejoinder to Hofstadter," *Journal of Politics,* XV (May 1962). Other useful collections are Morton Keller, ed., *The New Deal: What Was It?* * (1963), which contains mostly excerpts from books but also includes Arthur Schlesinger, Jr.'s "Sources of the New Deal: Reflections on the Temper of a Time," *Columbia University Forum,* II (Fall 1959); Bernard Sternsher, ed., *The New Deal: Doctrines and Democracy* * (1966), which includes Heinz Eulau's "Neither Ideology nor Utopia: The New Deal in Retrospect," *Antioch Review,* XIX (Winter 1959–60); Edwin Rozwenc, ed., *The New Deal, Revolution or Evolution* * (1949); Frank Warren and Michael Wreszin, eds., *The New Deal* * (1968); and Alonzo Hamby, ed., *The New Deal* * (1969).

The *New Deal: A Documentary History* * (1968), edited by William E. Leuchtenburg, and *The New Deal and the American People* * (1964), edited by Frank Freidel, are fine collections of materials gathered for students by two of the outstanding scholars of the New Deal. *The Public Papers and Addresses of Franklin D. Roosevelt,* 13 vols. (1938–50), edited by Samuel Rosenman, an important speechwriter of the President, provides the texts of press conferences, speeches, state papers, and other important public announcements. Elliott Roosevelt has edited *F.D.R.: His Personal Letters,* 4 vols. (1947–50), an uneven collection of materials. Among the other important primary sources on the New Deal are Harold L. Ickes' *The Secret Diary of Harold L. Ickes,* 3 vols. (1953–54), which expresses the self-righteousness of its author; *Roosevelt and Frankfurter: Their Correspondence, 1928–1945* (1968), edited by Max Freedman; and Eleanor Roosevelt's *This I Remember* (1949), the very selective memoirs by the former first lady. Frances Perkins' *The Roosevelt I Knew* (1946) is a friendly but not uncritical memoir by Roosevelt's former Secretary of Labor. Raymond Moley's *After Seven Years* (1939) is sharply critical of the President whom he had briefly served, and in *The First New Deal* (1967), Moley returned to similar themes.

WILLIAM E. LEUCHTENBURG

The Roosevelt Reconstruction:
Retrospect

INTRODUCTION

Liberals have always regarded the New Deal with a special fond-
ness. In their view it was the episode that both saved and human-
ized capitalism, redressed the social balance on behalf of the
lower classes, and curbed the excesses of big business. The best
single volume on the New Deal is William E. Leuchtenburg's
Franklin D. Roosevelt and the New Deal (1963), a history written
by a sophisticated liberal. Leuchtenburg, who is professor of history at Columbia University, is not blind to the limitations of the
New Deal, but he so admires its accomplishments and especially
its spirit that his overall assessment is highly favorable. Leuchtenburg's concluding chapter, which is reprinted below, is a

FROM William E. Leuchtenburg, *Franklin D. Roosevelt and the New Deal 1932–1940*,
pp. 326–48. Copyright © 1963 by William E. Leuchtenburg. Reprinted by permission of
Harper & Row, Publishers, Inc.

221

neat summary of his views on Roosevelt's presidency. As in the rest of his book, Leuchtenburg concedes weaknesses but chooses to emphasize strengths.

Yet the evidence so impressively collected in Leuchtenburg's volume could well support a more negative appraisal. The National Recovery Administration, Leuchtenburg writes, "prevented things from getting worse, but it did little to speed recovery, and probably actually hindered it by its support of restrictionism and price raising." He notes regretfully that the Agricultural Adjustment Agency curbed farm output at a time of hunger, that it worked to the disadvantage of tenant farmers, and that it did not succeed in raising farm income to the inadequate 1929 level until 1939. The Home Owners Loan Corporation helped refinance one-fifth of the mortgaged private dwellings in urban America, but HOLC later foreclosed on 100,000 mortgages of its own. The Social Security Act was a fundamental break with the frontier tradition, but its benefits were inadequate and regressively financed. Leuchtenburg concedes that the New Deal failed to redistribute wealth, that Roosevelt seriously erred in 1938 in resisting conversion to Keynesian ideas, and that only the Second World War ended the Depression. Leuchtenburg agrees with other students of the New Deal that Roosevelt operated as a broker dispensing favors to special interest groups, and that this system prevented any direct challenge to vested interests and penalized the unorganized.

It is not difficult to belittle Roosevelt's achievements. But nonetheless, in the 1930's the majority of Americans felt about the New Deal as Leuchtenburg did later. They appreciated the relief it dispensed to unemployed and hungry workers, the unions it helped make possible, the trees it planted, the public buildings it erected. They were enamored of the President and were attracted by the vigor of their government. They felt that the New Deal had rescued them from economic catastrophe, had given them courage to believe in the future, and had challenged outmoded myths and institutions. If one believes as Leuchtenburg did that the social order in the 1930's did not need significant restructuring, then Roosevelt's good works must be judged significant indeed.

*I*n eight years, Roosevelt and the New Dealers had almost revolutionized the agenda of American politics. "Mr. Roosevelt may have given the wrong answers to many of his problems," concluded the editors of *The Economist*. "But he is at least the first President of modern America who has asked the right questions." In 1932, men of acumen were absorbed to an astonishing degree with such questions as prohibition, war debts, and law enforcement. By 1936, they were debating social security, the Wagner Act, valley authorities, and public housing. The thirties witnessed a rebirth of issues politics, and parties split more sharply on ideological lines than they had in many years past. "I incline to think that for years up to the present juncture thinking Democrats and thinking Republicans had been divided by an imaginary line," reflected a Massachusetts congressman in 1934. "Now for the first time since the period before the Civil War we find vital principles at stake." Much of this change resulted simply from the depression trauma, but much too came from the force of Roosevelt's personality and his use of his office as both pulpit and lectern. "Of course you have fallen into some errors—that is human," former Supreme Court Justice John Clarke wrote the President, "but you have put a new face upon the social and political life of our country." [1]

Franklin Roosevelt re-created the modern Presidency. He took an office which had lost much of its prestige and power in the previous twelve years and gave it an importance which went well beyond what even Theodore Roosevelt and Woodrow Wilson had done. Clinton Rossiter has observed: "Only Washington, who made the office, and Jackson, who remade it, did more than [Roosevelt] to raise it to its present condition of strength, dignity, and independence." [2] Under Roosevelt, the White House became the focus of all government—the fountainhead of ideas, the initiator of action, the representative of the national interest.

Roosevelt greatly expanded the President's legislative functions. In the nineteenth century, Congress had been jealous of its prerogatives as the lawmaking body, and resented any encroachment on its domain by the Chief Executive. Woodrow Wilson and Theodore Roosevelt had broken new ground in sending actual drafts of bills to Congress and in using devices like the caucus to win enactment of measures they favored. Franklin Roosevelt made such constant use of these tools that he came to assume a legislative role not unlike that of a prime minister. He sent special messages to Congress, accompanied them with drafts of legislation prepared by his assistants, wrote letters to committee chairmen or members of Congress to urge passage of the proposals, and authorized men like Corcoran to lobby as presidential spokesmen on the Hill. By the end of Roosevelt's tenure in the White House, Congress looked automatically to the Executive for guidance; it expected the administration to have a "program" to present for consideration.[3]

---

[1] The Editors of the Economist, *The New Deal* (New York, 1937), p. 149; Representative Robert Luce to Herbert Claiborne Pell, November 14, 1934, Pell MSS., Box 7; Elliott Roosevelt (ed.), *F.D.R.: His Personal Letters, 1928–1945* (2 vols., New York, 1950), I, 723.

[2] Clinton Rossiter, *The American Presidency* (Signet edition, New York, 1956), p. 114.

[3] *Ibid.*, pp. 81–84; Edward S. Corwin, *The President: Office and Powers 1787–1957* (New York, 1957), pp. 274–275. Yet despite the growth of the Presidency, this was a

Roosevelt's most important formal contribution was his creation of the Executive Office of the President on September 8, 1939. Executive Order 8248, a "nearly unnoticed but none the less epoch-making event in the history of American institutions," set up an Executive Office staffed with six administrative assistants with a "passion for anonymity." [4] In 1939, the President not only placed obvious agencies like the White House Office in the Executive Office but made the crucial decision to shift the Bureau of the Budget from the Treasury and put it under his wing. In later years, such pivotal agencies as the Council of Economic Advisers, the National Security Council, and the Central Intelligence Agency would be moved into the Executive Office of the President. Roosevelt's decision, Rossiter has concluded,

> converts the Presidency into an instrument of twentieth-century government; it gives the incumbent a sporting chance to stand the strain and fulfill his constitutional mandate as a one-man branch of our three-part government; it deflates even the most forceful arguments, which are still raised occasionally, for a plural executive; it assures us that the Presidency will survive the advent of the positive state. Executive Order 8248 may yet be judged to have saved the Presidency from paralysis and the Constitution from radical amendment.[5]

Roosevelt's friends have been too quick to concede that he was a poor administrator. To be sure, he found it difficult to discharge incompetent aides, he procrastinated about decisions, and he ignored all the canons of sound administration by giving men overlapping assignments and creating a myriad of agencies which had no clear relation to the regular departments of government.[6] But if the test of good administration is not an impeccable organizational chart but creativity, then Roosevelt must be set down not merely as a good administrator but as a resourceful innovator. The new agencies he set up gave a spirit of excitement to Washington that the routinized old-line departments could never have achieved. The President's refusal to proceed through channels, however vexing at times to his subordinates, resulted in a competition not only among men but among ideas, and encouraged men to feel that their own beliefs might win the

---

period in which Congress had great influence. Much of the specific New Deal legislation was the consequence of the work of a Robert Wagner or a Robert La Follette, Jr. The expansion of the Presidency resulted in a reinvigoration of the whole political system.

[4] Luther Gulick, cited in Rossiter, *American Presidency*, p. 96.

[5] Rossiter, *American Presidency*, p. 100. Cf. Emile Giraud, *La Crise de la démocratie et le renforcement du pouvoir exécutif* (Paris, 1938).

[6] "At times Roosevelt acted as if a new agency were almost a new solution. His addiction to new organizations became a kind of nervous tic which disturbed even avid New Dealers." Arthur Schlesinger, Jr., *The Coming of the New Deal* (Boston, 1959), p. 535. Schlesinger has an excellent discussion of Roosevelt's administrative talent.

day. "You would be surprised, Colonel, the remarkable ideas that have been turned loose just because men have felt that they can get a hearing," one senator confided.[7] The President's "procrastination" was his own way both of arriving at a sense of national consensus and of reaching a decision by observing a trial by combat among rival theories. Periods of indecision —as in the spring of 1935 or the beginning of 1938—were inevitably followed by a fresh outburst of new proposals.[8]

Most of all, Roosevelt was a successful administrator because he attracted to Washington thousands of devoted and highly skilled men. Men who had been fighting for years for lost causes were given a chance: John Collier, whom the President courageously named Indian Commissioner; Arthur Powell Davis, who had been ousted as chief engineer of the Department of the Interior at the demand of power interests; old conservationists like Harry Slattery, who had fought the naval oil interests in the Harding era. When Harold Ickes took office as Secretary of the Interior, he looked up Louis Glavis—he did not even know whether the "martyr" of the Ballinger-Pinchot affair was still alive—and appointed him to his staff.[9]

The New Dealers displayed striking ingenuity in meeting problems of governing. They coaxed salmon to climb ladders at Bonneville; they sponsored a Young Choreographers Laboratory in the WPA's Dance Theatre; they gave the pioneer documentary film maker Pare Lorentz the opportunity to create his classic films *The Plow That Broke the Plains* and *The River*. At the Composers Forum-Laboratory of the Federal Music Project, William Schuman received his first serious hearing. In Arizona, Father Bernard Haile of St. Michael's Mission taught written Navajo to the Indians.[10] Roosevelt, in the face of derision from professional foresters and prairie states' governors, persisted in a bold scheme to plant a mammoth "shelterbelt" of parallel rows of trees from the Dakotas to the Panhandle. In all, more than two hundred million trees were planted—cottonwood and willow, hackberry and cedar, Russian olive and Osage orange; within six years, the President's visionary windbreak had won over his former critics.[11] The spirit behind such innovations generated a new excitement about the potentialities of government. "Once again," Roosevelt told a group of

---

[7] Elbert Thomas to Colonel E. LeRoy Bourne, January 6, 1934, Elbert Thomas MSS., Box 23.

[8] Richard Neustadt, *Presidential Power* (New York, 1960), pp. 156–158.

[9] In Roosevelt's first year in office, he signed an order restoring Glavis to the civil service status he had lost when President Taft fired him. Ironically, Ickes found Glavis as intolerable a subordinate as Taft had, and concluded that he had "been very unjust to Ballinger all of these years." *The Secret Diary of Harold Ickes* (3 vols., New York, 1954), III, 111.

[10] John Collier to Louis Brandeis, April 5, 1937, Brandeis MSS., SC 19.

[11] H. H. Chapman, "Digest of Opinions Received on the Shelterbelt Project," *Journal of Forestry*, XXXII (1934), 952–957; Bristow Adams, "Some Fence!" *Cornell Countryman*,

young Democrats in April, 1936, "the very air of America is exhilarating." [12]

Roosevelt dominated the front pages of the newspapers as no other President before or since has done. "Frank Roosevelt and the NRA have taken the place of love nests," commented Joe Patterson, publisher of the tabloid New York *Daily News.* At his very first press conference, Roosevelt abolished the written question and told reporters they could interrogate him without warning. Skeptics predicted the free and easy exchange would soon be abandoned, but twice a week, year in and year out, he threw open the White House doors to as many as two hundred reporters, most of them representing hostile publishers, who would crowd right up to the President's desk to fire their questions. The President joshed them, traded wisecracks with them, called them by their first names; he charmed them by his good-humored ease and impressed them with his knowledge of detail. [13] To a degree, Roosevelt's press conference introduced, as some observers claimed, a new institution like Britain's parliamentary questioning; more to the point, it was a device the President manipulated, disarmingly and adroitly, to win support for his program. [14] It served too as a classroom to instruct the country in the new economics and the new politics.

Roosevelt was the first president to master the technique of reaching people directly over the radio. In his fireside chats, he talked like a father discussing public affairs with his family in the living room. As he spoke, he seemed unconscious of the fact that he was addressing millions. "His head would nod and his hands would move in simple, natural, comfortable gestures," Frances Perkins recalled. "His face would smile and light up as though he were actually sitting on the front porch or in the parlor with them." Eleanor Roosevelt later observed that after the President's death people would stop her on the street to say "they missed the way the President used to talk to them. They'd say 'He used to talk to me about my government.' There was a real dialogue between Franklin and the people," she reflected. "That dialogue seems to have disappeared from the government since he died." [15]

XXXII (1934), 4; *Science News Letter,* CXXXIV (1938), 409; "Prairie Tree Banks," *American Forester,* CXLVII (1941), 177.

[12] Samuel Rosenman (ed.), *The Public Papers and Addresses of Franklin D. Roosevelt* (13 vols., New York, 1938–50), V, 165.

[13] Elmer Cornwell, Jr., "Presidential News: The Expanding Public Image," *Journalism Quarterly,* XXXVI (1959), 275–283; "The Chicago Tribune," *Fortune,* IX (May, 1934), 108; *Editor and Publisher,* March 4, 1933; Thomas Stokes, *Chip Off My Shoulder* (Princeton, 1940), p. 367.

[14] Erwin Canham, "Democracy's Fifth Wheel," *Literary Digest,* CXIX (January 5, 1935), 6; Douglass Cater, *The Fourth Branch of Government* (Boston, 1959), pp. 13–14, 142–155; James Pollard, *The Presidents and the Press* (New York, 1947), pp. 773–845.

[15] Frances Perkins, *The Roosevelt I Knew* (New York, 1946), p. 72; Bernard Asbell, *When F.D.R. Died* (New York, 1961), p. 161.

For the first time for many Americans, the federal government became an institution that was directly experienced. More than state and local governments, it came to be *the* government, an agency directly concerned with their welfare. It was the source of their relief payments; it taxed them directly for old age pensions; it even gave their children hot lunches in school. As the role of the state changed from that of neutral arbiter to a "powerful promoter of society's welfare," people felt an interest in affairs in Washington they had never had before.[16]

Franklin Roosevelt personified the state as protector. It became commonplace to say that people felt toward the President the kind of trust they would normally express for a warm and understanding father who comforted them in their grief or safeguarded them from harm. An insurance man reported: "My mother looks upon the President as someone so immediately concerned with her problems and difficulties that she would not be greatly surprised were he to come to her house some evening and stay to dinner." From his first hours in office, Roosevelt gave people the feeling that they could confide in him directly. As late as the Presidency of Herbert Hoover, one man, Ira Smith, had sufficed to take care of all the mail the White House received. Under Roosevelt, Smith had to acquire a staff of fifty people to handle the thousands of letters written to the President each week. Roosevelt gave people a sense of membership in the national community. Justice Douglas has written: "He was in a very special sense the people's President, because he made them feel that with him in the White House they shared the Presidency. The sense of sharing the Presidency gave even the most humble citizen a lively sense of belonging." [17]

When Roosevelt took office, the country, to a very large degree, responded to the will of a single element: the white, Anglo-Saxon, Protestant property-holding class. Under the New Deal, new groups took their place in the sun. It was not merely that they received benefits they had not had before but that they were "recognized" as having a place in the commonwealth. At the beginning of the Roosevelt era, charity organizations ignored labor when seeking "community" representation; at the end of the period, no fund-raising committee was complete without a union representative. While Theodore Roosevelt had founded a lily-white Progressive party in the South and Woodrow Wilson had introduced segregation into the federal government, Franklin Roosevelt had quietly brought the Negro into the New Deal coalition. When the distinguished Negro contralto Marian Anderson was denied a concert hall in Washington, Secretary Ickes ar-

---

16 Felix Frankfurter, "The Young Men Go to Washington," *Fortune*, XIII (1936), 61; E. W. Bakke, *Citizens Without Work* (New Haven, 1940), pp. 52–53.

17 Richard Neuberger, "They Love Roosevelt," *Forum and Century*, CI (1939), 15; Corwin, *The President*, p. 471; William O. Douglas, *Being an American* (New York, 1948), p. 88.

ranged for her to perform from the steps of Lincoln Memorial. Equal representation for religious groups became so well accepted that, as one priest wryly complained, one never saw a picture of a priest in a newspaper unless he was flanked on either side by a minister and a rabbi.

The devotion Roosevelt aroused owed much to the fact that the New Deal assumed the responsibility for guaranteeing every American a minimum standard of subsistence. Its relief programs represented an advance over the barbaric predepression practices that constituted a difference not in degree but in kind. One analyst wrote: "During the ten years between 1929 and 1939 more progress was made in public welfare and relief than in the three hundred years after this country was first settled." The Roosevelt administration gave such assistance not as a matter of charity but of right. This system of social rights was written into the Social Security Act. Other New Deal legislation abolished child labor in interstate commerce and, by putting a floor under wages and a ceiling on hours, all but wiped out the sweatshop.[18]

Roosevelt and his aides fashioned a government which consciously sought to make the industrial system more humane and to protect workers and their families from exploitation. In his acceptance speech in June, 1936, the President stated: "Governments can err, Presidents do make mistakes, but the immortal Dante tells us that divine justice weighs the sins of the cold-blooded and the sins of the warm-hearted in different scales.

"Better the occasional faults of a Government that lives in a spirit of charity than the constant omission of a Government frozen in the ice of its own indifference." Nearly everyone in the Roosevelt government was caught up to some degree by a sense of participation in something larger than themselves. A few days after he took office, one of the more conservative New Deal administrators wrote in his diary: "This should be a Gov't of humanity." [19]

The federal government expanded enormously in the Roosevelt years. The crisis of the depression dissipated the distrust of the state inherited from the eighteenth century and reinforced in diverse ways by the Jeffersonians and the Spencerians. Roosevelt himself believed that liberty in America was imperiled more by the agglomerations of private business than by the state. The New Dealers were convinced that the depression was the result not simply of an economic breakdown but of a political collapse; hence, they sought new political instrumentalities. The reformers of the 1930's accepted almost unquestioningly the use of coercion by the state

[18] Josephine Chapin Brown, *Public Relief 1929–1939* (New York, 1940), p. ix; Thomas Paul Jenkin, *Reactions of Major Groups to Positive Government in the United States, 1930–1940* (University of California Publications in Political Science [Berkeley and Los Angeles, 1945]), p. 284.

[19] *Public Papers*, V, 235; J. F. T. O'Connor MS. Diary, June 25, 1933.

to achieve reforms.[20] Even Republicans who protested that Roosevelt's policies were snuffing out liberty voted overwhelmingly in favor of coercive measures.[21]

This elephantine growth of the federal government owed much to the fact that local and state governments had been tried in the crisis and found wanting. When one magazine wired state governors to ask their views, only one of the thirty-seven who replied announced that he was willing to have the states resume responsibility for relief.[22] Every time there was a rumored cutback of federal spending for relief, Washington was besieged by delegations of mayors protesting that city governments did not have the resources to meet the needs of the unemployed.

Even more dramatic was the impotence of local governments in dealing with crime, a subject that captured the national imagination in a decade of kidnapings and bank holdups. In September, 1933, the notorious bank robber John Dillinger was arrested in Ohio. Three weeks later, his confederates released him from jail and killed the Lima, Ohio, sheriff. In January, 1934, after bank holdups at Racine, Wisconsin, and East Chicago, Indiana, Dillinger was apprehended in Tucson, Arizona, and returned to the "escape-proof" jail of Crown Point, Indiana, reputedly the strongest county prison in the country. A month later he broke out and drove off in the sheriff's car. While five thousand law officers pursued him, he stopped for a haircut in a barber shop, bought cars, and had a home-cooked Sunday dinner with his family in his home town. When he needed more arms, he raided the police station at Warsaw, Indiana.

Dillinger's exploits touched off a national outcry for federal action. State and local authorities could not cope with gangs which crossed and recrossed jurisdictional lines, which were equipped with Thompson submachine guns and high-powered cars, and which had a regional network of informers and fences in the Mississippi Valley. Detection and punishment of crime had always been a local function; now there seemed no choice but to call in the federal operatives. In July, 1934, federal agents shot down Dillinger outside a Chicago theater. In October, FBI men killed Pretty Boy Floyd near East Liverpool, Ohio; in November, they shot Baby Face Nelson, Public Enemy No. 1, near Niles Center, Illinois. By the end of 1934, the nation had a new kind of hero: the G-man Melvin Purvis and the chief

---

[20] Paul Carter has noted the change in the social gospel. The editors of *The Baptist*, he has written, "recognized that the transfer of social privilege involves the use of social coercion, a fact which the Right and Center of the old Social Gospel had not always faced up to." Carter, "The Decline and Revival of the Social Gospel" (unpublished Ph.D. dissertation, Columbia University, 1954).

[21] On the compulsory Potato Act, only six Republicans (and just nine Democrats) voted in opposition.

[22] *Today*, III (January 12, 1935), 4.

of the Division of Investigation of the Department of Justice, J. Edgar Hoover. By the end of that year, too, Congress had stipulated that a long list of crimes would henceforth be regarded as federal offenses, including holding up a bank insured by the Federal Deposit Insurance Corporation. The family of a kidnaped victim could call in the federal police simply by phoning National 7117 in Washington.[23]

Under the New Deal, the federal government greatly extended its power over the economy. By the end of the Roosevelt years, few questioned the right of the government to pay the farmer millions in subsidies not to grow crops, to enter plants to conduct union elections, to regulate business enterprises from utility companies to air lines, or even to compete directly with business by generating and distributing hydroelectric power. All of these powers had been ratified by the Supreme Court, which had even held that a man growing grain solely for his own use was affecting interstate commerce and hence subject to federal penalties.[24] The President, too, was well on his way to becoming "the chief economic engineer," although this was not finally established until the Full Employment Act of 1946. In 1931, Hoover had hooted that some people thought "that by some legerdemain we can legislate ourselves out of a world-wide depression." In the Roosevelt era, the conviction that government both should and could act to forestall future breakdowns gained general acceptance. The New Deal left a large legacy of antidepression controls—securities regulation, banking reforms, unemployment compensation—even if it could not guarantee that a subsequent administration would use them.[25]

In the 1930's, the financial center of the nation shifted from Wall Street to Washington. In May, 1934, a writer reported: "Financial news no longer originates in Wall Street." That same month, *Fortune* commented on a revolution in the credit system which was "one of the major historical events of the generation." "Mr. Roosevelt," it noted, "seized the Federal Reserve without firing a shot." The federal government had not only broken down the old separation of bank and state in the Reserve system but had gone into the credit business itself in a wholesale fashion under the aegis of the RFC, the Farm Credit Administration, and the housing agencies. Legislation in 1933 and 1934 had established federal regulation of Wall Street for the first time. No longer could the New York Stock Exchange operate as a private club free of national supervision. In 1935, Con-

---

[23] "The Marines Are Coming," *Fortune*, X (August, 1934), 56 ff.; *Literary Digest*, CXVII (May 5, 1934), 9; CXVIII (July 28, 1934), 6; CXVIII (December 8, 1934), 7; *Time*, XXIII (March 12, 1934), 14; *Public Papers*, III, 242 ff.

[24] Wickard v. Filburn, 317 U.S. 111 (1942).

[25] Sidney Hyman, *The American President* (New York, 1954), pp. 263–264; Carl Degler, *Out of Our Past* (New York, 1959), pp. 391–393. In a few pages, Degler has written the best analysis of the permanent significance of the New Deal.

gress leveled the mammoth holding-company pyramids and centralized yet more authority over the banking system in the federal government. After a tour of the United States in 1935, Sir Josiah Stamp wrote: "Just as in 1929 the whole country was Wall Street-conscious' now it is 'Washington-conscious.' " [26]

Despite this encroachment of government on traditional business prerogatives, the New Deal could advance impressive claims to being regarded as a "savior of capitalism." Roosevelt's sense of the land, of family, and of the community marked him as a man with deeply ingrained conservative traits. In the New Deal years, the government sought deliberately, in Roosevelt's words, "to energize private enterprise." The RFC financed business, housing agencies underwrote home financing, and public works spending aimed to revive the construction industry. Moreover, some of the New Deal reforms were Janus-faced. The NYA, in aiding jobless youth, also served as a safety valve to keep young people out of the labor market. A New Deal congressman, in pushing for public power projects, argued that the country should take advantage of the sea of "cheap labor" on the relief rolls. Even the Wagner Act and the movement for industrial unionism were motivated in part by the desire to contain "unbalanced and radical" labor groups. Yet such considerations should not obscure the more important point: that the New Deal, however conservative it was in some respects and however much it owed to the past, marked a radically new departure. As Carl Degler writes: "The conclusion seems inescapable that, traditional as the words may have been in which the New Deal expressed itself, in actuality it was a revolutionary response to a revolutionary situation." [27]

Not all of the changes that were wrought were the result of Roosevelt's own actions or of those of his government. Much of the force for change came from progressives in Congress, or from nongovernmental groups like the C.I.O., or simply from the impersonal agency of the depression itself. Yet, however much significance one assigns the "objective situation," it is difficult to gainsay the importance of Roosevelt. If, in Miami in February, 1933, an assassin's bullet had been true to its mark and John Garner rather than Roosevelt had entered the White House the next

---

[26] Ferdinand Lunberg, "Wall Street Dances to Washington's Tune," *Literary Digest*, CXVII (May 12, 1934), 46; "Federal Reserve," *Fortune*, IX (May, 1934), 65–66, 125; Sir Josiah Stamp, "Six Weeks in America," *The Times* (London), July 4, 1935.

[27] *Public Papers*, IX, 11; Walter Pierce to Bureau of Publicity, Democratic National Committee, January 4, 1940, Pierce MSS., File 7.1; Robert Wagner to Harold McCollom, April 24, 1935, Wagner MSS.; Sidney Lens, *Left, Right and Center* (Hinsdale, Ill., 1949), pp. 286 ff.; Degler, *Out of Our Past*, p. 416. Not only did the New Deal borrow many ideas and institutions from the Progressive era, but the New Dealers and the progressives shared more postulates and values than is commonly supposed. Nonetheless, the spirit of the 1930's seems to me to be quite different from that of the Progressive era.

month, or if the Roosevelt lines had cracked at the Democratic convention in 1932 and Newton Baker had been the compromise choice, the history of America in the thirties would have been markedly different.

At a time when democracy was under attack elsewhere in the world, the achievements of the New Deal were especially significant. At the end of 1933, in an open letter to President Roosevelt, John Maynard Keynes had written:

> You have made yourself the trustee for those in every country who seek to mend the evils of our condition by reasoned experiment within the framework of the existing social system. If you fail, rational change will be gravely prejudiced throughout the world, leaving orthodoxy and revolution to fight it out.

In the next few years, teams of foreigners toured the TVA, Russians and Arabs came to study the shelterbelt, French writers taxed Léon Blum with importing "Rooseveltism" to France, and analysts characterized Paul Van Zeeland's program in Belgium as a "New Deal." Under Roosevelt, observed a Montevideo newspaper, the United States had become "as it was in the eighteenth century, the victorious emblem around which may rally the multitudes thirsting for social justice and human fraternity." [28]

In their approach to reform, the New Dealers reflected the tough-minded, hard-boiled attitude that permeated much of America in the thirties. In 1931, the gangster film *Public Enemy* had given the country a new kind of hero in James Cagney: the aggressive, unsentimental tough guy who deliberately assaulted the romantic tradition. It was a type whose role in society could easily be manipulated; gangster hero Cagney of the early thirties was transformed into G-man hero Cagney of the later thirties. Even more representative was Humphrey Bogart, creator of the "private eye" hero, the man of action who masks his feelings in a calculated emotional neutrality.[29] Bogart, who began as the cold desperado Duke Mantee of *Petrified Forest* and the frightening Black Legionnaire, soon turned up on the right side of anti-Fascist causes, although he never surrendered the pose of noninvolvement. This fear of open emotional commitment and this admiration of toughness ran through the vogue of the "Dead End Kids," films like *Nothing Sacred*, the popularity of the St. Louis Cardinals' spike-

---

[28] *The New York Times*, December 31, 1933; Ludovic Naudeau, "Le Rooseveltisme ou la troisième solution," *L'Illustration*, XCCV (November 28, 1936), 375; Otto Veit, "Franklin Roosevelt's Experiment," *Die Neue Rundschau*, XLV (1934), 718–734; Nicholas Halasz, *Roosevelt Through Foreign Eyes* (Princeton, 1961); Donald Dozer, *Are We Good Neighbors?* (Gainesville, 1959), p. 30.

[29] Lewis Jacobs, *The Rise of the American Film* (New York, 1939), pp. 509–512; Lincoln Kirstein, "James Cagney and the American Hero," *Hound and Horn*, V (1932), 465–467; Alistair Cooke, *A Generation on Trial* (New York, 1950), p. 11.

flying Gas House Gang, and the "hard-boiled" fiction of writers like James Cain and Dashiell Hammett.

Unlike the earlier Progressive, the New Dealer shied away from being thought of as sentimental.[30] Instead of justifying relief as a humanitarian measure, the New Dealers often insisted it was necessary to stimulate purchasing power or to stabilize the economy or to "conserve manpower." The justification for a better distribution of income was neither "social justice" nor a "healthier national life," wrote Adolf Berle. "It remained for the hard-boiled student to work out the simple equation that unless the national income was pretty widely diffused there were not enough customers to keep the plants going." [31] The reformers of the thirties abandoned—or claimed they had abandoned—the old Emersonian hope of reforming man and sought only to change institutions.[32] This meant that they did not seek to "uplift" the people they were helping but only to improve their economic position. "In other words," Tugwell stated bluntly, "the New Deal is attempting to do nothing to *people,* and does not seek at all to alter their way of life, their wants and desires." [33]

Reform in the 1930's meant *economic* reform; it departed from the Methodist-parsonage morality of many of the earlier Progressives, in part because much of the New Deal support, and many of its leaders, derived from urban immigrant groups hostile to the old Sabbatarianism. While the progressive grieved over the fate of the prostitute, the New Dealer would have placed Mrs. Warren's profession under a code authority. If the archetypical progressive was Jane Addams singing "Onward, Christian Soldiers," the representative New Dealer was Harry Hopkins betting on the horses at Laurel Race Track. When directing FERA in late 1933, Hopkins announced: "I would like to provide orchestras for beer gardens to encourage people to sit around drinking their beer and enjoying themselves. It would be a great unemployment relief measure." "I feel no call to remedy evils," Raymond Moley declared. "I have not the slightest urge to be a reformer. Social workers make me very weary. They have no sense of humor." [34]

---

[30] A New Deal social worker, obviously moved by something she had seen, would preface her report apologetically: "At the risk of seeming slobbery . . ." Martha Gellhorn to Harry Hopkins, April 25, 1935, Hopkins MSS.

[31] A. A. Berle, Jr., "The Social Economics of the New Deal," *The New York Times Magazine,* October 29, 1933, pp. 4–5.

[32] Edgar Kemler, *The Deflation of American Ideals* (Washington, 1941), p. 69.

[33] Tugwell, *The Battle for Democracy* (New York, 1935), p. 319. "The excuse for us being in this thing," Aubrey Williams explained to NYA leaders, "is that we are trying to reform the structure of things rather than try to reform the people." National Advisory Committee, NYA, Minutes, August 15, 1937, Charles Taussig MSS., Box 6. In a speech to TVA employees, David Lilienthal derided "uplift." George Fort Milton to Lilienthal, July 10, 1936, Milton MSS., Box 20.

[34] *Time,* XXIII (January 1, 1934), 10; XXI (May 8, 1933), 10. Cf. Richard Hofstadter, *The Age of Reform* (New York, 1955), pp. 300–322.

Despite Moley's disclaimer, many of the early New Dealers like himself and Adolf Berle did, in fact, hope to achieve reform through regeneration: the regeneration of the businessman. By the end of 1935, the New Dealers were pursuing a quite different course. Instead of attempting to evangelize the Right, they mobilized massive political power against the power of the corporation. They relied not on converting industrial sinners but on using sufficient coercion. New Dealers like Thurman Arnold sought to ignore "moral" considerations altogether; Arnold wished not to punish wrongdoers but to achieve price flexibility. His "faith" lay in the expectation that "fanatical alignments between opposing political principles may disappear and a competent, practical, opportunistic governing class may rise to power." [35] With such expectations, the New Dealers frequently had little patience with legal restraints that impeded action. "I want to assure you," Hopkins told the NYA Advisory Committee, "that we are not afraid of exploring anything within the law, and we have a lawyer who will declare anything you want to do legal." [36]

In the thirties, nineteenth-century individualism gave ground to a new emphasis on social security and collective action.[37] In the twenties, America hailed Lindbergh as the Lone Eagle; in the thirties, when word arrived that Amelia Earhart was lost at sea, the New Republic asked the government to prohibit citizens from engaging in such "useless" exploits. The NRA sought to drive newsboys off the streets and took a Blue Eagle away from a company in Huck Finn's old town of Hannibal, Missouri, because a fifteen-year-old was found driving a truck for his father's business. Josef Hofmann urged that fewer musicians become soloists, Hollywood stars like Joan Crawford joined the Screen Actors Guild, and Leopold Stokowski canceled a performance in Pittsburgh because theater proprietors were violating a union contract.[38] In New York in 1933, after a series of meetings in Heywood Broun's penthouse apartment, newspapermen organized the American Newspaper Guild in rebellion against the dispiriting romanticism of Richard Harding Davis.[39] "We no longer care to develop the individual as a unique contributor to a democratic form," wrote the mordant Edgar Kemler. "In this movement each individual sub-man is im-

---

[35] Arnold, Symbols of Government, pp. 270–271. Cf. Sidney Hook, Reason, Social Myths and Democracy (New York, 1940), pp. 41–61.

[36] National Advisory Committee, NYA, Minutes, August 15, 1935, Charles Taussig MSS., Box 6.

[37] In Ernest Hemingway's To Have and Have Not, Harry Morgan says: "No matter how a man alone ain't got no bloody . . . chance." Hemingway, To Have and Have Not (New York, 1937), p. 225.

[38] New Republic, XCI (1937), 262; Time, XXIII (February 19, 1934), 14; Herbert Harris, American Labor (New Haven, 1938), p. 175.

[39] Cf. Editor and Publisher, LXVI (December 23, 1933), 7, 28.

portant, not for his uniqueness, but for his ability to lose himself in the mass, through his fidelity to the trade union, or cooperative organization, or political party." [40]

The liberals of the thirties admired intellectual activity which had a direct relation to concrete reality. Stuart Chase wrote of one government report: "This book is live stuff—wheelbarrow, cement mixer, steam dredge, generator, combine, power-line stuff; library dust does not gather here." [41] If the poet did not wish to risk the suspicion that his loyalties were not to the historic necessities of his generation, wrote Archibald MacLeish, he must "soak himself not in books" but in the physical reality of "by what organization of men and railroads and trucks and belts and book-entries the materials of a single automobile are assembled." [42] The New Dealers were fascinated by "the total man days per year for timber stand improvement," and Tugwell rejoiced in the "practical success" of the Resettlement Administration demonstrated by "these healthy collection figures." Under the Special Skills Division of the RA, Greenbelt was presented with inspirational paintings like *Constructing Sewers, Concrete Mixer,* and *Shovel at Work.* On one occasion, in attempting to mediate a literary controversy, the critic Edmund Wilson wrote: "It should be possible to convince Marxist critics of the importance of a work like 'Ulysses' by telling them that it is a great piece of engineering—as it is." [43] In this activist world of the New Dealers, the aesthete and the man who pursued a life of contemplation, especially the man whose interests centered in the past, were viewed with scorn. In Robert Sherwood's *The Petrified Forest,* Alan Squier, the ineffectual aesthete, meets his death in the desert and is buried in the petrified forest where the living turn to stone. He is an archaic type for whom the world has no place.

The new activism explicitly recognized its debt to Dewey's dictum of "learning by doing" and, like other of Dewey's ideas, was subject to exaggeration and perversion. The New Deal, which gave unprecedented authority to intellectuals in government, was, in certain important respects, anti-intellectual. Without the activist faith, perhaps not nearly so much would have been achieved. It was Lilienthal's conviction that "there is al-

---

[40] Kemler, *Deflation of Ideals,* pp. 109–110. Kemler, it hardly need be said, grossly overstated his argument.

[41] Stuart Chase, "Old Man River," *New Republic,* LXXXII (1935), 175. "I speak in dispraise of dusty learning, and in disparagement of the historical technique," declared Tugwell. "Are our plans wrong? Who knows? Can we tell from reading history? Hardly." Tugwell, *Battle for Democracy,* pp. 70–71.

[42] MacLeish, *A Time to Speak* (Boston, 1941), p. 45. Cf. MacLeish, "The Social Cant," *New Republic,* LXXIII (1932), 156–158.

[43] *The New York Times,* October 29, 1936; Paul Conkin, *Tomorrow a New World* (Ithaca, 1959), p. 196; Edmund Wilson, "The Literary Class War: I," *New Republic,* LXX (1932), 323.

most nothing, however fantastic, that (given competent organization) a team of engineers, scientists, and administrators cannot do today" that helped make possible the successes of TVA.[44] Yet the liberal activists grasped only a part of the truth; they retreated from conceptions like "tragedy," "sin," "God," often had small patience with the force of tradition, and showed little understanding of what moved men to seek meanings outside of political experience. As sensitive a critic as the poet Horace Gregory could write, in a review of the works of D. H. Lawrence: "The world is moving away from Lawrence's need for personal salvation; his 'dark religion' is not a substitute for economic planning." [45] This was not the mood of all men in the thirties—not of a William Faulkner, an Ellen Glasgow— and many of the New Dealers recognized that life was more complex than some of their statements would suggest. Yet the liberals, in their desire to free themselves from the tyranny of precedent and in their ardor for social achievement, sometimes walked the precipice of superficiality and philistinism.

The concentration of the New Dealers on public concerns made a deep mark on the sensibility of the 1930's. Private experience seemed self-indulgent compared to the demands of public life. "Indeed the public world with us has *become* the private world, and the private world has become the public," wrote Archibald MacLeish. "We live, that is to say, in a revolutionary time in which the public life has washed in over the dikes of private existence as sea water breaks over into the fresh pools in the spring tides till everything is salt." [46] In the thirties, the Edna St. Vincent Millay whose candle had burned at both ends wrote the polemical *Conversation at Midnight* and the bitter "Epitaph for the Race of Man" in *Wine from These Grapes*.

The emphasis on the public world implied a specific rejection of the values of the 1920's. Roosevelt dismissed the twenties as "a decade of debauch," Tugwell scored those years as "a decade of empty progress, devoid of contribution to a genuinely better future," Morris Cooke deplored the "gilded-chariot days" of 1929, and Alben Barkley saw the twenties as a "carnival" marred by "the putrid pestilence of financial debauchery." [47] The

---

[44] David Lilienthal, *TVA: Democracy on the March* (New York, 1944), p. 3.

[45] Waldo Frank, "Our Guilt in Fascism," *New Republic*, CII (1940), 603–608; Murray Kempton, *Part of Our Time* (New York, 1955); p. 2; Cushing Strout, "The Twentieth-Century Enlightenment," *American Political Science Review*, XLIX (1955), 321–339; Morton White, *Social Thought in America* (New York, 1949), p. 241; *New Republic*, LXXIII (1932), 133.

[46] MacLeish mocked "the nineteenth-century poet, the private speaker, the whisperer to the heart, the unworldly romantic, the quaint Bohemian, the understander of women, the young man with the girl's eyes." MacLeish, *A Time to Speak*, pp. 62, 88.

[47] *Public Papers*, V, 179; Tugwell, *Battle for Democracy*, p. 54; Morris Cooke to Louis Howe, July 3, 1933, Cooke MSS., Box 51; *Literary Digest*, CXXII (July 4, 1936), 27.

depression was experienced as the punishment of a wrathful God visited on a nation that had strayed from the paths of righteousness.[48] The fire that followed the Park Avenue party in Thomas Wolfe's *You Can't Go Home Again,* like the suicide of Eveline at the end of John Dos Passos' *The Big Money,* symbolized the holocaust that brought to an end a decade of hedonism.[49] In an era of reconstruction, the attitudes of the twenties seemed alien, frivolous, or—the most cutting word the thirties could visit upon a man or institution—"escapist." When Morrie Ryskind and George Kaufman, authors of the popular *Of Thee I Sing,* lampooned the government again in *Let 'em Eat Cake* in the fall of 1933, the country was not amused. The New York *Post* applauded the decision of George Jean Nathan and his associates to discontinue the *American Spectator:* "Nihilism, dadaism, smartsetism—they are all gone, and this, too, is progress." [50] One of H. L. Mencken's biographers has noted: "Many were at pains to write him at his new home, telling him he was a sophomore, and those writing in magazines attacked him with a fury that was suspect because of its very violence." [51]

Commentators on the New Deal have frequently characterized it by that much-abused term "pragmatic." If one means by this that the New Dealers carefully tested the consequences of ideas, the term is clearly a misnomer. If one means that Roosevelt was exceptionally anti-ideological in his approach to politics, one may question whether he was, in fact, any more "pragmatic" in this sense than Van Buren or Polk or even "reform" Presidents like Jackson and Theodore Roosevelt. The "pragmatism" of the New Deal seemed remarkable only in a decade tortured by ideology, only in contrast to the rigidity of Hoover and of the Left.

The New Deal was pragmatic mainly in its skepticism about utopias and final solutions, its openness to experimentation, and its suspicion of the dogmas of the Establishment. Since the advice of economists had so often

---

[48] "We were all miserable sinners," announced the Harvard economist Oliver Sprague. *The New York Times,* December 10, 1933. Cf. "Special Week of Penitence and Prayer, October 2–8," *Federal Council Bulletin,* XV (September, 1932), 14–15; Milton Garber, Radio Address, 1932, Garber MSS.

[49] Melvin Landsberg, "A Study of the Political Development of John Dos Passos from 1912 to 1936" (unpublished Ph.D. dissertation, Columbia University, 1959).

[50] Hiram Motherwell, "Political Satire Scores on the Stage," *Today,* II (July 28, 1934), 24; *The New York Times,* November 12, 1933; New York *Post, Press Time* (New York, 1936), pp. 317 ff.

[51] William Manchester, *Disturber of the Peace* (New York, 1951), p. 258. "Empty stomachs became more important than hurt sensibilities," commented one critic. "The vexations and hurt feelings of a Carol Kennecott or the spiritual frustration of an Amory Blaine in *This Side of Paradise,* or the frantic dash for personal freedom of a Janet Marsh seemed trifling themes when the dominant feature of the national scene was twelve million unemployed." Halford Luccock, *American Mirror* (New York, 1940), p. 36. Cf. Margaret Mitchell to Mrs. Julian Harris, April 28, 1936, Mitchell MSS.

been wrong, the New Dealers distrusted the claims of orthodox theory—
"All this is perfectly terrible because it is all pure theory, when you come
down to it," the President said on one occasion—and they felt free to try
new approaches.[52] Roosevelt refused to be awed by the warnings of economists and financial experts that government interference with the "laws" of
the economy was blasphemous. "We must lay hold of the fact that economic laws are not made by nature," the President stated. "They are made
by human beings." [53] The New Dealers denied that depressions were inevitable events that had to be borne stoically, most of the stoicism to be displayed by the most impoverished, and they were willing to explore novel
ways to make the social order more stable and more humane. "I am for experimenting . . . in various parts of the country, trying out schemes which
are supported by reasonable people and see if they work," Hopkins told a
conference of social workers. "If they do not work, the world will not come
to an end." [54]

Hardheaded, "anti-utopian," the New Dealers nonetheless had their
Heavenly City: the greenbelt town, clean, green, and white, with children
playing in light, airy, spacious schools; the government project at Long-
view, Washington, with small houses, each of different design, colored
roofs, and gardens of flowers and vegetables; the Mormon villages of Utah
that M. L. Wilson kept in his mind's eye—immaculate farmsteads on
broad, rectangular streets; most of all, the Tennessee Valley, with its model
town of Norris, the tall transmission towers, the white dams, the glistening
wire strands, the valley where "a vision of villages and clean small factories has been growing into the minds of thoughtful men." [55] Scandinavia
was their model abroad, not only because it summoned up images of the
countryside of Denmark, the beauties of Stockholm, not only for its experience with labor relations and social insurance and currency reform, but because it represented the "middle way" of happy accommodation of public

---

[52] *Public Papers,* II, 269. "In the months and years following the stock market crash,"
Professor Galbraith has concluded, "the burden of reputable economic advice was invariably on the side of measures that would make things worse." John Kenneth Galbraith,
The Great Crash (Boston, 1955), pp. 187–188. For a typical example, see N. S. B. Gras
to Edward Costigan, July 22, 1932, Costigan MSS., V.F. 1.

[53] *Public Papers,* I, 657. The Boston *Transcript* commented: "Two more glaring mis-
statements of the truth could hardly have been packed into so little space." J. Joseph
Huthmacher, *Massachusetts People and Politics, 1919–1933* (Cambridge, 1959), p. 244.
Cf. Eccles, *Beckoning Frontiers,* p. 73.

[54] *Public Papers,* II, 302; V, 497; Josephine Chapin Brown, *Public Relief,* p. 152. Cf.
Clarke Chambers, "FDR, Pragmatist-Idealist," *Pacific Northwest Quarterly, LII* (1961),
50–55; F. S. C. Northrop, *The Meeting of East and West* (New York, 1947), p. 152;
Jacob Cohen, "Schlesinger and the New Deal," *Dissent,* VIII (1961), 466–468.

[55] Tugwell, *Battle for Democracy,* p. 22. This is a vision caught, in different ways, in
the paintings of Paul Sample, Charles Sheeler, Grant Wood, and Joe Jones.

and private institutions the New Deal sought to achieve. "Why," inquired Brandeis, "should anyone want to go to Russia when one can go to Denmark?"[56]

Yet the New Deal added up to more than all of this—more than an experimental approach, more than the sum of its legislative achievements, more than an antiseptic utopia. It is true that there was a certain erosion of values in the thirties, as well as a narrowing of horizons, but the New Dealers inwardly recognized that what they were doing had a deeply moral significance however much they eschewed ethical pretensions. Heirs of the Enlightenment, they felt themselves part of a broadly humanistic movement to make man's life on earth more tolerable, a movement that might someday even achieve a co-operative commonwealth. Social insurance, Frances Perkins declared, was "a fundamental part of another great forward step in that liberation of humanity which began with the Renaissance."[57]

Franklin Roosevelt did not always have this sense as keenly as some of the men around him, but his greatness as a President lies in the remarkable degree to which he shared the vision. "The new deal business to me is very much bigger than anyone yet has expressed it," observed Senator Elbert Thomas. Roosevelt "seems to really have caught the spirit of what one of the Hebrew prophets called the desire of the nations. If he were in India today they would probably decide that he had become Mahatma—that is, one in tune with the infinite."[58] Both foes and friends made much of Roosevelt's skill as a political manipulator, and there is no doubt that up to a point he delighted in schemes and stratagems. As Donald Richberg later observed: "There would be times when he seemed to be a Chevalier Bayard, *sans peur et sans reproche*, and times in which he would seem to be the apotheosis of a prince who had absorbed and practiced all the teachings of Machiavelli." Yet essentially he was a moralist who wanted to achieve certain human reforms and instruct the nation in the principles of government. On one occasion, he remarked: "I want to be a *preaching President*—like my cousin."[59] His courtiers gleefully recounted his adroitness in trading and dealing for votes, his effectiveness on the stump, his

[56] Marquis Childs, *Sweden: The Middle Way* (New Haven, 1936); David Lilienthal to George Fort Milton, July 9, 1936; Milton to F.D.R., July 8, 1936, Milton MSS., Box 20; Irving Fisher to F.D.R., September 28, 1934, Fisher MSS.; John Commons to Edward Costigan, July 25, 1932, Costigan MSS., V.F. 1; Arthur Schlesinger, Jr., *The Politics of Upheaval* (Boston, 1960), p. 221.

[57] Frances Perkins, "Basic Idea Behind Social Security Program," *The New York Times*, January 27, 1935.

[58] Thomas to Colonel E. LeRoy Bourne, January 6, 1934, Elbert Thomas MSS.

[59] Donald Richberg, *My Hero* (New York, 1954), p. 279; Schlesinger, *Coming of the New Deal* (Boston, 1959), p. 558.

wicked skill in cutting corners to win a point. But Roosevelt's importance lay not in his talents as a campaigner or a manipulator. It lay rather in his ability to arouse the country and, more specifically, the men who served under him, by his breezy encouragement of experimentation, by his hopefulness, and—a word that would have embarrassed some of his lieutenants —by his idealism.

The New Deal left many problems unsolved and even created some perplexing new ones. It never demonstrated that it could achieve prosperity in peacetime. As late as 1941, the unemployed still numbered six million, and not until the war year of 1943 did the army of the jobless finally disappear. It enhanced the power of interest groups who claimed to speak for millions, but sometimes represented only a small minority.[60] It did not evolve a way to protect people who had no such spokesmen, nor an acceptable method for disciplining the interest groups. In 1946, President Truman would resort to a threat to draft railway workers into the Army to avert a strike. The New Deal achieved a more just society by recognizing groups which had been largely unrepresented—staple farmers, industrial workers, particular ethnic groups, and the new intellectual-administrative class. Yet this was still a halfway revolution; it swelled the ranks of the bourgeoisie but left many Americans—sharecroppers, slum dwellers, most Negroes—outside of the new equilibrium.

Some of these omissions were to be promptly remedied. Subsequent Congresses extended social security, authorized slum clearance projects, and raised minimum-wage standards to keep step with the rising price level. Other shortcomings are understandable. The havoc that had been done before Roosevelt took office was so great that even the unprecedented measures of the New Deal did not suffice to repair the damage. Moreover, much was still to be learned, and it was in the Roosevelt years that the country was schooled in how to avert another major depression. Although it was war which freed the government from the taboos of a balanced budget and revealed the potentialities of spending, it is conceivable that New Deal measures would have led the country into a new cycle of prosperity even if there had been no war. Marked gains had been made before the war spending had any appreciable effect. When recovery did come, it was much more soundly based because of the adoption of the New Deal program.

Roosevelt and the New Dealers understood, perhaps better than their critics, that they had come only part of the way. Henry Wallace remarked: "We are children of the transition—we have left Egypt but we have not yet arrived at the Promised Land." Only five years separated Roosevelt's inauguration in 1933 and the adoption of the last of the New Deal measures, the Fair Labor Standards Act, in 1938. The New Dealers perceived

---

[60] Henry Kariel, *The Decline of American Pluralism* (Stanford, 1961).

that they had done more in those years than had been done in any comparable period in American history, but they also saw that there was much still to be done, much, too, that continued to baffle them. "I believe in the things that have been done," Mrs. Roosevelt told the American Youth Congress in February, 1939. "They helped but they did not solve the fundamental problems. . . . I never believed the Federal government could solve the whole problem. It bought us time to think." She closed not with a solution but with a challenge: "Is it going to be worth while?" [61]

"This generation of Americans is living in a tremendous moment of history," President Roosevelt stated in his final national address of the 1940 campaign.

> The surge of events abroad has made some few doubters among us ask: Is this the end of a story that has been told? Is the book of democracy now to be closed and placed away upon the dusty shelves of time?
>
> My answer is this: All we have known of the glories of democracy—its freedom, its efficiency as a mode of living, its ability to meet the aspirations of the common man—all these are merely an introduction to the greater story of a more glorious future.
>
> We Americans of today—all of us—we are characters in the living book of democracy.
>
> But we are also its author. It falls upon us now to say whether the chapters that are to come will tell a story of retreat or a story of continued advance. [62]

---

[61] Henry Wallace, *The Christian Bases of World Order* (New York, 1943), p. 17; Dorothy Dunbar Bromley, "The Future of Eleanor Roosevelt," *Harper's*, CLXXX (1939), 136.

[62] *Public Papers*, IX, 545.

BARTON J. BERNSTEIN

The New Deal:
The Conservative Achievements
of Liberal Reform

INTRODUCTION

Using much the same evidence as William Leuchtenburg and other liberal historians, the so-called New Left historians have offered a more critical assessment of the New Deal. The differences between the liberal and radical historians do not lie simply in whether they admire or criticize the New Deal; much of the disagreement rests on the interpretation of the changes that did occur, why they occurred, and whether more could have occurred. The answers, as both liberal and radical historians acknowledge, depend ultimately on the analysis that reaches be-

FROM Barton J. Bernstein, ed., *Towards a New Past: Dissenting Essays in American History* (New York: Pantheon Books, 1968), pp. 263–88. Reprinted by permission of the author and publisher.

The author wishes to express his gratitude to David M. Potter, Allen J. Matusow, and Otis L. Graham for their generous criticism. This acknowledgment was accidentally omitted from the original and has been restored at the author's request.

yond the administration to the entire political and economic structure of the 1930's, and especially the ideology and power of various groups and political coalitions.

In the following essay, one of these radical historians, Barton J. Bernstein of Stanford University, stresses that the New Deal shored up the existing social and economic order with moderate reforms and thereby saved large-scale corporate capitalism. Some radical reforms, he asserts—including nationalization of banking—were possible, especially in the early years of the New Deal. But the administration was restricted by its ideology from such bold ventures; Roosevelt and some of his advisers were even less ambitious and daring than many Congressmen, as well as the radicals outside of government. Even in the later years, Bernstein notes, many of the New Deal's limitations resulted not from the conservative opposition but from the administration's conceptions of politics and ideology. His analysis acknowledges that there were inherent shortcomings in liberal democracy itself, and that many Americans did not seek a bold restructuring of the prevailing system, but his essay focuses primarily on the New Deal, and its achievements and shortcomings. In summary, he concludes that the New Deal could have achieved more—in redistributing income, in reshaping power relations, in restructuring the economy, and in extending meaningful representation and participation in the polity.

Even many of the New Deal's humane reforms, according to his analysis, "were generally faltering and shallow, of more value to the middle classes, of less value to organized workers, or even less to 'marginal men.' " He also contends that assistance to, and recognition of, organized labor and big agriculture were reforms of questionable value—"the integration of larger interest groups into a new political economy." What emerged, he implies, was a corporate liberalism in which potentially disruptive groups were integrated into the system without any substantial challenge to basic capitalist values or more than modifications in the nature of power relations. Unlike some radical analysts, however, he does not argue in this essay that powerful businessmen and the administration during the early New Deal supported unionism in order to squelch radicalism and gain a disciplined labor force.

Probably because the New Left analysis of the New Deal is still represented primarily by a few essays, it has drawn only a handful of published criticisms. One of the earliest, advanced by Jerold S. Auerbach ("New Deal, Old Deal, or Raw Deal: Some Thoughts on New Left Historiography," *Journal of Southern History,* XXXV [Feb. 1969]), attacks Bernstein and the others on three main grounds. First, if the New Deal did so little for the poor, the black, and the unemployed, why did these groups support Roosevelt with such enthusiasm and consistency? Auerbach rejects Bernstein's view that "the marginal men trapped in hopelessness were seduced by rhetoric," finds that the masses received concrete benefits from the New Deal, and concludes that both Roosevelt's supporters and enemies had a clear perception of their real self-interest. Given this criticism, Auerbach would probably also doubt the value of Bernstein's more recent call for an analysis of the mechanisms of hegemony in the New Deal and a reconsideration of the normal assumption that big business was bitterly hostile to the administration. Second, the New Left, Auerbach says, apparently believes that the New Deal was conservative because it saved capitalism and refused to abandon private property. But he points out that the public gave no mandate for a radical program and that by this standard, "every administration since Washington's is equally culpable." And third, the New Left, he charges, measures the New Deal by the standards of the 1960's, fails to study and assess it on its own terms and by the values of its own time, and therefore has abandoned history for propaganda. The reader is invited to examine Bernstein's essay, as well as the works of other New Left analysts, and to assess the merits of Auerbach's position.

Writing from a liberal democratic consensus, many American historians in the past two decades have praised the Roosevelt administration for its nonideological flexibility and for its far-ranging reforms. To many historians, particularly those who reached intellectual maturity during the depression,[1] the government's accomplishments, as well as the drama and passion, marked the decade as a watershed, as a dividing line in the American past.

---

[1] The outstanding examples are Arthur Schlesinger, Jr., Frank Freidel, Carl Degler, and William Leuchtenburg. Schlesinger, in *The Crisis of the Old Order* (Boston, 1957), emphasized the presence of reform in the twenties but criticized the federal government for its retreat from liberalism and condemned Hoover for his responses to the depression. The next two volumes of his *The Age of Roosevelt, The Coming of the New Deal* (Boston, 1958) and *The Politics of Upheaval* (Boston, 1960), praise the New Deal, but also contain information for a more critical appraisal. His research is quite wide and has often guided my own investigations. For his theory that the New Deal was likely even without the depression, see "Sources of the New Deal: Reflections on the Temper of a Time," *Columbia University Forum*, II (Fall 1959), 4–11. Freidel affirmed that the New Deal was a watershed (*American Historical Review*, October 1965, p. 329), but in *The New Deal in Historical Perspective* (Washington, 1959), he has suggested the conservatism of the New Deal as a reform movement. Degler, in *Out of Our Past* (New York, 1959), pp. 379–416, extolled the New Deal as a "Third American Revolution." But also see his "The Ordeal of Herbert Hoover," *Yale Review*, LII (Summer 1963), 565–83. Leuchtenburg, *Franklin D. Roosevelt and the New Deal, 1932–1940* (New York, 1963), offers considerable criticism of the New Deal, but finds far more to praise in this "half-way revolution." He cites Degler approvingly but moderates Degler's judgment (pp. 336–47). The book represents years of research and has often guided my own investigations.

Enamored of Franklin D. Roosevelt and recalling the bitter opposition to welfare measures and restraints upon business, many liberal historians have emphasized the New Deal's discontinuity with the immediate past. For them there was a "Roosevelt Revolution," or at the very least a dramatic achievement of a beneficent liberalism which had developed in fits and spurts during the preceding three decades.[2] Rejecting earlier interpretations which viewed the New Deal as socialism [3] or state capitalism,[4] they have also disregarded theories of syndicalism [5] or of corporate liberalism.[6] The New Deal has generally commanded their approval for such laws or institutions as minimum wages, public housing, farm assistance, the Tennessee Valley Authority, the Wagner Act, more progressive taxation, and social security. For most liberal historians the New Deal meant the replenishment of democracy, the rescuing of the federal government from the clutches of big business, the significant redistribution of political power. Breaking with laissez faire, the new administration, according to these interpretations, marked the end of the passive or impartial state and the beginning of positive government, of the interventionist state acting to offset concentrations of private power, and affirming the rights and responding to the needs of the unprivileged.

From the perspective of the late 1960s these themes no longer seem adequate to characterize the New Deal. The liberal reforms of the New Deal did not transform the American system; they conserved and protected American corporate capitalism, occasionally by absorbing parts of threatening programs. There was no significant redistribution of power in American society, only limited recognition of other organized groups, seldom of unorganized peoples. Neither the bolder programs advanced by New Dealers nor the final legislation greatly extended the beneficence of government

---

[2] Eric Goldman, *Rendezvous with Destiny* (New York, 1952); Henry Steele Commager, "Twelve Years of Roosevelt," *American Mercury*, LX (April 1945), 391–401; Arthur Link, *American Epoch* (New York, 1955), pp. 377–440. In his essay on "Franklin D. Roosevelt: the Patrician as Opportunist" in *The American Political Tradition* (New York, 1948), pp. 315–52, Richard Hofstadter was critical of the New Deal's lack of ideology but treated it as a part of the larger reform tradition. In *The Age of Reform* (New York, 1955), however, while chiding the New Deal for opportunism, he emphasized the discontinuity of the New Deal with the reform tradition of Populism and Progressivism.

[3] Edgar E. Robinson, *The Roosevelt Leadership, 1933–1945* (Philadelphia, 1955), the work of a conservative constitutionalist, does accuse the administration of having objectives approaching the leveling aims of communism (p. 376).

[4] Louis Hacker, *American Problems of Today* (New York, 1938).

[5] William Appleman Williams, *The Contours of American History* (Chicago, 1966), pp. 372–488; and his review, "Schlesinger: Right Crisis—Wrong Order," *Nation*, CLXXXIV (March 23, 1957), 257–60. Williams' volume has influenced my own thought.

[6] Ronald Radosh, "The Corporate Ideology of American Labor Leaders from Gompers to Hillman," *Studies on the Left*, VI (November–December 1966), 66–88.

beyond the middle classes or drew upon the wealth of the few for the needs of the many. Designed to maintain the American system, liberal activity was directed toward essentially conservative goals. Experimentalism was most frequently limited to means; seldom did it extend to ends. Never questioning private enterprise, it operated within safe channels, far short of Marxism or even of native American radicalisms that offered structural critiques and structural solutions.

All of this is not to deny the changes wrought by the New Deal—the extension of welfare programs, the growth of federal power, the strengthening of the executive, even the narrowing of property rights. But it is to assert that the elements of continuity are stronger, that the magnitude of change has been exaggerated. The New Deal failed to solve the problem of depression, it failed to raise the impoverished, it failed to redistribute income, it failed to extend equality and generally countenanced racial discrimination and segregation. It failed generally to make business more responsible to the social welfare or to threaten business's pre-eminent political power. In this sense, the New Deal, despite the shifts in tone and spirit from the earlier decade, was profoundly conservative and continuous with the 1920s.

[I]

Rather than understanding the 1920s as a "return to normalcy," the period is more properly interpreted by focusing on the continuation of progressive impulses, demands often frustrated by the rivalry of interest groups, sometimes blocked by the resistance of Harding and Coolidge, and occasionally by Hoover.[7] Through these years while agriculture and labor struggled to secure advantages from the federal government, big business flourished. Praised for creating American prosperity, business leaders easily convinced the nation that they were socially responsible, that they were fulfilling the needs of the public.[8] Benefiting from earlier legislation that had promoted economic rationalization and stability, they were opponents of federal benefits to other groups but seldom proponents of laissez faire.[9]

In no way did the election of Herbert Hoover in 1928 seem to challenge the New Era. An heir of Wilson, Hoover promised an even closer relationship with big business and moved beyond Harding and Coolidge by affirming federal responsibility for prosperity. As Secretary of Commerce,

---

[7] Arthur Link, "What Happened to the Progressive Movement?" *American Historical Review*, LXIV (July 1959), 833–51.

[8] James Prothro, *The Dollar Decade* (Baton Rouge, La., 1954).

[9] Louis Galambos, *Competition and Cooperation* (Baltimore, 1966), pp. 55–139; Link, "What Happened to the Progressive Movement?"

Hoover had opposed unbridled competition and had transformed his department into a vigorous friend of business. Sponsoring trade associations, he promoted industrial self-regulation and the increased rationalization of business. He had also expanded foreign trade, endorsed the regulation of new forms of communications, encouraged relief in disasters, and recommended public works to offset economic declines.[10]

By training and experience, few men in American political life seemed better prepared than Hoover to cope with the depression. Responding promptly to the crisis, he acted to stabilize the economy and secured the agreement of businessmen to maintain production and wage rates. Unwilling to let the economy "go through the wringer," the President requested easier money, self-liquidating public works, lower personal and corporate income taxes, and stronger commodity stabilization corporations.[11] In reviewing these unprecedented actions, Walter Lippmann wrote, "The national government undertook to make the whole economic order operate prosperously."[12]

But these efforts proved inadequate. The tax cut benefitted the wealthy and failed to raise effective demand. The public works were insufficient. The commodity stabilization corporations soon ran out of funds, and agricultural prices kept plummeting. Businessmen cut back production, dismissed employees, and finally cut wages. As unemployment grew, Hoover struggled to inspire confidence, but his words seemed hollow and his understanding of the depression limited. Blaming the collapse on European failures, he could not admit that American capitalism had failed. When prodded by Congress to increase public works, to provide direct relief, and to further unbalance the budget, he doggedly resisted. Additional deficits would destroy business confidence, he feared, and relief would erode the principles of individual and local responsibility.[13] Clinging to faith in voluntarism, Hoover also briefly rebuffed the efforts by financiers to secure the Reconstruction Finance Corporation (RFC). Finally endorsing the RFC,[14] he also supported expanded lending by Federal Land Banks, recommended home-loan banks, and even approved small federal

[10] Joseph Brandes, *Herbert Hoover and Economic Diplomacy* (Pittsburgh, 1962); Hofstadter, *American Political Tradition*, pp. 283–99.

[11] William S. Myers, ed., *The State Papers and Other Writings of Herbert Hoover* (New York, 1934), I, 84–88 (easier money), 137, 411, 431–33; II, 202 (public works); I, 142–43, 178–79 (lower taxes). The Commodity Stabilization Corporation was created before the crash.

[12] Lippmann, "The Permanent New Deal," *Yale Review*, XXIV (June 1935), 651.

[13] Myers, ed., *State Papers*, II, 195–201, 214–15, 224–26, 228–33 (on the budget); II, 405, 496–99, 503–5 (on relief).

[14] Gerald Nash, "Herbert Hoover and the Origins of the Reconstruction Finance Corporation," *Mississippi Valley Historical Review*, XLVI (December 1959), 455–68.

loans (usually inadequate) to states needing funds for relief. In this burst of activity, the President had moved to the very limits of his ideology.

Restricted by his progressive background and insensitive to politics and public opinion, he stopped far short of the state corporatism urged by some businessmen and politicians. With capitalism crumbling he had acted vigorously to save it, but he would not yield to the representatives of business or disadvantaged groups who wished to alter the government.[15] He was reluctant to use the federal power to achieve through compulsion what could not be realized through voluntary means. Proclaiming a false independence, he did not understand that his government already represented business interests; hence, he rejected policies that would openly place the power of the state in the hands of business or that would permit the formation of a syndicalist state in which power might be exercised (in the words of William Appleman Williams) "by a relatively few leaders of each functional bloc formed and operating as an oligarchy." [16]

Even though constitutional scruples restricted his efforts, Hoover did more than any previous American president to combat depression. He "abandoned the principles of laissez faire in relation to the business cycle, established the conviction that prosperity and depression can be publicly controlled by political action, and drove out of the public consciousness the old idea that depressions must be overcome by private adjustment," wrote Walter Lippmann.[17] Rather than the last of the old presidents, Herbert Hoover was the first of the new.

[II]

A charismatic leader and a brilliant politician, his successor expanded federal activities on the basis of Hoover's efforts. Using the federal government to stabilize the economy and advance the interests of the groups, Franklin D. Roosevelt directed the campaign to save large-scale corporate capitalism. Though recognizing new political interests and extending benefits to them, his New Deal never effectively challenged big business or the organization of the economy. In providing assistance to the needy and by rescuing them from starvation, Roosevelt's humane efforts also protected the established system: he sapped organized radicalism of its waning strength and of its potential constituency among the unorganized and discontented. Sensitive to public opinion and fearful of radicalism, Roosevelt acted from a mixture of motives that rendered his liberalism cautious and limited, his experimentalism narrow. Despite the flurry of activity, his gov-

---

[15] W. S. Myers and W. H. Newton, eds., *The Hoover Administration: A Documentary History* (New York, 1936), p. 119; "Proceedings of a Conference of Progressives," March 11–12, 1931, Hillman Papers, Amalgamated Clothing Workers (New York).

[16] *Contours of American History,* p. 428.

[17] Lippmann, "The Permanent New Deal," p. 651.

ernment was more vigorous and flexible about means than goals, and the goals were more conservative than historians usually acknowledge.[18]

Roosevelt's response to the banking crisis emphasizes the conservatism of his administration and its self-conscious avoidance of more radical means that might have transformed American capitalism. Entering the White House when banks were failing and Americans had lost faith in the financial system, the President could have nationalized it—"without a word of protest," judged Senator Bronson Cutting.[19] "If ever there was a moment when things hung in the balance," later wrote Raymond Moley, a member of the original "brain trust," "it was on March 5, 1933—when unorthodoxy would have drained the last remaining strength of the capitalistic system."[20] To save the system, Roosevelt relied upon collaboration between bankers and Hoover's Treasury officials to prepare legislation extending federal assistance to banking. So great was the demand for action that House members, voting even without copies, passed it unanimously, and the Senate, despite objections by a few Progressives, approved it the same evening. "The President," remarked a cynical congressman, "drove the money-changers out of the Capitol on March 4th—and they were all back on the 9th."[21]

Undoubtedly the most dramatic example of Roosevelt's early conservative approach to recovery was the National Recovery Administration (NRA). It was based on the War Industries Board (WIB) which had provided the model for the campaign of Bernard Baruch, General Hugh Johnson, and other former WIB officials during the twenties to limit competition through industrial self-regulation under federal sanction. As trade associations flourished during the decade, the FTC encouraged "codes of fair competition" and some industries even tried to set prices and restrict production. Operating without the force of law, these agreements broke down. When the depression struck, industrial pleas for regulation increased.[22] After the Great Crash, important business leaders including Henry I. Harriman of the Chamber of Commerce and Gerard Swope of

---

[18] For an excellent statement of this thesis, see Howard Zinn's introduction to his *New Deal Thought* (New York, 1966), pp. xv–xxxvi. So far historians have not adequately explored the thesis that F.D.R. frequently acted as a restraining force on his own government, and that bolder reforms were often thwarted by him and his intimates.

[19] Bronson Cutting, "Is Private Banking Doomed?" *Liberty*, XI (March 31, 1934), 10; cf. Raymond Moley, *The First New Deal* (New York, 1966), pp. 177–80.

[20] Moley, *After Seven Years* (New York, 1939), p. 155; Arthur Ballantine, "When All the Banks Closed," *Harvard Business Review*, XXVI (March 1948), 129–43.

[21] William Lemke, later quoted in Lorena Hickok to Harry Hopkins, November 23, 1933, Hopkins Papers, Franklin D. Roosevelt Library (hereafter called FDRL).

[22] Baruch to Samuel Gompers, April 19, 1924, Baruch Papers, Princeton University; Schlesinger, *Coming of the New Deal*, pp. 88–89; Gerald Nash, "Experiments in Industrial Mobilization: WIB and NRA," *Mid-America*, XLV (July 1963), 156–75.

General Electric called for suspension of antitrust laws and federal organization of business collaboration.[23] Joining them were labor leaders, particularly those in "sick" industries—John L. Lewis of the United Mine Workers and Sidney Hillman of Amalgamated Clothing Workers.[24]

Designed largely for industrial recovery, the NRA legislation provided for minimum wages and maximum hours. It also made concessions to pro-labor congressmen and labor leaders who demanded some specific benefits for unions—recognition of the worker's right to organization and to collective bargaining. In practice, though, the much-heralded Section 7a was a disappointment to most friends of labor.[25] (For the shrewd Lewis, however, it became a mandate to organize: "The President wants you to join a union.") To many frustrated workers and their disgusted leaders, NRA became "National Run Around." The clause, unionists found (in the words of Brookings economists), "had the practical effect of placing NRA on the side of anti-union employers in their struggle against trade unions. . . . [It] thus threw its weight against labor in the balance of bargaining power." [26] And while some far-sighted industrialists feared radicalism and hoped to forestall it by incorporating unions into the economic system, most preferred to leave their workers unorganized or in company unions. To many businessmen, large and independent unions as such seemed a radical threat to the system of business control.[27]

Not only did the NRA provide fewer advantages than unionists had anticipated, but it also failed as a recovery measure. It probably even retarded recovery by supporting restrictionism and price increases, concluded a Brookings study.[28] Placing effective power for code-writing in big business, NRA injured small businesses and contributed to the concentration of American industry. It was not the government-business partnership as envisaged by Adolf A. Berle, Jr., nor government managed as Rexford

[23] Gerard Swope, *The Swope Plan* (New York, 1931); Julius H. Barnes, "Government and Business," *Harvard Business Review*, X (July 1932), 411–19; Harriman, "The Stabilization of Business and Employment," *American Economic Review*, XXII (March 1932), 63–75; House Committee on Education and Labor, 73rd Cong., 1st Sess., *Thirty-Hour Week Bill, Hearings*, pp. 198–99.

[24] *Ibid.*, pp. 884–97; Hillman, "Labor Leads Toward Planning," *Survey Graphic*, LXVI (March 1932), 586–88.

[25] Irving Bernstein, *The New Deal Collective Bargaining Policy* (Berkeley, Cal., 1950), pp. 57–63.

[26] Quotes from Hofstadter, *American Political Tradition*, p. 336. "It is not the function of NRA to organize . . . labor," asserted General Hugh Johnson. "Automobile Code Provides for Thirty-Five Hour Week," *Iron Age*, CXXXII (August 3, 1933), 380.

[27] Richard C. Wilcock, "Industrial Management's Policy Toward Unionism," in Milton Derber and Edwin Young, eds., *Labor and the New Deal* (Madison, Wis., 1957), pp. 278–95.

[28] Leverett Lyon, *et al.*, *The National Recovery Administration* (Washington, 1935).

Tugwell had hoped, but rather, business managed, as Raymond Moley had desired.[29] Calling NRA "industrial self-government," its director, General Hugh Johnson, had explained that "NRA is exactly what industry organized in trade associations makes it." Despite the annoyance of some big businessmen with Section 7a, the NRA reaffirmed and consolidated their power at a time when the public was critical of industrialists and financiers.

[III]

Viewing the economy as a "concert of organized interests,"[30] the New Deal also provided benefits for farmers—the Agricultural Adjustment Act. Reflecting the political power of larger commercial farmers and accepting restrictionist economics, the measure assumed that the agricultural problem was overproduction, not underconsumption. Financed by a processing tax designed to raise prices to parity, payments encouraged restricted production and cutbacks in farm labor. With benefits accruing chiefly to the larger owners, they frequently removed from production the lands of sharecroppers and tenant farmers, and "tractored" them and hired hands off the land. In assisting agriculture, the AAA, like the NRA, sacrificed the interests of the marginal and the unrecognized to the welfare of those with greater political and economic power.[31]

In large measure, the early New Deal of the NRA and AAA was a "broker state." Though the government served as a mediator of interests and sometimes imposed its will in divisive situations, it was generally the servant of powerful groups. "Like the mercantilists, the New Dealers protected vested interests with the authority of the state," acknowledges William Leuchtenburg. But it was some improvement over the 1920s when business was the only interest capable of imposing its will on the government.[32] While extending to other groups the benefits of the state, the New Deal, however, continued to recognize the pre-eminence of business interests.

---

[29] The characterization of Berle, Tugwell, and Moley is from Schlesinger, *Coming of the New Deal*, pp. 181–84, and Johnson's address at the NAM is from NRA press release 2126, December 7, 1933, NRA Records, RG 9, National Archives.

[30] "Concert of interests" was used by F.D.R. in a speech of April 18, 1932, in Samuel Rosenman, ed., *The Public Papers and Addresses of Franklin D. Roosevelt* (13 vols.; New York, 1938–52), I, 627–39. (Hereafter referred to as *FDR Papers.*)

[31] M. S. Venkataramani, "Norman Thomas, Arkansas Sharecroppers, and the Roosevelt Agricultural Policies," *Mississippi Valley Historical Review*, XLVII (September 1960), 225–46; John Hutson, Columbia Oral History Memoir, pp. 114 ff.; Mordecai Ezekiel, Columbia Oral History Memoir, pp. 74 ff.

[32] Quoted from Leuchtenburg, *F.D.R.*, p. 87, and this discussion draws upon pp. 87–90; John Chamberlain, *The American Stakes* (Philadelphia, 1940): James MacGregor Burns, *Roosevelt: The Lion and the Fox* (New York, 1956), pp. 183–202.

The politics of the broker state also heralded the way of the future—of continued corporate dominance in a political structure where other groups agreed generally on corporate capitalism and squabbled only about the size of the shares. Delighted by this increased participation and the absorption of dissident groups, many liberals did not understand the dangers in the emerging organization of politics. They had too much faith in representative institutions and in associations to foresee the perils—of leaders not representing their constituents, of bureaucracy diffusing responsibility, of officials serving their own interests. Failing to perceive the dangers in the emerging structure, most liberals agreed with Senator Robert Wagner of New York: "In order that the strong may not take advantage of the weak, every group must be equally strong." [33] His advice then seemed appropriate for organizing labor, but it neglected the problems of unrepresentative leadership and of the many millions to be left beyond organization. [34]

In dealing with the organized interests, the President acted frequently as a broker, but his government did not simply express the vectors of external forces. [35] The New Deal state was too complex, too loose, and some of Roosevelt's subordinates were following their own inclinations and pushing the government in directions of their own design. [36] The President would also depart from his role as a broker and act to secure programs he desired. As a skilled politician, he could split coalitions, divert the interests of groups, or place the prestige of his office on the side of desired legislation.

In seeking to protect the stock market, for example, Roosevelt endorsed the Securities and Exchange measure (of 1934), despite the opposition of many in the New York financial community. His advisers split the opposition. Rallying to support the administration were the out-of-town exchanges, representatives of the large commission houses, including James Forrestal of Dillon, Read, and Robert Lovett of Brown Brothers, Harriman, and such commission brokers as E. A. Pierce and Paul Shields. Opposed to the Wall Street "old guard" and their companies, this group included those who wished to avoid more radical legislation, as well as others who had wanted earlier to place trading practices under federal legislation which they could influence. [37]

---

[33] Quoted from House Committee on Education and Labor, 74th Cong., 1st Sess., *National Labor Relations Board Hearings*, p. 35.

[34] For a warning, see Paul Douglas, "Rooseveltian Liberalism," *Nation*, CXXXVI (June 21, 1933), 702–3.

[35] Leuchtenburg, *F.D.R.*, p. 88, uses the image of "a parallelogram of pressures."

[36] For example see the Columbia Oral Histories of Louis Bean, Hutson, and Ezekiel.

[37] *New York Times*, January 30, 1934; House Interstate and Foreign Commerce Committee, 73rd Cong., 2nd Sess., House Report No. 1383, *Securities Exchange Bill of*

Though the law restored confidence in the securities market and protected capitalism, it alarmed some businessmen and contributed to the false belief that the New Deal was threatening business. But it was not the disaffection of a portion of the business community, nor the creation of the Liberty League, that menaced the broker state.[38] Rather it was the threat of the Left—expressed, for example, in such overwrought statements as Minnesota Governor Floyd Olson's: "I am not a liberal . . . I am a radical. . . . I am not satisfied with hanging a laurel wreath on burglars and thieves . . . and calling them code authorities or something else." [39] While Olson, along with some others who succumbed to the rhetoric of militancy, would back down and soften their meaning, their words dramatized real grievances: the failure of the early New Deal to end misery, to re-create prosperity. The New Deal excluded too many. Its programs were inadequate. While Roosevelt reluctantly endorsed relief and went beyond Hoover in support of public works, he too preferred self-liquidating projects, desired a balanced budget, and resisted spending the huge sums required to lift the nation out of depression.

[IV]

For millions suffering in a nation wracked by poverty, the promises of the Left seemed attractive. Capitalizing on the misery, Huey Long offered Americans a "Share Our Wealth" program—a welfare state with prosperity, not subsistence, for the disadvantaged, those neglected by most politicians. "Every Man a King": pensions for the elderly, college for the deserving, homes and cars for families—that was the promise of American life. Also proposing minimum wages, increased public works, shorter work weeks, and a generous farm program, he demanded a "soak-the-rich" tax program. Despite the economic defects of his plan, Long was no hayseed,

---

1934, p. 3; "SEC," *Fortune*, XXI (June 1940), 91–92, 120 ff.; Ralph De Bedts, *The New Deal's SEC* (New York, 1964), pp. 56–85.

[38] Frederick Rudolph, "The American Liberty League, 1934–1940," *American Historical Review*, LVI (October 1950), 19–33; George Wolfskill, *The Revolt of the Conservatives* (Boston, 1962). Emphasizing the Liberty League and focusing upon the rhetoric of business disaffection, historians have often exaggerated the opposition of the business communities. See the correspondence of James Forrestal, PPF 6367, FDRL, and at Princeton; of Russell Leffingwell, PPF 886, FDRL; of Donald Nelson, PPF 8615, FDRL, and at the Huntington Library; and of Thomas Watson, PPF 2489, FDRL. On the steel industry, see *Iron Age*, CXXXV (June 13, 1935), 44. For very early evidence of estrangement, however, see Edgar Mowrer to Frank Knox, November 8, 1933, Knox Papers, Library of Congress.

[39] Quoted from Donald McCoy, *Angry Voices: Left of Center Politics in the New Deal Era* (Lawrence, Kan., 1958), pp. 55, from *Farmer-Labor Leader*, March 30, 1934.

and his forays into the East revealed support far beyond the bayous and hamlets of his native South.[40] In California discontent was so great that Upton Sinclair, food faddist and former socialist, captured the Democratic nomination for governor on a platform of "production-for-use"—factories and farms for the unemployed. "In a cooperative society," promised Sinclair, "every man, woman, and child would have the equivalent of $5,000 a year income from labor of the able-bodied young men for three or four hours per day." [41] More challenging to Roosevelt was Francis Townsend's plan—monthly payments of $200 to those past sixty who retired and promised to spend the stipend within thirty days.[42] Another enemy of the New Deal was Father Coughlin, the popular radio priest, who had broken with Roosevelt and formed a National Union for Social Justice to lead the way to a corporate society beyond capitalism.

To a troubled nation offered "redemption" by the Left, there was also painful evidence that the social fabric was tearing—law was breaking down. When the truckers in Minneapolis struck, the police provoked an incident and shot sixty-seven people, some in the back. Covering the tragedy, Eric Sevareid, then a young reporter, wrote, "I understood deep in my bones and blood what fascism was." [43] In San Francisco union leaders embittered by police brutality led a general strike and aroused national fears of class warfare. Elsewhere, in textile mills from Rhode Island to Georgia, in cities like Des Moines and Toledo, New York and Philadelphia, there were brutality and violence, sometimes bayonets and tear gas.[44]

Challenged by the Left, and with the new Congress more liberal and more willing to spend, Roosevelt turned to disarm the discontent. "Boys— this is our hour," confided Harry Hopkins. "We've got to get everything we want—a works program, social security, wages and hours, everything— now or never. Get your minds to work on developing a complete ticket to provide security for all the folks of this country up and down and across the board." [45] Hopkins and the associates he addressed were not radicals: they did not seek to transform the system, only to make it more humane.

---

[40] Long, *My First Days in the White House* (Harrisburg, Pa., 1935).

[41] Quoted from Sinclair, *The Way Out* (New York 1933), p. 57. See Sinclair to Roosevelt, October 5 and 18, 1934, OF 1165, FDRL.

[42] Nicholas Roosevelt, *The Townsend Plan* (Garden City, N.Y., 1935). Not understanding that the expenditures would increase consumption and probably spur production, critics emphasized that the top 9 percent would have received 50 percent of the income, but they neglected that the top income-tenth had received (before taxes) nearly 40 percent of the national income in 1929. National Industrial Conference Board, *Studies in Enterprise and Social Progress* (New York, 1939), p. 125.

[43] Sevareid, *Not So Wild a Dream* (New York, 1946), p. 58.

[44] Sidney Lens, *Left, Right and Center* (Hinsdale, Ill., 1949), pp. 280–89.

[45] Quoted in Robert Sherwood, *Roosevelt and Hopkins,* rev. ed. (New York, 1950), p. 65.

They, too, wished to preserve large-scale corporate capitalism, but unlike Roosevelt or Moley, they were prepared for more vigorous action. Their commitment to reform was greater, their tolerance for injustice far less. Joining them in pushing the New Deal left were the leaders of industrial unions, who, while also not wishing to transform the system, sought for workingmen higher wages, better conditions, stronger and larger unions, and for themselves a place closer to the fulcrum of power.

The problems of organized labor, however, neither aroused Roosevelt's humanitarianism nor suggested possibilities of reshaping the political coalition. When asked during the NRA about employee representation, he had replied that workers could select anyone they wished—the Ahkoond of Swat, a union, even the Royal Geographical Society.[46] As a paternalist, viewing himself (in the words of James MacGregor Burns) as a "partisan and benefactor" of workers, he would not understand the objections to company unions or to multiple unionism under NRA. Nor did he foresee the political dividends that support of independent unions could yield to his party.[47] Though presiding over the reshaping of politics (which would extend the channels of power to some of the discontented and redirect their efforts to competition within a limited framework), he was not its architect, and he was unable clearly to see or understand the unfolding design.

When Senator Wagner submitted his labor relations bill, he received no assistance from the President and even struggled to prevent Roosevelt from joining the opposition. The President "never lifted a finger," recalls Miss Perkins. ("I, myself, had very little sympathy with the bill," she wrote.[48]) But after the measure easily passed the Senate and seemed likely to win the House's endorsement, Roosevelt reversed himself. Three days before the Supreme Court invalidated the NRA, including the legal support for unionization, Roosevelt came out for the bill. Placing it on his "must" list, he may have hoped to influence the final provisions and turn an administration defeat into victory.[49]

Responding to the threat from the Left, Roosevelt also moved during the Second Hundred Days to secure laws regulating banking, raising taxes, dissolving utility-holding companies, and creating social security. Building on the efforts of states during the Progressive Era, the Social Security Act marked the movement toward the welfare state, but the core of the mea-

---

[46] Roosevelt's press conference of June 15, 1934, *FDR Papers*, III, 301; cf., Roosevelt to John L. Lewis, February 25, 1939, Philip Murray Papers, Catholic University.

[47] Burns, *The Lion and the Fox*, pp. 217–19; quotation from p. 218.

[48] Perkins, Columbia Oral History Memoir, VII, 138, 147, quoted by Leuchtenburg, *F.D.R.*, p. 151.

[49] Irving Bernstein, *The New Deal Collective Bargaining Policy*, pp. 100–8; Burns, *The Lion and the Fox*, p. 219.

sure, the old-age provision, was more important as a landmark than for its substance. While establishing a federal-state system of unemployment compensation, the government, by making workers contribute to their old-age insurance, denied its financial responsibility for the elderly. The act excluded more than a fifth of the labor force leaving, among others, more than five million farm laborers and domestics without coverage.[50]

Though Roosevelt criticized the tax laws for not preventing "an unjust concentration of wealth and economic power,"[51] his own tax measure would not have significantly redistributed wealth. Yet his message provoked an "amen" from Huey Long and protests from businessmen.[52] Retreating from his promises, Roosevelt failed to support the bill, and it succumbed to conservative forces. They removed the inheritance tax and greatly reduced the proposed corporate and individual levies. The final law did not "soak the rich."[53] But it did engender deep resentment among the wealthy for increasing taxes on gifts and estates, imposing an excess-profits tax (which Roosevelt had not requested), and raising surtaxes. When combined with such regressive levies as social security and local taxes, however, the Wealth Tax of 1935 did not drain wealth from higher-income groups, and the top one percent even increased their shares during the New Deal years.[54]

[V]

Those historians who have characterized the events of 1935 as the beginning of a second New Deal have imposed a pattern on those years which most participants did not then discern.[55] In moving to social security, guarantees of collective bargaining, utility regulation, and progressive taxation, the government did advance the nation toward greater liberalism, but the shift was exaggerated and most of the measures accomplished far less than either friends or foes suggested. Certainly, despite a mild bill authorizing destruction of utilities-holding companies, there was no effort to atomize business, no real threat to concentration.

---

[50] Margaret Grant, *Old Age Security* (Washington, 1939), p. 217. Under social security, payments at sixty-five ranged from $10 a month to $85 a month, depending on earlier earnings.

[51] Roosevelt's message to Congress on June 19, 1935, *FDR Papers*, IV, 271.

[52] *New York Times*, June 20 and 21, 1935; *Business Week*, June 22, 1935, p. 5.

[53] John Morton Blum, *From the Morgenthau Diaries: Years of Crisis, 1928–1938* (Boston, 1959), pp. 302–4.

[54] Simon Kuznets, *Shares of Upper Income Groups in Income and Savings*, National Bureau of Economic Research, Occasional Paper 35 (New York, 1950), pp. 32–40.

[55] Otis L. Graham, Jr., "Historians and the New Deals: 1944–1960," *Social Studies*, LIV (April 1963), 133–40.

Nor were so many powerful businessmen disaffected by the New Deal. Though the smaller businessmen who filled the ranks of the Chamber of Commerce resented the federal bureaucracy and the benefits to labor and thus criticized NRA,[56] representatives of big business found the agency useful and opposed a return to unrestricted competition. In 1935, members of the Business Advisory Council—including Henry Harriman, outgoing president of the Chamber, Thomas Watson of International Business Machines, Walter Gifford of American Telephone and Telegraph, Gerard Swope of General Electric, Winthrop Aldrich of the Chase National Bank, and W. Averell Harriman of Union Pacific—vigorously endorsed a two-year renewal of NRA.[57]

When the Supreme Court in 1935 declared the "hot" oil clause and the NRA unconstitutional, the administration moved to measures known as the "little NRA." Re-establishing regulations in bituminous coal and oil, the New Deal also checked wholesale price discrimination and legalized "fair trade" practices. Though Roosevelt never acted to revive the NRA, he periodically contemplated its restoration. In the so-called second New Deal, as in the "first," government remained largely the benefactor of big business, and some more advanced businessmen realized this.[58]

Roosevelt could attack the "economic royalists" and endorse the TNEC investigation of economic concentration, but he was unprepared to resist the basic demands of big business. While there was ambiguity in his treatment of oligopoly, it was more the confusion of means than of ends, for his tactics were never likely to impair concentration. Even the antitrust program under Thurman Arnold, concludes Frank Freidel, was "intended less to bust the trusts than to forestall too drastic legislation." Operating through consent decrees and designed to reduce prices to the consumer, the program frequently "allowed industries to function much as they had in NRA days." In effect, then, throughout its variations, the New Deal had sought to cooperate with business.[59]

---

[56] *New York Times,* November 19, 1933; May 1, September 30, November 17, December 23, 1934; May 1, 3, 5, 28, 1935; "Chamber to Vote on NIRA," *Nation's Business,* XXII (December 1934), 51; "Business Wants a New NRA," *ibid.,* XXIII (February 1935), 60; "Listening in as Business Speaks," *ibid.,* XXIII (June 1935), 18, 20; William Wilson, "How the Chamber of Commerce Viewed the NRA," *Mid-America,* XLIII (January, 1962), 95–108.

[57] *New York Times,* May 3, 4, 12, 1935. On the steel industry see L. W. Moffet, "This Week in Washington," *Iron Age,* CXXXV (March 21, 1935), 41; *ibid.* (April 18, 1935), 49; "NRA Future Not Settled by Senate Committee's Action for Extension," *ibid.* (May 9, 1935), 58.

[58] Ellis W. Hawley, *The New Deal and the Problem of Monopoly* (Princeton, 1966), pp. 205–86.

[59] Freidel, *The New Deal,* pp. 18–19. On Arnold's efforts, see Wendell Berge Diary, 1938–1939, Berge Papers, Library of Congress; and Gene Gressley, "Thurman Arnold, Antitrust, and the New Deal," *Business History Review,* XXXVIII (Summer, 1964), 214–31. For characteristic Roosevelt rhetoric emphasizing the effort of his government

Though vigorous in rhetoric and experimental in tone, the New Deal was narrow in its goals and wary of bold economic reform. Roosevelt's sense of what was politically desirable was frequently more restricted than others' views of what was possible and necessary. Roosevelt's limits were those of ideology; they were not inherent in experimentalism. For while the President explored the narrow center, and some New Dealers considered bolder possibilities, John Dewey, the philosopher of experimentalism, moved far beyond the New Deal and sought to reshape the system. Liberalism, he warned, "must now become radical. . . . For the gulf between what the actual situation makes possible and the actual state itself is so great that it cannot be bridged by piecemeal policies undertaken *ad hoc*." [60] The boundaries of New Deal experimentalism, as Howard Zinn has emphasized, could extend far beyond Roosevelt's cautious ventures. Operating within very safe channels, Roosevelt not only avoided Marxism and the socialization of property, but he also stopped far short of other possibilities—communal direction of production or the organized distribution of surplus. The President and many of his associates were doctrinaires of the center, and their maneuvers in social reform were limited to cautious excursions. [61]

[VI]

Usually opportunistic and frequently shifting, the New Deal was restricted by its ideology. It ran out of fuel not because of the conservative opposition, [62] but because it ran out of ideas. [63] Acknowledging the end in 1939, Roosevelt proclaimed, "We have now passed the period of internal conflict in the launching of our program of social reform. Our full energies may now be released to invigorate the processes of recovery in order to preserve our reforms. . . ." [64]

---

to subdue "the forces of selfishness and of lust for power," see his campaign address of October 31, 1936, his press conference of January 4, 1938, and his message of April 29, 1938, in *FDR Papers*, V, 568–69, and VII, 11, 305–32.

[60] Dewey, *Liberalism and Social Action* (New York, 1935), p. 62.

[61] Howard Zinn, in *New Deal Thought*, pp. xxvi–xxxi, discusses this subject and has influenced my thought. Also consider those whom Zinn cites: Edmund Wilson, "The Myth of Marxist Dialectic," *Partisan Review*, VI (Fall, 1938), 66–81; William Ernest Hocking, "The Future of Liberalism," *The Journal of Philosophy*, XXXII (April 25, 1935), 230–47; Stuart Chase, "Eating Without Working: A Moral Disquisition," *Nation*, CXXXVII (July 22, 1933), 93–94.

[62] See James T. Patterson, "A Conservative Coalition Forms in Congress, 1933–1939," *Journal of American History*, LII (March 1966), 757–72.

[63] Hofstadter, *American Political Tradition*, p. 342; cf., Freidel, *The New Deal*, p. 20.

[64] Roosevelt's annual message to the Congress on January 4, 1939, *FDR Papers*, VIII, 7.

The sad truth was that the heralded reforms were severely limited, that inequality continued, that efforts at recovery had failed. Millions had come to accept the depression as a way of life. A decade after the Great Crash, when millions were still unemployed, Fiorello LaGuardia recommended that "we accept the inevitable, that we are now in a new normal." [65] "It was reasonable to expect a probable minimum of 4,000,000 to 5,000,000 unemployed," Harry Hopkins had concluded.[66] Even that level was never reached, for business would not spend and Roosevelt refused to countenance the necessary expenditures. "It was in economics that our troubles lay," Tugwell wrote. "For their solution his [Roosevelt's] progressivism, his new deal was pathetically insufficient. . . ." [67]

Clinging to faith in fiscal orthodoxy even when engaged in deficit spending, Roosevelt had been unwilling to greatly unbalance the budget. Having pledged in his first campaign to cut expenditures and to restore the balanced budget, the President had at first adopted recovery programs that would not drain government finances. Despite a burst of activity under the Civil Works Administration during the first winter, public works expenditures were frequently slow and cautious. Shifting from direct relief, which Roosevelt (like Hoover) considered "a narcotic, a subtle destroyer of the human spirit," the government moved to work relief.[68] ("It saves his skill. It gives him a chance to do something socially useful," said Hopkins.[69]) By 1937 the government had poured enough money into the economy to spur production to within 10 percent of 1929 levels, but unemployment still hovered over seven million. Yet so eager was the President to balance the budget that he cut expenditures for public works and relief, and plunged the economy into a greater depression. While renewing expenditures, Roosevelt remained cautious in his fiscal policy, and the nation still had almost nine million unemployed in 1939. After nearly six years of struggling with the depression, the Roosevelt administration could not lead the nation to recovery, but it had relieved suffering.[70] In most of America, starvation was no longer possible. Perhaps that was the most humane achievement of the New Deal.

Its efforts on behalf of humane *reform* were generally faltering and shallow, of more value to the middle classes, of less value to organized

[65] Fiorello LaGuardia to James Byrnes, April 5, 1939, Box 2584, LaGuardia Papers, Municipal Archives, New York City.

[66] Hopkins, "The Future of Relief," *New Republic,* XC (February 10, 1937), 8.

[67] Tugwell, *The Stricken Land* (Garden City, N.Y., 1947), p. 681.

[68] Roosevelt's speech of January 4, 1935, *FDR Papers,* IV, 19.

[69] Hopkins, "Federal Emergency Relief," *Vital Speeches,* I (December 31, 1934), 211.

[70] Broadus Mitchell, *Depression Decade: From New Era Through New Deal* (New York, 1947), pp. 37–54.

workers, of even less to the marginal men. In conception and in practice, seemingly humane efforts revealed the shortcomings of American liberalism. For example, public housing, praised as evidence of the federal government's concern for the poor, was limited in scope (to 180,000 units) and unfortunate in results.[71] It usually meant the consolidation of ghettos, the robbing of men of their dignity, the treatment of men as wards with few rights. And slum clearance came to mean "Negro clearance" and removal of the other poor. Of much of this liberal reformers were unaware, and some of the problems can be traced to the structure of bureaucracy and to the selection of government personnel and social workers who disliked the poor.[72] But the liberal conceptions, it can be argued, were also flawed for there was no willingness to consult the poor, nor to encourage their participation. Liberalism was elitist. Seeking to build America in their own image, liberals wanted to create an environment which they thought would restructure character and personality more appropriate to white, middle-class America.

While slum dwellers received little besides relief from the New Deal, and their needs were frequently misunderstood, Negroes as a group received even less assistance—less than they needed and sometimes even less than their proportion in the population would have justified. Under the NRA they were frequently dismissed and their wages were sometimes below the legal minimum. The Civilian Conservation Corps left them "forgotten" men—excluded, discriminated against, segregated. In general, what the Negroes gained—relief, WPA jobs, equal pay on some federal projects—was granted them as poor people, not as Negroes.[73] To many black men the distinction was unimportant, for no government had ever given them so much. "My friends, go home and turn Lincoln's picture to the wall," a Negro publisher told his race. "That debt has been payed in full." [74]

---

[71] Housing and Home Finance Agency, *First Annual Report* (Washington, 1947), pp. 24–25. Timothy McDonnell, *The Wagner Housing Act* (Chicago, 1957), pp. 53, 186–88, concludes that the Wagner bill would have passed earlier if Roosevelt had supported it.

[72] Jane Jacobs, *The Life and Death of Great American Cities* (New York, 1963). Racial policy was locally determined. U.S. Housing Authority, *Bulletin No. 18 on Policy and Procedure* (1938), pp. 7–8; Robert C. Weaver, "The Negro in a Program of Public Housing," *Opportunity*, XVI (July 1938), 1–6. Three fifths of all families, reported Weaver, were earning incomes "below the figure necessary to afford respectable living quarters without undue skimping on other necessities." (p. 4)

[73] Allen Kifer, "The Negro Under the New Deal, 1933–1941," (unpublished Ph.D. dissertation, University of Wisconsin, 1961), *passim*. The National Youth Agency was an exception, concludes Kifer, p. 139. For Negro protests about New Deal discrimination, John P. Davis, "What Price National Recovery?," *Crisis*, XL (December 1933), 272; Charles Houston and Davis, "TVA: Lily-White Construction," *Crisis*, XLI (October 1934), 291.

[74] Robert Vann of the *Pittsburgh Courier*, quoted in Joseph Alsop and William Kintner, "The Guffey," *Saturday Evening Post*, CCX (March 26, 1938), 6. Vann had offered this advice in 1932.

Bestowing recognition on some Negro leaders, the New Deal appointed them to agencies as advisers—the "black cabinet." Probably more dramatic was the advocacy of Negro rights by Eleanor Roosevelt. Some whites like Harold Ickes and Aubrey Williams even struggled cautiously to break down segregation. But segregation did not yield, and Washington itself remained a segregated city. The white South was never challenged, the Fourteenth Amendment never used to assist Negroes. Never would Roosevelt expend political capital in an assault upon the American caste system.[75] Despite the efforts of the NAACP to dramatize the Negroes' plight as second-class citizens, subject to brutality and often without legal protection, Roosevelt would not endorse the anti-lynching bill. ("No government pretending to be civilized can go on condoning such atrocities," H. L. Mencken testified. "Either it must make every possible effort to put them down or it must suffer the scorn and contempt of Christendom.") [76] Unwilling to risk schism with Southerners ruling committees, Roosevelt capitulated to the forces of racism.[77]

Even less bold than in economic reform, the New Deal left intact the race relations of America. Yet its belated and cautious recognition of the black man was great enough to woo Negro leaders and even to court the masses. One of the bitter ironies of these years is that a New Dealer could tell the NAACP in 1936: "Under our new conception of democracy, the Negro will be given the chance to which he is entitled. . . ." But it was true, Ickes emphasized, that "The greatest advance [since Reconstruction] toward assuring the Negro that degree of justice to which he is entitled and that equality of opportunity under the law which is implicit in his American citizenship, has been made since Franklin D. Roosevelt was sworn in as President. . . ." [78]

It was not in the cities and not among the Negroes but in rural America that Roosevelt administration made its (philosophically) boldest efforts: creation of the Tennessee Valley Authority and the later attempt to construct seven little valley authorities. Though conservation was not a new federal policy and government-owned utilities were sanctioned by munici-

---

[75] See Eleanor Roosevelt to Walter White, May 2, 29, 1934, April 21, 1938, White Papers, Yale University; Frank Freidel, *F.D.R. and the South* (Baton Rouge, La., 1965), pp. 71–102.

[76] Quoted from Senate Judiciary Committee, 74th Cong., 1st Sess., *Punishment for the Crime of Lynching, Hearings,* p. 23. Cf. Harold Ickes, "The Negro as a Citizen," June 29, 1936, Oswald Garrison Villard Papers, Harvard University.

[77] Roy Wilkins, Columbia Oral History Memoir, p. 98; Lester Granger, Columbia Oral History Memoir, p. 105, complains that Wagner had refused to include in his labor bill a prohibition against unions excluding workers because of race. When Wagner counseled a delay, Negroes felt, according to Granger, that the New Deal "was concerned with covering up, putting a fine cover over what there was, not bothering with the inequities."

[78] Ickes, "The Negro as a Citizen." Ickes had said, "since the Civil War."

pal experience, federal activity in this area constituted a challenge to corporate enterprise and an expression of concern about the poor. A valuable example of regional planning and a contribution to regional prosperity, TVA still fell far short of expectations. The agency soon retreated from social planning. ("From 1936 on," wrote Tugwell, "the TVA should have been called the Tennessee Valley Power Production and Flood Control Corporation.") Fearful of antagonizing the powerful interests, its agricultural program neglected the tenants and the sharecroppers.[79]

To urban workingmen the New Deal offered some, but limited, material benefits. Though the government had instituted contributory social security and unemployment insurance, its much-heralded Fair Labor Standards Act, while prohibiting child labor, was a greater disappointment. It exempted millions from its wages-and-hours provisions. So unsatisfactory was the measure that one congressman cynically suggested, "Within 90 days after appointment of the administrator, she should report to Congress whether anyone is subject to this bill." [80] Requiring a minimum of twenty-five cents an hour ($11 a week for 44 hours), it raised the wages of only about a half-million at a time when nearly twelve million workers in interstate commerce were earning less than forty cents an hour.[81]

More important than these limited measures was the administration's support, albeit belated, of the organization of labor and the right of collective bargaining. Slightly increasing organized workers' share of the national income,[82] the new industrial unions extended job security to millions who were previously subject to the whim of management. Unionization freed them from the perils of a free market.

By assisting labor, as well as agriculture, the New Deal started the institutionalization of larger interest groups into a new political economy. Joining business as tentative junior partners, they shared the consensus on the value of large-scale corporate capitalism, and were permitted to participate in the competition for the division of shares. While failing to redistribute income, the New Deal modified the political structure at the price of excluding many from the process of decision making. To many what was offered in fact was symbolic representation, formal representation. It was not the industrial workers necessarily who were recognized, but their unions and leaders; it was not even the farmers, but their organizations and

---

[79] Schlesinger, *Politics of Upheaval*, pp. 362–80; quotation from Tugwell, p. 371.

[80] Martin Dies, quoted by Burns, *Congress on Trial* (New York, 1949), p. 77.

[81] The law raised standards to thirty cents and forty-two hours in 1939 and forty cents and forty hours in 1945. U.S. Department of Labor, BLS, *Labor Information Bulletin* (April 1939), pp. 1–3.

[82] Arthur M. Ross, *Trade Union Wage Policy* (Berkeley, Cal., 1948), pp. 113–28.

leaders. While this was not a conscious design, it was the predictable result of conscious policies. It could not have been easily avoided, for it was part of the price paid by a large society unwilling to consider radical new designs for the distribution of power and wealth.

[VII]

In the deepest sense, this new form of representation was rooted in the liberal's failure to endorse a meaningful egalitarianism which would provide actual equality of opportunity. It was also the limited concern with equality and justice that accounted for the shallow efforts of the New Deal and left so many Americans behind. The New Deal was neither a "third American Revolution," as Carl Degler suggests, nor even a "half-way revolution," as William Leuchtenburg concludes. Not only was the extension of representation to new groups less than full-fledged partnership, but the New Deal neglected many Americans—sharecroppers, tenant farmers, migratory workers and farm laborers, slum dwellers, unskilled workers, and the unemployed Negroes. They were left outside the new order.[83] As Roosevelt asserted in 1937 (in a classic understatement), one third of the nation was "ill-nourished, ill-clad, ill-housed." [84]

Yet, by the power of rhetoric and through the appeals of political organization, the Roosevelt government managed to win or retain the allegiance of these peoples. Perhaps this is one of the crueler ironies of liberal politics, that the marginal men trapped in hopelessness were seduced by rhetoric, by the style and movement, by the symbolism of efforts seldom reaching beyond words. In acting to protect the institution of private property and in advancing the interests of corporate capitalism, the New Deal assisted the middle and upper sectors of society. It protected them, sometimes, even at the cost of injuring the lower sectors. Seldom did it bestow much of substance upon the lower classes. Never did the New Deal seek to organize these groups into independent political forces. Seldom did it risk antagonizing established interests. For some this would constitute a puzzling defect of liberalism; for some, the failure to achieve true liberalism. To others it would emphasize the inherent shortcomings of American liberal democracy. As the nation prepared for war, liberalism, by accepting private property and federal assistance to corporate capitalism, was not

---

[83] Leuchtenburg, *F.D.R.*, pp. 346–47. The Bankhead-Jones Farm Tenancy Act of 1937 provided some funds for loans to selected tenants who wished to purchase farms. In 1935, there were 2,865,155 tenants (about 42 percent of all farmers), and by 1941, 20,-748 had received loans. *Farm Tenancy: Report of the President's Committee* (Washington, February 1937), Table I, p. 89; *Report of the Administrator of the Farm Security Administration*, 1941 (Washington, 1941), p. 17.

[84] Roosevelt's Inaugural Address of January 20, 1937, *FDR Papers*, VI, 5.

prepared effectively to reduce inequities, to redistribute political power, or to extend equality from promise to reality.

SUGGESTED READING

Howard Zinn's analysis in Zinn, ed., *New Deal Social Thought* ° (1966); Paul Conkin's in *The New Deal* ° (1967); and Brad Wiley's in "The Myth of New Deal Reform," an ERAP pamphlet reprinted in Tom Christoffel *et al.*, eds., *Up Against the American Myth* (1970) have all been classified as radical or New Left interpretations. Conkin's book does not comfortably fit the classification, for much of his concern is that the New Deal lacked a coherent ideology, though he does note its shortcomings and suggest that much greater accomplishments were probably unlikely in America. A neglected review-essay, which some might deem radical or New Left, is Jacob Cohen's "Schlesinger and the New Deal," *Dissent*, VIII (Autumn 1961).

JOHN B. KIRBY

The Roosevelt Administration and Blacks: An Ambivalent Legacy

INTRODUCTION

Roosevelt's New Deal policies were under periodic attack from liberals outside the government who wanted the administration to be more forceful in combating the Depression, assisting organized labor, restraining business power, or changing the distribution of income. The problem of race relations did not attract the same liberal concern. Few white reformers devoted much energy to improving race relations or seeking government aid for the black man. In these years, liberalism had not yet developed much sensitivity to the difficulties confronted by blacks and was only slowly undergoing a redefinition that stressed opposition to racial discrimination and segregation. Not surprisingly, then, the plight of America's black citizens did not weigh heavily on the minds of most white citizens.

This essay was written especially for this volume.

The problems of black Americans remained only a peripheral concern for the New Deal. Confronting economic crisis and struggling to repair the economy, the government was not prepared to bestow much attention or to expend any political capital on the black man. "Roosevelt's actual commitments to the American Negro were slim," concludes Leslie Fishel, Jr. "He was more a symbol than an activist" ("The Negro in the New Deal Era," *Wisconsin Magazine of History,* XLVIII [Winter 1964–65], p. 111).

The President, as Roy Wilkins of the NAACP noted years later, befriended the black "only insofar as he refused to exclude [him] from the general policies that applied to the whole country" (Columbia University oral history memoir, p. 51). Some of the New Deal programs seriously disadvantaged blacks economically, and often contributed to discrimination and segregation. In most programs the number of blacks involved fell well below their need and sometimes even below their percentage in the population.

Even the best intentions of white liberals within the administration, explains John Kirby of Denison University in the following essay, were modified by racial considerations—real or feared racial antagonisms, the political weakness of blacks, and the ideological limitations of white liberals themselves. Kirby's most significant contribution is his analysis of the white liberal ideology. These liberals, he stresses, viewed the race problem primarily in economic terms and therefore concluded that improvement of the blacks' economic position would ultimately secure their equality in the society. For most liberals, the race problem was a class problem, and white prejudice was expected to crumble as blacks advanced economically. These liberals consequently counseled blacks to be patient and not to press for rights in ways that might intensify white passions and jeopardize federal programs assisting blacks economically. The New Deal liberals, as Kirby emphasizes, were blind to the deep-rooted racism that W. E. B. Du Bois had recognized in white America. They could not confront adequately the full dimensions of racism, and that inability hampered the success of New Deal race policies, created serious problems for blacks in understanding their own plight, and bestowed on future generations a mixed legacy in charting strategies to improve race relations.

The material assistance that the New Deal provided for blacks, as Kirby acknowledges, made it difficult for black intellectuals critical of the Roosevelt administration to establish successful organizations. Efforts by radicals to create black and white working-class solidarity foundered for various reasons, including the genial assumption that racisim would easily yield to class interest. Du Bois' more pessimistic counsel on the depths of white racism, as well as his emphases on community organization, racial pride, and a separate black community, also commanded little respect among the black masses.

In his analysis of New Deal policies and their effects on black understanding and strategies, Kirby chose not to investigate the reasons for the great affection of the black masses for Roosevelt. Perhaps their admiration for the man in the White House reflects their belief that half a loaf was better than none, and also their convictions that they had no share in the American dream and no right to expect equal treatment from the government. Perhaps the combination of racial and class oppression had left them with so little hope that they were grateful for the limited benefits bestowed on them. It is a fact that they could not be easily wooed by the Republicans, whom blacks in great numbers abandoned in the 1934 elections, or by radical groups. The GOP, which did not control access to federal coffers, could not court blacks with federal aid, and the strategy of the congressional party, which joined in the name of states rights with the Democratic South against antilynching and anti–poll tax measures, belied the comparatively strong promises of the party platform. Even radical groups, with richer hopes and more egalitarian conceptions than the New Deal's, could not gain a sympathetic hearing from most blacks in these years. What remains to be investigated is how the hegemony of white America shaped black expectations and loyalties, and how and why blacks were occasionally able to break free of the subtle ideological constraints to launch some protests against injustice and exploitation.

Few problems have caused liberal reformers greater difficulty than the issue of race. In almost every instance, racial considerations have constituted the limits or have become the exception to the general thrust of American reform. From Progressivism to the Great Society, the one ingredient that has never fit into the twentieth-century liberal reformers' package of social cures has been the color question—the plight of the Afro-American, the Indian, the Oriental, and the Mexican-American. The "color-line," as W. E. B. DuBois prophesied years ago, has been the major unsolved American problem.

At no time since the Reconstruction era were reform-minded men and women forced to face the "Negro problem" as they were in the Roosevelt years from 1933 to 1945. The manner in which they confronted that challenge and the success or failure of their endeavor has been the subject of much controversy among scholars and nonscholars, blacks as well as whites. In 1944, Gunnar Myrdal asserted in his now classic study, *An American Dilemma*, that the New Deal "had changed the whole configuration of the Negro problem." When "looked upon from the practical and political viewpoints," he argued, "the contrast between the present situation and the one prior to the New Deal is striking." [1]

But to what degree and in what sense was it "striking"? By 1945, black Americans remained, as they were in 1933, firmly segregated in American life. Not even the armed forces were integrated. Blacks continued to be confined to a separate and unequal status in most of the South, while in the North increasing numbers of black migrants swelled the urban slum ghettos. The one piece of legislation that the National Association for the Advancement of Colored People had fervently advocated since the 1920's, federal antilynching, was in 1945 still little more than a hopeful dream of its chief sponsor, Walter White. Race riots in Detroit, Los Angeles, and New York in 1943 manifested the frustration of blacks and the intransigence of whites. Despite the creation of the federal Fair Employment Practice Committee in 1941, and the later civil rights legislation of the Truman administration, it was not until the Supreme Court ruling against the "separate but equal" doctrine in 1954 that the legal structure of race segregation was directly challenged. And large numbers of white Americans were not forced to confront the true dimensions of their country's racial crisis until the late 1950's and early 1960's, when blacks took matters into their own hands and moved into the streets.

In light of the conditions and events after 1944, how is Myrdal's statement that the Roosevelt years transformed the "whole configuration" of the "Negro problem" to be understood? Myrdal believed that the growth of the federal welfare state was of central importance in altering the race issue. "Until the 1930s," he noted, the "practical Negro problem involved civil rights, education, charity and little more." Because of the New Deal's response to the depression, the problem was redefined "in pace with public policy in the 'new welfare state,'" and thus came to include not only civil rights but also "housing, nutrition, medicine, education, relief and social security, wages and hours, working conditions, child and woman labor." [2] The "great import of the New Deal to the Negro," he concluded, was that for the "first time in the history of the nation" the federal government had done "something substantial in a social way without excluding the Negro." Black people were thus given a "broader and more variegated front to defend and from which to push forward." [3]

The New Deal's meaning to black Americans can be most clearly as-

---

[1] Gunnar Myrdal, An American Dilemma: The Negro Problem and Modern Democracy, 2nd ed, Vol. I (New York, 1962), p. 74.

[2] Ibid.

[3] Ibid. Myrdal's view of the welfare state's importance to blacks has been restated by a number of later historians. See Leslie H. Fishel, Jr., "The Negro in the New Deal Era," Wisconsin Magazine of History, XLVIII (Winter 1964–65), 115–17; Arthur M. Schlesinger, Jr., The Politics of Upheaval (Boston, 1960), pp. 432–34; J. Saunders Reading, The Lonesome Road (Garden City, N.Y., 1958), pp. 260, 269–70; August Meier and El-

certained by asking two questions: first, did the liberal reform philosophy of the "new welfare state" truly transform the conditions of black people? Second, to what extent did the inclusion of the "Negro problem" in the general New Deal reform impulse affect the tactics by which blacks pursued their struggle for equality and human freedom? Unquestionably, Myrdal was right that the enormous influence of federal power in the 1930's and 1940's had a significant impact on the black population; but it remains to be fully determined what the ultimate value of that impact was and what its legacy is for blacks and whites in the 1970's.

Were white New Dealers actively involved in the improvement of the black situation in the 1930's and 1940's? In the sense of their presenting a concrete program directed specifically to blacks, the answer is no. President Roosevelt himself had little fundamental understanding of racial conditions and during his presidency indicated only vague concern for the plight of black America. Although at times he quietly lent support to individuals and governmental agencies who were involved in aiding blacks, he was unwilling to invest his considerable political prestige in confronting racism within his own party or within the country at large.[4] One scholar has recently stated that under FDR the New Deal had "no fixed policy with regard to the protection of black people."[5] What aid blacks received resulted from efforts by a small group of white New Dealers like Harold Ickes, Will Alexander, Aubrey Williams, Clark Foreman, Hallie Flanagan, and Eleanor Roosevelt who tried to insure the inclusion of blacks in the general reform programs. These public officials—particularly Ickes and

---

liot Rudwick, *From Plantation to Ghetto: An Interpretive History of American Negroes* (New York, 1966), p. 211; John Hope Franklin, *From Slavery to Freedom*, 2nd ed. (New York, 1967, pp. 527–40; and a lengthy, if somewhat confusing, discussion by Bernard Sternsher in Sternsher, ed., *The Negro in Depression and War: Prelude to Revolution, 1930–1945* (Chicago, 1969), pp. 3–6, 45–52.

[4] In respect to FDR's working behind the scenes, Robert K. Carr indicates that the President provided considerable support to the Civil Rights Section (CRS) of the Justice Department in prosecuting lynching cases involving blacks. "The interest of the CRS in the lynching problem was increased greatly in July, 1942," Carr notes, "when the Department of Justice received a directive from President Roosevelt ordering it to make an automatic investigation in all cases of Negro deaths where the suspicion of lynching is present" (*Federal Protection of Civil Rights: Quest for a Sword* [Ithaca, N.Y., 1947] pp. 163–64). I am indebted to Thomas A. Krueger for calling my attention to the Carr book and to this particular passage.

But James T. Patterson points out that "Roosevelt . . . assiduously avoided ruffling southern feelings on race problems. Though sympathetic to the plight of the Negro, he had not pressed for civil rights legislation and had tried to keep race issues out of Congress" (*Congressional Conservatism and the New Deal: The Growth of the Conservative Coalition in Congress, 1933–1939* [Lexington, Ky., 1967] p. 98).

[5] Raymond Wolters, *Negroes and the Great Depression: The Problem of Economic Recovery* (Westport, Conn., 1970), p. x. For a similar statement, see Benjamin Quarles, *The Negro in the Making of America* (New York, 1965), p. 209, and Allen Kifer, "The Negro Under the New Deal, 1933–1941," unpublished doctoral dissertation, University of Wisconsin, 1961, p. 272.

Mrs. Roosevelt—operated as the "conscience" of the government and served as an official link to the black community.[6]

But the absence of any fixed policy does not necessarily mean that there did not exist at the time a conceptual framework, one to which even the President gave official sanction, that related New Deal reformism to the "Negro problem." New Deal programs—from the National Recovery Administration to Social Security and wage-and-hour legislation—contained a common thesis that some white liberals frequently related to the black struggle in America. The essence of that thesis was stated by Harold Ickes to the NAACP in 1936 when he argued that the ultimate goal of the Roosevelt administration was to achieve "the greatest good for the greatest number" and under the New Deal's "conception of democracy, the Negro will be given the chance to which he is entitled—not because he will be singled out for special consideration but because he preeminently belongs to the class that the new democracy is designed especially to aid." [7]

The black man would be helped not because he was black but because he was an American. Sharing the same American values as whites, blacks would progress from the depths of poverty and oppression by way of programs aimed at every American whom "the new democracy" was "designed to aid." White liberals argued, in essence, that a combination of factors, emanating from the depression, had generated a host of new conditions that made the future of black people and black-white relations extremely hopeful. The economic collapse of 1929 signified to them the end of a distinctive phase in American life, a phase characterized predominantly by obsession with individualism.[8] Eleanor Roosevelt referred to it as the "era of the pioneer and rugged individualist"; Harold Ickes called it the era of the exploiter.[9] But the "frontier" had now passed; America had emerged, whether by choice or by necessity, a more constrained

---

[6] Kifer discusses some of the activities of these New Dealers; see especially his summary to "The Negro Under the New Deal," pp. 273–80. Also, Wolters, *Negroes and the Great Depression,* pp. 72–73, 196–97, 200, 203, 204–05; Schlesinger, Jr., *Politics of Upheaval,* pp. 432–36; William E. Leuchtenburg, *Franklin D. Roosevelt and the New Deal* (New York, 1963), pp. 186–87; and Tamara K. Hareven, *Eleanor Roosevelt: An American Conscience* (Chicago, 1968), pp. 114–24.

[7] Harold L. Ickes, "The Negro as Citizen," *The Crisis,* XLIII (August 1936), 23.

[8] See, for instance, Harold L. Ickes, *The New Democracy* (New York, 1934), written with Clark Foreman; Ickes, "The Social Implications of the Roosevelt Administration," *Congressional Digest,* XIII (June–July 1934), 170–72; Clark Foreman, in Chicago *Defender,* November 18, 1933, and New York *Times,* April 15, 1934; Hareven, *Eleanor Roosevelt,* pp. 130–32, and Eleanor Roosevelt's column in *Women's Home Companion,* LXI (November 1934), 14.

[9] Roosevelt, *Women's Home Companion,* LXI (November 1934), 14; Ickes, *New Democracy,* pp. 32, 43.

and closed society, economically and socially, as well as physically. The 1930's, liberals felt, were the "beginning of a new era"; one that no longer assumed that laissez-faire and individual liberty were the guiding American principles but that now stressed faith in planning, the need to enhance equality and the quality of American life. As Steven Kesselman had noted in a study of New Deal ideology, what inevitably followed from the "kind of thinking about the closing of the frontier" and the "end of economic expansion" was belief in the "need for, and the possibilities of, coordinated planning from above." [10]

"Coordinated planning" became the liberal strategy of the 1930's and 1940's, and many racial reformers believed it had a special importance to the black population. They interpreted the depression as a turning point in the black American experience. The "Negro problem" had always been at its root, they argued, an economic problem. Certainly the black man's situation had been complicated and made worse by political opportunism in the past and by the promulgation of unscientific theories regarding race "inferiority," but these were simply manifestations of the deeper dilemma; they were rationalizations for the economic oppression and exploitation of black people.[11] It was, as Eleanor Roosevelt stated, essentially because "colored people, not only in the South but in the North as well, have been economically at a low level . . . that they have been physically and intellectually at a low level." [12] What the depression had done, Mrs. Roosevelt and others believed, was to underline that fact by showing clearly the inherent economic instability of the black position in American life.

Liberals maintained further that the depression's devastation had the effect of transcending racial classifications and considerations. They argued that common adversity would create a common bond among diverse racial and ethnic groups as they became aware that they all suffered from similar deprivations and shared similar needs. Creation of a sense of shared values and goals was of prime importance in building the interdependency and the unity necessary for centralized government planning and for construc-

---

[10] Steven Kesselman, "The Frontier Thesis and the Great Depression," *Journal of the History of Ideas*, XXIX (April–June 1968), 264.

[11] The clearest statement of this is found in a number of speeches Harold Ickes gave before black groups in the 1930's. See, for example, Ickes' speech to the Chicago Urban League, February 26, 1936, and "The Negro Holds His Fate in His Own Hands," a speech intended for delivery at Wilberforce University, October 10, 1936, Franklin D. Roosevelt Library, Official File 6. Foreman's ideas are found in Chicago *Defender*, November 18, 1933, and New York *Times*, April 15, 1934; see also Will Alexander, "Our Conflicting Racial Policies," *Harper's Magazine*, CXC (January 1945), 172–79, Pittsburgh *Courier*, March 17, 1934; Eleanor Roosevelt, "The Negro and Social Change," *Opportunity*, XIV (January 1936), 22–23, and "Address," *National Conference on Fundamental Problems in the Education of Negroes, Washington, D.C., May 9–12, 1934* (Washington, D.C., U.S. Department of Interior, 1935), pp. 9–10.

[12] Roosevelt, "The Negro and Social Change," 22.

tion of the "new democracy." [13] New Dealers viewed the "Negro problem" as basically a class problem and believed that blacks and whites could overcome the "race conscious" stereotypes that had separated them in the past. They argued that government need spend less time concerning itself with the specific issue of race, since racial distinctions and hatreds would dissolve once New Deal economic and social reforms took firm root.[14] Harold Ickes noted that he had always been "interested in seeing that the Negro" had a "square deal"; but he had "never dissipated" his "strength against the particular stone wall of segregation." That wall would crumble, he was certain, "when the Negro has brought himself to a higher educational and economic status." [15]

For liberals like Ickes, then, the key to altering the traditional pattern of race relations in America lay in raising the "educational and economic status" of blacks through New Deal reform and recovery efforts and measures such as full employment.[16] Ickes and other white liberals assumed that white racial bias was based on a belief in the continued low level of black existence. Remove the source that nourished this attitude by elevating the economic and social status of blacks and no longer would there exist any rational basis for white bigotry; then all Americans, black and white, would see that they belonged to the "same human family," possessed the "same weaknesses," and were "capable of the same sacrifices and endowed with the same aspirations. . . ." [17] As Ickes's white assistant and the first New Deal advisor on "Negro Affairs," Clark Foreman, put it, under the Roosevelt administration "prejudice, unfair discrimination and exploitation" would be made "unprofitable." [18]

---

[13] Interdependency and unity were common themes of liberal New Dealers, particulary as they related administration reforms to changes within the black community and to the development of better relations between blacks and whites. Eleanor Roosevelt expressed a common belief when she stated that the "day of selfishness" was over; "the day of really working together has come, and we must learn to work together, all of us, regardless of race or creed or color. . . . We go ahead together or we go down together." ("Address," p. 10)

[14] This did not mean, of course, that New Dealers did not work to insure blacks inclusion within federal programs. But they felt that if this were achieved, if blacks could develop an economic base as a result of New Deal reforms, then the traditional racial divisions would gradually disappear.

[15] Harold L. Ickes, The Secret Diary of Harold L. Ickes, Vol. II (New York, 1954), p. 115.

[16] See Ickes, "To Have Jobs or to Have Not," Negro Digest, IV (January 1946), 73–75.

[17] Ickes' speech to the Chicago Urban League, Franklin D. Roosevelt Library, Official File 6. In 1946, Ickes stated that the "Negro problem merges into and becomes inseparable from the great problem of American citizens generally, who are at or below the line in decency and comfort from those who are not" (Ickes, "To Have Jobs or to Have Not," 73).

[18] Clark Foreman in Pittsburgh Courier, April 14, 1934. For a general critique of white New Deal racial thought containing much of the above discussion, see John B. Kirby,

Such optimistic theories provided the rationale by which liberal reformers emphasized the importance of the New Deal to the black community. But when they attempted to put these into practice as in the case of the early recovery measures, the results were less sanguine. The National Recovery Administration was designed to increase industrial production and to raise the wage and working standards of the average American laborer. Its effect on blacks was considerably different. NRA provided little real protection for black laborers caught up in the traditional squeeze between the discriminatory practices of trade unions and employer groups. NRA codes were often ignored in their case through devices such as occupational and geographical job classifications, wage loopholes, and simple lack of enforcement. When the minimum wage-and-hour standards were adequately enforced, the effects were equally harmful, as contemporary critics pointed out, since blacks were displaced by whites, primarily in the South, or lost their jobs when marginal industries, unable to compete in compliance with NRA wage levels, closed their doors. As consumers, black people were also "affected adversely . . . by the rise in the cost of living which occurred when businessmen passed along the higher cost of NRA wages for white workers." [19] The Agricultural Adjustment Administration's cotton subsidy or crop reduction program left black and white tenant farmers and sharecroppers at the mercy of racist land owners with no avenue for legal redress. Whatever the broad economic rationale behind it, AAA economic planning resulted in forcing large numbers of blacks off the land or reducing them to a peonage status, from which it was almost impossible for them to escape. Such a consequence was almost inevitable considering that the government allowed "both the formulation and administration of its cotton program to be controlled by those who were particularly sensitive to the power of southern congressmen and landowning farmers." [20]

In relief, employment, farm aid, and education, the New Deal had at best a mixed impact on the black community. Despite the frequent discrimination that took place at state and local levels, blacks did receive a

"The New Deal Era and Blacks; A Study of Black and White Race Thought, 1933–1945," unpublished doctoral dissertation, University of Illinois, 1971, pp. 17–105.

[19] Wolters, *Negroes and the Great Depression*, pp. 150–51; for a general description of the NRA's effect on blacks as workers and consumers, see also Wolters, pp. 83–215, especially, pp. 124–25, 148–55. For a contemporary account, see John P. Davis, "NRA Codifies Wage Slavery," *The Crisis*, XLI (October 1934), 298–99, 304; Davis, "What Price National Recovery?" *The Crisis*, XL (December 1933), 271–72, and Davis' testimony before the Finance Committee on the NRA, *Investigations of the National Recovery Administration*, April 13–18, 1935, 74th Congress, 1st Session, Senate Resolution 79 (Washington, D.C., 1935), pp. 2139–60.

[20] Wolters, *Negroes and the Great Depression*, p. 79. For studies dealing with a criticism of the AAA's effect on black and white farmers, see Charles Johnson, Edwin Embree, and Will Alexander, *The Collapse of Cotton Tenancy* (Chapel Hill, N.C., 1935); David Conrad, *The Forgotten Farmers: The Story of the Sharecroppers in the New Deal* (Urbana, Ill., 1965); and Wolters, pp. 3–55.

higher percentage of direct relief and relief work than their proportion of the population might have warranted.[21] As welcome as that undoubtedly was in the depression years, the increased numbers of blacks on federal welfare was less an indication of New Deal good will than it was the fact that whites were finding more job opportunities.[22] The same was true of the Civilian Conservation Corps. Although it discriminated against black applicants and often segregated them in its camps, black youth profited in considerable numbers from the existence of the CCC; after 1935, the ratio of blacks to whites increased even more.[23] But again, as was the case with relief, that fact simply underlined the difficulties young black men and women were experiencing in finding meaningful employment, while at the same time their white contemporaries were leaving the CCC for more permanent positions.[24]

One of the few attempts made to assure work opportunities for black Americans was carried out under Harold Ickes' Public Works Administration, through a labor quota system. Under this plan, based on the 1930 occupational census, local PWA contractors were required to employ a percentage of available skilled black workers. That plan was later carried over to the United States Housing Authority by black advisor Robert Weaver, who had originally helped to formulate it.[25] Yet Weaver later acknowledged that labor quotas were never intended to create additional jobs for blacks but to "regain lost ground; they were not designed to open new types of employment" since that would have been "most unrealistic . . . in a period when there was mass unemployment." [26]

Even if new jobs had been secured under the plan it would have affected only the handful of blacks who had skilled training. The same limitation also applied to the labor movement's importance to the black popu-

---

[21] Kifer, "The Negro Under the New Deal"; Richard Sterner, *The Negro's Share* (New York, 1943), pp. 239–46.

[22] See the perceptive comments of Forrester Washington, who briefly served as black advisor to the Federal Emergency Relief Administration, in "The Negro and Relief," *Proceedings*, National Conference of Social Work, 61st Annual Session, May 20–26, 1934, pp. 178–94. See also John P. Davis, *Let Us Build a National Negro Congress* (Washington, D.C., 1935), pp. 19–20.

[23] John A. Salmond, "The Civilian Conservation Corps and the Negro," *The Journal of American History*, LII (June 1965), 75–88; and Kifer, "The Negro Under the New Deal," pp. 5–75.

[24] Kifer, "The Negro Under the New Deal," pp. 67–68.

[25] Robert Weaver, "An Experiment in Negro Labor," *Opportunity*, XIV (October 1936), 296–97; Weaver, "Federal Aid, Local Control and Negro Participation," *Journal of Negro Education*, XI (January 1942), 47–59; Weaver, *Negro Labor: A National Problem* (New York, 1946), p. 11. Also, Wolters, *Negroes and the Great Depression*, pp. 200–03.

[26] Weaver, *Negro Labor*, pp. 13–15.

lation. Black people unquestionably benefited from the results of the Wagner Labor Relations Act and from the development of the less race conscious CIO, particularly during the war years. But they had to achieve their advantages for the most part without the help of the federal government, which capitulated to pressure from organized labor and accepted Section 7a of the NRA and the National Labor Relations Act without any guarantees against union racial discrimination.[27] More serious was the fact that neither the labor movement nor the New Deal took into account those who made up a large part of the black work force—farm laborers and household domestics. Both groups were left out of the union struggle and were excluded from coverage under the Social Security Act and the Fair Labor Standards Act.[28]

Race considerations constantly modified the best of liberal intentions. The politics of economic reform and recovery permitted real or feared racial antagonisms to dictate acquiescence to prevailing racial mores and folkways. Blacks received aid from the government but, in most instances, only within the bounds determined by white racial customs. Political capital was seldom exercised by the President or New Deal agencies in trying to overcome the antiblack attitudes that frequently influenced the administration's economic and welfare programs. The National Youth Administration, for instance, headed by southern white liberal Aubrey Williams and assisted by the charismatic black educator Mary McLeod Bethune funneled money directly to black college and graduate students and to black elementary and grammar school teachers, primarily in the South.[29] But

---

[27] For analysis of black reactions to section 7a, which gave labor collective bargaining rights, and the NLRA, see Wolters, *Negroes and the Great Depression*, pp. 169–92, and Wolters, "Closed Shop and White Shop: The Negro Response to Collective Bargaining, 1933–1935," in Milton Cantor, ed., *Black Labor in America* (Westport, Conn., 1969), pp. 137–52.

[28] See the discussion by a large cross section of black leaders at the 1937 and 1939 conferences sponsored by the National Youth Administration: *Report of the National Conference on the Problems of the Negro and Negro Youth* (Washington, D.C., 1937), *passim;* and National Conference on the Problems of the Negro and Negro Youth, *Proceedings of the Second Conference* (Washington, D.C., 1939), *passim.* Eleanor Roosevelt did call for the inclusion of domestics and farm laborers under Social Security and wage-and-hour legislation, see "Remarks," *Proceedings of the Second Conference*, p. 87. On blacks and the labor movement, see Marc Karson and Ronald Radosh, "The American Federation of Labor and Negro Workers, 1894–1949," and Sumner M. Rosen, "The CIO Era, 1935–1955," both in Julius Jacobson, ed., *The Negro and the American Labor Movement* (New York, 1968), pp. 155–208. Also, Alexander Saxton, "Race and the House of Labor," in Gary B. Nash and Richard Weiss, eds., *The Great Fear: Race in the Mind of America* (New York, 1970), pp. 98–120.

[29] "Final Report," National Youth Administration, National Archives, Record Group 119; Kifer, "The Negro Under the New Deal," pp. 136–38; George Philip Rawick, "The New Deal and Youth: The Civilian Conservation Corps, The National Youth Administration and the American Youth Congress," unpublished doctoral dissertation, University of Wisconsin, 1957, p. 250.

that assistance was made possible only through the NYA's sanction of the segregated southern school system and only by providing money on a separate basis. Still, John P. Davis, an informed black critic in the 1930's, charged that most of the assistance went essentially to middle-class youths, leaving the mass of black young people with little immediate or future support.[30]

Another example of the effect of racial bias was seen in the government's housing program. Of the forty-nine low-income projects built by the PWA between 1933 and 1937, fourteen were constructed for blacks alone and another seventeen for joint black and white occupancy. A little more than a third of the total housing units built under Ickes' direction were occupied by black people in 1940.[31] But the central consideration involved in the administration's housing scheme was more the stimulation of the economy than the improvement of relations between blacks and whites or the improvement of black and white ghetto existence. Instead of breaking down the barriers between the races, federal housing often increased them. Confronted by racist outcries from local officials and residents who protested against mixed housing proposals, Ickes, the PWA, and later the U.S. Housing Administration, generally capitulated. The result was that in the North almost all the housing projects that blacks occupied were built in all black neighborhoods. Weaver noted that "public housing prior to World War II, attempted to avoid the problem of residential segregation in the North by concentrating on slum sites and giving preference in tenant selection to the racial groups previously in the site and the surrounding neighborhood." [32] In the South, the tradition of separating the races was simply preserved by constructing separate black and white projects. Combined with the openly racist policies of the Federal Housing Administration, government housing in the long run had the effect of further confining black people to urban ghettos, though it may have been true for some that the living conditions in those ghettos were temporarily improved.[33]

Inability to overcome local hostility also plagued the highly respected Farm Security Administration. Created in part to deal with some of the social and economic problems either ignored or exacerbated by the

---

[30] Davis, *Let Us Build a National Negro Congress*, pp. 19–20; also, Rawick, "The New Deal and Youth," p. 250, and Kifer, "The Negro Under the New Deal," pp. 136–38.

[31] Sterner, *The Negro's Share*, p. 317.

[32] Robert Weaver, *The Negro Ghetto* (New York, 1948), p. 75.

[33] *Ibid.*, pp. 75, 179–80; Sterner, *The Negro's Share*, pp. 314–16, 319–21; Kifer, "The Negro Under the New Deal," p. 230. Commenting on New Deal housing programs, Sterner also noted that "the housing projects to a large extent serve income groups somewhat above the lowest levels. . . . Relief families may be admitted at the discretion of the local authorities, but the United States Housing Authority apparently does not count on reaching relief families unless the assistance is 'reasonably adequate'" (*The Negro's Share*, p. 321).

AAA, the FSA has generally been warmly praised for its efforts. With probably the best-known white racial liberal of the time, Will Alexander, administering Farm Security from 1937 to 1940, efforts were made to provide relief and loans to black farmers and to include black advisors throughout FSA's organization, national as well as state. Southern blacks made up about 24 percent of the entire southern population and they received 21 percent of the tenant purchase loans made in the 1930's.[34] Yet there existed serious limits to the FSA's commitment to blacks. In "matters of race," one scholar has argued, "the leaders of the FSA were careful. In their allocation of loan and grant funds, in their personnel appointments, in their cooperative and group enterprises, in their resettlement projects, and in their public information activities, they adhered fairly consistently to southern attitudes and practices regarding race." [35]

The gap between theory and practice in New Deal reform should not distract from the fact that under programs like FSA, PWA, WPA, NYA, and a host of others, black Americans were able to receive certain necessary material advantages. The importance of those benefits was indicated by the strong political support the black masses gave Franklin Roosevelt and the Democratic party. That support came despite criticisms made by numerous black leaders of the administration's policies, despite attempts made in the early 1940's to create an independent, nonpartisan political movement of black people, and despite efforts made by the Republican party and those on the far left to woo blacks to their particular causes. In every national election between 1936 and 1944, Republican presidential hopefuls took a more militant stand for racial equality than did President Roosevelt; during the same period, the Republican plank on civil rights was almost always more explicit and more encompassing than that found in the Democratic platform.[36] Both the Communist party and the Socialist

---

[34] Sidney Baldwin, *Poverty and Politics: The Rise and Decline of the Farm Security Administration* (Chapel Hill, N.C., 1968), pp. 279, 306–07, 332; Kifer, "The Negro Under the New Deal," pp. 207–09; Sterner, *The Negro's Share*, p. 300; Wolters, *Negroes and the Great Depression*, pp. 72–73, and Ralph J. Bunche, "Political Status of the Negro," unpublished memorandum for the Carnegie-Myrdal Study, New York, 1940, pp. 1309–1403. On percent of loans, see Sterner, pp. 305–07; Baldwin, pp. 196–97; Wolters, p. 67.

[35] Baldwin, *Poverty and Politics*, p. 279.

[36] For references to Alf Landon and blacks, see Donald R. McCoy, *Landon of Kansas* (Lincoln, Neb., 1966), pp. 45, 98, 103–05, 240, 277, 297, 311–12, 332–33, 420–21, 447, 507, 510; on the Republican and Democratic civil rights planks, see Kirk H. Porter and Donald Bruce Johnson, eds., *National Party Platforms, 1840–1956* (Urbana, Ill., 1956), pp. 381–87, 389–94, 402–04, 407–413. Also, Henry Lee Moon, *Balance of Power: The Negro Vote* (Garden City, N.Y., 1948), pp. 31–34. Attempts by blacks to form a national nonpartisan movement in 1944 are discussed in New York *Times*, April 30, 1944, and Chicago *Defender*, June 24, 1944; see also "A Declaration by Negro Voters," *The Crisis*, LI (January 1944), 16–17.

party of Norman Thomas, moreover, stressed issues considered of special importance to the black community; both groups made concerted efforts to attract blacks by denouncing racial segregation and discrimination in the federal government and the nation and by supporting black demands on a number of economic and social fronts.[37] But neither the Republican party nor the political left was able to convince many black Americans after 1934 that it had any meaningful alternative to Roosevelt reformism, whatever the New Deal's limitations in respect to racial matters.

Those limitations were inevitably increased by the existing political and economic realities of the time—the weak position of blacks as a political force, the inherent restrictions placed on the President and federal agencies to effect changes at state and local levels, even when they desired to do so, and the general difficulties experienced by the government in actually revitalizing a sick economy in the 1930's. But there were other reasons involved in the administration's ambivalent response to issues of a purely racial nature. The success of the liberal approach was dependent primarily on faith in the New Deal's power to achieve long range changes in black standards and white attitudes within a society "accustomed to discriminatory acts against Negroes." [38] Believing in the ultimate correctness of their approach, liberals could accept certain immediate disappointments that resulted from an unsympathetic Congress and from New Deal colleagues who did not share their same commitment, from periodic outbreaks of racial hostility, from local white resistance to their programs, and from the discriminatory treatment of blacks in defense industries and the armed forces during the 1940's. Convinced, however, that people's attitudes would change as black standards improved, they believed it important to caution blacks to be patient, to take advantage of the opportunities that were being created and not to push too hard for rights that were more social than economic and that might aggravate racial passions and complicate government efforts on their behalf.[39]

---

[37] There is a great need for a more extended study and objective analysis of the left (the Communist and Socialist parties) and its relationship to civil rights issues in the 1930's and 1940's, but for some references to the Communist party and blacks, see Wilson Record, *The Negro and the Communist Party* (Chapel Hill, N.C., 1951), especially pp. 64, 114–16, and Hugh T. Murray, Jr., "The NAACP Versus the Communist Party: The Scottsboro Rape Cases, 1931–1932," *Phylon*, XXVIII (Third Quarter 1967), 276–87. On the Socialist party's appeals to blacks, see Ernest Doerfler, "Socialism and the Negro Problem," *American Socialist Quarterly*, III (Summer 1933), 23–36; Margaret I. Lamont, "The Negro's Share in Socialism," *American Socialist Quarterly*, IV (March 1935), 41–51; Norman Thomas, "The Socialist's Way Out for the Negro," *Journal of Negro Education*, V (January 1936), 100–04; Thomas, *Human Exploitation in the United States* (New York, 1934), pp. 258–83. For an analysis of Thomas' views on the "Negro problem" in the 1930's, see Kirby, "The New Deal Era and Blacks," pp. 243–56.

[38] Kifer, "The Negro Under the New Deal," p. 280.

[39] In this regard, see Ickes' speeches to the Chicago Urban League and at Wilberforce University, Franklin D. Roosevelt Library, Official File 6, and his "The Negro as Citi-

Change would come but it would take time. People must be allowed, Mrs. Roosevelt wrote in 1943, to "think through and decide as individuals what they wish to do." [40] Ickes noted that it was impossible to "force people on each other who do not like each other" and the first lady affirmed that even the federal government could not "force people" to accept more blacks in its employment until there was "created opinion sufficiently strong to make people want to do the fair thing." [41] "I believe that your cheerful disposition, your faith, your loyalty and your lack of resentment," Ickes told the NAACP, "are some of the qualities that have brought you the success that already is yours." [42] To increase that success, he and other liberals called on black Americans to maintain those same qualities.

White New Dealers, in effect, tied the success of black equality to the fulfillment of the Roosevelt reform program. They identified their own faith in the New Deal's potential, their tolerance of white prejudice, their belief in economic priorities, and their acceptance of existing institutions and values with black needs, black endurance, black priorities, and continued black loyalty to the American way of life. The solution to the "Negro problem" ultimately hinged on a number of factors—expanded economic opportunities and security, the power of education to modify traditional beliefs, the steady rise in black standards, and the eventual decrease in white bigotry. But the government's efforts to effect these changes were limited by the degree to which the white population would accept the incorporation of blacks in the New Deal housing, labor, educational, and health programs, and white New Dealers felt they must operate within these limits if any assistance to black Americans was to be ever realized.

The ideas of the New Deal liberals on the racial problem not only affected their own activities but those of the black community as well. Since they considered the manner in which blacks carried on their protests to be of central importance to the ultimate success of the Roosevelt administration's efforts for racial equality, they spent considerable time and effort ad-

zen," 230–31, 242, 253; Roosevelt, "The Negro and Social Change," 22–23; Roosevelt, "Presentation of Spingarn Medal to Marian Anderson," *The Crisis*, XLVI (September 1939), 265–85; Roosevelt, "Freedom: Promise or Fact," *Negro Digest*, I (October 1943), 8–9; Alexander, "Our Conflicting Racial Policies," 172–79, *passim;* Alexander, "The Negro as a Human Person," *The Missionary Review of the World*, LIX (June 1936), 292–94; Alexander, "A Strategy for Negro Labor," *Opportunity*, XII (April 1934), 102–03.

[40] Roosevelt, "Freedom: Promise or Fact," 8. This article was written in the aftermath of the Detroit and New York riots. Sympathizing with black people's frustration and bitterness, Mrs. Roosevelt also cautioned them to determine what they felt were their "real rights as a citizen" and to begin to "work for those rights first, feeling that other things such as social relationships might well wait until certain people were given time to think through and decide as individuals what they wished to do."

[41] Ickes, *Secret Diary*, Vol. II, pp. 115; Roosevelt, "Remarks," *Proceedings of the Second Conference*, 1939, pp. 85–86.

[42] Ickes, "The Negro as Citizen," 231.

vising blacks on their responsibilities. And since they occupied the important positions within the government, it was inevitable that their philosophy would significantly influence the strategies and the general framework through which black people pursued their objectives.

Throughout the Roosevelt years, blacks followed two general courses of action: securing representation within the government and organizing pressure outside. The purpose of both strategies was the same—to influence administration policies and programs relevant to the needs of the black population. Neither activity, moreover, was exclusive of the other; the success of one was often dependent on the success of the other. But from the standpoint of winning approval for their actions from sympathetic whites in and outside the New Deal, and in achieving immediate relief from the effects of the Depression, the placing of blacks in the administration was considered most attractive. Pittsburgh *Courier* editor Robert Vann, Harvard-trained economist Robert Weaver, and Eugene Kinckle Jones, head of the National Urban League, joined the New Deal in 1933 as race advisors in the departments of Justice, Interior, and Commerce, respectively. From 1933 through the 1940's, a number of distinguished blacks like William Hastie, Forrester Washington, Mary McLeod Bethune, William J. Trent, and Frank J. Horne were added to the list of those who advised the government's departments and agencies on matters related to the black community.[43] Although the practice was not new (Republican administrations had been appointing blacks to positions such as in the Treasury Department and the Post Office ever since Reconstruction), Ralph Bunche, a strong critic of the New Deal in the 1930's, saw their selection as representing a "radical break with the past because of their novelty and the entirely different character of the appointee, as well as the method of appointment." [44] What Bunche and others noted as being novel was the essentially nonpolitical nature of the black appointments and the general high caliber of those black advisors selected to serve the government in the 1930's and 1940's.

It is difficult, however, to assess the importance that this group of black New Dealers, often referred to as the "black Cabinet," actually had in affecting government policy. Bunche pointed out that their strength

---

[43] Most studies dealing with the New Deal–black relationship make reference to the "black Cabinet" or black New Dealers. The best account of their numbers and their various involvements are Jane R. Motz, "The Black Cabinet: Negroes in the Administration of Franklin D. Roosevelt," unpublished Masters thesis, University of Delaware, 1964; Bunche, "The Political Status of the Negro," pp. 1392–1450; Roi Ottley, 'New World A-Coming': Inside Black America (Cleveland, 1943), pp. 254–66; Franklin, *Slavery to Freedom,* pp. 519–20; also, Henry Lee Moon, "Racial Aspects of Federal Public Relations Programs," *Phylon* (First Quarter 1943), 66–72, and Kirby, "The New Deal Era and Blacks," pp. 106–70.

[44] Bunche, "The Political Status of the Negro," p. 1361.

largely depended on the "liberality of administrative heads" who gave them the "latitude" to pursue their objectives.[45] Some, like Weaver and Mrs. Bethune, had considerable influence because they worked under whites who allowed ·them a measure of "latitude"; others, like Vann and Washington, frequently found their jobs frustrating and left the government after only a few months' or years' service.[46] Without their presence, it was probably true, as Bunche maintained, that thousands of dollars would not have gone to the black population. But there is also a tendency to overemphasize their importance. Even the most influential among them were seldom consulted on matters of policy-making in the "formative stages" and "their influence on the official process of decision-making at a high level was almost non-existent." In effect, most of the black advisors' achievements were "preventative" rather than innovative.[47]

The absence of a direct voice in important policy matters presented a troublesome dilemma for blacks as the activities of the federal government were expanded as a result of New Deal social and economic measures. In 1939, William H. Hastie, a black attorney and NAACP official who held a number of appointments under Roosevelt in the 1930's and 1940's, told a NAACP convention that since 1932 the federal government had "entered into the economic life of the nation and [had] undertaken to perform social services to an extent and over an area much larger than could have been forseen." By spending "billions to furnish jobs, housing, and recreation, to improve health, to provide credit, to subsidize education, to pension the aged," the government had "come to a position of enormous influence in the entire life of the nation." [48] Such an influence was, of course, a factor of both positive and negative consequence to black Americans. As Hastie noted, the "racial attitudes reflected in Government-financed enterprises of various types are potentially significant for the modification of the pattern of American life." [49] It was also true that the "countless projects represented problems of a variety and complexity" that truly staggered the imagination.

---

[45] *Ibid.*, p. 1455.

[46] Bethune was one of the few, perhaps the only, black advisor who actually administered programs directly for black Americans; most black New Dealers operated as simply advisors to whites who headed agencies or administration departments. Some advisors had little contact at all with those whom they were supposedly assisting, as was the case of Edgar Brown who worked under Robert Fechner in the CCC. See Bunche, "The Political Status of the Negro," p. 1398; Kifer, "The Negro Under the New Deal," p. 65; Motz, "The Black Cabinet," *passim.*

[47] Motz, "The Black Cabinet," p. 80.

[48] William H. Hastie, "A Look at the NAACP," *The Crisis,* XLVI (September 1939), 263–64.

[49] *Ibid.*

The job of keeping track of new proposals and analyzing them; the problems of learning the administrative procedures of a great many independent agencies; the bringing of pressure while administrative policies are in their formative stages; and the effort to correct abuses and injustices as varied as the ingenuity of man, make up a tremendous undertaking.[50]

That undertaking was made extremely difficult by the impotence of blacks within the government and the lack of black unity outside. During the 1930's and early 1940's, numerous black leaders and organizations, both new and old, struggled to come to grips with the New Deal's significance to black people.[51] Within the expanding northern black ghettos, economic boycott groups, such as the "Don't Buy Where You Can't Work" movement and the New Negro Alliance of Washington, D.C., sprang up in attempts to force more jobs for black residents. Traditional organizations like the NAACP and the Urban League lobbied in Congress, pressured public officials, supported coalitions such as the Joint Committee on Economic Recovery which tried to press for equitable treatment of blacks under NRA and AAA, agitated for antilynching legislation, and called for congressional investigations into federal discriminatory policies.[52] Those leaders who were dissatisfied with the NAACP and Urban League approaches and with the pace of New Deal reformism, and convinced of the necessity to construct a massive black response to the massive federal influence, created new organizations to advance their hopes. Most significant of these were the National Negro Congress (NNC), formed in 1936 by Ralph J. Bunche and John P. Davis, and the March on Washington Movement (MOWM), developed in 1940–41 in reaction to conditions surrounding the outbreak of the Second World War.[53]

---

[50] *Ibid.*, 264.

[51] For a discussion of black organizations and movements during this period see Charles Radford Lawrence, "Negro Organizations in Crisis: Depression, New Deal and World War II," unpublished doctoral dissertation, Columbia University, 1953; Ralph J. Bunche, "Extended Memorandum on the Programs, Ideologies, Tactics and Achievements of Negro Betterment and Interracial Organizations," unpublished memorandum for the Carnegie-Myrdal Study, New York, 1940; Bunche, "A Critical Analysis of the Tactics and Programs of Minority Groups," *Journal of Negro Education*, IV (July 1935), 308–20; Bunche, "The Programs of Organizations Devoted to the Improvement of the Status of the American Negro," *Journal of Negro Education*, VIII (July 1939), 539–50; Wolters, *Negroes and the Great Depression*, pp. 219–384.

[52] For a varied discussion of NAACP and Urban League activities, see Lawrence, "Negro Organizations in Crisis," *passim;* Bunche, "Extended Memorandum on Programs, Ideologies, Tactics and Achievements," pp. 23–300; Wolters, *Negroes and the Great Depression*, pp. 39–55, 139–92, 266–352; Robert L. Zangrando, "The NAACP and a Federal Anti-Lynching Bill, 1934–1940," *Journal of Negro History*, L (April 1965), 106–17.

[53] On the NNC and the MOWM, see Wolters, *Negroes and the Great Depression*, pp. 353–82; Harold Cruse, *The Crisis of the Negro Intellectual* (New York, 1967), pp.

Both the NNC and the MOWM presented extensive demands calling for stronger federal guarantees against race discrimination and segregation in every area affecting black Americans and demanding more expansive federal economic and social reforms. Both attempted to build a single, grass roots, mass-oriented organization within the black community. Significantly, both were initially headed by black labor leader A. Philip Randolph, who combined an appeal to black racial unity with black and white working class solidarity in seeking to construct a force that might be powerful enough to pressure the New Deal.[54] Yet neither organization was successful ultimately in forging a unified movement of black people. The NNC lost the support of the masses when it was unable to reconcile the divergent demands made by a variety of black interest groups and when it became dominated by the Communist party and the industrial unions in the late 1930's. The MOWM won an executive order creating a Fair Employment Practice Committee, but it was no more successful than NNC in sustaining a unified following and by 1942 it had lost support from traditional black and interracial organizations as well as from the black masses on which its future existence was dependent.[55]

With few exceptions, black organizations and leaders found themselves making the same "preventative" response as those within the Roosevelt administration. Confronted by the enormous influence of the federal government and with the many, often conflicting, needs and claims of their own people, black leaders were caught up in a process of sorting out in New Deal policies the good from the bad, of analyzing immediate and long term implications of numerous programs, and of finding a means by which they could gain leverage to affect administration policy-making. In desperate need of whatever aid and assistance the federal government could give them, the majority of blacks accepted the basic philosophy for racial prog-

---

171–80; Bunche, "Extended Memorandum on Programs, Ideologies, Tactics and Achievements," pp. 319–71; Lawrence S. Wittner, "The National Negro Congress: A Reassessment," *American Quarterly*, XXII (Winter 1970), 883–901; Richard M. Dalfiume, *Fighting on Two Fronts: Desegregation of the Armed Forces, 1939–1953* (Columbia, Mo., 1969), especially pp. 115–23; Dalfiume, "The 'Forgotten Years' of the Negro Revolution," *The Journal of American History*, LV (June 1968), 90–106; Herbert Garfinkel, *When Negroes March: The March on Washington Movement in the Organizational Politics for FEPC* (Glencoe, Ill., 1959).

[54] For the goals, programs, and strategies of NNC and MOWM and of Randolph's role, see Bunche, "Extended Memorandum of Programs, Ideologies, Tactics and Achievements," pp. 319–71; Garfinkel, *When Negroes March, passim*, but especially, pp. 102–49.

[55] Garfinkel, *When Negroes March,* pp. 107–59, 183; Dalfiume, *Fighting on Two Fronts,* pp. 116–23; Cruse, *The Crisis of the Negro Intellectual,* pp. 171–180; Wolters, *Negroes and the Great Depression,* pp. 368, 364; Bunche, "Extended Memorandum of Programs, Ideologies, Tactics and Achievements," pp. 350–71; Lawrence, "Negro Organizations in Crisis," pp. 350–51; Wittner, "The National Negro Congress," 897–901; Kirby, "The New Deal Era and Blacks," pp. 179–83, 219–27.

ress articulated by white liberals within the Roosevelt administration. They found it extremely difficult to criticize a government that provided some material improvement to their general welfare. The white liberals in the government, as was noted earlier, exercised strong influence over black protest activities and as a result, there were few direct challenges to the New Deal's theory of racial improvement. Not even radical Socialists like Norman Thomas questioned the New Deal philosophy on this point.

One of the few blacks, however, who did oppose the ideology of liberal racial reform was the civil rights advocate and former *Crisis* editor, W. E. B. DuBois, and it is indicative of DuBois' opposition that he found himself isolated from most of the reform and racial activities carried on during the Roosevelt years. DuBois argued that racism was deeply ingrained in the American psyche and it would continue to flourish despite changes in the economic, social, or political conditions that determined black standards or those of the country at large. He concluded that it was futile and ultimately disastrous for blacks to waste their energies and talents attacking New Deal discrimination or trying to build alliances with white leaders or white workers; racism could not be destroyed by educational appeals or liberal exhortations or by more generous federal economic policies. Whatever else the New Deal was doing, DuBois believed it was not nor was it capable of ever changing white racial beliefs through its present reform and recovery measures, contrary to what many blacks and whites at the time maintained. If blacks wanted to secure advantages from governmental programs, they should turn their attention, he stated, toward organizing their own community through emphasizing the institutional and cultural racial unity of black people. No lasting solution to the "Negro problem" would come, he asserted, unless there was a simultaneous assault on both white prejudice and the oppressive conditions existing within black communities; attacking one would not produce a favorable response to the other.[56]

DuBois's view found support in the 1940's from white novelist and native southerner Lillian Smith. Addressing "white liberals" in 1944, she maintained that "hard as it is to acknowledge, the simple truth is that the South's and the nation's racial problems cannot be solved by putting a loaf of bread, a book and a ballot in everyone's hand."[57] Although she recog-

---

[56] For an indication of DuBois's thought, see DuBois, "Does the Negro Need Separate Schools," *Journal of Negro Education*, IV (July 1935), 328–35; Dubois, "The NAACP and Race Segregation," *The Crisis*, XLI (February 1934), 52–53; DuBois, "A Negro Nation Within the Nation," *Current History*, XLII (June 1935), 265–70; DuBois, "The Position of the Negro in the American Social Order: Where Do We Go From Here?" *Journal of Negro Education*, VIII (July 1939), 451–70; and DuBois, *Dusk of Dawn: An Essay Toward an Autobiography of a Race Concept* (New York, 1940), especially Chapters 6 and 7. See also Wolters, *Negroes and the Great Depression*, pp. 230–65, and Kirby, "The New Deal Era and Blacks," pp. 202–11.

[57] Lillian Smith, "Addressed to White Liberals," *New Republic*, CLI (September 18, 1944), 332.

nized that such measures were necessary and important to black welfare, she was skeptical of their ultimate value to racial reform and of the motives that inspired white liberals to pursue them. It was, she felt, the "fear in the white man's heart that makes him more willing to work for specific, short range goals such as the vote, better schools, better jobs for Negroes, than to change his own attitudes toward himself and his white race." [58]

The reform spirit generated during the 1930's as well as the guarantees of racial and religious freedom commonly associated with the national defense effort in the 1940's did nevertheless provide an environment in which blacks and some of their white allies were given an opportunity to press more publicly for racial justice and equality. In the years between 1933 and 1945, new ideas were expressed and movements were founded with the aim of bringing racial change in America. In the long run, this may have constituted the most significant contribution of the Roosevelt era since, in the postwar period, it was considerably more difficult to keep the "Negro problem" hidden or to isolate racial issues from the broader questions that affected the American people. Inspired in part by the examples of New Deal whites like Harold Ickes, Eleanor Roosevelt, Will Alexander, and Clark Foreman, race equality assumed after 1945 a more central place in liberal ideology; prior to the New Deal, the "Negro problem" was never a major consideration of white reformers or reform philosophers.[59] Within the black community, older organizations underwent transformation and some, notably the NAACP and the National Urban League in the 1940's, saw their memberships and activities considerably increase.[60] New organizations also took root, employing tactics and developing strategies that were later utilized in the "Negro revolt" of the 1950's and 1960's.

But if American society seemed more receptive to the ideas of racial

---

[58] *Ibid.* For a general discussion of Smith's racial ideas, see Kirby, "The New Deal Era and Blacks," pp. 257–70.

[59] Only a few "Progressive" reformers showed concern over the problems of blacks or with the cause of racial prejudice in the early twentieth century. For a few critical assessments of progressivism and civil rights issues, see Dewey W. Grantham, "The Progressive Movement and the Negro," *South Atlantic Quarterly*, LIV (Oct. 1955), 461–77; Gilbert Osofsky, "Progressivism and the Negro: New York, 1900–1915," *American Quarterly*, XVI (Summer 1964), 153–68; Nancy J. Weiss, "The Negro and the New Freedom: Fighting Wilsonian Segregation," *Political Science Quarterly*, LXXXIV (Mar. 1969), 61–79; Howard W. Allen, Aage R. Clausen, and Jerome M. Clubb, "Political Reform and Negro Rights in the Senate, 1909–1915," *Journal of Southern History*, XXVII (May 1971), 191–212. During the Truman administration, civil rights became a more acceptable part of liberal thought, a fact clearly symbolized by the battle over the Democratic party's plank on civil rights at its 1948 convention and other issues. See in respect to Truman and blacks, Barton J. Bernstein, "The Ambiguous Legacy: The Truman Administration and Civil Rights," in Bernstein, ed., *Politics and Policies of the Truman Administration* (Chicago, 1970), pp. 269–314.

[60] Lawrence, "Negro Organizations," pp. 375–77. Lawrence states that the NAACP increased its membership sixfold during the war years. Also showing some revival were the National Business League and the National Council of Negro Women (Lawrence, p. 378).

reformers, many of the central dilemmas that had plagued the blacks as a people prior to 1933 remained unchanged. By 1940, whether the indices were unemployment, relief, or income, it was obvious that they were still disproportionally isolated from the mainstream of the nation's economic life.[61] One student has concluded that "it is probably safe to say that the Negro population was less an integral part of the basic American economy in 1940 than at any time since the invention of the cotton gin." [62] Black New Dealer Robert Weaver noted in 1946 that it "was generally conceded that the Negro was losing his quest for economic security and occupational advancement"; when the "defense program was launched the Negro had long been haunted by unemployment." [63] Black job opportunities did, of course, increase considerably during the boom years of the Second World War but since 1945, a high incidence of unemployment and relief and a low level of income have continued to be daily facts of black life.[64]

The inability to deal directly with the problem of racism lay at the bottom of the Roosevelt administration's tentative support provided black people in the 1930's and 1940's. For some New Dealers, that inability originated from a lack of real concern and sympathy for the plight of blacks; for others, those truly involved in the cause of racial progress, it derived more from a naive and "confused" understanding of the roots of the nation's racial dilemma. Though willing to acknowledge the presence of a "Negro problem," these latter reformers were unready to fully confront the racial as well as the economic and political patterns of American life that were responsible for that problem. The partial inclusion of blacks in the federal welfare programs and in the Roosevelt political coalition did alter, as Myrdal maintained, the nature of the black condition; however, it also tended to obscure from public view some of the more deep-seated features of that condition by instilling the notion that expanded governmental activity was

---

[61] Unemployment and relief figures vary tremendously but for a general discussion of both as well as black income figures up to 1942, see Sterner, *Negro's Share*, Chapters 2, 3, and 5. Myrdal noted in 1944 that public relief had "become one of the major Negro occupations; all through the thirties it was surpassed only by agriculture and possibly by domestic service" (Myrdal, *American Dilemma*, Vol. I, pp. 353–54); see also Lawrence, "Negro Organizations," p. 200. Lawrence quotes from the U.S. Census, 16th Census, *The Labor Force: Employment and Personal Characteristics* (1943), indicating that as of March, 1940, 26.6 percent of black urban males of working age were unemployed compared to 16.1 percent of the total male labor force in the cities (Lawrence, p. 208).

[62] Lawrence, "Negro Organizations," p. 200.

[63] Weaver, *Negro Labor*, p. 15.

[64] For illuminating analyses of recent black unemployment, relief, and income statistics, see Louis A. Ferman, Joyce L. Kornbluh, and J. A. Miller, eds., *Negroes and Jobs: A Book of Readings* (Ann Arbor, Mich. 1968); Leonard Broom and Norval D. Glenn, *Transformation of the Negro American* (New York, 1967), pp. 105–56; Rashi Fein, "An Economic and Social Profile of the Negro American," and Daniel Patrick Moynihan, "Employment, Income, and the Ordeal of the Negro Family," in Talcott Parsons and Kenneth B. Clark, eds., *The Negro American* (Boston, 1967), pp. 102–59.

synonymous with a successful eradication of racial oppression in America.[65] The New Deal's legacy to racial change was therefore ambivalent and the nature of that ambivalence was clearly evident in the mixed impact of Roosevelt administration reform policies and the frustrations experienced by blacks who tried to unravel its meaning to black people in the 1930's and 1940's and ever since then.[66]

SUGGESTED READING

Historians are only beginning to penetrate the complex relationship of the blacks and the New Deal. Raymond Wolters's *Negroes and the Great Depression* (1970) is a richly detailed study of the impact of the National Recovery Administration and the Agricultural Adjustment Administration on blacks, but the volume is chiefly important for its thoughtful analysis of the NAACP and the National Negro Congress. Leslie Fishel, Jr., in "The Negro in the New Deal Era," *Wisconsin Magazine of History*, XLVIII (Winter 1964–65), stresses the New Deal's contributions to the welfare of blacks, though he also notes Roosevelt's limited commitment in this area. In *F.D.R. and the South* (1965), Frank Freidel acknowledges the President's unwillingness to invest any political capital in obtaining black rights. Allan Morrison's "The Secret Papers of FDR," *Negro Digest*, IX (Jan. 1951), is a superficial but useful journalistic survey based on brief research in the Roosevelt papers.

Because the scholarship on blacks and the New Deal is still relatively sparse, contemporary black criticisms of the New Deal are especially important in analyzing the period. Among the more significant essays are Ralph Bunche's "A Critique of New Deal Planning as It Affects Negroes," *Journal of Negro Education*, V (Jan. 1936); John P. Davis' "A Black Inventory of the New Deal," *Crisis*, XLII (May 1935), and his "A Survey of the Problems of the Negro Under the New Deal," *Journal of Negro Education*, V (Jan. 1936); and Robert C. Weaver's "The New Deal and the Negro: A Look at the Facts," Op-

---

[65] In his conclusion on the status of blacks at the end of the Second World War, Charles Lawrence states that "there are false securities for Negroes in the present situation. War and the indefinitely prolongable garrison State have created an otherwise not securely-based state of relatively full employment. In this respect the United States has been the fortuitous beneficiary of a condition it did not entirely intend. . . . And, insofar as such a favorable economic condition is not securely based, the position of the Negro remains highly vulnerable" (Lawrence, "Negro Organizations," p. 388).

[66] For a recent critique of the liberal assumptions concerning race, particularly as expressed in Myrdal's *American Dilemma*, see Carl N. Degler, "The Negro in America— Where Myrdal Went Wrong," *The New York Times Magazine* (December 7, 1969), 64–65, 154–57, 159–60; and, from a somewhat different perspective, Leonard J. Fein, "The Limits of Liberalism," *Saturday Review*, LIII (June 20, 1970), 83–85, 95–96. On the New Deal legacy after the Second World War, see Bernstein, "The Ambiguous Legacy," pp. 269–314.

portunity, XIII (July 1935). Mary Bethune's "My Secret Talks with FDR," *Ebony*, IV (Apr. 1949) is a generous assessment.

Robert Zangrando, in "The NAACP and a Federal Anti-Lynching Bill, 1934–1940," *Journal of Negro History*, L (Apr. 1964), notes the NAACP's tactics of dramatizing the black's plight. Wilson Record's *Race Relations and Radicalism: The NAACP and the Communist Party in Conflict* ° (1964), and *The Negro and The Communist Party* (1951) are studies praising the black for his lack of receptivity to communism. Two important contemporary analyses by Ralph Bunche are "A Critical Analysis of the Tactics and Programs of Minority Groups," *Journal of Negro Education*, IV (July 1935), and "The Program of Organizations Devoted to the Improvement of the Status of the American Negro," *Journal of Negro Education*, VIII (July 1939). Francis Broderick's *W. E. B. Du Bois: Negro Leader in a Time of Crisis* ° (1959) and Elliott M. Rudwick's *W. E. B. Du Bois: A Study in Minority Group Leadership* ° (1960) are useful in understanding the shifting, critical thought of this great black intellectual. Harold Cruse's *The Crisis of the Negro Intellectual* ° (1967) is an often intemperate, but also challenging, analysis of the black man's failure to develop racial consciousness and solidarity.

John Salmond, in "The Civilian Conservation Corps and the Negro," *Journal of American History*, LII (June 1965), briefly examines one New Deal agency. This analysis constitutes part of his book *The Civilian Conservation Corps, 1933–1942: A New Deal Case Study* (1967). Sidney Baldwin, in *Poverty and Politics: The Rise and Decline of the Farm Security Administration* (1968), provides a useful analysis of the FSA and its responses to blacks and to the larger problem of rural poverty.

Southern agriculture and the collapse of Southern farm tenancy constitute one of the few well-explored subjects in black history during the 1920's and New Deal years. Among the better studies published during the New Deal are *The Collapse of Cotton Tenancy*, ° by Charles Johnson *et al.* (1935); *Preface to Peasantry*, by Arthur Raper (1933), and *Sharecroppers All*, by Raper and Ira DeA. Reid (1941). Two recent studies warranting consultation are David E. Conrad's *The Forgotten Farmers: The Study of Sharecroppers in the New Deal* (1965); and Donald H. Grubbs' *Cry From the Cotton: The Southern Tenant Farmers' Union and the New Deal* (1971). John Dollard's *Caste and Class in a Southern Town* ° (1937) and *Deep South: A Social Anthropological Study of Caste and Class* ° (1941) by Allison Davis *et al.* are classic, and still rewarding, studies of southern race relations. St. Clair Drake and Horace Cayton's *Black Metropolis: A Study of Negro Life in a Northern City* ° (1945) is a penetrating volume on Chicago.

Among the studies on black politics are James A. Harrell's "Negro Leadership in the Election Year 1936," *Journal of Southern History* (Nov. 1968); and John Allswang's "The Chicago Negro Voter and the Democratic Consensus: A Case Study, 1918–1936," *Journal of the Illinois State Historical Society*, LX (Summer 1967).

ELLIS W. HAWLEY

The New Deal
and the Problem of Monopoly

INTRODUCTION

Though the aims of big business during the New Deal have never
been systematically studied, Ellis W. Hawley, professor of history
at the University of Iowa, has made a start in gathering considerable evidence on the subject. He concludes that business rhetoric championing laissez faire frequently cloaked an enthusiasm
for industrial cooperation. Even after the Supreme Court declared
the National Recovery Administration unconstitutional in 1935,
"business supporters were in effect trying to maintain a private
NRA." As late as 1937, the Business Advisory Council—
composed of many of the nation's prominent businessmen—
proposed the establishment within each industry of price and
production controls, to be subject to federal approval. Though
this program foundered, Hawley finds that most major industries
were, nevertheless, able to eliminate price competition and

FROM "Conclusion: Retrospect and Prospect," in Ellis W. Hawley, *The New Deal and
the Problem of Monopoly* (copyright © 1969 by Princeton University Press; Princeton
Paperback, 1969), pp. 472–90. Reprinted by permission of Princeton University Press.

achieve stability through private controls and informal arrangements.

Hawley's book *The New Deal and the Problem of Monopoly*
(1966), from which the following essay is taken, is more concerned with the actual business policies of the New Deal than
with the aims of big business. He stresses administration twists
and turns in economic policy, from the NRA and federal support
of cartels and business planning to antitrust activity and an assault on rigid prices. But he also discerns an underlying *political*
"logic and consistency"—the need to balance antagonistic pressures and to make concessions both to those who wanted to increase competition and to those who wished to limit it. Roosevelt, responding to demands from antitrusters and critics of big
business, condemned monopoly and attacked the "economic royalists." Yet, while making "proper obeisance to the antitrust tradition," the administration also confronted demands for planning,
control, and rationalization, and therefore allowed "industrial
pressure groups to write their programs of market control into
law, particularly in areas where they could come up with the necessary lobbies and symbols."

Although Hawley does not analyze the political power of
business during the New Deal years, his study of the Government's shifting responses to the politically challenging problem
of monopoly is, nevertheless, impressive.

*T*wo souls dwell in the bosom of this Administration," wrote
Dorothy Thompson in 1938, "as indeed, they do in the bosom of the American people. The one loves the Abundant Life, as expressed in the cheap and
plentiful products of large-scale mass production and distribution. . . . The
other soul yearns for former simplicities, for decentralization, for the interests
of the 'little man,' revolts against high-pressure salesmanship, denounces
'monopoly' and 'economic empires,' and seeks means of breaking them up."
"Our Administration," she continued, "manages a remarkable . . . stunt of
being . . . in favor of organizing and regulating the Economic Empires to
greater and greater efficiency, and of breaking them up as a tribute to peren-
nial American populist feeling." [1]

Dorothy Thompson was a persistent critic of the Roosevelt Administration; yet her remarks did show considerable insight into the dilemma that
confronted New Dealers, and indeed, the dilemma that confronted industrial
America. The problem of reconciling liberty and order, individualism and
collective organization, was admittedly an ancient one, but the creation of a
highly integrated industrial system in a land that had long cherished its

---

[1] Dorothy Thompson, in *New York Herald Tribune*, Jan. 24, 1938.

liberal, democratic, and individualistic traditions presented the problem in a peculiarly acute form. Both the American people and their political leaders tended to view modern industrialism with mingled feelings of pride and regret. On one hand, they tended to associate large business units and economic organization with abundance, progress, and a rising standard of living. On the other, they associated them with a wide variety of economic abuses, which, because of past ideals and past standards, they felt to be injurious to society. Also, deep in their hearts, they retained a soft spot for the "little fellow." In moments of introspection, they looked upon the immense concentrations of economic power that they had created and accused them of destroying the good life, of destroying the independent businessman and the satisfactions that came from owning one's own business and working for oneself, of reducing Americans to a race of clerks and machine tenders, of creating an impersonal, mechanized world that destroyed man as an individual.[2]

The search in twentieth-century America, then, was for some solution that would reconcile the practical necessity with the individualistic ideal, some arrangement that would preserve the industrial order, necessarily based upon a high degree of collective organization, and yet would preserve America's democratic heritage at the same time. Americans wanted a stable, efficient industrial system, one that turned out a large quantity of material goods, insured full employment, and provided a relatively high degree of economic security. Yet at the same time they wanted a system as free as possible from centralized direction, one in which economic power was dispersed and economic opportunity was really open, one that preserved the dignity of the individual and adjusted itself automatically to market forces. And they were unwilling to renounce the hope of achieving both. In spite of periodic hurricanes of anti-big-business sentiment, they refused to follow the prophets that would destroy their industrial system and return to former simplicities. Nor did they pay much attention to those that would sacrifice democratic ideals and liberal traditions in order to create a more orderly and more rational system, one that promised greater security, greater stability, and possibly even greater material benefits.

There were times, of course, when this dilemma was virtually forgotten. During periods of economic prosperity, when Americans were imbued with a psychological sense of well-being and satiated with a steady outflow of material benefits, it was hard to convince them that their industrial organization was seriously out of step with their ideals. During such periods, the majority rallied to the support of the business system; so long as it continued to operate at a high level, they saw no need for any major reforms. So long as the competitive ideal was embodied in statutes and industrial and political lead-

---

[2] See Arthur R. Burns, in *AER*, June 1949, pp. 691–95; Burton R. Fisher and Stephen B. Withey, *Big Business as the People See It* (Ann Arbor: U. of Mich. Press, 1951), 21–22, 34–38; Rexford G. Tugwell, in *Western Political Quarterly*, Sept. 1950, pp. 392–400.

ers paid lip service to it, there was a general willingness to leave it at that. If there were troubled consciences left, these could be soothed by clothing collective organizations in the attributes of rugged individuals and by the assurances of economic experts that anything short of pure monopoly was "competition" and therefore assured the benefits that were supposed to flow from competition.

In a time of economic adversity, however, Americans became painfully aware of the gap between ideal and reality. Paradoxically, this awareness produced two conflicting and contradictory reactions. Some pointed to the gap, to the failure of business organizations to live by the competitive creed, and concluded that it was the cause of the economic debacle, that the breakdown of the industrial machine was the inevitable consequence of its failure to conform to competitive standards. Others pointed to the same gap and concluded that the ideal itself was at fault, that it had prevented the organization and conscious direction of a rational system that would provide stability and security. On one hand, the presence of depression conditions seemed to intensify anti-big-business sentiment and generate new demands for antitrust crusades. On the other, it inspired demands for planning, rationalization, and the creation of economic organizations that could weather deflationary forces. The first general effect grew directly out of the loss of confidence in business leadership, the conviction that industrial leaders had sinned against the economic creed, and the determination that they should be allowed to sin no more. The second grew out of the black fear of economic death, the urgent desire to stem the deflationary tide, and the mounting conviction that a policy of laissez-faire or real implementation of the competitive ideal would result in economic disaster.

During such a period, moreover, it would seem practically inevitable that the policy-making apparatus of a democracy should register both streams of sentiment. Regardless of their logical inconsistency, the two streams were so intermixed in the ideology of the average man that any administration, if it wished to retain political power, had to make concessions to both. It must move to check the deflationary spiral, to provide some sort of central direction, and to salvage economic groups through the erection of cartels and economic controls. Yet while it was doing this, it must make a proper show of maintaining competitive ideals. Its actions must be justified by an appeal to competitive traditions, by showing that they were designed to save the underdog, or if this was impossible, by an appeal to other arguments and other traditions that for the moment justified making an exception. Nor could antitrust action ever be much more than a matter of performing the proper rituals and manipulating the proper symbols. It might attack unusually privileged and widely hated groups, break up a few loose combinations, and set forth a general program that was presumably designed to make the competitive ideal a reality. But the limit of the program would, of necessity, be that point at which changes in business practice or business structures would cause serious economic dislocation. It could not risk the disruption of going concerns or a further shrinkage in employment and production, and it would not subject men to the logical working out of deflationary trends. To do so would amount to political suicide.

To condemn these policies for their inconsistency was to miss the point. From an economic standpoint, condemnation might very well be to the point. They were inconsistent. One line of action tended to cancel the other, with the result that little was accomplished. Yet from the political standpoint, this very inconsistency, so long as the dilemma persisted, was the safest method of retaining political power. President Roosevelt, it seems, never suffered politically from his reluctance to choose between planning and antitrust action. His mixed emotions so closely reflected the popular mind that they were a political asset rather than a liability.[3]

That New Deal policy was inconsistent, then, should occasion little surprise. Such inconsistency, in fact, was readily apparent in the National Industrial Recovery Act, the first major effort to deal with the problems of industrial organization. When Roosevelt took office in 1933, the depression had reached its most acute stage. Almost every economic group was crying for salvation through political means, for some sort of rationalization and planning, although they might differ as to just who was to do the planning and the type and amount of it that would be required. Pro-business planners, drawing upon the trade association ideology of the nineteen twenties and the precedent of the War Industries Board, envisioned a semi-cartelized business commonwealth in which industrial leaders would plan and the state would enforce the decisions. Other men, convinced that there was already too much planning by businessmen, hoped to create an order in which other economic groups would participate in the policy-making process. Even under these circumstances, however, the resulting legislation had to be clothed in competitive symbols. Proponents of the NRA advanced the theory that it would help small businessmen and industrial laborers by protecting them from predatory practices and monopolistic abuses. The devices used to erect monopolistic controls became "codes of fair competition." And each such device contained the proper incantation against monopoly.

Consequently, the NRA was not a single program with a single objective, but rather a series of programs with a series of objectives, some of which were in direct conflict with each other. In effect, the National Industrial Recovery Act provided a phraseology that could be used to urge almost any approach to the problem of economic organization and an administrative machine that each of the conflicting economic and ideological groups might

---

[3] See Adolf A. Berle, Jr., in *Virginia Quarterly Review*, Summer 1938, pp. 324–33; K. E. Boulding, in *QJE*, Aug. 1945, pp. 524, 529–42; Arthur M. Schlesinger, Jr., *The Politics of Upheaval* (Boston: Houghton Mifflin, 1960), 650–54.

possibly use for their own ends. Under the circumstances, a bitter clash over basic policies was probably inevitable.

For a short period these inconsistencies were glossed over by the summer boomlet of 1933 and by a massive propaganda campaign appealing to wartime precedents and attempting to create a new set of cooperative symbols. As the propaganda wore off, however, and the economic indices turned downward again, the inconsistencies inherent in the program moved to the forefront of the picture. In the code-writing process, organized business had emerged as the dominant economic group, and once this became apparent, criticism of the NRA began to mount. Agrarians, convinced that rising industrial prices were canceling out any gains from the farm program, demanded that businessmen live up to the competitive faith. Labor spokesmen, bitterly disillusioned when the program failed to guarantee union recognition and collective bargaining, charged that the Administration had sold out to management. Small businessmen, certain that the new code authorities were only devices to increase the power of their larger rivals, raised the ancient cry of monopolistic exploitation. Antitrusters, convinced that the talk about strengthening competition was sheer hypocrisy, demanded that this disastrous trust-building program come to a halt. Economic planners, alienated by a process in which the businessmen did the planning, charged that the government was only sanctioning private monopolistic arrangements. And the American public, disillusioned with rising prices and the failure of the program to bring economic recovery, listened to the criticisms and demanded that its competitive ideals be made good.

The rising tide of public resentment greatly strengthened the hand of those that viewed the NRA primarily as a device for raising the plane of competition and securing social justice for labor. Picking up support from discontented groups, from other governmental agencies, and from such investigations as that conducted by Clarence Darrow's National Recovery Review Board, this group within the NRA had soon launched a campaign to bring about a reorientation in policy. By June 1934 it had obtained a formal written policy embodying its views, one that committed the NRA to the competitive ideal, renounced the use of price and production controls, and promised to subject the code authorities to strict public supervision. By this time, however, most of the major codes had been written, and the market restorers were never able to apply their policy to codes already approved. The chief effect of their efforts to do so was to antagonize businessmen and to complicate the difficulties of enforcing code provisions that were out of line with announced policy.

The result was a deadlock that persisted for the remainder of the agency's life. Putting the announced policy into effect would have meant, in all probability, the complete alienation of business support and the collapse of the whole structure. Yet accepting and enforcing the codes for what they were would have resulted, again in all probability, in an outraged public and congressional opinion that would have swept away the whole edifice. Thus the NRA tended to reflect the whole dilemma confronting the New Deal. Admittedly, declared policy was inconsistent with practice. Admittedly, the NRA was accomplishing little. Yet from a political standpoint, if the agency were to continue at all, a deadlock of this sort seemed to be the only solution. If the Supreme Court had not taken a hand in the matter, the probable outcome would have been either the abolition of the agency or a continuation of the deadlock.

The practical effect of the NRA, then, was to allow the erection, extension, and fortification of private monopolistic arrangements, particularly for groups that already possessed a fairly high degree of integration and monopoly power. Once these arrangements had been approved and vested interests had developed, the Administration found it difficult to deal with them. It could not move against them without alienating powerful interest groups, producing new economic dislocations, and running the risk of setting off the whole process of deflation again. Yet, because of the competitive ideal, it could not lend much support to the arrangements or provide much in the way of public supervision. Only in areas where other arguments, other ideals, and political pressure justified making an exception, in such areas as agriculture, natural resources, transportation, and to a certain extent labor, could the government lend its open support and direction.

Moreover, the policy dilemma, coupled with the sheer complexity of the undertaking, made it impossible to provide much central direction. There was little planning of a broad, general nature, either by businessmen or by the state; there was merely the half-hearted acceptance of a series of legalized, but generally uncoordinated, monopolistic combinations. The result was not over-all direction, but a type of partial, piecemeal, pressure-group planning, a type of planning designed by specific economic groups to balance production with consumption regardless of the dislocations produced elsewhere in the economy.

There were, certainly, proposals for other types of planning. But under the circumstances, they were and remained politically unfeasible, both during the NRA period and after. The idea of a government-supported business commonwealth still persisted, and a few men still felt that if the NRA had really applied it, the depression would have been over. Yet in the political context of the time, the idea was thoroughly unrealistic. For one thing, there was the growing gap between businessmen and New Dealers, the conviction of one side that cooperation would lead to bureaucratic socialism, of the other that it would lead to fascism or economic oppression. Even if this quarrel had not existed, the Administration could not have secured a program that ran directly counter to the anti-big-business sentiment of the time. The monopolistic implications in such a program were too obvious, and there was little that could be done to disguise them. Most industrial leaders recognized the situation, and the majority of them came to the conclusion that a political program of this sort was no longer necessary. With the crisis past and the deflationary process checked, private controls and such governmental aids as tariffs, subsidies, and loans would be sufficient.

The idea of national economic planning also persisted. A number of New Dealers continued to advocate the transfer of monopoly power from businessmen to the state or to other organized economic groups. Each major economic group, they argued, should be organized and allowed to participate in the formulation of a central plan, one that would result in expanded production, increased employment, a more equitable distribution, and a better balance of prices. Yet this idea, too, was thoroughly impractical when judged in terms of existing political realities. It ran counter to competitive and individualistic traditions. It threatened important vested interests. It largely ignored the complexities of the planning process or the tendency of regulated interests to dominate their regulators. And it was regarded by the majority of Americans as being overly radical, socialistic, and un-American.

Consequently, the planning of the New Deal was essentially single-industry planning, partial, piecemeal, and opportunistic, planning that could circumvent the competitive ideal or could be based on other ideals that justified making an exception. After the NRA experience, organized business groups found it increasingly difficult to devise these justifications. Some business leaders, to be sure, continued to talk about a public agency with power to waive the antitrust laws and sanction private controls. Yet few of them were willing to accept government participation in the planning process, and few were willing to come before the public with proposals that were immediately vulnerable to charges of monopoly. It was preferable, they felt, to let the whole issue lie quiet, to rely upon unauthorized private controls, and to hope that these would be little disturbed by antitrust action. Only a few peculiarly depressed groups, like the cotton textile industry, continued to agitate for government-supported cartels, and most of these groups lacked the cohesion, power, and alternative symbols that would have been necessary to put their programs through.

In some areas, however, especially in areas where alternative symbols were present and where private controls had broken down or proven impractical, it was possible to secure a type of partial planning. Agriculture was able to avoid most of the agitation against monopoly, and while retaining to a large extent its individualistic operations, to find ways of using the state to fix prices, plan production, and regularize markets. Its ability to do so was attributable in part to the political power of the farmers, but it was also due to manipulation of certain symbols that effectively masked the monopolistic implications in the program. The ideal of the yeoman farmer—honest, independent, and morally upright—still had a strong appeal in America, and to many Americans it justified the salvation of farming as a "way of life," even at the cost of subsidies and the violation of competitive standards. Agriculture, moreover, was supposed to be the basic industry, the activity that supported all others. The country, so it was said, could not be prosperous unless its farmers were prosperous. Finally, there was the conservation argument, the great concern over conservation of the soil, which served to justify some degree of public planning and some type of production control.

Similar justifications were sometimes possible for other areas of the economy. Monopolistic arrangements in certain food-processing industries could be camouflaged as an essential part of the farm program. Departures from competitive standards in such natural resource industries as bituminous coal and crude oil production could be justified on the grounds of conservation. Public controls and economic cartelization in the fields of transportation and communication could be justified on the ground that these were "natural monopolies" in which the public had a vital interest. And in the distributive trades, it was possible to turn anti-big-business sentiment against the mass distributors, to brand them as "monopolies," and to obtain a series of essentially anti-competitive measures on the theory that they were designed to preserve competition by preserving small competitors. The small merchant, however, was never able to dodge the agitation against monopoly to the same extent that the farmer did. The supports granted him were weak to begin with, and to obtain them he had to make concessions to the competitive ideal, concessions that robbed his measures of much of their intended effectiveness.

In some ways, too, the Roosevelt Administration helped to create monopoly power for labor. Under the New Deal program, the government proceeded to absorb surplus labor and prescribe minimum labor standards; more important, it encouraged labor organization to the extent that it maintained a friendly attitude, required employer recognition of unions, and restrained certain practices that had been used to break unions in the past. For a time, the appeals to social justice, humanitarianism, and anti-big-business sentiment overrode the appeal of business spokesmen and classical economists to the competitive ideal and individualistic traditions. The doctrine that labor was not a commodity, that men who had worked and produced and kept their obligations to society were entitled to be taken care of, was widely accepted. Along with it went a growing belief that labor unions were necessary to maintain purchasing power and counterbalance big business. Consequently, even the New Dealers of an antitrust persuasion generally made a place in their program for social legislation and labor organization.

The general effect of this whole line of New Deal policy might be summed up in the word counterorganization, that is, the creation of monopoly power in areas previously unorganized. One can only conclude, however, that this did not happen according to any preconceived plan. Nor did it necessarily promote economic expansion or raise consumer purchasing power. Public support of monopolistic arrangements occurred in a piecemeal, haphazard fashion, in response to pressure from specific economic groups and as opportunities presented themselves. Since consumer organizations were weak and efforts to aid consumers made little progress, the benefits went primarily to producer groups interested in restricting production and raising prices. In the distributive trades, the efforts to help small merchants tended, insofar as they were successful, to impede technological changes, hamper mass distributors, and reduce consumer purchasing power. In the natural resource and transportation industries, most of the new legislation was designed to restrict production, reduce competition, and protect invested capital. And in the labor and agricultural fields, the strengthening of market controls was often at the expense of consumers and in conjunction with business groups. The whole tendency of interest-group planning, in fact, was toward the promotion of economic scarcity. Each group, it seemed, was trying to secure a larger piece from a pie that was steadily dwindling in size.

From an economic standpoint, then, the partial planning of the post-NRA type made little sense, and most economists, be they antitrusters, planners, or devotees of laissez-faire, felt that such an approach was doing more harm than good. It was understandable only in a political context, and as a political solution, it did possess obvious elements of strength. It retained the antitrust laws and avoided any direct attack upon the competitive ideal or competitive mythology. Yet by appealing to other goals and alternative ideals and by using these to justify special and presumably exceptional departures from competitive standards, it could make the necessary concessions to pressure groups interested in reducing competition and erecting government-sponsored cartels.[4] Such a program might be logically inconsistent and economically harmful. Perhaps, as one critic suggested at the time, it combined the worst features of both worlds, "an impairment of the efficiency of the competitive system without the compensating benefits of rationalized collective action."[5] But politically it was a going concern, and efforts to achieve theoretical consistency met with little success.

Perhaps the greatest defect in these limited planning measures was their tendency toward restriction, their failure to provide any incentive for expansion when an expanding economy was the crying need of the time. The easiest way to counteract this tendency, it seemed, was through government expenditures and deficit financing; in practice, this was essentially the path that the New Deal took. By 1938 Roosevelt seemed willing to accept the Keynesian arguments for a permanent spending program, and eventually, when war demands necessitated pump-priming on a gigantic scale, the spending solution worked. It overcame the restrictive tendencies in the economy, re-

---

[4] See Paul T. Homan, in AEA, *Readings in the Social Control of Industry* (Philadelphia: Blakiston, 1942), 242–46, 252–54; and in *Political Science Quarterly*, June 1936, pp. 169–72, 178–84; Berle, in *Virginia Quarterly Review*, Summer 1938, pp. 330–31; Ernest Griffith, *Impasse of Democracy* (N.Y.: Harrison-Hilton, 1939), 231.

[5] Homan, in *Political Science Quarterly*, June 1936, p. 181.

stored full employment, and brought rapid economic expansion. Drastic institutional reform, it seemed, was unnecessary. Limited, piecemeal, pressure-group planning could continue, and the spending weapon could be relied upon to stimulate expansion and maintain economic balance.

One major stream of New Deal policy, then, ran toward partial planning. Yet this stream was shaped and altered, at least in a negative sense, by its encounters with the antitrust tradition and the competitive ideal. In a time when Americans distrusted business leadership and blamed big business for the prevailing economic misery, it was only natural that an antitrust approach should have wide political appeal. Concessions had to be made to it, and these concessions meant that planning had to be limited, piecemeal, and disguised. There could be no over-all program of centralized controls. There could be no government-sponsored business commonwealth. And there could be only a minimum of government participation in the planning process.

In and of itself, however, the antitrust approach did not offer a politically workable alternative. The antitrusters might set forth their own vision of the good society. They might blame the depression upon the departure from competitive standards and suggest measures to make industrial organization correspond more closely to the competitive model. But they could never ignore or explain away the deflationary and disruptive implications of their program. Nor could they enlist much support from the important political and economic pressure groups. Consequently, the antitrust approach, like that of planning, had to be applied on a limited basis. Action could be taken only in special or exceptional areas, against unusually privileged groups that were actively hated and particularly vulnerable, in fields where one business group was fighting another, in cases where no one would get hurt, or against practices that violated common standards of decency and fairness.

This was particularly true during the period prior to 1938. The power trust, for example, was a special demon in the progressive faith, one that was actively hated by large numbers of people and one that had not only violated competitive standards but had also outraged accepted canons of honesty and tampered with democratic political ideals. For such an institution, nothing was too bad, not even a little competition; and the resulting battle, limited though its gains might be, did provide a suitable outlet for popular antitrust feeling. Much the same was also true of the other antitrust activities. Financial reform provided another outlet for antitrust sentiment, although its practical results were little more than regulation for the promotion of honesty and facilitation of the governmental spending program. The attacks upon such practices as collusive bidding, basing-point pricing, and block-booking benefited from a long history of past agitation. And the suits in the petroleum and auto-finance industries had the support of discontented business groups. The result of such activities, however, could hardly be more than marginal.

When the antitrusters reached for real weapons, when they tried, for example, to use the taxing power or make drastic changes in corporate law, they found that any thorough-going program was simply not within the realm of political possibilities.

Under the circumstances, it appeared, neither planning nor antitrust action could be applied in a thorough-going fashion. Neither approach could completely eclipse the other. Yet the political climate and situation did change; and, as a result of these changes, policy vacillated between the two extremes. One period might see more emphasis on planning, the next on antitrust action, and considerable changes might also take place in the nature, content, and scope of each program.

Superficially, the crisis of 1937 was much like that of 1933. Again there were new demands for antitrust action, and again these demands were blended with new proposals for planning, rationalization, and monopolistic controls. In some respects, too, the results were similar. There was more partial planning in unorganized areas, and eventually, this was accompanied by a resumption of large-scale federal spending. The big difference was in the greater emphasis on an antitrust approach, which could be attributed primarily to the difference in political circumstances. The alienation of the business community, memories of NRA experiences, and the growing influence of antimonopolists in the Roosevelt Administration made it difficult to work out any new scheme of business-government cooperation. These same factors, coupled with the direct appeal of New Dealers to the competitive ideal, made it difficult for business groups to secure public sanction for monopolistic arrangements. The political repercussions of the recession, the fact that the new setback had occurred while the New Deal was in power, made it necessary to appeal directly to anti-big-business sentiment and to use the administered price thesis to explain why the recession had occurred and why the New Deal had failed to achieve sustained recovery. Under the circumstances, the initiative passed to the anti-trusters, and larger concessions had to be made to their point of view.

One such concession was the creation of the Temporary National Economic Committee. Yet this was not so much a victory for the antitrusters as it was a way of avoiding the issue, a means of minimizing the policy conflict within the Administration and postponing any final decision. Essentially, the TNEC was a harmless device that could be used by each group to urge a specific line of action or no action at all. Antimonopolists hoped that it would generate the political sentiment necessary for a major breakthrough against concentrated economic power, but these hopes were never realized. In practice, the investigation became largely an ineffective duplicate of the frustrating debate that produced it, and by the time its report was filed, the circumstances had changed. Most of the steam had gone out of the monopoly issue, and antitrust sentiment was being replaced by war-induced patriotism.

The second major concession to antimonopoly sentiment was Thurman

Arnold's revival of antitrust prosecutions, a program that presumably was designed to restore a competitive system, one in which prices were flexible and competition would provide the incentive for expansion. Actually, the underlying assumptions behind such a program were of doubtful validity. Price flexibility, even if attainable, might do more harm than good. The Arnold approach had definite limitations, even assuming that the underlying theories were sound. It could and did break up a number of loose combinations; it could and did disrupt monopolistic arrangements that were no necessary part of modern industrialism. It could and, in some cases, did succeed in convincing businessmen that they should adopt practices that corresponded a bit more closely to the competitive model. But it made no real effort to rearrange the underlying industrial structure itself, no real attempt to dislodge vested interests, disrupt controls that were actual checks against deflation, or break up going concerns. And since the practices and policies complained of would appear in many cases to be the outgrowth of this underlying structure, the Arnold program had little success in achieving its avowed goals.

Even within these limits, moreover, Arnold's antitrust campaign ran into all sorts of difficulties. Often the combinations that he sought to break up were the very ones that the earlier New Deal had fostered. Often, even though the arrangements involved bore little relation to actual production, their sponsors claimed that they did, that their disruption would set the process of deflation in motion again and impair industrial efficiency. Arnold claimed that his activities enjoyed great popular support, and as a symbol and generality they probably did. But when they moved against specific arrangements, it was a different story. There they succeeded in alienating one political pressure group after another. Then, with the coming of the war, opposition became stronger than ever. As antitrust sentiment was replaced by wartime patriotism, it seemed indeed that the disruption of private controls would reduce efficiency and impair the war effort. Consequently, the Arnold program gradually faded from the scene.

It is doubtful, then, that the innovations of 1938 should be regarded as a basic reversal in economic policy. What actually happened was not the substitution of one set of policies for another, but rather a shift in emphasis between two sets of policies that had existed side by side throughout the entire period. Policies that attacked monopoly and those that fostered it, policies that reflected the underlying dilemma of industrial America, had long been inextricably intertwined in American history, and this basic inconsistency persisted in an acute form during the nineteen thirties. Policy might and did vacillate between the two extremes; but because of the limitations of the American political structure and of American economic ideology, it was virtually impossible for one set of policies to displace the other. The New Deal reform movement was forced to adjust to this basic fact. The practical outcome was an economy characterized by private controls, partial planning,

compensatory governmental spending, and occasional gestures toward the
competitive ideal.

SUGGESTED READING

George Wolfskill, in *The Revolt of the Conservatives* (1962), and
Frederick Rudolph, in "The American Liberty League, 1934–1940,"
American Historical Review, LVI (Oct. 1950), focus on the Liberty
League, a business group opposed to the New Deal, but fail to exam-
ine the business community in general and hence provide inadequate
analyses. Gene Gressley's "Thurman Arnold, Antitrust and the New
Deal," *Business History Review*, XXXVIII (Summer 1964); Ralph
DeBedts' *The New Deal's SEC: The Formative Years* (1964); Mi-
chael Parrish's *Securities Regulation and the New Deal* (1970);
Charles Jackson's *Food and Drug Legislation in the New Deal*
(1970); and Thomas P. Jenckin's *Reactions of Major Groups to Positive Government in the U.S., 1930–1940* (1945) are worth consulting.
William H. Wilson, in "How the Chamber of Commerce Viewed the
NRA: A Reexamination," *Mid-America*, XLIV (Apr. 1962), seeks to
correct Schlesinger's interpretation that the Chamber firmly supported
the National Recovery Administration.

There is still no volume that specifically treats the history of the
NRA, but Hugh Johnson's *The Blue Eagle from Egg to Earth* (1935)
and Donald Richberg's *The Rainbow* (1936) are useful works by two
administrators of the agency. Other contemporary evaluations may be
found in *The National Recovery Administration*, by Leverett Lyon *et
al.* (1935) and *The Economics of the Recovery Administration*, by
Douglas V. Brown *et al.* (1935).

James P. Johnson's "Drafting the NRA Code of Fair Competition
for the Bituminous Coal Industry," *Journal of American History*, LIII
(Dec. 1966), is a useful source on the coal industry; Louis Galambos'
Competition and Cooperation (1966) should be consulted for information regarding the cotton textile industry. Gerald Nash, in *United
States Oil Policy, 1890–1964: Business and Government in Twentieth-Century America* (1968), discusses efforts to restrict competition
during the New Deal years. Nash has also made a brief study of the
relation between the First World War mobilization and the NRA in
"Experiments in Industrial Mobilization: WIB and NRA," *Mid-America*, XLV (July 1963).

PAUL W. SCHROEDER

The Axis Alliance and Japanese-American Relations, 1941: An Appraisal of the American Policy

INTRODUCTION

In the last decade of the nineteenth century, both Japan and the United States began to manifest imperial intentions toward China. However, as Secretary of State John Hay made clear in a series of notes to the great powers in 1899 and 1900, the United States desired not territory in China but trade; Hay expected the other interested powers to assist America's commercial domination of China by maintaining the Open Door policy and respecting China's territorial integrity. Japan, in contrast, harbored a quite traditional, and thereby conflicting, notion of empire in China. Japan and the United States coexisted only unhappily as the great powers of the Pacific.

In 1931, when the Japanese Army defied John Hay's famous principles and ended the fiction of Chinese sovereignty in Manchuria, Japanese-American relations entered a particularly bitter period. To express the government's moral indignation at Japanese aggression in Manchuria, in January 1932, Secretary of State Henry Stimson withheld recognition of Manchukuo, the puppet kingdom established by Japan to replace the Chinese province. Stimson's doctrine of nonrecognition made clear America's disapproval, but his gesture, unaccompanied as it was by sanctions, merely poisoned Japanese-American relations without rendering assistance to the Chinese.

FROM Paul W. Schroeder, *The Axis Alliance and Japanese-American Relations, 1941*, pp. 200–16. Copyright © 1958 by American Historical Association. Reprinted by permission of the Cornell University Press.

When the Roosevelt administration came to power in 1933, it also refused to recognize Manchukuo, but it refrained from further moralistic denunciations. Relations improved markedly thereafter until 1937, when an accidental clash in North China between Chinese and Japanese troops expanded into full-scale war. The United States then resumed its condemnation of Japan. As the war dragged on, American hostility to Japan intensified, and in 1939 the administration began granting small loans to the Chinese government. At the end of the year, the United States abrogated its commercial treaty with Japan to allow for a possible embargo in the future.

When Hitler's stunning triumphs in Western Europe in May 1940 revealed how vulnerable the Dutch, French, and even British empires in the Pacific were, Japan decided to extend her imperial sway southward. In June, Japan forced the French colonial administration in Indochina to permit the Japanese Army to occupy the northern half of Vietnam. And in September, Japan concluded a military alliance with Germany and Italy to secure her position in world politics. These developments alarmed Roosevelt and led him to take a momentous step. He knew, of course, that exports of American oil and scrap metal were making Japanese war production possible; however, he feared that a total embargo might induce not moderation in Tokyo, but a Japanese invasion of the Dutch East Indies, whose natural resources could substitute for the American exports. On September 28, 1940, therefore, Roosevelt ended American shipments of scrap metal and iron to Japan, but he permitted the oil trade to continue.

After a brief, indecisive period, Japan moved in July 1941, into the south of Vietnam to complete the occupation of that country and to prepare an assault on the rest of Southeast Asia. Roosevelt on July 25 cut off Japan's supply of American oil. His decision left Japan with only two courses of action: she would have to either negotiate a settlement with the United States or obtain her own source of oil in Southeast Asia. Shrinking from the prospect of war with the Western powers, Prime Minister Konoye .in August of 1941 offered to meet with Roosevelt to work out the terms of settlement quickly at the highest level. But Roosevelt refused, acting on Secreatary of State Cordell Hull's advice that the President reject the meeting unless the Prime Minister offered in advance to make specific commitments about China. Konoye refused to make any such commitments and as a result negotiations had to continue through normal diplomatic channels. Because Roosevelt's rebuff strengthened the argument of Japanese expansionists and because Konoye was unable to find suitable terms of settlement, the Cabinet was forced to resign in October. The government was then turned over to the extremist General Hideki Tojo.

At the urging of the emperor, Tojo's Government made a last attempt at peace. On November 5, Japan offered the United

States a general settlement (Plan A); if that was refused, a temporary truce (Plan B) would be presented. If no agreement was achieved by November 25, the Japanese war machine would roll. Because the Japanese diplomatic code had been broken, Washington knew the contents of both plans in advance. Secretary of State Hull rejected Plan A out of hand: its implementation, he believed, would mean a sell-out in China. Plan B, which was subsequently offered, promised that Japan would not make new moves in Southeast Asia and the South Pacific, would draw her forces back to northern Vietnam, and would abandon Vietnam entirely at the conclusion of a general peace. In return the United States was to resume exports of oil to Japan and agree to a vaguely worded statement (Point 5) concerning China.

Point 5 stated, "The Government of the United States undertakes to refrain from such measures and actions as will be prejudicial to the endeavors for restoration of general peace between Japan and China." Hopelessly bogged down in China and desperate for a compromise solution, Japan believed that American aid to China was the major obstacle to a settlement. Though the meaning of Point 5 has been variously interpreted, Hull assumed that it required the immediate abandonment of China, and on November 26, 1941, he rejected Plan B.

Hull was by now so outraged at Japan for her disregard of international law that he would not countenance even temporary compromise over China, and he chose to uphold principle even if that meant war. He did have a general idea of the consequences of his decision, for as Roosevelt and Hull were studying Plan B, an incoming cable from Tokyo to the Japanese Ambassador was being deciphered. It said, "If you can bring about the signing of the pertinent notes we will wait till November 29. . . . After that things are automatically going to happen." It was only on December 7, 1941, that Hull learned the particulars.

The Japanese attack on Pearl Harbor extinguished the doubts of those Americans who had wished their nation to stay out of the war; they firmly supported their President's request on December 8 for a declaration of war against Japan. Three days later Hitler responded to Japan's request for a German declaration of war against the United States. When the President and Congress reciprocated, America entered the global conflict. Had Hull's inflexibility not provoked Japan's attack, it is at least possible, though not probable, that the United States might not have entered the European war and taken arms against Nazism, although Nazism was soon regarded by many Americans as a radical evil.

Paul W. Schroeder, professor of history at the University of Illinois and a proponent of the "realism" advocated by George Kennan, is perhaps the most effective "realist" critic of Hull's diplomacy. In *The Axis Alliance and Japanese-American Relations, 1941* (1958) Schroeder indicts the general assumptions of Ameri-

can policy as well as its execution. About Plan B, for instance, he
writes, "It is far from certain that Point 5 actually was a demand
for immediate cessation of aid [to China] or that the Japanese
would have insisted upon this as a *sine qua non* for agreement."
In the selection reprinted below from his book, he sums up his
appraisal of American foreign policy. By choosing to assess the
policy, he differs from historians, who, like Ernest May of Harvard, believe that diplomatic history should be neo-Rankean: the
description and analysis, not the criticism, of what happened.

Schroeder, although he moves beyond the limited enterprise endorsed by May, chooses to restrict his assignment in another important way: he does not analyze the reasons for Hull's
moral and legal inflexibility. Was it that Hull, along with many of
his fellow citizens, was so moralistic about foreign policy that he
was unable to accept "realist" conceptions of the national interest? Or did Hull and others believe that the concessions required
for peace represented a threat to America's national interest?

*I*n judging American policy toward Japan in 1941, it might be
well to separate what is still controversial from what is not. There is no longer
any real doubt that the war came about over China. Even an administration
stalwart like Henry L. Stimson and a sympathetic critic like Herbert Feis
concur in this.[1] Nor is it necessary to speculate any longer as to what could
have induced Japan to launch such an incredible attack upon the United
States and Great Britain as occurred at Pearl Harbor and in the south Pacific.
One need not, as Winston Churchill did in wartime, characterize it as "an
irrational act" incompatible "with prudence or even with sanity."[2] The
Japanese were realistic about their position throughout; they did not suddenly go insane. The attack was an act of desperation, not madness. Japan
fought only when she had her back to the wall as a result of America's diplomatic and economic offensive.

The main point still at issue is whether the United States was wise in
maintaining a "hard" program of diplomatic and economic pressure on Japan
from July 1941 on. Along with this issue go two subsidiary questions: the first,

---

[1] "If at any time the United States had been willing to concede Japan a free
hand in China, there would have been no war in the Pacific" (Henry Stimson and
McGeorge Bundy, *On Active Service* [New York: Harper & Row, 1948], 256). "Our full
induction into this last World War followed our refusal to let China fend for
itself. We had rejected all proposals which would have allowed Japan to remain in
China and Manchuria. . . . Japan had struck—rather than accept frustration"
(Herbert Feis, *The China Tangle* [Princeton: Princeton University Press, 1953], 3).

[2] Speech to U.S. Congress, Washington, Dec. 26, 1941, *War Speeches of Churchill*, II, 150.

whether it was wise to make the liberation of China the central aim of American policy and the immediate evacuation of Japanese troops a requirement for agreement; the second, whether it was wise to decline Premier Konoye's invitation to a meeting of leaders in the Pacific. On all these points, the policy which the United States carried out still has distinguished defenders. The paramount issue between Japan and the United States, they contend, always was the China problem. In her China policy, Japan showed that she was determined to secure domination over a large area of East Asia by force. Apart from the legitimate American commercial interests which would be ruined or excluded by this Japanese action, the United States, for reasons of her own security and of world peace, had sufficient stake in Far Eastern questions to oppose such aggression. Finally, after ten years of Japanese expansion, it was only sensible and prudent for the United States to demand that it come to an end and that Japan retreat. In order to meet the Japanese threat, the United States had a perfect right to use the economic power she possessed in order to compel the Japanese to evacuate their conquered territory. If Japan chose to make this a cause for war, the United States could not be held responsible.

A similar defense is offered on the decision to turn down Konoye's Leaders' Conference. Historians may concede, as do Langer and Gleason, that Konoye was probably sincere in wanting peace and that he "envisaged making additional concessions to Washington, including concessions on the crucial issue of the withdrawal of Japanese troops from China." But, they point out, Konoye could never have carried the Army with him on any such concession.[3] If the United States was right in requiring Japan to abandon the Co-Prosperity Sphere, then her leaders were equally right in declining to meet with a Japanese Premier who, however conciliatory he might have been personally, was bound by his own promises and the exigencies of Japanese politics to maintain this national aim. In addition, there was the serious possiblity that much could be lost from such a meeting—the confidence of China, the cohesiveness of the coalition with Great Britain and Russia. In short, there was not enough prospect of gain to merit taking the chance.

This is a point of view which must be taken seriously. Any judgment on the wisdom or folly of the American policy, in fact, must be made with caution—there are no grounds for dogmatic certainty. The opinion here to be developed, nonetheless, is that the American policy from the end of July to December was a grave mistake. It should not be necessary to add that this does not make it treason. There is a "back door to war" theory, espoused in various forms by Charles A. Beard, George Morgenstern, Charles C. Tansill, and, most recently, Rear Admiral Robert A. Theobald, which holds that the President chose the Far East as a rear entrance to the war in Europe and to

---

[3] William L. Langer and S. Everett Gleason, *The Undeclared War, 1940–1941* (New York: Harper & Row, 1953), 706–707.

that end deliberately goaded the Japanese into an attack.[4] This theory is quite different and quite incredible. It is as impossible to accept as the idea that Japan attacked the United States in a spirit of overconfidence or that Hitler pushed the Japanese into war. Roosevelt's fault, if any, was not that of deliberately provoking the Japanese to attack, but of allowing Hull and others to talk him out of impulses and ideas which, had he pursued them, might have averted the conflict. Moreover, the mistake (assuming that it was a mistake) of a too hard and rigid policy with Japan was, as has been pointed out, a mistake shared by the whole nation, with causes that were deeply organic. Behind it was not sinister design or warlike intent, but a sincere and uncompromising adherence to moral principles and liberal doctrines.

This is going ahead too fast, however; one needs first of all to define the mistake with which American policy is charged. Briefly, it was this. In the attempt to gain everything at once, the United States lost her opportunity to secure immediately her essential requirements in the Far East and to continue to work toward her long-range goals. She succeeded instead only in making inevitable an unnecessary and avoidable war—an outcome which constitutes the ultimate failure of diplomacy. Until July 1941, as already demonstrated, the United States consistently sought to attain two limited objectives in the Far East, those of splitting the Axis and of stopping Japan's advance southward. Both aims were in accordance with America's broad strategic interests; both were reasonable, attainable goals. Through a combination of favorable circumstance and forceful American action, the United States reached the position where the achievement of these two goals was within sight. At this very moment, on the verge of a major diplomatic victory, the United States abandoned her original goals and concentrated on a third, the liberation of China. This last aim was not in accord with American strategic interests, was not a limited objective, and, most important, was completely incapable of being achieved by peaceful means and doubtful of attainment even by war. Through her single-minded pursuit of this unattainable goal, the United States forfeited the diplomatic victory which she had already virtually won. The unrelenting application of extreme economic pressure on Japan, instead of compelling the evacuation of China, rendered war inevitable, drove Japan back into the arms of Germany for better or for worse, and precipitated the wholesale plunge by Japan into the South Seas. As it ultimately turned out, the United States succeeded in liberating China only at great cost and when it was too late to do the cause of the Nationalist Chinese much real good.

This is not, of course, a new viewpoint. It is in the main simply that of

---

[4] Charles A. Beard, *President Roosevelt and the Coming of the War, 1941* (New Haven: Yale University Press, 1948); George E. Morgenstern, *Pearl Harbor: The Story of the Secret War* (New York: Devin-Adair, 1947); Charles C. Tansill, *Back Door to War* (Chicago: Regnery, 1952); Rear Admiral Robert A. Theobald, *The Final Secret of Pearl Harbor* (New York: Devin-Adair, 1954).

Ambassador Grew, who has held and defended it since 1941. The arguments he advances seem cogent and sensible in the light of present knowledge. Briefly summarized, they are the following: First is his insistence on the necessity of distinguishing between long-range and immediate goals in foreign policy and on the folly of demanding the immediate realization of both.[5] Second is his contention that governments are brought to abandon aggressive policies not by sudden conversion through moral lectures, but by the gradual recognition that the policy of aggression will not succeed. According to Grew, enough awareness of failure existed in the government of Japan in late 1941 to enable it to make a beginning in the process of reversal of policy—but not nearly enough to force Japan to a wholesale surrender of her conquests and aims.[6] Third was his conviction that what was needed on both sides was time—time in which the United States could grow stronger and in which the tide of war in Europe could be turned definitely against Germany, time in which the sense of failure could grow in Japan and in which moderates could gain better control of the situation. A victory in Europe, Grew observed, would either automatically solve the problem of Japan or make that problem, if necessary, much easier to solve by force.[7] Fourth was his belief that Japan would fight if backed to the wall (a view vindicated by events) [8] and that a war at this time with Japan could not possibly serve the interests of the United States. Even if one considered war as the only final answer to Japanese militarism, still, Grew would answer, the United States stood to gain nothing by seeking a decision in 1941. The time factor was entirely in America's favor. Japan could not hope to gain as much from a limited relaxation of the embargo as the United States could from time gained for mobilization; Roosevelt and the military strategists were in fact anxious to gain time by a *modus vivendi*.[9]

There is one real weakness in Grew's argument upon which his critics have always seized. This is his contention that Konoye, faced after July 26 with the two clear alternatives of war or a genuine peace move, which would

---

[5] Joseph Grew, *Turbulent Era*, edited by Walter Johnson (Boston: Houghton Mifflin, 1952), II, 1255.

[6] *Ibid.*, 1290.

[7] *Ibid.*, 1268–1269, 1286.

[8] The opposite belief, that Japan would give way, not only was inconsonant with the best available political and military intelligence, but was also a bad estimate of Japanese national psychology and of expansionist psychology in general. F. C. Jones rightly criticizes it as "the folly of supposing that the rulers of a powerful nation, having committed themselves to an expansionist policy, will abandon or reverse that policy when confronted by the threat of war. So long as they see, or think they see, any possibility of success, they will elect to fight rather than face the humiliation and probable internal revolt which submission to the demands of their opponents would entail" (F. C. Jones, *Japan's New Order in East Asia* [Toronto: Oxford University Press, 1954], 461).

[9] Grew, *Turbulent Era*, II, 1276–1277.

of necessity include a settlement with China, had chosen the latter course and could have carried through a policy of peace had he been given the time. "We believed," he writes, "that Prince Konoye was in a position to carry the country with him in a program of peace" and to make commitments to the United States which would "eventually, if not immediately" meet the conditions of Hull's Four Points.[10] The answer of critics is that, even if one credits Konoye's sincerity and takes his assurances at face value, there is still no reason to believe that he could have carried even his own cabinet, much less the whole nation, with him on any program approximating that of Hull. In particular, as events show, he could not have persuaded the Army to evacuate China.[11]

The objection is well taken; Grew was undoubtedly over-optimistic about Konoye's capacity to carry through a peaceful policy. This one objection, however, does not ruin Grew's case. He countered it later with the argument that a settlement with Japan which allowed Japanese garrisons to remain in China on a temporary basis would not have been a bad idea. Although far from an ideal solution, it would have been better, for China as well, than the policy the United States actually followed. It would have brought China what was all-important—a cessation of fighting—without involving the United States, as many contended, in either a sacrifice of principle or a betrayal of China. The United States, Grew points out, had never committed herself to guaranteeing China's integrity. Further, it would not have been necessary to agree to anything other than temporary garrisons in North China which, in more favorable times, the United States could work to have removed. The great mistake was to allow American policy to be guided by a sentimental attitude toward China which in the long run could do neither the United States nor China any good. As Grew puts it:

> Japan's advance to the south, including her occupation of portions of China, constituted for us a real danger, and it was definitely in our national interest that it be stopped, by peaceful means if possible, by force of arms if necessary. American aid to China should have been regarded, as we believe it was regarded by our Government, as an indirect means to this end, and not from a sentimental viewpoint. The President's letter of January 21, 1941, shows that he then sensed the important issues in the Far East, and that he did not include China, purely for China's sake, among them. . . . The failure of the Washington Administration to seize the opportunity presented in August and September, 1941, to halt the southward advance by peaceful means, together with the paramount importance attached to the China question during the conversations in Washington, gives rise to the belief that not our Government

---

[10] *Ibid.*, 1263–1264.

[11] Herbert Feis, *Road to Pearl Harbor* (Princeton: Princeton University Press, 1950), 275–277; Jones, *Japan's New Order*, 457–458.

but millions of quite understandably sympathetic but almost totally unin-
formed American citizens had assumed control of our Far Eastern policy.[12]

There remains the obvious objection that Grew's solution, however
plausible it may now seem, was politically impracticable in 1941. No American government could then have treated China as expendable, just as no
Japanese government could have written off the China Affair as a dead loss.
This is in good measure true and goes a long way to explain, if not to justify,
the hard American policy. Yet it is not entirely certain that no solution could
have been found which would both have averted war and have been accepted by the American people, had a determined effort been made to find
one. As F. C. Jones points out, the United States and Japan were not faced in
July 1941 with an absolute dilemma of peace or war, of complete settlement
or open conflict. Hull believed that they were, of course; but his all-or-
nothing attitude constituted one of his major shortcomings as a diplomat.
Between the two extremes existed the possibility of a *modus vivendi*, an
agreement settling some issues and leaving others in abeyance. Had Roosevelt and Konoye met, Jones argues, they might have been able to agree on a
relaxation of the embargo in exchange for satisfactory assurances on the
Tripartite Pact and southward expansion, with the China issue laid aside.
The United States would not have had to cease aid, nor Japan to remove her
troops. The final settlement of the Far Eastern question, Jones concludes,

> would then have depended upon the issue of the struggle in Europe. If Ger-
> many prevailed, then the United States would be in no position to oppose
> Japanese ambitions in Asia; if Germany were defeated, Japan would be in no
> position to persist in those ambitions in the face of the United States, the
> USSR, and the British Commonwealth.[13]

Such an agreement, limited and temporary in nature, would have involved
no sacrifice of principle for either nation, yet would have removed the immediate danger of war. As a temporary expedient and as an alternative to otherwise inevitable and useless conflict, it could have been sold by determined
effort to the public on both sides. Nor would it have been impossible, in the
writer's opinion, to have accompanied or followed such an agreement with a
simple truce or standstill in the China conflict through American mediation.
    This appraisal, to be sure, is one based on realism. Grew's criticism of
Hull's policy and the alternative he offers to it are both characterized by fundamental attention to what is practical and expedient at a given time and to
limited objectives within the scope of the national interest. In general, the
writer agrees with this point of view, believing that, as William A. Orton

---

[12] Grew, *Turbulent Era*, II, 1367–1368.

[13] Jones, *Japan's New Order*, 459.

points out, it is foolish and disastrous to treat nations as morally responsible persons, "because their nature falls far short of personality," and that, as George F. Kennan contends, the right role for moral considerations in foreign affairs is not to determine policy, but rather to soften and ameliorate actions necessarily based on the realities of world politics.[14]

From this realistic standpoint, the policy of the State Department would seem to be open to other criticisms besides those of Grew. The criticisms, which may be briefly mentioned here, are those of inconsistency, blindness to reality, and futility. A notable example of the first would be the inconsistency of a strong no-compromise stand against Japan with the policy of broad accommodation to America's allies, especially Russia, both before and after the American entrance into the war.[15] The inconsistency may perhaps best be seen by comparing the American stand in 1941 on such questions as free trade, the Open Door in China, the territorial and administrative integrity of China, the maintenance of the prewar *status quo* in the Far East, and the sanctity of international agreements with the position taken on the same questions at the Yalta Conference in 1945.[16]

---

[14] William A. Orton, *The Liberal Tradition* (New Haven: Yale University Press, 1944), 239; George F. Kennan, *American Diplomacy, 1900–1950* (Chicago: University of Chicago Press, 1951), 95–103.

[15] One notes with interest, for example, a pre-Pearl Harbor statement by Senator Lister Hill of Alabama, a strong proponent of a radical anti-Japanese policy, as to America's attitude toward the Soviet Union: "It is not the business of this government to ask or to receive any assurance from Stalin about what he will do with regard to Finland after the war. . . . It is the business of this government to look out for and defend the vital interests of the United States" (*New York Times*, Nov. 5, 1941). If in the above quotation one reads "Tojo" for "Stalin" and "China" for "Finland," the result is a statement of the extreme isolationist position on the Far East which Hill and other supporters of the administration found so detestable.

[16] The writer has no desire to enter here into the controversy over the merits of the Yalta decisions, but only to draw a certain parallel. The standard defense for the Yalta policy on the Far East has been the contention that the United States conceded to Soviet Russia only what the U.S.S.R. could and would have seized without American leave, that the only alternative to aggreement would have been war with Russia, and that securing Russian entrance into the Far Eastern war was considered militarily necessary (George F. Lensen, "Yalta and the Far East," in John L. Snell, Forrest C. Pogue, Charles F. Delzell, and George F. Lensen, *The Meaning of Yalta: Big Three Diplomacy and the New Balance of Power* [Baton Rouge: Louisiana State University Press, 1956], 163–164). The argument may be quite sound, but surely it would serve equally well—indeed, much better, *mutatis mutandis*—to justify a policy of conciliation toward Japan in 1941. Applied to Japan, the argument would then read as follows: The United States would have conceded to Japan only the temporary possession of a part of what Japan had already seized without American leave; the only alternative to agreement would have been war with Japan; and preventing Japanese entrance into the European war was considered militarily necessary. The great difference between the two situations would seem to be that the concessions envisioned by Japan in 1941 were temporary and reversible; those gained by Russia in 1945 were not. The very necessity of pursuing the Yalta policy in 1945 casts doubt on the wisdom of the hard-and-fast stand of 1941. Felix Morley has put the parallel neatly: "To assert that the sudden and complete reversal of the long-established Far Eastern policy was justified was also to say, by implication, that the policy reversed was fundamentally

The blindness to reality may be seen in the apparent inability of American policy makers to take seriously into account the gravity of Japan's economic plight or the real exigencies of her military and strategic position, particularly as these factors would affect the United States over the long run.[17] Equally unrealistic and more fateful was the lack of appreciation on the part of many influential people and of wide sections of the public of the almost certain consequences to be expected from the pressure exerted on Japan—namely, American involvement in a war her military strategists considered highly undesirable. The attitude has been well termed by Robert Osgood, "this blind indifference toward the military and political consequences of a morally-inspired position." [18]

The charge of futility, finally, could be laid to the practice of insisting on a literal subscription to principles which, however noble, had no chance of general acceptance or practical application. The best example is the persistent demand that the Japanese pledge themselves to carrying out nineteenth-century principles of free trade and equal access to raw materials in a twentieth-century world where economic nationalism and autarchy, trade barriers and restrictions were everywhere the order of the day, and not the least in the United States under the New Deal. Not one of America's major allies would have subscribed whole heartedly to Hull's free-trade formula; what good it could have done to pin the Japanese down to it is hard to determine.[19]

---

faulty, that to fight a war with Japan in behalf of Chinese nationalism had been a dreadful mistake" (*The Foreign Policy of the United States* [New York: Alfred A. Knopf, 1951], 87–88). One may, as Morley does, reject both the above premise and the conclusion, or one may accept both; but it is difficult to see how one may affirm the premise and deny the conclusion. For those who believe that a vital moral difference existed between the two cases, the problem would seem to be how to show that it is morally unjustifiable to violate principle in order to keep a potential enemy out of a war, yet morally justifiable to sacrifice principle in order to get a potential ally into it. The dilemma appears insoluble.

[17] In his very interesting book, *America's Strategy in World Politics* (New York: Harcourt, Brace, 1942), Nicholas Spykman displays some of the insights which seem to have been lacking in the American policy of the time. He points out, for example, that Japan's economic and geographic position was essentially the same as that of Great Britain; that her position vis-à-vis the United States was also roughly equivalent to England's; that therefore it made little sense for America to aid Great Britain in maintaining a European balance of power, while at the same time trying to force Japan to give up all her buffer states in Asia; that the Japanese war potential could not compare to that of a revivified and unified China; and that one day (a striking prediction in 1942!) the United States would have to undertake to protect Japan from Soviet Russia and China (pp. 135–137, 469–470). Spykman saw then what is today so painfully evident—that without a Japanese foothold on the Asiatic mainland no real balance of power is possible in Asia.

[18] Robert E. Osgood, *Ideals and Self-Interest in America's Foreign Relations* (Chicago: University of Chicago Press, 1953), 361.

[19] A memorandum by the Chief of the State Department Division of Commercial Policy and Agreements (Hawkins) to Ballantine, Washington, Nov. 10, 1941, offers interesting comments on the extent and nature of the trade discriminations then being practiced against Japan by nations throughout the world, including the United States (*Foreign Relations, 1941*, IV, 576–577).

But these are all criticisms based on a realistic point of view, and to judge the American policy solely from this point of view is to judge it unfairly and by a standard inappropriate to it. The policy of the United States was avowedly not one of realism, but of principle. If then it is to be understood on its own grounds and judged by its own standards, the main question will be whether the policy was morally right—that is, in accord with principles of peace and international justice. Here, according to its defenders, the American policy stands vindicated. For any other policy, any settlement with Japan at the expense of China, would have meant a betrayal not only of China, but also of vital principles and of America's moral task in the world.

This, as we know, was the position of Hull and his co-workers. It has been stated more recently by Basil Rauch, who writes:

> No one but an absolute pacifist would argue that the danger of war is a greater evil than violation of principle. . . . The isolationist believes that appeasement of Japan without China's consent violated no principle worth a risk of war. The internationalist must believe that the principle did justify a risk of war.[20]

This is not an argument to be dismissed lightly. The contention that the United States had a duty to fulfill in 1941, and that this duty consisted in holding to justice and morality in a world given to international lawlessness and barbarism and in standing on principle against an unprincipled and ruthless aggressor, commands respect. It is not answered by dismissing it as unrealistic or by proscribing all moral considerations in foreign policy. An answer may be found, however, in a closer definition of America's moral duty in 1941. According to Hull, and apparently also Rauch, the task was primarily one of upholding principle. This is not the only possible definition. It may well be contended that the moral duty was rather one of doing the most practical good possible in a chaotic world situation and, further, that this was the main task President Roosevelt and the administration had in mind at least till the end of July 1941.

If the moral task of the United States in the Far East was to uphold a principle of absolute moral value, the principle of nonappeasement of aggressors, then the American policy was entirely successful in fulfilling it. The American diplomats proved that the United States was capable of holding to its position in disregard and even in defiance of national interests narrowly conceived. If, however, the task was one of doing concrete good and giving practical help where needed, especially to China, then the American policy falls fatally short. For it can easily be seen not only that the policy followed did not in practice help China, but also that it could not have been expected to. Although it was a pro-China and even a China-first policy in

---

[20] Basil Rauch, *Roosevelt, From Munich to Pearl Harbor* (Creative Age, 1950), 472.

principle, it was not in practical fact designed to give China the kind of help needed.

What China required above all by late 1941 was clearly an end to the fighting, a chance to recoup her strength. Her chaotic financial condition, a disastrous inflation, civil strife with the Communists, severe hunger and privation, and falling morale all enfeebled and endangered her further resistance. Chiang Kai-shek, who knew this, could hope only for an end to the war through the massive intervention of American forces and the consequent liberation of China. It was in this hope that he pleaded so strongly for a hard American policy toward Japan. Chiang's hopes, however, were wholly unrealistic. For though the United States was willing to risk war for China's sake, and finally did incur it over the China issue, the Washington government never intended in case of war to throw America's full weight against Japan in order to liberate China. The American strategy always was to concentrate on Europe first, fighting a defensive naval war in the Far East and aiding China, as before, in order to keep the Japanese bogged down. The possibility was faced and accepted that the Chinese might have to go on fighting for some years before eventual liberation through the defeat of Japan. The vehement Chinese protests over this policy were unavailing, and the bitter disillusionment suffered by the Chinese only helped to bring on in 1942 the virtual collapse of the Chinese war effort during the latter years of the war.[21]

As a realistic appraisal of America's military capabilities and of her world-wide strategic interests, the Europe-first policy has a great deal to recommend it. But the combination of this realistic strategy with a moralistic diplomacy led to the noteworthy paradox of a war incurred for the sake of China which could not then be fought for the sake of China and whose practical value for China at the time was, to say the least, dubious. The plain fact is that the United States in 1941 was not capable of forcing Japan out of China by means short of war and was neither willing nor, under existing circumstances, able to throw the Japanese out by war. The American government could conceivably have told the Chinese this and tried to work out the best possible program of help for China under these limitations. Instead, it yielded to Chinese importunities and followed a policy almost sure to eventuate in war, knowing that if the Japanese did attack, China and her deliverance would have to take a back seat. It is difficult to conceive of such a policy as a program of practical aid to China.

The main, though not the only, reason why this policy was followed is clearly the overwhelming importance of principle in American diplomacy,

---

[21] Werner Levi, *Modern China's Foreign Policy* (Minneapolis: University of Minnesota Press, 1953), 229–237. On the danger of internal collapse in China as early as 1940, see U.S. Department of State, *Foreign Relations of the United States: 1940*, vol. IV, *The Far East* (Washington: Government Printing Office, 1955), 672–677.

particularly the principle of nonappeasement of aggressors. Once most leaders in the administration and wide sections of the public became convinced that it was America's prime moral duty to stand hard and fast against aggressors, whatever the consequences, and once this conviction became decisive in the formulation of policy, the end result was almost inevitable: a policy designed to uphold principle and to punish the aggressor, but not to save the victim.[22]

It is this conviction as to America's moral duty, however sincere and understandable, which the writer believes constitutes a fundamental misreading of America's moral task. The policy it gave rise to was bad not simply because it was moralistic but because it was obsessed with the wrong kind of morality—with that abstract "Let justice be done though the heavens fall" kind which so often, when relentlessly pursued, does more harm than good. It would be interesting to investigate the role which this conception of America's moral task played in the formulation of the American war aims in the Far East, with their twin goals of unconditional surrender and the destruction of Japan as a major power, especially after the desire to vindicate American principles and to punish the aggressor was intensified a hundredfold by the attack on Pearl Harbor.[23] To pursue the later implications of this kind of morality in foreign policy, with its attendant legalistic and vindictive overtones, would, however, be a task for [a] volume.

In contrast, the different kind of policy which Grew advocated and toward which Roosevelt so long inclined need not really be considered immoral or unprincipled, however much it undoubtedly would have been

---

[22] It is Secretary of War Henry L. Stimson who gives evidence on how strong was the role of avenging justice in the prevailing picture of America's moral duty. He displays a striking anxiety to acquit the administration of the charge of being "soft" on Japan and to prove that the administration was always fully aware of the Japanese crimes and morally aroused by them. The nation's leaders, he insists in one place, were "as well aware as their critics of the wickedness of the Japanese." Avenging justice, too, plays an important role in the defense he makes of the postwar Nuremberg and Tokyo war crimes trials. These trials, he claims, fulfilled a vital moral task. The main trouble with the Kellogg Pact and the policy of nonrecognition and moral sanctions, according to Stimson, was that they named the international lawbreakers but failed to capture and punish them. The United States, along with other nations in the prewar world, had neglected "a duty to catch the criminal. . . . Our offense was thus that of the man who passed by on the other side." Now, this is a curious revision of the parable of the Good Samaritan, to which the Secretary here alludes. According to the Stimson version, the Good Samaritan should not have stopped to bind up the victim's wounds, put him on his beast of burden, and arranged for his care. Had he been cognizant of his real moral duty, he would rather have mounted his steed and rode off in hot pursuit of the robbers, to bring them to justice. This is only an illustration, but an apt one, of the prevailing concept of America's moral duty, with its emphasis on meting out justice rather than doing good (Stimson and Bundy, *On Active Service*, 384, 262).

[23] Admiral William D. Leahy (*I Was There* [New York: McGraw-Hill, 1950], 81) expresses his view of America's war aims in dubious Latin but with admirable forthrightness: "*Delenda est Japanico.*" He was, of course, not the only American leader to want to emulate Cato.

denounced as such. A limited *modus vivendi* agreement would not have required the United States in any way to sanction Japanese aggression or to
abandon her stand on Chinese integrity and independence. It would have
constituted only a recognition that the American government was not then in
a position to enforce its principles, reserving for America full freedom of action at some later, more favorable time. Nor would it have meant the abandonment and betrayal of China. Rather it would have involved the frank
recognition that the kind of help the Chinese wanted was impossible for the
United States to give at that time. It would in no way have precluded giving
China the best kind of help then possible—in the author's opinion, the offer
of American mediation for a truce in the war and the grant of fuller economic
aid to try to help the Chinese recover—and promising China greater assistance once the crucial European situation was settled. Only that kind of
morality which sees every sort of dealing with an aggressor, every instance of
accommodation or conciliation, as appeasement and therefore criminal
would find the policy immoral.[24]

What the practical results of such a policy, if attempted, would have
been is of course a matter for conjecture. It would be rash to claim that it
would have saved China, either from her wartime collapse or from the final
victory of communism. It may well be that already in 1941 the situation in
China was out of control. Nor can one assert with confidence that, had this
policy enabled her to keep out of war with Japan, the United States would
have been able to bring greater forces to bear in Europe much earlier, thus
shortening the war and saving more of Europe from communism. Since the
major part of the American armed forces were always concentrated in Europe and since in any case a certain proportion would have had to stand
guard in the Pacific, it is possible that the avoidance of war with Japan, however desirable in itself, would not have made a decisive difference in the
duration of the European conflict. The writer does, however, permit himself
the modest conclusions that the kind of policy advocated by Grew presented
real possibilities of success entirely closed to the policy actually followed and
that it was by no means so immoral and unprincipled that it could not have
been pursued by the United States with decency and honor.

SUGGESTED READING

Francis Jones's *Japan's New Order in East Asia, Its Rise and Fall,
1937–45* (1954) is also critical of the administration's policies in Asia,
but it should be supplemented by James Crowley's *Japan's Quest for*

---

[24] See the introductory remarks on the possibilities of appeasement, under certain circumstances, as a useful diplomatic tool, along with an excellent case study in the wrong use of
it, in J. W. Wheeler-Bennett, *Munich: Prologue to Tragedy* (London: Macmillan, 1948),
3–8.

Autonomy (1966). For the argument that the administration deliberately maneuvered the nation toward war, see Charles A. Beard's *American Foreign Policy in the Making, 1932–1940* (1946) and *President Roosevelt and the Coming of the War, 1941* (1948), which not only indict Roosevelt's policies but also emphasize the danger of presidential power in foreign relations and the Chief Executive's capacity to circumvent constitutional restraints.

Samuel Eliot Morison, who served as an official historian for the Navy during the war, savagely replies to Beard in "Did Roosevelt Start the War—History Through a Beard," *Atlantic Monthly,* CLXXXII (Aug. 1949). Other answers to Beard and early revisionism are provided by William L. Langer and S. Everett Gleason in *The Challenge to Isolation, 1937–1940* (1952), and *The Undeclared War, 1940–1941* (1953), histories written on the basis of privilieged access to restricted materials; Herbert Feis, in "War Came at Pearl Harbor: Suspicions Considered," *Yale Review,* XLV (Mar. 1956); Dexter Perkins, in "Was Roosevelt Wrong?," *Virginia Quarterly Review,* XXX (Summer 1954); and Robert Ferrell, in "Pearl Harbor and the Revisionists," *Historian,* XVII (Spring 1955). Dorothy Borg's *The United States and the Far Eastern Crisis of 1933–1938* (1964) should be examined on this earlier period along with Frederick C. Adams' "The Road to Pearl Harbor: A Reexamination of American Far Eastern Policy, July 1937–December 1938," *Journal of American History,* LVIII (June 1971).

Recent studies of the relation between Germany and the United States include James Compton's *The Swastika and The Eagle* (1967), and Alton Frye's *Nazi Germany and the American Hemisphere* (1967). Though acknowledging that there is no evidence of a German military plan to attack the United States, both Compton and Frye believe that Germany imperiled American security. Compton's evidence, however, supports the view of A. J. P. Taylor in *The Origins of the Second World War* ° (1962) that Hitler's ambitions were not global but continental (Europe) and that he lacked a grand design for world conquest. Bruce Russett's *No Clear and Present Danger: A Skeptical View of U.S. Entry Into World War II* ° (1972) also challenges the view that American security required intervention in the war. Robert Dallek's *Democrat: The Life of William E. Dodd* (1968), a study of the American ambassador to Germany from 1933 to 1938, emphasizes Dodd's opposition to fascism and argues that Roosevelt was not (privately) an isolationist between 1933 and 1937. Arnold A. Offner, in *American Appeasement, 1933–1938* (1969), finds that most policymakers, as well as Congressmen and citizens, did not understand the "threat of Nazi Germany" and persisted in the belief that that Germany's policy did not endanger the United States.

The best bibliographical survey is Wayne Cole's "American Entry into World War II: A Historiographical Appraisal," *Mississippi Valley Historical Review,* XLIII (Mar. 1957). Surveys of the period are found in Robert A. Divine's *The Reluctant Belligerent* ° (1965) and John Wiltz's *From Isolation to War, 1931–1941* ° (1968).

WILLIAM APPLEMAN WILLIAMS

The War for the American Frontier: World War II

INTRODUCTION

During the past half decade probably no volume on American foreign relations has been more influential in provoking a reexamination of the American experience than *The Tragedy of American
Diplomacy* (1959) by William Appleman Williams of Oregon State
University. Largely ignored when published, the book did not
begin to gain a wide audience until the late 1960's when the Vietnam War began to raise new questions about the sources and
nature of American foreign policy. Williams, influenced by the
later work of Charles A. Beard, interprets American policy as an
effort to protect and advance a world order in which liberal capitalism can flourish. He contends that American foreign policy is

FROM William Appleman Williams, *The Tragedy of American Diplomacy;* rev. ed., pp.
183–200. Copyright © 1959, 1962 by William Appleman Williams. Reprinted by permission of the World Publishing Company.

based on a particular conception of political economy (a *Weltan-schauung* or ideology), and he questions the traditional analysis of events that separates politics from economics.

He locates in American society since at least the 1890's widely-shared impulses for economic expansion abroad and concludes that most policy-makers and most major businessmen believed that America's democracy and economy required this expansion and the establishment of an international liberal capitalist order. "America's freedom and prosperity," they thought, "depend upon the continued expansion of its economic and ideological systems through the policy of the open door" (p. 303). They sought to impose on the world a system that would block revolutions, break down colonialism, extend democracy, and maintain equal access for all nations to markets and outlets for investment (the Open Door policy).

According to Williams, they thought American economic expansion would be most secure in a liberal capitalist world. And expansion was necessary for maintaining America's domestic prosperity. Depression at home, they feared, could mean turmoil, class division, maybe even the destruction of democracy. International trade and investments required international stability and depended on law and order; consequently, revolutions (especially left-wing movements) were contrary to American interests. They also assumed that democracy was preferable to other forms of government.

Through the policy of the open door, America, with its preponderant economic strength, "would enter and dominate all underdeveloped areas of the world." The result was the Open Door empire—or what is called informal empire or the imperialism of free trade. Williams explains that "when an advanced industrial nation plays, or tries to play, a controlling or one-sided role in the development of a weaker economy, then the policy of the more industrial country can . . . only be described as imperial" (p. 47). While according to Williams the Open Door policy was self-serving, he acknowledges that policy-makers believed sincerely that American trade and investment would also benefit other peoples both directly (as recipients) and indirectly (by expanding world trade). Put simply, what was in America's interest was also in the world's interest. Americans did not intend exploitation but mutual benefit. But, as Williams contends, by the middle of the twentieth century, this empire created antagonisms and challenged American foreign policy, thereby contributing to the crisis of our times.

Williams goes on to explain that this American ideology, because of its contradictions, led to the tragedy of American foreign policy. "Americans believed in the right of self-determination, in helping others solve their problems, and that other people cannot *really* solve their problems and improve their lives unless they go about it in the same way" (p. 9). Or, as Dean Acheson put it after the Second World War: "We are willing to help people who believe the way we do, to continue to live the way they want to live" (p. 10). The result, Williams contends, is that America sought to coerce other peoples into adopting American patterns, especially capitalism and also our form of government.

The Spanish-American War, the Open Door notes, the imperialism of Roosevelt and Taft, the policies of Wilson, the diplomacy of the 1920's and 1930's, and the Cold War all fit into Williams' analysis. In the case of the Spanish-American War, for example, he concludes that policy-makers, externalizing danger and interpreting events in economic terms, embarked on war with Spain primarily in order to "clean up the Cuban mess so that domestic *and other foreign policy* issues could be dealt with efficiently and effectively" (p. 29). This was an indication of their belief that America's frontier lay outside her territorial boundaries. It was the "frontier-expansionist explanation of American democracy and prosperity" (p. 308). The battle over the annexation of the Philippines was not about imperialism, but about colonialism, and many of the so-called antiimperialists were simply urging a different strategy for economic expansion. The colonialists won the battle but lost the war, for the Open Door empire was the policy of the future. The Open Door notes, according to Williams, constitute an astute strategy designed to maintain American economic opportunity in China and to prevent foreign imperialist powers from barring American economic penetration.

Williams points out that for Woodrow Wilson intervention in Mexico was justifiable because dictatorship and social upheaval were threatening to the liberal capitalist order that Wilson so greatly valued and deemed essential to America's welfare. Williams offers a similar analysis of America's entry into the First World War and the making of the peace. Wilson, he notes, tied the American economy to the Allies in order to avoid a depression at home, and that decision "reinforced the bias of Wilson's ideology and morality toward defining German naval warfare as the most important diplomatic issue of the war." Pushed by submarine warfare, the President entered the war (as Wilson put it) "to do justice and assert the rights of mankind" and to fight until Germany established "a government we can trust." "Making the world safe for democracy" in Wilson's terms, Williams explains, meant creating a liberal capitalist system. Idealism and materialism merge in this framework, for, according to Williams' conception of Wilson, there was no conflict. The Treaty of Versailles, Williams notes, was shaped with the specter of Bolshevik Russia hovering over the meetings, and the final version expressed Wilson's eagerness to use American power to maintain the *status quo* in the world. Williams contends that the American debate over the League of Nations was not for the most part a controversy between isolationists and internationalists but a dispute over the appropriate tactics for extending American power and advancing the national interest.

Even the foreign relations of the 1920's, according to Williams, meant not isolationism (a false "legend"), but participation and involvement in foreign affairs to promote economic expansion and a liberal capitalist order. "Our investments and trade relations," as President Calvin Coolidge said in 1928, "are such that it is almost impossible to conceive of any conflict anywhere on earth which would not affect us injuriously."

Williams argues that the strategy of the Open Door also led to the Second World War: American conceptions of the requirements for prosperity at home created policies that ultimately embroiled the nation first in the undeclared naval war with Germany, and then in war with Japan. A complete embargo on trade with the belligerents in the years before Pearl Harbor, he contends, was considered impossible by policy-makers and businessmen because of the damage to the American economy. In addition, he finds that Germany's economic penetration of Latin America made American leaders more hostile toward the Axis powers. In the case of Japan, he stresses that her attack on China was a dramatic and frightening threat to this "frontier of America's ideological and economic expansion." War, which had been viewed as a great threat to the American system, came to seem less troubling than the alternatives. Ultimately the problem was (as businessmen admitted) that the United States could not surrender its neutral rights, adopt economic containment, or acquiesce to Japanese demands in the Orient. Compromise then became impossible and the result was war.

Williams does not closely analyze most of the major events and decisions that led to the undeclared war with Germany or the shooting war with Japan. Rather, he focuses on the main themes of development and shows how these can be explained in terms of the ideology of policy-makers and the leaders of America's corporate economic system. His interpretation, then, offers the ideology within which leaders acted, but he does not try to examine closely, in most cases, the interaction of events, perceptions, and ideology.

In his section on the coming of the Second World War, his analysis also does not specifically deal with larger questions that warrant consideration. Was Hitler bent on world conquest and, therefore, did he constitute a military threat to the United States? Did policy-makers accept this view? Even if, as Williams suggests, his mandate is to analyze primarily policies in the Far East because that is where war started, some critics might contend that he should offer a general explanation of American policy-maker's hostility to Naziism. Was it based on more than the fears that Germany was disrupting the peace and therefore the international economy, and that she was autarchic and threatening the liberal capitalist order? Was it not that she was also anti-democratic? Americans did not necessarily oppose Germany primarily because she was totalitarian, but this may have been a consideration influencing American responses. In fact, given the suppleness of Williams' general framework of explaining American foreign policy, perhaps such hostility can also be explained in terms of the American desire to establish a world made "safe for democracy"—the American Century. Since Williams' framework is generally broader than his analysis of this segment of the American past, perhaps the use of that framework can extend the analysis considerably beyond his own effort in *The Tragedy of American Diplomacy.*

Despite the impact of Williams' theory on the interpretation of American history, there has been no published, extended criticism of his analysis. Judging from reviews and occasional comments on his work, it seems that the most common criticism by historians is that he has imposed on policy-makers and others a centrality of vision and concern with the political economy of capitalism that the evidence does not adequately support.

A few historians on the left, however, suggest the contrary. They contend that he exaggerates the policy-makers' concern for democracy and hostility to trade barriers, and thereby does not fully acknowledge America's double standard (state trading for the United States *but* opposition to other nation's state trading) and the preeminent concern with markets for trade, investment, and sources of raw material. To some radicals, Williams is in fact too liberal: he does not recognize that imperialism is essential to the American economy and the structure of power.

Some critics note that Williams' work is occasionally ambiguous about whether the Open Door policy is a tactic or a preeminent value, and his definition of ideology sometimes seems too vague, evading any analysis of a hierarchy of values. At times, Williams has been wrongly interpreted as being an economic determinist or as arguing that foreign policy is governed by economics. Actually he links economics and politics within an ideology of political economy and suggests that policy-makers have developed a dysfunctional ideology that can be corrected. In *The Roots of the Modern American Empire* (1969), he has called for a transformation of the American system that will be free of the felt need for an "informal empire."

*A*merican policy-makers . . . discovered, . . . in a way contrary to its axioms and expectations, that the strategy of the open door did lead to war. None of them wanted war. They did not plot to involve the

United States in armed conflict with the Axis. Indeed, and as symbolized by Roosevelt's support of the Munich Agreement of 1938 between Nazi Germany and Great Britain, they tried very seriously and persistently to accomplish their objectives without war. But given their *Weltanschauung*, their explanation of how the prosperity and welfare of the United States was to be achieved and maintained, they had no recourse but war. And as it happened, the United States was engaged in a shooting conflict with Germany before Japan struck Hawaii. The question of how and when that combat would have formally been joined if the Japanese had not attacked Pearl Harbor is fascinating but nevertheless irrelevant to an understanding of how American leaders came to accept the necessity of violence. It is also possible, perhaps even probable, that they would have reached that decision even if they had not entertained a frontier-expansionist conception of history. But again, and however pertinent it may be for later consideration, that hypothetical question is not germane to an explanation of how the United States did actually become involved in World War II.

Perhaps the most helpful way to approach that problem is by reviewing the attitudes toward foreign policy that existed after Roosevelt had been in office two full years. Encouraged by the economic revival that seemed in 1935 to herald a general recovery from the depression, the community of public and private decision-makers looked ahead to a continuing extension of overseas economic activities. Those men also reasserted their conviction that such expansion would prevent foreign revolutions (and future depressions in the United States itself) and that peace was essential to recovery at home and profitable operations abroad.

Beyond those areas of agreement, however, the policy-makers split into differing—and often bitterly antagonistic—groups. Two main features of their dialogue and argument must be kept in mind if the evolution of policy is to be understood.

First: these divisions over policy not only cut across political lines, but also across what was by then an increasingly artificial boundary between private economic (including labor) leadership and formal office holders. The decision-making community at all times included men of great power and influence outside the government as well as those inside the nation's official establishment. Thus the support for a given policy always came from men in both groups. The natural corollary was that both the private leadership and the government bureaucracy disagreed among themselves as well as with members of the other bloc. One striking result of this hammering out of a consensus on policy between 1935 and 1941 was that a consolidated corporate group emerged under the banner of bipartisanship for security and prosperity. That coalition came to enjoy a very extensive measure of control over foreign policy. Often, for example, their internal debates were not even known to—let alone participated in by—their critics or the general public. And their broad authority over both private and official information and news media further closed down the discussion of alternatives.

It is vital to understand this pattern of power if the role and the authority of the military itself is not to be exaggerated. Beginning in 1938 and 1939, the evolving corporate coalition of private and official leaders called in the military to execute a policy that they—*the civilians*—were formulating and adopting. *It was the civilians who defined the world in military terms, not the military who usurped civilian powers.* Once the military had been called in, they quite naturally gained more influence because the situation had been defined in a way that put a premium on their particular knowledge and experience. But a change in the definition of reality would decrease the power of the military. Even granting a generous measure of new authority, the military had not even by 1962 established themselves in an independent and superior position. Along with recognizing that fact, it is essential to remember that it was the civilians who called in the military, and that they did so between 1935 and 1941.

Second: the argument within the policy-making community developed around four issues. At the outset, by 1935, the debate concerned whether or not it was possible to work out some compromise with the Axis powers. That discussion shaded into an argument about whether the effort to remain neutral in another war would lead to an economic depression through the loss of overseas markets. Then, in 1937, the majority, who still held feasible some kind of accommodation without war, began to divide over whether or not to coerce the Axis into an acceptable settlement by using economic sanctions and the threat of military force (if not its actual use in combat short of a formal declaration of war). Finally, and beginning in 1939 after the Nazi victory over Poland, there opened a final argument over whether or not it would be necessary for the United States to become a total and formal belligerent. Though that angry debate was settled by the Japanese, it seems apparent that the policy-makers and the public were reaching, however reluctantly, the conclusion that war was necessary.

The detailed reconstruction of that evolution into trial by arms has yet to be made by any historian or group of historians.[1] But it is possible to characterize the changing attitudes of various groups and personalities within the corporate leadership of the country, and to outline the main phases of the debate. One of these was the argument over neutrality policy that began early in the 1930's with a discussion of blocking the sale of mu-

---

[1] The two volumes by W. L. Langer and S. E. Gleason, *The Challenge to Isolation*, and *The Undeclared War* (New York: Harper and Bros., 1952, 1953), have a general but undeserved reputation as being the last word. Another approach, fairly represented in a collective volume edited by H. E. Barnes, *Perpetual War for Perpetual Peace* (Caxton, Idaho: Caxton Printers, Ltd., 1953), is challenging but by no means definitive. The best single volume is P. W. Schroeder, *The Axis Alliance and Japanese-American Relations* (Ithaca: Cornell University Press, 1958).

nitions to belligerents in another war. American leaders (and the public at large) generally agreed on the wisdom of that restriction, but they rapidly drew back from any commitment to full neutrality when it became apparent that such a policy would undercut existing and prospective overseas economic expansion.

Along with the strikingly frightened reaction of American leaders to the threat posed to exports and foreign investments by the outbreak of World War I, this marked fear in the 1930's about the economic consequences of real neutrality offers impressive proof of the degree to which Americans *thought* their domestic welfare depended upon overseas economic activity.[2] Theoretical and statistical arguments concerning the actual extent of that dependence are of course relevant, particularly in connection with any consideration of alternate foreign policies, but this idea about its great importance is the crucial factor in understanding and interpreting American foreign policy in the 1930's—and in subsequent decades. Americans thought and believed that such expansion was essential, and their actions followed from that supposition.

This became apparent early in the discussion which developed around the ideas of Charles Warren, an international lawyer who had served President Wilson as an Assistant Attorney General prior to 1917. Warren argued that the only way to avoid involvement in a future war was to abandon all claims to neutral rights and rest content with whatever trade the belligerents would permit. In the face of prompt opposition, he shortly modified his original proposal by suggesting that trade with belligerents be limited to the average amount carried on during a five year period prior to the outbreak of hostilities.

Secretary Hull and other key advisors in the State Department, and such quasi-official figures in the corporation community as Allen Dulles, continued to criticize even Warren's revised plan as a surrender of traditional rights and as a body blow to American commerce. As might have been expected, many businessmen joined the attack on Warren. No doubt influenced by Senator Gerald P. Nye's investigation of the traffic in munitions at the time of World War I, and even in the period of peace thereafter, the pro-trade group accepted the need for an arms embargo. But everyone actually involved in the debate, if not all those who followed it in the popular press, knew that the commerce in arms was not the central issue.

The crucial point involved trade in other manufactured goods, and in raw or semi-processed materials. Not only were those the products sought

---

[2] Some of the most revealing evidence concerning this response to the World War I situation is to be found in the *Hearings before the Special Senate Committee Investigating the Munitions Industry* (39 parts: Washington: Government Printing Office, 1934–1936).

by belligerents, but they were the items that Americans wanted to sell abroad. Senator Nye understood and defined the dilemma as early as 1935. "My own belief," he concluded, "is that a complete embargo on trade is the only absolute insurance against the United States being drawn into another prolonged major war between great powers. I am convinced that drastic legislation to accomplish this could not be passed even in time of peace." [3]

Nye had strong reasons for reaching such a conclusion. Secretary Hull and Herbert Feis of the State Department argued quite openly that restrictions of that kind on American overseas economic activity would be extremely harmful if not disastrous to the nation's economy. In a typical bit of calculated understatement, for example, the Secretary observed that a general embargo would be "undesirable." The bipartisan nature of this resistance to real economic neutrality was indicated by the agreement of Henry Cabot Lodge, Jr. And Roosevelt was warned in 1935 by the President of the New York Chamber of Commerce that "exporters and merchants on our eastern seaboard are now more interested in the freedom of the seas for American ships than at any time since the World War." The same view was advanced by General Motors, the giant cotton firm of Anderson, Clayton, and even by the Business Advisory Council of the Department of Commerce.

One of the bluntest analyses of these economic considerations was offered by Edwin Borchard, an outstanding professor of international law at Yale who was deeply concerned to strengthen American neutrality. Commenting in 1936 on proposed legislation that followed some of Warren's early ideas, Borchard warned that "we are likely to begin to lose our markets the minute this bill is passed." "Nobody," he feared, "has apparently thought through the full effects of this legislation." Those consequences would be "revolutionary" because they involved the issue of "self-sufficiency." Neutrality of that kind was dangerous because it would "incite disorders and distress at home."

Senator Key Pittman's judgment of the situation in 1936 made it clear that Borchard underestimated the extent to which government and business leaders had in fact very carefully "thought through the full effects of this legislation." "The necessity for foreign commerce is so great and political pressure at this particular time is so strong," Pittman explained, that it

---

[3] This analysis and interpretation was originally prepared from materials in the National Archives, manuscript collections of such figures as President Roosevelt and Senator Borah, the *Congressional Record*, and the various investigations into neutrality undertaken by the Congress during the late 1920's and the 1930's. Just as this manuscript was going to press, however, I had the good fortune to receive an advance copy of R. A. Divine, *The Illusion of Neutrality* (Chicago: University of Chicago Press, 1962), which deals with the fight over neutrality within a similar framework. I have borrowed this quotation from Nye, and a later one from Pittman, from Professor Divine, who found them during his research in the manuscript files of the congressional committees.

was unrealistic to expect real neutrality legislation. The compromise was Cash-and-Carry Neutrality, a concept and an idea apparently conceived by Bernard Baruch. The long-term result of that approach was clear even at the time of its adoption by the Congress—it created an economic alliance between the United States and Great Britain.

Even before that implicit connection led to formal political and military discussions and agreements, however, American leaders were defining the Axis powers as dangerous economic rivals in Latin America. That conflict played an early and significant role in the thinking of decision-makers about the possibilities and probabilities of war with Germany and Italy, and even with Japan. Much of the shift toward a policy of vigorous opposition short of formal belligerence took place in connection with Axis activities in Latin America. In the intellectual and emotional sense, that is to say, an important number of American leaders began to go to war against the Axis in the Western Hemisphere.

This attitude was intensified in those who already held it, and adopted by others, as a result of two events during 1937–1938. One was the Spanish Civil War, and the other was the Japanese attack in China. Although the Spanish conflict generated more emotional involvement and more vociferous agitation, particularly in the populous Eastern part of the country, the Japanese action made a more significant impact within the policy-making community. This was in part due to the triumph in Spain of General Francisco Franco, who was openly supported by Germany and Italy. His total victory liquidated the issue. If the Republican Government had held out for a longer period, as did the Chinese, it is possible that the Spanish Civil War would have brought the United States into a general European coalition against Germany before Japan attacked Pearl Harbor. That is possible but not very probable. Spain served to arouse and involve two rival groups in the United States, but they were quite unevenly matched in power and influence. The reformers who opposed fascism and thought it was time to slow or halt its ideological, political, and military momentum did mount a dynamic public campaign in behalf of their policy. But it is highly doubtful that a majority of those reformers favored direct American intervention. The opposition in the debate, especially the hierarchy of the Catholic Church and a broad segment of private and public Protestant leaders, enjoyed much more influence. As a result, the Roosevelt Administration followed a policy of strict and formal neutrality which weakened the Republican Government. American policy in its deeper nature is rather well characterized by a bit of chronology: Franco captured Madrid on March 28, 1939, and the United States recognized his government on April 1, 1939.

Japan's attack in China on July 7, 1937, which followed upon its withdrawal from the London Naval Conference in 1936, had a far greater effect on the entire community of American policy-makers. Several considerations explain this difference. The most important of these was the emphasis on Asia as the Eldorado of America's overseas economic expansion ever since the time of the Sino-Japanese War in 1894, which had led to the strategy of the Open Door Policy. This had always been focused on China, even though tactical and other considerations had prompted economic and political dealings with Japan that sometimes seemed to create a different impression. It is at most a slight exaggeration to say that China was by 1937 firmly established in the minds of most American policy-makers, *and even below the level of conscious thought,* as the symbol of the new frontier of America's ideological and economic expansion. This was as true for those who advocated working through and with Japan as it was for others who persistently agitated for a stronger direct effort in China. The commitment to China was much greater than the identification with any European power except England—and possibly France. This cast of mind and emotion, this utopian image, was strengthened and infused with new substance between 1935 and 1937 by very practical economic developments. A significant number of private and official decision-makers became convinced during those years that the long-awaited blossoming of China as a market was finally under way. There was, as one of them phrased it, a "new spirit" of confidence that the open door was about to lead to something big and profitable.

This enthusiasm was the offspring of two economic facts. One involved the way that China had actually begun to modernize its own system; that meant it was buying more and more industrial goods and services from the United States. The other concerned American trade with China. After a slump during the 1920's, it began to increase very rapidly. In 1932, for the first time in over a decade, American-Chinese trade totalled more than Chinese-Japanese trade. That exciting trend continued, moreover, through the next two years. This led, in 1935, to a little remembered but very significant liaison between the National Foreign Trade Council and various people and groups (including a bloc in the State Department) who held official positions in the Roosevelt Administration. The result was two-fold. Men inside the government who favored implementing the Open Door Policy by dealing directly with China and taking a firmer stand against Japan became more active in policy discussions. And the N.F.T.C. organized a quasi-official American Economic Mission to the Far East. Headed by W. Cameron Forbes, it visited Japan and China for the purpose of gathering data upon which to base future policy.

Upon his return, Forbes announced that there was little enthusiasm for the mission in Japan. "In China, on the other hand," he reported, "American participation and American investment along all lines was sought." He then spelled out the implications by reminding American businessmen that in 1935 they had outscored Japan in trade with China to the amount of some $22,000,000. Finally, he made it clear that it was time to use firm pressure to keep the door open. "This policy of the open door does not seem to have been observed in the conduct of affairs in Manchuria." Should that Japanese conduct be extended to more of China, he warned, "there will inevitably be built up a greater and greater resistance." Japan's attack was particularly disturbing to Forbes and men who shared his outlook because it came at a time when American economic activity in China "was considered especially bright." "Probably never in its history," Forbes remarked in his judgment on the assault, "has China offered greater promise for its future trade, industry, and general economic progress than . . . just prior to the outbreak of the present hostilities." Nor were the implications limited to China, or to Forbes and his followers. In 1937, for example, Asia furnished 51.5 per cent of all raw and crude materials imported into the United States. British Malaya and the Dutch East Indies supplied 86 per cent of its crude rubber and 87 per cent of its tin. Asia provided, in addition, 85 per cent of its tungsten, a third of its mica, 99 per cent of its jute, and 98 per cent of its shellac.

This confrontation between, on the one hand, America's specific and general economic interests and expectations and, on the other hand, Japan's move south into China, affected the posture and the policy of the United States very directly. Through September and October 1937, the issue was debated very vigorously within the State Department in preparation for the Brussels Conference on the Far East. The argument took the traditional form: some wanted to make a strong stand with China, a smaller group suggested working with the Russians, and others reiterated that it was necessary to follow the tactic of trying to control Japan.

At this juncture, the Soviet Union renewed the traditional Russian bid for an entente with the United States. Its spokesmen warned American officials at Brussels that, while the offer was wholly sincere, it might well represent the last stand of those in the Kremlin who advocated collaboration with the Western Powers against the Axis. Russia felt it "had taken some terrible beatings" while striving to work out such an alliance, and it might very soon change its policy and emphasize unilateral moves to insure its own security. (The general assumption that the Soviets can never be trusted in such situations is not borne out by the Brussels experience. The failure of the conference did verify the warnings given to American policy-makers. The decline in influence of Maxim Litvinov, and of the pro-Western views he advocated, can be dated from that time. American policy-makers continued to make this kind of error in dealing with the Soviet Union, however, right down to 1962.)

Roosevelt seems to have considered, however briefly, a more positive response to this overture. But his final instructions followed the pro-Japanese line. He defended his choice by arguing that, short of war, Japan could be stopped only by arranging a truce in China. Even so, the American policy at Brussels was based on extracting extensive concessions from

China. It may be that the President had even then concluded that war was all but inevitable, and was only buying time with a down payment provided by the Chinese. It seems more probable, however, that Roosevelt and Hull felt that unilateral American economic and military pressure would force the Japanese to retreat. They were no doubt encouraged in this traditional assumption behind the strategy of the Open Door Policy by the speed with which Japan accepted American demands for an apology, reparations, and promises for the future in connection with the sinking of the Navy river gunboat *Panay* in December 1937.

There is no doubt, in any event, that the United States proceeded very quickly after the Brussels Conference to reassert and act upon both its frontier-expansionist outlook and its traditional strategy of the Open Door Policy. Hull clarified that with one blunt remark on February 19, 1938, shortly after the administration had asked for a huge increase in naval construction. "There can be no military disarmament," he explained, "without economic appeasement. . . . Only healthy international trade will make possible a full and stable domestic economy." And by "healthy international trade," Hull obviously and exclusively meant trade defined in American terms.

Assistant Secretary Sayre reviewed the events of 1937 and 1938 a bit more laconically: "The economic world became a battlefield in which the issues were sometimes political as well as economic." And military as well as political, he might have added. But the most classic explanation of the crisis was offered by William S. Culbertson, who had begun his service as an economic advisor and policy-maker on trade matters under President Wilson, had continued to exercise such influence in the 1920's, and was still active in the New Deal period. "Our economic frontiers," he remarked, "are no longer coextensive with our territorial frontiers." No one ever offered a more succinct description and interpretation of the single most important aspect of twentieth-century American diplomacy—either in general, or pertaining explicitly to the nation's involvement in World Wars I and II.

Administration leaders in Congress made the same point in less striking style during the consideration in the late winter of 1938 of Roosevelt's bill for the expansion of the Navy. In a long debate that was far more revealing of the nature of American foreign policy than were the arguments over the Neutrality Acts of 1935, 1936, and 1937, New Deal Senators David I. Walsh and Tom Connally stressed two factors. They began by pointing to German and Japanese activity in Latin America and cautioned that it was necessary to be "very careful" about such competition. Their conclusion was a warning that the danger might rapidly become greater.

Then they compared the American economic system to the British Empire. "We, too, have trade routes," Walsh explained. "It is estimated by our experts that unless we are able to keep open certain trade routes the

United States could not maintain itself more than two years without being defeated by a powerful enemy." Any delay in building a big Navy would court final surrender. "We cannot build battleships in time of war unless we keep the trade routes open to bring in manganese. We cannot make munitions in time of war unless we keep the trade routes open to bring in certain essential raw materials." Backed by such leadership and logic, the bill passed the House of Representatives 294 to 100, and the Senate 56 to 28.

Armed with this steel in his diplomatic glove, Secretary Hull called for a moral embargo on shipments to Japan in June 1938. Six months later the United States loaned China $25,000,000. And in July 1939, it renounced its commercial treaty with Japan. One segment of the policy-making community which had access to governmental authority was clearly moving to stop the Japanese by economic pressure and the threat of force. A spokesman of that group who was also an active member of the Council on Foreign Relations put it very bluntly. "Seen in its Far Eastern setting," William Diebold, Jr., explained, "our concept of commercial policy expands. . . . It becomes our most potent instrument of foreign policy, a long-range weapon with which to settle the fate of nations."

That intensity and tempo of opposition was not apparent, however, in dealings with Germany in 1938 and 1939. And it slacked off for more than a year in affairs with Japan. The reason for this lies in the ambivalence and the split within the community of American policy-makers. Fears of war and hopes of compromise with the Axis were still very strong. John L. Lewis and other leaders in the C.I.O., for example, manifested that combination of attitudes very clearly. Aware and concerned by 1939 that the United States was "gradually being driven out of trade relationships with the various markets of the world," Lewis did not turn to war or preparations for war as a solution. He first accepted the reality that "the open door is no more" in Asia. Then he advocated an increased effort in Latin America to take up the slack. Government loans should be granted to provide the peons with buying power. Lewis shared the feeling of the steel workers that foreign policy should not "be formulated or made dependent upon the protection of the vested or property interests in foreign countries of the large corporations in this country." Of course, labor leaders feared such preparations for war as the draft, because the government—and its industrial contractors—could then control the conditions and the market for labor. Lewis saw the squeeze and disliked it. "Unless substantial economic offsets are provided to prevent this nation from being wholly dependent upon the war expenditures," he cried out in anguish in 1940, "we will sooner or later come to the dilemma which requires either war or depression."

Corporation leaders and their associates were caught in the same corner, as were other policy-makers who held positions in the government.

The great majority of American leaders emerged from World War I fearing war as the midwife of international revolution and domestic unrest. A good many of them remained unconvinced even by 1939 that it was the greater part of wisdom to make war in order to make peace. Worried about "world-wide ruin," and frightened of the political and social consequences of "another generation of misery," such leaders opposed war as a "great destroyer and unsettler of their affairs." Bernard Baruch, for example, thought that "the institutions of government, as we have known them, [would] fall down . . . and that the whole moral attitude of the world would change." Many corporation leaders and a significant though probably smaller number of national politicians extended that line of reasoning on through the 1930's. They argued that serious preparation for war would subvert the kind of political economy they equated with freedom and democracy. "As certain as night follows day," asserted the editors of *Iron Age* in 1939, "while we were fighting to crush dictatorships abroad, we would be extending one at home."

"It is fairly certain," agreed a corporation executive who was prominent in the financial and policy affairs of the America First Committee, "that capitalism cannot survive American participation in this war." Others broadened the analysis, seeing American intervention as leading "to the end of capitalism all over the world" with a resulting "spread of communism, socialism, or fascism in Europe and even in the United States." Winthrop W. Aldrich spoke from a similar estimate in his remarks to the National Foreign Trade Council shortly after the Munich Agreement of 1938 had been signed. "We ought to take full advantage of the opportunity for the continuance of peace which has resulted from the events of the last few weeks," he advised in very strong terms. "It is of paramount importance that the efforts of the diplomats and of the heads of governments should speedily be reinforced by measures of economic appeasement." The depth and power of the cross-currents within the community of policymakers is clearly revealed by Aldrich's remarks. He was head of the Chase National Bank, which not only was a very powerful element in the Federal Reserve System, but also handled most of the Soviet Union's transactions in the United States. He was advising conciliation with the Axis while Secretary of State Hull was militantly fighting the pressures for such economic appeasement.

Tormented by their estimates of the consequences of intervention, leaders of the Aldrich bent argued, when pressed to the wall, that America could and should avoid war by building and integrating an impregnable empire in the Western Hemisphere or that it could and should assert America's ultimate supremacy by waiting for the belligerents to exhaust themselves. Senator Harry S. Truman was one of the politicians who inclined toward the latter proposal. "The role of this great Republic," he explained in October 1939, "is to save civilization; we must keep out of war."

Later, after the Nazis attacked Russia, he went so far as to suggest aiding both of them in such a way as to promote their mutual exhaustion.

The way those attitudes began to change was nicely revealed in the course of a discussion among leading businessmen held late in 1939 under the auspices of *Fortune* magazine. The participants formally and vigorously rejected entry into the war. But almost everything else they said indicated either that they expected American involvement or that they were still trying with considerable success to avoid facing the fact that the things they did want could not be obtained short of war. No war, they agreed, and then voted "unanimously" to oppose giving way to Japan's New Order in Asia. No war, they reiterated, and then flatly refused even to discuss the possibility of a more self-contained economy. Overseas economic expansion was mandatory. No war, they repeated, and then agreed that the Philippines had to be defended in order to protect "the rich resources" of Southeast Asia. No war, they concluded, and proceeded to reject "abandonment of the U.S. world position through surrendering neutral rights, adopting economic self-containment, or acquiescing in Japanese demands in the Orient."

The contradictions became somewhat blatant when they went on to discuss "the important tasks confronting the next peace." "What interests us primarily," the businessmen explained in perfect candor, "is the longer-range question of whether the American capitalist system could continue to function if most of Europe and Asia should abolish free enterprise." Their conclusion was not too surprising: the next peace settlement would have "to organize the economic resources of the world so as to make possible a return to the system of free enterprise in every country."

It required very little more Axis expansion to push men who were that ambivalent over to the side of intervention. They were further exhorted and encouraged by industrial leaders like James A. Farrell of the steel industry, who had been agitating for more expansion, and more militant opposition to the Axis, for at least two years. "Our internal economy," Farrell explained in 1938, "is geared to export trade on an increasingly higher level. . . . We must be prepared," therefore, "to increase our outlets abroad for manufactured products or make adjustments of far-reaching consequences." Hence to Farrell it was "imperative that business interests and government agencies act together to assure American business a proportionate and equitable share in the [world's] trade. . . . The door of equal opportunity to all trading areas should be kept open." Farrell strongly implied that war would come: "It suffices to say that no compromise seems possible between [economic] doctrines so wide apart in principle."

The Business Advisory Council of the Roosevelt Administration gave Farrell the assurances he wanted. "An enlargement of our opportunities for trade and investment in foreign countries is *now essential* to maximum national prosperity." In addition, many of those who had in 1938 and 1939 feared the totalitarian consequences of going to war had by 1940 turned the argument upside down. They began to assert that staying out of the war would bring the end of free enterprise and democracy. Lewis W. Douglas, who had served as Budget Director in the early days of the New Deal, typified such thinking. "To retreat to the cyclone cellar here means, ultimately, to establish a totalitarian state at home."

Such a convergence of thinking within the corporate community of policy-makers encouraged the administration to act more openly. It continued to lie about, and in other ways conceal, some of its key policy decisions. But Roosevelt and Hull felt strong enough by September 1940, to embargo aviation gasoline and end iron shipments to Japan. Germany's rapid conquest of France brought even more support for their policies. Hitler might be said to have provided the deciding vote that passed the first peacetime draft in the same month of September. Thereafter events and decisions moved in an ever-accelerating spiral downward into war. Within a year, on September 4, 1941, the United States was engaged in undeclared naval warfare with Germany. Japan attacked three months later.

The final explanation of the tragedy at Pearl Harbor has yet to be made. It most certainly lies in some combination of American arrogance and negligence and of Japanese brilliance. But there is no doubt about the final convergence of thought between the Roosevelt Administration and the leaders of America's corporate economic system. For by mid-1943, when the issue of postwar foreign policy came to the fore and was thrashed out in Congressional hearings and departmental discussions, it was apparent that the Roosevelt Administration was dominated by men whose personal experience and intellectual outlook were conditioned by their careers as leaders or agents or students of the large corporation. Dean Acheson, Averell Harriman, Donald M. Nelson, Edward Stettinius, Adolf A. Berle, Jr., John Foster Dulles, Eric Johnson, Paul Hoffman, William C. Foster, and James Forrestal are but the most obvious names from the top layer of American leadership in foreign affairs.

These men symbolized a consensus that had been foreshadowed in the winter of 1939–1940, when American economic leaders began to support Roosevelt's policy toward the Axis. By January 1940, key leaders of America's large corporations were defining crucial problems in terms of economic stagnation at home and postwar peace terms. Having had the central issue spelled out for them in that fashion, the editors of *Fortune* devoted their attention to the questions of "The Dispossessed" at home and a redefinition of "The U.S. Frontier."

From the candid admission that the American system was in serious trouble ("For nearly one-fourth of the population there is no economic system—and from the rest there is no answer"), the editors of *Fortune* drew three major conclusions. First, they acknowledged that "the U.S.

economy has never proved that it can operate without the periodic injection of new and real wealth. The whole frontier saga, indeed, centered around this economic imperative." Second, and in consequence of this fact, the editors defined two new frontiers. A new emphasis on enlarged consumer sales at home would have to be paralleled by a tremendous expansion of "foreign trade and foreign investment." Secretary of State Hull's trade agreements program was "a step in the right direction," but to "open up real frontiers, under a general policy of raising the standard of living of other countries, we shall have to go much further."

In outlining its conception of such a program, *Fortune* argued that "the analogy between the domestic frontier in 1787, when the Constitution was formed, and the present international frontier is perhaps not an idle one. The early expansion of the U.S. was based upon firm political principles; and it may be that further expansion must be based upon equally firm —and equally revolutionary—international principles." *Fortune's* third point concerned the importance of having more and more corporation leaders enter the Roosevelt Administration and subsequent governments.

As they devoted more of their attention and energy to the challenge of extending the new American frontier, many economic leaders became enthusiastic converts to the mission to reform the world. The convergence of a sense of economic necessity and a moral calling transformed the traditional concept of open door expansion into a vision of an American Century. In this fashion, the United States entered and fought World War II. Americans were convinced that they were defending an anticolonial democracy charged with a duty to regenerate the world. They also had come firmly to believe that their own prosperity and democracy depended upon the continued expansion of their economic system under the strategy of the open door.

SUGGESTED READING

Although *The Tragedy of American Diplomacy* went unreviewed by the historical journals, Williams' most recent volume, *The Roots of the Modern American Empire* ° (1970), evoked reviews in some political journals and in the major historical journals. The most extended examination of *The Roots of the Modern American Empire*, which spilled over into a discussion of Williams' other works, was by Howard Zinn, Michael Harrington, and Arthur Schlesinger, Jr., in "America II," *Partisan Review*, XXXVII (No. 4, 1970), which provoked a reply by Williams, and rejoinders by the others, "America II, Continued," *Partisan Review*, XXXVIII (No. 1, 1971). Carl Degler also reviewed the book in *American Historical Review*, LXXV (Oct. 1970) from a liberal perspective, and Barton J. Bernstein, in "The Roots of Empire," *Progressive* XXIII (June 1970), reviewed it from a radical perspective. Robert W. Tucker's *The Radical Left and American Foreign Policy* ° (1971), a book primarily devoted to assessing and rebutting radical analyses of the Cold War, presents some critical comments on Williams' general framework.

One of Williams' students, Lloyd Gardner, in "From New Deal to New Frontiers: 1937–1941," *Studies on the Left*, I (Fall 1959), and in *Economic Aspects of New Deal Diplomacy* ° (1964), also emphasizes the role of American ideology, and its concern for expanding markets, in interpreting responses to Japanese and German actions. A similar thesis is advanced by another former student influenced by Williams, Robert F. Smith, in Barton J. Bernstein, ed., *Towards a New Past* ° (1968). Gerhard Weinberg, *The Foreign Policy of Hitler's Germany* (1970), Chapter IV, provides some evidence for this thesis in the 1933–36 period, for Weinberg stresses that Germany's economic nationalism deeply troubled American policy-makers.

The related issue of the relationship of American businessmen to the coming of the war has not been adequately explored. In "American Business and the Approach of War, 1935–1941," *Journal of Economic History*, XIII (Winter 1953), Roland Stromberg concludes that "business played no independent role [but] . . . was dragged along in the wake of circumstances, like everyone else." This analysis has been sharply criticized by Gabriel Kolko in "American Business and Germany, 1930–1941," *Western Political Quarterly*, XV (December 1962), who faults Stromberg for relying on the rhetoric of business publications and for neglecting behavior—especially key cartel and contractual agreements between Germany and twenty-six of the top one hundred American industrial corporations. These cartel agreements also raise serious questions about whether major businessmen, as Williams contends, sought the preservation or maintenance of the Open Door. Additional information on business is available in Barton J. Bernstein's "The Automobile Industry and the Coming of the Second World War," *Southwestern Social Science Quarterly* (June 1966), which finds that automobile producers before Pearl Harbor were generally reluctant to convert to the manufacture of war goods.

IV

The Era of the Cold War

Until the Vietnam War, the American people in the era of the Cold War were united by common perceptions of the world in which they lived. In the belief that communism was expansionary and that it could be contained abroad only by American military power, the nation accepted the necessity for a large permanent army, established worldwide military alliances, fought the Korean War, and spent huge sums for foreign aid and intercontinental ballistic missiles. At home Americans looked with satisfaction on the apparent disappearance of poverty, the equitable distribution of national wealth, and the benign character of the modern business corporation. Thankful that a half-century of reform had established social justice, most Americans were content to leave their institutions just as they were.

Before the Vietnam War only two movements of dissent against this consensus attained mass proportions. In the years immediately following the end of the Second World War, Henry A. Wallace, Roosevelt's Vice President in his third term, rallied left-wing Americans to fight for expansion of the New Deal and rejection of Truman's anticommunist foreign policy. By the time of his crushing defeat in 1948 as a third party presidential candidate,

Wallace's crusade was already disintegrating. The other movement of dissent rallied those on the American right. Fighting for fiscal orthodoxy and individual liberty, Senator Robert A. Taft, Republican of Ohio, led a losing effort to curb not only the federal bureaucracy but also such internationalist policies as foreign aid and entangling alliances, policies that Taft feared would create trouble rather than security for the United States. By 1950 reverses in China and evidence of communist subversion at home broadened the discontent with the Democratic administration. At this point Senator Joseph R. McCarthy, Republican of Wisconsin, assumed command of the right wing and appealed mainly to Taft's earlier constituency as he led a movement against communist influences inside America. Although McCarthy succeeded for a time in disrupting the nation's political life, his impact ultimately proved ephemeral, and organized right-wing power declined rapidly after 1955. A right-wing minority in the Republican party succeeded in nominating Barry Goldwater for President in 1964, but his disastrous showing merely demonstrated the impotence of the right in national politics of this period.

Intellectuals played an important role in shaping the national consensus in the early Cold War era, for their writings reinforced the general public's tendency to praise American life. Some intellectuals initially had reservations about the waging of a Cold War, but the brutal communist coup in Czechoslovakia in 1948 and the Berlin Blockade of the same year convinced the skeptical that Soviet Communism was no less malevolent than Nazism and just as expansionary in its intentions. Liberal intellectuals became, in fact, among the most strident advocates of a large military establishment and nuclear deterrents. When Senator Joseph McCarthy assaulted established institutions, intellectuals rallied to defend them with explicitly conservative justifications of the existing social order. The vogue of the "new conservatism" in the mid–1950's reflected not merely revulsion against the so-called radical right but also a genuine belief that American society was amply providing freedom and justice for its citizens. Theorists of countervailing power and pluralism in the social order (for example, John K. Galbraith, Seymour M. Lipset, and Daniel Bell) recognized the existing distribution of power as the best way of protecting the separate interests composing American society. Since McCarthyism had seemed a popular uprising, many intellectuals became distrustful of the masses and sympathetic to leadership by the elite.

Liberal intellectuals conceded that the second-class citizenship of the blacks was a regrettable exception to their optimistic analysis but noted approvingly that the civil rights victories of the mid–1950's and early 1960's were establishing legal equality for black men. (Curiously, the poverty and serious unemployment in the black community remained largely unnoticed until the ghetto revolt of the mid–1960's). Intellectuals had reservations only about the quality of national culture and the tastes of the public. Why should the common man, seemingly emancipated at last from drudgery, still prefer football and cowboys to Kafka and Kant?

During the liberal administration of John F. Kennedy, the intellectuals received recognition and even some power. With their help, the government sought to mobilize the energy, enthusiasm, and humanitarianism of youth through the establishment of the Peace Corps. More significantly, the government strengthened the military, implemented the concept of counterinsurgency and applied force to keep communism out of the Caribbean and Southeast Asia, and created the Alliance for Progress to promote economic growth and counteract revolution in Latin America. At home the New Frontier saw as its main task the maintenance of consumer demand to advance prosperity and to keep private corporations productive and profitable. To the Kennedy circle, reform meant technical adjustments in the American economy. The Kennedy liberals proposed no basic alteration in the social order.

But in the years of the Johnson administration the consensus broke down. The continuing conflict in Vietnam alarmed the intellectuals and provoked a reassessment of the Cold War, causing some liberals to reexamine their nation's foreign policy since the Second World War and to question the morality and wisdom of that policy. Rampaging ghetto blacks made a mockery of exercises in social apology by liberals. The resulting ferment revived the dormant old left, created a New Left, produced the movement of Eugene McCarthy and the third party of George Wallace, and unleashed a powerful criticism against American society. By the end of the Johnson administration, the celebration of American life was over and the nation was convulsed by internal struggles more severe than anything known in this country since the Civil War.

With the election of Richard Nixon to the presidency, dramatic eruptions of protest became increasingly less frequent. The problems of the 1960's had hardly disappeared, but the mood among the dissenting opposition changed from activism to sullen despair. The new President slowly withdrew U.S. ground troops from South Vietnam but continued the devastating air war in Southeast Asia. Students staged protests against the allied invasions of Laos and Cambodia and then surrendered to despair or exhaustion. Nixon weakened the nation's commitment to fight segregation and gutted the war on poverty. But even as conditions deteriorated in the ghetto, the black masses quieted down. As evidenced by Nixon's reversal of America's China policy, the Cold War had obviously begun to wane: yet expenditures for new weapon systems continued to consume huge portions of the national wealth. Social problems that had seemed solvable in the mid–1960's now appeared bafflingly complex and intractable. But despair was not acquiescence, and the critique of America generated in the 1960's still commanded widespread adherence in the early 1970's. Intellectuals in general continued to oppose corporate greed and what increasingly they viewed as American imperialism. And the so-called counterculture lost little of its attraction to great numbers of the young. It began to appear that the rebellion of the 1960's might not be merely an ephemeral development—a cyclical phenomenon soon to vanish without historical trace. For if social values indeed were changing, then many thought that institutional changes might follow.

SUGGESTED READING

There are no scholarly volumes that examine in depth general American history from 1940 or 1945 well into the early 1970's. Dewey Grantham, in *The United States Since 1945* (1967), surveys some of the major literature on parts of this period. Gaddis Smith's *American Diplomacy During the Second World War, 1941–1945* * (1965) is a brief study of the war years. James MacGregor Burns's *Roosevelt: The Soldier of Freedom* (1970) is a broad biography of the wartime President, of his policies at home and abroad, and of the society. John Spanier's *American Foreign Policy Since World War II,** 4th rev. ed. (1971), is a thoughtful volume written from a realist perspective, as is Norman Graebner's perceptive *Cold War Diplomacy, 1945–1960* * (1961). John Lukacs' *A New History of the Cold War,** rev. ed. (1962), is worth consulting; see also Paul Y. Hammond's *American Foreign Policy Since 1945* * (1969). *Cold War: Ideological Conflict or Power Struggle,** edited by Norman Graebner (1963), is a collection of useful essays and excerpts from books on the Cold War. More recent collections are Thomas G. Paterson, ed., *The Origins of the Cold War* * (1970), the best of the group and with a substantial bibliography; and James Compton, ed., *America and the Origins of the Cold War* * (1972). Walter La Feber's *America, Russia, and the Cold War, 1945–1971* * (1972) and Stephen Ambrose's *The Rise to Globalism* * (1971) are the best general revisionist surveys of the Cold War.

Scholars are just beginning to explore the history of domestic America during the war and early postwar years. Richard Polenberg's *War and Society, 1941–1945* * (1972) is a useful survey of the wartime period based on some work in the archival materials. A more limited and critical analysis is Barton J. Bernstein's "America in War and Peace: The Test of Liberalism," in Bernstein, ed., *Towards A New Past* * (1968). Race relations and black attitudes during the war are examined by Richard Dalfiume, in "The 'Forgotten Years' of the Negro Revolution," *Journal of American History,* LV (June 1968); and by Harvard Sitkoff, in "Racial Militancy and Interracial Violence in the Second World War," *Journal of American History,* LVIII (Dec. 1971). Jim Heath, in "Domestic America During World War II: Research Opportunities for Historians," *Journal of American History,* LVIII (Sept. 1971), surveys the literature on the wartime period.

Eric Goldman's *The Crucial Decade and After, 1945–1960* * (1961) is a breezy survey, critical of the tone and style of much of postwar domestic politics, but full of respect for the early foreign policy of containment. Rexford G. Tugwell, in *Off Course* (1971), assesses the postwar Presidents and gives low marks to Truman, Eisenhower, and Johnson. Walter Johnson, in *1600 Pennsylvania Avenue* (1963), analyzes the politics of the years 1929–1960 from a liberal perspective. Essays on the elections of 1948 (Richard S. Kirkendall), 1952 (Barton J. Bernstein), 1956 (Malcolm Moos), 1960 (Richard Goodwin), and 1964 (John B. Martin) are in the fourth volume of Arthur Schlesinger, Jr., ed., *History of American Presidential Elections,* 4 vols. (1971). Cabell Phillips' superficial *The Truman Presidency* * (1966) unfortunately remains the best volume on the subject. *The Truman Period as a Research Field,* edited by Richard S. Kirkendall (1967), contains five uneven historiographical essays on the war and postwar years. Richard Neustadt's *Presidential Power: The Politics of Leadership* (1960), a perceptive essay based on events in the Truman and Eisenhower years, emphasizes the subtle restraints on the President's exercise of his formal powers. Barton J. Bernstein and Allen J. Matusow, editors of *The Truman Administration: A Documentary History* * (1966), include reprints of some manuscript materials in their survey of the period.

Richard Neustadt, former assistant to both Truman and Kennedy, has published a sympathetic assessment of the Truman Administration in "Congress and the Fair Deal: A Legislative Balance Sheet," in Carl Friedrich and John K. Galbraith, eds., *Public Policy,* Vol. 5 (1954). Jonathan Daniels' *The Man of Independence* (1950) is a flattering study by one of Truman's early assistants. Richard Rovere's "President Harry," *Harper's,* CXCVII (July 1948), and "Truman After Seven Years," *Harper's,* CCIV (May 1952), are contemporary evaluations. The President's own memoirs, *Year of Decisions* * (1955) and *Years of Trial and Hope* * (1956), are rich but—like most partly ghostwritten recollections—not always reliable.

The Politics and Policies of the Truman Administration, * edited by Barton J. Bernstein (1970), includes essays critical of the administration's policies in civil rights and civil liberties. William C. Berman, in *The Politics of Civil Rights in the Truman Administration* (1970) also critically examines the administration. Athan Theoharis' *Seeds of Repression: Harry S. Truman and the Origins of McCarthyism* * (1971) stresses the administration's responsibility for McCarthyism. Richard Freeland, in *The Truman Doctrine and the Origins of McCarthyism* (1972), emphasizes the administration's exaggeration of the Soviet "menace" and also holds leaders responsible for McCarthyism. Alan D. Harper's *The Politics of Loyalty* (1969) is more favorable to the administration and views it as responding to real problems and to right-wing pressures. *The Radical Right,* * edited by Daniel Bell (1963), originally issued as *The New American Right* (1955), traced McCarthyism back to the Populist tradition and sought to explain the movement in the 1950's in terms of status politics and authoritarianism. The most penetrating critique of these theories is Michael P. Rogin's *The Intellectuals and McCarthy* * (1967). *The Meaning of McCarthyism,* * edited by Earl Latham (1965), is a useful, but badly dated, anthology that appeared before radical criticisms of the liberal theories, and of liberal responsibility for McCarthyism, emerged. A wider-ranging, more recent collection is *Joseph R. McCarthy,* * edited by Allen J. Matusow (1970). Earl Latham, in *The Communist Controversy in Washington* * (1966), concludes that significant communist espionage in the Federal government did exist.

Irwin Ross's *The Loneliest Campaign* (1968) is a superficial account of the 1948 election. Samuel Lubell's *The Future of American Politics,** rev. ed. (1956), is a fine analysis of ethnic groups, politics, and the Truman administration. Allen J. Matusow, in *Farm Politics and Policies of the Truman Years* (1967), is critical of the administration, but Richard C. Davies, in *Housing Reform During the Truman Administration* (1966), is more favorable.

Eisenhower as President,* edited by Dean Albertson (1963), is a fine collection of essays and portions of books that assess the administration. Aida DiPace Donald, editor of *John F. Kennedy and the New Frontier* * (1967), has compiled useful appraisals of Kennedy. Edward Flash, in *Economic Advice and Presidential Leadership* (1965), covers the activities of the Council of Economic Advisers through the Kennedy years. Bert G. Hickman's *Growth and Stability of the Postwar Economy* (1960) examines factors of the economy up to 1958, and Harold Vatter's *The U.S. Economy in the Fifties* * (1963) surveys the economic trends of that decade. In *Wealth and Power in America* * (1962), Gabriel Kolko argues that wealth and power have remained concentrated within certain groups since before the New Deal.

Rowland Evans and Robert Novak, in *Lyndon B. Johnson: The Exercise of Power* * (1966), concentrate on Johnson's Senate career and are occasionally critical of his tactics, although they endorse his policies in the Dominican Republic and Vietnam. Marvin Gettleman and David Mermelstein, editors of *The Great Society Reader* * (1967), include statements by the administration as well as harsh assessments of contemporary liberalism.

James Gilbert's *Writers and Partisans* (1968), focusing on *Partisan Review,* traces some of the literary radicals into 1948. Christopher Lasch's *The New Radicalism in America* * (1965) analyzes a selected group of intellectuals in the postwar period, and his "Cultural Cold War," in Barton J. Bernstein, ed., *Towards a New Past* * (1968), severely criticizes the Congress for Cultural Freedom for its anticommunism. Philip Green, in "Science, Government, and the Case of RAND: A Singular Pluralism," *World Politics,* XX (Jan. 1968), emphasizes the shortcomings of "defense intellectuals." Ronald Berman's *America in the Sixties* (1968) is harshly critical of the liberal and radical intellectual currents of the decade. William O'Neill's *Coming Apart* (1971), surveying the politics from Eisenhower to Nixon, is critical of the counterculture.

John Higham, in "The Cult of the Consensus," *Commentary,* XXXVII (Feb. 1959), criticizes the dominant American historiography of the postwar years, and Irwin Unger, in "The 'New Left' and American History: Some Recent Trends in United States Historiography," *American Historical Review,* LXXII (June 1967), analyzes and attacks several so-called New Left historians.

BARTON J. BERNSTEIN

American Foreign Policy and the Origins of the Cold War

INTRODUCTION

By the mid–1960's the trauma of Vietnam had begun to inspire a major reassessment of American history and institutions. The best scholarly illustration of this impulse was a growing movement among historians to take a fresh look at the origins of the

FROM Barton J. Bernstein, ed., *Politics and Policies of the Truman Administration* (Chicago: Quadrangle Books, 1970), pp. 15–43, 49–77. Reprinted by permission of the author and the publisher.

The author wishes to express his gratitude for generous counsel to Gar Alperovitz, H. Stuart Hughes, Gabriel Kolko, Walter LaFeber, Lloyd Gardner, Allen J. Matusow, Thomas G. Paterson, Athan Theoharis, and Samuel Williamson. Research was conducted with the assistance of grants from the Rabinowitz Foundation, the American Philosophical Society, the Harry S Truman Library Institute, the Charles Warren Center of Harvard University, and the Institute of American History at Stanford University. Portions of this paper were presented at the Warren Center in November 1967, at the John F. Kennedy Institute at Harvard in 1967–1968, and at the annual meeting of the Southern Historical Association in November 1968.

Cold War. Some scholars who had once accepted their government's version of events in the early postwar period looked again and found in Soviet behavior a cautious design that posed no real threat to American security. Stalin, it seemed, was bent not on world domination but merely on creating a sphere of influence in Eastern Europe to act as a buffer against the Germans. Liberals who argue this thesis usually blame the Cold War on a regrettable failure of perception—on a breakdown in communication in which each side was led by its suspicions into misreading the real and limited intentions of the other. Scholars on the resurgent American left have a quite different explanation, one that places responsibility for the Cold War primarily or exclusively on American imperialism. In the view of these historians the U.S. failed to acquiesce in Stalin's sphere because America sought to extend the frontiers of its system even into Eastern Europe.

Radical critics of America's role in the Cold War are by no means agreed on all major historical or theoretical issues. The most fundamental disagreement lies in whether the capitalist system actually *needs* continuing overseas economic expansion, as Gabriel Kolko, Harry Magdoff, and David Horowitz contend, or whether policy-makers and big businessmen simply (and wrongly) think that the system needs this expansion, as William A. Williams, Lloyd Gardner, and Walter La Feber conclude. Despite this dispute over theory, both groups of radical historians agree that both policy-makers and big businessmen believe that the great menace to the prosperity of the capitalist system is the surpluses that it supposedly generates—surpluses that cannot be absorbed in the home market because the mass of consumers have too little income. To avoid depressions without resorting to radical reform, business and government leaders turn abroad for markets. As the radicals see it, American foreign policy is intended to foster a noncolonial empire for American trade. To protect the empire from the menace posed by the world left, the United States is committed to containing Russia and China and putting down revolutions in the third world. Maintaining access to the underdeveloped world and protecting American investments there has meant supporting undemocratic governments friendly to the United States and condemning countries that produce raw materials to economic subservience.

The relationship of the Open Door policy (equal access to markets and materials) to economic expansion and American ideology is also in dispute. For Kolko and others, the Open Door is primarily a *tactic* for reconstructing the world economy and facilitating American economic penetration. In *The Politics of War* (1968), Kolko stressed the Open Door vision of Secretary of State Cordell Hull and noted the contradictions between this vision and state-trading, cartels, and some of the desires of big business, but he did not clarify whether he considered the Open Door a tactic or an ideology. But in the *Roots of American Foreign Policy* (1969), he endorsed the "tactic" interpretation and stressed America's "dual standard"—the Open Door in most other places *but* not at home. Williams, Gardner, and La Feber, however, despite their occasional ambivalent comments, view the Open Door as part of the ideology. In their books, state-trading, cartels, and other departures from Open Door activities by the United States receive little attention.

The third issue on which there is disagreement also involves the nature of American imperialism. For Kolko, Magdoff, and Horowitz, among others, the successful operation of the American system often requires the self-conscious exploitation of foreign peoples. To Williams and his associates, however, policy-makers and businessmen have evolved an ideology that both serves their material needs and endows their acts with high moral purpose. Policy-makers, say these radicals usually fail to recognize that this ideology is rooted in a particular history and economy. Instead, they mistakenly believe their vision to be transcendently good and universally applicable. In the ideal world order cherished in American official circles, liberal governments dedicated to capitalism and democracy would offer reforms to their peoples. They would regulate their affairs with each other according to international law. All nations could participate in an international economy open to the free flow of goods and private capital. Such a world order would simultaneously achieve the stability necessary for American business expansion and bring the blessings of the American way of life to the rest of mankind. According to Williams and his associates, Americans are blinded by this peculiar perspective and fail to see the exploitative character of the empire they maintain.

On a fourth issue—the structure of power—there is, surprisingly, little open disagreement, though some radical analysts of the Cold War avoid dealing explicitly with the problem. Kolko and Williams stress the class domination of foreign policy and deny the importance of the military-industrial complex, contending that the military has remained subordinate to civilian leaders. Most radical analysts, including Williams and Kolko, are not especially interested in examining the federal bureacracy, which they assume serves (and may also come from) the dominant class, or in studying decision-making beneath the elite level. Put simply, they locate the important decisions at the top. For these historians, the liberals' assumption of an independent, often self-serving, bureaucracy disregards the concentration of power and focuses on the wrong men and probably also on the wrong issues.

On the historical roots of imperialism and the breadth of support for it in the postwar years there is also little disagreement, though again many radicals skirt these problems. Kolko, for example, only offers a few suggestions on the first and nothing explicit on the second. Kolko, like many other radical historians, traces imperialism back at least to the Wilsonian world view, but never discusses when or if this conception became a part of general American convictions. In contrast, Williams, who initially located the sources of expansion in the industrial economy of the 1890's, has recently traced the imperialistic impulse to the agrarians of earlier generations; he has long contended that the belief has been widely held by Americans regardless of class. Williams consequently concludes that policy-makers, by appealing to common American assumptions that support an expansionist foreign policy, can manipulate the electorate without analyzing publicly the basic issues. His is but one—though probably the most popular—of several possible explanations of a phenomenon that most radicals have noted and lamented—the postwar bipartisan consensus on the Cold War, the capacity of the administration repeatedly to use scare tactics and militant anticommunism to promote the programs of containment (such as the Truman Doctrine, the Marshall Plan, and NATO), and the success of the administration and its Congressional allies of both parties in blocking the challenges of right-wing Republicans who questioned the emerging "mythology" of the Cold War.

In the article reprinted below, Barton J. Bernstein of Stanford University finds American policy-makers largely responsible for the beginning of the Cold War. He contends that the United States ignored Russia's security and economic needs, flirted with "atomic diplomacy," provoked the impasse over Germany, relied on a double standard in judging American and Soviet behavior, refused at various junctures to negotiate in good faith, and even wrongly interpreted the revolution in Greece. Stalin, in contrast, behaved conservatively, sought primarily the sphere of influence conceded him in 1944 by Churchill and later by Roosevelt, and even followed counterrevolutionary policies.

Bernstein's analysis is cast within the radical framework. But because he is primarily interested in examining specific events, the framework is often implicit. The result is that he skirts some important theoretical problems. For example, who is ultimately responsible for United States foreign policy? Is there an elite or class that consciously seeks the health of large corporations and manipulates the public? Was American policy also an expression of a national ideology, partly predating the large corporation and reflecting a popular hatred of radicalism? Except for an inconclusive discussion in the last footnote, Bernstein does not deal explicitly in this essay with the problems of who has the power to make foreign policy and how the administration led the American public to accept the Cold War.

As for the issue of ideology, Bernstein discusses it most fully late in the essay and then primarily in connection with containment and the Truman Doctrine. But the role of ideology in the earlier disagreements over Eastern Europe remains ambiguous. He does not clarify the fact that the United States sought to pry Eastern Europe out of the Soviet orbit partly because she wished to reintegrate this area into the Western European economy, whose health was essential to the world and also the American economy. In his later discussion of ideology, Bernstein emphasizes the felt American need for markets, their assumed relationship to democracy and order, and the consequent pursuit of the Open Door, but he does not clearly resolve the problem of whether the Open Door was a tactic or an ideology and whether the economy actually needed expansion.

Bernstein's analysis conflicts at numerous points with the views of many nonradical historians. First of all, defenders of American policy often dispute his view of Stalin, arguing that the dictator's apparent moderation in 1945 and 1946 merely cloaked malicious intentions or that his actions were not really moderate and that he needed the Cold War, and the external enemy it provided, in order to maintain his grip on the Soviet Union. Also, some historians deny that Roosevelt ever accepted temporary, much less permanent, spheres of influence. Among this group are Kolko, Williams, and Lloyd Gardner, who believe that Roosevelt did. not back away from his grand design of using foreign policy as an instrument for opening both the British and Soviet empires to American and Western European economic penetration.

Most nonradical historians of the early Cold War years deny that the atomic bomb played an important role in influencing American policy in 1945 and 1946. Minimizing the scattered evidence in the Potsdam Papers (Department of State, *The Conference of Berlin,* 2 vols. [1955]) and in other collections, they conclude that there is no direct evidence of the bomb's influence on such crucial policies as the American position on German reparations at Potsdam. Bernstein disagrees, citing as one piece of evidence an entry in the diary of Joseph Davies, former Soviet ambassador to the Soviet Union, written in Potsdam on July 28, 1945: "Had a talk this morning with Jim Byrnes. He was still having a hard time over reparations. The details as to the success of the Atomic Bomb, which he had just received, gave him confidence that the Soviets would agree as to these difficulties." In analyzing the post-Potsdam period, many nonradical historians deny that the United States used "atomic diplomacy" even though, as Bernstein points out, Secretary Stimson recorded in his diary that Byrnes wanted to retain the bomb to push through his program at the London Conference, the Soviets twitted Byrnes for brandishing the bomb, and various reports from Europe noted Soviet fears of the bomb and Communist denials that they would succumb to America's "nuclear blackmail."

Even most historians who disagree with Bernstein and the

other radicals on many issues of interpretation are probably now willing to acknowledge that American wartime policy was not innocent, naive, or unconcerned about Soviet policy and power, and that the Cold War had begun by at least 1945, not 1947. Many nonradical historians are also reassessing earlier notions that the primary cause of the Cold War was the threat of imminent Soviet expansion into Western Europe: the radical analysis seems to have established that most American policy-makers did not fear or anticipate such aggression in the early postwar years.

There is no nation which has attitudes so pure that they cannot be bettered by self-examination.
—John Foster Dulles (1946)

We are forced to act in the world as it is, and not in the world as we wish it were, or as we would like it to become.
—Henry L. Stimson (1947)

*D*espite some dissents, most American scholars have reached a general consensus on the origins of the Cold War. As confirmed internationalists who believe that Russia constituted a threat to America and its European allies after World War II, they have endorsed their nation's acceptance of its obligations as a world power in the forties and its desire to establish a world order of peace and prosperity. Convinced that only American efforts prevented the Soviet Union from expanding past Eastern Europe, they have generally praised the containment policies of the Truman Doctrine, the Marshall Plan, and NATO as evidence of America's acceptance of world responsibility. While chiding or condemning those on the right who opposed international involvement (or had even urged preventive war), they have also been deeply critical of those on the left who have believed that the Cold War could have been avoided, or that the United States shared substantial responsibility for the Cold War.[1]

Whether they are devotees of the new realism or open admirers of

---

[1] For the most notable dissents, see D. F. Fleming, *The Cold War and Its Origins* (Garden City, 1961, 2 vols.); William Appleman Williams, *American-Russian Relations, 1781–1947* (New York, 1952), and *The Tragedy of American Diplomacy* (New York, 1962, rev. ed.); Gar Alperovitz, *Atomic Diplomacy* (New York, 1965); Walter La Feber, *America, Russia and the Cold War, 1945–1966* (New York, 1967); Gabriel Kolko, *The Politics of War* (New York, 1968); and Walter Lippmann, *The Cold War* (New York, 1947). My own interpretations have been influenced particularly by the work of Williams and Lippmann. It appears that some scholars who generally accepted the consensus may be moving to a new position. See Arthur M. Schlesinger, Jr., "Origins of the Cold War," *Foreign Affairs,* XLVII (October 1967), 22–51, which accepts portions of recent reinterpretations before abruptly moving back to the more traditional position.

moralism and legalism in foreign policy, most scholars have agreed that the United States moved slowly and reluctantly, in response to Soviet provocation, away from President Franklin D. Roosevelt's conciliatory policy. The Truman administration, perhaps even belatedly, they suggest, abandoned its efforts to maintain the Grand Alliance and acknowledged that Russia menaced world peace. American leaders, according to this familiar interpretation, slowly cast off the shackles of innocence and moved to courageous and necessary policies.

Despite the widespread acceptance of this interpretation, there has long been substantial evidence (and more recently a body of scholarship) which suggests that American policy was neither so innocent nor so non-ideological; that American leaders sought to promote their conceptions of national interest and their values even at the conscious risk of provoking Russia's fears about her security. In 1945 these leaders apparently believed that American power would be adequate for the task of reshaping much of the world according to America's needs and standards.[2]

By overextending policy and power and refusing to accept Soviet interests, American policy-makers contributed to the Cold War. There was little understanding of any need to restrain American political efforts and desires. Though it cannot be proved that the United States could have achieved a *modus vivendi* with the Soviet Union in these years, there is evidence that Russian policies were reasonably cautious and conservative, and that there was at least a basis for accommodation. But this possibility slowly slipped away as President Harry S Truman reversed Roosevelt's tactics of accommodation. As American demands for democratic governments in Eastern Europe became more vigorous, as the new administration delayed in providing economic assistance to Russia and in seeking international control of atomic energy, policy-makers met with increasing Soviet suspicion and antagonism. Concluding that Soviet-American cooperation was impossible, they came to believe that the Soviet state could be halted only by force or the threat of force.[3]

The emerging revisionist interpretation, then, does not view American actions simply as the necessary response to Soviet challenges, but instead tries to understand American ideology and interests, mutual suspicions and misunderstandings, and to investigate the failures to seek and achieve accommodation.

---

[2] Among the major collections are the Henry Stimson and Arthur Bliss Lane Papers at Yale University; the Joseph Grew Papers at Harvard University; the William Leahy, Joseph Davies, Laurence Steinhardt, J. Robert Oppenheimer, and Robert P. Patterson Papers at the Library of Congress; and the Bernard Baruch, Harry Dexter White, and James Forrestal Papers at Princeton University; the William Clayton Papers at Rice University; and the Papers of Harry S Truman and many of his advisers and subordinates at the Truman Library.

[3] Williams, *Tragedy*, pp. 204–226, concludes that Roosevelt's ideology would have led to similar results.

[1]

During the war Allied relations were often marred by suspicions and doubts rooted in the hostility of earlier years. It was only a profound "accident"—the German attack upon the Soviet Union in 1941—that thrust that leading anti-Bolshevik, Winston Churchill, and Marshal Josef Stalin into a common camp. This wartime alliance, its members realized, was not based upon trust but upon necessity; there was no deep sense of shared values or obvious similarity of interests, only opposition to a common enemy. "A coalition," as Herbert Feis has remarked, "is heir to the suppressed desires and maimed feelings of each of its members." Wartime needs and postwar aims often strained the uneasy alliance. In the early years when Russia was bearing the major burden of the Nazi onslaught, her allies postponed for two years a promised second front which would have diverted German armies. In December 1941, when Stalin requested recognition of 1941 Russian borders as they had been before the German attack (including the recently annexed Baltic states), the British were willing to agree, but Roosevelt rebuffed the proposals and aroused Soviet fears that her security needs would not be recognized and that her allies might later resume their anti-Bolshevik policies. So distrustful were the Allies that both camps feared the making of a separate peace with Germany, and Stalin's suspicions erupted into bitter accusations in March 1945, when he discovered (and Roosevelt denied) that British and American agents were participating in secret negotiations with the Germans. In anger Stalin decided not to send Vyacheslav Molotov, the Foreign Minister, to San Francisco for the April meeting on the founding of the United Nations Organization.[4]

So suspicious were the Americans and British that they would not

[4] Herbert Feis, *Churchill-Roosevelt-Stalin* (Princeton, 1957), p. 22. On the postponed second front, see Robert Sherwood, *Roosevelt and Hopkins* (New York, 1948), pp. 562–565, 618–620, 638–642; *Stalin's Correspondence with Roosevelt and Truman* (New York, 1965), pp. 33, 51–52, 74–76 (hereafter *Stalin's Corr.* I); *Stalin's Correspondence with Churchill and Attlee* (New York, 1965), pp. 60–62, 105–106, 131–135 (hereafter *Stalin's Corr.* II); Cordell Hull, *Memoirs*, II, 1173–1184, 1231–1280; Winston Churchill, *The Hinge of Fate* (Boston, 1952), pp. 479–487. On Russian borders and early fears, see Cordell Hull, *Memoirs* (New York, 1948), II, 1165–1175, 1247–1254; Churchill, *The Grand Alliance* (Boston, 1950), pp. 621–630, 695; Sherwood, *Roosevelt and Hopkins*, pp. 708–716; Anthony Eden, *The Memoirs of Anthony Eden: The Reckoning* (Boston, 1965), pp. 330–347. On the separate peace and negotiations, see *Stalin's Corr.* I, pp. 195–214; II, pp. 313–314, 316–318; Churchill, *Triumph and Tragedy* (Boston, 1953), pp. 441–442; John Ehrman, *Grand Strategy* (London, 1956), pp. 122–128; Allen W. Dulles, *The Secret Surrender* (New York, 1966); Henry Stimson Diary, March 13, 1945, Yale University; Alperovitz, *Atomic Diplomacy*, pp. 256–260. There were already bad feelings about the Russian encouragement of the uprising of the Polish resistance movement, which the Russians then abandoned without aid, and of Russian treatment of liberated American and British prisoners. Also see Davies Diary, September 16, 1946.

inform the Soviet Union that they were working on an atomic bomb. Some American leaders even hoped to use it in postwar negotiations with the Russians. In wartime, American opposition to communism had not disappeared, and many of Roosevelt's advisers were fearful of Soviet intentions in Eastern Europe. In turn, Soviet leaders, recalling the prewar hostility of the Western democracies, feared a renewed attempt to establish a *cordon sanitaire* and resolved to establish a security zone in Eastern Europe.

Though Roosevelt's own strategy often seems ambiguous, his general tactics are clear: they were devised to avoid conflict. He operated often as a mediator between the British and Russians, and delayed many decisions that might have disrupted the wartime alliance. He may have been resting his hopes with the United Nations or on the exercise of America's postwar strength, or he may simply have been placing his faith in the future. Whatever future tactics he might have been planning, he concluded that America's welfare rested upon international peace, expanded trade, and open markets:

> . . . it is our hope, not only in the interest of our own prosperity, but in the interest of the prosperity of the world, that trade and commerce and access to materials and markets may be freer after this war than ever before in the history of the world. . . . Only through a dynamic and soundly expanding world economy can the living standards of individual nations be advanced to levels which will permit a full realization of our hopes for the future.

His efforts on behalf of the postwar world generally reflected this understanding.[5]

During the war Roosevelt wavered uneasily between emphasizing the postwar role of the great powers and minimizing their role and seeking to extend the principles of the Atlantic Charter. Though he often spoke of the need for an open postwar world, and he was reluctant to accept spheres of influence (beyond the Western hemisphere, where American influence was pre-eminent), his policies gradually acknowledged the pre-eminence of the great powers and yielded slowly to their demands. By late 1943 Roosevelt confided to Archbishop Francis Spellman (according to Spellman's notes)

---

[5] On Roosevelt's use of American economic power to gain Soviet concessions, see John Morton Blum, *From the Morgenthau Diaries* (Boston, 1967), III, 304–306; James Byrnes, *All in One Lifetime* (New York, 1958), pp. 309–310; Williams, *American-Russian Relations*, p. 274, and *Tragedy*, pp. 218–225; Hull to Roosevelt, June 2, 1944, OF5528, Franklin D. Roosevelt Library. Quotes from Roosevelt's speech of January 6, 1945, in Samuel Rosenman, ed., *Public Papers and Addresses of Franklin D. Roosevelt* (New York, 1952, 13 vols.), XIII, 502–503, and his speech of June 29, 1944, *ibid.*, XIII, 186. Also see his speeches of January 11, 1944, and March 26, 1945, *ibid.*, XIII, 32–43, 595–600; Hull, *Memoirs*, II, 970–977; Edward Stettinius, *Department of State Bulletin* (hereafter *SDB*), XII (April 1, 1945), 531–533; Will Clayton, *ibid.* (April 8, 1945), p. 620. State Department officials, in *SDB*, XII (March 11, 1945), 401–407.

that "the world will be divided into spheres of influence: China gets the Far East; the U.S. the Pacific; Britain and Russia, Europe and Africa." The United States, he thought, would have little postwar influence on the continent, and Russia would probably "predominate in Europe," making Austria, Hungary, and Croatia "a sort of Russian protectorate." He acknowledged "that the European countries will have to undergo tremendous changes in order to adapt to Russia; but he hopes that in ten or twenty years the European influence would bring the Russians to become less barbarous." [6]

In 1944 Roosevelt recognized the establishment of zones of influence in Europe. The Italian armistice of the year before had set the pattern for other wartime agreements on the control of affairs of liberated and defeated European nations. When Stalin requested the creation of a three-power Allied commission to deal with the problems of "countries falling away from Germany," Roosevelt and Churchill first rebuffed the Russian leader and then agreed to a joint commission for Italy which would be limited to information gathering. By excluding Russia from sharing in decision-making in Italy, the United States and Great Britain, later concluded William McNeill, "prepared the way for their own exclusion from any but a marginal share in the affairs of Eastern Europe." [7]

When Roosevelt refused to participate in an Anglo-American invasion of southeastern Europe (which seemed to be the only way of restricting Russian influence in that area), Churchill sought other ways of dealing with Russian power and of protecting British interests in Greece. In May 1944 he proposed to Stalin that they recognize Greece as a British "zone of influence" and Rumania as a Russian zone; but Stalin insisted upon seeking Roosevelt's approval and refused the offer upon learning that the United

---

[6] "Atlantic Charter" is in *A Decade of American Foreign Policy*, 81st Cong., 1st sess., S. Doc. 123, pp. 1–2. Churchill declared that it did not apply to the British Empire. (Speech to House of Commons, September 9, 1941, *House of Commons Debates*, 5th series, CCLXXIV, 68–69.) The Soviet Union, though not a signatory, endorsed the principles with the reservation that their "practical application . . . will necessarily adapt itself to the circumstances, needs, and historical peculiarities of particular countries." (I. M. Maisky, Soviet ambassador to Britain. Report of Proceedings, *Inter-Allied Meeting Held in London at St. James Palace on September 24, 1941* [London, 1941], p. 6315.) On Soviet fears that the Atlantic Charter was directed against the Soviet Union, see Eden, *Reckoning*, pp. 335–344. Quotes are from a memorandum prepared by Spellman after his meeting of September 3, 1943, with Roosevelt, in Robert Gannon, *The Cardinal Spellman Story* (Garden City, 1962), pp. 222–224.

[7] On Stalin's request, see *Stalin's Corr.* I, p. 84; II, pp. 148–149. On Italy, *ibid.*, I, pp. 85–102; II, pp. 149–170; "Military Armistice" and "Allied Control Commission" documents, *Decade of Foreign Policy*, pp. 456–459; William McNeill, *America, Britain, and Russia* (London, 1953), p. 310; cf. Herbert Feis, *Churchill-Roosevelt-Stalin*, pp. 182–188. For warnings about the Italian precedent, see *Foreign Relations of the United States* (hereafter *FR*), 1943, III, 26, 556.

States would not warmly endorse the terms. When the Soviets liberated Rumania in September they secured temporarily the advantages that Churchill had offered. They simply followed the British-American example in Italy, retained all effective power, and announced they were "acting in the interests of all the United Nations." From the Soviet Union, W. Averell Harriman, the American ambassador, cabled, "The Russians believe, I think, that we lived up to a tacit understanding that Rumania was an area of predominant Soviet interest in which we should not interfere. . . . The terms of the armistice give the Soviet command unlimited control of Rumania's economic life" and effective control over political organization.[8]

With Russian armies sweeping through the Balkans and soon in a position to impose similar terms on Hungary and Bulgaria, Churchill renewed his efforts. "Winston," wrote an associate, "never talks of Hitler these days; he is always harping on the dangers of Communism. He dreams of the Red Army spreading like a cancer from one country to another. It has become an obsession, and he seems to think of little else." In October Churchill journeyed to Moscow to reach an agreement with Stalin. "Let us settle our affairs in the Balkans," Churchill told him. "Your armies are in Rumania and Bulgaria. We have interests, missions and agents there. Don't let us get at cross-purposes in small ways." Great Britain received "90 per cent influence" in Greece, and Russia "90 per cent influence" in Rumania, "80 per cent" in Bulgaria and Hungary, and "50 per cent" in Yugoslavia.[9]

In the cases of Hungary and Bulgaria the terms were soon sanctioned by armistice agreements (approved by the United States) which left effective power with the Soviets. "The Russians took it for granted," Cordell Hull, then Secretary of State, wrote later, "that . . . Britain and the United States had assigned them a certain portion of the Balkans, including Rumania and Bulgaria, as their spheres of influence." In December Stalin even confirmed the agreement at a considerable price: he permitted British troops to put down a rebellion in Greece. "Stalin," wrote Churchill later, "adhered strictly and faithfully to our agreement . . . and during all the

---

[8] On the rejected invasion, see Hull, *Memoirs*, II, 1231. For early negotiations, see *Stalin's Corr*. II, pp. 235–236, 238; Churchill, *Triumph and Tragedy*, pp. 74–81; Hull, *Memoirs*, II, 1456–1459. Hull wrongly concludes that the agreement then went into effect. On the agreement, see also Davies Diary, October 9, 18, 1945. Armistice agreements for three nations are in *Decade of Foreign Policy*, pp. 486–500; Feis, *Churchill-Roosevelt-Stalin*, pp. 415–419. Quoted from Harriman's cable of September 15, 1944, in *FR, Diplomatic Papers, 1944* (Washington, D.C., 1966), IV, 234–236. On earlier U.S. reluctance to become involved, see Eden, *Reckoning*, p. 542.

[9] Quoted from Charles Wilson, *Churchill: Taken from the Diaries of Lord Moran* (Boston, 1966), p. 185. Churchill, from his *Triumph and Tragedy*, pp. 226–227. Percentages from Llewelyn Woodward, *British Foreign Policy in the Second War*, p. 308; Churchill, *Triumph and Tragedy*, p. 227. For Harriman's correspondence with Washington, see *FR, 1944*, IV, 1003–1014.

long weeks of fighting the communists in the streets of Athens, not one word of reproach came from *Pravda* or *Izvestia.*" [10]

At Yalta in February 1945 Roosevelt did not seem to challenge Soviet dominance in east central Europe, which had been established by the Churchill-Stalin agreement and confirmed by the armistices and by British action in Greece. What Roosevelt did seek and gain at Yalta was a weak "Declaration on Liberated Europe"—that the powers would consult "where in their judgment conditions require" assistance to maintain peace or to establish democratic governments. By requiring unanimity the declaration allowed any one power to veto any proposal that seemed to threaten that power's interests. In effect, then, the declaration, despite its statements about democratic governments, did not alter the situation in Eastern Europe. The operative phrases simply affirmed the principle that the three powers had already established: they could consult together when all agreed, and they could act together when all agreed. At Yalta the broadly phrased statement provoked little discussion—only a few pages in the official proceedings. Presumably the Russians did not consider it a repudiation of spheres of influence, only as rhetoric that Roosevelt wanted for home consumption. Despite later official American suggestions, the Yalta agreement was not a product of Roosevelt's misunderstanding of the Soviet meaning of "democracy" and "free elections." Rather, it ratified earlier agreements, and the State Department probably understood this.[11]

While accepting the inevitable and acknowledging Russian influence in these areas, Roosevelt had not been tractable on the major issue con-

---

[10] Agreements are in *Decade of Foreign Policy,* pp. 482–486, 494–499. On the agreements, see Department of State, *Conference of Berlin (Potsdam)* (Washington, D.C., 1960), I, 215; Feis, *Churchill-Roosevelt-Stalin,* pp. 450–453. On the understanding of the agreements, see Hull, *Memoirs,* II, 1459; *Stalin's Corr.* I, 164–167; Sherwood, *Roosevelt and Hopkins,* pp. 833–837; Davies Diary, January 2, 1945. For other evidence that American officials understood the implications of the armistice agreements, see *FR, 1944,* III, 438–439, 455–456, 463, 469–470, 472–473, 475–478, 482–483, 941–943, 951, 963, 969–972; IV, 243, 275–277; *ibid., 1945,* IV, 151–152. The Churchill quote is from *Triumph and Tragedy,* p. 293. See also Churchill to Roosevelt, March 8, 1945, in *FR, 1945,* V, 505–506; Department of State, *The Conferences at Malta and Yalta* (Washington, D.C., 1955), pp. 105–106.

[11] For the text, see *Yalta Conference,* pp. 977–978. On discussions and revisions, *ibid.,* pp. 854, 860–863, 873, 899, 908, 913, 918–924, 948. On later suggestions, see James F. Byrnes, *Speaking Frankly* (New York, 1947), pp. 32–33. A State Department draft which Roosevelt had rejected did not require unanimity for consultation, only for action. The results would have been largely the same. (*Yalta Conference,* pp. 97–109, and for warnings by W. A. Harriman, see pp. 64–66; also see Edward Stettinius, Jr., *Roosevelt and the Russians* [Garden City, 1949], pp. 88–89; Byrnes, *Speaking Frankly,* pp. 32–33.) Churchill also acted on the basis that the earlier "spheres of influence" agreement continued to operate. (*Triumph and Tragedy,* pp. 560–561, 636. Cf. McNeill, *America, Britain, and Russia,* p. 559; and Alperovitz, *Atomic Diplomacy,* pp. 132–135.) For State Department views of the Balkans, see *Yalta Conference,* pp. 234–249, and 234–236 on economic power. For State Department understanding of the declaration, see *FR, 1945,* V, 515–516, 520–524, 835–836.

fronting the three powers: the treatment of postwar Germany. All three leaders realized that the decisions on Germany would shape the future relations of Europe. A dismembered or permanently weakened Germany would leave Russia without challenge on the continent and would ease her fears of future invasion. As Anthony Eden, the British Foreign Minister, explained, "Russia was determined on one thing above all others, that Germany would not again disturb the peace of Europe. . . . Stalin was determined to smash Germany so that it would never again be able to make war." A strong Germany, on the other hand, could be a partial counterweight to Russia and help restore the European balance of power on which Britain had traditionally depended for protection. Otherwise, as Henry Morgenthau once explained in summarizing Churchill's fears, there would be nothing between "the white snows of Russia and the white cliffs of Dover." [12]

The Allied policy on Germany had been in flux for almost two years. At Teheran in 1943 the Allies had agreed in principle (despite Churchill's reluctance) that Germany should be dismembered, and in 1944 Roosevelt and a reluctant Churchill, much to the distress of Foreign Minister Anthony Eden, had agreed on a loosely phrased version of the Morgenthau Plan for the dismemberment and pastoralization of Germany. Not only would the plan have eliminated German military-industrial potential and thereby allayed Russian fears, but by stripping Germany it would also have provided the resources for Russian economic reconstruction. Churchill, despite his fear of Russia and his desire for Germany as a counterweight on the continent, had temporarily agreed to the plan because it seemed to be a prerequisite for increased American economic aid and promised to eliminate German industry as a postwar rival for the trade that the debt-ridden British economy would need. Many in the State and War Departments charged that the plan was economic madness, that it would leave not only Germany but also much of war-torn Western Europe (which would need postwar German production) without the means for economic reconstruction. (Secretary of the Treasury Morgenthau concluded after discussion with many officials that they wanted a strong Germany as a "bulwark against Bolshevism.") Yielding to the pleas of the War and State Departments, Roosevelt decided upon a plan for a stronger postwar Germany, and Churchill, under pressure from advisers, also backed away from his earlier endorsement of the Morgenthau Plan and again acted upon his fears of an unopposed Russia on the continent. At Yalta, he resisted any agreement on the dismemberment of Germany. Stalin, faced with Anglo-American solidarity on this issue, acceded. The final communiqué patched over this fundamental dispute by announcing that the three

---

[12] Eden is quoted in Department of State, *The Conferences at Cairo and Teheran* (Washington, D.C., 1961), p. 882; Churchill is quoted in *Morgenthau Diaries*, III, 277.

powers had pledged to "take such steps including the complete disarmament, demilitarization, and dismemberment of Germany as they deem requisite for future peace and security." The strategy of postponement had triumphed. Unable to reach a substantive agreement, the Big Three agreed to submit these problems (and the related, vital issues of reparations and boundaries) to three-power commissions.[13]

Though Yalta has come to represent the triumph of the strategy of postponement, at the time it symbolized Allied accord. Stalin accepted a limitation of the veto power on certain quasi-judicial issues in the U.N. Security Council; Roosevelt conceded to Russia the return of the Kurile Islands, which stretched between Japan and Siberia, and special rights in Dairen and Port Arthur in Manchuria; Stalin promised to enter the Pacific war within three months of the end of the European conflict. "Stalin," as William McNeill explained, "had conceded something to the British in Yugoslavia; and Churchill had yielded a good deal in Poland." [14]

[II]

Roosevelt's successor was less sympathetic to Russian aspirations and more responsive to those of Roosevelt's advisers, like Admiral William Leahy, Chief of Staff to the Commander in Chief; Harriman; James Forrestal, Secretary of the Navy; and James F. Byrnes, Truman's choice for Secretary of State, who had urged that he resist Soviet efforts in Eastern Europe. As an earlier self-proclaimed foe of Russian communism, Truman mistrusted Russia. ("If we see that Germany is winning the war," advised Senator Truman after the German attack upon Russia in 1941, "we ought to help Russia, and if Russia is winning we ought to help Germany and in that way kill as many as possible.") Upon entering the White House, he did not seek to follow Roosevelt's tactics of adjustment and accommodation. Only eleven days in the presidency and virtually on the eve of the United Nations con-

---

[13] On Germany and Roosevelt's shift, see John Snell, "What to Do with Germany?" in Snell, ed., *The Meaning of Yalta* (Baton Rouge, 1956), pp. 43–49; Kolko, *Politics of War*, pp. 324–333, 352–356. For Churchill, see Wilson, *Churchill*, pp. 190–192; Eden, *Reckoning*, pp. 552–553; Blum, *Morgenthau Diaries*, III, 369–372; cf. Churchill, *Triumph and Tragedy*, p. 157. For Morgenthau, see Blum, *Morgenthau Diaries*, III, 394–395; for State and Hull, see Hull, *Memoirs*, II, 1602–1629. For Stimson and War, see Henry Stimson and McGeorge Bundy, *On Active Service in Peace and War* (New York, 1948), pp. 568–582. For Robert Murphy, later General Lucius Clay's political adviser in Germany, see Davies Diary, July 13, 1945. On Yalta, see *Yalta Conference*, pp. 299–309, 874–882; Stettinius, *Roosevelt and the Russians*, pp. 41, 230–231; Byrnes, *Speaking Frankly*, p. 26; Churchill, *Triumph and Tragedy*, pp. 349–353; *Yalta Conference*, pp. 978–979.

[14] *Yalta Conference*, pp. 975–984; McNeill, *America, Britain, and Russia*, pp. 538–566, and quote from p. 564. This analysis, unlike later right-wing charges of a "sell-out," does not assume a conspiracy nor an enthusiasm for acceding to Russian power.

ference, Truman moved to a showdown with Russia on the issue of Poland.[15]

Poland became the testing ground for American foreign policy, as Truman later said, "a symbol of the future development of our international relations." At Yalta the three powers had agreed that the Soviet-sponsored Lublin Committee (the temporary Polish government) should be "reorganized on a broader democratic basis with the inclusion of democratic leaders from Poland itself and from Poland abroad." The general terms were broad: there was no specific formula for the distribution of power in the reorganized government, and the procedures required consultation and presumably unanimity from the representatives of the three powers. The agreement, remarked Admiral Leahy, was "so elastic that the Russians can stretch it all the way from Yalta to Washington without ever technically breaking it." ("I know, Bill—I know it. But it's the best I can do for Poland at this time," Roosevelt replied.) [16]

For almost two months after Yalta the great powers haggled over Poland. The Lublin Committee objected to the Polish candidates proposed by the United States and Great Britain for consultation because these Poles had criticized the Yalta accord and refused to accept the Soviet annexation of Polish territory (moving the eastern boundary to the Curzon Line). In early April Stalin had offered a compromise—that about 80 per cent of the cabinet posts in the new government should be held by members of the Lublin Committee, and that he would urge the committee to accept the leading Western candidates if they would endorse the Yalta agreement (including the Curzon Line). By proposing a specific distribution of power, Stalin cut to the core of the issue that had disrupted negotiations for nearly three months, and sought to guarantee the victory he probably expected in Poland. Roosevelt died before replying, and it is not clear whether he would have accepted this 4 to 1 representation; but he had acknowledged that he was prepared to place "somewhat more emphasis on the Lublin Poles." [17]

Now Truman was asked to acknowledge Soviet concern about countries on her borders and to assure her influence in many of these countries

---

[15] On resistance to the Soviets, see Truman, *Memoirs*, I, 69–82; William Leahy, *I Was There* (New York, 1950), pp. 347–355; Walter Millis, ed., *The Forrestal Diaries* (New York, 1951), pp. 35–51; and Harriman's cables, April 4, 6, 1945, in *FR, 1945*, V, 817–820, 821–824. Truman is quoted in *New York Times*, June 24, 1941.

[16] Quotes from Truman are in *Memoirs* (Garden City, 1955, 2 vols.), I, 76; "Protocol," *Yalta Conference*, p. 980; Leahy, *I Was There*, pp. 315–316. On Yalta and Poland, see Adam B. Ulam, *Expansion and Coexistence* (New York, 1968), pp. 373–377.

[17] On the dispute, see *Stalin's Corr.* I, pp. 201–204, 211–222; II, 309–316, 322–325; *FR, 1945*, V, 123, 157, 180–182, 194, and 189, the source of the quote from FDR (message to Churchill, March 29, 1945). On April 1 Roosevelt warned Stalin against "a thinly disguised continuance of the present Warsaw regime."

by granting her friendly (and probably nondemocratic) governments, and even by letting her squelch anti-communist democrats in countries like Poland. To the President and his advisers the issue was (as Truman later expressed Harriman's argument) "the extension of Soviet control over neighboring states by independent action; we were faced with a barbarian invasion of Europe." The fear was not that the Soviets were about to threaten all of Europe but that they had designs on Eastern Europe, and that these designs conflicted with traditional American values of self-determination, democracy, and open markets.[18]

Rushing back to Washington after Roosevelt's death, Harriman found most of FDR's advisers (now Truman's) sympathetic to a tougher approach. At a special White House meeting Harriman outlined what he thought were the Soviet Union's two policies—cooperation with the United States and Great Britain, and the creation of a unilateral security ring through domination of its border states. These policies, he contended, did not seem contradictory to Russian leaders, for "certain elements around Stalin" misinterpreted America's generosity and desire to cooperate as an indication of softness and concluded "that the Soviet Government could do anything that it wished without having any trouble with the United States." Before Roosevelt's death, Harriman had cabled:

> It may be difficult . . . to believe, but it still may be true that Stalin and Molotov considered at Yalta that by our willingness to accept a general wording of the declaration on Poland and liberated Europe, by our recognition of the need of the Red Army for security behind its lines, and of the predominant interest of Russia in Poland as a friendly neighbor and as a corridor to Germany, we understood and were ready to accept Soviet policies already known to us.[19]

Harriman wanted the American government to select a few test cases and make the Russians realize they could not continue their present policies. Such tactics, he advised, would place Russian-American relations on a more realistic basis and compel the Soviet Union to adhere to the American interpretation of the issues in dispute. Because the Soviet government "needed our [economic assistance] . . . in their reconstruction," and because Stalin did not wish to break with the United States, Harriman

---

[18] Truman's paraphrase and quotation from Harriman are from Truman, *Memoirs*, I, 70–72. On the meeting of April 20, also see *FR, 1945*, V, 231–234. See *Forrestal Diaries*, p. 47, for fears of ideological expansion, and Stimson Diary, July 15, 1945, for Harriman's fears that Russia would even monopolize trade in Manchuria. Also see *FR, 1944*, IV, 283–289, 1025; *Conference of Yalta*, pp. 234–237, 243–246, and for Harriman's fears of continued Soviet penetration, see *FR, 1945*, V, 821, 841–843.

[19] *FR, 1945*, V, 231–234, and 232 is the source of the first two quotes. Similar message is in Harriman's cable of April 6, 1945, *ibid., 1945*, V, 821–826, the source of the last quote.

thought Truman "could stand firm on important issues without running serious risks." As early as January 1944 Harriman had emphasized that "the Soviet Government places the utmost importance on our cooperation" in providing economic assistance, and he had concluded: "it is a factor which should be integrated into the fabric of our overall relations." In early April Harriman had proposed that unless the United States were prepared "to live in a world dominated largely by Soviet influence, we must use our economic power to assist those countries that are naturally friendly to our concepts." In turn, he had recommended "tying our economic assistance directly into our political problems with the Soviet Union." [20]

General George Marshall, the Army Chief of Staff, and Secretary of War Henry Stimson, however, recommended caution. Stimson observed "that the Russians perhaps were being more realistic than we were in regard to their own security," and he feared "that we would find ourselves breaking our relations with Russia on the most important and difficult question which we and Russia have gotten between us." Leahy, though supporting a firm policy, admitted that the Yalta agreement "was susceptible to two interpretations." Secretary of State Edward Stettinius read aloud the Yalta decision and concluded "that this was susceptible of only one interpretation." [21]

Having heard his advisers' arguments, Truman resolved to force the Polish question: to impose his interpretation of the Yalta agreement even if it destroyed the United Nations. He later explained that this was the test of Russian cooperation. If Stalin would not abide by his agreements, the U.N. was doomed, and, anyway, there would not be enough enthusiasm among the American electorate to let the United States join the world body. "Our agreements with the Soviet Union so far . . . [have] been a one-way street." That could not continue, Truman told his advisers. "If the Russians did not wish to join us, they could go to hell." ("FDR's appeasement of Russia is over," joyously wrote Senator Arthur Vandenberg, the Republican leader on foreign policy.) Continuing in this spirit at a private conference with Molotov, the new President warned that economic aid would depend

---

[20] Truman's paraphrase of Harriman is from Truman, *Memoirs*, I, 70. See also *FR, 1945*, V, 232. On the issue of economic assistance to Russia, see *FR, 1944*, IV, 1032–1078. Other quotes are from Harriman's message to Secretary of State, January 9, 1944, in *FR, 1944*, IV, 1035; and Harriman's message of April 4, 1945, *ibid., 1945*, V, 819–820.

[21] Paraphrase of Stimson is quoted from Bohlen's notes on meeting of April 23, 1945, *FR, 1945*, V, 254; and also in Truman, *Memoirs*, I, 78. The second Stimson quote is from Stimson Diary, April 23, 1945. Leahy's statement is from paraphrase in Bohlen's notes. All the sources—Truman, *Memoirs*, I, 70–78; Leahy Diary, April 23, in Library of Congress; Leahy, *I Was There*, pp. 351–353; *Forrestal Diaries*, pp. 48–51; and Stimson Diary, April 23—agree on the substance, and Forrestal and Truman both mention that Leahy used the phrase "two interpretations." Stettinius is also from paraphrase in Bohlen's notes.

upon Russian behavior in fulfilling the Yalta agreement. Brushing aside the diplomat's contention that the Anglo-American interpretation of the Yalta agreement was wrong, the President accused the Russians of breaking agreements and scolded the Russian Foreign Minister. When Molotov replied, "I have never been talked to like that in my life," Truman warned him, "Carry out your agreement and you won't get talked to like that." [22]

At the United Nations conference in San Francisco, when Anthony Eden, the British Foreign Minister, saw a copy of Truman's "blunt message" about Poland to Stalin, "he could scarcely believe his eyes . . . and cheered loudly," reported Vandenberg. But the policy of firmness was not immediately successful. American-Russian relations were further strained by the disputes at the meeting to create the U.N.—over the veto, the admission of fascist Argentina, and the persistent question of Poland. Despite Soviet objections and Roosevelt's promise at Yalta to exclude Argentina from the U.N., the United States supported the Latin American state's candidacy for membership. In committee Molotov, whom Stalin had sent to establish good will with the new President, tried to block the admission of Argentina until the Lublin Poles were also admitted, but his proposed bargain was overwhelmingly defeated. Later in the plenary session, when only three nations voted with Russia, the Soviets found additional evidence for their fears of an American bloc directed against their interests. The Truman administration's action also gave the Soviets more reason to doubt America's explanations that her interests in Poland were inspired simply by a desire to guarantee representative, democratic governments. Moreover, because of the American bloc and Soviet fears that the U.N. (like the League of Nations) might be used against her, Molotov was at first unwilling to accede to the demands of the United States and the smaller nations who wished to exclude procedural questions before the Security Council from the great-power veto.[23]

The Soviets were further embittered when the United States abruptly curtailed lend-lease six days after V-E Day. Though Truman later explained this termination as simply a "mistake," as policy-making by subordinates, his recollection was incomplete and wrong. Leo Crowley, the

---

[22] Truman, quoted from Bohlen's notes of April 23, 1945, meeting, *FR, 1945*, V, 253. Vandenberg in his diary entry of April 24, Arthur H. Vandenberg, Jr., ed., *The Private Papers of Senator Vandenberg* (Boston, 1952), p. 176. Truman's second statement is quoted from his *Memoirs*, I, 82, and see 80–82. For corroboration, Davies Diary, April 30, 1945. Cf. Bohlen's notes of April 23 meeting, in *FR, 1945*, V, 256–258. For a similar economic threat by Stettinius, see entry of April 24 in *Vandenberg Papers*, p. 176.

[23] Quoted from entry of April 24, *Vandenberg Papers*, p. 176; for a summary of these disputes, see McNeill, *America, Britain, and Russia*, pp. 591–603. On Argentina, see *FR, 1945*, I, 36, 199–201, 396–398, 483–488, 500–501. In part, the United States believed that it had to yield to Latin America's wishes in return for its support of admission for the Ukraine and White Russia.

director of lend-lease, and Joseph Grew, the Under Secretary of State, the two subordinates most closely involved, had repeatedly warned the President of the likely impact of such action on relations with Russia, and the evidence suggests that the government, as Harriman had counseled, was seeking to use economic power to achieve diplomatic means. Termination of lend-lease, Truman later wrote, "should have been done on a gradual basis which would not have made it appear as if somebody had been deliberately snubbed." Yet, despite this later judgment, Truman had four days after signing the order in which to modify it before it was to be implemented and announced, and the lend-lease administrator (in the words of Grew) had made "sure that the President understands the situation." The administrator knew "that we would be having difficulty with the Russians and did not want them to be running all over town for help." After discussing the decision with Truman, Grew, presumably acting with the President's approval, had even contrived to guarantee that curtailment would be a dramatic shock. When the Soviet chargé d'affaires had telephoned Grew the day before the secret order was to become effective, the Under Secretary had falsely denied that lend-lease to Russia was being halted. Harriman, according to Grew's report to the Secretary of State, "said that we would be getting 'a good tough slashback' from the Russians but that we would have to face it." [24]

Presumably to patch the alliance, Truman dispatched to Moscow Harry Hopkins, Roosevelt's former adviser and a staunch advocate of Soviet-American friendship. Hopkins denied that Truman's action was an American effort to demonstrate economic power and coerce Russia ("pres-

---

[24] For Truman's later explanation, see Truman, *Memoirs*, I, 225. On Truman's knowledge, see Grew, "Memorandum of [Telephone] Conversation" with Leo Crowley, May 11; for other evidence on this subject, see Grew, "Conference with the President," May 11; "Memorandum of [Telephone] Conversation" with Stettinius, McCloy, Harriman, May 12; and "Memorandum of Telephone Conversation" with Crowley, May 12. For the phone conversation, see Grew, "Memorandum of [Telephone] Conversation" with the Soviet chargé d'affaires, May 12, 1945; and for Harriman, see Grew, "Memorandum of [Telephone] Conversation" with Harriman, Stettinius, McCloy, May 12. All of the preceding in Grew Papers. On Harriman, see his cable to State Department, April 11, and parts of *Forrestal Diaries*, pp. 39–40, and *FR, 1945*, V, 998–1000, 1018–1021. On lend-lease and Russia, see also Stimson Diary, May 14, 1945. On the fear of using lend-lease for reconstruction, in violation of promises to Congress, see Harold Smith Diary, April 26, 1945, Smith Papers, Bureau of the Budget Library; Leo Crowley to Bernard Baruch, February 13, Baruch Papers. On the strategy behind termination, cf. Herbert Feis, *Between War and Peace: The Potsdam Conference* (Princeton, 1960), pp. 28–30, 101. The mistake, it appears, was not cutting off lend-lease abruptly but turning around the ships at sea that were carrying lend-lease; that was the decision of subordinates. See "Minutes of Meeting of Soviet Protocol Subcommittee on Shipping," May 12, 1945, Edgerton folder, Director of Matériel, Records of Army Service Forces, National Archives. George Herring, "Lend-Lease to Russia and the Origins of the Cold War, 1944–1945" (unpublished manuscript, 1968), emphasizes the legal and domestic political reasons for termination, and argues that subordinates misinterpreted the administration's intentions.

sure on the Russians to soften them up," as Stalin charged). Instead he emphasized that "Poland had become a symbol of our ability to work out our problems with the Soviet Union." Stalin acknowledged "the right of the United States as a world power to participate in the Polish question," but he stressed the importance of Poland to Soviet security. Within twenty-five years the "Germans had twice invaded Russia via Poland," he emphasized. "All the Soviet Union wanted was that Poland should not be in a position to open the gates to Germany," and that required a government friendly to Russia. There was "no intention," he promised, "to interfere in Poland's internal affairs" or to Sovietize Poland.[25]

Through the Hopkins mission, Truman and Stalin reached a compromise: 70 per cent of the new Polish government (fourteen of twenty ministers) should be drawn from the Lublin Committee. At the time there was reason to believe that such heavy communist influence would not lead to Soviet control. Stalin had reaffirmed the pledge of free elections in Poland, and Stanislaw Mikolajczyk, former Prime Minister of the exile government in London and Deputy Prime Minister in the new coalition government, was optimistic. He hoped (in Harriman's words) that

> a reasonable degree of freedom and independence can be preserved now and that in time after conditions in Europe can become more stable and [as] Russia turns her attention to her internal development, controls will be relaxed and Poland will be able to gain for herself her independence of life as a nation even though he freely accepts that Poland's security and foreign policy must follow the lead of Moscow.[26]

Truman compromised and soon recognized the new Polish government, but he did not lose his hopes of rolling back the Soviets from their spheres of influence in Eastern Europe. Basing most of his case on the Yalta "Declaration on Liberated Europe" (for which he relied on State Department interpretations), Truman hoped to force Russia to permit representative governments in its zones, and expected that free elections would diminish, perhaps even remove, Soviet authority. Refusing to extend diplomatic recognition to Rumania and Bulgaria, he emphasized that these governments were "neither representative of nor responsive to the will of the people."[27]

"The opportunities for the democratic elements in Rumania and Bul-

---

[25] Quoted from paraphrases of conversations, *Conference of Berlin*, I, 33–39.

[26] Based on Harriman to Secretary of State, June 21, 1945, *FR, 1945*, V, 352–354, and his message of June 28, in *Conference of Berlin*, I, 727–728. Alperovitz, *Atomic Diplomacy*, 75n, concludes two-thirds. Harriman is quoted from *Conference of Berlin*, I, 728. Also see *FR, 1945*, V, 372–374.

[27] *Conference of Berlin*, I, · 357–434, and quote is from Truman's message, 358n. For earlier advice on recognition, see Harriman to State, May 30, 1945, *FR, 1945*, V, 548.

garia are not less than, say, in Italy, with which the Governments of the United States and the Soviet Union have already resumed diplomatic relations," replied Stalin, who was willing to exaggerate to emphasize his case. The Russians were demanding a *quid pro quo,* and they would not yield. At Potsdam, in late July, when Truman demanded "immediate reorganization" of the governments of Hungary and Bulgaria to "include representatives of all significant democratic elements" and three-power assistance in "holding . . . free and unfettered elections," Stalin pointed to Greece, again to remind Truman of the earlier agreements. The Russians were "not meddling in Greek affairs," he noted, adding that the Bulgarian and Rumanian governments were fulfilling the armistice agreements while in Greece "terrorism rages . . . against democratic elements." (One member of the American delegation later claimed that Stalin at one point made his position clear, stating that "any freely elected government [in Eastern Europe] would be anti-Soviet and that we cannot permit.") In effect, Stalin demanded that the United States abide by his construction of earlier agreements, and that Truman acknowledge what Roosevelt had accepted as the terms of the sphere-of-influence agreements—that democratic forms and anti-communist democrats of Eastern Europe be abandoned to the larger cause of Russian-American concord.[28]

Though the Allies at Potsdam were not able to settle the dispute over influence in Eastern Europe, they did reach a limited agreement on other European issues. In a "package" deal the Soviets accepted Italy in the U.N. after a peace treaty could be arranged; the United States and Great Britain agreed to set the temporary western border of Poland at the Oder-Neisse line; and the Soviets settled for far less in reparations than they had expected. The decisions on Germany were the important settlements, and the provision on reparations, when linked with American avoidance of offering Russia economic aid, left Russia without the assistance she needed for the pressing task of economic reconstruction.[29]

---

[28] Quotes, in order, are from *Stalin's Corr.* I, 244; State Department proposals, *Conference of Berlin,* II, 53, 643–644; Churchill's paraphrase, *Triumph and Tragedy,* 636; Soviet proposals, *Conference of Berlin,* II, 1044; Philip Mosely, "Hopes and Failures: American Policy Towards East Central Europe, 1941–1947," in Stephen Kertesz, ed., *The Fate of East Central Europe* (South Bend, Ind., 1956), p. 40.

[29] Byrnes insisted upon the "package." *Conference of Berlin,* II, 491–492. On aid, see *Conference of Berlin,* II, 1477–1497. However, the OSS Report, *Russian Reconstruction and Postwar Foreign Trade Developments,* September 9, 1944, enclosure with Samuel Lubell to Baruch [about March 1945], Baruch Papers, concluded that Russia could rebuild its economy by 1948 if the war ended in 1944, and that reconstruction "will depend very little on foreign loans." For a similar position, see *Yalta Conference,* pp. 321–322; cf. *FR, 1945,* V, 935–936, which notes that a loan of $6 billion "would speed up the Soviet economic development by at least two years, and probably more." Based on these reports, America's offer of credits seemed to be a useful but limited bargaining point. Cf. Martin Herz, *Beginnings of the Cold War* (Bloomington, Ind., 1966), pp. 153–174; and Albert Z. Carr, *Truman, Stalin, and Peace* (Garden City, 1950), p. 41.

Russia had long been seeking substantial economic aid, and the American failure to offer it seemed to be part of a general strategy. Earlier Harriman had advised "that the development of friendly relations [with Russia] would depend upon a generous credit," and recommended

> that the question of the credit should be tied into our overall diplomatic relations with the Soviet Union and at the appropriate time the Russians should be given to understand that our willingness to cooperate wholeheartedly with them in their vast reconstruction problem will depend upon their behavior in international matters.

In January 1945 Roosevelt had decided not to discuss at Yalta the $6 billion credit to the Soviet Union, explaining privately, "I think it's very important that we hold this back and don't give them any promises until we get what we want." (Secretary Morgenthau, in vigorous disagreement, believed that both the President and Secretary of State Stettinius were wrong, and "that if they wanted to get the Russians to do something they should . . . do it nice. . . . Don't drive such a hard bargain that when you come through it does not taste good.") In future months American officials continued to delay, presumably using the prospect of a loan for political leverage. Shortly before Potsdam, the administration had secured congressional approval for a $1 billion loan fund which could have been used to assist Russia, but the issue of "credits to the Soviet Union" apparently was never even discussed.[30]

Shunting aside the loan, the United States also retreated from Roosevelt's implied agreement at Yalta that reparations would be about $20 billion (half of which the Soviets would receive); Truman's new Secretary of State, James F. Byrnes, pointed out that the figures were simply the "basis" for discussion. (He was technically correct, but obviously Roosevelt had intended it as a general promise and Stalin had so understood it. Had it not been so intended, why had Churchill refused to endorse this section of the Yalta agreement?) Because Byrnes was unwilling to yield, the final agreement on reparations was similar to the terms that would have prevailed if there had been no agreement: the Soviet Union would fill her claims largely by removals from her own zone. That was the substance of the Potsdam agreement. The Russians also surrendered any hopes of partici-

---

[30] Harriman is quoted from his dispatch, *Yalta Conference*, p. 313, and for his earlier thoughts, see *FR, 1944*, IV, 1032–1035. FDR is quoted from Morgenthau's notes on the President's comments and the Secretary's reaction, in Blum, *Morgenthau Diaries*, III, 305. On German reparations and political leverage, see *FR, 1945*, III, 1186, 1211–1213; *New York Times*, January 24, 1945; Grew, "Memorandum of Conversation with Morgenthau," January 24, 1945, Grew Papers; *Yalta Conference*, p. 319; Harriman cable of April 11, 1945; on the loan, see Fred Vinson to Truman, July 14, 1945, Central Files, Box 29, Office of War Mobilization and Reconversion (OWMR) Records, National Archives (NA); *Conference of Potsdam*, I, 181; *New York Times*, February 14, 1950.

pating in control of the heavily industrialized Ruhr, and confirmed the earlier retreat from the policy of dismemberment of Germany. They settled for an agreement that they could trade food and raw materials from their zone for 15 per cent of such industrial capital equipment from the Western Zones "as is unnecessary for the German peace economy," and that the allies would transfer from the Western Zones "10 per cent of such industrial capital equipment as is unnecessary for the German peace economy"—but the agreement left undefined what was necessary for the economy.[31]

Potsdam, like Yalta, left many of the great questions unresolved. "One fact that stands out more clearly than others is that nothing is ever settled," wrote Lord Alanbrooke, Chief of the British Staff, in his diary. As he observed, neither the United States nor Russia had yielded significantly. Russia had refused to move from the areas that her armies occupied, and the United States had been vigorous in her efforts, but without offering economic assistance to gain concessions. Though the atomic bomb may not have greatly influenced Truman's actions in the months before Potsdam, the bomb certainly influenced his behavior at Potsdam. When he arrived he still wanted (and expected) Russian intervention in the Japanese war. During the conference he learned about the successful test at Alamogordo. With Russian intervention no longer necessary, Truman's position hardened noticeably. As sole possessor of the bomb, he had good reason to expect easier future dealings with Stalin. For months Stimson had been counseling that the bomb would be the "master card," and Truman, acting on Stimson's advice, even delayed the Potsdam Conference until a time when he would know about the bomb. On the eve of the conference the President had confided to an adviser, "If it explodes, as I think it will, I'll certainly have a hammer on those boys [the Russians]." [32]

---

[31] Byrnes is quoted from paraphrase, *Conference of Berlin*, II, 474. On Churchill, see *Yalta Conference*, p. 983. *Conference of Berlin*, II, 1481–1487, for the final agreement; *ibid.*, II, 490–491, 520–521, 291, 450, 473, 476, 485–492, 822, 827, 932, for their understanding on reparations; and cf. *ibid.*, 944, and *FR, 1945*, III, 1253–1254, for a later American interpretation. On earlier negotiations, see *Yalta Conference*, pp. 808–809, 822, 874.

[32] Diary entry of July 23, Arthur Bryant, *Triumph in the West* (based on the diaries of Lord Alanbrooke), (Garden City, 1959), p. 364; Churchill, *Triumph and Tragedy*, p. 668. "This is some conference. We are getting some good things from it," wrote Truman to Henry Wallace, July 27, 1945, OF27-B, Truman Papers. On economic assistance, see *Conference of Berlin*, I, 181; Alperovitz, *Atomic Diplomacy*, pp. 129–131; Williams, *Tragedy*, pp. 244–252. On the influence of the bomb before Potsdam, Alperovitz, *Atomic Diplomacy*, argues a different thesis. My position is very close to that of Athan Theoharis, "Review of Atomic Diplomacy," *New University Thought*, V (May–June 1967), 12 ff. Cf. Kolko, *Politics of War*, pp. 532–543, 556–567, 595–598. For evidence that Truman delayed the Potsdam Conference until he expected to have knowledge about the bomb, see Stimson Diary, June 6, 1945; Davies Diary, May 21, 1945. On Truman's arrival, see Truman, *Memoirs*, I, 417. On the bomb, see Stimson Diary, July 23 and 24, 1945. On Truman's reaction, see Stimson Diary, July 22, 23, 24, 1945. On Stimson's concern about the bomb and its value in diplomacy, see Stimson Diary, April

[III]

At Potsdam President Truman was "delighted" when Stimson brought him the news about the bomb on July 16. Upon learning more about the results of the test, Truman (according to Stimson) said "it gave him an entirely new feeling of confidence and he thanked me for having come to the conference and being present to help him in this way." The President's enthusiasm and new sense of power were soon apparent in his meetings with the other heads of state, for as Churchill notes (in Stimson's words), "Truman was evidently much fortified by something that had happened and . . . he stood up to the Russians in a most emphatic and decisive manner." After reading the full report on the Alamogordo explosion, Churchill said, "Now I know what happened to Truman yesterday. I couldn't understand it. When he got to the meeting after having read this report he was a changed man. He told the Russians just where they got off and generally bossed the whole meeting." [33]

"From that moment [when we learned of the successful test] our outlook on the future was transformed," Churchill explained later. Forced earlier to concede parts of Eastern Europe to the Russians because Britain did not have the power to resist Soviet wishes and the United States had seemed to lack the desire, Churchill immediately savored the new possibilities. The Prime Minister (Lord Alanbrooke wrote in his diary about Churchill's enthusiasm)

> was completely carried away . . . we now had something in our hands which would redress the balance with the Russians. The secret of this explosive and the power to use it would completely alter the diplomatic equilibrium. . . . Now we had a new value which redressed our position (push-

---

24 and 25, May 10, 14, 15, 16, March 15, 1945. Truman is quoted by Jonathan Daniels, *The Man of Independence* (Philadelphia, 1950), p. 266. My analysis does not rest upon this quotation, and I have purposely avoided relying upon later statements that may be rather dubious: for example, such statements as Truman's paraphrase in 1955 (in his partly "ghosted" memoirs) of Byrnes's statements of April 1945 that "the bomb might well put us in a position to dictate our own terms at the end of the war" (*Memoirs*, I, 87). When relying upon post-Hiroshima sources for evidence of pre-Hiroshima attitudes, I have particularly avoided using their phrasing as precise expressions of earlier attitudes or conversations. In seeking to interpret attitudes toward the atomic bomb, it is important to rely *primarily* upon those sources—contemporaneous manuscripts and published diaries (which seem faithfully to use contemporaneous materials)—which cannot, or are unlikely to, represent post-Hiroshima attitudes or, still worse, Cold War attitudes of 1947 and after.

[33] First quote from Stimson Diary, July 16, 1945; second from *ibid.*, July 21, and others from *ibid.*, July 22; also see *ibid.*, July 18.

ing out his chin and scowling); now we could say, "If you insist on doing this or that well . . . And then where were the Russians!" [34]

Stimson and Byrnes had long understood that the bomb could influence future relations with Russia, and, after the successful test, they knew that Russian entry was no longer necessary to end the Japanese war. Upon Truman's direction, Stimson conferred at Potsdam with General Marshall and reported to the President that Marshall no longer saw a need for Russian intervention. "It is quite clear," cabled Churchill from Potsdam, "that the United States do not at the present time desire Russian participation in the war against Japan." [35]

"The new explosive alone was sufficient to settle matters," Churchill reported. The bomb had displaced the Russians in the calculations of American policy-makers. The combat use of the bomb, then, was not viewed as the only way to end the Far Eastern war promptly. In July there was ample evidence that there were other possible strategies—a noncombat demonstration, a warning, a blockade. Yet, before authorizing the use of the bomb at Hiroshima, Truman did not try *any* of the possible strategies, including the three most likely: guaranteeing the position of the Japanese Emperor (and hence making surrender conditional), seeking a Russian declaration of war (or announcement of intent), or waiting for Russian entry into the war.[36]

---

[34] Churchill from his speech of August 16, 1945, House of Commons Debates, 5th Series, CDXIII, 78–79; Alanbrooke in his diary entry of July 23; *Triumph in the West,* pp. 363–364. Lord Cherwell had recognized earlier (in Margaret Gowing's words) "that whoever possessed . . . [atomic capability] would be able to dictate terms to the rest of the world" (*Britain and Atomic Energy* [London, 1964], pp. 100–105). Sir John Anderson expressed similar thoughts (Samuel Pickersgill, *The Mackenzie King Record* [Chicago, 1960], p. 532).

[35] On Byrnes, see Leahy Diary, May 20, 1945; Richard Hewlett and Oscar Anderson, Jr., *The New World* (University Park, 1962), pp. 354–357; J. W. Wheeler-Bennett, *King George VI* (New York, 1958), p. 644; Byrnes, *Speaking Frankly,* pp. 261–262; *All in One Lifetime,* p. 300; Stimson Diary, July 17, 24, 1945; Davies Diary, July 28, 1945. All this evidence indicates strongly that Byrnes understood the significance for Russia, but the clearest evidence (though unfortunately from post-1945) is Leo Szilard, "A Personal History of the Atomic Bomb," University of Chicago *Roundtable,* 601 (September 25, 1949), 14–15; and "Was A-Bomb on Japan a Mistake?" *U.S. News and World Report* (August 15, 1960), 65–71. On Russian entry as unnecessary, see Stimson Diary, July 20–24, 1945. On Marshall's report, *ibid.,* June 24. Churchill's cable of July 25, 1945, in Ehrman, *Grand Strategy,* p. 292. Churchill had reached this conclusion after a discussion with Byrnes (Hewlett and Anderson, *The New World,* p. 391).

[36] Churchill is quoted from entry of July 23 (paraphrase by Alanbrooke of conversation with Churchill), in *Triumph in the West.* On the warning, see Alice K. Smith, "Behind the Decision to Use the Atomic Bomb," *Bulletin of the Atomic Scientists,* XIV (October 1958), 288–312; John J. McCloy, *The Challenge to American Foreign Policy* (Cambridge, Mass., 1953), pp. 40–44. Shortly after the Interim Committee's approval of combat use of the bomb, Ralph Bard, Under Secretary of the Navy, had dissented and suggested other alternatives—a warning about the bomb, a warning about Russia's likely

As an invasion of the Japanese mainland was not scheduled until about November 1, and as Truman knew that the Japanese were sending out "peace feelers" and that the main obstacle to peace seemed to be the requirement of unconditional surrender (which threatened the position of the Emperor), he could wisely have revised the terms of surrender. At first Under Secretary of State Grew and then Stimson had urged Truman earlier to revise the terms in this way, and he had been sympathetic. But at Potsdam Stimson found that Truman and Byrnes had rejected his advice. As a result the proclamation issued from Potsdam by the United States, Great Britain, and China retained the demand for unconditional surrender when a guarantee of the Emperor's government might have removed the chief impediment to peace.[37]

---

entry into the war, and relaxation of the requirement of unconditional surrender (Bard memorandum of June 27, 1945, reprinted in "Was A-Bomb on Japan a Mistake?" p. 64). Admiral Ernest King claims that he had pointed out many times that a naval blockade could have been successful (King and Walter Muir Whitehall, *Fleet Admiral King* [New York, 1952], p. 621). Of course, King's views reflect the pride of the Navy and could easily and not unreasonably have been discounted on those grounds. Generals Henry Arnold and Curtis LeMay of the Air Force believed that continued bombing of Japan would have been successful (Wesley Craven and James Cate, eds., *The Army Air Forces in World War II* [Chicago, 1953, 6 vols.], V, 711, 726, 747). These judgments were not after the fact, but there was no good evidence that saturation bombing would have had the very prompt results expected of the atomic bomb. The employment of heavy bombing and a blockade had been accepted earlier as complementary tactics and as preliminaries to invasion (Department of Defense, *The Entry of the Soviet Union into the War Against Japan* [mimeographed, 1955], pp. 78–83).

[37] The invasion of Kyushu was scheduled for the fall, but the full-scale invasion was not scheduled until the spring, so there was no reason to fear losses of 500,000 or 1,000,000 in the autumn, as later statements by officials charged. Indeed, the estimates were about 31,000 for the first thirty days on Kyushu (*Entry of the Soviet Union*, pp. 64–66, 79–83; Truman, *Truman Speaks* [New York, 1960], p. 67; Stimson, "The Decision to Use the Atomic Bomb," *Harper's*, CXCIV [February 1947], 97–107; Churchill's speech of August 16, 1945). On Truman's knowledge, see *Conference of Berlin*, I, 873–876, II, 87, 1262–1263, 1264–1267; on the knowledge of policy-makers, see *Forrestal Diaries*, pp. 74–76, and *Conference of Berlin*, II, 1265–1267; Byrnes, *All in One Lifetime*, p. 297, and see in general, *Conference of Berlin*, I, 873–948, II, 1248, 1376. On May 28 Grew suggested to the President that he should guarantee the position of the Emperor, and Truman directed the Under Secretary to discuss the issue with military leaders. Stimson, Forrestal, and Marshall "were all in accord with the principle but for certain military reasons, not divulged, it was considered inadvisable for the President to make such a statement now," recorded Grew. "The question of timing was the nub of the whole matter according to the views present" ("Memorandum of Conversation," May 29, 1945, Grew Papers). Years later Stimson claimed that "the difficulty at the time was that we were having considerable trouble with the Japanese . . . on Okinawa and some of us were afraid that any possible concession at that time might be taken as an indication of weakness" (Stimson to Grew, June 19, 1947, Grew Papers). But Grew regarded Stimson's letter as "no less disingenuous than his article in Harper's," and pointed out that, by the end of May, "the fighting on Okinawa was practically over, or at least the issue was no longer in doubt" (Grew to Eugene H. Dooman, June 30, 1947. Cf. Grew, *Turbulent Era* [Boston, 1952, 2 vols.], II, 1421–1431.) On attempts at revision of the formula, see Stimson Diary, June 19, July 24; *Conference of Berlin*, I, 889–894, II,

Nor was Truman willing to seek a Russian declaration of war (or even an announcement of intent). Even though American advisers had long believed that the *threat* of Russian entry might be sufficient to compel Japanese capitulation, Truman did not invite Stalin to sign the proclamation, which would have constituted a statement of Russian intent. There is even substantial evidence that Truman sought to delay Russian entry into the war.[38]

Pledging to maintain the position of the Emperor, seeking a Russian declaration of war (or announcement of intent), awaiting Russian entry—each of these options, as well as others, had been proposed in the months before Hiroshima and Nagasaki. Each was available to Truman. Why did he not try one or more? No *definite* answer is possible. But it is clear that Truman was either incapable or unwilling to reexamine his earlier assumption (or decision) of using the bomb. Under the tutelage of Byrnes and Stimson, Truman had come to assume by July that the bomb should be used, and perhaps he was incapable of reconsidering this strategy because he found no compelling reason not to use the bomb. Or he may have consciously rejected the options because he wanted to use the bomb. Perhaps he was vindictive and wished to retaliate for Pearl Harbor and other atrocities. (In justifying the use of the bomb against the Japanese, he wrote a few days after Nagasaki, "The only language they seem to understand is the one we have been using to bombard them. When you have to deal with a beast you have to treat him as a beast.") Or, most likely, Truman agreed with Byrnes that using the bomb would advance other American policies: it would end the war before the Russians could gain a hold in Manchuria, it would permit the United States to exclude Russia from the occupation government of Japan, and it would make the Soviets more manageable in

---

1265–1267; *Soviet Entry into the War*, pp. 87–88. On Stimson, see also Stimson Diary, July 17, 24, 1945. Despite the use of the term "unconditional surrender," the proclamation did make certain promises about the future treatment of Japan (*Conference of Berlin*, II, 1280). On the Japanese response, see *Conference of Berlin*, I, 1292–1293; Katzu Kawai, " 'Mokusatsu', Japan's Response to the Potsdam Declaration," *Pacific Historical Review*, XIX (November 1950), 409–414; Robert Butow, *Japan's Decision to Surrender* (Stanford, 1954), pp. 140–149.

[38] There had been considerable discussion of the "shock" of Soviet entry into the war, and sometimes policy-makers felt that a declaration or announcement might have the same effect. *Conference of Berlin*, I, 173, 891–897, 905; II, 36; *Entry of the Soviet Union*, pp. 78–80. On expectations of Soviet entry, see *New York Times*, April 6, 1945; *Soviet Entry into the War*, pp. 70–72; Leahy Diary, May 11, July 17, 24, 1945; Alpeovitz, *Atomic Diplomacy*, pp. 91–128. On Russia and the proclamation, see Byrnes, *Speaking Frankly*, pp. 207–213. Also see Davies Diary, July 27, 1945. On delaying Russian entry, see Churchill cable of July 23, in Ehrman, *Grand Strategy*, p. 292; Byrnes, *All in One Lifetime*, pp. 290–298; *Speaking Frankly*, pp. 68, 205–209; *Conference of Berlin*, II, 1585–1588. On Truman's order to use the bomb, see Feis, letter to the editor, *American Historical Review*, LXVIII (October 1962), 309–310; Patterson to Stimson, December 11, 1946, Patterson Papers, No. 22.

Eastern Europe. It would enable the United States to shape the peace according to its own standards.[39]

At minimum, then, the use of the bomb reveals the moral insensitivity of the President—whether he used it because the moral implications did not compel a reexamination of assumptions, or because he sought retribution, or because he sought to keep Russia out of Manchuria and the occupation government of Japan, and to make her more manageable in Eastern Europe. In 1945 American foreign policy was not innocent, nor was it unconcerned about Russian power, nor did it assume that the United States lacked the power to impose its will on the Russian state, nor was it characterized by high moral purpose or consistent dedication to humanitarian principles.

[IV]

Both Secretary of War Stimson and Secretary of State Byrnes had foreseen the importance of the bomb to American foreign policy. To Stimson it had long promised to be the "master card" for diplomacy. After Hiroshima and Nagasaki Byrnes was eager to use the bomb as at least an "implied threat" in negotiations with Russia, and Truman seems to have agreed to a vigorous course in trying to roll back Russian influence in Eastern Europe.[40]

---

[39] For Truman's statement, see Truman to Samuel McCrea Cavert, August 11, 1945, OF692-A, Truman Papers. Perhaps there were also racist impulses behind this statement. Also see Alperovitz, *Atomic Diplomacy*, p. 190n. "Byrnes said he was most anxious to get the Japanese affair over with before the Russians got in, with particular reference to Dairen" (*Forrestal Diaries* [July 28], p. 78). For agreement, see "Was A-Bomb on Japan a Mistake?" p. 66. On the other hand, General Marshall had concluded (in Stimson's words) "that even if we went ahead in the war without the Russians, and compelled the Japanese to surrender to our terms, that would not prevent the Russians from marching into Manchuria anyhow and striking, thus permitting them to get virtually what they wanted in surrender terms" (Stimson Diary, July 23, 1945). Norman Cousins and Thomas Finletter, "A Beginning for Sanity," *Saturday Review*, XXIX (June 15, 1946), 5–9 ff.; and P. M. S. Blackett, *Fear, War and the Bomb* (New York, 1949), pp. 127–143, conclude that *political* considerations led to the use of the bomb—the desire to keep Russia out of Manchuria and to exclude Russia from decision-making in the occupation of Japan. For earlier consideration of breaking the Yalta agreement on the Far East, see Edward Stettinius, "Memorandum for the Secretary of War," May 12, 1945, Stettinius Papers, University of Virginia. In 1949 Szilard reported his conversation of May 1945 with Byrnes: "Mr. Byrnes did not argue that it was necessary to use the bomb against the cities of Japan in order to win the war. . . . [He believed] that our possessing and demonstrating the bomb would make Russia more manageable in Europe" ("Personal History," pp. 14–15). Williams, *Tragedy*, p. 254, and Alexander Werth, *Russia at War* (London, 1964), pp. 936–942, conclude that this was the purpose, and Alperovitz, *Atomic Diplomacy*, believes that "the evidence strongly suggests" that Byrnes's view (as recalled by Szilard) "was an accurate statement of policy." Cf. Herbert Feis, *The Atomic Bomb and the End of World War II* (Princeton, 1966), *passim*, and pp. 194–195. My own study of the decision to use the bomb has benefited from the work of Blackett, Williams, and Alperovitz.

[40] Stimson Diary, August 12, September 3, 4, 5, 1945.

Truman seemed to be rejecting Stimson's recommendations that international control of atomic energy be traded for important Russian concessions—"namely the settlement of the Polish, Rumanian, Yugoslavian, and Manchurian problems." In his report on the Potsdam Conference the day after the second bomb, the President asserted that Rumania, Bulgaria, and Hungary "are not to be spheres of influence of any one power" and at the same time proclaimed that the United States would be the "trustees" of the atomic bomb.[41]

Following Truman's veiled threat, Byrnes continued his efforts to roll back the Soviet Union's influence. Assisted by a similar protest by the British, who clearly recognized the power of the bomb, he gained postponement of the Bulgarian elections, charging that the government was not "adequately representative of important elements . . . of democratic opinion" and that its arrangements for elections "did not insure freedom from the fear of force or intimidation." In Hungary, Russia also acceded to similar Anglo-American demands and postponed the scheduled elections. It is not unreasonable to conclude that the bomb had made the Russians more tractable. "The significance of Hiroshima was not lost on the Russians," Alexander Werth, British correspondent in the Soviet Union, later reported. "It was clearly realized that this was a New Fact in the world's power politics, that the bomb constituted a threat to Russia. . . . Everybody . . . believed that although the two [atomic] bombs had killed or maimed [the] . . . Japanese, their real purpose was, first and foremost, to intimidate Russia."[42]

Perhaps encouraged by his successes in Bulgaria and Hungary, Byrnes "wished to have the implied threat of the bomb in his pocket during the [September] conference" of foreign ministers in London. Stimson confided to his diary that Byrnes

---

[41] Quoted from Stimson Diary, June 6, 1945; Truman's address of August 9, 1945, in *Public Papers of the Presidents: Harry S. Truman* (hereafter *Truman Papers*), (Washington, D.C., 1961), 1945, pp. 210–213.

[42] Byrnes's note of August 13 is in *SDB*, XIII (August 19, 1945), 274. On American maneuvering and the British reversal, see *FR, 1945*, IV, 282–385. *Conference of Berlin*, II, 689–690, 1494–1495, includes the revision of administrative procedures for the Allied Control Council in Hungary. For revisions on Bulgaria and Rumania, see *Conference of Berlin*, I, 406–408; II, 690–692, 1494–1495. Fleming, *Cold War*, I, 308–357, suggests, and Williams, *Tragedy*, pp. 252–261, and Alperovitz, *Atomic Diplomacy*, pp. 188–225, conclude that the administration used atomic diplomacy. But Alperovitz, p. 205, also suggests that Russia might have yielded on Hungary anyway. Lend-lease was quickly terminated after the Japanese surrendered, and Alperovitz, p. 223, sees the decision as part of a larger strategy; cf. Leahy Diary, August 17, 1945. On Soviet responses see Werth, *Russia at War*, pp. 934, 940, the source of quotes; *FR, 1945*, II, 82–84. Cf. Ulam, *Expansion and Coexistence*, p. 414. The termination of lend-lease shocked and dismayed British leaders, and made Britain more dependent upon, and more anxious for, a large American loan; see Richard Gardner, *Sterling-Dollar Diplomacy* (Oxford, 1956), p. 185.

was very much against any attempt to cooperate with Russia. His mind is full of his problems with the coming meeting . . . and he looks to having the presence of the bomb in his pocket . . . as a great weapon to get through the thing he has. He also told me of a number of acts of perfidy . . . of Stalin which they had encountered at Potsdam and felt in the light of those that we would not rely upon anything in the way of promises from them." [43]

The London conference ended in deadlock, disbanding without even a joint communiqué. Despite American possession of the bomb, Molotov would not yield to American demands to reorganize the governments of Bulgaria and Rumania. In turn, he demanded for Russia a role in the occupation government of Japan, but Byrnes rebuffed the proposal. Unprepared for this issue, Byrnes was also unwilling or unable to understand Soviet anxieties about the security of their frontiers, and he pressed most vigorously for the reorganization of the Rumanian government. He would not acknowledge and perhaps could not understand the dilemma of his policy: that he was supporting free elections in areas (particularly in Rumania) where the resulting governments would probably be hostile to the Soviet Union, and yet he was arguing that democracy in Eastern Europe was compatible with Soviet demands for security. Unable to accept that Byrnes might be naive, Molotov questioned the Secretary's sincerity and charged that he wanted governments unfriendly to the Soviet Union. From this, Byrnes could only conclude later, "It seemed that the Soviet Union was determined to dominate Europe." [44]

While the United States in the cases of these Eastern European nations chose to support traditional democratic principles and neither to acknowledge its earlier agreements on spheres of influence nor to respect Russian fears, Byrnes would not admit the similarity between Russian behavior in Rumania and British action in Greece. As part of the terms of his agreement with Churchill, Stalin had allowed the British to suppress a revolutionary force in Greece, and as a result the Greek government could not be accurately interpreted as broadly representative nor as a product of democratic procedures. Yet, as Molotov emphasized, the United States had not opposed British action in Greece or questioned the legitimacy of that government, nor was the United States making a reversal of British imperialism in Greece a condition for the large loan that Britain needed.[45]

---

[43] John McCloy is quoted from Stimson Diary, August 12, September 3, 1945. Stimson from Stimson Diary, September 4, 1945.

[44] On Rumania, see Henry Roberts, *Rumania* (New Haven, 1951), p. 269; McNeill, *America, Britain, and Russia*, pp. 698–702. On Byrnes and Molotov, see *FR, 1945*, II, 243–245. The quote is from Byrnes, *Speaking Frankly*, p. 99.

[45] On Greece, see William McNeill, *The Greek Dilemma* (Philadelphia, 1947), pp. 162–173; Todd Gitlin, "Counter-Insurgency: The Myth and Reality in Greece," in

Some American observers, however, were aware of this double standard. In the northern Pacific and in Japan, America was to have the deciding voice, but in Eastern Europe, emphasized Walter Lippmann, "we invoke the principle that this is one world in which decisions must not be taken unilaterally." Most Americans did not see this paradox, and Byrnes probably expressed crystallizing national sentiment that autumn when he concluded that the dispute with Russia was a test of whether "we really believed in what we said about one world and our desire to build collective security, or whether we were willing to accept the Soviet preference for the simpler task of dividing the world into two spheres of influence." [46]

Despite Byrnes's views, and although he could not secure a reorganization of the Rumanian government, communist influence was weakened in other parts of Eastern Europe. In Budapest free elections were held and the Communist party was routed; and early in November, just two days after the United States recognized Hungary, the Communists lost in the national elections there. In Bulgaria elections took place in "complete order and without disturbance," and, despite American protests, a Communist-dominated single ticket (representing most of the political parties) triumphed. [47]

While the Soviet Union would not generally permit in Eastern Europe conditions that conformed to Western ideals, Stalin was pursuing a cautious policy and seeking accommodation with the West. He was willing to allow capitalism but was suspicious of American efforts at economic penetration which could lead to political dominance. Though by the autumn of 1945 the governments in Russia's general area of influence were subservient in foreign policy, they varied in form and in degree of independence—democracy in Czechoslovakia (the only country in this area with a democratic tradition), free elections and the overthrow of the Communist party in Hungary, a Communist-formed coalition government in Bulgaria, a broadly based but Communist-dominated government in Poland, and a Soviet-imposed government in Rumania (the most anti-Russian of these nations). In all of these countries Communists controlled the ministries of interior (the police) and were able to suppress anti-Soviet groups, including anti-communist democrats. [48]

Those who have attributed to Russia a policy of inexorable expansion

---

David Horowitz, ed., *Containment and Revolution* (Boston, 1967). On Molotov, see *FR, 1945*, II, 197, 246–247. Also see *FR, 1946*, VI, 681–682.

[46] Lippmann, *New York Herald Tribune*, October 21, 1945. Byrnes, *Speaking Frankly*, p. 105. See also *FR, 1946*, VI, 681–682.

[47] On the election in Budapest, see *FR, 1945*, IV, 883. Quoted from *New York Times*, November 21, 1945. Some opponents of the Communists had withdrawn from the election when the Communists and the major parties agreed upon a single ticket. *FR, 1945*, IV, 374–375.

[48] V. M. Molotov, *Problems of Foreign Policy: Speeches and Statements* (Moscow, 1949), pp. 44–45, 116–117, 213–214. On American policy, see *Conference of Berlin*, I,

have often neglected this immediate postwar period, or they have interpreted it simply as a necessary preliminary (a cunning strategy to allay
American suspicions until the American Army demobilized and left the
continent) to the consolidation and extension of power in east-central Europe. From this perspective, however, much of Stalin's behavior becomes
strangely contradictory and potentially self-defeating. If he had planned to
create puppets rather than an area of "friendly governments," why (as
Isaac Deutscher asks) did Stalin "so stubbornly refuse to make any concessions to the Poles over their eastern frontiers?" Certainly, also, his demand
for reparations from Hungary, Rumania, and Bulgaria would have been
unnecessary if he had planned to take over these countries. (America's insistence upon using a loan to Russia to achieve political goals, and the
nearly twenty-month delay after Russia first submitted a specific proposal
for assistance, led Harriman to suggest in November that the loan policy
"may have contributed to their [Russian] avaricious policies in the countries occupied or liberated by the Red Army.") [49]

Russian sources are closed, so it is not possible to prove that Soviet
intentions were conservative; nor for the same reason is it possible for
those who adhere to the thesis of inexorable Soviet expansion to prove
their theory. But the available evidence better supports the thesis that
these years should be viewed not as a cunning preliminary to the harshness
of 1947 and afterward, but as an attempt to establish a *modus vivendi* with
the West and to protect "socialism in one country." This interpretation explains more adequately why the Russians delayed nearly three years before
ending dissent and hardening policies in the countries behind their own
military lines. It would also explain why the Communist parties in France
and Italy were cooperating with the coalition governments until these parties were forced out of the coalitions in 1947. The American government
had long hoped for the exclusion of these Communist parties, and in Italy,
at least, American intimations of greater economic aid to a government
without Communists was an effective lever. At the same time Stalin was
seeking to prevent the revolution in Greece.[50]

179, 186, 366, 369, 370–373, 420–426, 715, 786–787; II, 477; *Conference of Yalta*,
234–235, 237, 243, 246; *FR, 1945*, IV, 889–890, 908, 915–916, 922–925; II, 236–238.

[49] On Soviet policy, see Mark Ethridge and C. E. Black, "Negotiating on the Balkans,"
in Raymond Dennett and Joseph Johnson, eds., *Negotiating with the Russians* (Boston,
1951), pp. 203–204. Cf. George Kennan, *Memoirs* (Boston, 1967), pp. 255–258, and his
memorandum in *FR, 1945*, V, 853–860. Isaac Deutscher, *Stalin* (New York, 1960), pp.
536–541., Harriman in "Certain Factors Underlying Our Relations with the Soviet
Union," November 14, 1945, Harriman Papers, cited by Paterson, "The Abortive Russian Loan" (unpublished manuscript, 1967). On Stalin and Greece, see Milovan Djilas,
Conversations with Stalin (New York, 1962), pp. 181–184, 246–247.

[50] Deutscher, *Stalin*, pp. 518, 536–547, offers a similar thesis and has influenced my
thought. Also see Blackett, Fear, War, pp. 80–81; Alperovitz, "How Did the Cold War
Begin?" *New York Review*, VIII (March 23, 1967), 6–12; and Williams, *Tragedy*, pp.
259–276. On Czechoslovakia, see Hubert Ripka, *Czechoslovakia Enslaved*, pp. 304–310.

If the Russian policy was conservative and sought accommodation (as now seems likely), then its failure must be explained by looking beyond Russian actions. Historians must reexamine this period and reconsider American policies. Were they directed toward compromise? Can they be judged as having sought adjustment? Or did they demand acquiescence to the American world view, thus thwarting real negotiations?

There is considerable evidence that American actions clearly changed after Roosevelt's death. Slowly abandoning the tactics of accommodation, they became even more vigorous after Hiroshima. The insistence upon rolling back Soviet influence in Eastern Europe, the reluctance to grant a loan for Russian reconstruction, the inability to reach an agreement on Germany, the maintenance of the nuclear monopoly—all of these could have contributed to the sense of Russian insecurity. The point, then, is that in 1945 and 1946 there may still have been possibilities for negotiations and settlements, for accommodations and adjustments, if the United States had been willing to recognize Soviet fears, to accept Soviet power in her areas of influence, and to ease anxieties.

[V]

In October 1945 President Truman delivered what Washington officials called his "getting tough with the Russians" speech. Proclaiming that American policy was "based firmly on fundamental principles of righteousness and justice," he promised that the United States "shall not give our approval to any compromise with evil." In a veiled assault on Soviet actions in Eastern Europe, he declared, "We shall refuse to recognize any government imposed on any nation by the force of any foreign power." Tacitly opposing the bilateral trading practices of Russia, he asserted as a principle of American foreign policy the doctrine of the "open door"—all nations "should have access on equal terms to the trade and the raw materials of the world." At the same time, however, Truman disregarded the fact of American power in Latin America and emphasized that the Monroe Doctrine (in expanded form) remained a cherished part of American policy there: ". . . the sovereign states of the Western Hemisphere, without interference from outside the Western Hemisphere, must work together as good neighbors in the solution of their common economic problems." [51]

"Soviet current policy," concluded a secret report by the Deputy Director of Naval Intelligence a few months later, "is to establish a Soviet

---

On Italy, see H. Stuart Hughes, *The United States and Italy* (Cambridge, Mass., 1965, rev. ed.), p. 135; on France, see Philip Williams, *Politics in Post-War France* (New York, 1954), pp. 16–20. On the Communist party in France, see *FR, 1946*, V, 471–477.

[51] First quote from interview with Chester Bowles, September 13, 1962. Truman address of October 27, 1945, is in *Truman Papers 1945*, pp. 433–434; cf. transcript of conversation between McCloy and Stimson, May 8, 1945, Stimson Papers.

Monroe Doctrine for the area under her shadow, primarily and urgently for security, secondarily to facilitate the eventual emergence of the USSR as a power which could not be menaced by any other world combination of powers." The report did not expect the Soviets ". . . to take any action during the next five years which might develop into hostilities with Anglo-Americans," but anticipated attempts to build up intelligence and potential sabotage networks, "encouragement of Communist parties in all countries potentially to weaken antagonists, and in colonial areas to pave the way for 'anti-imperialist' disorders and revolutions as a means of sapping the strength of . . . chief remaining European rivals, Britain and France." "Present Soviet maneuvers to control North Iran," the report explained, were conceived to "push . . . from their own oil . . . and closer to the enemy's oil." There was no need to fear military expansion beyond this security zone, suggested the report, for the Soviet Union was economically exhausted, its population undernourished and dislocated, its industry and transportation "in an advanced state of deterioration." Despite suggestions that Soviet policy was rather cautious, Truman was reaching a more militant conclusion. "Unless Russia is faced with an iron fist and strong language," asserted Truman to his Secretary of State in January, "another war is in the making. Only one language do they understand—'How many divisions have you' . . . I'm tired of babying the Soviets." [52]

During the winter months Byrnes, Senator Vandenberg, and John Foster Dulles, a Republican adviser on foreign policy, publicly attacked Russian policies. Vandenberg warned "our Russian ally" that the United States could not ignore "a unilateral gnawing away at the status quo." After these attacks, Churchill, accompanied by the President, delivered at Fulton, Missouri, a speech that announced the opening of the Cold War. "From Stettin in the Baltic to Trieste in the Adriatic, an iron curtain has

---

[52] Thomas Inglis (Deputy Director, Office of Naval Intelligence), "Memorandum of Information," January 21, 1946. On Harriman, see *FR, 1945*, V, 901–908; Leahy Diary, February 21, 1946. On Iran, see George Kirk, *The Middle East, 1945–1950* (London, 1954), pp. 56–105; LaFeber, *America, Russia*, pp. 28–29, and McNeill, *America, Britain, and Russia*, pp. 560, 561, 608, 626, 711–714; *FR, 1945*, II, 629–631, 685–687. N. S. Fatemi, *Oil Diplomacy* (New York, 1954), pp. 6, 59–60, 99–125, 233–288. Truman memo of January 5, 1946, which he allegedly read to Byrnes (*Memoirs*, I, 605–606; cf. Byrnes, *All in One Lifetime*, p. 403). Though the interpretations of Soviet actions *supra* are dated after Truman's memo, there is no reason to assume that they are uncharacteristic of secret reports during this period. Some scholars have cited Stalin's speech of February 9, 1946, as evidence that the Soviets believed that war between the U.S. and the USSR was inevitable, but actually his speech was far more conservative. He did emphasize the likelihood of war between capitalist nations and also called for an economic build-up to insure the country "against any eventuality." For the text, see Morray, *Yalta to Disarmament*, pp. 339–349, and for Molotov's speech of February 6, see Molotov, *Problems of Foreign Policy*, pp. 21–36. For interpretations of Stalin's speech as bellicose, see *Forrestal Diaries*, pp. 134–135, and Walter Bedell Smith, *My Three Years in Moscow* (Philadelphia, 1950), p. 62. For Soviet estimates of an Anglo-American clash, see *FR, 1946*, VI, 683–685.

descended across the Continent," declared the former British war leader. Condemning the establishment of "police governments" in Eastern Europe and warning of "Communist fifth columns or . . . parties elsewhere," Churchill, with Truman's approval, called for an Anglo-American alliance to create "conditions of freedom and democracy as rapidly as possible in all [these] countries." The Soviet Union, he contended, did not want war, only "the fruits of war and the indefinite expansion of their power and doctrines." Such dangers could not be removed "by closing our eyes to them . . . nor will they be removed by a policy of appeasement." While he said that it was "not our duty *at this time* . . . to interfere forcibly in the internal affairs" of Eastern European countries, Churchill implied that intervention was advisable when Anglo-American forces were strengthened. His message was clear: ". . . the old doctrine of the balance of power is unsound. We cannot afford . . . to work on narrow margins, offering temptations to a trial of strength." [53]

This was, as James Warburg later wrote, the early "idea of the containment doctrine . . . [and] the first public expression of the idea of a 'policy of liberation,'" which Dulles would later promulgate. Truman's presence on the platform at Fulton implied that Churchill's statement had official American endorsement, and though the President lamely denied afterward that he had known about the contents of the speech, he had actually discussed it with Churchill for two hours. Despite official denials and brief, widespread popular opposition to Churchill's message (according to public opinion polls), American policy was becoming clearly militant. It was not responding to a threat of immediate military danger; it was operating from the position of overwhelming power, and in the self-proclaimed conviction of righteousness.[54]

Undoubtedly Truman had also agreed with the former Prime Minister when Churchill said at Fulton:

---

[53] On Byrnes, see *SDB*, XIII (March 10, 1946), 355–358; on Vandenberg, see *Vital Speeches*, XII (March 15, 1946), 322–326; on Dulles, see *New York Times*, March 2, 1946. All quotes from Churchill's speech are from *Congressional Record*, 79th Cong., 2nd sess., pp. 45–47, but emphasis is added.

[54] James P. Warburg, *Germany: Key to Peace* (Cambridge, Mass., 1953), pp. 36–37. On Truman, see President's Press Conference, March 8, 1946, Truman Library. On responses, see Fleming, *Cold War*, I, 348–357. For his knowledge, see Leahy Diary, February 10, 1946; Official Appointment Book, February 10, 1946, Truman Library; Davies Diary, February 11, 1946. For estimates of Soviet capability, see Inglis, "Memorandum," and Leahy Diary, February 21, 1946. In May General Joseph McNarney, anticipating a communist uprising in France, secured permission from Truman (despite Acheson's opposition) to move troops into France if necessary (Leahy Diary, May 3, 1946). By late spring the Truman administration judged that its military strength in Germany and Italy was inadequate to stop a Soviet attack or even to permit evacuation of troops in case of an attack. But top leaders believed (in Leahy's words) "that the Soviet government did not wish to start a war in the early future" (Leahy Diary, May 28, June 11, 1946). Also see *FR, 1946*, V, 435–438.

It would . . . be wrong and imprudent to intrust the secret knowledge of experience of the atomic bomb, which the United States, Great Britain and Canada now share, to the world organization. . . . No one in any country has slept less well in their beds because this knowledge and the method and raw material to apply it are at present . . . in American hands. I do not believe that we should all have slept so soundly had the positions been reversed and some Communist or neo-Fascist state monopolized, for the time being, these dread agencies. . . . Ultimately, when the essential brotherhood of man is truly embodied and expressed in a world organization, these powers may be confided to it.

Here, in classic form, was a theme that would dominate the American dialogue on the Cold War—the assertion of the purity of Anglo-American intentions and the assumption that the opposing power was malevolent and had no justifiable interests, no justifiable fears, and should place its trust in a Pax Americana (or a Pax Anglo-Americana). Under Anglo-American power the world could be transformed, order maintained, and Anglo-American principles extended. Stalin characterized Churchill's message as, "Something in the nature of an ultimatum: 'Accept our rule voluntarily, and then all will be well; otherwise war is inevitable.' " [55]

. . . .

[VI]

As the great powers moved toward a stalemate on atomic energy, the dispute over Germany contributed to the growing mistrust. At the root of many of the difficulties were the French. Though not a signatory to the Potsdam declaration, they had a zone in Germany and were frustrating efforts at cooperation. They feared a revived Germany, preferred to weaken their enemy of the last three wars, and hoped also to profit at her expense. Seeking to annex territory west of the Rhine, they also wanted to participate in control of the Ruhr and to dismember Germany. When the French were blocked in the four-power council, they vetoed proposals for interzonal trade and economic unification. The other Western powers tolerated these obstructions, but the Russians believed the actions were American-inspired. "After six months of French obstruction," a high Russian official told James Warburg in the summer of 1946, "we began to suspect that this was a put-up-job—that you did not like the bargain you had made at Potsdam and that you are letting the French get you out of it." [56]

---

[55] Quoted from *Pravda* interview of March 13, 1946, in Morray, *Yalta to Disarmament*, p. 50. For earlier Soviet responses, see *FR, 1946*, V, 712–713.

[56] Quoted from Warburg, *Germany*, p. 22, and this paragraph relies on pp. 17–25. For explanations of why U.S. economic aid was not used to coerce France to reverse her German policy, see *FR, 1946*, V, 413, 505–511, 516–520.

"Our first break with Soviet policy in Germany came over reparations," later wrote Lieutenant General Lucius Clay, Deputy Military Governor of the American zone. With the German economy in disorder and the United States and Britain contributing food to their zones while the Soviet Union made its zone live on its own resources and pay reparations, Clay in May terminated reparations deliveries to the Russians from the American zone. "This situation could not be permitted to continue as it represented indirect payment for deliveries to the Soviet Union." This, Clay wrongly contended, violated the Potsdam agreement by withdrawing reparations from a deficient economy. (Despite the provision in the Potsdam protocol that Germany would be treated as "one economic unit," the poorly worded, rather muddled agreement also provided that the Russians should take reparations from their own zone and that these reparations were not contingent upon the import-export balance of the Western zones. In arguing for the plan adopted at Potsdam, Byrnes had explained that the Russians "would have no interest in exports and imports from our zone.") [57]

Lashing out at the United States after Clay's decision, the Russians charged that the Potsdam agreement had been violated. And Russian policy toward Germany soon changed. On July 10, the day after Molotov attacked the Western zonal authorities for failing to destroy fascism and its economic base, the cartels and landed estates, he reversed his tactics and made a bid for German support. Implying that the Morgenthau plan still shaped Western policy, he urged the development of peaceful basic industries in a politically unified Germany. The sudden emphasis on greater industrialization followed abruptly upon Soviet demands for less industrialization. Perhaps the reversal was simply a cynical response to fears of continuing Western violations. Whatever its inspiration, the speech seemed to be an attempt to kindle antagonism against the West.[58]

Byrnes promptly countered with a proposal for economic (but not political) unification, which the Russians could not accept without halting reparations. When France and Russia refused to participate, the British and Americans moved to create a bizonal economy. Because of the failure

---

[57] Quoted from Clay, *Decision in Germany* (Garden City, 1950), p. 122. Paraphrase of Byrnes's statement, *Conference of Berlin,* II, 491. See Manuel Gottlieb, *The German Peace Settlement and the Berlin Crisis* (New York, 1960), pp. 35–42; John Gimbel, *The American Occupation of Germany* (Stanford, 1968), pp. 58–62; E. F. Penrose, *Economic Planning for the Peace* (Princeton, 1953), pp. 282–291; Edward Mason, in House Special Committee on Postwar Economic Policy and Planning, *Statistical Analyses of the Economic Conditions of Selected Countries of Europe and the Middle East* (February 7, 1946), H. Report 1527, 79th Cong., 2nd sess., p. 68. On reparations, also see Patterson, "Notes on a Cabinet Meeting," June 27, 194(6?), Patterson Papers, No. 19. For the dispute on reparations, see *FR, 1946,* V, 520–521, 538, 545–556.

[58] Molotov, speeches of July 9 and 10, in Molotov, *Problems of Foreign Policy,* pp. 55–71. On Soviet policy, see Vladimir Rudolph, in Robert Slusser, ed., *Soviet Economic Policy in Postwar Germany* (New York, 1953), pp. 18–86. *FR, 1946,* V, 576–577.

to establish a unified economy, explained Byrnes in his famous Stuttgart speech of September, the United States no longer felt bound by the earlier agreement to maintain a low level of industry. He emphasized that a prosperous Germany was essential to European recovery. In addition, he called into question the temporary Neisse River boundary with Poland and implied that the United States would support a return of the eastern territory to Germany. By affirming that the United States would stay in Germany "as long as there is an occupation army," he declared in effect that the country would not be abandoned to Russia. The government of Germany, he promised, would be returned to the people so that there could be a "peaceful, democratic" nation which would remain free and independent. "It is not in the interest of the German people or in the interest of world peace that Germany should become a pawn or a partner in a military struggle for power between the East and West," concluded the Secretary. Yet, as the Potsdam agreement crumbled and the United States and Russia quarreled, Germany would remain a key issue in the Cold War struggle.[59]

[VII]

How do American actions since V-J Day appear to other nations? I mean by actions the concrete things like $13 billion for the War and Navy departments, the Bikini tests of the atomic bomb [begun just before Baruch presented his proposal at the U.N.] and continued production of bombs, the plan to arm Latin America with our weapons, production of B-29s and planned production of B-36s, and the effort to secure air bases spread over half the globe from which the other half of the globe can be bombed.

. . . it follows that to the Russians all of the defense and security measures of the Western powers seem to have an aggressive intent. Our actions to expand our military security system . . . appear to them as going far beyond the requirements of defense. I think we might feel the same if the United States were the only capitalistic country in the world, and the principal socialistic countries were creating a level of armed strength far exceeding anything in their previous history. From the Russian point of view, also, the granting of a loan to Britain and the lack of tangible results on their request to borrow for rehabilitation purposes may be regarded as another evidence of the strengthening of an anti-Soviet bloc.

Finally, our resistance to her attempts to obtain . . . her own security system in the form of "friendly" neighboring states seems, from the Russian point of view, to clinch the case. . . . Our interest in establishing democracy in Eastern Europe, where democracy by and large has never existed, seems to her an attempt to re-establish the encirclement of unfriendly

---

[59] Clay, *Decision in Germany,* pp. 130–132. Byrnes's speech of September 6, 1946, *Decade of Foreign Policy,* pp. 522–536. On French and Soviet responses, see *FR, 1946,* V, 584–585, 600–605.

neighbors which was created after the last war and which might serve as a springboard for still another effort to destroy her.[60]

Wallace could not reverse the course of American policy, and Truman was not sympathetic to the letter, later claiming that Wallace had proposed "surrendering" to the Soviet Union. In September the Secretary of Commerce openly criticized the administration's policies while Byrnes was in Paris negotiating peace treaties for the Balkan states. Calling for cooperation between the two great powers, Wallace warned against a " 'get tough with Russia' policy. . . . The tougher we get the tougher the Russians will get." While recommending "an open door for trade throughout the world" as the way to promote peace and prosperity, he contended that the United States should recognize that "we have no more business in the *political* affairs of Eastern Europe than Russia has in the *political* affairs of Latin America, Western Europe, and the United States." [61]

Perhaps Wallace was naive to think that economics and politics could be so easily separated, and clearly he did not understand that Russia, particularly after American efforts to use a loan to pry open trade, feared Western economic penetration of Eastern Europe. "In the situation which is likely to prevail in Poland and the Balkan states . . . the United States can hope to make its influence felt only if some degree of equal opportunity in trade [and] investment . . . is preserved," the State Department had advised earlier. Though trade need not lead to political dominance, the Soviets not unreasonably expressed fears of American economic power. (At Potsdam Stalin had thwarted Truman's attempts to open the Danube to free navigation and to create a multination commission for the river with American representation.) If the " 'principles of equality' are applied in international life," Molotov had argued, "the smaller states will be governed by the orders, injunctions, and instructions of strong foreign trusts and monopolies." Molotov had already seen the United States withhold aid from Poland when it would not accede to American demands for the "open door," and the State Department had insisted that the Czech government in order to be eligible for a loan must accept "the United States proposals for the expansion of world trade and employment." And Molotov knew that the United States had tried to use its economic power to coerce the Soviet Union into creating an "open door" in Eastern Europe and changing her own state-regulated trade. While negotiating a loan of

---

[60] Wallace to Truman, July 23, 1946, also Wallace to Truman, March 15, 1946, Office of the Secretary, Department of Commerce Record, National Archives. For Truman's reply of March 20, see Ronald Radosh, "The Economic and Political Thought of Henry A. Wallace" (unpublished M.A. thesis, University of Iowa, 1960), p. 99.

[61] Truman, *Memoirs*, I, 557. Wallace speech of September 12, 1946, is in Alfred Schindler Papers, Truman Library, emphasis in original. For evidence that Wallace believed Truman had read and endorsed the speech, see Davies Diary, September 11, 1946.

$3.75 billion for Great Britain, at a low interest rate and without demanding liquidation of the Empire, the United States had falsely claimed to have lost for five months the Soviet request for a loan of $1 billion. The Truman administration belatedly offered in February to consider the Soviet Union's request, then insisted upon more stringent terms than for the British loan—Russia would have to reject state-trading and bilateralism, accept multilateralism, join the American-dominated World Bank and International Monetary Fund, reveal secret information about her economy, and disclose the terms of the favorable trade treaties that she had imposed on the nations of Eastern Europe.[62]

Though Wallace never seemed to understand specifically why these demands were unacceptable to the Soviet Union, he did not want to use American economic power to coerce the Russians. Freer trade, he believed, would advance world peace and prosperity only if nations negotiated agreements without economic blackmail. As early as March he had sufficiently distrusted the American negotiators on the loan to urge the President to appoint a group more sympathetic to the Soviet Union. Truman, by his later admission, "ignored" Wallace's request, and in July, just before Wallace's lengthy lecture, the President had foreclosed the possibility of a loan.[63]

---

[62] Briefing paper, *Yalta Conference*, p. 235. Molotov speech of October 10, 1946, in *Problems of Foreign Policy*, pp. 213–214; and see pp. 125–127, for similar sentiments on August 15, and pp. 117–119 for August 13. On the Polish loan, see Arthur Bliss Lane, *I Saw Poland Betrayed*, pp. 225–239, 318–320; *New York Times,* June 23 and 27, 1946; *FR, 1945,* V, 388, 402–403, 411, 419. On the Czech loan, see James Riddleberger to Laurence Steinhardt, December 2, 1946, Francis Williamson to Laurence Steinhardt, July 1 and August 1, 1946, Box 51, Steinhardt Papers. Department of State, *Proposals for the Expansion of World Trade and Employment* (Washington, D.C., 1945). The United States had also ended the United Nations Relief and Rehabilitation Administration (to which the U.S. had contributed about 70 per cent of the funds) in favor of using relief as a lever to achieve political and diplomatic goals. *SDB*, XV (August 1, 1946), 249; Senate, Committee on Foreign Relations, *Hearings, Assistance to Greece and Turkey*, 80th Cong., 1st sess., p. 37. For earlier U.S. efforts to use aid for political purposes, see Bela Gold, *Wartime Planning in Agriculture* (New York, 1953), pp. 434–454; Stimson memorandum of conversation with Herbert Hoover, May 13, 1945; and Stimson to Truman, July 22, 1945, Stimson Papers. On the loan request, see *FR, 1945,* V, 878, 881, 1034, and *ibid.*, pp. 1048, 1049, for evidence that it was not lost. On later "negotiations," see *New York Times*, March 2 and 3, April 11, 18, 21, May 18, 1946. On the loan, also see House Special Committee on Postwar Economic Policy and Planning, *Postwar Economic Policy and Planning*, 8th Report, H. Rept. 1205 (November 12, 1945), 79th Cong., 2nd sess., pp. 9–10, 29–32, 44–45. For a smaller credit on lend-lease orders, see *FR, 1945,* V, 1048. The United States was also trying to pry open the British system for American trade and sought to move the British toward multilateralism. See William Clayton to Bernard Baruch, April 26, 1946, Baruch Papers; Richard Gardner, *Sterling-Dollar Diplomacy*. Additional information on the Russian loan is in *FR, 1946,* VI, 820–853.

[63] Wallace to Truman, March 15, 1946; Truman, *Memoirs*, I, 556. President's News Conference, July 18, 1946. For Stalin's later interest in the loan, see *New York Times*, October 29, 1946; and also see House Special Committee on Postwar Economic Policy and Planning, Supplement to 11th Report, H. Rept. 2737 (December 30, 1946), pp. 24–28.

Still believing that Truman was an unknowing captive of Secretary Byrnes and his cohorts, Wallace sought to carry the battle on foreign policy into the public forum. But, often naive and perhaps foolishly optimistic, he could not provoke a dialogue within the administration on a policy that had long been endorsed by the President. Eight days after his speech Wallace was fired for publicly criticizing foreign policy, and the last dissenter against Truman's foreign policy left the cabinet. By then, negotiations on atomic energy were proving useless, and the American staff was casting about for new ways to compel Russian approval. A much-respected foreign service officer, George Kennan, offered his analysis. The Russians, he suggested, had probably concluded "that we will do nothing" if they did not agree to the American proposal. Under such circumstances he proposed that the United States "begin a series of moves designed to convince the Russians of our serious intent and of the consequences if they choose to continue their present course." [64]

[VIII]

As early as February 1946 Kennan had formulated the strategy—later called "containment"—which became acknowledged official policy in 1947 and was dramatically expressed in the Truman Doctrine. In explaining Soviet behavior Kennan expressed the emerging beliefs of American leaders about Soviet irrationality and the impossibility of achieving agreements. Kennan disregarded the history of Western hostility to the Soviet Union and concluded that Soviet policy was *unreasonably* based upon a fear of Western antagonism. Russian leaders, he warned, had a "neurotic view of world affairs. And they have learned to seek security only in patient but deadly struggle for total destruction of rival power, *never in compacts and compromises with it.*" [65]

Soviet power, however, "is neither schematic nor adventuristic," he said. "It does not take unnecessary risks. For this reason it can easily withdraw—and usually does—when strong resistance is encountered at any point. Thus, if the adversary has sufficient force and makes clear his readiness to use it, he rarely has to do so." (In an extended development of the same theme in 1947, Kennan warned that the Soviets move "inexorably along the prescribed path, like a persistent toy automobile wound up and headed in a given direction, stopping only when it meets unanswerable force." It was necessary to "confront the Russians with unalterable counter-

---

[64] Quoted from paraphrase of Kennan's comments, Franklin Lindsay to staff, November 12, 1946; Baruch Papers. See also *FR, 1945*, V, 884.

[65] Kennan to State Department, February 22, 1946, Forrestal Papers; also source of first quotation in next paragraph, emphasis added.

force at any point where they show signs of encroaching," to stop the Russians with "superior force.") [66]

Read eagerly by policy-makers, Kennan's message seemed to represent only a slight shift in emphasis from Byrnes's policies. In 1945 and early 1946 the Secretary sought through diplomacy (and apparently "implied threats") to roll back Soviet influence in Eastern Europe. Kennan apparently accepted the situation in Eastern Europe, seemed to recommend military resistance to future expansion, and, by implication, supported a stronger military force and foreign bases. In late 1946, as Byrnes moved reluctantly toward accepting the governments of Eastern Europe, he seemed temporarily to accede to Soviet power there. But he never surrendered his hope of pushing the Soviets back, and he was prepared to resist Soviet expansion. The containment doctrine, by urging continued pressure and predicting that Soviet power would either mellow or disintegrate, promised the success that Byrnes sought; but the doctrine, according to Kennan's conception, did not emphasize the heavy reliance upon armaments and alliances that developed. (Though Kennan never explicitly discussed in his famous cable the issue of economic aid to the Soviet Union, it was clear from his analysis and from his other recommendations that disintegration could be speeded by denying economic assistance.) To the goals that Byrnes and most American officials shared, Kennan added a tactic—patience.[67]

The policies of Byrnes and Kennan were based upon what Walter Lippmann diagnosed as "a disbelief in the possibility of a settlement of the issues raised by . . . [the Cold War. The government] has reached the conclusion that all we can do is 'to contain' Russia until Russia changes." This conclusion, wrote Lippmann, was unwarranted and dangerous. "The history of diplomacy is the history of relations among rival powers which did not enjoy political intimacy and did not respond to appeals to common purposes. Nevertheless, there have been settlements . . . to think that rival and unfriendly powers cannot be brought to a settlement is to forget what diplomacy is about." [68]

---

[66] George Kennan, "The Sources of Soviet Conduct," *Foreign Affairs*, XXV (July 1947), 566–582.

[67] On the message, see *Forrestal Diaries*, pp. 135–140. On Byrnes, see George Curry, "James F. Byrnes," in Robert Ferrell, ed., *The American Secretaries of State and their Diplomacy* (New York, 1965), XIV, 191–297; *Forrestal Diaries*, pp. 233–235, 262; Byrnes, *Speaking Frankly*, p. 203; cf. Alperovitz, *Atomic Diplomacy*, p. 234. Truman had confided to Leahy that he had not known that his government was recognizing Yugoslavia until he read about it in the newspaper (Leahy Diary, January 4, 1946). On Kennan's later interpretation, see *Memoirs*, pp. 268–270.

[68] Quoted from Lippmann, *The Cold War*, p. 60, in which he is specifically discussing "Mr. X's" (Kennan's) thought. For similar thoughts, see Clifford to Truman, "American Relations with the Soviet Union," September 1946, Clifford Papers.

Giving up diplomacy, the government prepared to declare publicly a war of ideologies—the struggle between the forces of light and darkness. On March 12, just a year after Churchill's Iron Curtain speech, the President officially proclaimed the containment policy as the Truman Doctrine: ". . . it must be the policy of the United States to support free peoples who are resisting subjugation by armed minorities or by outside pressures." In urging financial aid for Greece and Turkey, the administration relied upon arguments that would become a familiar part of the American Cold War rhetoric. Truman justified opposition to the Greek revolution by defining it not as a revolution but as a struggle between totalitarianism and freedom. The insurgents, he believed, were communist-directed and represented part of the Soviet scheme for expansion. Their victory in Greece would probably lead to the victory of communism in other European countries, and the spread of communism automatically undermined the foundations of world peace and hence the security of the United States.[69]

Though there is still considerable controversy about the situation in Greece, it was a dangerous oversimplification to view the conflict as a struggle between freedom and totalitarianism. Greece, as many American liberals then emphasized, was not a free, democratic nation, and indeed many of the guerrillas were not communists. Rather than being part of the Soviet design for expansion (as American policy-makers wrongly believed), the revolution was opposed by Stalin and it apparently continued despite his opposition. In effect the United States was blocking a revolutionary group, often led by communists and aided by neighboring communist states, which was seeking to overthrow a corrupt, harsh, British-imposed government.[70]

---

[69] Truman's address of March 12, in *Truman Papers, 1947*, pp. 76–80, and quote at pp. 79–80. As a spokesman for the administration, Dean Acheson, Under Secretary of State, later backed away from this open-ended commitment. He tried to limit the objectives to Greece and Turkey, leaving open the issue of policy in future cases (Senate, Committee on Foreign Relations, *Hearings, Assistance to Greece and Turkey*, 80th Cong., 1st sess., p. 42). Opposing an earlier and more temperate draft of the presidential message, Kennan did not endorse aid to Turkey, wanted small military aid to Greece, but objected most to the tone and ideological content of the message. "The Russians might even reply by declaring war!" (Paraphrase of Kennan by Joseph Jones, *Fifteen Weeks* [New York, 1955], pp. 154–155). For earlier evidence of British financial difficulties and the cutback of aid to Greece, see *New York Times*, January 26, February 4, 1947. On earlier American involvement in and commitments to Greece, see Stephen Xydis, *Greece and the Great Powers* (Thessaloniki, 1963), pp. 91–100, 143–160, 187–189, 257–265, 317–318, 379–396, 400–401, 433, 513–514, 652; Byrnes, *Speaking Frankly*, pp. 300–302. On Turkey and the rebuff to Russian efforts to share control of the Dardanelles, see LaFeber, *America, Russia*, pp. 28–29. Truman's address of March 12; Acheson in Senate, *Assistance to Greece and Turkey*, p. 24; and State Department answers, in House, Committee on Foreign Affairs, *Assistance to Greece and Turkey*, 80th Cong., 2nd sess., pp. 341–386.

[70] On Greece, see L. S. Stavrianos, *Greece: American Dilemma and Opportunity* (Chicago, 1952); Frank Smothers, *et al., Report on the Greeks* (New York, 1948); D. G. Kousoulas, *Revolution and Defeat* (London, 1965); Xydis, *Greece*.

Partly because American policy-makers wrongly viewed communism as monolithic and Soviet-directed, they preferred a repressive but anti-communist regime to a pro-communist or communist regime. Because many were coming to view communism as a radical evil, as simply a totalitarianism of the left (and identifying it with Hitler's Nazism), they felt justified in taking vigorous action to halt its advance. Their vaguely formulated assumption seemed to be that communism, once it gained control, would never relax its grip or even ease restraints on liberty; but other forms of repression were milder and would probably yield, ultimately conforming more closely to American democratic aspirations. Significantly, though there were occasional admissions that Greece was not really democratic, American policy-makers did not broaden the public dialogue and adequately explain that they were supporting counter-insurgency to keep open the options for democracy. Rather, in terms reminiscent of the earlier discussion about the Balkans, they publicly discussed the conflict in unreal terms distorted by ideology, as a struggle between freedom and tyranny.[71]

There were of course other reasons why the administration was concerned about Greece and Turkey, for these nations controlled the sea trade to the Middle East and were close to important oil resources on which Anglo-American interests depended. The United States wanted to retain access to these vital resources and to keep them out of the Soviet sphere of influence. "These raw materials have to come over the sea," Forrestal explained privately, and "that is *one* reason why the Mediterranean must remain a free highway." In an earlier draft of Truman's speech, advisers had stressed that Greece and Turkey were areas of great natural resources which "must be accessible to all nations and must not be under the exclusive control or domination of any single nation." But, significantly, this theme was removed from the speech, and neither the private nor public arguments that followed generally emphasized such a narrow conception of national economic interest. Instead, American policy-makers painted a larger and more frightening picture: a defeat in Greece, by sapping the will of anti-communists elsewhere and encouraging their communist enemies, would lead to the collapse of governments in Western Europe and, through a mixture of infiltration, subversion, and indirect aid, even to the fall of Africa and Asia. "If Greece and then Turkey succumb, the whole Middle East will be lost," explained William Clayton, the Under Secretary of State for Economic Affairs. "France may then capitulate to the Communists. As France goes, all Western Europe and North Africa will go."[72]

---

[71] This is an attempt to reconstruct the thought of the administration as reflected particularly, but not exclusively, in: Truman's address of March 12; Acheson in Senate, *Assistance to Greece and Turkey*, p. 10; and State Department answers, House, *Assistance to Greece and Turkey*, pp. 850–865.

[72] Forrestal quoted from transcript of his phone conversation with Paul Smith, March 19, 1947, in Forrestal Papers No. 91. Second quote from "Draft" (of Truman Doctrine

The specter of expanding communism did not simply outrage American humanitarianism; more seriously, it seemed to threaten the national interest in the largest sense. For some it simply meant that world resources—populations and materials for war—would fall to the enemy and might give it the strength to conquer the United States. (During the years when America relied upon a nuclear monopoly for protection, this view was certainly unrealistic in the short run and dubious even in the long run.) For others there was another and more subtle fear, not of attacks on the United States but of the menace of expanding communism to the American economy: it could cut off supplies of raw materials for America and curtail trade, eliminating markets for investment capital and for surpluses.[73]

Such restrictions would compel a drastic readjustment of the Ameri-

---

speech), March 10, 1947, Clark Clifford Papers (used while in his possession but now at Truman Library). Also see Acheson's private explanations in Joseph Jones, *The Fifteen Weeks*, pp. 139–142; Address of May 5, 1947, by Henry Villard, Deputy Director of Office of Near Eastern and African Affairs, Joseph Jones Papers, Truman Library; House, *Assistance to Greece and Turkey*, pp. 375–376; Forrestal, telephone conversation with Paul Shields, March 20, 1947, Forrestal Papers No. 91. Third quote is from Clayton, Memorandum, March 5, 1947, Clayton Papers, Rice University, and it is almost identical to Acheson's words, as reported in Patterson, "Memorandum on Cabinet Meeting," March 7, 1947, Patterson Papers, No. 19.

[73] For the largest sense, see Jones, *Fifteen Weeks*, pp. 139–142. Ambassador W. B. Smith, according to Leahy, did not anticipate a war in the near future, but "he was convinced that the Soviet government confidently expects to conduct a successful war against the capitalistic governments . . . at some time in the future" (Leahy Diary, October 17, 1947). Harriman agreed that the Soviets "will not take any steps which they feel would bring them into a major conflict in the foreseeable future" ("Statement Before President's Air Policy Commission," September 8, 1947, Commission Papers, Truman Library). Kennan, *Memoirs, passim,* expressed fears of the Russians' gaining more resources for war and overturning the balance. The most overt public statement of the threat to the U.S. economy (in connection with communism) is by Clayton in Senate, *Assistance to Greece and Turkey*, p. 81. Also see Dean Acheson, House Committee on Postwar Policy and Planning, 79th Cong., 1st sess., p. 1082; Truman's statement of March 4, 1946, in *Truman Papers, 1946*, p. 140; and Truman's address of March 6, 1947, in *Truman Papers, 1947*, pp. 167–172; Clayton, House, Committee on Banking and Currency, *Anglo-American Financial Agreement,* pp. 191–192, and in *SDB,* XII (April 22, 1945), 760–762; Fred Vinson, *ibid.,* pp. 2–4; Byrnes, in *SDB,* XIII (November 18, 1945), 783–786; Clair Wilcox, in *ibid.,* XV (October 6, 1946), 640. Also, for similar views, see Research Committee of Committee on Economic Development (including Donald David, Gardner Cowles, Chester Davis, Beardsley Ruml, Ernest Kanzler, Eric Johnston, and Paul Hoffman), "International Trade, Foreign Investment and Domestic Employment, Including Bretton Woods Proposals," May 29, 1945; U.S. Chamber of Commerce, "Wartime National Foreign Trade Week" (1945); "Report to the President on Activities of the National Advisory Council on International Monetary and Financial Problems" (about March 1946), OF85E, Truman Library; Herbert Hoover to Baruch (between May 10 and August 5, 1945), Baruch Papers; Charles Taft, in *SDB,* XII, April 25, 1945), 826–831, and in *ibid.* (May 20, 1945), pp. 942–946. For a similar analysis, see Williams, *Tragedy, passim,* and Kolko, *Politics of War,* pp. 242–279. On economic needs, see Kolko, *The Roots of American Foreign Policy* (Boston, 1969), pp. 48–87.

can economy and greatly reduce the standard of living. Unless communism was halted, according to this view, it might economically encircle the United States and disorder the American economic system. "If these countries [Greece and Turkey] and the other countries should adopt closed economies," warned Clayton, "you can imagine the effect that it would have on our foreign trade . . . it is important that we do everything we can to retain those export markets." Looking at the economic crises in the world in early 1947, Joseph Jones, a major draftsman of the Truman Doctrine speech, explained the fears of the administration. If the British Empire, Greece, France, and China "are allowed to spiral downwards into economic anarchy, then at best they will drop out of the United States orbit and try an independent nationalistic policy; at worst they will swing into the Russian orbit." The result, he predicted, would be a disastrous depression, far worse than the Great Depression.[74]

"A large volume of soundly based international trade is essential if we are to achieve prosperity, build a durable structure of world economy and attain our goal of world peace and security," explained Harry S Truman. Linking national prosperity to international peace and prosperity, American leaders acknowledged their nation's overwhelming economic power and assumed that it was essential to the advancement of world peace and prosperity. According to this analysis, the conditions necessary for American economic expansion also promoted international economic and political good health, *directly* (through the flow of benefits from America) and *indirectly* (because other economies would emulate the American). In turn, however, nations like Russia, which engaged in state-trading and bilateralism, endangered the world economy and the American econ-

---

[74] Quoted from Senate, *Assistance to Greece and Turkey*, p. 81. This view also entails concern about communism's developing in *any one country* because of the effect on American trade with that country; but the larger fear cannot be proved unreasonable or unlikely simply by establishing that relations with *that country* are not in themselves economically significant to the American economy. Normally, those who expressed concern about communism in a *particular country* shared the larger fear, but they often emphasized the *specific* problem at hand. Consider, for example, Stimson and Harriman on maintaining the "open door" in Manchuria (Stimson Diary, July 15, 1945). Of course, businessmen with interests in a particular country may limit their concern to threats to those interests without considering larger issues. (This analysis has been influenced by Williams, *Tragedy*.) In turn, businessmen, once convinced of the danger of international communism, have been willing to halt or trim trade with communist states. Between 1944 and 1947 businessmen slowly moved from enthusiasm for trade with Russia to willingness, and sometimes enthusiasm, for cutting trade with the Soviet bloc. See *Nation's Business*, XXXII (October 1944), 21–22; *Fortune*, XXXII (September 1945), 238; Baruch, draft of speech, July 21, 1947, Baruch Papers; *Steel*, CXX (June 9, 1947), 64; *Report of the Thirty-Fourth National Foreign Trade Convention* (New York, 1947), p. 457. For the quote, see Joseph Jones to William Benton, February 26, 1947, Jones Papers. Significantly, when Jones discussed in *Fifteen Weeks* the thought behind the Truman Doctrine, he neglected this theme.

omy. "Nations which act as enemies in the marketplace," explained Clayton, "cannot long be friends at the council table." [75]

"If, by default, we permit free enterprise to disappear in the other nations of the world, the very existence of our own economy and our own democracy will be threatened . . ."—these were the words penned by some of Truman's assistants in an earlier draft of the Truman Doctrine speech. Not only did most American leaders believe that communism threatened the American economy, but they often expressed the belief that traditional freedoms rested upon the prevailing forms of the economy. "Under a different system in this country," explained Dean Acheson,

> you could use the entire production of the country in the United States. If you wished to control the entire trade and income of the United States, which means the life of the people, you could probably fix it so that everything produced here would be consumed here, but that would completely change our Constitution, our relations to property, human liberty, our very conceptions of law. [76]

"Foreign trade is vitally necessary to an expanding American economy," Truman explained. "Our system cannot survive in a contracting economy." Less than a week before announcing the Truman Doctrine, the President offered a more complete analysis of the American political economy, of the relation of cherished freedoms to corporate capitalism:

> There is one thing that Americans value even more than peace. It is freedom. Freedom of worship—freedom of speech—freedom of enterprise. It must be true that the first two of these freedoms are related to the third. . . . So our devotion to free enterprise has deeper roots than a desire to protect the profits of ownership. It is part and parcel of what we call American.
> . . . The pattern of trade that is *least* conducive to freedom of enterprise is one in which decisions are made by governments.
> . . . If this [international] trend is not reversed, the Government of the United States will be under pressure . . . to fight for markets and raw materials. And if the Government were to yield to this pressure, it would shortly find itself in the business of allocating foreign goods among import-

---

[75] Truman statement of July 23, 1946, in *Truman Papers, 1946*, pp. 353–354. Clayton in *SDB*, XII (May 27, 1945), 979. Not all, however, who accepted the theory of peace and prosperity emphasized Russian restrictions on trade as necessarily hostile to the world or to America.

[76] Quoted from "Draft" (of Truman Doctrine speech), March 10, 1947. Dean Acheson directed that this statement be deleted because it gave undue public attention to economic factors (Jones, *Fifteen Weeks*, pp. 156–157). For Acheson, see *Postwar Policy and Planning*, p. 1082.

ers and foreign markets among exporters, and telling every trader what he could buy or sell. . . . It is not the American way.[77]

Opposition among policy-makers to communist expansion in the immediate postwar years sprang from a cluster of related attitudes— humanitarianism, expectation of military attack in the short or long run, and the fear of economic encirclement. It is this fear of economic danger, so closely linked to the political economy of American liberalism, which has often constituted much of the basis for American intervention in other lands. American efforts, as William Appleman Williams has emphasized, have frequently been directed toward maintaining an economic open door. To do so, at times the United States has been compelled to subdue or limit challenges, and in the postwar years the most serious challenges were communist. The justification usually offered—that these challenges are totalitarian—is not false but, rather, often incomplete.[78]

[IX]

The fear of communism, often mixed with a misunderstanding of Munich and the sense that compromise may be appeasement, has led policy-makers generally to be intransigent in their response to communism. They have allowed their fears to distort their perceptions and their ideology to blur

---

[77] First quote is from statement of March 4, 1946. Long quote is from speech of March 6, 1947. Cf. Allen J. Matusow, *Farm Policies and Politics in the Truman Years* (Cambridge, Mass., 1967), pp. 79–110, for the defeat of free trade by others in the government. Also see James Warburg, *Put Yourself in Marshall's Place* (New York, 1948), pp. 12–46. On economic relations with the nations within the Soviet sphere, see McNeill, *America, Britain, and Russia*, pp. 690–699; Byrnes, *Speaking Frankly*, pp. 116, 142–144.

[78] By design, this essay has sought to analyze American policy and the ideology of policy-makers and only to suggest (in these closing paragraphs) the influence upon public understanding. It is clear that the *public* fear of Soviet communism and the commitment to internationalism (in the forms of intervention, economic assistance, or even concern about international economic relations) lagged behind the concern of policy-makers in 1945–1947. It may be a false question to ask whether the public's increasing fear of communism was a result of the efforts of American policy-makers *or* of the publicity about communist action. The two are so intimately linked as to make definitive analysis difficult, if not impossible. On general public attitudes, see *Public Opinion Quarterly* (1945–1948) for polls. The essay does not attempt to analyze congressional-executive relations on foreign policy, but my research indicates that Vandenberg and the internationalist wing of the Republican party provided sufficient votes and support for the administration's general foreign policy in this period to substantiate the conventional characterization of a bipartisan policy. Of course, bipartisanship did not eliminate the need for minor concessions to Vandenberg, nor did it prevent squabbles about details, and Vandenberg and his followers did constitute a strong anti-Soviet force which would have politically restricted the administration if it had sought a compromise with the Soviet Union after the autumn of 1945.

reality. This is part of the legacy of the Truman administration in the development of the Cold War.

In these years American liberal democracy became visibly defensive. Though espousing humanitarian ideals and proclaiming the value of self-determination, Americans have often failed to exhibit a tolerance or understanding of the methods of other people in pursuing social change and establishing governments in their own (non-American) way. Revolutions have been misunderstood, seldom accepted, never befriended. Fearing violence, respecting private property, and believing in peaceful reform, Americans have become captives of an ideology which interprets revolution as dysfunctional and dangerous to American interests. Opposing these radical movements in the name of freedom, America has turned often to oligarchies and dictators instead. By falsely dividing the world into the free and the unfree, and by making alliances in the name of freedom (not security) with the enemies of freedom, America has often judged world events by the standards of the crusade against communism, and thus it has been unable to understand the behavior and problems of the underdeveloped nations. It is this defective world view, so visible in the early Cold War, that has led some to lament that the American self-conception has lost its utopian vision.

SUGGESTED READING

The first contemporary revisionist study of the Cold War was Carl Marzani's *We Can Be Friends: Origins of the Cold War* (1952), which is being reissued with a critical introduction by Barton J. Bernstein. William Appleman Williams' *American-Russian Relations, 1781–1947* (1952), the first significant revisionist interpretation of the Cold War by a scholar, includes a brief chapter on Soviet-American relations after 1941 and relies on the framework later developed in *The Tragedy of American Diplomacy*. Lloyd Gardner's *Economic Aspects of New Deal Diplomacy* ° (1964) extends into the war years and employs the Williams framework. Gardner's *Architects of Illusion: Men and Ideas in American Foreign Policy, 1941–1949* ° (1970) focuses on U.S. policy, not Soviet policy, and examines especially the activities of the wartime Presidents, three secretaries of state, and some military leaders.

Denna F. Fleming's *The Cold War and Its Origins*, 2 vols. (1961), is an ambivalent, early revisionist study that shifts from lamenting the departures from Wilsonianism to offering an analysis similar to Williams. David Horowitz, in *The Free World Colossus* ° (1965), following Fleming, is rooted in the same framework but reaches into the Johnson years. Horowitz later moved to a radical analysis of the Cold War in his *Empire and Revolution* ° (1969) and this orientation is also evident in a volume he edited, *Corporations and the Cold War* (1969). *Containment and Revolution* ° (1967), another useful collection of essays edited by Horowitz, includes a fine study of the origins of the Cold War by John Bagguley.

Gabriel Kolko and Joyce Kolko have written *The Limits of Power: The World and United States Foreign Policy* ° (1972), which extends his analysis into the Eisenhower years, stresses the inability of the United States to shape the world according to her design, broadens the examination beyond the problem of Soviet-American relations, examines Congressional-Executive relations, and contends that the executive often used "crises" to gain Congressional support for Cold War programs. Harry Magdoff's *The Age of Imperialism: The Economics of U.S. Foreign Policy* ° (1969) is a brief examination of the sources of the "American empire." K. T. Fann and Donald C. Hedges have edited *Readings in U.S. Imperialism* ° (1971), a fine collection of essays.

Among other revisionist volumes on the Cold War are Kenneth Ingram's *History of the Cold War* (1955); Richard J. Barnet and Marcus Raskin's *After 20 Years: Alternatives to the Cold War in Europe* (1965); Barnet's *Intervention and Revolution* ° (1969); Joseph P. Morray's *From Yalta to Disarmament: Cold War Debate* (1961); Gar Alperovitz' *Cold War Essays* ° (1970); Ronald Steel's *Pax Americana* ° (1967) and *Imperialists and Other Heroes: A Chronicle of the American Empire* (1971); *Politics and Policies of the Truman Administration,*° edited by Barton J. Bernstein (1970); *Cold War Critics,*° edited by Thomas G. Peterson (1971); *Struggle Against History,*° edited by N. D. Houghton (1968); Diane Shaver Clemens' *Yalta* (1971); Ronald Radosh's *American Labor and United States Foreign Policy* (1970); and David Green's *The Containment of Latin America* (1971). Isaac Deutscher's *Stalin* ° (1949) is a harsh criticism of the Soviet leader by a Marxist who emphasizes the conservatism of Stalin's foreign policy in the early postwar period. Christopher Lasch's "The Cold War, Revisited and Re-visioned," *New York Times Magazine* (Jan. 14, 1968) is a useful summary of revisionism.

Herbert Feis's "Political Aspects of Foreign Loans," *Foreign Affairs,* XXIII (July 1945), and his "The Conflict over Trade Ideologies," *Foreign Affairs,* XXV (Jan. 1947), are important analyses of economic policy. E. F. Penrose's *Economic Planning for the Peace* (1953) is a thoughtful study by a State Department adviser. George Herring in "Lend-Lease to Russia and the Origins of the Cold War, 1944–1945," *Journal of American History,* LVI (June 1969), having had privileged access to restricted materials, argues that the brief termination of lend-lease to Russia in May was not intended to coerce the Russians but that it occurred for legal reasons. According to Herring, the order was misunderstood by some officials who took more extreme action than was desired by the President and his close advisers. In disagreement, Thomas G. Paterson, in "The Abortive Loan to Russia and the Origins of the Cold War, 1943–1946," *Journal of*

American History, LVI (June 1969), writing without benefit of the restricted sources, concludes that the loan was used to coerce the Russians and that lend-lease was halted in May for the same reason.

Manuel Gottlieb, a former economic adviser who had access to valuable and generally unused sources, provides a study of American policy in Germany in *The German Peace Settlement and the Berlin Crisis* (1960). John Snell, in *Wartime Origins of the East-West Dilemma over Germany* (1959), and John Gimbel, in *The American Occupation of Germany* (1970), present differing interpretations. Klaus Epstein's "The German Problem, 1945–50," *World Politics*, XX (Jan. 1968), is an excellent review-essay on important recent literature. Bruce Kuklick's "The Division of Germany and American Policy on Reparations," *Western Political Quarterly*, XXIII (June 1970), an outgrowth of his doctoral thesis under Kolko, should also be consulted.

George Kennan's "The Sources of Soviet Conduct," *Foreign Affairs*, XXXV (July 1947), is the first explicit *public* statement of containment. The text of the telegram of February 1946, on which Kennan's article is based, is reprinted in his *Memoirs, 1925–1950* (1967); Kennan struggles unconvincingly in this volume to retreat from the military implications of containment. Walter Lippmann's *The Cold War* (1947), based on a series of newspaper columns, is a penetrating contemporary criticism of what containment seemed to mean then.

GAR ALPEROVITZ

Why We Dropped the Bomb

INTRODUCTION

In the decade after Hiroshima, only a few Americans were troubled by their nation's use of atomic weapons against Japan, and those who expressed doubts usually confined them to moral considerations. Most citizens seemed content to agree with President Harry S Truman that the bomb "saved millions of lives," including perhaps a million American soldiers who would otherwise have died in the invasion of Japan.

Though Truman's explanation may have allayed doubts for some at that time, it also obscured chronology and glossed over important facts. In July and August of 1945, the alternative ways for ending the war with Japan were not simply the atomic bomb or imminent invasion. There were also the possibilities of pursuing peace feelers from the Japanese or awaiting Russian entry into the Pacific war, which might have induced the Japanese to surrender. And the invasion of Japan in which MacArthur anticipated only "light casualties," was planned not for August, but for early November. (The large-scale invasion, which Truman cited as justification for using the bomb, was not scheduled until the following spring.) Thus Truman never confronted what now seems to be the relevant question: Why did the United States *rush* to use the bomb without first trying other alternatives? In 1948, P. M. S. Blackett, British Nobel Laureate in physics, contended "that the dropping of the atomic bombs was not so much the last military act of the second World War, as the first major

FROM Gar Alperovitz, "Why We Dropped the Bomb," *The Progressive* (Aug. 1965), pp. 11–14. Another version of this essay appears in *Atomic Diplomacy: Hiroshima and Potsdam.* Copyright © 1965 by Gar Alperovitz. Reprinted by permission of Simon & Schuster, Inc.

operation of the cold diplomatic war with Russia" (*Fear, War and the Bomb* [1948]). He argued that the bomb was unnecessary to end the Japanese war, and that American policy-makers had not pursued other paths to peace. Blackett concluded that the administration rushed to use the bomb in order to end the war before Russian armies could gain a toehold in Manchuria and to prevent Russia from demanding an equal voice in the postwar occupation of Japan.

Critics at the time of the publication of Blackett's book rightly pointed out that much of his argument rested on conjecture, that it imposed on complex decisions a rationality rarely present, and that it conflicted with published recollections by the decision-makers, especially with the influential article by former Secretary of War Henry L. Stimson, under whose department the atomic bomb project operated ("The Decision to Use the Atomic Bomb," *Harper's*, CLCIV [Feb. 1947]). Only later did some manuscript material supporting Blackett's view become available. For instance, in his diary on July 28, 1945, Secretary of the Navy James Forrestal reported that Secretary of State James F. Byrnes "said he was most anxious to get the Japanese affair over with before the Russians got in, with particular reference to Dairen and Port Arthur. Once in there, he felt, it would not be easy to get them out" (Walter Millis, ed., *The Forrestal Diaries* [1956], p. 78). Another source rich in evidence that the decision to drop the bomb was affected by relations with Russia is the collection of Stimson's papers, now at Yale University.

Gar Alperovitz relied on the Stimson papers in the early 1960's in writing his important book *Atomic Diplomacy* (1965). Rather than focusing directly on the question of why the bomb was used, Alperovitz concentrated on a more subtle problem: Did the bomb influence the formation of American policy during the months between Truman's taking office and the actual dropping of the bombs on Hiroshima and Nagasaki? The article printed below was adapted by Alperovitz from his book. Ascribing to Truman a mastery of details and skill as a diplomatic strategist that most other revisionist historians of this period would deny, Alperovitz found in the seemingly convoluted policies of the administration an underlying pattern of intelligence. He argues that Truman, following Stimson's advice, delayed a meeting of the Big Three and even a confrontation with Stalin over Poland until he knew that the bomb was a success because he expected that the Russians would then become more tractable. At Potsdam, Truman delayed again—this time awaiting the use of the bomb against Japan.

Alperovitz' thesis has frequently been misunderstood by unfriendly critics, but even more sympathetic scholars have also raised some difficult questions. Why, for example, did Truman, when he was still unsure about the bomb, yield on Poland and thereby accede to what the administration had opposed and

could not politically afford at home: the "loss" of Poland? Alperovitz' use of sources has also been criticized. Much of his evidence about the administration's general strategy rests on the
Stimson papers, and it is doubtful that they constitute a reliable
source of information on Truman's intentions. Evidence exists indicating that the President, who greatly respected Stimson, often
deferred to the Secretary in his presence but actually was not
relying on his counsel. Indeed, at Potsdam, where, according to
Alperovitz, the bomb shaped Truman's responses, Stimson
tagged along with Truman's retinue and was shunted to the side-
lines. The President did not rely on his Secretary's advice. In addition, much of Alperovitz's other evidence comes not from documents that were contemporary with the events but often from
articles and books written after the Cold War had hardened—for
example, Truman's *Memoirs* (1955), Byrnes's *Speaking Frankly*
(1947), and a speech by Leo Szilard, "A Personal History of the
Atomic Bomb," University of Chicago *Roundtable,* No. 601 (Sept.
25, 1949).

But even those who would reject certain parts of Alperovitz's argument must now acknowledge on the basis of his evidence that the bomb did have some influence on American foreign policy before Potsdam. And there are additional materials in
manuscript collections—such as the papers of Joseph Davies,
former ambassador to Russia—that Alperovitz did not exploit
that support some of his contentions. For example, on May 21,
1945, Truman confided to Davies that he was postponing the
Potsdam conference until July, when he expected to know
whether the atomic bomb worked. And there is ample evidence
of the state of mind of Secretary of State James F. Byrnes—far
more so than of that of Truman. At Potsdam, for example, on July
29, 1945, Davies recorded, "Byrnes suggested that the New Mexico situation [the bomb] had given us great power, and that in
the last analysis, it would control." For Byrnes and the President,
the bomb, by early summer, was a possible panacea—a weapon
whose power might compel the Russians to become tractable.

In Alperovitz's book, and more clearly in the following article, he goes beyond the question of "the influence of the bomb
on certain questions of diplomacy," although he wrote in his
book "I do not believe that the reverse question—the influence
of diplomacy upon the decision to use the bomb—can be answered on the basis of the presently available evidence." What
he implies in much of his book, however, is clearly expressed in
the last sentence of this essay: the assumption that the bomb
would be used was not challenged because (as Leo Szilard in
1949 recalled Byrnes saying in 1945) "our possessing and demonstrating the bomb would make Russia more manageable in Europe."

But Alperovitz neglects an issue that should be investigated
in any analysis of why the bomb was used: the origin of the as-

sumption that the bomb was a legitimate weapon and would be used against Japan. In the preface to his book, Alperovitz claims that this is precisely what he set out to discover. But the answer to that question begins with the Roosevelt administration—which Alperovitz virtually ignores on this issue—and not with the Truman administration that inherited assumptions that it did not and would have found difficult to revise. A historian wishing to understand these assumptions must examine the thought and actions of Roosevelt, of Stimson, of the Secretary's close advisers, and of the policy-making scientists like Vannevar Bush and James Conant, as well as the environment in which they operated. It is not simply a matter of diplomatic history, but of studying the social, personal, and institutional forces that defined their world. How able were they to break out of older molds of thought and to consider issues freshly in the face of an overwhelming bureaucracy? What were their attitudes toward the mass killing of civilians in war? Was there, as Gabriel Kolko suggests, an insensitivity to death, a moral callousness? And what is the significance of the fact that Bush and Conant, long before Roosevelt's death, were concerned about the bomb's influence on postwar relations with the Soviet Union and earnestly tutored Stimson on this matter? They saw that it could be useful for bargaining, and along with Winston Churchill they also understood that it could be a counterweight to Soviet conventional military forces.

Moving to Truman, we may ask a new question: Was there any reason *not* to use the bomb? Given the inherited assumptions from Roosevelt's administration, Truman probably saw many reasons to use the bomb and no significant reason *not* to use it or even to reexamine these assumptions. Truman's own thoughts are further illumined by a letter (that Alperovitz did not see) he sent to a prominent churchman a few days after Nagasaki to justify his use of nuclear weapons:

> Nobody is more disturbed over the use of Atomic bombs than I am but I was greatly disturbed over the unwarranted attack by the Japanese on Pearl Harbor. The only language they seem to understand is the one we have been using to bombard them. When you have to deal with a beast you have to treat him as a beast. It is most regrettable but nevertheless true.

That letter to the churchman may suggest some of the reasons why the administration found it unnecessary to reconsider the assumptions that it had inherited.

Dear Mr. President,

I think it is very important that I should have a talk with you as soon as possible on a highly secret matter. I mentioned it to you shortly after you took office, but have not urged it since on account of the pressure you have been under. It, however, has such a bearing on our present foreign relations and

has such an important effect upon all my thinking in this field that I think you
ought to know about it without much further delay.

—SECRETARY OF WAR HENRY L.
STIMSON TO PRESIDENT TRUMAN,
APRIL 24, 1945

*T*his note was written twelve days after Franklin Delano
Roosevelt's death and two weeks before World War II ended in Europe. The
following day Secretary Stimson advised President Truman that the "highly
secret matter" would have a "decisive" effect upon America's postwar foreign policy. Stimson then outlined the role the atomic bomb would play in
America's relations with other countries. In diplomacy, he confided to his
diary, the weapon would be a "master card."

In the spring of 1945, postwar problems unfolded as rapidly as the
Allied armies converged in Central Europe. During the fighting which preceded Nazi surrender the Red Army conquered a great belt of territory
bordering the Soviet Union. Debating the consequences of this fact, American policy-makers defined a series of interrelated problems: What political
and economic pattern was likely to emerge in Eastern and Central Europe?
Would Soviet influence predominate? Most important, what power—if any
—did the United States have to effect the ultimate settlement on the very
borders of Russia?

Roosevelt, Churchill, and Stalin had attempted to resolve these issues
of East-West influence at the February, 1945, Yalta Conference. With the
Red Army clearly in control of Eastern Europe, the West was in a weak bargaining position. It was important to reach an understanding with Stalin before American troops began their planned withdrawal from the European
continent. Poland, the first major country intensely discussed by the Big
Three, took on unusual significance; the balance of influence struck between
Soviet-oriented and Western-oriented politicians in the government of this
one country could set a pattern for big-power relationships in the rest of
Eastern Europe.

Although the Yalta Conference ended with a signed accord covering
Poland, within a few weeks it was clear that Allied understanding was more
apparent than real. None of the heads of government interpreted the somewhat vague agreement in the same way. Churchill began to press for more
Western influence; Stalin urged less. True to his well-known policy of cooperation and conciliation, Roosevelt attempted to achieve a more definite
understanding for Poland and a pattern for East-West relations in Europe.
Caught for much of the last of his life between the determination of Churchill
and the stubbornness of Stalin, Roosevelt at times fired off angry cables to
Moscow, and at others warned London against an "attempt to evade the fact
that we placed, as clearly shown in the agreement, somewhat more emphasis
. . . [on Soviet-oriented Polish politicians in the government]."

President Roosevelt died on April 12, 1945, only two months after

Yalta. When President Truman met with Secretary Stimson to discuss the "bearing" of the atomic bomb upon foreign relations, the powers were deeply ensnarled in a tense public struggle over the meaning of the Yalta agreement. Poland had come to symbolize *all* East-West relations. Truman was forced to pick up the tangled threads of policy with little knowledge of the broader, more complex issues involved.

Herbert Feis, a noted expert on the period, has written that "Truman made up his mind that he would not depart from Roosevelt's course or renounce his ways." Others have argued that "we tried to work out the problems of the peace in close cooperation with the Russians." It is often believed that American policy followed a conciliatory course, changing—in reaction to Soviet intransigence—only in 1947 with the Truman Doctrine and the Marshall Plan. My own belief is somewhat different. It derives from the comment of Mr. Truman's Secretary of State, James F. Byrnes, that by early autumn of 1945 it was "understandable" that Soviet leaders should feel American policy had shifted radically after Roosevelt's death: It is now evident that, far from following his predecessor's policy of cooperation, shortly after taking office President Truman launched a powerful foreign policy initiative aimed at reducing or eliminating Soviet influence in Europe.

The ultimate point of this study is not, however, that America's approach to Russia changed after Roosevelt. Rather it is that the atomic bomb played a role in the formulation of policy, particularly in connection with President Truman's only meeting with Stalin, the Potsdam Conference of late July and early August, 1945. Again, my judgment differs from Feis's conclusion that "the light of the explosion 'brighter than a thousand suns' filtered into the conference rooms at Potsdam only as a distant gleam." I believe new evidence proves not only that the atomic bomb influenced diplomacy, but that it determined much of Mr. Truman's shift to a tough policy aimed at forcing Soviet acquiescence to American plans for Eastern and Central Europe.

The weapon "gave him an entirely new feeling of confidence," the President told his Secretary of War, Henry L. Stimson. By the time of Potsdam, Mr. Truman had been advised on the role of the atomic bomb by both Secretary Stimson and Secretary of State Byrnes. Though the two men differed as to tactics, each urged a tough line. Part of my study attempts to define how closely Truman followed a subtle policy outlined by Stimson, and to what extent he followed the straight forward advice of Byrnes that the bomb (in Mr. Truman's words) "put us in a position to dictate our own terms at the end of the war."

Stalin's approach seems to have been cautiously moderate during the brief few months here described. It is perhaps symbolized by the Soviet-sponsored free elections which routed the Communist Party in Hungary in the autumn of 1945. I do not attempt to interpret this moderation, nor to explain how or why Soviet policy changed to the harsh totalitarian controls characteristic of the period after 1946.

The judgment that Truman radically altered Roosevelt's policy in mid-1945 nevertheless obviously suggests a new point of departure for interpretations of the cold war. In late 1945, General Dwight D. Eisenhower observed in Moscow that "before the atom bomb was used, I would have said, yes, I was sure we could keep the peace with Russia. Now I don't know . . . People are frightened and disturbed all over. Everyone feels insecure again." To what extent did postwar Soviet policies derive from insecurity based upon a fear of America's atom bomb and changed policy? I stop short of this fundamental question, concluding that further research is needed to test Secretary Stimson's judgment that "the problem of our satisfactory relations with Russia [was] not merely connected with but [was] virtually dominated by the problem of the atomic bomb."

Similarly, I believe more research and more information are needed to reach a conclusive understanding of why the atomic bomb was used. The common belief is that the question is closed, and that President Truman's explanation is correct: "The dropping of the bombs stopped the war, saved millions of lives." My own view is that available evidence shows the atomic bomb was not needed to end the war or to save lives—and that this was understood by American leaders at the time.

General Eisenhower recently recalled that in mid-1945 he expressed a similar opinion to the Secretary of War: "I told him I was against it on two counts. First, the Japanese were ready to surrender and it wasn't necessary to hit them with that awful thing. Second, I hated to see our country be the first to use such a weapon . . ." To go beyond the limited conclusion that the bomb was unnecessary is not possible at present.

Perhaps the most remarkable aspect of the decision to use the atomic bomb is that the President and his senior political advisers do not seem ever to have shared Eisenhower's "grave misgivings." They simply assumed that they would use the bomb, never really giving serious consideration to not using it. Hence, to state in a precise way the question, "Why was the atomic bomb used?" is to ask why senior political officials did *not* seriously question its use, as General Eisenhower did.

The first point to note is that the decision to use the weapon did not derive from overriding military considerations. Despite Mr. Truman's subsequent statement that the weapon "saved millions of lives," Eisenhower's judgment that it was "completely unnecessary" as a measure to save lives was almost certainly correct. This is not a matter of hindsight; *before the atomic bomb was dropped each of the Joint Chiefs of Staff advised that it was highly likely that Japan could be forced to surrender "unconditionally," without use of the bomb and without an invasion.* Indeed, this characterization of the position taken by the senior military advisers is a conservative one.

General George C. Marshall's June 18 appraisal was the most cautiously phrased advice offered by any of the Joint Chiefs: "The impact of Russian entry on the already hopeless Japanese may well be the decisive action levering them into capitulation. . . ." Admiral William D. Leahy was absolutely certain there was no need for the bombing to obviate the necessity of an invasion. His judgment after the fact was the same as his view before the bombing: "It is my opinion that the use of this barbarous weapon at Hiroshima and Nagasaki was of no material assistance in our war against Japan. The Japanese were already defeated and ready to surrender. . . ." Similarly, through most of 1945, Admiral Ernest J. King believed the bomb unnecessary, and Generals Henry H. Arnold and Curtis E. LeMay defined the official Air Force position in this way: Whether or not the atomic bomb should be dropped was not for the Air Force to decide, but explosion of the bomb was not necessary to win the war or make an invasion unnecessary.

Similar views prevailed in Britain long before the bombs were used. General Hastings Ismay recalls that by the time of Potsdam, "for some time past it had been firmly fixed in my mind that the Japanese were tottering." Ismay's reaction to the suggestion of the bombing was, like Eisenhower's and Leahy's, one of "revulsion." And Churchill, who as early as September, 1944, felt that Russian entry into the war with Japan was likely to force capitulation, has written: "It would be a mistake to suppose that the fate of Japan was settled by the atomic bomb. Her defeat was certain before the first bomb fell. . . ."

The military appraisals made before the weapons were used have been confirmed by numerous post-surrender studies. The best known is that of the United States Strategic Bombing Survey. The Survey's conclusion is unequivocal: "Japan would have surrendered even if the atomic bombs had not been dropped, even if Russia had not entered the war, and even if no invasion had been planned or contemplated."

That military considerations were not decisive is confirmed—and illuminated—by the fact that the President did not even ask the opinion of the military adviser most directly concerned. General Douglas MacArthur, Supreme Commander of Allied Forces in the Pacific, was simply informed of the weapon shortly before it was used at Hiroshima. Before his death he stated on numerous occasions that, like Eisenhower, he believed the atomic bomb was completely unnecessary from a military point of view.

Although military considerations were not primary, unquestionably political considerations related to Russia played a major role in the decision; from at least mid-May in 1945, American policy-makers hoped to end the hostilities before the Red Army entered Manchuria. For this reason they had no wish to test whether Russian entry into the war would force capitulation—as most thought likely—long before the scheduled November Allied invasion of Japan. Indeed, they actively attempted to delay Stalin's declaration of war.

Nevertheless, it would be wrong to conclude that the atomic bomb was used simply to keep the Red Army out of Manchuria. Given the desperate efforts of the Japanese to surrender, and President Truman's willingness to offer assurances to the Emperor, it is entirely possible that the war could have been ended by negotiation before the Red Army had begun its attack. But after history's first atomic explosion at Alamogordo neither the President nor his senior political advisers were interested in exploring this possibility.

One reason may have been their fear that if time-consuming negotiations were once initiated, the Red Army might attack in order to seize Manchurian objectives. But, if this explanation is accepted, once more one must conclude that the bomb was used primarily because it was felt to be politically important to prevent Soviet domination of the area.

Such a conclusion is difficult to accept, for American interests in Manchuria, although historically important to the State Department, were not of great significance. The further question therefore arises: Were there other political reasons for using the atomic bomb? In approaching this question, it is important to note that most of the men involved at the time who since have made their views public always mention *two* considerations which dominated discussions. The first was the desire to end the Japanese war quickly, which was not primarily a military consideration, but a political one. The second is always referred to indirectly.

In June, for example, a leading member of President Truman's Advisory Interim Committee's scientific panel, A. H. Compton, advised against the Franck report's suggestion of a technical demonstration of the new weapon: Not only was there a possibility that this might not end the war promptly, but failure to make a combat demonstration would mean the "loss of the opportunity to impress the world with the national sacrifices that enduring security demanded." The general phrasing that the bomb was needed "to impress the world" has been made more specific by J. Robert Oppenheimer. Testifying on this matter some years later he stated that the second of the two "overriding considerations" in discussions regarding the bomb was "the effect of our actions on the stability, on our strength, and the stability of the postwar world." And the problem of postwar stability was inevitably the problem of Russia. Oppenheimer has put it this way: "Much of the discussion revolved around the question raised by Secretary Stimson as to whether there was any hope at all of using this development to get less barbarous relations with the Russians."

Vannevar Bush, Stimson's chief aide for atomic matters, has been quite explicit: "That bomb was developed on time. . . ." Not only did it mean a quick end to the Japanese war, but "it was also delivered on time so that there was no necessity for any concessions to Russia at the end of the war."

In essence, the second of the two overriding considerations seems to have been that a combat demonstration was needed to convince the Russians to accept the American plan for a stable peace. And the crucial point of this effort was the need to force agreement on the main questions in dispute: the American proposals for Central and Eastern Europe. President Truman may well have expressed the key consideration in October, 1945; publicly urging the necessity of a more conventional form of military power (his proposal for universal military training), in a personal appearance before Congress, the President declared: "It is only by strength that we can impress the fact upon possible future aggressors that we will tolerate no threat to peace. . . ."

If indeed the "second consideration" involved in the bombing of Hiroshima and Nagasaki was the desire to impress the Russians, it might explain the strangely ambiguous statement by Mr. Truman that not only did the bomb end the war, but it gave the world "a chance to face the facts." It would also accord with Stimson's private advice to Assistant Secretary of War John J. McCloy: "We have got to regain the lead and perhaps do it in a pretty rough and realistic way. . . . We have coming into action a weapon which will be unique. Now the thing [to do is] . . . let our actions speak for themselves."

Again, it would accord with Stimson's statement to Mr. Truman that the "greatest complication" would occur if the President negotiated with Stalin before the bomb had been "laid on Japan." It would tie in with the fact that from mid-May, strategy toward all major diplomatic problems was based upon the assumption the bomb would be demonstrated. Finally, it might explain why none of the highest civilian officials seriously questioned the use of the bomb as Eisenhower did; for, having reversed the basic direction of diplomatic strategy *because* of the atomic bomb, it would have been difficult indeed for anyone subsequently to challenge an idea which had come to dominate all calculations of high policy.

It might also explain why the sober and self-controlled Stimson reacted so strongly when General Eisenhower objected to the bombing: "The Secretary was deeply perturbed by my attitude, almost angrily refuting the reasons I gave. . . ." Stimson's post-Hiroshima reversal, and his repeated references to the gravity of the moral issues raised by the new weapon, are evidence of his own doubts. General Eisenhower's searching criticism may well have touched upon a tender point—namely, Stimson's undoubted awareness that Hiroshima and Nagasaki were to be sacrificed primarily for political, not military, reasons.

At present no final conclusion can be reached on this question. But the problem can be defined with some precision: Why did the American government refuse to attempt to exploit Japanese efforts to surrender? Or, alternatively, why did it refuse to test whether a Russian declaration of war would force capitulation? Were Hiroshima and Nagasaki bombed primarily to impress the world with the need to accept America's plan for a stable and lasting peace—that is, primarily, America's plan for Europe? The evidence strongly suggests that the view which the President's personal representative offered to one of the atomic scientists in May, 1945, was an accurate statement of policy: "Mr. Byrnes did not argue that it was necessary to use the bomb against the cities of Japan in order to win the war. . . . Mr. Byrnes's . . . view [was] that our possessing and demonstrating the bomb would make Russia more manageable in Europe. . . ."

SUGGESTED READING

Norman Cousins and Thomas Finletter, in "A Beginning of Sanity," *Saturday Review of Literature*, XXIX (June 5, 1946), first suggested that the bomb was used to end the war before the Russians could intervene. Blackett's analysis is in *Fear, War and the Bomb* (1948). Louis Morton's "The Decision to Use the Atomic Bomb," *Foreign Affairs*, XXXV (Jan. 1957), is an essay by a military historian who generally disagrees with the Cousins-Finletter suggestion and Blackett's analysis, but admits in passing that there may well have been political motives (including that of stopping the Soviets in Eastern Europe) for some policy-makers affecting the decision to drop the bomb. Rudolph Winnacker, also a military historian, defends the realistic morality behind the decision to drop the bomb in "The Debate About Hiroshima," *Military Affairs*, XI (Spring 1947).

Herbert Feis's *Japan Subdued: The Atomic Bomb and the End of the War in the Pacific* (1961), for a time considered the definitive volume on the A-bomb decision, concluded that "the impelling reason for the decision to use [the bomb] was military." Feis unaccountably either failed to use the Stimson papers or to acknowledge the evidence in these papers of intense concern before and during Potsdam about the bomb and Russia. In his first edition there is only a paragraph of conjecture about this theme. But in a revised edition, *The Atomic Bomb and the End of World War II °* (1966), perhaps provoked by Alperovitz, Feis treats the issue at greater length in a revised paragraph of conjecture that leans toward conceding a portion of Alperovitz' argument, but still avoids confronting the important questions directly. In a later printing of the first edition Feis acknowledges the existence of Alperovitz' book and bluntly denies its validity. Alperovitz' "The Trump Card," *New York Review of Books* (June 15, 1967), is a harsh critical review of Feis's revised volume.

Gabriel Kolko, in *The Politics of War °* (1968), and Barton J. Bernstein, in Bernstein, ed., *The Politics and Policies of the Truman Administration °* (1970), an essay which is reprinted in this section, dissent from Alperovitz' analysis of the bomb's *great* influence on American policy before Hiroshima. Bernstein concludes that Truman did delay the Potsdam conference because of the bomb, but Kolko denies this. Kolko also sharply disagrees with Alperovitz' interpretation of why the bomb was used, points out that the bomb raised no moral issues for policy-makers, denies that they viewed it as an alternative to Soviet entry into the war, and concludes that they never believed that the bomb would cause the Russians to "cower." Bernstein, in contrast, modifies Alperovitz' thesis by stressing that there was probably no compelling reason to reconsider the decision to use the bomb and that there were also political advantages to using it. For reviews of Alperovitz' book, see Michael Amrine's "The Day the Sun Rose

Twice," *Book Week* (July 18, 1965), and Athan Theoharis' review, in *New University Thought,* V (May–June 1967). Alperovitz responded in that same issue to the criticisms by Theoharis. Kenneth Glazier's "The Decision to Use Atomic Weapons Against Hiroshima and Nagasaki," *Public Policy,* XVIII (1970), based on a Harvard honors thesis that assails Alperovitz' interpretation and pointedly criticizes his use of evidence and conclusions, barely mentions Alperovitz, referring more often to Blackett and William Appleman Williams. Glazier acknowledges political influences on the decision to drop the bomb, but contends that anticipated Russian entry was viewed as an *alternative* to the use of the bomb, not as a *cause* for its use. He stresses the marginal influence of Stimson on Truman, emphasizes bureaucratic struggles, and notes that policy alternatives to using the bomb (Russian entry and clarification of surrender terms) were not fully explored. He concludes that "the decision to use atomic weapons was made, therefore, without any systematic consideration of either the political implications or the alternatives to that decision." Martin Sherwin's "The Atomic Bomb as History: An Essay Review," *Wisconsin Magazine of History* (Winter 1969–70), is also critical of Alperovitz and calls wisely for an examination of the Roosevelt period (covered in his doctoral thesis) to explain the sources and processes for the assumption that the bomb would be used. Walter Schoenberger's *Decision of Destiny* (1969) is a loosely wrought, frequently uncritical study of the decision to use the bomb.

Alice K. Smith, in *A Peril and A Hope: The Scientists' Movement in America, 1945–47* (1965), and Richard Hewlett and Oscar Anderson, Jr., in *The New World,* Vol. I, *A History of the United States Atomic Energy Commission* (1962), provide important background on the A-bomb decision; Hewlett and Anderson's book contains information on Byrnes's postwar design for the bomb. Henry Stimson and McGeorge Bundy's *On Active Service in Peace and War* (1948), an "autobiography" of Stimson, includes most of the article from *Harper's* but, strangely, excludes nearly all the evidence in the manuscript diaries that Stimson stressed to Truman (before Hiroshima) the impact of the bomb on future Russian relations. Elting E. Morison, in *Turmoil and Tradition* ° (1960), a biography of Stimson, notes some of this evidence. *The Atomic Bomb: The Great Decision,* ° edited by Paul Baker (1968), and *Hiroshima: The Decision to Use the Bomb,*° edited by Edwin Fogelman (1964), are useful collections of essays and excerpts from books on the bomb.

ARTHUR SCHLESINGER, JR.

Origins of the Cold War

INTRODUCTION

Dedicated to the liberalism of the "vital center," Arthur Schlesinger, Jr., celebrates moderate, nonideological reform, and in his
studies of the Roosevelt and Kennedy years has found much to
praise in the efforts of these liberal administrations. A scholar
who has won honors in the world of public affairs and the profession of history, Schlesinger was a founding member of the Americans for Democratic Action, wrote campaign speeches for Adlai
E. Stevenson and John F. Kennedy, and served the latter as a
special assistant during the thousand days. Staying with the
Johnson administration for six months after Kennedy's death,
Schlesinger at first ardently defended the administration's policy
in Vietnam. Not until late in 1966 did he publicly dissent from the
continued escalation of the war, and in criticizing American policy in Vietnam, he at first located the error not in American ideology but simply in a number of petty mistakes that had led policy-
makers astray.

   Now professor of history at the City University of New York,
Schlesinger has become distressed in the past few years by the
revisionist analyses of the early Cold War. In an outburst in 1966
that he later good-naturedly labeled "intemperate," he wanted to
"blow the whistle" (Letter, *New York Review,* Oct. 20, 1966) on
revisionism, and in 1967 he offered his own vigorous counterar-
gument. Though his essay, which follows, was intended as a
reply to the revisionists, the first four-fifths of the argument does
not differ markedly from the moderate revisionist case advanced
by Staughton Lynd in 1960 ("How the Cold War Began," *Commentary,* XXX [Nov. 1960]). Schlesinger concedes that the United

FROM Arthur Schlesinger, Jr., "Origins of the Cold War," *Foreign Affairs,* XLVI (Oct.
1967), pp. 22–52. Copyright © 1967 by the Council on Foreign Relations, Inc., New
York. Reprinted by special permission.

States made mistakes that contributed to the Cold War, and that Soviet policies were cautious and simply directed at creating a security zone. "In other words," writes Schlesinger of Stalin, "his initial objectives were very probably not world conquest but Russian security."

But Schlesinger abruptly retreats from his incipient revisionism. Citing "the intransigence of Leninist ideology, the sinister dynamics of a totalitarian society and the madness of Stalin," Schlesinger retreats from much of his earlier analysis and concludes that even different American policies could not have avoided the Cold War and achieved an accommodation with the Soviet Union. This argument, aside from its assumption about Stalin's paranoia, is strikingly similar in substance and sometimes in phrasing to part of Schlesinger's *Vital Center* (1949), though there he also forecast that "so long as America remains a capitalist democracy, no American policy can win basic Soviet confidence; every American initiative is poisoned from the source" (pp. 99–100)—a judgment that he has since altered.

William A. Williams, one of the founders of Cold War "revisionism," wrote a brief reply to Schlesinger ("The Cold War Revisionists," *Nation,* CCV [Nov. 13, 1967]). Questioning Schlesinger's psychiatric judgments, Williams pointed out that "no major American policy-maker between 1943 and 1948 defined and dealt with the Soviet Union in those [psychiatric] terms." Why invoke paranoia to explain Soviet reactions when there is ample evidence of American hostility? asks Williams. He criticizes Schlesinger for overlooking anti-Bolshevik attitudes that had existed since 1917, and for neglecting to admit that American "universalism" (that is, Wilsonianism) was implicitly anticommunist. Rather than exhibiting paranoia or succumbing to rigid ideology, Stalin's attempts to create a security zone as protection against the West were not unreasonable, concludes Williams, in view of earlier capitalist hostility and America's nuclear monopoly in the early postwar years. Critics who accept Williams' contention that Stalin sought a rapprochement with the West, may also challenge Schlesinger's assertion that a totalitarian Soviet state could not afford harmony with the United States without contributing to the destruction of the Soviet dictatorship.

Schlesinger points to a public letter of April 1945 by Jacques Duclos, the Comintern official responsible for Western Communist parties, as evidence of Soviet hostility to the West and the impossibility of accommodation. Schlesinger interprets the letter as a militant call for subversion and preparation for revolution, but it can also be understood as a call for independent electoral politics in the West (Gar Alperovitz argues the latter interpretation in *New York Review* [Oct. 20, 1966]). In view of the participation of the French and Italian Communist parties in coalition governments until 1947, when they were forced out with

American approval (and perhaps at America's urging) this interpretation seems more consistent with the evidence.

As Williams argues, Schlesinger overlooks the fact that
American policy-makers in 1945 did not fear imminent Russian
expansion into Western Europe. In addition, he skirts the issues
raised by the atomic bomb, naively accepts the official American
claims about the lost Russian request for a loan and termination
of lend-lease, and disregards evidence in manuscript collections
that would have compelled a more direct confrontation with the
revisionist arguments.

*T*he Cold War in its original form was a presumably mortal antagonism, arising in the wake of the Second World War, between two rigidly
hostile blocs, one led by the Soviet Union, the other by the United States. For
nearly two somber and dangerous decades this antagonism dominated the
fears of mankind; it may even, on occasion, have come close to blowing up the
planet. In recent years, however, the once implacable struggle has lost its
familiar clarity of outline. With the passing of old issues and the emergence
of new conflicts and contestants, there is a natural tendency, especially on
the part of the generation which grew up during the Cold War, to take a fresh
look at the causes of the great contention between Russia and America.

Some exercises in reappraisal have merely elaborated the orthodoxies
promulgated in Washington or Moscow during the boom years of the Cold
War. But others, especially in the United States (there are no signs, alas, of
this in the Soviet Union), represent what American historians call "revisionism"—that is, a readiness to challenge official explanations. No one should
be surprised by this phenomenon. Every war in American history has been
followed in due course by skeptical reassessments of supposedly sacred
assumptions. So the War of 1812, fought at the time for the freedom of the
seas, was in later years ascribed to the expansionist ambitions of Congressional war hawks; so the Mexican War became a slaveholders' conspiracy. So
the Civil War has been pronounced a "needless war," and Lincoln has even
been accused of manœuvring the rebel attack on Fort Sumter. So too the
Spanish-American War and the First and Second World Wars have, each in
its turn, undergone revisionist critiques. It is not to be supposed that the
Cold War would remain exempt.

In the case of the Cold War, special factors reinforce the predictable
historiographical rhythm. The outburst of polycentrism in the communist
empire has made people wonder whether communism was ever so monolithic as official theories of the Cold War supposed. A generation with no
vivid memories of Stalinism may see the Russia of the forties in the image of
the relatively mild, seedy and irresolute Russia of the sixties. And for this
same generation the American course of widening the war in Viet Nam—
which even non-revisionists can easily regard as folly—has unquestionably

stirred doubts about the wisdom of American foreign policy in the sixties which younger historians may have begun to read back into the forties.

It is useful to remember that, on the whole, past exercises in revisionism have failed to stick. Few historians today believe that the war hawks caused the War of 1812 or the slaveholders the Mexican War, or that the Civil War was needless, or that the House of Morgan brought America into the First World War or that Franklin Roosevelt schemed to produce the attack on Pearl Harbor. But this does not mean that one should deplore the rise of Cold War revisionism.[1] For revisionism is an essential part of the process by which history, through the posing of new problems and the investigation of new possibilities, enlarges its perspectives and enriches its insights.

More than this, in the present context, revisionism expresses a deep, legitimate and tragic apprehension. As the Cold War has begun to lose its purity of definition, as the moral absolutes of the fifties become the moralistic clichés of the sixties, some have begun to ask whether the appalling risks which humanity ran during the Cold War were, after all, necessary and inevitable; whether more restrained and rational policies might not have guided the energies of man from the perils of conflict into the potentialities of collaboration. The fact that such questions are in their nature unanswerable does not mean that it is not right and useful to raise them. Nor does it mean that our sons and daughters are not entitled to an accounting from the generation of Russians and Americans who produced the Cold War.

The orthodox American view, as originally set forth by the American government and as reaffirmed until recently by most American scholars, has been that the Cold War was the brave and essential response of free men to communist aggression. Some have gone back well before the Second World War to lay open the sources of Russian expansionism. Geopoliticians traced the Cold War to imperial Russian strategic ambitions which in the nineteenth century led to the Crimean War, to Russian penetration of the Balkans and the Middle East and to Russian pressure on Britain's "lifeline" to India. Ideologists traced it to the Communist Manifesto of 1848 ("the violent overthrow of the bourgeoisie lays the foundation for the sway of the proletariat"). Thoughtful observers (a phrase meant to exclude those who speak in Dullese about the unlimited evil of godless, atheistic, militant communism) concluded that classical Russian imperialism and Pan-Slavism, compounded after 1917 by Leninist messianism, confronted the West at the end of the Second World War with an inexorable drive for domination.[2]

---

[1] As this writer somewhat intemperately did in a letter to *The New York Review of Books*, October 20, 1966.

[2] Every student of the Cold War must acknowledge his debt to W. H. McNeill's remarkable account, *America, Britain and Russia: Their Cooperation and Conflict, 1941–1946* (New York, 1953) and to the brilliant and indispensable series by Herbert Feis: *Churchill, Roosevelt, Stalin: The War They Waged and the Peace They Sought* (Princeton, 1957); *Between War and Peace: The Potsdam Conference* (Princeton, 1960); and *The Atomi*

The revisionist thesis is very different.[3] In its extreme form, it is that, after the death of Franklin Roosevelt and the end of the Second World War, the United States deliberately abandoned the wartime policy of collaboration and, exhilarated by the possession of the atomic bomb, undertook a course of aggression of its own designed to expel all Russian influence from Eastern Europe and to establish democratic-capitalist states on the very border of the Soviet Union. As the revisionists see it, this radically new American policy—or rather this resumption by Truman of the pre-Roosevelt policy of insensate anti-communism—left Moscow no alternative but to take measures in defense of its own borders. The result was the Cold War.

These two views, of course, could not be more starkly contrasting. It is therefore not unreasonable to look again at the half-dozen critical years between June 22, 1941, when Hitler attacked Russia, and July 2, 1947, when the Russians walked out of the Marshall Plan meeting in Paris. Several things

---

Bomb and the End of World War II (Princeton, 1966). Useful recent analyses include André Fontaine, *Histoire de la Guerre Froide* (2 v., Paris, 1965, 1967); N. A. Graebner, *Cold War Diplomacy, 1945–1960* (Princeton, 1962); L. J. Halle, *The Cold War as History* (London, 1967); M. F. Herz, *Beginnings of the Cold War* (Bloomington, 1966) and W. L. Neumann, *After Victory: Churchill, Roosevelt, Stalin and the Making of the Peace* (New York, 1967).

[3] The fullest statement of this case is to be found in D. F. Fleming's voluminous *The Cold War and Its Origins* (New York, 1961). For a shorter version of this argument, see David Horowitz, *The Free World Colossus* (New York, 1965); the most subtle and ingenious statements come in W. A. Williams' *The Tragedy of American Diplomacy* (rev. ed., New York, 1962) and in Gar Alperowitz's *Atomic Diplomacy: Hiroshima and Potsdam* (New York, 1965) and in subsequent articles and reviews by Mr. Alperowitz in *The New York Review of Books*. The fact that in some aspects the revisionist thesis parallels the official Soviet argument must not, of course, prevent consideration of the case on its merits, nor raise questions about the motives of the writers, all of whom, so far as I know, are independent-minded scholars.

I might further add that all these books, in spite of their ostentatious display of scholarly apparatus, must be used with caution. Professor Fleming, for example, relies heavily on newspaper articles and even columnists. While Mr. Alperowitz bases his case on official documents or authoritative reminiscences, he sometimes twists his material in a most unscholarly way. For example, in describing Ambassador Harriman's talk with President Truman on April 20, 1945, Mr. Alperowitz writes, "He argued that a reconsideration of Roosevelt's policy was necessary" (p. 22, repeated on p. 24). The citation is to p. 70–72 in President Truman's *Years of Decision*. What President Truman reported Harriman as saying was the exact opposite: "Before leaving, Harriman took me aside and said, 'Frankly, one of the reasons that made me rush back to Washington was the fear that you did not understand, as I had seen Roosevelt understand, that Stalin is breaking his agreements.'" Similarly, in an appendix (p. 271) Mr. Alperowitz writes that the Hopkins and Davies missions of May 1945 "were opposed by the 'firm' advisers." Actually the Hopkins mission was proposed by Harriman and Charles E. Bohlen, who Mr. Alperowitz elsewhere suggests were the firmest of the firm—and was proposed by them precisely to impress on Stalin the continuity of American policy from Roosevelt to Truman. While the idea that Truman reversed Roosevelt's policy is tempting dramatically, it is a myth. See, for example, the testimony of Anna Rosenberg Hoffman, who lunched with Roosevelt on March 24, 1945, the last day he spent in Washington. After luncheon, Roosevelt was handed a cable. "He read it and became quite angry. He banged his fists on the arms of his wheelchair and said, 'Averell is right; we can't do business with Stalin. He has broken every one of the promises he made at Yalta.' He was very upset and continued in the same vein on the subject."

should be borne in mind as this reëxamination is made. For one thing, we have thought a great deal more in recent years, in part because of writers like Roberta Wohlstetter and T. C. Schelling, about the problems of communication in diplomacy—the signals which one nation, by word or by deed, gives, inadvertently or intentionally, to another. Any honest reappraisal of the origins of the Cold War requires the imaginative leap—which should in any case be as instinctive for the historian as it is prudent for the statesman— into the adversary's viewpoint. We must strive to see how, given Soviet perspectives, the Russians might conceivably have misread our signals, as we must reconsider how intelligently we read theirs.

For another, the historian must not overindulge the man of power in the illusion cherished by those in office that high position carries with it the easy ability to shape history. Violating the statesman's creed, Lincoln once blurted out the truth in his letter of 1864 to A. G. Hodges: "I claim not to have controlled events, but confess plainly that events have controlled me." He was not asserting Tolstoyan fatalism but rather suggesting how greatly events limit the capacity of the statesman to bend history to his will. The physical course of the Second World War—the military operations undertaken, the position of the respective armies at the war's end, the momentum generated by victory and the vacuums created by defeat—all these determined the future as much as the character of individual leaders and the substance of national ideology and purpose.

Nor can the historian forget the conditions under which decisions are made, especially in a time like the Second World War. These were tired, overworked, aging men: in 1945, Churchill was 71 years old, Stalin had governed his country for 17 exacting years, Roosevelt his for 12 years nearly as exacting. During the war, moreover, the importunities of military operations had shoved postwar questions to the margins of their minds. All—even Stalin, behind his screen of ideology—had became addicts of improvisation, relying on authority and virtuosity to conceal the fact that they were constantly surprised by developments. Like Eliza, they leaped from one cake of ice to the next in the effort to reach the other side of the river. None showed great tactical consistency, or cared much about it; all employed a certain ambiguity to preserve their power to decide big issues; and it is hard to know how to interpret anything any one of them said on any specific occasion. This was partly because, like all princes, they designed their expressions to have particular effects on particular audiences; partly because the entirely genuine intellectual difficulty of the questions they faced made a degree of vacillation and mind-changing eminently reasonable. If historians cannot solve their problems in retrospect, who are they to blame Roosevelt, Stalin and Churchill for not having solved them at the time?

Peacemaking after the Second World War was not so much a tapestry as it was a hopelessly raveled and knotted mess of yarn. Yet, for purposes of clarity, it is essential to follow certain threads. One theme indispensable to an understanding of the Cold War is the contrast between two clashing views of world order: the "universalist" view, by which all nations shared a common interest in all the affairs of the world, and the "sphere-of-influence" view, by which each great power would be assured by the other great powers of an acknowledged predominance in its own area of special interest. The universalist view assumed that national security would be guaranteed by an international organization. The sphere-of-interest view assumed that national security would be guaranteed by the balance of power. While in practice these views have by no means been incompatible (indeed, our shaky peace has been based on a combination of the two), in the abstract they involved sharp contradictions.

The tradition of American thought in these matters was universalist— *i.e.* Wilsonian. Roosevelt had been a member of Wilson's subcabinet; in 1920, as candidate for Vice President, he had campaigned for the League of Nations. It is true that, within Roosevelt's infinitely complex mind, Wilsonianism warred with the perception of vital strategic interests he had imbibed from Mahan. Morever, his temperamental inclination to settle things with fellow princes around the conference table led him to regard the Big Three —or Four—as trustees for the rest of the world. On occasion, as this narrative will show, he was beguiled into flirtation with the sphere-of-influence heresy. But in principle he believed in joint action and remained a Wilsonian. His hope for Yalta, as he told the Congress on his return, was that it would "spell the end of the system of unilateral action, the exclusive alliances, the spheres of influence, the balances of power, and all the other expedients that have been tried for centuries—and have always failed."

Whenever Roosevelt backslid, he had at his side that Wilsonian fundamentalist, Secretary of State Cordell Hull, to recall him to the pure faith. After his visit to Moscow in 1943, Hull characteristically said that, with the Declaration of Four Nations on General Security (in which America, Russia, Britain and China pledged "united action . . . for the organization and maintenance of peace and security"), "there will no longer be need for spheres of influence, for alliances, for balance of power, or any other of the special arrangements through which, in the unhappy past, the nations strove to safeguard their security or to promote their interests."

Remembering the corruption of the Wilsonian vision by the secret treaties of the First World War, Hull was determined to prevent any sphere-of-influence nonsense after the Second World War. He therefore fought all proposals to settle border questions while the war was still on and, excluded as he largely was from wartime diplomacy, poured his not inconsiderable moral energy and frustration into the promulgation of virtuous and spacious general principles.

In adopting the universalist view, Roosevelt and Hull were not indulging personal hobbies. Sumner Welles, Adolf Berle, Averell Harriman,

Charles Bohlen—all, if with a variety of nuances, opposed the sphere-of-influence approach. And here the State Department was expressing what seems clearly to have been the predominant mood of the American people, so long mistrustful of European power politics. The Republicans shared the true faith. John Foster Dulles argued that the great threat to peace after the war would lie in the revival of sphere-of-influence thinking. The United States, he said, must not permit Britain and Russia to revert to these bad old ways; it must therefore insist on American participation in all policy decisions for all territories in the world. Dulles wrote pessimistically in January 1945, "The three great powers which at Moscow agreed upon the 'closest coöperation' about European questions have shifted to a practice of separate, regional responsibility."

It is true that critics, and even friends, of the United States sometimes noted a discrepancy between the American passion for universalism when it applied to territory far from American shores and the preëminence the United States accorded its own interests nearer home. Churchill, seeking Washington's blessing for a sphere-of-influence initiative in Eastern Europe, could not forbear reminding the Americans, "We follow the lead of the United States in South America;" nor did any universalist of record propose the abolition of the Monroe Doctrine. But a convenient myopia prevented such inconsistencies from qualifying the ardency of the universalist faith.

There seem only to have been three officials in the United States Government who dissented. One was the Secretary of War, Henry L. Stimson, a classical balance-of-power man, who in 1944 opposed the creation of a vacuum in Central Europe by the pastoralization of Germany and in 1945 urged "the settlement of all territorial acquisitions in the shape of defense posts which each of these four powers may deem to be necessary for their own safety" in advance of any effort to establish a peacetime United Nations. Stimson considered the claim of Russia to a preferred position in Eastern Europe as not unreasonable: as he told President Truman, "he thought the Russians perhaps were being more realistic than we were in regard to their own security." Such a position for Russia seemed to him comparable to the preferred American position in Latin America; he even spoke of "our respective orbits." Stimson was therefore skeptical of what he regarded as the prevailing tendency "to hang on to exaggerated views of the Monroe Doctrine and at the same time butt into every question that comes up in Central Europe." Acceptance of spheres of influence seemed to him the way to avoid "a head-on collision."

A second official opponent of universalism was George Kennan, an eloquent advocate from the American Embassy in Moscow of "a prompt and clear recognition of the division of Europe into spheres of influence and of a policy based on the fact of such division." Kennan argued that nothing we could do would possibly alter the course of events in Eastern Europe; that we were deceiving ourselves by supposing that these countries had any future but Russian domination; that we should therefore relinquish Eastern Europe to the Soviet Union and avoid anything which would make things easier for the Russians by giving them economic assistance or by sharing moral responsibility for their actions.

A third voice within the government against universalism was (at least after the war) Henry A. Wallace. As Secretary of Commerce, he stated the sphere-of-influence case with trenchancy in the famous Madison Square Garden speech of September 1946 which led to his dismissal by President Truman:

> On our part, we should recognize that we have no more business in the *political* affairs of Eastern Europe than Russian has in the *political* affairs of Latin America, Western Europe, and the United States. . . . . Whether we like it or not, the Russians will try to socialize their sphere of influence just as we try to democratize our sphere of influence. . . . The Russians have no more business stirring up native Communists to political activity in Western Europe, Latin America, and the United States than we have in interfering with the politics of Eastern Europe and Russia.

Stimson, Kennan and Wallace seem to have been alone in the government, however, in taking these views. They were very much minority voices. Meanwhile universalism, rooted in the American legal and moral tradition, overwhelmingly backed by contemporary opinion, received successive enshrinements in the Atlantic Charter of 1941, in the Declaration of the United Nations in 1942 and in the Moscow Declaration of 1943.

The Kremlin, on the other hand, thought *only* of spheres of interest; above all, the Russians were determined to protect their frontiers, and especially their border to the west, crossed so often and so bloodily in the dark course of their history. These western frontiers lacked natural means of defense—no great oceans, rugged mountains, steaming swamps or impenetrable jungles. The history of Russia had been the history of invasion, the last of which was by now horribly killing up to twenty million of its people. The protocol of Russia therefore meant the enlargement of the area of Russian influence. Kennan himself wrote (in May 1944), "Behind Russia's stubborn expansion lies only the age-old sense of insecurity of a sedentary people reared on an exposed plain in the neighborhood of fierce nomadic peoples," and he called this "urge" a "permanent feature of Russian psychology."

In earlier times the "urge" had produced the tsarist search for buffer states and maritime outlets. In 1939 the Soviet-Nazi pact and its secret protocol had enabled Russia to begin to satisfy in the Baltic states, Karelian Finland and Poland, part of what it conceived as its security requirements in Eastern Europe. But the "urge" persisted, causing the friction between Russia and Germany in 1940 as each jostled for position in the area which separated them. Later it led to Molotov's new demands on Hitler in November

1940—a free hand in Finland, Soviet predominance in Rumania and Bulgaria, bases in the Dardanelles—the demands which convinced Hitler that he had no choice but to attack Russia. Now Stalin hoped to gain from the West what Hitler, a closer neighbor, had not dared yield him.

It is true that, so long as Russian survival appeared to require a second front to relieve the Nazi pressure, Moscow's demand for Eastern Europe was a little muffled. Thus the Soviet government adhered to the Atlantic Charter (though with a significant if obscure reservation about adapting its principles to "the circumstances, needs, and historic peculiarities of particular countries"). Thus it also adhered to the Moscow Declaration of 1943, and Molotov then, with his easy mendacity, even denied that Russia had any desire to divide Europe into spheres of influence. But this was guff, which the Russians were perfectly willing to ladle out if it would keep the Americans, and especially Secretary Hull (who made a strong personal impression at the Moscow conference) happy. "A declaration," as Stalin once observed to Eden, "I regard as algebra, but an agreement as practical arithmetic. I do not wish to decry algebra, but I prefer practical arithmetic."

The more consistent Russian purpose was revealed when Stalin offered the British a straight sphere-of-influence deal at the end of 1941. Britain, he suggested, should recognize the Russian absorption of the Baltic states, part of Finland, eastern Poland and Bessarabia; in return, Russia would support any special British need for bases or security arrangements in Western Europe. There was nothing specifically communist about these ambitions. If Stalin achieved them, he would be fulfilling an age-old dream of the tsars. The British reaction was mixed. "Soviet policy is amoral," as Anthony Eden noted at the time; "United States policy is exaggeratedly moral, at least where non-American interests are concerned." If Roosevelt was a universalist with occasional leanings toward spheres of influence and Stalin was a sphere-of-influence man with occasional gestures toward universalism, Churchill seemed evenly poised between the familiar realism of the balance of power, which he had so long recorded as an historian and manipulated as a statesman, and the hope that there must be some better way of doing things. His 1943 proposal of a world organization divided into regional councils represented an effort to blend universalist and sphere-of-interest conceptions. His initial rejection of Stalin's proposal in December 1941 as "directly contrary to the first, second and third articles of the Atlantic Charter" thus did not spring entirely from a desire to propitiate the United States. On the other hand, he had himself already reinterpreted the Atlantic Charter as applying only to Europe (and thus not to the British Empire), and he was, above all, an empiricist who never believed in sacrificing reality on the altar of doctrine.

So in April 1942 he wrote Roosevelt that "the increasing gravity of the war" had led him to feel that the Charter "ought not to be construed so as to deny Russia the frontiers she occupied when Germany attacked her." Hull, however, remained fiercely hostile to the inclusion of territorial provisions in the Anglo-Russian treaty; the American position, Eden noted, "chilled me with Wilsonian memories." Though Stalin complained that it looked "as if the Atlantic Charter was directed against the U.S.S.R.," it was the Russian season of military adversity in the spring of 1942, and he dropped his demands.

He did not, however, change his intentions. A year later Ambassador Standley could cable Washington from Moscow: "In 1918 Western Europe attempted to set up a *cordon sanitaire* to protect it from the influence of bolshevism. Might not now the Kremlin envisage the formation of a belt of pro-Soviet states to protect it from the influences of the West?" It well might; and that purpose became increasingly clear as the war approached its end. Indeed, it derived sustenance from Western policy in the first area of liberation.

The unconditional surrender of Italy in July 1943 created the first major test of the Western devotion to universalism. America and Britain, having won the Italian war, handled the capitulation, keeping Moscow informed at a distance. Stalin complained:

> The United States and Great Britain made agreements but the Soviet Union received information about the results . . . just as a passive third observer. I have to tell you that it is impossible to tolerate the situation any longer. I propose that the [tripartite military-political commission] be established and that Sicily be assigned . . . as its place of residence.

Roosevelt, who had no intention of sharing the control of Italy with the Russians, suavely replied with the suggestion that Stalin send an officer "to General Eisenhower's headquarters in connection with the commission." Unimpressed, Stalin continued to press for a tripartite body; but his Western allies were adamant in keeping the Soviet Union off the Control Commission for Italy, and the Russians in the end had to be satisfied with a seat, along with minor Allied states, on a meaningless Inter-Allied Advisory Council. Their acquiescence in this was doubtless not unconnected with a desire to establish precedents for Eastern Europe.

Teheran in December 1943 marked the high point of three-power collaboration. Still, when Churchill asked about Russian territorial interests, Stalin replied a little ominously, "There is no need to speak at the present time about any Soviet desires, but when the time comes we will speak." In the next weeks, there were increasing indications of a Soviet determination to deal unilaterally with Eastern Europe—so much so that in early February 1944 Hull cabled Harriman in Moscow:

> Matters are rapidly approaching the point where the Soviet Government will have to choose between the development and extension of the foundation of international cooperation as the guiding principle of the postwar world as against the continuance of a unilateral and arbitrary method of dealing with its special problems even though these problems are admittedly of more direct interest to the Soviet Union than to other great powers.

As against this approach, however, Churchill, more tolerant of sphere-of-influence deviations, soon proposed that, with the impending liberation of the Balkans, Russia should run things in Rumania and Britain in Greece. Hull strongly opposed this suggestion but made the mistake of leaving Washington for a few days; and Roosevelt, momentarily free from his Wilsonian conscience, yielded to Churchill's plea for a three-months' trial. Hull resumed the fight on his return, and Churchill postponed the matter.

The Red Army continued its advance into Eastern Europe. In August the Polish Home Army, urged on by Polish-language broadcasts from Moscow, rose up against the Nazis in Warsaw. For 63 terrible days, the Poles fought valiantly on, while the Red Army halted on the banks of the Vistula a few miles away, and in Moscow Stalin for more than half this time declined to coöperate with the Western effort to drop supplies to the Warsaw Resistance. It appeared a calculated Soviet decision to let the Nazis slaughter the anti-Soviet Polish underground; and, indeed, the result was to destroy any substantial alternative to a Soviet solution in Poland. The agony of Warsaw caused the most deep and genuine moral shock in Britain and America and provoked dark forebodings about Soviet postwar purposes.

Again history enjoins the imaginative leap in order to see things for a moment from Moscow's viewpoint. The Polish question, Churchill would say at Yalta, was for Britain a question of honor. "It is not only a question of honor for Russia," Stalin replied, "but one of life and death. . . . Throughout history Poland had been the corridor for attack on Russia." A top postwar priority for any Russian régime must be to close that corridor. The Home Army was led by anti-communists. It clearly hoped by its action to forestall the Soviet occupation of Warsaw and, in Russian eyes, to prepare the way for an anti-Russian Poland. In addition, the uprising from a strictly operational viewpoint was premature. The Russians, it is evident in retrospect, had real military problems at the Vistula. The Soviet attempt in September to send Polish units from the Red Army across the river to join forces with the Home Army was a disaster. Heavy German shelling thereafter prevented the ferrying of tanks necessary for an assault on the German position. The Red Army itself did not take Warsaw for another three months. None the less, Stalin's indifference to the human tragedy, his effort to blackmail the London Poles during the ordeal, his sanctimonious opposition during five precious weeks to aerial resupply, the invariable coldness of his explanations ("the Soviet command has come to the conclusion that it must dissociate itself from the Warsaw adventure") and the obvious political benefit to the Soviet Union from the destruction of the Home Army—all these had the effect of suddenly dropping the mask of wartime comradeship and displaying to the West the hard face of Soviet policy. In now pursuing what he grimly regarded as the minimal requirements for the postwar security of his country, Stalin was inadvertently showing the irreconcilability of both his means and his ends with the Anglo-American conception of the peace.

Meanwhile Eastern Europe presented the Alliance with still another crisis that same September. Bulgaria, which was not at war with Russia, decided to surrender to the Western Allies while it still could; and the English and Americans at Cairo began to discuss armistice terms with Bulgarian envoys. Moscow, challenged by what it plainly saw as a Western intrusion into its own zone of vital interest, promptly declared war on Bulgaria, took over the surrender negotiations and, invoking the Italian precedent, denied its Western Allies any role in the Bulgarian Control Commission. In a long and thoughtful cable, Ambassador Harriman meditated on the problems of communication with the Soviet Union. "Words," he reflected, "have a different connotation to the Soviets than they have to us. When they speak of insisting on 'friendly governments' in their neighboring countries, they have in mind something quite different from what we would mean." The Russians, he surmised, really believed that Washington accepted "their position that although they would keep us informed they had the right to settle their problems with their western neighbors unilaterally." But the Soviet position was still in flux: "the Soviet Government is not one mind." The problem, as Harriman had earlier told Harry Hopkins, was "to strengthen the hands of those around Stalin who want to play the game along our lines." The way to do this, he now told Hull, was to

> be understanding of their sensitivity, meet them much more than half way, encourage them and support them wherever we can, and yet oppose them promptly with the greatest of firmness where we see them going wrong. . . . The only way we can eventually come to an understanding with the Soviet Union on the question of non-interference in the internal affairs of other countries is for us to take a definite interest in the solution of the problems of each individual country as they arise.

As against Harriman's sophisticated universalist strategy, however, Churchill, increasingly fearful of the consequences of unrestrained competition in Eastern Europe, decided in early October to carry his sphere-of-influence proposal directly to Moscow. Roosevelt was at first content to have Churchill speak for him too and even prepared a cable to that effect. But Hopkins, a more rigorous universalist, took it upon himself to stop the cable and warn Roosevelt of its possible implications. Eventually Roosevelt sent a message to Harriman in Moscow emphasizing that he expected to "retain complete freedom of action after this conference is over." It was now that Churchill quickly proposed—and Stalin as quickly accepted—the celebrated division of southeastern Europe: ending (after further haggling between Eden and Molotov) with 90 percent Soviet predominance in Rumania, 80 percent in Bulgaria and Hungary, fifty-fifty in Jugoslavia, 90 percent British predominance in Greece.

Churchill in discussing this with Harriman used the phrase "spheres of influence." But he insisted that these were only "immediate wartime arrangements" and received a highly general blessing from Roosevelt. Yet, whatever Churchill intended, there is reason to believe that Stalin construed the percentages as an agreement, not a declaration; as practical arithmetic, not algebra. For Stalin, it should be understood, the sphere-of-influence idea did not mean that he would abandon all efforts to spread communism in some other nation's sphere; it did mean that, if he tried this and the other side cracked down, he could not feel he had serious cause for complaint. As Kennan wrote to Harriman at the end of 1944:

> As far as border states are concerned the Soviet government has never ceased to think in terms of spheres of interest. They expect us to support them in whatever action they wish to take in those regions, regardless of whether that action seems to us or to the rest of the world to be right or wrong. . . . I have no doubt that this position is honestly maintained on their part, and that they would be equally prepared to reserve moral judgment on any actions which we might wish to carry out, i.e., in the Caribbean area.

In any case, the matter was already under test a good deal closer to Moscow than the Caribbean. The communist-dominated resistance movement in Greece was in open revolt against the effort of the Papandreou government to disarm and disband the guerrillas (the same Papandreou whom the Greek colonels have recently arrested on the claim that he is a tool of the communists). Churchill now called in British Army units to crush the insurrection. This action produced a storm of criticism in his own country and in the United States; the American Government even publicly dissociated itself from the intervention, thereby emphasizing its detachment from the sphere-of-influence deal. But Stalin, Churchill later claimed, "adhered strictly and faithfully to our agreement of October, and during all the long weeks of fighting the Communists in the streets of Athens not one word of reproach came from *Pravda* or *Izvestia*," though there is no evidence that he tried to call off the Greek communists. Still, when the communist rebellion later broke out again in Greece, Stalin told Kardelj and Djilas of Jugoslavia in 1948, "The uprising in Greece must be stopped, and as quickly as possible."

No one, of course, can know what really was in the minds of the Russian leaders. The Kremlin archives are locked; of the primary actors, only Molotov survives, and he has not yet indicated any desire to collaborate with the Columbia Oral History Project. We do know that Stalin did not wholly surrender to sentimental illusion about his new friends. In June 1944, on the night before the landings in Normandy, he told Djilas that the English "find nothing sweeter than to trick their allies. . . . And Churchill? Churchill is the kind who, if you don't watch him, will slip a kopeck out of your pocket. Yes, a kopeck out of your pocket! . . . Roosevelt is not like that. He dips in his hand only for bigger coins." But whatever his views of his colleagues it is not unreasonable to suppose that Stalin would have been satisfied at the end of the war to secure what Kennan has called "a protective glacis along Russia's western border," and that, in exchange for a free hand in Eastern Europe, he was prepared to give the British and Americans equally free hands in their zones of vital interest, including in nations as close to Russia as Greece (for the British) and, very probably—or at least so the Jugoslavs believe—China (for the United States). In other words, his initial objectives were very probably not world conquest but Russian security.

It is now pertinent to inquire why the United States rejected the idea of stabilizing the world by division into spheres of influence and insisted on an East European strategy. One should warn against rushing to the conclusion that it was all a row between hard-nosed, balance-of-power realists and starry-eyed Wilsonians. Roosevelt, Hopkins, Welles, Harriman, Bohlen, Berle, Dulles and other universalists were tough and serious men. Why then did they rebuff the sphere-of-influence solution?

The first reason is that they regarded this solution as containing within itself the seeds of a third world war. The balance-of-power idea seemed inherently unstable. It had always broken down in the past. It held out to each power the permanent temptation to try to alter the balance in its own favor, and it built this temptation into the international order. It would turn the great powers of 1945 away from the objective of concerting common policies toward competition for postwar advantage. As Hopkins told Molotov at Teheran, "The President feels it essential to world peace that Russia, Great Britain and the United States work out this control question in a manner which will not start each of the three powers arming against the others." "The greatest likelihood of eventual conflict," said the Joint Chiefs of Staff in 1944 (the only conflict which the J.C.S., in its wisdom, could then glimpse "in the foreseeable future" was between Britain and Russia), ". . . would seem to grow out of either nation initiating attempts to build up its strength, by seeking to attach to herself parts of Europe to the disadvantage and possible danger of her potential adversary." The Americans were perfectly ready to acknowledge that Russia was entitled to convincing assurance of her national security—but not this way. "I could sympathize fully with Stalin's desire to protect his western borders from future attack," as Hull put it. "But I felt that this security could best be obtained through a strong postwar peace organization."

Hull's remark suggests the second objection: that the sphere-of-influence approach would, in the words of the State Department in 1945, "militate against the establishment and effective functioning of a broader system of general security in which all countries will have their part." The United Nations, in short, was seen as the alternative to the balance of power. Nor did the universalists see any necessary incompatibility between the Russian desire for "friendly governments" on its frontier and the American desire for self-determination in Eastern Europe. Before Yalta the State Department judged the general mood of Europe as "to the left and strongly in favor of far-reaching economic and social reforms, but not, however, in favor of a

left-wing totalitarian regime to achieve these reforms." Governments in
Eastern Europe could be sufficiently to the left "to allay Soviet suspicions"
but sufficiently representative "of the center and *petit bourgeois* elements"
not to seem a prelude to communist dictatorship. The American criteria were
therefore that the government "should be dedicated to the preservation of
civil liberties" and "should favor social and economic reforms." A string of
New Deal states—of Finlands and Czechoslovakias—seemed a reasonable
compromise solution.

Third, the universalists feared that the sphere-of-interest approach
would be what Hull termed "a haven for the isolationists," who would advocate America's participation in Western Hemisphere affairs on condition that
it did not participate in European or Asian affairs. Hull also feared that
spheres of interest would lead to "closed trade areas or discriminatory systems" and thus defeat his cherished dream of a low-tariff, freely trading
world.

Fourth, the sphere-of-interest solution meant the betrayal of the principles for which the Second World War was being fought—the Atlantic
Charter, the Four Freedoms, the Declaration of the United Nations. Poland
summed up the problem. Britain, having gone to war to defend the independence of Poland from the Germans, could not easily conclude the war by surrendering the independence of Poland to the Russians. Thus, as Hopkins told
Stalin after Roosevelt's death in 1945, Poland had "become the symbol of our
ability to work out problems with the Soviet Union." Nor could American
liberals in general watch with equanimity while the police state spread into
countries which, if they had mostly not been real democracies, had mostly
not been tyrannies either. The execution in 1943 of Ehrlich and Alter, the
Polish socialist trade union leaders, excited deep concern. "I have particularly in mind," Harriman cabled in 1944, "objection to the institution of
secret police who may become involved in the persecution of persons of truly
democratic convictions who may not be willing to conform to Soviet
methods."

Fifth, the sphere-of-influence solution would create difficult domestic
problems in American politics. Roosevelt was aware of the six million or more
Polish votes in the 1944 election; even more acutely, he was aware of the
broader and deeper attack which would follow if, after going to war to stop
the Nazi conquest of Europe, he permitted the war to end with the communist conquest of Eastern Europe. As Archibald MacLeish, then Assistant Secretary of State for Public Affairs, warned in January 1945, "The wave of disillusionment which has distressed us in the last several weeks will be increased
if the impression is permitted to get abroad that potentially totalitarian provisional governments are to be set up without adequate safeguards as to the
holding of free elections and the realization of the principles of the Atlantic
Charter." Roosevelt believed that no administration could survive which
did not try everything short of war to save Eastern Europe, and he was the
supreme American politician of the century.

Sixth, if the Russians were allowed to overrun Eastern Europe without argument, would that satisfy them? Even Kennan, in a dispatch of May 1944, admitted that the "urge" had dreadful potentialities: "If initially successful, will it know where to stop? Will it not be inexorably carried forward, by its very nature, in a struggle to reach the whole—to attain complete mastery of the shores of the Atlantic and the Pacific?" His own answer was that there were inherent limits to the Russian capacity to expand—"that Russia will not have an easy time in maintaining the power which it has seized over other people in Eastern and Central Europe, unless it receives both moral and material assistance from the West." Subsequent developments have vindicated Kennan's argument. By the late forties, Jugoslavia and Albania, the two East European states farthest from the Soviet Union and the two in which communism was imposed from within rather than from without, had declared their independence of Moscow. But, given Russia's success in maintaining centralized control over the international communist movement for a quarter of a century, who in 1944 could have had much confidence in the idea of communist revolts against Moscow?

Most of those involved therefore rejected Kennan's answer and stayed with his question. If the West turned its back on Eastern Europe, the higher probability, in their view, was that the Russians would use their security zone, not just for defensive purposes, but as a springboard from which to mount an attack on Western Europe, now shattered by war, a vacuum of power awaiting its master. "If the policy is accepted that the Soviet Union has a right to penetrate her immediate neighbors for security," Harriman said in 1944, "penetration of the next immediate neighbors becomes at a certain time equally logical." If a row with Russia were inevitable, every consideration of prudence dictated that it should take place in Eastern rather than Western Europe.

Thus idealism and realism joined in opposition to the sphere-of-influence solution. The consequence was a determination to assert an American interest in the postwar destiny of all nations, including those of Eastern Europe. In the message which Roosevelt and Hopkins drafted after Hopkins had stopped Roosevelt's initial cable authorizing Churchill to speak for the United States at the Moscow meeting of October 1944, Roosevelt now said, "There is in this global war literally no question, either military or political, in which the United States is not interested." After Roosevelt's death Hopkins repeated the point to Stalin: "The cardinal basis of President Roosevelt's policy which the American people had fully supported had been the concept that the interests of the U.S. were worldwide and not confined to North and South America and the Pacific Ocean."

For better or worse, this was the American position. It is now necessary to attempt the imaginative leap and consider the impact of this position on the leaders of the Soviet Union who, also for better or for worse, had reached the bitter conclusion that the survival of their country depended on their unchallenged control of the corridors through which enemies had so often invaded their homeland. They could claim to have been keeping their own side of the sphere-of-influence bargain. Of course, they were working to capture the resistance movements of Western Europe; indeed, with the appointment of Oumansky as Ambassador to Mexico they were even beginning to enlarge underground operations in the Western Hemisphere. But, from their viewpoint, if the West permitted this, the more fools they; and, if the West stopped it, it was within their right to do so. In overt political matters the Russians were scrupulously playing the game. They had watched in silence while the British shot down communists in Greece. In Jugoslavia Stalin was urging Tito (as Djilas later revealed) to keep King Peter. They had not only acknowledged Western preëminence in Italy but had recognized the Badoglio régime; the Italian Communists had even voted (against the Socialists and the Liberals) for the renewal of the Lateran Pacts.

They would not regard anti-communist action in a Western zone as a *casus belli*; and they expected reciprocal license to assert their own authority in the East. But the principle of self-determination was carrying the United States into a deeper entanglement in Eastern Europe than the Soviet Union claimed as a right (whatever it was doing underground) in the affairs of Italy, Greece or China. When the Russians now exercised in Eastern Europe the same brutal control they were prepared to have Washington exercise in the American sphere of influence, the American protests, given the paranoia produced alike by Russian history and Leninist ideology, no doubt seemed not only an act of hypocrisy but a threat to security. To the Russians, a stroll into the neighborhood easily became a plot to burn down the house: when, for example, damaged American planes made emergency landings in Poland and Hungary, Moscow took this as attempts to organize the local resistance. It is not unusual to suspect one's adversary of doing what one is already doing oneself. At the same time, the cruelty with which the Russians executed their idea of spheres of influence—in a sense, perhaps, an unwitting cruelty, since Stalin treated the East Europeans no worse than he had treated the Russians in the thirties—discouraged the West from accepting the equation (for example, Italy = Rumania) which seemed so self-evident to the Kremlin.

So Moscow very probably, and not unnaturally, perceived the emphasis on self-determination as a systematic and deliberate pressure on Russia's western frontiers. Moreover, the restoration of capitalism to countries freed at frightful cost by the Red Army no doubt struck the Russians as the betrayal of the principles for which *they* were fighting. "That they, the victors," Isaac Deutscher has suggested, "should now preserve an order from which they had experienced nothing but hostility, and could expect nothing but hostility . . . would have been the most miserable anti-climax to their great 'war of liberation.'" By 1944 Poland was the critical issue; Harriman later said that "under instructions from President Roosevelt, I talked about Poland with

Stalin more frequently than any other subject." While the West saw the point of Stalin's demand for a "friendly government" in Warsaw, the American insistence on the sovereign virtues of free elections (ironically in the spirit of the 1917 Bolshevik decree of peace, which affirmed "the right" of a nation "to decide the forms of its state existence by a free vote, taken after the complete evacuation of the incorporating or, generally, of the stronger nation") created an insoluble problem in those countries, like Poland (and Rumania) where free elections would almost certainly produce anti-Soviet governments.

The Russians thus may well have estimated the Western pressures as calculated to encourage their enemies in Eastern Europe and to defeat their own minimum objective of a protective glacis. Everything still hung, however, on the course of military operations. The wartime collaboration had been created by one thing, and one thing alone: the threat of Nazi victory. So long as this threat was real, so was the collaboration. In late December 1944, von Rundstedt launched his counter-offensive in the Ardennes. A few weeks later, when Roosevelt, Churchill and Stalin gathered in the Crimea, it was in the shadow of this last considerable explosion of German power. The meeting at Yalta was still dominated by the mood of war.

Yalta remains something of an historical perplexity—less, from the perspective of 1967, because of a mythical American deference to the sphere-of-influence thesis than because of the documentable Russian deference to the universalist thesis. Why should Stalin in 1945 have accepted the Declaration on Liberated Europe and an agreement on Poland pledging that "the three governments will jointly" act to assure "free elections of governments responsive to the will of the people"? There are several probable answers: that the war was not over and the Russians still wanted the Americans to intensify their military effort in the West; that one clause in the Declaration premised action on "the opinion of the three governments" and thus implied a Soviet veto, though the Polish agreement was more definite; most of all that the universalist algebra of the Declaration was plainly in Stalin's mind to be construed in terms of the practical arithmetic of his sphere-of-influence agreement with Churchill the previous October. Stalin's assurance to Churchill at Yalta that a proposed Russian amendment to the Declaration would not apply to Greece makes it clear that Roosevelt's pieties did not, in Stalin's mind, nullify Churchill's percentages. He could well have been strengthened in this supposition by the fact that *after* Yalta, Churchill himself repeatedly reasserted the terms of the October agreement as if he regarded it, despite Yalta, as controlling.

Harriman still had the feeling before Yalta that the Kremlin had "two approaches to their postwar policies" and that Stalin himself was "of two minds." One approach emphasized the internal reconstruction and development of Russia; the other its external expansion. But in the meantime the fact which dominated all political decisions—that is, the war against Germany

—was moving into its final phase. In the weeks after Yalta, the military situation changed with great rapidity. As the Nazi threat declined, so too did the need for coöperation. The Soviet Union, feeling itself menaced by the American idea of self-determination and the borderlands diplomacy to which it was leading, skeptical whether the United Nations would protect its frontiers as reliably as its own domination in Eastern Europe, began to fulfill its security requirements unilaterally.

In March Stalin expressed his evaluation of the United Nations by rejecting Roosevelt's plea that Molotov come to the San Francisco conference, if only for the opening sessions. In the next weeks the Russians emphatically and crudely worked their will in Eastern Europe, above all in the test country of Poland. They were ignoring the Declaration on Liberated Europe, ignoring the Atlantic Charter, self-determination, human freedom and everything else the Americans considered essential for a stable peace. "We must clearly recognize," Harriman wired Washington a few days before Roosevelt's death, "that the Soviet program is the establishment of totalitarianism, ending personal liberty and democracy as we know and respect it."

At the same time, the Russians also began to mobilize communist resources in the United States itself to block American universalism. In April 1945 Jacques Duclos, who had been the Comintern official responsible for the Western communist parties, launched in *Cahiers du Communisme* an uncompromising attack on the policy of the American Communist Party. Duclos sharply condemned the revisionism of Earl Browder, the American Communist leader, as "expressed in the concept of a long-term class peace in the United States, of the possibility of the suppression of the class struggle in the postwar period and of establishment of harmony between labor and capital." Browder was specifically rebuked for favoring the "self-determination" of Europe "west of the Soviet Union" on a bourgeois-democratic basis. The excommunication of Browderism was plainly the Politburo's considered reaction to the impending defeat of Germany; it was a signal to the communist parties of the West that they should recover their identity; it was Moscow's alert to communists everywhere that they should prepare for new policies in the postwar world.

The Duclos piece obviously could not have been planned and written much later than the Yalta conference—that is, well before a number of events which revisionists now cite in order to demonstrate American responsibility for the Cold War: before Allen Dulles, for example, began to negotiate the surrender of the German armies in Italy (the episode which provoked Stalin to charge Roosevelt with seeking a separate peace and provoked Roosevelt to denounce the "vile misrepresentations" of Stalin's informants); well before Roosevelt died; many months before the testing of the atomic bomb; even more months before Truman ordered that the bomb be dropped on Japan. William Z. Foster, who soon replaced Browder as the leader of the

American Communist Party and embodied the new Moscow line, later boasted of having said in January 1944, "A post-war Roosevelt administration would continue to be, as it is now, an imperialist government." With ancient suspicions revived by the American insistence on universalism, this was no doubt the conclusion which the Russians were reaching at the same time. The Soviet canonization of Roosevelt (like their present-day canonization of Kennedy) took place after the American President's death.

The atmosphere of mutual suspicion was beginning to rise. In January 1945 Molotov formally proposed that the United States grant Russia a $6 billion credit for postwar reconstruction. With characteristic tact he explained that he was doing this as a favor to save America from a postwar depression. The proposal seems to have been diffidently made and diffidently received. Roosevelt requested that the matter "not be pressed further" on the American side until he had a chance to talk with Stalin; but the Russians did not follow it up either at Yalta in February (save for a single glancing reference) or during the Stalin-Hopkins talks in May or at Potsdam. Finally the proposal was renewed in the very different political atmosphere of August. This time Washington inexplicably mislaid the request during the transfer of the records of the Foreign Economic Administration to the State Department. It did not turn up again until March 1946. Of course this was impossible for the Russians to believe; it is hard enough even for those acquainted with the capacity of the American government for incompetence to believe; and it only strengthened Soviet suspicions of American purposes.

The American credit was one conceivable form of Western contribution to Russian reconstruction. Another was lend-lease, and the possibility of reconstruction aid under the lend-lease protocol had already been discussed in 1944. But in May 1945 Russia, like Britain, suffered from Truman's abrupt termination of lend-lease shipments—"unfortunate and even brutal," Stalin told Hopkins, adding that, if it was "designed as pressure on the Russians in order to soften them up, then it was a fundamental mistake." A third form was German reparations. Here Stalin in demanding $10 billion in reparations for the Soviet Union made his strongest fight at Yalta. Roosevelt, while agreeing essentially with Churchill's opposition, tried to postpone the matter by accepting the Soviet figure as a "basis for discussion"—a formula which led to future misunderstanding. In short, the Russian hope for major Western assistance in postwar reconstruction foundered on three events which the Kremlin could well have interpreted respectively as deliberate sabotage (the loan request), blackmail (lend-lease cancellation) and pro-Germanism (reparations).

Actually the American attempt to settle the fourth lend-lease protocol was generous and the Russians for their own reasons declined to come to an agreement. It is not clear, though, that satisfying Moscow on any of these financial scores would have made much essential difference. It might have persuaded some doves in the Kremlin that the U.S. government was genuinely friendly; it might have persuaded some hawks that the American anxiety for Soviet friendship was such that Moscow could do as it wished without inviting challenge from the United States. It would, in short, merely have reinforced both sides of the Kremlin debate; it would hardly have reversed deeper tendencies toward the deterioration of political relationships. Economic deals were surely subordinate to the quality of mutual political confidence; and here, in the months after Yalta, the decay was steady.

The Cold War had now begun. It was the product not of a decision but of a dilemma. Each side felt compelled to adopt policies which the other could not but regard as a threat to the principles of the peace. Each then felt compelled to undertake defensive measures. Thus the Russians saw no choice but to consolidate their security in Eastern Europe. The Americans, regarding Eastern Europe as the first step toward Western Europe, responded by asserting their interest in the zone the Russians deemed vital to their security. The Russians concluded that the West was resuming its old course of capitalist encirclement; that it was purposefully laying the foundation for anti-Soviet régimes in the area defined by the blood of centuries as crucial to Russian survival. Each side believed with passion that future international stability depended on the success of its own conception of world order. Each side, in pursuing its own clearly indicated and deeply cherished principles, was only confirming the fear of the other that it was bent on aggression.

Very soon the process began to acquire a cumulative momentum. The impending collapse of Germany thus provoked new troubles: the Russians, for example, sincerely feared that the West was planning a separate surrender of the German armies in Italy in a way which would release troops for Hitler's eastern front, as they subsequently feared that the Nazis might succeed in surrendering Berlin to the West. This was the context in which the atomic bomb now appeared. Though the revisionist argument that Truman dropped the bomb less to defeat Japan than to intimidate Russia is not convincing, this thought unquestionably appealed to some in Washington as at least an advantageous side-effect of Hiroshima.

So the machinery of suspicion and counter-suspicion, action and counter-action, was set in motion. But, given relations among traditional national states, there was still no reason, even with all the postwar jostling, why this should not have remained a manageable situation. What made it unmanageable, what caused the rapid escalation of the Cold War and in another two years completed the division of Europe, was a set of considerations which this account has thus far excluded.

Up to this point, the discussion has considered the schism within the wartime coalition as if it were entirely the result of disagreements among national states. Assuming this framework, there was unquestionably a failure of communication between America and Russia, a misperception of signals and, as time went on, a mounting tendency to ascribe ominous motives to the other side. It seems hard, for example, to deny that American postwar policy created genuine difficulties for the Russians and even assumed a threatening aspect for them. All this the revisionists have rightly and usefully emphasized.

But the great omission of the revisionists—and also the fundamental explanation of the speed with which the Cold War escalated—lies precisely in the fact that the Soviet Union was *not* a traditional national state.[4] This is where the "mirror image," invoked by some psychologists, falls down. For the Soviet Union was a phenomenon very different from America or Britain: it was a totalitarian state, endowed with an all-explanatory, all-consuming ideology, committed to the infallibility of government and party, still in a somewhat messianic mood, equating dissent with treason, and ruled by a dictator who, for all his quite extraordinary abilities, had his paranoid moments.

Marxism-Leninism gave the Russian leaders a view of the world according to which all societies were inexorably destined to proceed along appointed roads by appointed stages until they achieved the classless nirvana. Moreover, given the resistance of the capitalists to this development, the existence of any non-communist state was *by definition* a threat to the Soviet Union. "As long as capitalism and socialism exist," Lenin wrote, "we cannot live in peace: in the end, one or the other will triumph—a funeral dirge will be sung either over the Soviet Republic or over world capitalism."

Stalin and his associates, whatever Roosevelt or Truman did or failed to do, were bound to regard the United States as the enemy, not because of this deed or that, but because of the primordial fact that America was the leading capitalist power and thus, by Leninist syllogism, unappeasably hostile, driven by the logic of its system to oppose, encircle and destroy Soviet Russia. Nothing the United States could have done in 1944–45 would have abolished this mistrust, required and sanctified as it was by Marxist gospel— nothing short of the conversion of the United States into a Stalinist despotism; and even this would not have sufficed, as the experience of Jugoslavia and China soon showed, unless it were accompanied by total subservience to Moscow. So long as the United States remained a capitalist democracy, no American policy, given Moscow's theology, could hope to win basic Soviet confidence, and every American action was poisoned from the source. So long as the Soviet Union remained a messianic state, ideology compelled a steady expansion of communist power.

---

[4] This is the classical revisionist fallacy—the assumption of the rationality, or at least of the traditionalism, of states where ideology and social organization have created a different range of motives. So the Second World War revisionists omit the totalitarian dynamism of Nazism and the fanaticism of Hitler, as the Civil War revisionists omit the fact that the slavery system was producing a doctrinaire closed society in the American South. For a consideration of some of these issues, see "The Causes of the Civil War: A Note on Historical Sentimentalism" in my *The Politics of Hope* (Boston, 1963).

It is easy, of course, to exaggerate the capacity of ideology to control events. The tension of acting according to revolutionary abstractions is too much for most nations to sustain over a long period: that is why Mao Tse-tung has launched his Cultural Revolution, hoping thereby to create a permanent revolutionary mood and save Chinese communism from the degeneration which, in his view, has overtaken Russian communism. Still, as any revolution grows older, normal human and social motives will increasingly reassert themselves. In due course, we can be sure, Leninism will be about as effective in governing the daily lives of Russians as Christianity is in governing the daily lives of Americans. Like the Ten Commandments and the Sermon on the Mount, the Leninist verities will increasingly become platitudes for ritual observance, not guides to secular decision. There can be no worse fallacy (even if respectable people practiced it diligently for a season in the United States) than that of drawing from a nation's ideology permanent conclusions about its behavior.

A temporary recession of ideology was already taking place during the Second World War when Stalin, to rally his people against the invader, had to replace the appeal of Marxism by that of nationalism. ("We are under no illusions that they are fighting for us," Stalin once said to Harriman. "They are fighting for Mother Russia.") But this was still taking place within the strictest limitations. The Soviet Union remained as much a police state as ever; the régime was as infallible as ever; foreigners and their ideas were as suspect as ever. "Never, except possibly during my later experience as ambassador in Moscow," Kennan has written, "did the insistence of the Soviet authorities on isolation of the diplomatic corps weigh more heavily on me . . . than in these first weeks following my return to Russia in the final months of the war. . . . [We were] treated as though we were the bearers of some species of the plague"—which, of course, from the Soviet viewpoint, they were: the plague of skepticism.

Paradoxically, of the forces capable of bringing about a modification of ideology, the most practical and effective was the Soviet dictatorship itself. If Stalin was an ideologist, he was also a pragmatist. If he saw everything through the lenses of Marxism-Leninism, he also, as the infallible expositor of the faith, could reinterpret Marxism-Leninism to justify anything he wanted to do at any given moment. No doubt Roosevelt's ignorance of Marxism-Leninism was inexcusable and led to grievous miscalculations. But Roosevelt's efforts to work on and through Stalin were not so hopelessly naïve as it used to be fashionable to think. With the extraordinary instinct of a great political leader, Roosevelt intuitively understood that Stalin was the *only* lever available to the West against the Leninist ideology and the Soviet system. If Stalin could be reached, then alone was there a chance of getting the Russians to act contrary to the prescriptions of their faith. The best evidence is that Roosevelt retained a certain capacity to influence Stalin to the end; the nominal Soviet acquiescence in American universalism as late as Yalta was perhaps an indication of that. It is in this way that the death of Roosevelt was crucial—not in the vulgar sense that his policy was then reversed by his successor, which did not happen, but in the sense that no other American could hope to have the restraining impact on Stalin which Roosevelt might for a while have had.

Stalin alone could have made any difference. Yet Stalin, in spite of the impression of sobriety and realism he made on Westerners who saw him during the Second World War, was plainly a man of deep and morbid obsessions and compulsions. When he was still a young man, Lenin had criticized his rude and arbitrary ways. A reasonably authoritative observer (N. S. Khrushchev) later commented, "These negative characteristics of his developed steadily and during the last years acquired an absolutely insufferable character." His paranoia, probably set off by the suicide of his wife in 1932, led to the terrible purges of the mid-thirties and the wanton murder of thousands of his Bolshevik commrades. "Everywhere and in everything," Khrushchev says of this period, "he saw 'enemies,' 'double-dealers' and 'spies.'" The crisis of war evidently steadied him in some way, though Khrushchev speaks of his "nervousness and hysteria . . . even after the war began." The madness, so rigidly controlled for a time, burst out with new and shocking intensity in the postwar years. "After the war," Khrushchev testifies,

> the situation became even more complicated. Stalin became even more capricious, irritable and brutal; in particular, his suspicion grew. His persecution mania reached unbelievable dimensions. . . . He decided everything, without any consideration for anyone or anything.
>
> Stalin's wilfulness showed itself . . . also in the international relations of the Soviet Union. . . . He had completely lost a sense of reality; he demonstrated his suspicion and haughtiness not only in relation to individuals in the USSR, but in relation to whole parties and nations.

A revisionist fallacy has been to treat Stalin as just another Realpolitik statesman, as Second World War revisionists see Hitler as just another Stresemann or Bismarck. But the record makes it clear that in the end nothing could satisfy Stalin's paranoia. His own associates failed. Why does anyone suppose that any conceivable American policy would have succeeded?

An analysis of the origins of the Cold War which leaves out these factors—the intransigence of Leninist ideology, the sinister dynamics of a totalitarian society and the madness of Stalin—is obviously incomplete. It was these factors which made it hard for the West to accept the thesis that Russia was moved only by a desire to protect its security and would be satisfied by the control of Eastern Europe; it was these factors which charged the debate between universalism and spheres of influence with apocalyptic potentiality.

Leninism and totalitarianism created a structure of thought and behavior which made postwar collaboration between Russia and America—in any normal sense of civilized intercourse between national states—inherently impossible. The Soviet dictatorship of 1945 simply could not have survived such a collaboration. Indeed, nearly a quarter-century later, the Soviet régime, though it has meanwhile moved a good distance, could still hardly survive it without risking the release inside Russia of energies profoundly opposed to communist despotism. As for Stalin, he may have represented the only force in 1945 capable of overcoming Stalinism, but the very traits which enabled him to win absolute power expressed terrifying instabilities of mind and temperament and hardly offered a solid foundation for a peaceful world.

The difference between America and Russia in 1945 was that some Americans fundamentally believed that, over a long run, a modus vivendi with Russia was possible; while the Russians, so far as one can tell, believed in no more than a short-run modus vivendi with the United States.

Harriman and Kennan, this narrative has made clear, took the lead in warning Washington about the difficulties of short-run dealings with the Soviet Union. But both argued that, if the United States developed a rational policy and stuck to it, there would be, after long and rough passages, the prospect of eventual clearing. "I am, as you know," Harriman cabled Washington in early April, "a most earnest advocate of the closest possible understanding with the Soviet Union so that what I am saying relates only to how best to attain such understanding." Kennan has similarly made it clear that the function of his containment policy was "to tide us over a difficult time and bring us to the point where we could discuss effectively with the Russians the dangers and drawbacks this status quo involved, and to arrange with them for its peaceful replacement by a better and sounder one." The subsequent careers of both men attest to the honesty of these statements.

There is no corresponding evidence on the Russian side that anyone seriously sought a modus vivendi in these terms. Stalin's choice was whether his long-term ideological and national interests would be better served by a short-run truce with the West or by an immediate resumption of pressure. In October 1945 Stalin indicated to Harriman at Sochi that he planned to adopt the second course—that the Soviet Union was going isolationist. No doubt the succession of problems with the United States contributed to this decision, but the basic causes most probably lay elsewhere: in the developing situations in Eastern Europe, in Western Europe and in the United States.

In Eastern Europe, Stalin was still for a moment experimenting with techniques of control. But he must by now have begun to conclude that he had underestimated the hostility of the people to Russian dominion. The Hungarian elections in November would finally convince him that the Yalta formula was a road to anti-Soviet governments. At the same time, he was feeling more strongly than ever a sense of his opportunities in Western Europe. The other half of the Continent lay unexpectedly before him, politically demoralized, economically prostrate, militarily defenseless. The hunting would be better and safer than he had anticipated. As for the United States, the alacrity of postwar demobilization must have recalled Roosevelt's offhand remark at Yalta that "two years would be the limit" for keeping American troops in Europe. And, despite Dr. Eugene Varga's doubts about the imminence of American economic breakdown, Marxist theology assured Stalin that the United States was heading into a bitter postwar depression and would be consumed with its own problems. If the condition of Eastern Europe made unilateral action seem essential in the interests of Russian security, the condition of Western Europe and the United States offered new temptations for communist expansion. The Cold War was now in full swing.

It still had its year of modulations and accommodations. Secretary Byrnes conducted his long and fruitless campaign to persuade the Russians that America only sought governments in Eastern Europe "both friendly to the Soviet Union and representative of all the democratic elements of the country." Crises were surmounted in Trieste and Iran. Secretary Marshall evidently did not give up hope of a modus vivendi until the Moscow conference of foreign secretaries of March 1947. Even then, the Soviet Union was invited to participate in the Marshall Plan.

The point of no return came on July 2, 1947, when Molotov, after bringing 89 technical specialists with him to Paris and evincing initial interest in the project for European reconstruction, received the hot flash from the Kremlin, denounced the whole idea and walked out of the conference. For the next fifteen years the Cold War raged unabated, passing out of historical ambiguity into the realm of good versus evil and breeding on both sides simplifications, stereotypes and self-serving absolutes, often couched in interchangeable phrases. Under the pressure even America, for a deplorable decade, forsook its pragmatic and pluralist traditions, posed as God's appointed messenger to ignorant and sinful man and followed the Soviet example in looking to a world remade in its own image.

In retrospect, if it is impossible to see the Cold War as a case of American aggression and Russian response, it is also hard to see it as a pure case of Russian aggression and American response. "In what is truly tragic," wrote Hegel, "there must be valid moral powers on both the sides which come into collision. . . . Both suffer loss and yet both are mutually justified." In this sense, the Cold War had its tragic elements. The question remains whether it was an instance of Greek tragedy—as Auden has called it, "the tragedy of necessity," where the feeling aroused in the spectator is "What a pity it had to be this way"—or of Christian tragedy, "the tragedy of possibility," where the feeling aroused is "What a pity it was this way when it might have been otherwise."

Once something has happened, the historian is tempted to assume that it had to happen; but this may often be a highly unphilosophical assumption. The Cold War could have been avoided only if the Soviet Union had not been possessed by convictions both of the infallibility of the communist word and of the inevitability of a communist world. These convictions transformed an impasse between national states into a religious war, a tragedy of possibility into one of necessity. One might wish that America had preserved the poise and proportion of the first years of the Cold War and had not in time succumbed to its own forms of self-righteousness. But the most rational of American policies could hardly have averted the Cold War. Only today, as Russia begins to recede from its messianic mission and to accept, in practice if not yet in principle, the permanence of the world of diversity, only now can the hope flicker that this long, dreary, costly contest may at last be taking on forms less dramatic, less obsessive and less dangerous to the future of mankind.

SUGGESTED READING

Adam Ulam, in *Expansion and Co-Existence* ° (1968), is occasionally ambivalent in his analysis of the Cold War, noting both that it was rooted in competing state systems and ideologies and that it was the inevitable result of Stalin's need to remain in power "as the ruler of a totalitarian society and as the supreme head of a movement that seeks security through constant expansion." In *The Rivals: America and Russia Since World War II* (1971), Ulam looks more closely at the American society, but still without the benefit of any examination of the archival materials. In "Re-Reading the Cold War," *Interplay,* III (Mar. 1969), he offers a harsh assessment of revisionism.

Robert Tucker's *The Radical Left and American Foreign Policy* ° (1971) is a critique of radical analyses (most often those of Kolko and Williams) of U.S. foreign policy, and primarily of the Cold War. It represents a modification of Tucker's earlier, more sanguine views about U.S. foreign policy. Charles Maier, in "Revisionism and the Interpretation of Cold War Origins," *Perspectives in American History,* IV (1970), is less effective but still thoughtful in his criticism of the revisionists. Both Tucker's and Maier's studies represent evidence that radical history is being taken seriously for the first time since at least the Second World War. "Origins of the Post-war Crisis," *Journal of Contemporary History,* III (Apr. 1968) is a loose-knit symposium generally critical of the revisionism to that date. Paul Seabury and Brian Thomas offer useful critiques in "Cold War Origins," *Journal of Contemporary History,* III (Jan. 1968), but they focus on Alperovitz, Horowitz, and Fleming, and neglect Williams. Henry Pachter's "Revisionist Historians and the Cold War," *Dissent* (Nov.–Dec. 1968) is an intemperate and flawed attack on revisionism. Hans Morgenthau and Arthur Schlesinger examine the Cold War and reply to Lloyd Gardner's revisionist analysis in Gardner *et al., The Origins of the Cold War* (1970). Morgenthau also tried to deal with revisionism in his troubled review of Kolko's *Politics of War,* "The Cold War as History," *New York Review of Books* (July 10, 1969). George Lichteim's

Imperialism ° (1971) is a hasty analysis that includes a critical section on the left and Cold War revisionism. John Snell's "The Cold War: Four Contemporary Appraisals," *American Historical Review*, LXVIII (Oct. 1962), is a vigorous attack on Fleming and Morray especially.

George Kennan's *Memoirs, 1925–1950* (1967) is a beautifully literate, often personal statement about the early Cold War; it reveals how unsuccessful the author was in freeing himself from the very moralism that he has decried in his call for a foreign policy based on the national interest. Dean Acheson's *Present at The Creation: My Years in the State Department* ° (1969) is often smug in defense of the Truman administration and its foreign policy, and admits no serious errors by the President or the author. W. Averell Harriman, in *America and Russia in a Changing World* (1970), includes a useful discussion of wartime and early postwar foreign policy. *The Transformation of American Foreign Policy* (1969), by Charles Bohlen, a former State Department official, is remarkably conventional in celebrating the Truman administration's triumphs, but does provide some important information on the Marshall Plan. In *The Cold War as History* (1967), Louis Halle, a member of the Policy Planning Staff in Truman's State Department, wavers in his judgments on the Cold War between historical inevitability (and Olympian perspective) and uneasy moralism.

Walt W. Rostow's *The United States in the World Arena* (1960) is a representative view of the early Cold War by a Kennedy liberal writing during the Eisenhower years. Philip Mosely's *The Kremlin and World Politics: Studies in Soviet Policy & Action* ° (1960) and Marshall Shulman's *Stalin's Foreign Policy Reappraised* ° (1963) are analyses by two former State Department advisers.

In "Henry A. Wallace, the Liberals, and Soviet-American Relations," *Review of Politics*, XXX (Apr. 1968), Alonzo Hamby is close to Schlesinger's position. For Schlesinger's thought, see *The Vital Center* ° (1949), a passionate defense of liberalism and anticommunism; *The Age of Roosevelt,* ° 3 vols. (1957–1960), which views the New Deal as the triumph of the middle way; *A Thousand Days* ° (1965), which emphasizes the value of tough liberalism; *The Bitter Heritage* ° (1966), a brief volume critical of administration policies in Vietnam; and "Vietnam and the End of the Age of the Superpowers," *Harper's* (May 1969), which blames the "tragedy of Vietnam" partly on a "warrior class" and explains the tragedy as "the catastrophic overextension . . . of valid principles."

RICHARD ROVERE

Eisenhower Revisited— A Political Genius? A Brilliant Man?

INTRODUCTION

During the Eisenhower years, liberal intellectuals were fond of chiding Americans for the blandness of their culture and their President for his addiction to golf and westerns. They deplored Eisenhower's mangled syntax, his homilies and platitudes, and his distrust of intellectuals. They criticized him for eschewing leadership, for failing to be an active and innovative president —like Franklin D. Roosevelt or even Harry S Truman. Ike fell drastically short of their standards for presidential greatness. He neither sought to expand the powers of his office nor tried generally to extend American power abroad. Nor did he inspire the nation or move it toward a more noble vision. Indeed, his was a

FROM Richard Rovere, "Eisenhower Revisited—A Political Genius? A Brilliant Man?" *The New York Times Magazine*, February 7, 1971, pp. 14, 15, 54, 58, 59, 62. Copyright ©1971 by The New York Times Company. Reprinted by permission.

businessman's government, his liberal critics complained, and they found it crass, dull, unimaginative. The Eisenhower years, William Shannon charged shortly before the General's departure from the White House, "have been years of flabbiness and self-satisfaction and gross materialism," and the President was both symptom and cause. Complacency and conformity defined the era.

His achievements, according to these critics, were modest. As leader of a party that had been out of the White House for two decades and had periodically threatened to repeal the New Deal at home and collective security abroad, Eisenhower had managed to control the GOP's worst impulses, to make his party responsible, and to keep the nation on an even keel. He was the great conservator. He consolidated the gains of the Democratic past and adapted that legacy to the 1950's.

It was a holding action, his critics concluded. Shannon, for example, labeled this period the "Great Postponement" and Eisenhower a modern-day James Buchanan who failed to resolve the dilemmas of his time or to anticipate the problems and needs of the society. Shannon's indictment was long and ranged from the general to the specific. Eisenhower did not act to improve the quality of American life or significantly to advance civil rights. He even allowed recessions, was slow in responding with counter-cyclical fiscal policies, and did not maintain an adequate rate of economic growth. "No national problem, whether it be education, housing, urban revitalization, agriculture, or inflation," concluded Shannon, "will have been advanced importantly toward solution nor its dimensions significantly altered" ("Eisenhower as President: A Critical Appraisal of the Record," *Commentary*, XXVI [Nov. 1958], p. 390).

Eisenhower's major failures, according to his critics, were in the realm of foreign policy. They assailed him for letting Secretary of State John Foster Dulles dominate foreign policy, for allowing Dulles' self-acknowledged "brinkmanship," and for relying on moralism in foreign affairs. The administration, they charged, sacrificed military strength and flexibility (in the form of nonnuclear weapons and forces) to fiscal orthodoxy and squandered American prestige. Eisenhower also failed to bring articulated goals in foreign policy into line with the limits of American power.

This last theme—the limitations of American power—is central to the foreign policy criticisms of the realists: Hans Morgenthau, George Kennan, Walter Lippmann, and Norman Graebner. Along with many others, they criticized the Eisenhower administration for a rhetoric that overreached its power and for words that promised more than the government could or would deliver. For example, the promise of liberation of Soviet satellites was fraudulent, and massive retaliation ("more bang for the buck") was dangerous and impractical. These critics lamented the fact that the administration never educated the American public on the realities of the Cold War, on the impossibilities of clear-cut victories, on the termination of American omnipotence. Put simply, the Eisenhower administration left Americans in innocence.

Looking back on this administration in 1962, Richard Rovere, liberal columnist for the *New Yorker* and author of *Affairs of State: The Eisenhower Years* (1956) offered a friendlier, though critical, appraisal of the period. He concluded that in Eisenhower's first term a new consensus was reached and tensions eased. Eisenhower, partly because he was a Republican, was able to do "many of the things that needed doing and that could not have been done by a Democratic administration." He ended the Korean War—which neither Truman nor Stevenson, fearing charges of appeasement, could have done. In addition, Eisenhower led the Republican party to support collective security and established a policy that, despite the heady rhetoric about Quemoy and Matsu and Formosa and Chiang Kai-shek, "probably saved us from some bloody and pointless engagements in the Far East." He also contributed to the political destruction of Senator Joseph McCarthy, though, Rovere noted, Eisenhower could probably be faulted for not acting more forcefully, or at least for not using more of his prestige earlier in this matter. But Rovere was quick to defend the President from charges that the use of presidential powers could have stopped McCarthy much earlier at small cost to Eisenhower.

Rovere, though finding "little to regret" in Eisenhower's first term, found the second term sharply disappointing and endorsed many of Shannon's criticisms: Eisenhower avoided supporting civil rights, often relied on mediocre advisors (especially after the death of Dulles), praised "the simple-minded . . . semiliterate political economy" of Secretary of the Treasury George Humphrey, and was unresponsive to charges that the nation was militarily unprepared for limited warfare, especially paramilitary action. In concluding, Rovere suggested that the tragedy was that "we did not have a President who wanted to keep abreast of the more salutary developments within American society—the intellectual ferment, the technological ferment, the struggles for equality" ("Eisenhower Over the Shoulder," *American Scholar*, XXXI [Spring 1962]).

Beginning about five years after Rovere's appraisal, some journalists and historians, writing amid hostility to the Vietnam War, offered a higher estimation of Eisenhower and his accomplishments. Murray Kempton, Richard Rhodes, I. F. Stone, Garry Wills, William L. O'Neill, and Barton J. Bernstein have contributed to this new assessment. Kempton, a liberal supporter of the New Deal–Fair Deal who moved recently into the left-liberal camp, wrote one of the earliest, and perhaps the most enthusiastic, of the reassessments ("The Underestimation of Dwight D. Eisenhower," *Esquire,* LXXII [Sept. 1967]).

Kempton sees the former President as shrewd and even ruthless, a man of masks. His protective coloration was the appearance of being amiable and innocent. He disguised his thoughts, his motives, and his actions. Even Eisenhower's mangled syntax, Kempton contends, was not a flaw of mind but a skillful strategem of concealment, confusion, and evasion that allowed him to maintain control of situations. When, for example, the President did not want to explain his policy on Formosa to reporters, he smilingly told his advisers that he would simply confuse the press and thereby avoid a commitment that would narrow his options. In Eisenhower's memoirs, which most liberal critics found dreary and simple-minded, Kempton found brief flashes of the "true" Eisenhower, whom he described as "the President most superbly equipped for truly consequential decision we may have ever had, a mind neither rash nor hesitant, free of the slightest concern for how things might look, indifferent to any sentiment. . . ." For Kempton, who stressed foreign policy in his assessment, the administration's policies in Korea, Lebanon, and Indochina illustrate Eisenhower's techniques and skills.

Consider, for example, Kempton's version (which relies on the memoirs) of Eisenhower's policy in Korea; a quick trip to Korea by the President-elect led to his discovery that the enemy could not be easily dislodged through conventional warfare, and he decided to settle the war. Another example of this diplomatic skill is the carefully-conceived, limited intervention in Lebanon in 1958. Kempton quotes from Eisenhower's memoirs:

> The basic mission of United States forces in Lebanon was not primarily to fight. Every effort was made to have our landing be as much of a garrison as possible. . . . The decision to occupy only the airfield and capital was a political one I adhered to over the recommendations of some of the military. If the Lebanese army were unable to subdue the rebels when we had secured their capital and protected their government, I felt that we were backing up a government with so little popular support that we probably should not be there.

Underlying Kempton's analysis is his assumption that Eisenhower was too wise, too cautious, too aware of the necessary relationship between limited resources and goals, to allow himself to be sucked into the commitment in Vietnam that Lyndon Johnson directed and defended.

In 1954, even before the French defeat, Eisenhower concluded that the French plan to place 10,000 troops in Dien Bien Phu was a classic military blunder. He refused to be drawn into the Indochina war, Kempton stresses, because he contended that

American air strikes could not support the French and that American intervention would (in Ike's words) "entail the risk of a loss." He feared also—in what some might regard as great vision —that American intervention would "draw off our resources and . . . weaken our over-all defense position."

Eisenhower, according to Kempton, relied on rational and cautious deviousness in order to maintain control and avoid risks and liabilities. The President wore masks. He let underlings take the blame for his unpleasant decisions or stake out risky advance positions. He lied when necessary but retreated when he was found out. As part of the strategy of avoiding unnecessary challenges, he "always gave an enemy an exit, and never gave an ally his head." In summary, Ike was a genius as a politician and as a Chief Executive, even though, as Kempton did not mention but would undoubtedly acknowledge, the President's social vision on domestic matters (especially race relations, the economy and poverty, and urban problems) was very limited.

Rovere, provoked by what he considers the extravagant claims for Eisenhower, offers in the essay reprinted below his own estimate of the President, which is slightly more favorable than his assessment in 1962, and uses this new position as a basis for criticizing the Eisenhower admirers. Rovere, rightly, notes that they are overly influenced by the fact that of all postwar chief executives, only Eisenhower managed to keep the nation out of war. But was he lucky or skillful? Probably both, concludes Rovere, while admitting that he leans toward the "luck" theory. He points out that it was Eisenhower who articulated the "domino" theory. He also entertained the possibility of intervention in Vietnam, but set criteria that required willing allies (who proved unwilling), and ended by rejecting intervention for military, and also diplomatic, reasons. Rovere also stresses that going to the "brink"—to use Dulles' politically inept word—was "an indispensable part of the [Eisenhower] strategy."

Perhaps, however, Rovere should have devoted more attention to explaining why and how the President, despite Dulles' claims of brinkmanship, actually did avoid war. Kempton suggests that the administration managed every situation in such a way that it could quietly back down and carefully redefine the conditions in order to avoid conflict. For example, if we can believe Eisenhower, the administration obliquely used nuclear blackmail on China to end the Korean War. There was no open confrontation, no dramatic public test of American credibility. It was a skillfully devised threat that did not commit the United States to action. In the case of intervention in Vietnam, one can contend that the President established criteria that he knew were unlikely to be met and also allowed military weaknesses to deter him. Because the nation lacked the forces for limited war (precisely what the liberals demanded), America could not afford to

commit troops to Indochina. In view of this restriction, it is interesting that Rovere in 1971 dropped his 1962 indictment of Eisenhower for failing to develop a limited war capacity.

Eisenhower, his defenders maintain, did what John F. Kennedy tried to do but often failed to accomplish: Eisenhower kept
his options open and maintained greater freedom for maneuver
without risking prestige at home or abroad. His small-scale
interventions—in Guatemala under the CIA, in Lebanon in a very
closely defined situation, and in Vietnam with a few hundred
advisers—were shrewdly designed to minimize risks. The Bay of
Pigs adventure, had Eisenhower remained in office, might have
been an exception. Or, as some of his admirers think, it might
never have been launched under Eisenhower. Unlike Kennedy,
the General had more reason to distrust intelligence agencies
(having suffered the debacle of the U–2), and he did not have to
prove his toughness. He had already demonstrated that the military could not coerce him, and he was politically invulnerable to
their threats and actions. Perhaps, in summary, Eisenhower did
know how to retain control of decisions and command of events.
Perhaps, too, he had a splendid sense of the relationship between power and goals—precisely what the realists desired and
found wanting in his administration.

Rovere, in assessing Eisenhower's domestic policy, still relies heavily on his analysis of 1962. In challenging the probably
exaggerated estimates of Eisenhower as a "genius," Rovere uses
liberal standards as the basis for his judgments and therefore
does not disagree so much on what happened as on what it
meant. (Along the way, he shifts attention from the views of
Kempton, Stone, and Walter Cronkite to attack the grandiose
claims advanced by Nixon, whom no commentator would take seriously on this matter. Kempton and the others have made no
claims for Ike's moral vision in civil rights or civil liberties.) For
Rovere, Eisenhower at home presided over the Great Postponement: a failure of vision, even of moral vision. His stand on civil
rights is the most dramatic example. He gave the mass of voters
what they wanted, not what Rovere and liberal reformers thought
they should want.

Rovere's judgments raise some interesting methodological
problems that often appear in assessments of recent history. His
liberal analysis of the Great Postponement, students should note,
is strikingly familiar in form (not content) to the interpretation
that some New Left historians have presented of the New Deal—
and that liberal historians have sometimes judged ahistorical or
anachronistic. Some New Left critics of the New Deal have lamented the restrictions of ideology in Roosevelt and his associates that made them unable to conceive of bolder reforms, and
also have concluded that the New Deal therefore lost the opportunity for reshaping (or at least more substantially reforming)

America. The Great Postponement thesis also finds the President's vision wanting, but on the basis of liberal, not radical,
standards. In the liberal critique of Eisenhower (as in the New
Left critique of Roosevelt), there is a presumption that far more
could have been accomplished if the President had desired. In
neither the New Left analysis of the New Deal nor in the Great
Postponement thesis is this notion of much greater flexibility in
the political system developed at adequate length.

Rovere's analysis also raises the plaguing question of
whether Eisenhower still clung to an image of the nation formed
in Kansas circa 1910. Certainly, as Rovere claims, Eisenhower's
statements, filled with platitudes and pieties and optimism and
earnestness, suggest that turn-of-the-century Kansas was always
his world. But if, as Kempton contends, Eisenhower was a man of
masks, then we must ask whether his words were not also an important part of the roles he played in the public forum. For Ike
was a man whose life symbolized the triumph of organization. He
was not a traditional hero but, as Rovere admits, an "organizer of
victory." He had most surely learned modern industrial values
of management, of bureaucracy, of efficiency—values of a later
urban, industrial America, not of little Abilene circa 1910. When
he was president of a major university, he knew that his task was
public relations and money-raising, not educational leadership,
for he understood the modern division of labor, the bureaucratic
way of life, and the role and use of image-making. In his personal
life, he managed to project the useful, anticosmopolitan image of
the happily-married, faithful husband, and of the church-going,
God-fearing man. His network of friendships was not (as in the
case of Truman) composed of old buddies from the army or his
hometown and state; rather, he often chose powerful, wealthy
businessmen, frequently men he met after 1945. Was he, then, so
much the innocent, the naive? Or was he shrewd, calculating, astute in foreign affairs and politics, but morally backward (by liberal standards) on civil rights and civil liberties and intellectually
backward on economic matters? Was he, perhaps, a modern-day
American Machiavelli capable of coldly defining and achieving
his—not the liberals'—goals?

*I*t has been slightly more than a decade since Robert Frost
greeted the dawn of a "next Augustan age . . . of poetry and power" and
Dwight D. Eisenhower, ex-President, left Washington for Gettysburg—still
an immensely popular figure who, had the law permitted and the spirit and
the flesh been willing, could easily have been the man taking the oath of office on January 20, 1961, thus deferring the Augustan age for at least four
more years. Eisenhower was held in high esteem for the rest of his life, but

throughout most of the sixties those amateurs who sit in more or less professional judgment on Presidents—other politicians, historians, journalists —came more and more into agreement that his eight years in the White House had been a period of meager accomplishment and lackadaisical leadership. The greatest failure, the consensus seemed to be, was one of anticipation. What a prescient statesman could have foreseen in the fifties, the argument runs, was that the ship of state was headed for a sea of troubles, and this the 34th President conspicuously failed to perceive. He lacked foresight and imagination and thus bore considerable responsibility for the difficulties of the three men who succeeded him in the sixties.

Many of those who judged him most harshly until only a few years ago are now having second and third thoughts about the man and his Presidency—thoughts that should ring most agreeably in the ears of those whose faith had never never wavered. Such nay-sayers on the left as Murray Kempton and I. F. Stone are finding virtues in him they failed to detect while he served, and others are making claims for him that not even his partisans made when he sought office or held it. Garry Wills, the eminent Nixonologist, advises us in *Nixon Agonistes* that Eisenhower was "a political genius." Walter Cronkite, who first knew Eisenhower in France during the war and saw him often in subsequent years, recently said that he never thought highly of Eisenhower "either as a general or a President" but that in the post–White House years he discovered that Eisenhower was in actuality a "brilliant" man—indeed, "more brilliant than many brilliant men I have met."

A political genius? A brilliant man? Who ever said or thought that about Eisenhower in his own time? Certainly not Eisenhower himself. It was not that he was lacking in vanity; he had his share, but there is no evidence that he ever thought of himself as possessing a great talent for politics or a towering intellect, and the aspect of his "genius" that Wills calls "realism" would have deterred him from this kind of self-appraisal. He was, and we can be sure that he knew he was, no slouch politically (had he been below average in this respect, he would not have risen in the Army), and he was certainly not lacking in intelligence. But his real strengths lay elsewhere, and the Wills and Cronkite superlatives seem, one has to say, silly.

In the case of Garry Wills, the judgment supports a theory. Wills maintains that Eisenhower all along saw Richard Nixon in the light in which Wills today sees him. In Cronkite's case, the delayed but nonetheless dazzling illumination appeared in the course of many meetings he had with Eisenhower while taping some television interviews in the mid-sixties. He asserts his discovery of the ex-President's "brilliance" but does not tell us how it was made manifest.

For my part, I think the revisionist phenomenon as a whole can be rather easily accounted for—though I do not wish to suggest that new judgments are erroneous simply because they are new or, at least as I see it, obvious in their origins. Seen from 1971, the most important single thing about Dwight D. Eisenhower was that, through luck or good management or some combination of both, *we did not go to war while he was President.* To be sure, we came close on occasion, and his Secretary of State practiced a brand of cold-war diplomacy in which what was called "brinkmanship" at the time—risking war, including nuclear war—was an indispensable strategy. It can also be argued that Dulles's and Eisenhower's Indochina policy made Kennedy's and Johnson's and Nixon's all but inevitable and that, had Eisenhower held office for a third term, he would have found himself at war in Vietnam. The contrary can also be argued, but it does not matter; we were at war when he came to office, and six months later we were out of it, and we did not enter another war during his tenure. Eight years of Eisenhower: seven and a half years of peace. Ten years of Kennedy, Johnson, Nixon: almost ten solid years of war.

What else is there to celebrate about the Eisenhower years? I can think of a few things, but they are of far less consequence and, moreover, they are not blessings of the sort that can be appreciated only in hindsight —unless one chooses to include among them such engineering projects as the St. Lawrence Seaway and the interstate highway system. Though I have myself altered some of my views about Eisenhower over the years, I have felt since 1958 or thereabouts that the country benefited from his first term but would have been better off if he had not had a second. I think I can defend this view in 1971. By 1953 we had made our point in Korea—the expulsion of the invading armies—and it was time for a settlement. It required a Republican President (not necessarily Eisenhower, though of course it helped that he was a successful military man) to end that war on terms short of the "victory" for which Gen. Douglas MacArthur said there was "no substitute." As Harry Truman was to say, he or any other Democrat would have been "lynched" for agreeing to the settlement Eisenhower so cheerfully accepted. It also required a Republican in the White House (though, again, not necessarily Eisenhower) to bring about the downfall of Senator Joe McCarthy.

Eisenhower, to be sure, never took the initiative against McCarthy. He declined to "get into the gutter" with the demagogue, and he tolerated, for a while, a certain amount of high-level appeasement. But the fact remains that 15 months after Eisenhower took office McCarthy was done for. With an active, militant President, the job might have been done somewhat sooner and with less loss of dignity all around. However, a Republican President did not have to be an activist to draw McCarthy's fire. Though nominally a Republican, McCarthy was bound by the nature of his mission in American political life to attack *any* administration, and when in time he attacked his own party's stewardship of affairs, resistance was bound to be offered. It tends now to be forgotten that McCarthy scored most of his triumphs when the Democrats controlled both the White House and Congress, and he would probably have been more difficult to deal with had they remained in control. It has always seemed to me that the election of Adlai Stevenson in 1952, however desirable it might have been in certain respects, would have prolonged both the Korean war and McCarthyism, and I have reason to think that, in later years, Stevenson believed this, too. The country was bitterly divided in 1952, and 20 years of Democratic governance was one of the causes of disunity.

Putting Eisenhower in the White House seemed a way of promoting national unity, which, though hardly the highest of political values, is not one to be disregarded. But by 1956 Eisenhower had achieved just about all that it was in his power to achieve. The war was over, McCarthy was a spent force and the President had, at the Geneva Summit Conference of 1955, helped negotiate a limited but nonetheless helpful *détente* in the cold war.

The second term was anticlimax almost all the way. It was also rather melancholy and at times squalid. The President was not a well man. The Democrats, growing in power in the Congress and knowing that no one would ever again ride Eisenhower's coattails, were openly seeking to embarrass him and passing bills he felt he had to veto. In midterm, he lost the two men he had relied on most heavily. John Foster Dulles left office and soon died, and Sherman Adams, who was general manager at the White House, had to retire because of a clear conflict of interest. Eisenhower began on his own to practice some of Dulles's peripatetic diplomacy, but it didn't work. In 1960, he started for another summit meeting, in Paris, but Nikita Khrushchev refused to make the final ascent because of the unpleasantness over the U-2 affair. Eisenhower set out for Japan, but for security reasons (rioting anti-American students, etc.) was advised to turn around and go home.

There is more to being a President than entering or ending wars—and more than instituting or failing to institute political and social change. Style and character are important and closely related aspects of leadership. Eisenhower came to us as a hero—not in the old sense of a man who had displayed great valor but in the newer sense of having been an organizer of victory. His style, though, was anything but heroic. It was in part fatherly, in larger part avuncular. He was not an exhorter—except now and then in campaigns—and as a counselor his performance was as a rule inadequate. He had difficulties with language, particularly when he extemporized. Readers of press-conference texts found his syntax all but impenetrable and often concluded that his thinking was as muddled as the verbatim transcripts. Actually, he was seldom as unclear as he appeared to be when encountered in cold type. Those who listened and watched as he talked were rarely in doubt as to what he was saying. Inflection and expression conveyed much of what seemed missing or mixed up in print. But he was never, to put it mildly, eloquent, never a forceful persuader. He never influenced, or sought to influence, American thought.

Eulogizing Eisenhower in April, 1969, President Nixon said of his late mentor: "For more than a quarter of a century, he spoke with a moral authority seldom equaled in American public life." Nixon did not explain how, when or where the impact of this "moral authority" was felt. Eisenhower was an upright man, a believer in the Protestant ethic he seemed to embody. But the man he twice defeated was no less honorable, and Stevenson had a moral vision that seemed somewhat broader, deeper and less simplistic than Eisenhower's. Do any survivors recall the Eisenhower years as a period notable for elevated standards of morality in public life or elsewhere? In our public life, there were two issues full of "moral" content— McCarthyism and race. On neither did the President personally exercise any of the kind of authority Nixon attributed to him. He was not a McCarthyite or a racist, but he conspicuously failed to engage his personal prestige or that of his office in the struggles against demagogy and racial injustice.

A President can also provide leadership by improving the quality of public life—the quality of the people he appoints and associates himself with, the quality of the acts he and they perform, the quality of the ideas his administration espouses. If in the future, the brief Presidency of Eisenhower's successor is well regarded, it will be largely because of his quest for "excellence." Kennedy brought many first-rate people to Washington, and if one of the lessons they taught us is that first-rate people can sometimes mess things up as badly as third-raters or fourth-raters, it is nevertheless true that some of them performed brilliantly and should continue to serve the Republic for some years to come. No such praise, so far as I am aware, accrues to Eisenhower—except in the case of one institution, the Supreme Court.

He appointed a Chief Justice and four Associate Justices, and all but one of the five (Charles Whittaker, who sat only briefly) served with high distinction. In this respect, Eisenhower's record may be as good as any in history. There was about it, though, a kind of inadvertent quality—as if some architect had achieved splendor while seeking only mediocrity. The President was surprised and in some cases hugely disappointed by the performance of the institution he had created.

In the executive branch, mediocrity was the rule. The one Cabinet member of stature was John Foster Dulles, an imposing man in many ways but also a stiff, self-righteous Calvinist who intensified the cold war as an ideological conflict and sometimes seemed bent on making it a theological one as well—making, as he put it, "the moral force of Christendom . . . felt in the conduct of nations." Nevertheless, Dulles was a man of some intellectual prowess, and nothing of the sort could be said for anyone else in the upper echelons. Eisenhower's measure of expertise in any field was that of the Bitch Goddess: success, usually financial success. Especially in the early days, it was a businessman's administration—to a degree that bred misgivings even in the mind of the first Senator Robert Taft of Ohio, who made no bones about being a spokesman for business but said, when he heard of the first appointments, "I don't know of any reasons why success in business should mean success in public service. . . . Anyone who thinks he can just transfer business methods to government is going to have to learn that it isn't so." Eisenhower's appointments were uninspired and uninspiring; one cannot think of any major office holder whose example might have led any young man or young woman to feel that public life might be a high calling. On the White House staff, there were from time to time highly gifted younger men—Maxwell Rabb, Emmet Hughes, Malcolm Moos—but for the most part they lacked power and visibility, though Moos exerted an influence of a kind when he wrote the line about the "military-industrial complex" into Eisenhower's farewell address.

Still and all, who in 1971 wouldn't exchange a trainload of mediocrities, incompetents and even pickpockets for a speedy end to the war in Vietnam and to the rancor and discord it has created? There may be some survivors of the better-dead-than-Red set, but even a number of these, one suspects, no longer see the conflict in Vietnam as one that compels a choice between extinction and the surrender of American independence. There was peace under Eisenhower, and the question of historical interest to those of us who survived the ensuing decade is whether this indisputable fact is to be ascribed to his stewardship or to luck or to some combination of both. I lean toward the combination theory, with perhaps a heavier emphasis on luck than others might care to make.

The opportunities for military involvement during his tenure were fully as numerous as those of the Kennedy, Johnson and Nixon years. In Asia, there were Korea, the Formosa Strait and Indochina; in Europe, Germany and Hungary; in the Middle East, Suez and Lebanon, and in our own hemisphere, Cuba. In some of these troubled areas, intervention was seriously contemplated; in others, it seemed out of the question from the start. In the Suez crisis of 1956, our policy from the onset was to stay out militarily; we made our disapproval so clear to the British and the French that we were not consulted in the planning stages. Nor was there ever much likelihood of our doing anything about Hungary, which erupted just after Suez in the closing days of the Presidential campaign; the Dulles line on Eastern Europe was always that we stood ready to help in the task of "liberation," but it was never much more than a line, and in moments of crisis behind the Iron Curtain—except when there was trouble in Berlin— we looked the other way. In 1958 in Lebanon, we did, at the request of its beleaguered President, land combat-ready Marine and Army units, but there was no combat and the troops spent their time girl-watching on the beaches they had stormed.

But elsewhere the risks were large. Even before his inauguration, Eisenhower went to Korea in search of peace, and in a matter of months a welcome (though far from satisfactory) settlement was made. Politically, in this country, the credit was all his, and if the whole truth is ever known—it will probably never be—it might turn out that he deserves it all. From what is currently known, his principal strategy seems to have been nuclear blackmail—a threat conveyed to our adversaries that if they dragged their feet much longer in the truce talks while pressing on with the war, this country would not consider itself bound to a reliance on conventional weapons. (Eisenhower was never opposed to the use of atomic weapons on moral grounds. He regarded them simply as explosives, suitable for some demolition jobs and not for others. His later assertions about general wars being "unthinkable" in the atomic age were based not on a moral judgment but a military one. He saw no point in a war no one would survive. But tactical "nukes" were another matter.) Maybe that did it, and maybe not. The truth could only come from the other side, and about all we now have on any other factor is Khrushchev's memory of Chou En-lai later explaining that the Chinese losses in Korea had become militarily insupportable. In any case, with all due respect for and gratitude to Eisenhower, one is compelled to wonder what would have happened—what *could* have happened—if the Communists had said that they weren't afraid of our bombs and intended to carry on with the war. Did he have a fallback position? If so, was it credible? Or did he, as seems so out of character, stake everything on a wildly dangerous threat of holocaust? These are questions that await answers that may never come. We know only that the war was terminated the following summer.

In Formosa we have what is perhaps the clearest case of prudent management during the Eisenhower Presidency. The danger was that we would be suckered into at least an air and sea war against Communist China, which was, as it still is, insisting on the rightness of its claim to sovereignty over Formosa and all the islands between it and the mainland. Eisenhower was, in 1954 and 1955, under enormous pressure from his own military and diplomatic advisers, among them Dulles, from Congressional Republicans and from many prominent Americans who had supported his candidacy (Henry Luce, for example) to give Chiang Kai-shek every form of assistance he asked for and to help in the defense of every rock in the Formosa Strait—not only to help keep the Generalissimo in his fortress but to aid in preparations for a return to the mainland by the Nationalist armies that had been driven out half a decade earlier. Eisenhower quite clearly had no taste for the entire enterprise. He knew that Chiang alone could never dislodge the Communists, no matter how much matériel we gave him, and he knew, too, that Mao Tse-tung's forces, no matter how many shells they lobbed at the close-in islands, were unequipped for an amphibious invasion of Formosa. So he jollied Chiang with hardware and money and high-level visitors, meanwhile protecting himself with a Congressional resolution and a treaty that pledged direct military assistance to Chiang only if we—not he—determined that Peking's maneuvers in the Formosa Strait were unmistakably preparatory to an assault on Formosa itself.

Had Admiral Radford, then Chairman of the Joint Chiefs, been in control, he might have made that fateful determination a dozen times over. Eisenhower read the cables and studied the maps and found no occasion for invoking those parts of the agreements that could have led to war. His methods were in certain ways dubious—there were questions about the constitutionality of the treaty and the resolution—but at least in the perspective of the present he found a way of averting a war that could have been far costlier than the one we have been in for most of the last decade. There can be little doubt that this was his will and his doing, for, as far as Communist China was concerned, he was the only "dove" in his administration.

Indochina—as always, it is the most complicated of matters. Eisenhower did not get involved militarily, but he may, by his patronage of his Secretary of State and by other words and acts, have made subsequent intervention all but unavoidable. It was Eisenhower who articulated the "domino theory" for Southeast Asia, and we know from his memoirs that on several occasions he seriously considered intervention and was deterred not primarily by political or moral considerations but by military and, to some extent, diplomatic ones. An obvious restraint was our lack of troops and weapons suitable for fighting the kind of war he quite correctly judged it to be. He gave thought to the use of nuclear weapons, and two carriers whose planes had nuclear bombs were in the Tonkin Gulf. But, as Earl Ravenal writes in *Foreign Affairs*, he "could not identify an appropriate enemy or target to fit the massive nuclear response [and] narrowly declined to intervene."

He considered using ground troops to aid the French but stipulated that under no circumstances would he go it alone—that is, without Asian and European allies. Dulles looked for suitable allies but found none. Had Eisenhower found either the appropriate targets for nuclear retaliation or willing partners in intervention, he might still have come up with an excuse for staying out, for nonintervention seemed almost always his preference; his distaste for war was general and a consistent factor in his reasoning. But it was indisputably under Eisenhower that we made heavy commitments to the powers that were and were to be in Saigon, and it was with Eisenhower's blessing that Dulles set up the Southeast Asia Treaty Organization, at once a political joke and a political disaster.

During his time, Eisenhower was not called upon to make good on any of Dulles's commitments in the region. I think it quite conceivable, however, that had he held office in the early sixties he might have found himself a prisoner of his own past and of then-current events and have followed pretty much the course of his successors. One advantage he had over his successors, though, was confidence in his own military judgment, and this might have saved him, us and the Vietnamese from the horrors that were soon to come.

Eisenhower's two terms fell between the two great Berlin crises—the one brought on by the blockade of the Western Sector in 1948 and the one brought on by the Berlin Wall 10 years ago. There was continuous tension over Germany throughout the fifties, but the dangers of war lessened as NATO, whose supreme command he had left to seek the Presidency, grew in strength and as circumspection seemed increasingly to prevail in the Kremlin. These were the early days of the world of two nuclear superpowers, and the "balance of terror" would probably have held under any leadership save that of a madman. Though in Europe Dulles made a good many enemies for himself and for his Government, his European diplomacy was always more traditional and more prudent, as witness the Austrian treaty, than his diplomacy elsewhere in the world, and it would, I think, be rather difficult to fault Eisenhower for his handling of American policy in Germany.

In his memoirs, Eisenhower wrote of the Bay of Pigs as a "fiasco" for which "indecision and untimely counterorders" were "apparently responsible." He did not elaborate. But whatever he meant by Kennedy's "indecision," the original conclusion that we should sponsor an invasion came out of the Eisenhower, not the Kennedy, Administration. As he acknowledged, his military and intelligence people had, with his encouragement, armed and trained the forces in exile and, as we learned in the aftermath, completion of the scheme was urged on the new President by such holdovers as Allen Dulles of the C.I.A. and Gen. Lyman Lemnitzer, Chairman of the Joint Chiefs of Staff. Kennedy took responsibility for the bad show of which Eisenhower was the original producer. Eisenhower was lucky enough to be out of office when the rehearsals were over and the performers were ready for the opening. We can only conjecture as to whether he would have called off the whole business or gone about it in some other way. But he surely bears some responsibility for the policy and for the crucial failure of intelligence which led the executors of the policy to believe that the Cuban people would welcome the invaders as liberators and would take up arms to join them.

I have been somewhat surprised in thinking and writing about the Eisenhower years a decade later to discover that we know a good deal less about the Eisenhower Administration than about most recent ones. The historians haven't got around to it yet, and the few memoirists it produced haven't revealed very much except about themselves. Eisenhower's two large volumes were put together mainly with scissors and paste. Richard

Nixon's *Six Crises* is all about Richard Nixon. Sherman Adams's *First-Hand Report* is not first-hand at all but second- and third-hand—dealing extensively with large events, such as Indochina and Formosa, about which he knew little and, despite his closeness to the President, was seldom if ever consulted. Robert Murphy's *Diplomat Among Warriors* is a stiff-necked but instructive work, only part of which bears on the Eisenhower period. Emmet Hughes's *Ordeal of Power* is a thoughtful, critical work, but Hughes's experience was limited to two brief tours in the White House as a speechwriter and political consultant. A few journalists—notably Robert J. Donovan in *Eisenhower: The Inside Story*—produced creditable works, more useful on the whole than the memoirs, but the literature by and large is thin.

"The President of the United States," Alfred Kazin wrote in reviewing the first volume of Eisenhower's memoirs, "had to look up the public record that most of us more or less knew in order to find out what happened during his Administration." This, I think, comes close to the heart of the matter about Eisenhower. For eight years as President, he presided in the most literal dictionary sense—he occupied the seat of authority. But he exercised authority only when there was no other choice. He headed an administration but he rarely administered. In foreign affairs, he stepped in only on certain European questions and when, as Commander in Chief, he was required to make command decisions. In domestic affairs his temperament was in line with his economics—laissez-faire. Whenever possible, he let the Government run itself—and it was possible a good part of the time.

In fairness, though, it must be recalled that Eisenhower never offered himself as an activist. He never pledged innovation or any sort of basic reform. One cannot quite contend that he was the product of a political "draft," but, at least as much as any chief executive in this century, he had the office thrust upon him. His style was well known to those who engineered his nomination and to those who elected and reelected him. Whatever else may be said in dispraise, he did not betray his trust. He construed it rather narrowly, but in doing so he embodied a long tradition and a specifically Republican tradition.

His command decisions seem, in retrospect, to have been generally wise. He was clear about the hazards of intervention in Asia. However, he deputized Dulles to contract military alliances all over the place—confident, perhaps, that in crises he could prevail as he had in Korea. He deputized much to the other Dulles, Allen, too—and it was under him that the C.I.A. became a force in world affairs and undertook such missions as the overturn of Governments in Iran and Guatemala. Eisenhower was anything but an empire builder—he was by almost any definition an anti-imperialist—but it was while he presided that this country began, if not to acquire new holdings overseas, to use its power in an imperial manner far beyond the Americas.

Domestically, he and we marked time. In the first few years, this was more or less defensible. The country might not have sustained him if he had tried to remake it. Once the Korean war was over and McCarthy's fangs had been drawn, complacency was the dominant American mood, and very few Americans were aware of the large structural faults in many of our institutions. In 1954, the Supreme Court ruled that if we were to be true to ourselves and our pretensions, racism had to be deinstitutionalized, but this was about the only blow to complacency until, in the second term, Sputnik went aloft and made some Americans wonder about our educational system. With hindsight, we can see that practically all the problems that bedeviled us in the sixties had been worsening in the fifties. It can be said, to be sure, that nearly all of them predated the fifties by decades, even centuries, and that Eisenhower was no more to blame in such matters than most of his predecessors. And this is only just. He was not a cause of any of our present domestic disorders. Neither, though, did he perceive them or heed the prophets of his time—and there were several—who did perceive them.

What Eisenhower clearly lacked—and this was due as much to the education and experience that had been his lot as a servant of his country as to any deficiency of mind or spirit—was the kind of knowledge of the American condition he might have gained if his background had been in politics rather than in the military. He went through most of the fifties and on into the sixties with an image of this country formed in Kansas *circa* 1910. Nowhere is this so dismayingly clear as in the closing words of the second volume of his memoirs, which was published in a dreadful year for this country, 1965—after his successor had met violent death in Dallas, at a time when violence increasingly characterized our race relations, when the generation gap was widening alongside the credibility gap, when our sons were marching by the tens of thousands into the Vietnam quagmire. In that year, he could bring himself to this apostrophe:

> I have unshakable faith that the ideals and the way of life that Western civilization has cherished . . . will flourish everywhere to the infinite benefit of mankind . . . At home . . . our level of education constantly rises . . . Opportunity for the properly ambitious boy or girl increases daily. Prospects for the good life were never better, provided only that each continues to feel that he, himself, must earn and deserve these advantages.
>
> Imbued with sense and spirit we will select future leaders [who will] keep a firm, sure hand on the rudder of this splendid ship of state, guiding her through future generations to the great destiny for which she was created.

A good man? Of course. A "brilliant" man? Hardly. "A political genius"? If so, the evidence remains concealed. A good President? Better than average, perhaps, and very useful in his early years. But by and large not what the times required.

SUGGESTED READING

The papers of the Eisenhower administration have been open to scholars only since the late 1960's, and so far little research on that government's domestic activities exists. As a result, the bulk of the literature is composed of journalistic accounts written during these years or memoirs recorded at the end of the administration.

Among the few scholarly studies of domestic policies are Aaron Wildavsky's *Dixon-Yates: A Study in Power Politics* (1962), which covers a major controversy in the administration; Robert Griffith's *The Politics of Fear: Joseph R. McCarthy and The Senate* (1970), which briefly examines the McCarthy-Eisenhower administration relationship; James L. Sundquist's *Politics and Policy: The Eisenhower, Kennedy, and Johnson Years* (1968); and David Frier's, *Conflict of Interest in the Eisenhower Administration* (1969). Heinz Eulau's *Class and Party in the Eisenhower Years* (1962) is useful on voting patterns.

Samuel Lubell's *The Revolt of the Moderates* (1956) is an analysis of the "new politics" and is often critical of Eisenhower. Marquis Childs, in *Eisenhower: Captive Hero* (1958), expresses the unhappiness of liberals with the tone, style, and accomplishments of the man and his administration. Merlo Pusey, in *Eisenhower: The President* (1956), aided by White House staff members, is appreciative of the administration and offers a favorable judgment of the President. Robert J. Donovan's *Eisenhower: The Inside Story* (1956) is a generally flattering account based on privileged access to private papers.

Among the recent favorable estimates of the administration and the President are Richard Rhodes' "Ike: An Artist in Iron," *Harper's*, CCXLI (July 1970); William O'Neill's *Coming Apart: An Informal History of America in the 1960's* (1971), which begins with a chapter surveying Eisenhower's presidency; and Garry Wills's *Nixon Agonistes* (1970), a clever journalistic analysis of Nixon which also examines Eisenhower.

Dwight D. Eisenhower's *The White House Years: Mandate for Change, 1953–1956* ° (1963) and *The White House Years* ° (1965) have biases but also contain valuable information and often remarkably candid admissions useful for an assessment of the Eisenhower administration. Even more revealing of the man is his *At Ease: Stories I Tell My Friends* (1967). In *Ordeal of Power* ° (1963), Emmet John Hughes, an Eisenhower speech-writer and liberal Republican, reveals his disillusionment with the administration. This view contrasts sharply with that of Arthur Larson in *Eisenhower: The President Nobody Knew* (1968), a shrewd, favorable assessment by a liberal Republican; and that of Sherman Adams in *Firsthand Report* ° (1961), the memoir by Eisenhower's "executive secretary," who was dismissed for unethical business dealings. Among the other sources by members of the administration are Ezra Taft Benson's *Cross Fire: The Eight Years with Eisenhower* (1962); Allen Dulles' *The Craft of Intelligence* ° (1963); Richard Nixon's *Six Crises* ° (1962); E. Frederic Morrow's *Black Man in the White House* (1963); and Lewis Strauss's *Men and Decisions* (1962).

Herman Finer's *Dulles over Suez* (1964) is a savage indictment of the Secretary's policies. Louis Gerson, in *John Foster Dulles* (1967), offers more moderate judgments. The early military strategy of the administration has been examined by Glenn Snyder in Warner Schilling *et al.*, eds., *Strategy, Politics, and Defense Budgets* (1962).

The foreign policy of right-wing Republicans, the so-called isolationists, has never been sympathetically analyzed. Norman Graebner, in *The New Isolationism* (1956), stresses their pro-Asian orientation and their ambivalence about withdrawing the United States from foreign involvements abroad or using military power to triumph in disputes abroad. Henry Berger, in essays in David Horowitz, ed., *Containment and Revolution* ° (1967), and in Thomas G. Paterson, ed., *Cold War Critics* ° (1971), contends that the most prominent of the isolationists in the early postwar years offered a substantial critique of overextending American power.

GEORGE KATEB

Kennedy As Statesman

INTRODUCTION

Since John F. Kennedy's tragic death in November of 1963, liberal
politicians have vied with one another to wear his mantle, and his
name has become a symbol of hope and vitality, of toughness and
idealism, of compassion and wisdom. Beginning with his presidential campaign in 1960, Kennedy demonstrated the power to excite
the public and mobilize the energies of the young. He capitalized
on vague discontents in promising the nation renewed purpose,
economic growth, a stronger and more flexible military defense,
and a restoration of prestige in the Cold War—in short, a New
Frontier.

　　During the campaign, Kennedy had pledged vigorous domestic reform, but his slim plurality over Richard Nixon forced him to
take a more cautious approach when in office. Even so, he could

FROM George Kateb, "Kennedy as Statesman," *Commentary*, XLIV (June, 1966), pp. 54–
60. Copyright © 1966 by the American Jewish Committee. Reprinted from *Commentary*, by permission.

neither coerce nor cajole Congress to do his bidding in domestic
affairs, particularly in regard to civil rights legislation and the tax
cut. It was not Kennedy but his successor who would see enacted
many of the programs that the departed President had initiated during his brief period in office. His contemporaries, however, believe
that Kennedy left his mark not in domestic policy, but in foreign
policy. The "disasters" of the first year—the Bay of Pigs invasion
and the Berlin Wall crisis—were followed by "triumphs"—the
Cuban missile crisis, the nuclear test ban treaty, and the détente
with the Soviet Union.

It is Kennedy's foreign policy that George Kateb, who
teaches political theory at Amherst College, critically examines in
the following essay, written in 1966, when the Vietnam conflict
had begun to drain American dollars and lives at an alarming
rate. Kateb, unlike many of Kennedy's liberal admirers, stresses
the defects and questionable achievements of Kennedy's foreign
policy. He points out that the Kennedy administration unwisely
reversed Eisenhower's decision and implemented counterinsurgency, thus making possible large-scale American intervention in
Vietnam.

Citing Kennedy's own words, Kateb also raises serious questions about whether the President's response to the presence of
Russian missiles was necessary, since the balance of military
power was not actually threatened. In defense of Kennedy, it can be
pointed out that the missiles in Cuba trapped him in the cruel dilemma inherent in the theory of nuclear deterrence. This theory
claims that deterrence is effective only if the enemy believes that a
nation possesses the necessary weapons and means of delivery
and, just as important, that it has the will to resort to nuclear warfare. It was Kennedy's will, his credibility, that seemed threatened
by the installation of Soviet missiles in Cuba. To preserve credibility in order to prevent war, a nation may actually have to run a serious risk of war. There is another dimension to the missile crisis
that Kateb overlooks. How candid in spirit and words was President
Kennedy in his talk to the nation on the evening of October 22,
1962, when he reported that the Soviet Union had surreptitiously
overturned the balance of power and planted "offensive" weapons
ninety miles from Florida? If the danger was not as imminent as he
suggested, did he not mislead the nation?

The missile crisis, the Bay of Pigs, and the armed intervention in Vietnam raise profound questions about the nature of and
restraints on presidential power. The conduct of American foreign
policy leaves to the President great discretion that allows him to
bypass constitutional requirements. Without formal congressional
approval, he can plunge the nation into armed conflict—as Truman did in Korea and Kennedy and Johnson did in Vietnam. The
dangers of expanded presidential authority in the Cold War have
come to seem so serious in recent years that historians are begin-

ning to reappraise their criteria for measuring the success of Presidents, and some have recently expressed doubts that vigorous action in foreign affairs necessarily constitutes evidence of greatness. Kateb, though never explicitly raising these issues, seems to share these doubts.

*T*he dream of the political outsider is to know why men of state are doing what they do. There are, of course, some resources available to the diligent student: he can rely on the New York *Times* for an accumulation of indispensable detail, he can infer motive on the basis of a general theory of political behavior, he can immerse himself in the reading of history for the sake of plucking rough analogies from the inexhaustible record of the crimes and follies of mankind. But a nagging sense of insufficiency is always there. Detail, inference, analogy do not quite add up to the real thing. How can the student be sure that he is not catching at shadows, that he is not lost in the maze of his own imaginings, that he does not see a plot where there is only confusion or an impulse where there is in fact calculation? To be sure, his occupational hazard is paranoid suspicion, dirty-mindedness, motive-mongering; and his self-administered therapy is to take refuge in the epilogues to *War and Peace,* or in a desperate skepticism, or finally in an acceptance of things at face value. The lust to know what really is happening, however, cannot be checked. The voices of consolation or derision will inevitably be drowned out. The truth must be pursued. He will cling to the belief—perhaps it is a delusion—that secrecy is the one great obstacle between him and his goal, which is to perceive the time in which he lives.

So it is with enormous expectations that one opens the pages of the two recent books on John F. Kennedy by Theodore Sorensen [*Kennedy* (Harper & Row, 1966)] and Arthur Schlesinger, Jr. [*A Thousand Days* (Houghton Mifflin, 1966)]. Obviously, the whole truth will not be contained in them. Allowance must be made for tact and for national security. No single chronicler can have at his disposal more than a small amount of the raw ingredients of countless Presidential and bureaucratic decisions. For all that, both Sorensen and Schlesinger were close to the center; both would want to fill in the picture; Schlesinger especially could be expected to befriend the academic inquirer by letting him in on the daily actuality of the Kennedy administration. The events covered are not yet cold: we are now locked in their ramifications. Surely the intimate truth about the years 1961–1963 will make the immediate present more intelligible?

Neither book disappoints; each deepens our understanding of the Kennedy years. It would not be correct to say that any startling revelations are made; it may even be that a few vain readers will come away from these books (especially Sorensen's) with the feeling that there is nothing at all new in them, and that what the *Times* and a few journals had not already reported and disclosed, political shrewdness could supply. So be it. The fact remains that, at the very least, *Kennedy* and *A Thousand Days* put a great many things together, and by their very inclusiveness, permit a more definite sense of the recent past to emerge.

Truly, the sense that emerges is not the sense intended. The aim of both writers is naturally to praise—not indiscriminately, but for one main trait: newness. In the eyes of Sorensen and Schlesinger, Kennedy stood for a break with the past, and a break that was all to the good. He injected vitality into a stagnant nation, while striving to direct that vitality away from cold-war bellicosity, toward the deepest problems of the age, toward hunger, backwardness, and the craving for peace. Who can doubt that if it were only a question of Kennedy's abstract intention, this description of him would be perfectly accurate? What is so awful is that in case after case, as these two narratives (in spite of themselves) make clear, Kennedy's abstract intention gave way before pressures of one sort or another. Even more, Kennedy's initiative, in the absence of immediate pressures, was sometimes in direct contradiction to his abstract intention. To put the matter briefly: the break that Kennedy effected with the past resulted in an intensification of cold-war bellicosity, not in its lessening. Sometimes he acted deliberately; sometimes he acted as he did because he thought he could not act in any other way. The tendency of his actions, however, was to change the direction of Eisenhower's policy, and prepare the way for Johnson's activism. A good part of the story is found in these two books.

The story begins with the adoption of the so-called "McNamara strategy." This was a deliberate act of policy on the part of the Kennedy administration; a free choice, so to speak. It is certain that if Rockefeller had been President, the same strategy would have been adopted.[1] It is probable that if Nixon had been elected, he would have moved in the same direction as Kennedy. It is likely that only Stevenson, among the leading Democrats, would at least have tried, as President, to resist the adoption of the "McNamara strategy." Among the Republicans it had been, in fact, none other than Eisenhower who prevented its earlier acceptance, thereby causing the resignations of Ridgway, Gavin, and Maxwell Taylor. Which is to say that Kennedy's position represented no new departure in principle, but rather was faithful to widespread assumptions—assumptions shared by men wanting a more vigorous and extended American involvement in the struggle against Communism. From the very start of his administration, then, Kennedy was

---

[1] Sorensen says that in mid-1961, when McNamara's views were assuming final shape, Kennedy thought that Rockefeller was the most likely Republican opponent in 1964. "Nor was [Kennedy] unmindful of the fact that . . . Rockefeller . . . was criticizing the administration's complacency on civil defense in much the same terms Kennedy had applied to the 'missile gap' in earlier years."

determined to make American capacities more powerful because more refined, even though he sincerely believed, and had believed for a long time,
that the affairs of the world perhaps needed an altogether different approach.

The McNamara strategy was meant to repeal the principal military
theory of the Eisenhower administration, the doctrine of massive retaliation.
Under this doctrine, the Soviet Union was to be held directly responsible for
any Leninist coup or insurrection anywhere in the world, and would stand to
suffer an overwhelming nuclear attack as punishment for its imputed responsibility. Furthermore, the response to any Soviet conventional military move
would also be an overwhelming nuclear attack. The doctrine needs only to
be stated to be convicted of monstrous absurdity; but there were doubtless
numerous officials who accepted it in its full absurdity. It is impossible, however, to believe that either Eisenhower or Dulles ever took their own theory
literally. It may even be possible to believe that by talking about massive
retaliation, Eisenhower was indirectly saying two things. First, American
opposition to coups and insurrections would have to take essentially non-
military forms, like bribery, good works, economic pressure, and backstage
conspiracy. Second, the old cold war was over, and no overt Russian military move was foreseen. In any case, the development of American anti-
guerrilla forces and, more important, the buildup of conventional forces, in
the name of open American engagement, were ruled out. The costs were
prohibitive; the effort provocative; the consequences treacherously uncertain. Schlesinger says half in humor, "Eisenhower could never find the use
of local aggression to which nuclear warfare seemed a sensible response."
But the joke is now on Schlesinger.

Kennedy initiated the abandonment of that policy. He embraced, as
Schlesinger neatly puts it, ". . . the strong view taken by the service whose
mission, money and traditions were most threatened by the . . . doctrine
[of massive retaliation]—the Army." In his first months, he added six billion
dollars to the last Eisenhower military budget. A large fraction went to the
nuclear deterrent: McNamara was, and is, a firm believer in something called
"flexible response": nuclear weapons must be so diverse and sophisticated as
to permit selectivity and gradation in their use. This is another phantom, and
I need not chase it now. The important point is that great sums were allo-
cated to the buildup of anti-guerrilla and conventional forces. Sorensen gives
the rationale: ". . . if this country was to be able to confine a limited challenge to the local and non-nuclear level, without permitting a Communist
victory—then it was necessary to build our own non-nuclear forces to the
point where any aggressor would be confronted with the same poor choice
Kennedy wanted to avoid: humiliation or escalation. A limited Communist
conventional action, in short, could best be deterred by a capacity to respond
effectively in kind." The only trouble with this rationale, in regard to Russia,
is that the buildup of conventional forces was much more a provocation than
a deterrence. Who could take seriously the possibility that Russia would in-

vade Western Europe or the Near East—who except the army and its intellectuals? What was there to deter? The trouble with this rationale, in regard
to revolutionary movements, is that the inability of conventional and anti-
guerrilla forces to deter would soon become apparent, and America would be
tempted to use its strength to destroy what it could not deter. The counterrevolutionary career would be launched in earnest, with no end in sight. A
task more huge, more hopeless, could not be conceived. The view of Communism as a monolithic force was retained from the old theory of massive
retaliation; but now the ambition of meeting it in all its forms became entirely serious. Containment became a universal and undiscriminating principle of foreign policy. The threats to American security were seen as infinite.

Kennedy's vision of the world comes out most clearly in his conversations with Khrushchev at Vienna in June 1961. Schlesinger's report is fuller
than Sorensen's, though Sorensen's is also quite valuable. Tension over Berlin, the Laotian crisis, and the Bay of Pigs episode were the background to
the conference. But the great theme was the balance of power throughout the
world, and the relation of "wars of national liberation" to that balance. Deli-
cately but insistently, Kennedy tried to get Khrushchev to see the world as he
saw it. War between the two great powers was out of the question; the use of
nuclear weapons was too terrible to contemplate. But each great power had
vital interests which had to be respected; let there be no miscalculation concerning the determination of either side to protect its vital interests. The effort to impose Communism by force of arms in any country would obviously
imperil the balance of power in the world. The United States and the Soviet
Union would compete peacefully, and allow the uncommitted world to
choose freely its way of life.

Obviously, Khrushchev did not accept the responsibility that Kennedy
seemed to wish to thrust on him. Sorensen paraphrases his reply: "Was the
President saying that Communism should exist only in Communist countries,
that its development elsewhere would be regarded by the U.S. as a hostile act
by the Soviet Union? The United States wants the U.S.S.R., he said, to sit like
a schoolboy with hands on the table, but there is no immunization against
ideas. . . . [Khrushchev] returned time and again to the thesis that the Soviet Union could not be held responsible for every spontaneous uprising or
Communist trend. . . . Castro was not a Communist but U.S. policy could
make him one. . . ."

It is apparent from the reports that Khrushchev alternated between
two responses. Either the Soviet Union could not be held responsible for the
surge of revolutionary discontent throughout the world, or the Soviet Union
could not be expected to withhold aid, when asked, to insurgent movements
and new regimes. It is hard to see what else Khrushchev could have said: he
was, in effect, describing the role of the Soviet Union in world affairs analo-

gously to that of the United States. He nowhere said that the Soviet Union would export revolution in the old Trotskyist sense: not by Soviet arms, or by Soviet instigation in an otherwise tranquil situation. That there would be uncontrolled revolutionary movements could not be denied; but Soviet responsibility could not possibly extend to them.

Kennedy's words at Vienna, and the policies he followed, show that he accepted the view that all insurgencies in which Communists take part are inspired by and directed from Moscow. In turn, the triumph of any such insurgency represents a shift in the balance of power between the great power-blocs, a defeat for the West, a serious impairment of its security. As Sorensen says, "The extent of U.S. commitment and of Communist power involvement differed from one to the other, but the dilemma facing John Kennedy in each one was essentially the same: how to disengage the Russians from the 'liberation' movement and prevent a Communist military conquest without precipitating a major Soviet-American military confrontation." The way out of the seeming dilemma was to increase the American anti-guerrilla and conventional capacity.

Sooner or later that capacity would be used. Political moves are determined by the means on hand as much as by anything else: men do all they can. One would like to praise Kennedy unreservedly for apparently limiting American military involvement in the Laotian crisis of 1961–62 to dramatic but empty gestures, despite intense pressure put on him by his military advisers to land American troops in Laos. (Sorensen says his "posture . . . combined bluff with real determination in proportions he made known to *no one*. . . .) But the praise must be qualified. First, Kennedy was strongly inclined to intervene: he saw the Laotian crisis as a manifestation of the world Communist conspiracy rather than as the product of local antagonisms, in which local Communists played a part; and he thought that a Communist victory in Laos would imperil the security of the United States and its major allies.[2] Second, the reason for staying out of Laos was, in part, the Bay of Pigs affair. " 'Thank God the Bay of Pigs happened when it did,' he would say to me [Sorensen] in September. . . . 'Otherwise we'd be in Laos by now— and that would be a hundred times worse.' " Kennedy told Schlesinger the same thing. It took one fiasco to prevent another. As it turned out, the Pathet Lao stopped short of total victory: Khrushchev, appalled at the prospect of American military intervention, managed to police an insurgency he had no part in starting and little part in sustaining. By acting as he did, Khrushchev must have lent credibility to the view that all insurgencies were his to turn on and off. The nature of his act was not seen for what it was.

---

[2] There was also a political consideration. Schlesinger says, "Kennedy told Rostow that Eisenhower could stand the political consequences of Dien Bien Phu and the expulsion of the West from Vietnam in 1954 because the blame fell on the French; 'I can't take a 1954 defeat today.' "

The stage was set for a reversal of Eisenhower's policy in Vietnam. In May 1961, Vice-President Johnson reported to Kennedy, according to Schlesinger, ". . . the basic decision in Southeast Asia is here. We must decide whether to help these countries to the best of our ability or throw in the towel in the area and pull back our defenses to San Francisco and a 'Fortress America' concept." In October, General Maxwell Taylor made a three-week visit to Vietnam and urged positive action on Kennedy. Once again, Kennedy was induced to see a local struggle as an element in a greater struggle. Schlesinger says, ". . . given the truculence of Moscow, the Berlin crisis and the resumption of nuclear testing, the President unquestionably felt that an American retreat in Asia might upset the whole world balance." Sorensen says, "What was needed, Kennedy agreed with his advisers, was a major counterinsurgency effort—the first ever mounted by this country. . . . Formally, Kennedy never made a final negative decision on troops. In typical Kennedy fashion, he made it difficult for any of the pro-intervention advocates to charge him privately with weakness." Gradually, almost insensibly, the American commitment grew and became irreversible. This is not to say that Kennedy would necessarily have permitted the expansion of American force which Johnson has permitted. It is impossible to speculate; one must simply acknowledge that by the end of 1963 "only" 15,500 American soldiers were in Vietnam. Nevertheless, it is hard to imagine Johnson's commitment having been made without Kennedy's prior one, and without the wholehearted support Kennedy gave to the development of American non-nuclear capability—to the McNamara strategy. When anti-guerrilla activity fails (as it must in conditions like those in Vietnam), a next step can be taken. There will be many to say that it must be taken. Guerrilla warfare will be changed into conventional warfare, so that American technical superiority can be brought into play.

The idea that the power of the West and the Communist bloc were in a balance that required constant vigilance to be preserved drove Kennedy not only to look on insurgencies as suitable for American military involvement, but also led him to invest every direct Soviet-American problem with a high degree of passion. The passion was of a special sort: an intense desire to avoid giving the impression of weakness. Let it be noted that this desire is not the same as the desire to give the impression of overbearing strength. No one could ever accuse Kennedy of enjoying the role of bully. The matter is more sad, more complicated. In his early book, *Why England Slept,* he expressed the belief that democracies were inherently pacific and self-absorbed, and that they had to have "shocks" to keep them alert to the dangers surrounding them. Being alert, they would not give the appearance of weakness; they would thereby dissuade aggressors from rashness. In line with this aim, Kennedy wanted to raise taxes in 1961 in order to enhance a sense of sacrifice and impress on Americans the gravity of world affairs. His ill-considered support of fallout shelters was part of the same purpose. More than that, all one can briefly say is that Kennedy seems to have had a naturally agonistic conception of world politics. He did not look for fights; rather he thought that they were inevitable, that crisis was the normality of international relations, even in the nuclear age. (He shocked Stevenson by referring to disarmament proposals as "propaganda.") Beyond the conflict of aims that always exists between nations, Kennedy saw a contest of wills, an almost formal antagonism in which the prize was pride at least as much as any substantive outcome. In discussing Dean Acheson's advice during the Berlin crisis of 1961, Schlesinger says, "[Khrushchev's] object, as Acheson saw it, was not to rectify a local situation but to test the general American will to resist; his hope was that, by making us back down on a sacred commitment, he could shatter our world power and influence. This was a simple conflict of wills, and, until it was resolved, any effort to negotiate the Berlin issue per se would be fatal. . . . For Acheson the test of will seemed almost an end in itself rather than a means to a political end." Schlesinger and Sorensen both make it clear that the tone of Kennedy's military advisers was practically identical to Acheson's. What is so troubling is that Kennedy's reasons for policy, on numerous occasions, were similar. They prominently included the wish to appear to be accepting a challenge. He was inclined to define the world as the "realists" defined it, though possessed of a self-doubt and a magnanimity foreign to them. Fortunately, one could probably say that the United States under Kennedy never yielded in a contest of wills, was never bested. But the precedents perhaps established, the opportunities perhaps missed, are not easily dismissed.

It would be heavy-handed to make much of the Bay of Pigs affair. Kennedy regretted the failure; he may even have regretted the effort. (The one time Sorensen raises his voice in censure of Kennedy is when he is reporting this event.) But the analysis made by Sorensen of Kennedy's mood before he allowed the expedition to get under way is fairly depressing: "He did not regard Castro as a direct threat to the United States, but neither did he see why he should 'protect' Castro from Cubans embittered by the fact that their revolution had been sold out to the Communists. Cancellation of the plan at that stage, he feared, would be interpreted as an admission that Castro ruled with popular support and would be around to harass Latin America for many years to come. His campaign pledges to aid anti-Castro rebels had not forced his hand, as some suspected, but he did feel that his disapproval of the plan would be a show of weakness inconsistent with his general stance." Anxiety was piled on anxiety, but the sharpest of them all was the fear of having himself or his country thought weak. Appearances were accorded great weight; the United States was constantly having to prove itself. But why? Who was in a position to put this country on trial, who doubted its resolve, who was ignorant of its strength, who, indeed, was not terrified of its strength (the Soviet Union and China included)?

Again, in the case of the Berlin crisis in 1961, the same anxieties are disclosed. After a while, it becomes hard to keep on worrying about Berlin; any problem loses some of its reality through continuous exposure. One does not mean to be callous; but is a mutually satisfactory settlement out of the reach of human wit? Or is the problem useful to all parties as a source of manipulable tension? Before the U-2 incident, it seemed as if Eisenhower and Khrushchev were about to reach some accord. No accord, of course, was reached. Kennedy inherited Khrushchev's dissatisfaction, and the rigid incompetence of the imbecile East German regime. Schlesinger informs us that Kennedy "used to wonder later what had gone wrong in the spring of 1961. He thought at times that the March and May messages calling for an increased American defense effort might have sounded too threatening." The intended deterrence to crisis had helped bring one about. What, now, to do? Kennedy's advisers, led by Acheson, as we have already seen, refused to countenance any negotiations: the possibility that Khrushchev had perhaps a troublesome situation on his hands was not granted. The exact status-quo had to be maintained; some alternative to staying put on the old terms or getting out in a humiliating way was disregarded. Kennedy was determined, Sorensen says, ". . . to make [the Berlin crisis] not only a question of West Berlin's rights—on which U.S., British, French, and West German policies were not always in accord [3]—but a question of direct Soviet-American confrontation over a shift in the balance of power." The bondage to the cold war could not be relinquished. The result was, once more, dramatic gesture: ". . . draft calls were doubled, tripled, enlistments were extended and the Congress promptly and unanimously authorized the mobilization of up to 250,000 men. . . ." The Wall was built, the crisis faded. Only the people of East Berlin had lost, securely imprisoned as they were now to become. It will not do to place, as Sorensen does, the full responsibility for the stiffness of American policy on the inertia or philo-Germanism of the State Department. Kennedy had other sources of opinion—for example, Sorensen and Schlesinger. In reflecting on the crisis, Sorensen cannot forbear from remarking, ". . . no one knew when either side, convinced that the other would back down, might precipitate a situation from which neither could back down." Only flexibility, only an avoidance of seeing one's total position implicated in every situation, only a willingness to give up the ideology of confrontation, could help to insure that intolerable situations would not emerge. The Berlin crisis uselessly impaired Soviet-American relations, and prevented (temporarily, to be sure) certain kinds of cooperation with the Soviets.

The American decision of March 1962 to resume atmospheric testing of nuclear weapons is yet another example of the politics of appearances. Russia had itself resumed testing in September 1961, and had made, Sorensen says, "important weapons progress." That is, at the time they resumed, they must

---

[3] How sly Sorensen sometimes is!—G.K.

have felt that the nuclear buildup implemented by McNamara had weakened their security; the arms race had taken another leap forward. As both Sorensen and Schlesinger make clear, Kennedy's decision to resume derived primarily from considerations having little to do with American military needs. Sorensen says, "Nearly all the principal advisers involved favored resuming atmospheric tests (though a few days before the tests began, McNamara startled Rusk and Bundy at lunch by suggesting that they were not really necessary)." Schlesinger says, "Jerome Wiesner maintained in December that it remained basically a political question: 'While these tests would certainly contribute to our military strength, they are not critical or even very important to our over-all military posture.' " Schlesinger indicates that Kennedy agreed more or less. Sorensen says that Kennedy ". . . still had doubts about the value of his test series (although not about the necessity of his decision). . . . Privately he speculated that fears of Soviet nuclear test progress might have been akin to previous fears of a Soviet 'bomber gap' and 'missile gap.' . . ." But still the order to resume was given. In reply to Harold Macmillan's impassioned plea to avoid resumption, Kennedy said (in Sorensen's paraphrase) that the Soviets ". . . would be more likely to attribute such a decision to weakness rather than goodwill. . . ." To Adlai Stevenson, he was equally emphatic: "What choice did we have? . . . [Khrushchev] has had a succession of apparent victories—space, Cuba, [the Berlin Wall]. . . . He wants to give out the feeling that he has us on the run. . . ." Feeling challenged, fearing to be thought fearful, Kennedy decided to do what he hated to do, and had little faith in. He could not escape the tyranny of appearances.

The Cuban missile crisis, the greatest of all crises in the Kennedy years, also contained this same obsession. Kennedy's most desperate anguish came at a moment when he felt that appearances were not to be endured; his most stunning victory came at a moment when he succeeded in altering appearances. It would be foolish to reduce the crisis to this single element of appearances; but to ignore its possibly *preponderant* role would also be foolish.

In a wonderfully lucid exposition, Sorensen describes the several theories suggested by the President's advisers to explain Khrushchev's move. (One of the most fascinating small aspects of this affair was the response of the Chinese, who accused Khrushchev of "adventurism" in trying to place missiles in Cuba—and of cowardice for removing them.) The theories mentioned by Sorensen are (1) that Khrushchev was testing the will of the United States, and hoped to make the United States look weak, irresolute, and faithless to its sworn commitments; (2) that Khrushchev hoped to induce us to invade Cuba in order to disgrace us in the eyes of the world; (3) that Khrushchev was genuinely concerned for Cuba's security,[4] (4) that Khrushchev

---

[4] Sorensen says, "It should be noted that the Soviet Union stuck throughout to this position. Mikoyan claimed in a conversation with the President weeks after it was all over that the weapons were purely defensive, that they had been justified by threats of invasion voiced by Richard Nixon and Pentagon generals, and that the Soviets intended to inform

was bargaining, and hoped to trade off the Cuban bases for a Berlin settle-ment or American bases overseas; and (5) that Khrushchev was desirous of improving his strategic nuclear position. Sorensen says that Kennedy's own analysis ". . . regarded the third and fifth theories as offering likely but in-sufficient motives and he leaned most strongly to the first." That is, Kennedy interpreted the move as primarily an affront to the United States, a calcu-lated probe of weakness, a contest of wills. He increasingly insisted to his ad-visers that the entire matter be defined as a Soviet-American confrontation. Irrespective of interpretation, however, Kennedy insisted that the missiles "would have to be removed by the Soviets in response to direct American action." In a television interview on December 16, 1962, to which Sorensen makes only a brief allusion, Kennedy gave a splendidly candid account of his reasons for taking any risk to prevail. He said, ". . . [the Russians] were planning in November to open to the world the fact that they had these mis-siles so close to the United States; not that they were intending to fire them, because if they were going to get into a nuclear struggle, they have their own missiles in the Soviet Union. But it would have politically changed the bal-ance of power. It would have appeared to, and appearances contribute to reality."

Harold Macmillan could wonder "what all the fuss was about"; after all, Europe was used to living under the nuclear threat. He seems to have missed the point, namely that there was no military threat but instead a threat to America's reputation as a world power. Largely for the sake of great-power reputation (though other reasons, including the reputation of the Democratic party, figured), the world was brought close to a terrible event. (One assumes that this is so, but *The Penkovskiy Papers* say that Kennedy knew the Soviet nuclear capacity to be unready for action, and that Kennedy was therefore quite free to be as tough as he wanted and not incur grave risks.) Appearances do contribute to reality: reputation for power is a source of power: you are if they think you are. But was America's reputation so fragile? The irony is that America's very strength permitted Kennedy to act out of fear of being thought weak. Its very strength, however, should have permitted him to mitigate this fear. He did not carry his consciousness of American power far enough—as far as Eisenhower, before him, had carried it. And a relentless pursuit of right appearances can be catastrophic. In this instance, the pursuit was not catastrophic, but what guarantee was there? Kennedy later told Sorensen that "The odds that the Soviets would go all the way to war seemed to him then 'somewhere between one out of three and even.'" A nuclear war to eliminate a nuclear installation—can such thoughts be entertained?

---

the United States of these weapons immediately after the elections to prevent the matter from affecting the American political campaign." Sorensen acknowledges that the admin-istration in 1962 had been ". . . readying a plan of military action in the knowledge that an internal revolt, a Berlin grab or some other action might someday require it. . . ."

The alternative was not mortified acceptance, but negotiation before the crisis escaped control. Stevenson, according to Schlesinger, proposed the removal of the missiles in exchange for a UN presence in Cuba, an American non-invasion guarantee, and relinquishment of the base at Guantanamo. This program struck Kennedy as premature, and some of his advisers ". . . felt strongly that the thought of negotiations at this point would be taken as an admission of the moral weakness of our case and the military weakness of our posture." The blockade was declared; unless Khrushchev backed down, ". . . the United States would have had no real choice but to take action against Cuba the next week." The implications of invasion were understood: Kennedy said that "If we had invaded Cuba . . . I am sure the Soviets would have acted. They would have to, just as we would have to. I think there are certain compulsions on any major power." Khrushchev did back down, and was freely granted a guarantee against the invasion of Cuba. But he did back down; he refused to breach the blockade; he agreed to withdraw the missiles. How is his decision to be assessed? Was it cowardice or was it sanity? Did he not also win a victory of sorts in the realm of appearances by emerging as a champion of rationality? As such, did not his reputation improve, and indirectly with it, the power of the Soviet Union?

Redefinition of radical revolution as Muscovite conspiracy, redefinition of every problem as a great-power confrontation affecting the global balance of power, the adoption of the McNamara strategy in order to have the means to act on the basis of these redefinitions—can this be all that Kennedy bequeathed us in foreign policy? The answer is, of course, no. Who can repress nostalgia for those days in late 1962 and early 1963, when Kennedy, abetted by Pope John and Khrushchev, seemed to recapture the spirit of his inaugural address and of many of his earlier speeches? Surely this was the real Kennedy who, hitherto distracted from his mission and victimized by the foreign-policy establishment, had finally struggled free. The Cuban missile crisis may have petrified Khrushchev; it seems to have altered Kennedy. The very next morning after Khrushchev's capitulation, Kennedy told Schlesinger that ". . . he was afraid that people would conclude from this experience that all we had to do in dealing with the Russians was to be tough and they would collapse." After a shrewd analysis of the affair, he went on to say, "They were in the wrong and knew it. So, when we stood firm, they had to back down. But this doesn't mean at all that they would back down when they felt that they were in the right and had vital interests involved." But these words do not capture the full transformation. After the Cuban crisis, Schlesinger says, Kennedy's feelings ". . . underwent a qualitative change . . . a world in which nations threatened each other with nuclear weapons now seemed to him not just an irrational but an intolerable and impossible world." The proof of this sentiment came in the form of strenuous negotiation to produce the Nuclear Test Ban Treaty. The fact is that much of the strenuousness was spent on Kennedy's own military advisers. Once again, the passion for right appearances was exhibited by the Chiefs of Staff. Maxwell Taylor told the Senate Foreign Relations Committee that "the most serious reservations of the military had to do with the fear of a euphoria in the West which will eventually reduce our vigilance." Only this time Kennedy, after making some concessions to the military, rejected the logic of appearances and went ahead with the treaty.

The real victory that Kennedy won in Cuba was over his own advisers. Some would like to say that he had softened up Khrushchev: that a show of strength and determination, on such a scale and under such trying conditions, had so demoralized the Russian leader that he had no choice but to feign moderation and accept Kennedy's overtures of peace. It would be equally plausible to say that Kennedy's show of strength and determination had (for the time being) won him so much prestige and brought him so much self-confidence that he could at last prevail even over his bellicose aides, and pursue a policy that he (and Khrushchev) wanted from the beginning. Not out of a good heart, but out of cold prudence, out of dread of American power, Khrushchev had been straining to be compliant. Success in Cuba accidentally made it possible for Kennedy to take advantage of Khrushchev's wishes. Kennedy's sense of reality shone through. If he had lived, would he have imposed that sense on the men around him? One wants to believe that he would.

SUGGESTED READING

Literature on the Kennedy administration is already substantial. The two most important books are quite flattering and by assistants of the late President: Theodore Sorensen's *Kennedy* ° (1965), and Arthur M. Schlesinger, Jr.'s *A Thousand Days* ° (1965). On the 1960 election, see Theodore White, *The Making of the President, 1960* ° (1961); the invaluable analysis by Philip E. Converse, Angus Campbell, *et al.*, "Stability and Change in 1960: A Reinstating Election," *American Political Science Review*, LV (June 1961); V. O. Key, Jr.'s "Interpreting Election Results," in Paul T. David, ed., *The Presidential Election and Transition, 1960–1961* (1961); and Russel Middleton's "The Civil Rights Issue and Presidential Voting among Southern Negroes and Whites," *Social Forces*, XL (Mar. 1962).

On national economic policy, see the useful book by the chairman of Kennedy's Council of Economic Advisers, Walter Heller, *New Dimensions in Political Economy* ° (1966). Herbert Stein, a Republican economist, offers insights into the relation of politics and economics in Kennedy's fiscal policies in *The Fiscal Revolution in America* (1969), Chapters 15–17. Less helpful and more technical is E. Ray Canterbery's *Economics on a New Frontier* (1968). See also the partisan defense by Seymour Harris, *Economics of the Kennedy*

Years (1964). Useful material by another of Kennedy's economic advisers, James Tobin, is contained in his *National Economic Policy* (1966). Two books on business-government relations are Jim F. Heath's *John F. Kennedy and the Business Community* (1969), and Hobart Rowen's *The Free Enterprisers: Kennedy, Johnson, and the Business Establishment* ° (1964). On the steel crisis of 1962, the best book is Grant McConnell's *Steel and the Presidency* ° (1962). In *The Real Voice* (1964), Richard Harris presents a critical account of Kennedy's role in the passage of drug legislation in 1962.

By 1963 President Kennedy regarded civil rights for blacks as his main domestic problem. Howard Zinn, in *SNCC: The New Abolitionists* ° (1964), attacked the administration for failing to protect civil rights workers; Burke Marshall, Assistant Attorney General for Civil Rights, defended the administration in *Federalism and Civil Rights* (1964). Edwin Guthman, in *We Band of Brothers* (1971), tells of his experiences in the Justice Department, working with Robert F. Kennedy. See also Victor Navasky's *Kennedy Justice* (1971), and Alexander Bickel's *Politics and the Warren Court* (1965), pp. 49–115.

The best single volume on Kennedy's foreign policy is unfortunately still Roger Hilsman's *To Move a Nation* ° (1967). Hilsman, an adviser to the President, served in the Defense and State Departments. Jerome Levinson and Juan de Onis, in *The Alliance that Lost Its Way* ° (1970), conclude that the Alliance for Progress failed. Kennedy's ambassador to India, John Kenneth Galbraith, recounts his diplomatic adventures in *Ambassador's Journal* (1969). Chester Bowles, in *Promises to Keep* (1971), tells about his short and unhappy tenure as Under Secretary of State. See also Arthur Dean's *The Test Ban and Disarmament* ° (1966) and William Kaufman's *The McNamara Strategy* ° (1964). American policy toward Cuba is severely criticized by Robert Scheer and Maurice Zeitlin in *Cuba: Tragedy in our Hemisphere* ° (1963) and generally defended by Theodore Draper in *Castro's Revolution, Myths and Realities* ° (1962) and in *Castroism, Theory and Practice* ° (1965). Haynes Johnson, in *The Bay of Pigs: The Leaders' Story* (1964), and Karl E. Meyer and Tad Szulc, in *The Cuban Invasion* ° (1962), cover the events of the Bay of Pigs.

The Cuban missile crisis is perhaps the crucial episode of the Kennedy administration. A journalistic narrative is provided by Elie Abel, *The Missile Crisis* (1966). See also Robert F. Kennedy's memoir, *Thirteen Days* ° (1969). Arnold Horelick argues the strategic importance of the Cuban missiles in "The Cuban Missile Crisis: An Analysis of Soviet Calculations and Behavior," *World Politics*, XVI (Apr. 1964). Horelick's analysis is disputed by Roger Hagan and Bart Bernstein, in "Military Value of Missiles in Cuba," *Bulletin of the Atomic Scientists*, XIX (Feb. 1963). See also Graham Allison's "Conceptual Models and the Cuban Missile Crisis," *American Political Science Review*, LXIII (1969). Some of the literature on the crisis has been collected in *The Cuban Missile Crisis*,° edited by Robert Divine (1971).

LESLIE H. GELB

Vietnam: The System Worked

INTRODUCTION

Vietnam proved a major embarrassment for American liberals. Liberal Presidents, after all, bore primary responsibility for the tragedy, and many well-known liberals had helped to plan and promote the war. When the failure of U.S. policy became apparent in the late 1960's, most pro-war liberals recanted. Vietnam, they now said, had been a mistake, though one arising out of no malevolent purpose or misconceived grand strategy. The classic liberal explanation for American involvement was Arthur Schlesinger's *The Bitter Heritage* (1967). "In retrospect," Schlesinger wrote,

> Vietnam is a triumph of the politics of inadvertence. We have achieved our present entanglement, not after due and deliberate consideration, but through a series of small decisions. . . . Each step in

FROM Leslie H. Gelb, "Vietnam: The System Worked," *Foreign Policy* (Summer 1971), pp. 140–67. Copyright © 1971 by National Affairs, Inc. Reprinted by permission.

the deepening of the American commitment was reasonably regarded as the last that would be necessary. Yet, in retrospect, each step led only to the next, until we find ourselves entrapped today in that nightmare of American strategists, a land war in Asia—a war which no President, including President Johnson, desired or intended. The Vietnam story is a tragedy without villains.

In variations on this general theme, some formerly pro-war liberals stress the responsibility of the military in leading liberal administrations to increase the nation's involvement in Vietnam but emphasize that the military simply erred in its estimates.

Leslie Gelb, the Defense Department official who directed the compilation of the famous Pentagon Papers for Secretary McNamara, has recently offered a variant of the liberal interpretation of U.S. involvement in Vietnam. Gelb contends that the Presidents who made the war were not moral fanatics bent on victory over communism. Each President did indeed increase U.S. involvement by a series of small decisions, but each one acted with few illusions and knew what he was doing. The Presidents knew that the long-range prospects in Vietnam were not good and sought only to buy time to avoid defeat. Defeat, they believed, would weaken America's overall position in international affairs and invite politically damaging charges at home of softness on communism. Gelb portrays American Presidents as pragmatic and moderate politicians, taking minimum steps not to win the war but to stave off ruin. Until midway through Lyndon Johnson's presidency, Gelb says, the policy worked.

Gelb's view of presidential intentions in Vietnam does not easily fit the known facts. President Kennedy's policy is a case in point. Thanks to memoirs, Gelb's own Pentagon Papers, and the exhaustive researches of Ralph Stavins (see *Washington Plans an Aggressive War* [1971]), we have a reasonably good grasp on Kennedy's Vietnam policy. For all Presidents, victory has meant only one thing—securing the permanence of the noncommunist government in South Vietnam. This victory was Kennedy's objective, and he sought it by means of gradual escalation. Escalation would stiffen the will to resist in the South and, more importantly, convey to the North the warning that further resistance risked worse punishment. When the North bowed to superior force, the task of saving the South would be achievable. Kennedy was less worried about the domestic political consequences of failure than he was about the probable unwillingness of the public to support military assistance to the repressive Diem regime of South Vietnam. Kennedy, therefore, chose to fight a "private war," whose true military character was hidden from his own people. When Walt Whitman Rostow and General Maxwell Taylor proposed in October 1961, that the U.S. send 8,000 combat troops to Vietnam to bolster Diem, Kennedy demurred. To avoid public scrutiny, he

instead dispatched small groups of "advisers" whose numbers
grew to 16,500 by 1963. Contrary to the government's assurances
to American citizens, these troops were actively engaged in combat operations. Moreover, the U.S. was secretly sponsoring guerrilla raids and amphibious landings against North Vietnam. However reluctant he was to fight in Vietnam, Kennedy chose to do
so in the conviction that it was right policy and that victory was
eventually possible.

The chief weakness in liberal analyses of Vietnam, according to radicals, is the tendency to view U.S. intervention there as
an aberration. Intervention against leftist revolutions, the radicals
contend, has been characteristic of American foreign policy
since the end of the Second World War. Truman gave aid to the
Nationalist Chinese until 1949 in their civil war against the communists, assisted the counterrevolution in Greece, and helped
put down the Huk insurgency in the Philippines. Under Eisenhower the United States covertly aided in the overthrow of leftist
regimes in Iran and Guatemala, landed Marines in Lebanon to
quiet unrest in the Middle East, and overthrew a neutralist government in Laos. Kennedy tried unsuccessfully to remove Castro
from Cuba by force, engaged in a sophisticated intervention
against the left in the Congo, sent U.S. Special Forces to assist
in defeating guerrillas in Colombia, and succeeded in bringing
down a Marxist premier in British Guiana through the machina-
tions of the CIA. Before President Johnson openly sent combat
troops to save South Vietnam, he sent troops into the Dominican
Republic to prevent a left-wing victory in the civil war there.
American intervention in Vietnam fits a consistent pattern of
American foreign policy and differed from other intervention
only in that it occasioned disaster. Policy-makers in the postwar era have viewed left-wing revolutions anywhere as inimical
to American security, dangerous to the American economy, and
contrary to American principles. As the champion of the liberal
ideology in world politics, America has used economic aid, military equipment, and soldiers to extinguish leftist revolutions in
the Third World. Viewed in this context, involvement in Vietnam
is hardly an isolated mistake requiring special explanation. Instead, what is necessary, according to radicals, is an analysis
of the ideological and social bases for the belief by America's
leaders that left-wing revolutions, even in remote parts of the
world, threaten the American system. Is the leaders' belief, radicals ask, an astute or a flawed judgment about the kind of world
that must exist in order to maintain the security and prosperity
of this system?

The story of United States policy toward Vietnam is either far
better or far worse than generally supposed. Our Presidents and most of

those who influenced their decisions did not stumble step by step into Vietnam, unaware of the quagmire. U.S. involvement did not stem from a failure to foresee consequences.

Vietnam was indeed a quagmire, but most of our leaders knew it. Of course there were optimists and periods where many were genuinely optimistic. But those periods were infrequent and short-lived and were invariably followed by periods of deep pessimism. Very few, to be sure, envisioned what the Vietnam situation would be like by 1968. Most realized, however, that "the light at the end of the tunnel" was very far away—if not finally unreachable. Nevertheless, our Presidents persevered. Given international compulsions to "keep our word" and "save face," domestic prohibitions against "losing," and their personal stakes, our leaders did "what was necessary," did it about the way they wanted, were prepared to pay the costs, and plowed on with a mixture of hope and doom. They "saw" no acceptable alternative.

Three propositions suggest why the United States became involved in Vietnam, why the process was gradual, and what the real expectations of our leaders were:

First, U.S. involvement in Vietnam is not mainly or mostly a story of step by step, inadvertent descent into unforeseen quicksand. It is primarily a story of why U.S. leaders considered that it was vital not to lose Vietnam by force to Communism. Our leaders believed Vietnam to be vital not for itself, but for what they thought its "loss" would mean internationally and domestically. Previous involvement made further involvement more unavoidable, and, to this extent, commitments were inherited. But judgments of Vietnam's "vitalness"—beginning with the Korean War—were sufficient in themselves to set the course for escalation.

Second, our Presidents were never actually seeking a military victory in Vietnam. They were doing only what they thought was minimally necessary at each stage to keep Indochina, and later South Vietnam, out of Communist hands. This forced our Presidents to be brakemen, to do less than those who were urging military victory and to reject proposals for disengagement. It also meant that our Presidents wanted a negotiated settlement without fully realizing (though realizing more than their critics) that a civil war cannot be ended by political compromise.

Third, our Presidents and most of their lieutenants were not deluded by optimistic reports of progress and did not proceed on the basis of wishful thinking about winning a military victory in South Vietnam. They recognized that the steps they were taking were not adequate to win the war and that unless Hanoi relented, they would have to do more and more. Their strategy was to persevere in the hope that their will to continue—if not the practical effects of their actions—would cause the Communists to relent.

Each of these propositions is explored below.

I. Ends: "We Can't Afford to Lose"

Those who led the United States into Vietnam did so with their eyes open, knowing why, and believing they had the will to succeed. The deepening involvement was not inadvertent, but mainly deductive. It flowed with sureness from the perceived stakes and attendant high objectives. U.S. policy displayed remarkable continuity. There were not dozens of likely "turning points." Each postwar President inherited previous commitments. Each extended these commitments. Each administration from 1947 to 1969 believed that it was necessary to prevent the loss of Vietnam and, after 1954, South Vietnam by force to the Communists. The reasons for this varied from person to person, from bureaucracy to bureaucracy, over time and in emphasis. For the most part, however, they had little to do with Vietnam itself. A few men argued that Vietnam had intrinsic strategic military and economic importance, but this view never prevailed. The reasons rested on broader international, domestic, and bureaucratic considerations.

Our leaders gave the *international* repercussions of "losing" as their dominant explicit reason for Vietnam's importance. During the Truman Administration, Indochina's importance was measured in terms of French-American relations and Washington's desire to rebuild France into the centerpiece of future European security. After the cold war heated up and after the fall of China, a French defeat in Indochina was also seen as a defeat for the policy of containment. In the Eisenhower years, Indochina became a "testing ground" between the Free World and Communism and the basis for the famous "domino theory" by which the fall of Indochina would lead to the deterioration of American security around the globe. President Kennedy publicly reaffirmed the falling domino concept. His primary concern, however, was for his "reputation for action" after the Bay of Pigs fiasco, the Vienna meeting with Khrushchev, and the Laos crisis, and in meeting the challenge of "wars of national liberation" by counterinsurgency warfare. Under President Johnson, the code word rationales became Munich, credibility, commitments and the U.S. word, a watershed test of wills with Communism, raising the costs of aggression, and the principle that armed aggression shall not be allowed to succeed. There is every reason to assume that our leaders actually believed what they said, given both the cold war context in which they were all reared and the lack of contradictory evidence.

With very few exceptions, then, our leaders since World War II saw Vietnam as a vital factor in alliance politics, U.S.-Soviet-Chinese relations, and deterrence. This was as true in 1950 and 1954 as it was in 1961 and 1965. The record of United States military and economic assistance to fight Communism in Indochina tells this story quite clearly. From 1945 to 1951, U.S. aid to France totaled over $3.5 billion. Without this, the French position in Indochina would have been untenable. By 1951, the U.S. was paying about 40 percent of the costs of the Indochina war and our share was going up. In 1954, it is estimated, U.S. economic and technical assistance amounted to $703 million and military aid totaled almost $2 billion. This added up to almost 80 percent of the total French costs. From 1955 to 1961, U.S. military aid averaged about $200 million per year. This made South Vietnam the second largest recipient of such aid, topped only by Korea. By 1963, South Vietnam ranked first among recipients of military assistance. In economic assistance, it followed only India and Pakistan.

The *domestic* repercussions of "losing" Vietnam probably were equally important in Presidential minds. Letting Vietnam "go Communist" was undoubtedly seen as:

· opening the floodgates to domestic criticism and attack for being "soft on Communism" or just plain soft;

· dissipating Presidential influence by having to answer these charges;

· alienating conservative leadership in the Congress and thereby endangering the President's legislative program;

· jeopardizing election prospects for the President and his party;

· undercutting domestic support for a "responsible" U.S. world role; and

· enlarging the prospects for a right-wing reaction—the nightmare of a McCarthyite garrison state.

U.S. domestic politics required our leaders to maintain both a peaceful world and one in which Communist expansion was stopped. In order to have the public support necessary to use force against Communism, our leaders had to employ strong generalized, ideological rhetoric. The price of this rhetoric was consistency. How could our leaders shed American blood in Korea and keep large numbers of American troops in Europe at great expense unless they were also willing to stop Communism in Vietnam?

Bureaucratic judgments and stakes were also involved in defining U.S. interests in Vietnam. Most bureaucrats probably prompted or shared the belief of their leaders about the serious repercussions of losing Vietnam. Once direct bureaucratic presence was established after the French departure, this belief was reinforced and extended. The military had to prove that American arms and advice could succeed where the French could not. The Foreign Service had to prove that it could bring about political stability in Saigon and "build a nation." The CIA had to prove that pacification would work. AID had to prove that millions of dollars in assistance and advice could bring political returns.

The U.S. commitment was rationalized as early as 1950. It was set in 1955 when we replaced the French. Its logic was further fulfilled by President Kennedy. After 1965, when the U.S. took over the war, it was immeasurably hardened.

There was little conditional character to the U.S. commitment—except for avoiding "the big war." Every President talked about the ultimate responsibility resting with the Vietnamese (and the French before them). This "condition" seems to have been meant much more as a warning to our friends than a real limitation. In every crunch, it was swept aside. The only real limit applied to Russia and China. Our leaders were not prepared to run the risks of nuclear war or even the risks of a direct conventional military confrontation with the Soviet Union and China. These were separate decisions. The line between them and everything else done in Vietnam always held firm. With this exception, the commitment was always defined in terms of the objective to deny the Communists control over all Vietnam. This was further defined to preclude coalition governments with the Communists.

The importance of the objective was evaluated in terms of cost, and the perceived costs of disengagement outweighed the cost of further engagement. Some allies might urge disengagement, but then condemn the U.S. for doing so. The domestic groups which were expected to criticize growing involvement always were believed to be outnumbered by those who would have attacked "cutting and running." The question of whether our leaders would have started down the road if they knew this would mean over half a million men in Vietnam, over 40,000 U.S. deaths, and the expenditure of well over $100 billion is historically irrelevant. Only Presidents Kennedy and Johnson had to confront the possibility of these large costs. The point is that each administration was prepared to pay the costs it could foresee for itself. No one seemed to have a better solution. Each could at least pass the baton on to the next.

Presidents could not treat Vietnam as if it were "vital" without creating high stakes internationally, domestically, and within their own bureaucracies. But the rhetoric conveyed different messages:

To the Communists, it was a signal that their actions would be met by counteractions.

To the American people, it set the belief that the President would ensure that the threatened nation did not fall into Communist hands—although without the anticipation of sacrificing American lives.

To the Congress, it marked the President's responsibility to ensure that Vietnam did not go Communist and maximized incentives for legislators to support him or at least remain silent.

To the U.S. professional military, it was a promise that U.S. forces would be used, if necessary and to the degree necessary, to defend Vietnam.

To the professional U.S. diplomat, it meant letting our allies know that the U.S. cared about their fate.

To the President, it laid the groundwork for the present action and showed that he was prepared to take the next step to keep Vietnam non-Communist.

Words were making Vietnam into a showcase—an Asian Berlin. In the process, Vietnam grew into a test case of U.S. credibility—to opponents, to allies, but perhaps most importantly, to ourselves. Public opinion polls seemed to confirm the political dangers. Already established bureaucratic judgments about the importance of Vietnam matured into cherished convictions and organizational interests. The war dragged on.

Each successive President, initially caught by his own belief, was further ensnarled by his own rhetoric, and the basis for the belief went unchallenged. Debates revolved around how to do things better, and whether they could be done, not whether they were worth doing. Prior to 1961, an occasional senator or Southeast Asian specialist would raise a lonely and weak voice in doubt. Some press criticism began thereafter. And later still, wandering American minstrels returned from the field to tell their tales of woe in private. General Ridgway as Chief of Staff of the Army in 1954 questioned the value of Vietnam as against its potential costs and dangers, and succeeded in blunting a proposed U.S. military initiative, although not for the reasons he advanced. Under Secretary of State George Ball raised the issue of international priorities in the summer of 1965 and lost. Clark Clifford as Secretary of Defense openly challenged the winnability of the war, as well as Vietnam's strategic significance, and argued for domestic priorities. But no systematic or serious examination of Vietnam's importance to the United States was ever undertaken within the government. Endless assertions passed for analysis. Presidents neither encouraged nor permitted serious questioning, for to do so would be to foster the idea that their resolve was something less than complete. The objective of a non-Communist Vietnam, and after 1954 a non-Communist South Vietnam, drove U.S. involvement ever more deeply each step of the way.

II. Means: "Take the Minimal Necessary Steps"

None of our Presidents was seeking total victory over the Vietnamese Communists. War critics who wanted victory always knew this. Those who wanted the U.S. to get out never believed it. Each President was essentially doing what he thought was minimally necessary to prevent a Communist victory during his tenure in office. Each, of course, sought to strengthen the anti-Communist Vietnamese forces, but with the aim of a negotiated settlement. Part of the tragedy of Vietnam was that the compromises our Presidents were prepared to offer could never lead to an end of the war. These preferred compromises only served to reinforce the conviction of both Communist and anti-Communist Vietnamese that they had to fight to the finish in their civil war. And so, more minimal steps were always necessary.

Our Presidents were pressured on all sides. The pressures for victory came mainly from the inside and were reflected on the outside. From inside the administrations, three forces almost invariably pushed hard. *First,* the military establishment generally initiated requests for broadening and intensifying U.S. military action. Our professional military placed great weight on the strategic significance of Vietnam; they were given a job to do; their prestige was involved; and of crucial importance (in the 1960's) —the lives of many American servicemen were being lost. The Joint Chiefs of Staff, the MAAG (Military Assistance Advisory Group) Chiefs and later the Commander of U.S. forces in Vietnam were the focal points for these pressures. *Second,* our Ambassadors in Saigon, supported by the State Department, at times pressed for and often supported big steps forward. Their reasons were similar to those of the military. *Thirdly,* an ever-present group of "fixers" was making urgent demands to strengthen and broaden the Saigon government in order to achieve political victory. Every executive agency had its fixers. They were usually able men whose entire preoccupation was to make things better in Vietnam. From outside the administration, there were hawks who insisted on winning and hawks who wanted to "win or get out." Capitol Hill hawks, the conservative press, and, for many years, Catholic organizations were in the forefront.

The pressures for disengagement and for de-escalation derived mostly from the outside with occasional and often unknown allies from within. Small for most of the Vietnam years, these forces grew steadily in strength from 1965 onward. Isolated congressmen and senators led the fight. First they did so on anticolonialist grounds. Later their objections developed moral aspects (interfering in a civil war) and extended to nonwinnability, domestic priorities, and the senselessness of the war. Peace organizations and student groups in particular came to dominate headlines and air time. Journalists played a critical role—especially through television reports. From within each administration, opposition could be found: (1) among isolated military men who did not want the U.S. in an Asian land war; (2) among some State Department intelligence and area specialists who knew Vietnam and believed the U.S. objective was unattainable at any reasonable price; and (3) within the civilian agencies of the Defense Department and isolated individuals at State and CIA, particularly after 1966, whose efforts were trained on finding a politically feasible way out.

Our Presidents reacted to the pressures as brakemen, pulling the switch against both the advocates of "decisive escalation" and the advocates of disengagement. The politics of the Presidency largely dictated this role, but the personalities of the Presidents were also important. None were as ideological as many persons around them. All were basically centrist politicians.

Their immediate aim was always to prevent a Communist takeover. The actions they approved were usually only what was minimally necessary to that aim. Each President determined the "minimal necessity" by trial and error and his own judgment. They might have done more and done it more rapidly if they were convinced that: (1) the threat of a Communist takeover were more immediate, (2) U.S. domestic politics would have been more permissive, (3) the government of South Vietnam had the requisite political stability and military potential for effective use, and (4) the job really would have gotten done. After 1965, however, the minimal necessity became the maximum they could get given the same domestic and international constraints.

The tactic of the minimally necessary decision makes optimum sense for the politics of the Presidency. Even our strongest Presidents have tended to shy away from decisive action. It has been too uncertain, too risky. They derive their strength from movement (the image of a lot of activity) and building and neutralizing opponents. Too seldom has there been forceful moral leadership; it may even be undemocratic. The small step that maintains the momentum gives the President the chance to gather more political support. It gives the appearance of minimizing possible mistakes. It allows time to gauge reactions. It serves as a pressure-relieving valve against those who want to do more. It can be doled out. Above all, it gives the President something to do next time.

The tactic makes consummate sense when it is believed that nothing will fully work or that the costs of a "winning" move would be too high. This was the case with Vietnam. This decision-making tactic explains why the U.S. involvement in Vietnam was gradual and step by step.

While the immediate aim was to prevent a Communist victory and improve the position of the anti-Communists, the longer-term goal was a political settlement. As late as February 1947, Secretary of State Marshall expressed the hope that "a pacific basis of adjustment of the difficulties" between France and the Vietminh could be found.[1] After that, Truman's policy hardened, but there is no evidence to suggest that until 1950 he was urging the French not to settle with the Vietnamese Communists. Eisenhower, it should be remembered, was the President who tacitly agreed (by not intervening in 1954) to the creation of a Communist state in North Vietnam. President Kennedy had all he could do to prevent complete political collapse in South Vietnam. He had, therefore, little basis on which to compromise. President Johnson inherited this political instability, and to add to his woes, he faced in 1965 what seemed to be the prospect of a Communist military victory. Yet, by his standing offer for free and internationally supervised elections, he apparently was prepared to accept Communist participation in the political life of the South.

By traditional diplomatic standards of negotiations between sovereign states, these were not fatuous compromises. One compromise was, in effect, to guarantee that the Communists could remain in secure control of North Vietnam. The U.S. would not seek to overthrow this regime. The

---

[1] *New York Times*, February 8, 1947.

other compromise was to allow the Communists in South Vietnam to seek power along the lines of Communist parties in France and Italy, i.e. to give them a "permanent minority position."

But the real struggle in Vietnam was not between sovereign states. It was among Vietnamese. It was a civil war and a war for national independence.

Herein lies the paradox and the tragedy of Vietnam. Most of our leaders and their critics did see that Vietnam was a quagmire, but did not see that the real stakes—who shall govern Vietnam—were not negotiable. Free elections, local sharing of power, international supervision, cease-fires —none of these could serve as a basis for settlement. What were legitimate compromises from Washington's point of view were matters of life and death to the Vietnamese. For American leaders, the stakes were "keeping their word" and saving their political necks. For the Vietnamese, the stakes were their lives and their lifelong political aspirations. Free elections meant bodily exposure to the Communist guerrillas and likely defeat to the anti-Communists. The risk was too great. There was no trust, no confidence.

The Vietnam war could no more be settled by traditional diplomatic compromises than any other civil war. President Lincoln could not settle with the South. The Spanish Republicans and General Franco's Loyalists could not have conceivably mended their fences by elections. None of the post–World War II insurgencies—Greece, Malaya, and the Philippines— ended with a negotiated peace. In each of these cases, the civil differences were put to rest—if at all—only by the logic of war.

It is commonly acknowledged that Vietnam would have fallen to the Communists in 1945–46, in 1954, and in 1965 had it not been for the intervention of first the French and then the Americans. The Vietnamese Communists, who were also by history the Vietnamese nationalists, would not accept only part of a prize for which they had paid so heavily. The anti-Communist Vietnamese, protected by the French and the Americans, would not put themselves at the Communists' mercy.

It may be that our Presidents understood this better than their critics. The critics, especially on the political left, fought for "better compromises," not realizing that even the best could not be good enough, and fought for broad nationalist governments, not realizing there was no middle force in Vietnam. Our Presidents, it seems, recognized that there was no middle ground and that "better compromises" would frighten our Saigon allies without bringing about a compromise peace. And they believed that a neutralization formula would compromise South Vietnam away to the Communists. So the longer-term aim of peace repeatedly gave way to the immediate needs of the war and the next necessary step.

III. Expectations: "We Must Persevere"

Each new step was taken not because of wishful thinking or optimism about its leading to a victory in South Vietnam. Few of our leaders thought that they could win the war in a conventional sense or that the Communists would be decimated to a point that they would simply fade away. Even as new and further steps were taken, coupled with expressions of optimism, many of our leaders realized that more—and still more—would have to be done. Few of these men felt confident about how it would all end or when. After 1965, however, they allowed the impression of "winnability" to grow in order to justify their already heavy investment and domestic support for the war.

The strategy always was to persevere. Perseverance, it seemed, was the only way to avoid or postpone having to pay the domestic political costs of failure. Finally, perseverance, it was hoped, would convince the Communists that our will to continue was firm. Perhaps, then, with domestic support for perseverance, with bombing North Vietnam, and with inflicting heavy casualties in the South, the Communists would relent. Perhaps, then, a compromise could be negotiated to save the Communists' face without giving them South Vietnam.

Optimism was a part of the "gamesmanship" of Vietnam. It had a purpose. Personal-organizational optimism was the product of a number of motivations and calculations:

· Career services tacitly and sometimes explicitly pressured their professionals to impart good news.

· Good news was seen as a job well done; bad news as personal failure.

· The reporting system was set up so that assessments were made by the implementors.

· Optimism bred optimism so that it was difficult to be pessimistic this time if you were optimistic the last time.

· People told their superiors what they thought they wanted to hear.

· The American ethic is to get the job done.

Policy optimism also sprang from several rational needs:

· To maintain domestic support for the war.

· To keep up the morale of our Vietnamese allies and build some confidence and trust between us and them.

· To stimulate military and bureaucratic morale to work hard.

There were, however, genuine optimists and grounds for genuine optimism. Some periods looked promising: the year preceding the French downfall at Dienbienphu; the years of the second Eisenhower Presidency when most attention was riveted on Laos and before the insurgency was stepped up in South Vietnam; 1962 and early 1963 before the strategic hamlet pacification program collapsed; and the last six months of 1967 before the 1968 Tet offensive.

Many additional periods by comparison with previous years yielded a sense of real improvement. By most conventional standards—the size and firepower of friendly Vietnamese forces, the number of hamlets pacified, the number of "free elections" being held, the number of Communists killed, and so forth—reasonable men could and did think in cautiously optimistic terms.

But comparison with years past is an illusory measure when it is not coupled with judgments about how far there still is to go and how likely it is that the goal can ever be reached. It was all too easy to confuse short-term breathing spells with long-term trends and to confuse "things getting better" with "winning." Many of those who had genuine hope suffered from either a lack of knowledge about Vietnam or a lack of sensitivity toward politics or both.

The basis for pessimism and the warning signals were always present. Public portrayals of success glowed more brightly than the full range of classified reporting. Readily available informal and personal accounts were less optimistic still. The political instability of our Vietnamese allies—from Bao Dai through Diem to President Thieu—has always been apparent. The weaknesses of the armed forces of our Vietnamese allies were common knowledge. Few years went by when the fighting did not gain in intensity. Our leaders did not have to know much about Vietnam to see all this.

Most of our leaders saw the Vietnam quagmire for what it was. Optimism was, by and large, put in perspective. This means that many knew that each step would be followed by another. Most seemed to have understood that more assistance would be required either to improve the relative position of our Vietnamese allies or simply to prevent a deterioration of their position. Almost each year and often several times a year, key decisions had to be made to prevent deterioration or collapse. These decisions were made with hard bargaining, but rapidly enough for us now to perceive a preconceived consensus to go on. Sometimes several new steps were decided at once, but announced and implemented piecemeal. The whole pattern conveyed the feeling of more to come.

With a tragic sense of "no exit," our leaders stayed their course. They seemed to hope more than expect that something would "give." The hope was to convince the Vietnamese Communists through perseverance that the U.S. would stay in South Vietnam until they abandoned their struggle. The hope, in a sense, was the product of disbelief. How could a tiny, backward Asian country *not* have a breaking point when opposed by the might of the United States? How could they not relent and negotiate with the U.S.?

And yet, few could answer two questions with any confidence: Why should the Communists abandon tomorrow the goals they had been paying so dear a price to obtain yesterday? What was there really to negotiate? No one seemed to be able to develop a persuasive scenario on how the war could end by peaceful means.

Our Presidents, given their politics and thinking, had nothing to do but persevere. But the Communists' strategy was also to persevere, to make the U.S. go home. It was and is a civil war for national independence. It was and is a Greek tragedy.

IV. After Twenty-Five Years

A quick review of history supports these interpretations. To the Roosevelt Administration during World War II, Indochina was not perceived as a "vital" area. The United States defeated Japan without Southeast Asia, and Indochina was not occupied by the allies until *after* Japan's defeat. FDR spoke informally to friends and newsmen of placing Indochina under United Nations trusteeship after the war, but—aware of French, British, and U.S. bureaucratic hostility to this—made no detailed plans and asked for no staff work prior to his death. For all practical purposes, Truman inherited *no* Southeast Asia policy.

In 1946 and 1947, the U.S. acquiesced in the re-establishment of French sovereignty. Our policy was a passive one of hoping for a negotiated settlement of the "difficulties" between Paris and the Vietminh independence movement of Ho Chi Minh. To the south, in Indonesia, we had started to pressure the Dutch to grant independence and withdraw, and a residue of anticolonialism remained in our first inchoate approaches to an Indochina policy as well.

But events in Europe and China changed the context from mid-1947 on. Two important priorities were to rearm and strengthen France as the cornerstone of European defense and recovery in the face of Russian pressure, and to prevent a further expansion of victorious Chinese Communism. The Truman Doctrine depicted a world full of dominoes. In May 1950, before Korea, Secretary of State Acheson announced that the U.S. would provide military and economic assistance to the French and their Indochinese allies for the direct purpose of combating Communist expansion.[2] After years of hesitating, Truman finally decided that anti-Communism was more important than anticolonialism in Indochina.

Acheson admits that U.S. policy was a "muddled hodgepodge":

> The criticism, however, fails to recognize the limits on the extent to which one may successfully coerce an ally. . . . Furthermore, the result of withholding help to France would, at most, have removed the colonial power. It could not have made the resulting situation a beneficial one either for Indo-

---

[2] *Department of State Bulletin,* May 1950, p. 821.

china or for Southeast Asia, or in the more important effort of furthering the stability and defense of Europe. So while we may have tried to muddle through and were certainly not successful, I could not think then or later of a better course. One can suggest, perhaps, doing nothing. That might have had merit, but as an attitude for the leader of a great alliance toward an important ally, indeed one essential to a critical endeavor, it had its demerits, too.[3]

Several months after the Korean War began, Acheson recalled the warning of an "able colleague": "Not only was there real danger that our efforts would fail in their immediate purpose and waste valuable resources in the process, but we were moving into a position in Indochina in which 'our responsibilities tend to supplant rather than complement those of the French'." Acheson then remembers: "I decided, however, that having put our hand to the plow, we would not look back."[4] He decided this despite the fact that he "recognized as no longer valid an earlier French intention to so weaken the enemy before reducing French forces in Indochina that indigenous forces could handle the situation."[5]

V. The Eisenhower Administration

President Eisenhower inherited the problem. Although, with Vietminh successes, the situation took on graver overtones, he, too, pursued a policy of "minimum action" to prevent the total "loss" of Vietnam to Communism. Sherman Adams, Eisenhower's assistant, explains how the problem was seen in the mid-1950's:

> If the Communists had pushed on with an aggressive offensive after the fall of Dienbienphu, instead of stopping and agreeing to stay out of Southern Vietnam, Laos and Cambodia, there was a strong possibility that the United States would have moved against them. A complete Communist conquest of Indochina would have had far graver consequence for the West than a Red victory in Korea.[6]

Apparently the President felt he could live with Communist control in the restricted area of North Vietnam, away from the rest of Southeast Asia.

Eisenhower did not take the minimal necessary step to save *all* of Indochina, but he did take the necessary steps to prevent the loss of most of

---

[3] Dean Acheson, *Present at the Creation* (New York: W. W. Norton, 1969), p. 673.

[4] *Ibid.*, p. 674.

[5] *Ibid.*, p. 676–77.

[6] Sherman Adams, *Firsthand Report* (New York: Harper & Row, 1961), p. 120.

Indochina. He paid almost all the French war cost, increased the U.S. military advisory mission, supplied forty B-26's to the French, and continued the threat of U.S. intervention, first by "united action" and then by forming SEATO. In taking these actions, Eisenhower was deciding against Vice-President Nixon and Admiral Radford, Chairman of the Joint Chiefs of Staff, who favored U.S. intervention in force, and against General Ridgway, Chief of the Army Staff, who opposed any action that could lead to an Asian land war. He was treading the well-worn middle path of doing just enough to balance off contradictory domestic, bureaucratic, and international pressures. The Vietnamese Communists agreed to the compromise, believing that winning the full prize was only a matter of time.

In public statements and later in his memoirs, President Eisenhower gave glimpses of his reasoning. At the time of Dienbienphu, he noted, ". . . we ought to look at this thing with some optimism and some determination . . . long faces and defeatism don't win battles." [7] Later he wrote, "I am convinced that the French could not win the war because the internal political situation in Vietnam, weak and confused, badly weakened their military position." [8] But he persevered nevertheless, believing that "the decision to give this aid was almost compulsory. The United States had no real alternative unless we were to abandon Southeast Asia." [9]

The Geneva Conference of 1954 was followed by eighteen bleak and pessimistic months as official Washington wondered whether the pieces could be put back together. Despite or perhaps because of the pessimism, U.S. aid was increased. Then, in the fall of 1956, Dulles could say: "We have a clean base there now, without a taint of colonialism. Dienbienphu was a blessing in disguise." [10] The years of "cautious optimism" had begun.

President Eisenhower kept the U.S. out of war because he allowed a territorial compromise with the Communists. More critically, he decided to replace the French and maintain a direct U.S. presence in Indochina. With strong rhetoric, military training programs, support for Ngo Dinh Diem in his refusal to hold the elections prescribed by the Geneva accords, and continuing military and economic assistance, he made the new state or "zone" of South Vietnam an American responsibility. Several years of military quiet in South Vietnam did not hide the smoldering political turmoil

---

[7] *Public Papers of the Presidents, Eisenhower, 1954*, p. 471. This remark was made on May 12, 1954.

[8] Dwight D. Eisenhower, *Mandate for Change* (New York: Doubleday, 1963), p. 372.

[9] *Ibid.*, p. 373.

[10] Emmet John Hughes, *The Ordeal of Power* (New York: Dell, 1962), p. 182. Eisenhower himself wrote that in 1954 "The strongest reason of all for United States refusal to respond by itself to French pleas was our tradition of anti-colonialism." (in *Mandate for Change*, p. 373)

in that country nor did it obscure the newspaper headlines which regularly proclaimed that the war in Indochina had shifted to Laos.

VI. The Kennedy Administration

The Administration of John F. Kennedy began in an aura of domestic sacrifice and international confrontation. The inauguration speech set the tone of U.S. responsibilities in "hazardous and dangerous" times.

Vietnam had a special and immediate importance which derived from the general international situation. Kennedy's predictions about dangerous times came true quickly—and stayed true—and he wanted to show strength to the Communists. But it was also the precarious situation in Laos and the "neutralist" compromise which Kennedy was preparing for Laos that were driving the President deeper into Vietnam. In Sorensen's words, Kennedy was "skeptical of the extent of our involvement [in Vietnam] but unwilling to abandon his predecessor's pledge or permit a Communist conquest. . . ." [11]

Kennedy had to face three basic general decisions. First, was top priority to go to political reform or fighting the war? On this issue the fixers, who wanted to give priority to political reform, were arrayed against the military. Second, should the line of involvement be drawn at combat units? On this issue the fixers were more quiet than in opposition. The military and the Country Team pushed hard—even urging the President to threaten Hanoi with U.S. bombing. Some counterweight came from State and the White House staff. Third, should the President make a clear, irrevocable, and open-ended commitment to prevent a Communist victory? Would this strengthen or weaken the U.S. hand in Saigon? Would it frighten away the Communists? What would be the domestic political consequences?

Kennedy's tactics and decisions—like Eisenhower's—followed the pattern of doing what was minimally necessary. On the political versus military priority issue, Kennedy did not make increasing military assistance definitively contingent on political reform, but he pointed to the absence of reform as the main reason for limiting the U.S. military role. On the combat unit issue, according to biographer Sorensen, "Kennedy never made a final negative decision on troops. In typical Kennedy fashion, he made it difficult for any of the pro-intervention advocates to charge him privately with weakness." [12] On the third issue, he avoided an open-ended commitment, but escalated his rhetoric about the importance of Vietnam. While he did authorize an increase of U.S. military personnel from 685 to

---

[11] Theodore Sorensen, *Kennedy* (New York: Harper & Row, 1965), p. 639.

[12] *Ibid.*, p. 654.

16,000, he did so slowly, and not in two or three big decisions. He continually doled out the increases. He gave encouragement to bureaucratic planning and studying as a safety valve—a valve he thought he could control. He kept a very tight rein on information to the public about the war. In Salinger's words, he "was not anxious to admit the existence of a real war. . . ." [13] By minimizing U.S. involvement, Kennedy was trying to avoid public pressures either to do more or to do less.

The President would make it "their" war until he had no choice but to look at it in a different light. He would not look at it in another light until Diem, who looked like a losing horse, was replaced. He would not gamble on long odds. But it is not clear what he expected to get as a replacement for Diem.

With the exception of much of 1962, which even the North Vietnamese have called "Diem's year," the principal Kennedy decisions were made in an atmosphere of deterioration, not progress, in Vietnam. This feeling of deterioration explains why Kennedy dispatched so many high-level missions to Vietnam. As Kennedy's biographers have written, the President was not really being told he was winning, but how much more he would have to do.

Writing in 1965, Theodore Sorensen summed up the White House view of events following the Diem coup in November 1963:

> The President, while eager to make clear that our aim was to get out of Vietnam, had always been doubtful about the optimistic reports constantly filed by the military on the progress of the war. . . . The struggle could well be, he thought, this nation's severest test of endurance and patience. . . . He was simply going to weather it out, a nasty, untidy mess to which there was no other acceptable solution. Talk of abandoning so unstable an ally and so costly a commitment "only makes it easy for the Communists," said the President. "I think we should stay." [14]

VII. The Johnson Administration

Lyndon Johnson assumed office with a reputation as a pragmatic politician and not a cold war ideologue. His history on Southeast Asia indicated caution and comparative restraint. And yet it was this same man who as President presided over and led the U.S. into massive involvement.

Three facts conspired to make it easier for Johnson to take the plunge on the assumed importance of Vietnam than his predecessors. First, the world was a safer place to live in and Vietnam was the only continuing cri-

---

[13] Pierre Salinger, *With Kennedy* (New York: Doubleday, 1966), pp. 319–29.

[14] Sorensen, *op. cit.*, p. 661.

sis. Europe was secure. The Sino-Soviet split had deepened. Mutual nuclear deterrence existed between the two superpowers. Second, the situation in Vietnam was more desperate than it ever had been. If the U.S. had not intervened in 1965, South Vietnam would have been conquered by the Communists. Third, after years of effort, the U.S. conventional military forces were big enough and ready enough to intervene. Unlike his predecessors, Johnson had the military capability to back up his words.

In sum, Vietnam became relatively more important, it was in greater danger, and the U.S. was in a position to do something about it.

At Johns Hopkins in April 1965, the President told the American people what he would do: "We will do everything necessary to reach that objective [of no external interference in South Vietnam], and we will do only what is absolutely necessary." But in order to prevent defeat and in order to keep the faith with his most loyal supporters, the minimum necessary became the functional equivalent of gradual escalation. The Air Force and the Commander in Chief, Pacific (CINPAC) pressed hard for full systems bombing—the authority to destroy 94 key North Vietnamese targets in 16 days. Johnson, backed and pressured in the other direction by Secretary McNamara, doled out approval for new targets over three years in a painstaking and piecemeal fashion. Johnson accommodated dovish pressure and the advice of the many pragmatists who surrounded him by making peace overtures. But these overtures were either accompanied with or followed by escalation. Johnson moved toward those who wanted three-quarters of a million U.S. fighting men in Vietnam, but he never got there. Guided by judgments of domestic repercussion and influenced again by McNamara, the President made at least eight separate decisions on U.S. force levels in Vietnam over a four-year period.[15] For the "fixers" who felt that U.S. conduct of the war missed its political essence and for the doves who wanted to see something besides destruction, Johnson placed new emphasis on "the other war"—pacification, nation-building, and political development—in February 1966. Johnson referred to this whole complex of actions and the air war in particular as his attempt to "seduce not rape" the North Vietnamese.

The objective of the Johnson Administration was to maintain an independent non-Communist South Vietnam. In the later years, this was rephrased: "allowing the South Vietnamese to determine their own future without external interference." As the President crossed the old barriers in pursuit of this objective, he established new ones. While he ordered the bombing of North Vietnam, he would not approve the bombing of targets which ran the risk of confrontation with China and Russia. While he permitted the U.S. force level in Vietnam to go over one-half million men, he

---

[15] See the Chronology in U.S. Senate Foreign Relations Committee, *Background Information Relating to Southeast Asia and Vietnam*, March 1969.

would not agree to call up the Reserves. While he was willing to spend $25 billion in one year on the war, he would not put the U.S. economy on a wartime mobilization footing. But the most important Johnson barrier was raised against invading Cambodia, Laos, and North Vietnam. This limitation was also a cornerstone in the President's hopes for a compromise settlement. He would agree to the permanent existence of North Vietnam—even help that country economically—if North Vietnam would extend that same right to South Vietnam.

In order to sustain public and bureaucratic support for his policy, Johnson's method was to browbeat and isolate his opponents. To the American people, he painted the alternatives to what he was doing as irresponsible or reckless. In either case, the result would be a greater risk of future general war. The bureaucracy used this same technique of creating the bug-out or bomb-out extremes in order to maintain as many of its own members in "the middle road." The price of consensus—within the bureaucracy and in the public at large—was invariably a middle road of contradictions and no priorities for action.

President Johnson was the master of consensus. On Vietnam this required melding the proponents of negotiations with the proponents of military victory. The technique for maintaining this Vietnam consensus was gradual escalation punctuated by dramatic peace overtures. As the war was escalated without an end in sight, the numbers of people Johnson could hold together diminished. The pressures for disengagement or for "decisive military action" became enormous, but with the "hawks" always outnumbering and more strategically placed than the "doves."

Johnson knew he had inherited a deteriorating situation in Vietnam. Vietcong military successes and constant change in the Saigon government from 1964 to 1966 were not secrets to anyone. Throughout the critical year of 1965, he struck the themes of endurance and more-to-come. In his May 4, 1965 requests for Vietnam Supplemental Appropriations he warned: "I see no choice but to continue the course we are on, filled as it is with peril and uncertainty." In his July 28, 1965 press conference he announced a new 125,000 troop ceiling and went on to say: "Additional forces will be needed later, and they will be sent as requested."

Talk about "turning corners" and winning a military victory reached a crescendo in 1967. At the same time a new counterpoint emerged— "stalemate." [16] The message of the stalemate proponents was that the U.S. was strong enough to prevent defeat, but that the situation defied victory. Hanoi would continue to match the U.S. force build-up and would not "cry uncle" over the bombing. The Saigon government and army had basic political and structural problems which they were unlikely to be able to over-

---

[16] R. W. Apple, "Vietnam: The Signs of Stalemate," *New York Times*, August 7, 1967.

come. Stalemate, it was urged, should be used as a basis for getting a compromise settlement with Hanoi.

These arguments were not lost on the President. At Guam in March 1967, while others around him were waxing eloquent about progress, the President was guardedly optimistic, speaking of "a favorable turning point, militarily and politically." But after one of the meetings he was reported to have said: "We have a difficult, a serious, long-drawn-out, agonizing problem that we do not have an answer for." [17] Nor did the President overlook the effects of the 1968 Tet offensive, coming as it did after many months of virtually unqualified optimism by him and by others. He stopped the bombing partially, increased troop strength slightly, made a peace overture, and announced his retirement.

In November 1963, Johnson is quoted as saying: "I am not going to be the President who saw Southeast Asia go the way China went." [18] In the spring of 1965, Lady Bird Johnson quoted him as saying: "I can't get out. I can't finish it with what I have got. So what the Hell can I do?" [19] President Johnson, like his predecessors, persevered and handed the war on to his successor.

VIII. Where Do We Go from Here?

If Vietnam were a story of how the system failed, that is, if our leaders did not do what they wanted to do or if they did not realize what they were doing or what was happening, it would be easy to package a large and assorted box of policy-making panaceas. For example: Fix the method of reporting from the field. Fix the way progress is measured in a guerrilla war. Make sure the President sees all the real alternatives. But these are all third-order issues, because the U.S. political-bureaucratic system did not fail; it worked.

Our leaders felt they had to prevent the loss of Vietnam to Communism, and they have succeeded so far in doing just that. Most of those who made Vietnam policy still believe that they did the right thing and lament only the domestic repercussions of their actions. It is because the price of attaining this goal has been so dear in lives, trust, dollars, and priorities, and the benefits so intangible, remote, and often implausible, that these leaders and we ourselves are forced to seek new answers and new policies.

Paradoxically, the way to get these new answers is not by asking why did the system fail, but why did it work so tragically well. There is, then,

---

[17] Quoted in Henry Brandon, *Anatomy of Error* (Boston: Gambit, 1969), p. 102.

[18] Tom Wicker, *JFK and LBJ* (New York: Penguin Books, 1968), p. 208.

[19] Lady Bird Johnson, *A White House Diary* (New York: Holt, Rinehart and Winston, 1970), p. 248.

only one first-order issue—how and why does our political-bureaucratic system decide what is vital and what is not? By whom, in what manner, and for what reasons was it decided that all Vietnam must not fall into Communist hands?

Almost all of our leaders since 1949 shared this conviction. Only a few voices in the wilderness were raised in opposition. Even as late as mid-1967, most critics were arguing that the U.S. could not afford to lose or be "driven from the field," that the real problem was our bombing of North Vietnam, and that this had to be stopped in order to bring about a negotiated settlement. Fewer still were urging that such a settlement should involve a coalition government with the Communists. Hardly anyone was saying that the outcome in Vietnam did not matter.

There is little evidence of much critical thinking about the relation of Vietnam to U.S. security. Scholars, journalists, politicians, and bureaucrats all seem to have assumed either that Vietnam was "vital" to U.S. national security or that the American people would not stand for the loss of "another" country to Communism.

Anti-Communism has been and still is a potent force in American politics, and most people who were dealing with the Vietnam problem simply believed that the Congress and the public would "punish" those who were "soft on Communism." Our leaders not only anticipated this kind of public reaction, but believed that there were valid reasons for not permitting the Communists to take all of Vietnam by force. In other words, they believed in what they were doing on the national security "merits." The domino theory, which was at the heart of the matter, rested on the widely shared attitude that security was indivisible, that weakness in one place would only invite aggression in others.

What can be done?

The President can do more than Presidents have in the past to call his national security bureaucracy to task. He can show the bureaucracy that he expects it to be more rigorous in determining what is vital or important or unimportant. Specifically, he can reject reasoning which simply asserts that security is indivisible, and he can foster the belief that while the world is an interconnected whole, actions can be taken in certain parts of the world to compensate for actions which are not taken elsewhere. For example, if the real concern about Vietnam were the effect of its loss on Japan, the Middle East, and Berlin, could we not take actions in each of these places to mitigate the "Vietnam fallout"?

None of these efforts with the bureaucracy can succeed, however, unless there is a change in general political attitudes as well. If anti-Communism persists as an overriding domestic political issue it will also be the main bureaucratic issue. Altering public attitudes will take time, education, and political courage—and it will create a real dilemma for the President. If the President goes "too far" in re-educating public and congressional opinions about Communism, he may find that he will have little support for threatening or using military force when he believes that our security really is at stake. In the end, it will still be the President who is held responsible for U.S. security. Yet, if our Vietnam experience has taught us anything, it is that the President must begin the process of re-education despite the risks.

SUGGESTED READING

Joseph Buttinger's *The Smaller Dragon: A Political History of Vietnam* ° (1958) surveys Vietnamese history from ancient times to 1900; Buttinger's *Vietnam: A Dragon Embattled*, 2 vols. (1967), continues the history from 1900 to the end of the Diem regime. Ellen Hammer's *The Struggle for Indochina, 1940–1955* ° (1956) is useful on French policies from 1946 to 1953. Jean Lacouture, in *Vietnam Between Two Truces* ° (1966), emphasizes the indigenous and independent nature of the guerrilla movement. Douglas Pike's *Viet Cong* ° (1966) is a sometimes inconsistent account by a USIA employee asserting the primacy of Hanoi in the rebellion. John T. McAlister, Jr., and Paul Mus, in *The Vietnamese and Their Revolution* (1970), examine the cultural base of Vietnamese politics.

The most respected scholar of the Vietnamese war was Bernard Fall, a writer whose views on crucial questions underwent constant revision. His books include *The Two Viet-Nams: A Political and Military History*, ° 5th rev. ed. (1965), an encyclopedic collection of useful information that is, unfortunately, extremely difficult to read; *Street without Joy*, 4th rev. ed. (1964), on the French war against the Vietminh; *Hell in a Very Small Place* (1966), on the fall of Dien Bien Phu; *Viet-Nam Witness, 1953–66* ° (1966), a fine collection of some of Fall's articles; and *Last Reflections on War* ° (1967), a collection of articles and interviews published after his tragic death in Vietnam.

Useful surveys of American involvement in Vietnam are Robert Shaplen's *The Lost Revolution* ° (1965); Theodore Draper's *The Abuse of Power* ° (1966); George Kahin and John Lewis' *The United States in Vietnam* (1965); and Marvin Kalb and Elie Abel's *Roots of Involvement* ° (1971). Chester Cooper's *The Lost Crusade* (1970) is a disappointing survey by a man who helped make policy.

Edward Drachman's *United States Policy Toward Vietnam, 1940–1945* (1970) examines the war years. Victor Bator's *Vietnam: A Diplomatic Tragedy* (1965) contains a critical analysis of Dulles' diplomacy. Roger Hilsman, in *To Move a Nation* ° (1967) discusses Kennedy's Vietnam policy in detail. Anthony Austin, in *The President's War* (1971), exposes official deception on the Tonkin Gulf episode of 1964. The publication of the *Pentagon Papers* ° (1971) supplied important documentary material on the history of American involvement. Using this and other sources, Ralph Stavins wrote a highly critical account of American policy from 1954 to the time of President Johnson's withdrawal from the presidency. Stavin's extended essay is published in *Washington Plans an Aggressive War* (1971), which includes less useful pieces by Richard J. Barnet and Marcus G. Raskin. Don Oberdorfer's *Tet!* (1971) tells of the crucial battle in February 1968, that contributed much to American revulsion against the war. Townsend Hoopes's *The Limits of Intervention* ° (1969) is an inside account by the Under Secretary of the Air Force of the events in March 1968, leading to the decision not to escalate further. A differing account of the same events is offered by Lyndon Johnson in *The Vantage Point: Perspectives of the Presidency* (1971). On the presidential election of 1968, in which the war issue played a large role, see Eugene J. McCarthy's *The Year of the People* (1969) and Theodore H. White's *The Making of the President, 1968* ° (1969). President Johnson's press secretary George Christian tells in *The President Steps Down* (1970) of the decision to halt the bombing in November 1968. Seymour M. Hersh's *My Lai* (1970) tells the story ·of the tragic massacre.

The government case for involvement was presented by the State Department in *Aggression from the North: The Record of North Vietnam's Campaign to Conquer South Vietnam* (1965). Frank Trager, in *Why Viet Nam?* (1966), supports the views of the government. *Can We Win in Vietnam?* (1968), a publication in the Hudson Institute Series on National Security and International Order, presents the views of five essayists, three of whom support American intervention. The wisdom of the American commitment is both defended and attacked in the classic *Vietnam Hearings* ° (1966), a collection of testimony before the Senate Foreign Relations Committee. *Viet-Report* (1965–68), a special magazine established by critics of administration policy, and *I. F. Stone's Weekly* (later a bi-weekly, published until 1972) were deeply hostile to the war. Since 1968 the *Bulletin of Concerned Asian Scholars* has published many essays critical of American policy in Asia. The best academic critic of U.S. policy has been Noam Chomsky. See his *American Power and the New Mandarins* ° (1967) and *At War With Asia* ° (1969). Gabriel Kolko, a radical historian, offers his view in *Roots of American Foreign Policy* ° (1969).

Gelb, himself, has been challenged in a limited way by two critics, whose letters, along with his reply, appear in "Letters-1," *Foreign Policy*, I (Fall 1971). Gelb's views were also criticized by Arthur Schlesinger, Jr., in "Eyeless in Indochina," *New York Review* (Oct. 21, 1971), which provoked Gelb to respond in *New York Review* (Dec. 2, 1971).

ALLEN J. MATUSOW

From Civil Rights to Black Power: The Case of SNCC, 1960–1966

INTRODUCTION

In 1954 when the Supreme Court declared laws requiring racial segregation in public schools to be unconstitutional, American liberals rejoiced and looked forward to the achievement of racial integration. They believed that the major struggles would be waged in the South, and they rested their hopes on the willingness of the federal executive and judiciary to compel compliance with the law of the land. Although the slowness of school desegregation in the late 1950's dampened their expectations for quick success, the liberals still clung comfortably to the heady principles that destruction of legal segregation and increased mingling between blacks and whites would solve America's racial problems.

Martin Luther King symbolized their hopes. His courage and philosophy inspired respect, and his tactics seemed to hold the

This essay was written especially for the first edition of this volume.

promise of ultimate success. Preaching and practicing nonviolence, he offered love to his enemies and relied on the coercive power of local black economic boycotts and outraged liberal sentiment beyond the South to force changes in Dixie.

The black civil rights movement of 1960, beginning with the sit-ins at Woolworth counters, self-consciously adhered to the tactics of King and shared the liberal faith in the desirability and likelihood of establishing racial equality in America. The Student Nonviolent Coordinating Committee (SNCC) was formed from the 1960 sit-in movement and dedicated its energies to gaining for black Americans in the South a place in white middle-class life. Yet within a few years the betrayals of civil rights by white liberals and the freshly uncovered depths of racial misunderstanding and mistrust dramatically challenged earlier optimistic liberal assumptions and compelled healthy introspection among whites and blacks who toiled for civil rights in the South. (In SNCC, unlike in King's Southern Christian Leadership Conference, the fears and attractions of interracial sex also rose to the surface, indicating that the gap between the races had been narrowed but that a chasm still separated them.) Blacks and even some whites in SNCC were deciding by 1966 that black power offered a more appropriate strategy and philosophy for "liberating the blacks from white oppression." The history of SNCC, concludes Allen J. Matusow, professor of history at Rice University, discloses the roots of black power and charts "the sad fate of the whole civil rights movement."

Matusow considers the black man's recognition of racism and paternalism among whites to be healthy, but he is critical of the doctrine of black power as expressed by Stokely Carmichael, its first prominent spokesman. Emphasizing that Carmichael seeks a radical reconstruction of American society, Matusow challenges his claim that black power is largely traditional ethnic-bloc politics practiced by a new group. "Its greatest weakness," Matusow further argues, "is its failure to propose adequate solutions," for he regards as unrealistic the hopes of a socialist alliance of poor whites and poor blacks. He sees as more realistic the liberal-labor-civil rights coalition proposed by Bayard Rustin, a former aide of King. This coalition has been eagerly endorsed by some white liberals who view it as a way of redeeming American society for racial integration and equality and saving the society from continued violence.

What Matusow does not directly confront, his critics would contend, is whether this alliance and its program of $100 billion for social justice are possible, or whether the earlier liberal betrayals and the continued power of Southern conservatives in Congress can be taken as evidence that the political system cannot become truly responsive to the aspirations and needs of the blacks and other disadvantaged Americans.

*T*he transformation of black protest in the 1960's from civil rights to black power has seemed in retrospect an inevitable development. When the inherent limitations of the civil rights movement finally became apparent and when the expectations that the movement created met frustration, some kind of militant reaction in the black community seemed certain. However predictable this development may have been, it tells little about the concrete events that led to the abandonment of the civil rights program and to the adoption of a doctrine that is in many ways its opposite. For black power was not plucked whole from impersonal historical forces; nor was its content the only possible expression of rising black militancy. Rather, black power both as a slogan and a doctrine was in large measure the creation of a small group of civil rights workers who in the early 1960's manned the barricades of black protest in the Deep South. The group was called the Student Nonviolent Coordinating Committee (SNCC). Through its spokesman, Stokely Carmichael, SNCC first proclaimed black power and then became its foremost theoretician. Others would offer glosses on black power that differed from SNCC's concept, but because SNCC had contributed so much to the civil rights movement, no other group could speak with so much authority or command a comparable audience. Although SNCC borrowed freely from many sources to fashion black power into a doctrine, the elements of that doctrine were in the main the results of SNCC's own history. An examination of that history reveals not only the roots of black power but also the sad fate of the whole civil rights movement.

Founded in 1960, SNCC was an outgrowth of the historic sit-in movement, which began in Greensboro, North Carolina, on February 1 of that year. Four freshmen from a local Negro college attempted to desegregate the lunch counter at a Woolworth's five and ten store. The example of these four sent shock waves through the black colleges of the South and created overnight a base for a campaign of massive civil disobedience. The new generation of black students seemed suddenly unwilling to wait any longer for emancipation at the hands of the federal courts and in the next months supplied most of the recruits for the nonviolent army of 50,000 that rose spontaneously and integrated public facilities in 140 Southern cities. For the students on the picket lines, the prophet of the sit-in movement was Dr. Martin Luther King, the leader of the successful Montgomery bus boycott of 1955–56. The students found in King's nonviolent philosophy a ready-made ethic, a tactic, and a conviction of righteousness strong enough to sustain them on a sometimes hazardous mission.[1] It was King's organization, the

---

[1] For accounts of the sit-ins see Howard Zinn, *SNCC: The New Abolitionists* (Beacon, 1965), Chapter 2; Jack Newfield, *A Prophetic Minority* (Signet, 1966), Chapter 3; August

Southern Christian Leadership Conference (SCLC), that first suggested the need for some central direction of the sit-in movement. At the invitation of SCLC's executive secretary, some 300 activist students from throughout the South met in Raleigh, North Carolina, in April 1960, to discuss their problems. The students agreed to form a coordinating body, which became SNCC, and in May 1960, hired a secretary and opened an office in Atlanta. In October the organization decided to become a permanent one, and 235 delegates approved a founding statement inspired by King's philosophy:

> We affirm the philosophical or religious ideal of nonviolence as the foundation of our purpose, the presupposition of our belief, and the manner of our action. . . . Through nonviolence, courage displaces fear. Love transcends hate. Acceptance dissipates prejudice; hope ends despair. Faith reconciles doubt. Peace dominates war. Mutual regards cancel enmity. Justice for all overwhelms injustice. The redemptive community supersedes immoral social systems.[2]

In truth, the Christian rhetoric of SNCC's founding statement was not appropriate. The author of the statement was James Lawson, a young minister who never actually belonged to SNCC.[3] Most of the students who rallied to the sit-ins in 1960 accepted King's teachings more out of convenience than conviction and respected his courage more than his philosophy. For while King believed that Christian love was an end in itself and that Negro nonviolence would redeem American society, the students preferred to participate in America rather than to transform it. Sociologists who examined the attitudes of protesters in the black colleges found not alienation from American middle-class values but a desire to share fully in middle-class life.[4] In a perceptive piece written for *Dissent*, Michael Walzer supported these findings from his own first-hand impressions of the sit-ins. Walzer concluded that the students were materialistic as well as moral, were "willing to take risks in the name of both prosperity and virtue," and had as their goal "assimilation into American society." As for nonviolence, Walzer wrote, "I

Meier, "The Successful Sit-Ins in a Border City: A Study in Social Causation," *The Journal of Intergroup Relations*, II (Summer, 1961), 230–37; Charles U. Smith, "The Sit-Ins and the New Negro Student," *ibid.*, 223–29; James Peck, *Freedom Ride* (Simon & Schuster, 1962), Chapter 6.

[2] Quoted in Newfield, *A Prophetic Minority*, p. 47.

[3] Emily Schottenfeld Stoper, "The Student Nonviolent Coordinating Committee: The Growth of Radicalism in a Civil Rights Organization," unpublished dissertation, Harvard University, 1968, pp. 35–36.

[4] Ruth Searles and J. Allen Williams, Jr., "Negro College Students' Participation in Sit-Ins," *Social Forces*, (Dec., 1966), 215–20.

was told often that 'when one side has all the guns, then the other side is non-violent.' " [5]

In the beginning, the philosophical inconsistencies of the sit-ins did not trouble SNCC, for it stood at the forefront of a movement whose ultimate triumph seemed not far distant. But within months, as mysteriously as it began, the sit-in movement vanished. By the spring of 1961 the black campuses had lapsed into their customary quiescence, their contribution to the civil rights movement at an end. As for SNCC, since October 1960, the student representatives from each Southern state had been meeting monthly to squander their energies trying to coordinate a movement that was first too amorphous and then suddenly moribund. SNCC's attempts in early 1961 to raise up new hosts of students proved ineffectual, and lacking followers, the organization seemed without a future.[6] Then in May 1961, the Freedom Rides restored a sense of urgency to the civil rights movement and gave SNCC a second life.

On May 14, 1961, members of the Congress of Racial Equality (CORE) began the Freedom Rides to test a Supreme Court decision outlawing segregation in transportation terminals. On May 20, after one of CORE's integrated buses was bombed near Anniston, Alabama, and another was mobbed in Birmingham, CORE decided to call off its rides. But amid sensational publicity, students from Nashville and Atlanta, many associated with SNCC, rushed to Birmingham to continue the journey to New Orleans. After mobs assaulted this second wave of riders, the Federal Government stepped in to protect them, and they were permitted to go as far as Jackson, where local authorities put them in jail for defying segregation ordinances. Throughout the summer of 1961 some 300 citizens from all over America took Freedom Rides that brought them to the jails of Jackson.[7] For SNCC the Freedom Rides provided a temporary outlet for activism and, more important, inspired radical changes in the structure and purpose of the organization.

Perhaps the most important result of the Freedom Rides for SNCC was to focus its attention on the Deep South. Most of the sit-ins had occurred in the cities and larger towns of the Upper South, and the victories there had come with relative ease. Now the magnitude of the task confronting the civil

---

[5] Michael Walzer, "The Politics of the New Negro," *Dissent*, VII (Summer, 1960), 235–43.

[6] Anne Braden, "The Southern Freedom Movement in Perspective," *Monthly Review*, XVII (July–Aug., 1965), 31–32; also James Howard Laue, "Direct Action and Desegregation: Toward a Theory of the Rationalization of Protest," unpublished dissertation, Harvard University, 1965, p. 128.

[7] For accounts of the Freedom Rides, see Zinn, *SNCC*, Chapter 3; and Peck, *Freedom Ride*, Chapters 8 and 9.

rights movement became clearer. As some in SNCC had already perceived, sit-ins to desegregate public places offered no meaningful benefits to poverty-stricken tenant farmers in, say, Mississippi. In order to mobilize the black communities in the Deep South to fight for their rights, sporadic student demonstrations would be less useful than sustained efforts by full time field workers.[8] In the summer of 1961, as SNCC was beginning to grope toward the concept of community action, the Federal Government stepped in with an attractive suggestion.

Embarrassed by the Freedom Rides, Attorney General Robert F. Kennedy moved to direct the civil rights movement into paths that, in his view, were more constructive. Kennedy suggested that the civil rights organizations jointly sponsor a campaign to register Southern black voters. Such a drive, its proponents argued, would be difficult for even extreme segregationists to oppose and eventually might liberalize the Southern delegation in Congress. When the Justice Department seemed to offer federal protection for registration workers and when white liberals outside the Administration procured foundation money to finance anticipated costs, the civil rights groups agreed to undertake the project.[9] Within SNCC, advocates of direct action fought acceptance of the project, but the issue was compromised and a threatened split was averted. SNCC's decision to mobilize black communities behind efforts to secure political rights decisively changed the character of the organization. It thereafter ceased to be an extracurricular activity of student leaders and became instead the vocation of dedicated young men and women who temporarily abandoned their careers to become full time paid workers (or "field secretaries") in the movement. Moreover, as SNCC workers drifted away from the black campuses and began living among Deep South blacks, they cast aside the middle-class goals that had motivated the sit-ins of 1960 and put on the overalls of the poor. Begun as middle-class protest, SNCC was developing revolutionary potential.[10]

In Mississippi the major civil rights groups (NAACP, SCLC, CORE, and SNCC) ostensibly joined together to form the Council of Federated Organizations (COFO) to register black voters. But in reality, except for one Mississippi congressional district where CORE had a project of its own, COFO was manned almost entirely by SNCC people. The director of COFO was SNCC's now legendary Robert Moses, a product of Harlem with a Masters degree in philosophy from Harvard, whose courage and humanity made him the most respected figure in the organization. Moses had entered Pike

---

[8] Laue, "Direct Action and Desegregation," pp. 154, 160, 167–68.

[9] On origins of the voter registration drive, see Pat Watters and Reece Cleghorn, *Climbing Jacob's Ladder* (Harcourt, Brace & World, 1967), pp. 44–59; and Louis Lomax, *The Negro Revolt* (Signet, 1963), pp. 246–50.

[10] Braden, "Southern Freedom Movement," p. 36; Laue, "Direct Action and Desegregation," p. 171; Stoper, "The Student Nonviolent Coordinating Committee," pp. 6 and 8.

County, Mississippi, alone in 1961, stayed on in spite of a beating and a jail term, and in the spring of 1962 became COFO's director in charge of voting projects in Vicksburg, Cleveland, Greenwood, and a few other Mississippi towns.[11] Although SNCC also had registration projects in Arkansas, Alabama, and Georgia, it concentrated on Mississippi, where the obstacles were greatest.

Throughout 1962 and into 1963 SNCC workers endured assaults, offered brave challenges to local power structures, and exhorted local blacks to shake off fear and stand up for freedom. But SNCC scored no breakthroughs to sustain morale, and while its goals remained outwardly unchanged, its mood was turning bitter. To SNCC the hostility of local racists was not nearly so infuriating as the apparent betrayal that it suffered at the hands of the Justice Department. SNCC believed that in 1961 the Kennedy Administration had guaranteed protection to registration workers, but in Mississippi in 1962 and 1963, SNCC's only contact with federal authority consisted of the FBI agents who stood by taking notes while local policemen beat up SNCC members. SNCC and its supporters insisted that existing law empowered the Federal Government to intervene, but the Justice Department contended that it was in fact powerless. SNCC doubted the sincerity of the Government's arguments and became convinced that the Kennedys had broken a solemn promise for political reasons.[12] Thus by 1963 SNCC was already becoming estranged from established authority and suspicious of liberal politicians.

SNCC's growing sense of alienation cut it off even from other civil rights organizations and most importantly from Dr. King, who by 1963 had become a fallen idol for SNCC workers. They believed that King was too willing to compromise, wielded too much power, and too successfully monopolized the funds of the movement. Doubts about King had arisen as early as the Freedom Rides, when students turned to him for advice and leadership and received what they considered only vague sympathy. In fact, after CORE called off the first ride, King privately supported Robert Kennedy's plea for a "cooling-off" period. But much to SNCC's annoyance, when militant voices prevailed and the rides continued, the press gave King all the credit.[13] In Albany, Georgia, in December 1961, after SNCC aroused the black population to pack the local jails for freedom, King came to town, got arrested, monopolized the headlines, and almost stole the leadership of the Albany campaign from SNCC.[14] In SNCC's view, dependence on King's

---

[11] For an account of Moses in Mississippi, see Zinn, SNCC, Chapter 4.

[12] See *ibid.*, Chapter 10; and Watters and Cleghorn, *Climbing Jacob's Ladder*, p. 58.

[13] Laue, "Direct Action and Desegregation," pp. 179, 338.

[14] Stoper, "The Student Nonviolent Coordinating Committee," p. 104; *New York Times* (Dec. 24, 1961), section IV, 5.

charisma actually weakened the civil rights movement, for it discouraged development of leadership at the grass-roots level. Why, SNCC asked, did King use his huge share of civil rights money to maintain a large staff in Atlanta, and why did he never account for the funds that he so skillfully collected? [15] As King lost influence on SNCC, dissenting attitudes about nonviolence, implicit since 1960, came to be frankly articulated. When Robert Penn Warren asked Robert Moses what he thought of King's philosophy, Moses replied,

> We don't agree with it, in a sense. The majority of the students are not sympathetic to the idea that they have to love the white people that they are struggling against. . . . For most of the members, it is tactical, it's a question of being able to have a method of attack rather than to be always on the defensive.[16]

During the March on Washington in August 1963, the nation almost caught a glimpse of SNCC's growing anger. John Lewis, the chairman of SNCC and one of the scheduled speakers, threatened to disrupt the harmony of that happy occasion by saying what he really thought. Only with difficulty did moderates persuade Lewis to delete the harshest passages of his address. So the nation did not know that SNCC scorned Kennedy's civil rights bill as "too little and too late." Lewis had intended to ask the 250,000 people gathered at the Lincoln Memorial,

> What is there in this bill to insure the equality of a maid who earns $5 a week in the home of a family whose income is $100,000 a year? . . . This nation is still a place of cheap political leaders who build their careers on immoral compromises and ally themselves with open forms of political, economic, and social exploitation. . . . The party of Kennedy is also the party of Eastland. The party of Javits is also the party of Goldwater. Where is *our* party? . . . We cannot depend on any political party, for the Democrats and the Republicans have betrayed the basic principles of the Declaration of Independence.

In those remarks that he never delivered, Lewis used both the language of Christian protest and images alive with the rage of SNCC field workers. "In the struggle we must seek more than mere civil rights; we must work for the community of love, peace, and true brotherhood." And,

> the time will come when we will not confine our marching to Washington. We will march through the South, through the heart of Dixie, the way Sherman did. We shall pursue our "scorched earth" policy and burn Jim Crow to

---

[15] "Integration: Hotter Fires," *Newsweek*, LXII (July 1, 1963), 19–21.

[16] Robert Penn Warren, *Who Speaks for the Negro* (Random House, 1965), p. 91.

the ground—nonviolently. We shall fragment the South into a thousand pieces and put them back together in the image of democracy.[17]

The crucial milestone of SNCC's road to radicalism was the Freedom Summer of 1964. Freedom Summer grew out of a remarkable mock election sponsored by SNCC in the autumn of 1963. Because the mass of Mississippi's black population could not legally participate in choosing the state's governor that year, Robert Moses conceived a freedom election to protest mass disfranchisement and to educate Mississippi's blacks to the mechanics of the political process. COFO organized a new party called the Mississippi Freedom Democrats, printed its own ballots, and in October conducted its own poll. Overwhelming the regular party candidates, Aaron Henry, head of the state NAACP and Freedom Democratic nominee for governor, received 70,000 votes, a tremendous protest against the denial of equal political rights. One reason for the success of the project was the presence in the state of 100 Yale and Stanford students, who worked for two weeks with SNCC on the election. SNCC was sufficiently impressed by the student contribution to consider inviting hundreds more to spend an entire summer in Mississippi. Sponsors of this plan hoped not only for workers but for publicity that might at last focus national attention on Mississippi.[18] By the winter of 1963–64, however, rising militancy in SNCC had begun to take on the overtones of black nationalism, and some of the membership resisted the summer project on the grounds that most of the volunteers would be white.

Present from the beginning, by mid-1964 whites made up one-fifth of SNCC's approximately 150 full time field secretaries. Though whites had suffered their fair share of beatings, some blacks in SNCC were expressing doubts about the role of white men in a movement for black freedom. At a staff meeting at Greenville, Mississippi, in November 1963, a debate on the proposed Freedom Summer brought the issue of white-black relations into the open. In his book *SNCC: The New Abolitionists*, Howard Zinn, who attended this meeting, summarizes the views of the militants:

> Four or five of the Negro staff members now urged that the role of whites be limited. For whites to talk to Mississippi Negroes about voter registration, they said, only reinforced the Southern Negro's tendency to believe that whites were superior. Whites tended to take over leadership roles in the movement, thus preventing Southern Negroes from being trained to lead. Why didn't whites just work in the white Southern community? One man noted that in Africa the new nations were training black Africans to take over all important government positions. Another told of meeting a Black Muslim

---

[17] Quoted in Watters and Cleghorn, *Climbing Jacob's Ladder*, pp. xiv–xv.

[18] On freedom ballot, see Len Holt, *The Summer That Didn't End* (William Morrow, 1965), pp. 35–36, 152–53.

in Atlanta who warned him that whites were taking over the movement. "I had the feeling inside. I felt what he said was true."

But Fannie Lou Hamer disagreed. Mrs. Hamer had been a time-keeper on a cotton plantation and was one of the local Mississippi blacks whom SNCC discovered and elevated to leadership. Speaking for the majority of the meeting, she said, "If we're trying to break down this barrier of segregation, we can't segregate ourselves." Thus in February 1964, SNCC sent an invitation to Northern college students to spend their summer vacation in Mississippi.[19]

In retrospect, the summer of 1964 was a turning point in the civil rights movement. When the summer began, SNCC was still operating within the framework of liberal America, still committed to integration and equal political rights for all citizens. But by the end of the summer of 1964, the fraying cords that bound SNCC to liberal goals and values finally snapped. In a sense, much of later black power thought was merely a postscript to SNCC's ill-fated summer project.

In June 1964, more than 700 selected students, judged by a staff psychiatrist at MIT to be "an extraordinarily healthy bunch of kids," [20] came to Oxford, Ohio, for two week-long orientation sessions conducted by veteran SNCC workers. The atmosphere in Oxford, tense from the outset, became on June 22 pervaded with gloom. Robert Moses quietly told the volunteers that three workers had gone into Neshoba county in Mississippi the day before and had not been heard from since. One was Michael Schwerner, a CORE staff member; the second was James Chaney, a black SNCC worker from Mississippi; and the third was Andrew Goodman, a student volunteer who had finished his orientation in Ohio a few days before.[21] (In August the bodies of these three were discovered in their shallow graves near Philadelphia, Mississippi.)

The volunteers in Ohio had to face not only their own fear but also unanticipated hostility from the SNCC workers whom they had come to assist. Tensions between black workers and white volunteers seethed under the surface for some days and then finally erupted. One night SNCC showed a film of a grotesque voting registrar turning away black applicants. When the student audience laughed at the scene, six SNCC people walked out, enraged at what they considered an insensitive response. There followed an exchange between the workers and the volunteers, in which the students

---

[19] Zinn, SNCC, pp. 8–9, 186–88; see also Calvin Trillin, "Letter from Jackson," New Yorker, XL (Aug. 29, 1964), 80–105.

[20] Quoted in James Atwater, "If We Can Crack Mississippi . . . ," Saturday Evening Post, CCXXXVII (July 25, 1964), 16.

[21] Sally Belfrage, Freedom Summer (Viking, 1965), p. 11.

complained that the staff was distant, uncommunicative, and "looked down on us for not having been through what they had." A SNCC worker replied,

> If you get mad at us for walking out, just wait until they break your head in, and see if you don't have something to get mad about. Ask Jimmy Travis over there what he thinks about the project. What does he think about Mississippi? He has six slugs in him, man, and the last one went right through the back of his neck when he was driving a car outside Greenwood. Ask Jesse here—he has been beaten so that we wouldn't recognize him time and time and time and time again. If you don't get scared, pack up and get the hell out of here because we don't need any favors of people who don't know what they are doing here in the first place.

The bitter words seemed to have a cathartic effect, and the meeting culminated in emotional singing. Said one volunteer a bit too optimistically, "The crisis is past, I think." [22]

From one perspective the story of the two months that followed is one of the human spirit triumphant. Though three more people were killed, eighty others were beaten, thirty-five churches were burned, and thirty other buildings bombed, few turned back; black and white together, the civil rights workers in Mississippi worked for racial justice.[23] The student volunteers taught in Freedom Schools, where 3,000 children were given their first glimpse of a world beyond Mississippi. They organized the disfranchised to march on county courthouses to face unyielding registrars. Most importantly, they walked the roads of Mississippi for the Freedom Democratic Party (FDP). Denying the legitimacy of the segregated Democratic party, COFO opened the FDP to members of all races and declared the party's loyalty to Lyndon Johnson. The goal of the FDP in the summer of 1964 was to send a delegation to the Democratic convention in Atlantic City to challenge the credentials of the regular Democrats and cast the state's vote for the party's nominees. To mount this challenge against the racist Democrats of Mississippi, COFO enrolled 60,000 members in the FDP and then organized precinct, county, and state conventions to choose 68 integrated delegates to go north. The FDP, in which tens of thousands of black Mississippi citizens invested tremendous hopes, was a true grass-roots political movement and the greatest achievement of Freedom Summer.[24]

Although the FDP brought to Atlantic City little more than a sense of moral outrage, it nevertheless managed to transform its challenge of the Mississippi regulars into a major threat to the peace of the national party. Mrs.

---

[22] Elizabeth Sutherland, ed., *Letters from Mississippi* (McGraw-Hill, 1965), pp. 5–6.

[23] Watters and Cleghorn, *Climbing Jacob's Ladder*, p. 139.

[24] Holt, *The Summer That Didn't End*, Chapter 8; Zinn, *SNCC*, p. 251.

Hamer helped make this feat possible by her electrifying (and televised) testimony before the credentials committee on how Mississippi policemen had beaten her up for trying to register to vote. As Northern liberals began rallying to the FDP, the managers of the convention sought a compromise that would satisfy the liberals and at the same time keep the bulk of the Southern delegations in the convention. President Johnson favored a proposal to seat all the Mississippi regulars who pledged their loyalty to the party, to deny any voting rights to the FDP delegates, but to permit them to sit on the floor of the convention. In addition, he proposed that at future conventions no state delegations chosen by racially discriminatory procedures would be accredited. But because this compromise denied the FDP's claims of legitimacy, the FDP and many liberals declared it unacceptable and threatened to take their case to the floor of the convention, a prospect that greatly displeased the President. Johnson then sent Senator Hubert Humphrey to Atlantic City to act as his agent in settling the controversy. Unsubstantiated rumors had it that if Humphrey's mission failed, the President would deny the Senator the party's vice-presidential nomination. In close touch with both the White House and the credentials committee, Humphrey proposed altering the original compromise by permitting two FDP delegates to sit in the convention as delegates at large with full voting rights. This was as far as Johnson would go, and at the time it seemed far enough. Though the Mississippi white regulars walked out, no Southern delegations followed them, and, at the same time, most liberals felt that the Administration had made a genuine concession. Black leaders, including Dr. King, pleaded with the FDP to accept Humphrey's compromise. But the FDP denied that the compromise was in any sense a victory.[25] Angered at Humphrey's insistence that he alone choose the two at-large delegates, the FDP announced that it had not come to Atlantic City "begging for crumbs." [26] Mrs. Hamer, by now a minor national celebrity, said of Humphrey's efforts, "It's a token of rights on the back row that we get in Mississippi. We didn't come all this way for that mess again." [27]

To the general public the FDP appeared to be a band of moral zealots hostile to reasonable compromise and ungrateful for the real concession that the party had offered. The true story was more complicated. Aware that total victory was impossible, the FDP had in fact been quite willing to accept any proposal that recognized its legitimacy. At the beginning of the controversy Oregon's Congresswoman Edith Green offered a compromise that the FDP found entirely acceptable. Mrs. Green proposed that the convention seat

[25] Holt, *The Summer That Didn't End,* pp. 16–17; Watters and Cleghorn, *Climbing Jacob's Ladder,* pp. 290–92; *New York Times* (Aug. 25, 1964), 23.

[26] William McCord, *Mississippi: The Long Hot Summer* (Norton, 1965), p. 117.

[27] Mrs. Hamer is quoted in Holt, *The Summer That Didn't End,* p. 174.

every member of both delegations who signed a pledge of loyalty and that Mississippi's vote be divided between the two groups according to the number of seated delegates in each. Since only eleven members of the credentials committee (10 percent of the total) had to sign a minority report to dislodge the Green compromise from committee, the FDP seemed assured that its case would reach the convention floor, where many believed that the Green compromise would prevail over Johnson's original proposal. FDP's hopes for a minority report rested chiefly on Joseph Rauh, a member of the credentials committee, leader of the Democratic party in the District of Columbia, veteran of innumerable liberal crusades, and, happily, adviser and legal counsel of the FDP. But Rauh was also a friend of Hubert Humphrey and an attorney for Humphrey's strong supporter, Walter Reuther. After Humphrey came on the scene with his compromise, Rauh backed away from the minority report.

In his semi-official history of the Mississippi Summer Project, *The Summer That Didn't End*, Len Holt presents the FDP and SNCC interpretation of what happened. Presumably pressured by his powerful friends, Rauh broke a promise to the FDP and would not support the Green compromise. One by one the FDP's other allies on the committee backed away—some to protect jobs, others to keep alive hopes for federal judgeships, and one because he feared the loss of a local antipoverty program. In the end the FDP failed to collect the needed signatures, and there was no minority report. The angry rhetoric that the FDP delegates let loose in Atlantic City was in reality inspired less by Humphrey's compromise than by what the FDP regarded as its betrayal at the hands of the white liberals on the credentials committee. By the end of the Democratic convention SNCC was convinced that membership in the Democratic coalition held little hope for Southern blacks and that, lacking power, they would always be sold out by the liberals. In Atlantic City the phrase "white power structure" took on concrete meaning. Freedom Summer, which began with SNCC fighting for entrance into the American political system, ended with the radical conviction that that system was beyond redemption.[28]

In the end the Freedom Summer Project of 1964 not only destroyed SNCC's faith in the American political system; it also undermined its commitment to integration. Within the project racial tensions between white and black workers were never successfully resolved. Though many white volunteers established warm relationships with the local black families that housed them,[29] healthy communication between students and veteran SNCC workers proved difficult at best. Staff members resented the officious

---

[28] *New York Times* (Aug. 25, 1964), 23; Holt, *The Summer That Didn't End*, pp. 171–78; see also Zinn, *SNCC*, pp. 251–56; and Stoper, "The Student Nonviolent Coordinating Committee," pp. 74, 77–79, 81.

[29] See, for instance, Sutherland, *Letters from Mississippi*, p. 48.

manner of better-educated volunteers and feared that the white students were taking over the movement. "Several times," one volunteer wrote, "I've had to completely re-do press statements or letters written by one of them." [30] Said a SNCC worker, "Look at those fly-by-night freedom fighters bossing everybody around." [31] SNCC people found it hard to respect the efforts of volunteers who they knew would retreat at the end of the summer to their safe middle-class world. One sensitive white female volunteer wrote that SNCC workers "were automatically suspicious of us, the white volunteers; throughout the summer they put us to the test, and few, if any, could pass. . . . It humbled, if not humiliated, one to realize that *finally they will never accept me.*" [32] By the end of the summer a spirit akin to black nationalism was rising inside the SNCC organization.

The overall failure of Freedom Summer administered a blow to SNCC's morale from which the organization almost did not recover. In November 1964, Robert Coles, a psychiatrist who had worked closely with SNCC, wrote about the tendency of veteran workers to develop battle fatigue. Even heroic temperaments, he said, could not escape the depression that inevitably results from long periods of unremitting dangers and disappointments. But by the fall of 1964 battle fatigue was no longer just the problem of individual SNCC members; it was pervading the entire organization. One patient told Coles,

> I'm tired, but so is the whole movement. We're busy worrying about our position or our finances, so we don't do anything. . . . We're becoming lifeless, just like all revolutions when they lose their first momentum and become more interested in preserving what they've won than going on to new challenges. . . . Only with us we haven't won that much, and we're either holding to the little we have as an organization, or we get bitter, and want to create a new revolution. . . . You know, one like the Muslims want which is the opposite of what we say we're for. It's as if we completely reverse ourselves because we can't get what we want.[33]

Uncertain of their purpose, SNCC workers in the winter of 1964–65 grew introspective. Months were consumed in discussing the future of whites in the movement and the proper structure of the organization. Fresh from a trip to Africa where he met the black nationalist Malcolm X, John Lewis, Chairman of SNCC, spoke for the majority in early 1965 when he demanded

---

[30] Quoted in *ibid.*, p. 202.

[31] Quoted in Pat Watters, *Encounter with the Future* (Southern Regional Council, May, 1965), p. 32.

[32] Belfrage, *Freedom Summer*, p. 80.

[33] Robert Coles, "Social Struggle and Awareness," *Psychiatry*, XXVII (Nov., 1964), 305-15.

that blacks lead their own movement.[34] At the same time, quarrels over organization almost tore SNCC apart. Some workers became "high on freedom" and advocated a romantic anarchism that rejected bureaucratic structure and leadership. Robert Moses, for instance, believed that SNCC workers should "go where the spirit say go, and do what the spirit say do." Moses was so disturbed by his own prestige in the movement that he changed his name, drifted into Alabama, and thereafter was only vaguely connected with SNCC. Meanwhile SNCC's field work tended to fall into neglect.[35]

In the summer of 1965 SNCC brought 300 white volunteers into Mississippi for its second and last summer project. The result was a shambles. Racial tensions caused some projects to break up and prevented serious work in others. Problems only dimly perceived a year before assumed stark clarity, and SNCC's resentment of the volunteers became overt and unambiguous. At staff meetings blacks would silence white students with such remarks as "How long have you been here?" and "How do you know what it's like being black?" and "if you don't like the way we do it, get the hell out of the state." [36] Not all the blame for the final breakdown of race relations in SNCC, however, belonged to the black staff. The questionable motivation of some of the white students led Alvin Poussaint, a black psychiatrist close to SNCC, to add a new neurosis to medical terminology—the white African Queen or Tarzan complex. The victim of this neurosis harbored repressed delusions of himself as an "intelligent, brave, and handsome white man or woman, leading the poor down-trodden and oppressed black men to freedom and salvation." [37]

But the most serious obstacle to healthy race relations inside SNCC was sex, and in this dimension, as really in all others, the villain was neither black worker nor white student, but rather the sad and twisted history of race relations in America. The white girl who came South to help SNCC found herself, according to Dr. Poussaint, "at the center of an emotionally shattering crossfire of racial tensions that have been nurtured for centuries." [38] In the summer of 1965 a veteran black civil rights worker in SCLC tried to warn

[34] Watters, *Encounter with the Future*, pp. 29–31; see also Lerone Bennett, Jr., "SNCC, Rebels with a Cause," *Ebony*, XX (July, 1965), 146–53.

[35] For the Moses quote, see Gene Roberts, "From Freedom High to 'Black Power,'" *New York Times Magazine* (Sept. 25, 1966), 21; see also Bruce Payne, "The Student Nonviolent Coordinating Committee: An Overview Two Years Later," *The Activist* (Nov., 1965), 6–7; and Stoper, "Student Nonviolent Coordinating Committee," pp. 126–27.

[36] These quotations are from transcripts of informal taped interviews conducted in the South in 1965 by students of Stanford University. The tapes are stored at Stanford.

[37] Alvin F. Poussaint, "Problems of White Civil Rights Workers in the South," *Psychiatric Opinion*, III (Dec., 1966), 21.

[38] Alvin F. Poussaint, "The Stresses of the White Female Worker in the Civil Rights Movement in the South," *American Journal of Psychiatry*, CXXIII (Oct., 1966), 401.

white girls of the perils that awaited them in their dealings with black men in the movement:

> What you have here is a man who had no possible way of being a man in the society in which he lives, save one. And that's the problem. The only way or place a Negro man has been able to express his manhood is sexually and so you find a tremendous sexual aggressiveness. And I say quite frankly, don't get carried away by it and don't get afraid of it either. I mean, don't think it's because you're so beautiful and so ravishing that this man is so enamoured of you. It's not that at all. He's just trying to find his manhood and he goes especially to the places that have robbed him of it. . . . And so, in a sense, what passes itself as desire is probably a combination of hostility and resentment—because he resents what the society has done to him and he wants to take it out on somebody who symbolizes the establishment of society.[39]

At the end of the summer a white girl spoke of her experiences:

> Well, I think that the white female should be very well prepared before she comes down here to be bombarded. And she also has to be well prepared to tell them to go to hell and be prepared to have them not give up. . . . I've never met such forward men as I have in Mississippi.[40]

The problem was complicated by the jealousy of black girls toward their white rivals, and by neurotic whites who sought to ease their guilt by permitting blacks to exploit them sexually and financially.[41] On leaving their projects to go home, a few white girls told Poussaint, "I hate Negroes." [42] By the end of the summer of 1965 no one could any longer doubt that the blacks reciprocated the feeling.

The year 1965 was a lost one for SNCC. For the first time since its founding, it was no longer on the frontier of protest, no longer the keeper of the nation's conscience, no longer the driving force of a moral revolution. The civil rights acts of 1964 and 1965 brought the civil rights movement, for which SNCC had suffered so much, to a triumphant conclusion, but SNCC had lost interest in integrated public accommodations and equal political rights. SNCC seemed to be losing its sense of mission and after years of providing heroes for the black protest movement, it now needed a hero of its own. Significantly it chose Malcolm X, the black nationalist who had been assassinated by Muslim rivals in February 1965.[43] Only a few years before,

---

[39] Taped by Stanford students in 1965.

[40] *Ibid.*

[41] Poussaint, "Problems of White Civil Rights Workers in the South," 20–21.

[42] Pousaint, "Stresses of the White Female Worker," 404.

[43] On influence of Malcolm X on SNCC, see Stoper, "The Student Nonviolent Coordinating Committee," p. 181.

SNCC and Malcolm X had seemed to occupy opposite poles of black protest. Thus while SNCC's John Lewis was toning down his speech at the March on Washington, Malcolm X w̧as saying,

> Who ever heard of angry revolutionists all harmonizing "We Shall Overcome . . . Suum Day . . ." while tripping and swaying along arm-in-arm with the very people they were supposed to be angrily revolting against? Who ever heard of angry revolutionists swinging their bare feet together with their oppressors in lily-pad park pools, with gospels and guitars and "I Have a Dream" speeches? [44]

While policemen were clubbing SNCC workers in Mississippi, Malcolm X was saying, "If someone puts a hand on you, send him to the cemetery." [45] While SNCC was pondering the meaning of Atlantic City, Malcolm X was saying, "We *need* a Mau Mau. If they don't want to deal with the Mississippi Freedom Democratic Party, then we'll give them something else to deal with." While black nationalists were still a minority in SNCC, Malcolm X was calling for black control of black politicians in black communities, black ownership of ghetto businesses, and black unity "to lift the level of our community, to make our society beautiful so that we will be satisfied in our own social circles and won't be running around here trying to knock our way into a social circle where we're not wanted." [46] This was the language that had made Malcolm X the hero of the urban ghetto, and it was the language appropriate in 1965 to SNCC's militant mood. In a certain sense Malcolm X was the link that connected SNCC with the black radicalism that was arising in the North.

Unlike SNCC, the ghetto masses never had to disabuse themselves of the colorblind assumptions of the civil rights movement. Trapped permanently in their neighborhoods, the poor blacks of the North have always been painfully conscious of their racial separateness. As Essien-Udom, a historian of black nationalism, has written, blackness "is the stuff of their lives and an omnipresent, harsh reality. For this reason the Negro masses are instinctively 'race men.'" [47] But the civil rights movement nevertheless had its consequences in the ghetto. The spectacle of Southern blacks defying their white tormentors apparently inspired among Northern blacks race pride and resurgent outrage at the gap between American ideals and black realities. Thus the civil rights movement had the ironic effect of feeding the nationalist tendency in the ghetto to turn inward, to separate, and to identify the white

---

[44] *The Autobiography of Malcolm X* (Grove Press, 1966), pp. 280–81.

[45] *Malcolm X Speaks: Selected Speeches and Statements* (Merit, 1965), p. 12.

[46] *Ibid.*, 38–39.

[47] E. U. Essien-Udom, *Black Nationalism* (Univ. of Chicago Press, 1962), p. 3.

men outside as the enemy. SNCC's frustrations exploded intellectually in the formulation of black power doctrines, but ghetto rage took the form of riot.

The riot of August 1965, in Watts (the sprawling ghetto of Los Angeles) dwarfed the violent outbursts of the previous year and awakened America to the race crisis in her big cities. A social trauma of the first order, the Watts riot resulted in 35 deaths, 600 burned and looted buildings, and 4,000 persons arrested.[48] Above all it revealed the dangerous racial hatred that had been accumulating unnoticed in the nation's black ghettos. The official autopsy of Watts denied by implication that it was a revolt against white oppression. The McCone Commission (after its chairman, John McCone), appointed by California's Governor Pat Brown to investigate the riot, estimated that only 10,000 Watts residents, or 2 percent of the population in the riot area, had actually been on the streets during the uprising. This minor fraction, the Commission contended, was not protesting specific grievances, which admittedly existed in abundance, but was engaged in an "insensate rage of destruction" that was "formless, quite senseless." [49] Critics of the McCone report have ably challenged these findings. (For example, Robert Fogelson points out that "to claim that only 10,000 Negroes rioted when about 4,000 were arrested is to presume that the police apprehended fully 40 percent of the rioters.") [50] In reality, a rather large minority of the riot-age population in Watts was on the streets during the riot, and as one of the Commission's own staff reports revealed, the riot had significant support inside the ghetto, especially in the worst slum areas.[51]

On the crucial question of the riot's causes, observers on the scene agreed that the rioters were animated by a common anger against whites.[52] Robert Blauner, a staff member for the McCone Commission and its severest ciritic, has written,

> Most of the actions of the rioters appear to have been informed by the desire to clear out an alien presence, white men, rather than to kill them. . . . It was primarily an attack on property, particularly white-owned businesses. . . .

---

[48] A Report by the Governor's Commission on the Los Angeles Riot, *Violence in the City —An End or a Beginning?* (Dec. 2, 1965), pp. 1–2. (Referred to heareafter as the McCone Report.)

[49] McCone Report, pp. 1, 4–5.

[50] Robert M. Fogelson, "White on Black: A Critique of the McCone Commission Report on the Los Angeles Riots," *Political Science Quarterly*, LXXXII (Sept., 1967), 345.

[51] E. Edward Ransford, *Attitudes and Other Characteristics of Negroes in Watts, South Central, and Crenshaw Areas of Los Angeles* (a staff study prepared for the McCone Commission), p. 2.

[52] See, for instance, Robert Conot, *Rivers of Blood, Years of Darkness* (Bantam Books, 1967), p. 204.

The spirit of the Watts rioters appears similar to that of anti-colonial crowds demonstrating against foreign masters.[53]

Said Bayard Rustin, a moderate black intellectual who was in Watts during the riot, "The whole point of the outburst in Watts was that it marked the first major rebellion of Negroes against their masochism and was carried on with the express purpose of asserting that they would no longer quietly submit to the deprivation of slum life." [54] Thus in 1965, for different reasons, both the ghetto masses and the members of SNCC were seized by militant anti-white feelings, and it was this congruence of mood that would shortly permit SNCC to appeal to a nation-wide black audience.

After a year on the periphery of the black protest movement, SNCC in 1966 moved again to the forefront. In May 1966, at a time when the organization was apparently disintegrating, 135 staff members (25 of them white) met in Nashville to thrash out their future. Early in the emotional conference, by a vote of 60 to 22, John Lewis, the gentle advocate of nonviolence, retained the chairmanship of SNCC by defeating the challenge of the militant Stokely Carmichael. But as the conference went on, the arguments of the militants began to prevail. When the staff voted to boycott the coming White House conference on civil rights, Lewis announced that he would attend anyway, and the question of the chairmanship was then reopened. This time SNCC workers chose Carmichael as their new leader by a vote of 60 to 12. The conference next issued a statement calling, among other things, for "black Americans to begin building independent political, economic, and cultural institutions that they will control and use as instruments of social change in this country." [55]

A few weeks later the full meaning of Carmichael's election became clear to the whole nation. The occasion was the famous Meredith march through Mississippi in June of 1966. James Meredith, the man who integrated the University of Mississippi in 1962 with the help of the United States Army, embarked on a 200-mile walk from Memphis to Jackson to show the black people of Mississippi that they could walk to the voting booths without fear. On June 6, 28 miles out of Memphis, a white man felled Meredith with buckshot. Erroneously believing that Meredith had been killed, civil rights leaders immediately flew to Mississippi to continue his walk against fear. So it was that arm in arm, Martin Luther King of SCLC, Floyd McKissick of

[53] Quoted in Robert Blauner, "Whitewash over Watts: The Failure of the McCone Commission Report," *Transaction*, III (March–April, 1966), 9.

[54] Bayard Rustin, "The Watts 'Manifesto' and the McCone Report," *Commentary*, XLI (March, 1966), 30.

[55] This account of Carmichael's election and the quotations from SNCC's statement are from Newfield, *A Prophetic Minority*, pp. 75–77.

CORE, and Stokely Carmichael of SNCC marched down U.S. Highway 51.

Early efforts of the three leaders to maintain surface unity rapidly broke down. Significantly, the first issue that divided them was the role of white people in the Meredith march. King's workers publicly thanked Northern whites for joining the procession. McKissick also thanked the Northerners but announced that black men must now lead the civil rights movement. And Carmichael mused aloud that maybe the whites should go home. As the column moved onto the back roads and Southern white hostility increased, the leadership of the march failed to agree on how to respond to violence. In Philadelphia, Mississippi, Dr. King conducted a memorial service for Goodman, Chaney, and Schwerner and told a crowd of 300 jeering whites that the murderers of the three men were no doubt "somewhere around me at this moment." Declaring that "I am not afraid of any man," King then delivered a Christian sermon. But after the service was over and local whites got rough, the marchers returned punch for punch.

The real spokesman for the march, it soon developed, was not King but Stokely Carmichael. In one town, after spending a few hours in jail, Carmichael told a crowd, "I ain't going to jail no more. I ain't going to jail no more," and he announced, "Every courthouse in Mississippi ought to be burned down to get rid of the dirt." Carmichael then issued the cry that would make him famous. Five times he shouted "Black Power!" and, the *New York Times* reported, "each time the younger members of the audience shouted back, 'Black Power.'" Informed of this new slogan, Dr. King expressed disapproval, and SCLC workers exhorted crowds to call not for black power but for "freedom now." Nevertheless, by the end of the Meredith march, black power had become a force to reckon with.[56]

At its inception in June, 1966, black power was not a systematic doctrine but a cry of rage. In an article in the *New York Times Magazine*, Dr. Poussaint tried to explain the psychological origin of the anger expressed in the new slogan:

> I remember treating Negro workers after they had been beaten viciously by white toughs or policemen while conducting civil rights demonstrations. I would frequently comment, "You must feel pretty angry getting beaten up like that by those bigots." Often I received a reply such as: "No, I don't hate those white men, I love them because they must really be suffering with all that hatred in their souls. Dr. King says the only way we can win our freedom is through love. Anger and hatred has never solved anything."
>
> I used to sit there and wonder, "Now, what do they really do with their rage?"

---

[56] For the Meredith march, see *New York Times*, June 7, 1966, p. 1; June 8, pp. 1 and 26; June 9, p. 1; June 12, pp. 1 and 82; June 17, p. 1; June 21, p. 30; June 22, p. 25.

Poussaint reported that after a while these workers vented their mounting rage against each other.

> While they were talking about being nonviolent and "loving" the sheriff that just hit them over the head, they rampaged around the project houses beating up each other. I frequently had to calm Negro civil rights workers with large doses of tranquilizers for what I can describe clinically only as acute attacks of rage.

In time the civil rights workers began to direct their anger against white racists, the Federal Government, and finally white people in the movement. Said Poussaint:

> This rage was at a fever pitch for many months, before it became crystallized in the "Black Power" slogan. The workers who shouted it the loudest were those with the oldest battle scars from the terror, demoralization, and castration which they experienced through continual direct confrontation with Southern white racists. Furthermore, some of the most bellicose chanters of the slogan had been, just a few years before, examples of nonviolent, loving passive resistance in their struggle against white supremacy. These workers appeared to be seeking a sense of inner psychological emancipation from racists through self-assertion and release of aggressive angry feelings.[57]

In the months following the Meredith march, SNCC found itself at the center of a bitter national controversy and spokesman for an enlarged constituency. The anger implicit in the slogan "black power" assured SNCC a following in the ghettos of the North and ended its regional confinement. Through its leader, Stokely Carmichael, SNCC labored through 1966 and into 1967 to give intellectual substance to the black power slogan, seeking especially to frame an analysis that would be relevant to black Americans of all sections. Although his speeches were often inflammatory, Carmichael in his writing attempted serious, even restrained, argument suitable for an educated audience. But the elements of black power were not, in truth, derived from rational reflection but from wretched experience—from the beatings, jailhouses, and abortive crusades that SNCC veterans had endured for six years. SNCC had tried nonviolence and found it psychologically destructive. (The "days of the free head-whipping are over," Carmichael and his collaborator Charles Hamilton wrote. "Black people should and must fight back." [58]) SNCC, for example, had believed in integration and tried it within its own organization, but black and white together had not worked. (In-

---

[57] Alvin F. Poussaint, "A Negro Psychiatrist Explains the Negro Psyche," *New York Times Magazine* (Aug. 20, 1967), 55 ff.

[58] Stokely Carmichael and Charles V. Hamilton, *Black Power: The Politics of Liberation* (Vintage, 1967), p. 52.

tegration, said Carmichael, "is a subterfuge for the maintenance of white supremacy" and "reinforces, among both black and white, the idea that 'white' is automatically better and 'black' is by definition inferior."[59]) SNCC had allied with white liberals in the Democratic party and had come away convinced that it had been betrayed. (In dealing with blacks, Carmichael said, white liberals "perpetuate a paternalistic, colonial relationship."[60]) SNCC had struggled for equal political rights but concluded finally that political inequality was less oppressive than economic exploitation. In 1966 SNCC felt it was necessary to go beyond the assertion of these hard conclusions and to attempt to impose on them systematic form. So it was that after years of activism divorced from ideology, SNCC began to reduce its field work and concentrate on fashioning an intellectual rationale for its new militancy. At a time when the black protest movement was floundering and its future direction was uncertain, SNCC stepped forward to contribute the doctrines of black power, which were really the culmination of its career. No history of SNCC would be complete, therefore, without some consideration of those doctrines.

According to Stokely Carmichael, the black masses suffer from two different but reinforcing forms of oppression: class exploitation and white racism. To illustrate this point, he relies on an analogy apparently inspired by Franz Fanon's *Wretched of the Earth*, a book with considerable influence in black power circles. The black communities of contemporary America, Carmichael says, share many of the characteristics of African colonies under European rule. Thus as Africa once enriched its imperialist masters by exporting valuable raw materials to Europe, so now do the American ghettos "export" their labor for the profit of American capitalists. In both Africa and America, white men own local businesses and use them to drain away any wealth somehow possessed by the subject population. As in Africa, there exists in the ghetto a white power structure that is no abstraction, but is a visible and concrete presence—the white landlords, for instance, who collect rent and ignore needed repairs, the city agencies and school systems that systematically neglect black people, the policemen who abuse black citizens and collect payoffs from white racketeers. By far the most insidious method devised by the white imperialists for perpetuating class exploitation has been the use of race as a badge of inferiority. Colonial masters, says Carmichael, "purposely, maliciously, and with reckless abandon relegated the black man to a subordinated, inferior status in society. . . . White America's School of Slavery and Segregation, like the School of Colonialism, has taught the subject to hate himself and deny his humanity." As the colonies of Africa have done, black Americans must undergo "political

---

[59] Stokely Carmichael, "What We Want," *New York Review of Books* (Sept. 22, 1966), 6.

[60] Carmichael and Hamilton, *Black Power*, p. 65.

modernization," liberate their communities, and achieve self-determination. And like Africa, the ghetto must win the struggle by its own effort.[61]

For Carmichael, liberation begins with eradication of the effects of white racism. To overcome the shame of race bred in them by white men, blacks must develop a cultural identity, rediscover the rich African civilization from which they originally came, and learn from their history that they are a "vibrant, valiant people." [62] Freed of their damaging self-image, they can begin to challenge the capitalist values that have enslaved them as a class. The white middle class, says Carmichael, has fostered esteem for "material aggrandizement," is "without a viable conscience as regards humanity," and constitutes "the backbone of institutional reason in this country." Black men, however, will develop values emphasizing "the dignity of man, not . . . the sanctity of property," "free people," not "free enterpise." [63] "The society we seek to build among black people, then, is not a capitalist one. It is a society in which the spirit of community and humanistic love prevail." [64] To complete the process of liberation, black men will have to purge the ghetto of exploiting institutions and develop structures that conform to their new values.

The reconstruction of the black community, Carmichael contends, should be in the hands of black people in order to "convey the revolutionary idea . . . that black people are able to do things themselves." Among other acts of liberation that they can perform, ghetto blacks should conduct rent strikes against slum landlords and boycotts against the ghetto merchant who refuses to " 'invest' say forty to fifty percent of his net profit in the indigenous community." Governmental structures that have violated the humanity of blacks will have to be either eliminated from the ghetto or made responsive to their black constituency. The school system must be taken from professionals, most of whom have demonstrated "insensitivity to the needs and problems of the black child" and given to black parents, who will control personnel and curriculum. The indifference of the existing political parties to black people necessitates formation of separate (parallel) black organizations, both in the 110 Southern counties with black majorities and in the ghettos of the North.[65] According to Carmichael, it is simply naive to think that poor and powerless blacks have anything in common with the other components of the Democratic coalition. White liberals inevitably fall under the "overpowering influence" of their racist environment, and their demands for civil

---

[61] For the colonial analogy, see *ibid.*, Chapter 1.

[62] *Ibid.*, pp. 37–39.

[63] *Ibid.*, pp. 40–4 .

[64] Carmichael, "What We Want," 7.

[65] Carmichael and Hamilton, *Black Power*, Chapter 8 and p. 166.

rights are "doing for blacks." Labor unions accept the existing order and, in the case of the AFL, even discriminate against black workers. Black political parties, Carmichael believes, will alone be devoted to real change and will in fact make possible emancipation from dominant American values and power centers.[66]

Carmichael professes to believe that black power is not really a departure from American practice. "Traditionally," he writes, "for each new ethnic group, the route to social and political integration into America's pluralistic society has been through the organization of their own institutions with which to represent their communal needs within the larger society." [67] Once in possession of power, blacks then could reenter the old coalitions for specific goals. But "let any ghetto group contemplating coalition be so tightly organized, so strong, that . . . it is an 'undigestible body' which cannot be absorbed or swallowed up." Given Carmichael's scheme for a radical reconstruction of American society, it is not surprising that the only group that he someday hopes to make his ally is the poor whites.[68]

As several critics have pointed out,[69] Carmichael's version of black power is hardly more than a collection of fragments, often lacking in clarity, consistency, and conviction. Thus, for example, Carmichael talks about the need for parallel institutions but offers only one example—black political organizations. He claims that these organizations can regenerate the entire political system but typically neglects to explain concretely how this regeneration is to be achieved. He calls for radical rejection of American values and institutions but at the same time portrays the black community as merely another ethnic group turning temporarily inward to prepare for later integration into American society. According to Carmichael, ghetto blacks are an exploited proletariat kept in bondage to enrich America's capitalist class; yet black workers seem more like a *lumpenproletariat* threatened with loss of economic function and forced to the margin of the American economy. Carmichael fails to reveal the mechanisms by which big business keeps the black man exploited, and indeed it seems doubtful that big business especially profits from the depressed condition of such a large group of potential consumers. But the real criticism of black power is not that as a body of thought it lacks coherence and sustained argument. Its greatest weakness is its failure to propose adequate solutions.

---

[66] *Ibid.*, pp. 60–66.

[67] Stokely Carmichael, "Toward Black Liberation," *The Massachusetts Review*, VII (Autumn, 1966), 642.

[68] Carmichael and Hamilton, *Black Power*, pp. 80, 82.

[69] For critiques of black power, see, for instance, Paul Feldman, "The Pathos of 'Black Power,' " *Dissent* (Jan.–Feb., 1967), 69–79; Bayard Rustin, " 'Black Power' and Coalition Politics," *Commentary*, XLII (Sept., 1966), 35–40; Christopher Lasch, "The Trouble with Black Power," *New York Review of Books*, X (Feb. 29, 1968), 4 ff.

Carmichael began his argument by maintaining that black men suffer from two separate but related forms of discrimination—racial and economic. When Carmichael proposes ways for black men to undo the effects of racism, he makes good sense. Certainly black men should uncover their cultural roots and take pride in what has been of worth in their heritage. Certainly liberal paternalism is now anachronistic and black men should lead their own organizations. Nonviolence probably *was* psychologically damaging to many who practiced it, and integration into a hostile white society is not only an unrealistic goal but demeaning to a self-respecting people. Furthermore, some middle-class values, as Carmichael maintains, are less than ennobling, and elements of the black man's life style do have intrinsic merit. But it is doubtful whether black self-respect can ever be achieved without a solution of the second problem confronting ghetto blacks, and it is here that Carmichael's version of black power is most deficient.

Concerned primarily with humanizing social and governmental structures inside the ghetto, Carmichael has little to say about ending poverty in black America. Although more responsive policemen and schoolteachers and less dishonest slum lords and merchants will no doubt be a great step forward, these aspects of ghetto life are of less consequence than unemployment or poverty wages. Within the ghetto the resources for economic reconstruction are simply not available, and since Carmichael rejects coalitions outside the ghetto, he is barred from offering a realistic economic strategy. It is this weakness that led the black intellectual and long-time civil rights leader Bayard Rustin to oppose black power. Pointing to the futility of separatist politics in a society in which the black man is a minority, Rustin calls for "a liberal-labor-civil rights coalition which would work to make the Democratic party truly responsive to the aspirations of the poor, and which would develop support for programs (specifically those outlined in A. Philip Randolph's $100 billion Freedom Budget) aimed at the reconstruction of American society in the interest of greater social justice." [70] Rustin's goals are considerably less apocalyptic than Carmichael's, but they are far more realistic. Carmichael's radical ruminations about a socialist alliance of poor whites and poor blacks seem fantasies irrelevant to American social realities. Although Carmichael's vision holds out hope for some distant time, it offers no meaningful proposals for the present.

The true significance of black power lies not in the doctrines into which it evolved but in the historical circumstances that gave it birth. The real message of black power is that after years of struggle to make America an open and just society, an important group of civil rights workers, instructed by the brute facts of its own history, gave up the fight. Black power was a cry of rage directed against white bigots who overcame righteous men by force, a cry of bitterness against white liberals who had only a stunted comprehen-

---

[70] Bayard Rustin, " 'Black Power' and Coalition Politics," 36.

sion of the plight of the black poor, and a cry of frustration against gains that seemed meager when compared to needs. It is possible, however, that even rage can perform a useful function, and if the black power slogan brings about a constructive catharsis and helps rouse the black masses from apathy, then the intellectual shortcomings of black power doctrines may seem of little consequence, and what began as a cry of despair may yet play a creative role in the black protest movement. Therefore, whether the history of SNCC in this decade will be considered triumph or tragedy depends on events yet to occur.

SUGGESTED READING

Though much of the literature on the black protest movement of recent years has been more journalistic than scholarly, a few books have proved of value. Useful surveys include Arthur I. Waskow's *From Race Riot to Sit-In* ° (1966), which begins its story in 1919, and Anthony Lewis' *Portrait of a Decade* ° (1964), a study of the fight against segregation from 1954 to 1964. An excellent statement of the race problem as of the mid–1960's is Charles E. Silberman's *Crisis in Black and White* ° (1964), which is remarkable for its sensitivity to developing trends. For an illuminating public opinion survey containing material on the initial impact of black power, see William Brink and Louis Harris' *Black and White* ° (1966). Especially valuable for its statistical information is the *Report of the National Advisory Commission on Civil Disorders* ° (1968). Nixon's policies on race are attacked by Leon E. Panetta in *Bring Us Together: The Nixon Team and Civil Rights* (1971).

Studies with important implications for the student of black power are Charles Eric Lincoln's *The Black Muslims in America* (1961); Lee Rainwater and William Yancey's *The Moynihan Report and the Politics of Controversy* (1967), which reprints Moynihan's famous study of the black family and many of the reactions that the study provoked; Eldridge Cleaver's *Soul on Ice* (1968); William H. Grier and Price M. Cobbs's *Black Rage* (1968), a study by two psychiatrists that is too impressionistic to be convincing; and Jerry Cohen and William S. Murphy's *Burn, Baby, Burn* ° (1966), which comments on the Watts riot. On the failure of civil rights movements, see U.S. Commission on Civil Rights, *Federal Civil Rights Enforcement Effort: A Report of the U.S. Commission on Civil Rights* (1970). See also *Black Protest in the Sixties,* edited by August Meier and Elliott Rudwick (1970); August Meier's *The Transformation of Activism: Black Experience* (1970); and Benjamin Muse's *The American Negro Revolution: From Nonviolence to Black Power, 1963–1967* (1968).

Vincent Harding's "Black Radicalism: The Road from Montgomery," in Alfred Young, ed., *Dissent: Explorations in the History of*

American Radicalism ° (1968), is a sensitive study by a young black scholar. For a Marxist's defense of black power, see Eugene Genovese's "The Legacy of Slavery and the Roots of Black Nationalism," *Studies on the Left* (1967); for a negative reaction on the white left, see Christopher Lasch's "The Trouble with Black Power," *New York Review of Books,* X (Feb. 29, 1968); and for a study of the problems that black power posed for the white liberal, see Hugh D. Graham's "The Storm over Black Power," *Virginia Quarterly Review,* XLIII (Autumn 1967). Martin Duberman, in "Black Power in America," *Partisan Review,* XXXV (Winter 1968), finds parallels between the development of black power and both abolitionism and anarchism. *The Black Power Revolt* ° (1968) and *The Black Seventies* (1970), both edited by Floyd Barbour, are useful collections of statements on black aspirations and diagnoses. Gary Marx's *Protest and Prejudice* ° (1968) is a sociological study of beliefs in the black community.

KENNETH KENISTON

Revolution or Counterrevolution?

INTRODUCTION

College students were so indifferent to political and social problems in the 1950's that some of their elders feared for the future
of the republic. But in the early 1960's young people on the campus surprised the country by flocking to the Peace Corps and
providing the shock troops for the civil rights movement. Though
the campus mood in the early Kennedy years was idealistic,
hopeful, and liberal, a small minority was already groping toward
a radical critique of American society. At Port Huron, Michigan,
in 1962, fifty-nine members of the Students for a Democratic Society issued a manifesto of the New Left. It was neither Marxist
nor liberal; neither a program nor a seasoned social analysis. But

FROM *Youth and Dissent: The Rise of a New Opposition,* © 1971 by Kenneth Keniston.
Reprinted by permission of Harcourt Brace Jovanovich, Inc.

it expressed the incohate discontent that would grow in future years into the prevalent mood on campus. The Port Huron statement protested the powerlessness of the individual, the meaninglessness of most work in industrial society, and the "cumbersome academic bureaucracy" that imposed irrelevant curricula on students. And it pleaded for a real American democracy that would give every citizen some control over his own life.

At the University of California at Berkeley in 1964, the Free Speech Movement used these ideas to help mobilize students in an epochal confrontation with the university. Mario Savio, leader of the Free Speech Movement, told the students,

> There is a time when the operations of the machine become so odious, make you so sick at heart, that you can't take part. . . . And you've got to put your bodies upon the gears and upon the wheels, upon the levers, upon all the apparatus, and you've got to make it stop. And you've got to indicate to the people who own it . . . that unless you're free the machine will be prevented from working at all.

The sit-in at Berkeley following Savio's speech resulted in the arrest of eight hundred students.

It was Vietnam, however, that did most to create a sympathetic student audience for the radicals. In 1965 SDS first turned its attention to the war, organizing a march of twenty-five hundred people in Washington as well as the first antiwar teach-ins. When SDS began this attack on American foreign policy it had only twelve hundred members in 30 chapters. By 1967 it had six thousand in 227 chapters, and tens of thousands more willing to follow radical leadership. As the decade proceeded, the New Left critique of America became more strident, more pointed, more hostile. America's corporate capitalism, the radicals said, fostered injustice at home and imperialism abroad. Liberal intellectuals and politicians were servants of this capitalism, as were the universities and the military. This view of the social order proved compelling enough to inspire a young people's crusade against some of the most cherished institutions of traditional American society.

In addition to political radicals, the college generation of the 1960's produced hippies, drop-outs, Young Americans for Freedom, and students who merely wanted their degrees. Observers of the youth scene found the variety and contradictions of student life baffling, and most interpreters dealt in clichés and oversimplification. One who did not was Kenneth Keniston, professor of psychology at Yale Medical School. In 1965 Keniston published *The Uncommitted,* a book about alienated students based on extended observation of a small number of subjects. Keniston's students were not the committed radicals of SDS but young people whose rejection of contemporary life and values

left them isolated, ready to drop out, and without personal or political goals. They were, in short, a breed of youth soon to be
known as hippies. Keniston found that his alienated sample of
the young tended to have weak or absent fathers, and mothers
who tried to compensate for disappointments in their lives by over-
investing in the lives of their sons. Competing with their fathers
for their mothers' attention during early childhood, these sons
won victories that deprived them of fathers to emulate and mothers who would love them without making overwhelming demands.
In consequence, these young people rejected competition, aggressiveness, initiative, and rivalry. But Keniston was not content
with merely psychological explanations and looked for sources
of youth alienation in contemporary society. The pace of change,
he argued, was so rapid that individuals were threatened with detachment from history and tended to overemphasize present experience. The technological values of contemporary society dangerously subordinated the emotional aspect of human nature.
Social fragmentation deprived men of the support of community
and made it difficult to achieve psychological integration. And
the decline of Utopia and the rise of technological values made it
difficult for the young to find meaning for their lives.

In 1967 Keniston turned his attention to a different kind of
rebel. His subjects this time were the leaders of Vietnam Summer, young radicals interested in educating America on the issue
of the war. The result of Keniston's observation was a book
called *Young Radicals*. Keniston disputed the popular notion that
radicals were maladjusted failures in revolt against parental and
other authority. His subjects had close and rewarding relations
with their achievement-demanding mothers. And they admired
their fathers for their ethics and idealism, though finding them in
some respects unsuccessful, acquiescent, and weak. These radicals had become interested in the issues that they now found of
paramount concern long before they had come to full political
consciousness. Their conversion to radicalism at the end of troubled adolescence was gradual and the result in part of personal
confrontation with social inequity. Keniston found the leaders of
Vietnam Summer open, dedicated, and psychologically healthy,
and he obviously admired them.

By 1971, when Keniston wrote the following essay, the era
of the disruptive campus demonstration had begun to wane, but
the ideological opposition of a large portion of the young was
more thoroughgoing than ever. Keniston here critically examines
both the "counter-culture" and its neo-liberal critics, finding substantial merit in the position of each. Though sympathetic to the
values of the counterculture, Keniston borrows his analysis of the
social forces in contemporary society from the neo-liberals. Like
the liberals, Keniston assigns the central role in contemporary
society to the "knowledge sector," and in so doing he ignores

what may be the real locus of power in America. Power, it may more persuasively be argued, is primarily located now, as it has been throughout the twentieth century, in the large corporations. To a large extent they own or control the knowledge sector and use its outposts, including the universities and the mass media, for their own ends. If this is a more accurate view of power in America than Keniston's, then his hope for the future rests on error.

No issue today divides the public or intellectual community so deeply as does the "counterculture," the "new culture," "consciousness III"—what I will call the new youthful opposition. Hawks and doves on the youth question debate campus unrest with an intensity and heat generally reserved only for the weightiest ideological matters. The mildest criticism of the youthful romance with violence or the gentlest critique of radical mindlessness evokes epithets like "reactionary," "counterrevolutionary," or, worst of all, "liberal" from the passionate defenders of the youthful opposition. But conversely, hawks on the youth question feel that the expression of guarded optimism about the decency of students or the claim that most young people act from idealistic motives makes the speaker a sycophant, a Pied Piper, or an "apologist."

Merely to deride this debate would blind us to the real importance of the issues raised. However fashionable it has become to laud or lambaste the dissenting young, serious issues lie hidden behind the current polemics in little magazines. For the debate about the oppositional young ultimately involves a debate about the nature of man and society, and requires that we examine our basic assumptions about both. I suspect that this debate, which crosscuts and confounds the traditional distinctions between conservatives and liberals, may well define the basic terms of intellectual inquiry, controversy, and creativity during the decades ahead.

The debate is important because no event is quite so interesting theoretically as an event that we were led to believe could not occur. A scientific experiment that confirms a prediction is ultimately of far less importance than an experiment that fails. For if our predictions are merely confirmed, we are only re-enforced in our attachment to the ways of thinking that led us to anticipate correctly what was going to happen. But when prediction fails, we are obliged to re-examine the theories upon which the prediction was based, so as to explain, at least in retrospect, the events we failed to anticipate.

The emergence of a youthful opposition is an instance of an historical event that was predicted by no one twenty years ago. Marxist theorists either continued to cherish hopes of a working-class revolt in the capitalist nations, or else devoted their theoretical energies to explaining how monopoly capitalism had successfully co-opted the potentially revolutionary spirit of the working class. Even the most sophisticated neo-Marxists did not predict that those who apparently benefited most from capitalist societies would help lead a new attack upon them. In a comparable way, what I will group together as "liberal theories" not only failed to anticipate the emergence of the youthful revolt, but predicted that such a revolt would become progressively *less* likely as affluence and higher education spread. To understand the theoretical importance of the current debate over the meaning of the youthful opposition therefore requires us to examine in broad outline the widely shared theoretical assumptions of liberal thinkers in the 1950's and early 1960's.

The "Liberal" Analysis

Liberal theories of man have usually started from the malleability or plasticity of human nature. The cultural anthropologists' discovery of the enormous variety of human belief and behavior in primitive cultures led to the view that man was almost totally adaptable to his social environment. Even psychoanalysis, with its heavy initial emphasis upon innate biological factors in development, was modified so as to place far greater stress on environmental influences in shaping the child's personality, and to minimize the importance of innate developmental sequences.

Given this implicit or explicit assumption of human plasticity, psychology as a field concentrated upon the processes by which human beings are influenced, shaped, and molded. For example, among the most highly developed areas in social psychology are the study of attitude change and small-group behavior. Attitude-change studies stressed the way convictions, beliefs, and values could be changed through experimental manipulation. Small-group studies explored how groups influence their members. In general, psychologists attempted to discover the "laws" that governed the molding and alteration of men's feelings, beliefs, convictions, and behavior.

If liberal psychology emphasized human plasticity and the techniques by which human conviction and behavior can be molded and modified, liberal social theories stressed equilibrium, stability, and the mechanisms of social control. The basic model of human society was the model of the "social system," constantly seeking to reach "dynamic equilibrium." The major theoretical effort of liberal sociologists went into explaining precisely *how* this equilibrium, harmony, lack of conflict, or absence of revolution had been guaranteed.

Many of the most powerful liberal theories in politics and economics can also be understood as efforts to explain the mechanisms of social equilibrium. Political theorists emphasized the stabilizing effects of competing interest groups, each with "veto power" over the others. The importance of pluralistic tolerance, of "democratic consensus," and of "liberal personality" was extensively studied. Still others examined how social conflicts are routinized—channeled into institutional forms that minimize social disruption and encourage compromise and reconciliation. For their part, some economists have emphasized the "countervailing powers" that prevent the domination of the economy by any one set of monopolistic interests. Even Keynesianism can be seen as an effort to define the means whereby a stable economy might be guaranteed. Experts on labor relations scrutinized the way highly organized trade unions and the institutions of collective bargaining minimized class struggle, promoting peaceful "conflict resolution." In virtually all areas of scholarly endeavor, then, the major theoretical emphasis was upon explaining that stability which was considered the goal and norm of societal existence.

The liberal assumptions of human plasticity and sociopolitical equilibrium were joined explicitly in the theory of socialization and acculturation. Malleable man was said to be related to stable society through a series of special socializing institutions like the family and the education system, whose primary function was to "integrate" the individual into society. Specifically, families' and schools' chief job was to teach children the social roles and cultural values necessary for adult life in that society. Key societal norms, symbolic systems, values, and role models were said to be "internalized" during the socialization process, and their internalization resulted in adults who were "adjusted"—who "functioned" with the symbols, values, and roles expected by their society.

The family is seen as the primary socializing and acculturating institution. But with the advent of early and prolonged schooling, formal education has increasingly supplemented the family as an agency of socialization. In highly industrialized states, it was argued, prolonged education is inevitable, for the skills required to operate a complex industrial state take many years to learn. Similarly, each of the higher vocations, occupations, and professions has its own set of specialized norms and ethics, its own methods and techniques, its own body of knowledge. So even the far reaches of higher education—graduate and professional school—have generally been described in terms of "professional socialization." Indeed, a generation of studies of the impact of higher education on students has been almost exclusively organized around the single concept of socialization.

Liberal social theorists did not naïvely confuse stability with stasis. A society in a state of basic equilibrium might still be a society that was changing rapidly: the equilibrium might still be a society that was changing rapidly: the equilibrium could be "dynamic." Social change created social strains and psychological stresses; but if all went well, it did not finally upset the basic social equilibrium. Between social strain and social disequilibrium stood a series of "mechanisms of social control," ranging from the police force to the practice of psychotherapy, which served to reduce societal tension by resocializing or isolating deviant individuals and by encapsulating or co-opting deviant social movements. The ideal kind of social change was seen as incremental—slow, quantitative, gradual, and nonrevolutionary. Indeed, some social changes like rising economic prosperity or increasing education were believed to increase the stability of the societies in which they occurred. Increasing prosperity meant that more human needs could be met by society, while prolonging education provided more individuals with a lengthier and more thorough socialization experience.

Nor were liberal social theorists ignorant of the fact that revolutions, social convulsions, and dramatic upheavals abound in history. But convulsive social upheavals were almost always seen as symptoms of a breakdown of the system of social control, and as regressive or destructive in their consequences. "Meaningful social change" was thought most likely to occur through "gradualism" and "piecemeal social reform." Nor have liberal theorists blinded themselves to the existence within every society of murderers, artists, radicals, racists, inventors, crackpots, and geniuses—*i.e.*, of "unsocialized" or "deviant" men and women. But individual behavior that deviated markedly from the norm was seen as the result of aberrant or deviant socialization, generally during the years of early childhood.

In principle, there is no reason why functional failures—e.g., breakdown in mechanisms of social control—should be deemed undesirable. Nazi Germany abounded with mechanisms of social control, from the Gestapo on down. Had they failed from a functional point of view, we might well have deemed this failure ideal from a broader ethical or political point of view. Nor is there any logical reason why societal equilibrium should be maintained: it is conceivable in principle that sudden and dramatic revolutions might result in human betterment. Similarly, there is no *a priori* reason to equate individual "deviance" with sin or pathology. In fact, individual "deviants" are the wellsprings of art, philosophy, religion, and all constructive ideological innovation: one might applaud rather than deplore "deviance."

But in practice, liberal social theories have tended to identify functional "failures" with undesirable moral failures. The collapse of the French Revolution into Bonapartism or of the Russian Revolution into Stalinism was used to demonstrate the general undesirability of revolutions, and to confirm the implication that social change involving naked conflict was the undesirable result of a "breakdown" in the system of social control. Similarly, the study of psychological deviance has largely been a study of criminals, psychopaths, delinquents, or other "desocialized" or "unsocialized" individuals whose behavior resulted in patently undesirable consequences.

The internal logic of liberal theories thus pushes them toward psychological explanations of both individual deviance and social revolution. At an individual level, criminals, artists, and rebels are seen as the products of anomalies in childhood experience. Psychoanalytic theory was extensively adapted in order to explain—and to explain away—radicalism, innovation, creativity, homosexuality, delinquency, and so on in terms of the alleged childhood origins. But since, by definition, the deviant individual must be the product of deviant socialization, the sophisticated liberal never blamed the deviant himself for his deviance. Instead, he blamed the deviant's early environment—especially his family—and aimed his reformist efforts at changing the family circle that was said to produce deviance. Thus, for example, one characteristic liberal solution to racial tensions was to reform the "inadequate" Negro family, which allegedly bred so much suffering and crime. At a collective level, mass revolutionary movements like fascism, Nazism, or communism were often traced to the special conditions of childhood socialization in the nations where these movements prospered. Psychological "strains" transmitted to individuals through their families were thought to culminate in bizarre or irrational collective behavior: e.g., the authoritarian German family led indirectly to Nazism; early swaddling contributed to the totalitarian Russian character, and so on.

In looking to the future, liberal theorists naturally enough foresaw more of what their theories led them to view as normal, desirable, and inevitable: more industrial productivity, more technologization, more piecemeal reform, higher education, more stability, and more effective management. Admittedly, problems were anticipated—for example, the problem of avoiding political apathy when most major social and ideological problems had been solved. Most liberal writers urged that new ways must be found to involve the young in the political future of their nation, and most deplored the "privatism" of the "silent generation" of the 1950's. Other problems were also foreseen: the problems of mass culture, of the lonely crowd, of the use of leisure time, of the organization man, of rapid job obsolescence, and so on. But compared with the old problems of scarcity, economic depression, class warfare, and ideological conflict, these new problems seemed minor. It was persuasively argued by writers like Daniel Bell, Seymour Martin Lipset, and Edward Shils that the age of ideology was over, and that the remaining problems of Western civilization could be defined as largely instrumental—as problems of "how" and not of "what." As a result, it was believed that these problems would eventually yield to scientific knowledge, professional expertise, and technical know-how.

Theories like these attempted to explain—indeed they *did* explain—the relative domestic stability of the Western democracies in the 1950's, along with the general acceptance, acquiescence, or apathy of educated youth. But in retrospect, they were too airtight and too historically parochial. We can now see that they took a particular historical moment—one that today seems abnormal in its tranquillity—and constructed theories that elevated this particular moment into the natural state of affairs. And among other things, this liberal system of ideas—it would be fair to call it an ideology—effectively prevented us from anticipating, much less understanding, what was increasingly to happen among a growing minority of the youth during the 1960's. Like Marxist theories, liberal theories demonstrated the *impossibility* of wide-scale dissent by the educated, privileged young in the highly industrialized democracies.

We cannot, however, simply deprecate the achievements, the usefulness, or the enduring power of the diverse points of view that share what I have called "liberal" assumptions. Men and women are indeed malleable in many ways, and readily influenced. Societies do often exhibit stability and employ powerful resources to preserve equilibrium. And men and women are indeed socialized to the society in which they live from the moment they draw their first breath. It is easy to caricature, criticize, and mock liberal social thought, but it will be the work of a generation to develop a view of the world that does a better job. In the meanwhile, we had best admit that we are all at least partly liberals in our theoretical bases, sometimes the more so as we insist on our radicalism.

Yet in its treatment of the relationship of youth to society, liberal social thought, like Marxism, predicted precisely the opposite of what has actually happened. And that fact alone should impel us to question and redefine the basic assumptions from which liberalism began. The emergence of a youthful opposition, then, demands new theories not only of youthfulness, but of human nature, of society, and of their relationship. Theoretically, this is perhaps the prime significance of the youthful revolt.

Two Current Theories

Given the failure of liberal theories to anticipate the growing disaffection of the affluent young, it was inevitable that other views would emerge. Most of these views are not worthy of serious consideration: they select some single factor like parental permissiveness, the war in Vietnam, the idealism of youth, faculty instigation, Communist conspiracy, or the Oedipus complex as satisfactory explanations of what is happening. But two new analyses of the youthful opposition are emerging that have theoretical depth, scope, and profundity: they properly attempt to understand the new opposition in terms of a broader theory of man and society. The first theory, which is an adaptation of liberal theories, asserts in essence that the youth movement in the industrialized nations is historically a counterrevolutionary movement, a reaction against the more basic forces involved in the growth of a new technological society. The second theory counters by claiming that the dissenting young are true revolutionaries; an historical vanguard that is defining a new and better society. It is worth examining each theory in greater detail.

Youth as a counterrevolutionary force.   Consider first the "counterrevolutionary" theory of youth. The most thoughtful proponents of this view are men like Zbigniew Brzezinski, Lewis Feuer, and, in very different ways, Raymond Aron, Daniel Bell, Alvin Toffler, Bruno Bettelheim, and Herman Kahn. These thinkers differ on a great many key issues, and it does each an injustice to group them together without also underlining their differences. But they are usually in essential agreement on several major points.

First, they agree that we are in the midst of a major social transformation that is taking us out of an industrial society into the postindustrial, technological, postmodern, superindustrial, or, in Brzezinski's terms, "technetronic" society of the future. The new society will be highly rationalized. It will be characterized by high productivity, automation, increased leisure time, more individual choices, better social planning, greater opportunities for the expression of individual interests, rapid rates of social change, more rational administration, and the demand for enormously high levels of education among those who occupy positions of leadership. It will be a society of complex large-scale organizations, global communications, and a basically technical approach to the solution of human problems. In this society, power will lie increasingly not with those who possess economic capital, but with those who possess educational "capital." In the technetronic society, the "knowledge industry," centered above all in the professoriate and in the universities, will be the central industry of society and the central motor of historical change.

The second assumption common to the counterrevolutionary theory of youth is that periods of basic historical transition are inevitably marked by social disturbances. The introduction of factories in Europe and America in the nineteenth century was marked by growing class conflict and the Luddite Movement, which led displaced agricultural workers to try to destroy the factories that were depriving them of work. Today, the transition into the technetronic age is marked by an equally violent revulsion by those whose skills and values are made obsolete by the new social revolution.

Specifically, a postindustrial society imposes what Daniel Bell terms a heavy "organizational harness" upon the young: it requires them to study for many years, to acquire highly specialized technical skills, to stay in school, and to postpone gratification well into biological adulthood. Equally important, this new society renders obsolete a large number of traditional values, skills, and outlooks. A technetronic society above all needs skilled executives, systems analysts, computer programmers, trained administrators, and high-level scientists. Those who possess these skills are in the forefront of historical change: their talents are needed; their outlooks are valued. But those identified with "traditional" fields like the humanities and the social sciences find that their values and skills are becoming increasingly unnecessary, irrelevant, and obsolete; they are today's neo-Lud-dites. The ideals of romanticism, expressiveness, and traditional humanism may dominate the contemporary youth culture, but they do not dominate the social structure—the specific institutions that are changing our lives. One consequence, then, is what Bell terms the disjuncture between the culture—specifically the adversary culture of intellectuals and many students—and the dominant social structure of large-scale organization, technology, mass communications, and electronics.

The conclusion that the revolt of the young is essentially counterrevo-lutionary follows from the first two points. According to this theory, the hu-manistic young are rebelling because of their latent awareness of their own obsolescence. The "organizational harness" around their necks is too tight and heavy for them to endure. An ever-larger group of young men and women feel that they have no place in the modern world, for they lack sal-able skills, basic character styles, and value orientations that are adaptable to the emergent postindustrial society. They are, as Bruno Bettelheim puts it, "obsolete youth." They rebel in a blind, mindless, and generally destruc-tive way against rationalism, intellect, technology, organization, discipline, hierarchy, and all of the requisites of a postindustrial society. Sensing their historical obsolescence, they lash out like the Luddites against the comput-ers and managers that are consigning them into the "dustbin of history." It is predictable that they will end with bombing, terrorism, and anarchy, for the obsolete young are desperately pitting themselves against historical forces that they cannot stop. But students of engineering, business adminis-tration, and so on—students in the fields most rewarded in the techne-tronic society—do not protest or rebel; instead, it is the obsolescent hu-manist and social scientist who lead the counterculture.

Although theorists differ as to precisely *which* unconscious forces are expressed in student dissent, the logic of the conterrevolutionary argument makes a recourse to psychologism almost mandatory. For if the manifest is-sues of student unrest are seen as pseudo issues, disguises, and rationaliza-tions, then we are forced into the realm of the not-conscious in our search to locate the "real" motives behind the youthful opposition. And in today's post-Freudian age, such explanations are likely to involve recourse to con-cepts like unconscious Oedipal feelings, adolescent rebellion, castration anxiety, and the "acting out" of feelings that originate in the early family.

As a result, the counterrevolutionary view of youth is associated with an interpretation of psychoanalysis that sees Oedipal urges as driving forces for student rebellion. To be sure, theorists do not agree about the exact nature of the Oedipal forces that are acted out. Some like Feuer see a simple re-enactment of the jealous child's hatred of his powerful father; others see a blind striking out against surrogates for a father who was not powerful *enough* to inoculate his son against excessive castration anxieties; another psychoanalyst has pointed to insufficient parental responsiveness as a causative factor in radicalism; early family permissiveness or failure to set limits has also been blamed. But whatever the precise irrational forces behind the youthful revolt are said to be, the counterrevolutionary theory, by denying the validity of the youth movement's own explanations of its acts, is forced to hypothesize unconscious motivations as the "real" motives behind the revolt.

A final conclusion follows from this argument: no matter how destructive the revolt of the young may be in the short run, that revolt is historically foredoomed to failure in the long run. The technetronic society, the postindustrial world, the superindustrial state—these forces are unstoppable. The liberal democratic state is being basically transformed, but the rantings and rampagings of the young, devoted to obsolescent ideas of self-expression, anarchism, romanticism, direct democracy, liberation, and the expansion of consciousness, cannot stop this transformation. The revolt of the young may indeed be, in Daniel Bell's phrase, the emergent "class conflict" of postindustrial society. But from Bell's analysis, it follows that students are a neo-Luddite, counterrevolutionary class, and that their counterrevolution will fail. Increasingly, power will be held by those who have more successfully acquired the capital dispensed by the knowledge industry. The counterculture is, in Brzezinski's words, the "death rattle" of the historically obsolete.

The counterrevolutionary theory of the youth revolt is a reformulation of liberal theory, modified to make room for the convulsions of the last decade. Within any social equilibrium theory, there must be room for the possibility that the system will temporarily get "out of balance." The assumption of thinkers like Brzezinski is that we have entered a period of imbalance that accompanies the transition from an industrial to a technetronic society. In this transitional period, traditional mechanisms of social control, older forms of integration between social structure and culture, and previous forms of socialization have ceased to function adequately. But in the future, it is assumed, equilibrium can once again be regained. Upon arrival in the technetronic society, the postindustrial society, or the world of the year 2000, the temporary storm squalls on the weatherfront between industrial and postindustrial society will have dissipated, and we will once again be in a state of relative social equilibrium. If we can only wait out the transition, maintaining and repairing our basic institutions, we can build a new equilibrium—one that will grind under the youthful opposition just as triumphant industrialism destroyed the Luddites. In the meanwhile we must fight to preserve decency, civilization, rationality, and higher education from the depredations of the mindless young.

Youth as a revolutionary force.   The second major theory holds that the dissenting young are historically a revolutionary force. This theory views that counterculture as a regenerative culture, and interprets those forces that oppose it as ultimately counterrevolutionary. This view is expressed in different forms in the works of Theodore Roszak and Charles Reich, in the writings of members of the counterculture like Tom Hayden and Abbie Hoffman, and, most convincingly of all, by Philip Slater. Let us consider the basic assumptions of the revolutionary view of the youth culture.

First, this theory also accepts the notion that industrialized societies are in a period of major cultural, institutional, and historical transition. But it alleges that the thrust of the liberal democratic state has exhausted itself. What is variously termed "corporate liberalism," the "establishment," or the "welfare-warfare state" is seen as fundamentally bankrupt. Admittedly, industrial states have produced unprecedented wealth. But they have not been able to distribute it equitably, nor have they found ways to include large minorities in the mainstream of society. Furthermore, their basic assumptions have led directly to disastrous "neoimperialistic" wars like the American involvement in Southeast Asia. Corporate liberalism has produced a highly manipulated society, in which "real" human needs and interests are neglected in the pursuit of political power, the merchandising of products, or the extension of overseas markets. Large-scale organizations have dehumanized their members, depriving men of participation in the decisions that affect their lives. The electronic revolution merely provides the rulers of the corporate state with more effective means of manipulating the populace. Corporate liberalism has today revealed its bankruptcy.

The second assumption of this theory is that the economic successes and moral failures of liberal industrial societies today make possible and necessary a new kind of consciousness, new values, new aspirations, and new life styles—in short, a new culture. The old industrial state was founded upon the assumption of scarcity. It was organized to reduce poverty, to increase production, to provide plenitude. But today it has largely succeeded in this goal, and as a result, a new generation has been born in affluence and freed from the repressed character structure of the scarcity culture. In an era of abundance, the niggardly, inhibited psychology of saving, scrupulosity, and repression is no longer necessary. Alienated relationships between people who view each other as commodities are no longer inevitable. The "objective consciousness" of the scientist or technician is becoming obsolete. In brief, the material successes and moral failures of corporate liberalism permit and require the emergence of a new and truly revolutionary generation with a new consciousness, a postscarcity outlook, and a new vision of the possibilities of human liberation.

It follows from this analysis that the new oppositional culture is not an atavistic and irrational reaction against the old culture but a logical outgrowth of it—an expression of its latent possibilities, a rational effort to remedy its failings, in some sense its logical fulfillment. If the central goal of the old culture was to overcome want and if that goal has been largely achieved, then the counterculture stands on the shoulders of the old culture, fulfilling, renewing, and expressing that culture's latent hopes. Far from being historical reactionaries, the counterculturists are the historical vanguard. Their alleged anarchism and anti-intellectualism are but efforts to express the desire for human liberation whose roots lie in the postponed dreams of the old culture. As the British philosopher Stuart Hampshire has recently suggested, the dissenting young are not against reason, but only against a constricted definition of reason as a quantitative calculus that ignores human values and needs.

The revolutionary theory of youth also entails a definite view of the psychology of young rebels and revolutionaries. It asks that we take them completely at their word when they state the reasons for their protests, disruptions, dropouts, or rejections. The dissenting young are seen as miraculously healthy products of the irrational, dangerous, and unjust world they inherited. Their motives are noble, idealistic, and pure, while their statements of their goals are to be taken at face value. They are not animated by their childhood pasts, but by a vision (which they may, however, find it difficult to articulate) of a freer, more peaceful, more liberated, and more just society. As for the Oedipus complex, to discuss the psychological motives of the members of the youthful opposition at all is seen as a typically "liberal" way of distracting attention from the real issues. Thus, even if the dissenting young behave in an undemocratic, dogmatic, or violent way, one "understands" their behavior by discussing the undemocratic, dogmatic, and violent society to which they are objecting.

This view of the psychology of the youthful opposition follows logically from the assumption that the young are in the historical vanguard. For in general, historical vanguards must be endowed with ordinary wisdom and prescience, and with a special freedom from that gnawingly irrational attachment to the personal or historic past that plagues most non-vanguard groups. In the views of one theorist, "radical man" is the highest possible form of human development; another political theorist has argued that only rebellion can attest to human freedom, and that among today's young, only those who rebel are truly free. The argument that the youthful revolt arises from psychopathology is here encountered by its opposite—by the claim that the new opposition springs from the extraordinary insight, maturity, high consciousness, and "positive mental health" of its members.

Finally, as is by definition true of any historical vanguard, the triumph of this vanguard is seen as ultimately inevitable. With rising abundance, new recruits to the counterculture are being created daily. It is the old, then, who are obsolete, not the young. The locomotive of history, so to speak, has the youth movement sitting on the front bumper, scattering its opponents in a relentless rush into the future. Eventually the opponents of progressive change will be defeated or will die of old age—only then will the truly liberating potentials of the postscarcity era be actualized in society.

In many respects the theory of the youth movement as revolutionary is embryonic and incomplete. The counterrevolutionary theory builds upon the highly developed resources of liberal social thought. But the "revolutionary" view, rejecting both liberalism and Marxism, presents us more with a vision of what the counterculture might be at its best than with a complex or thorough social analysis. Only in the work of Philip Slater do we have the beginnings of a critical examination of liberal theory, a task so enormous that it is obviously beyond the capabilities of any one man, much less one book. Other writers who view the counterculture as revolutionary largely limit themselves to a vision that is more literary than descriptive and that makes little attempt to connect the emergence of the counterculture to the structural changes emphasized by writers like Bell, Brzezinski, or Kahn. In this sense, the revolutionary theory of the new opposition remains more of a promise than a fulfillment.

The Limits of Both Theories

My presentation of two polar theories obviously does scant justice to the complexity of the specific theorists who have seriously considered the counterculture. There is no unity, much less membership in a "school," either among those who oppose or among those who support the youthful opposition. Among its critics, for example, Feuer and Bettelheim concentrate upon the psychopathology that allegedly animates its members, while Brzezinski or Kahn focuses upon the structural or social conditions that make the youthful opposition obsolete. Similarly, there is an enormous difference between the romantic portrait of "consciousness III" presented by Reich and the more careful social-psychological analysis offered by Slater in his *The Pursuit of Loneliness*.

But no matter how oversimplified this account of the revolutionary and the counterrevolutionary theories, if either interpretation of youthful dissent were fundamentally adequate, this discussion could end. It therefore behooves us to examine each of these theories critically.

We should first acknowledge that each of these views has its highly persuasive points. Those who view the new opposition as historically counterrevolutionary are correct in underlining the increasing importance of technology, complex social organizations, and education in the most industrialized nations. They have pointed accurately to the new role of a highly educated and technologically trained elite. And they seem to help us explain why youthful dissenters are virtually absent among potential engineers, computer specialists, and business administrators, but disproportionately drawn from the ranks of social scientists and humanists.

Above all, however, the opponents of the youthful opposition are accurate in their criticism of that opposition. They rightly argue that the counterculture almost completely neglects the institutional side of modern life. Thus the call for liberation, for the expansion of consciousness, and for the expression of impulse has not been matched by the creation or even by the definition of institutions whereby these purposes could be achieved and sustained. Furthermore, in its cultural wing, the new opposition has often been callous to continuing injustice, oppression, and poverty in America and abroad. In its political wing, the counterculture has been vulnerable to despair, to apocalyptic but transient fantasies of instant revolution, to superficial Marxism, and to a romance with violence. Finally, the youthful opposition as a whole has never adequately confronted or understood its own derivative relationship to the dominant society. Perhaps as a result, it has too often been a caricature rather than a critique of the consumption-oriented, manipulative, technocratic, violent, electronic society that it nominally opposes. In pointing to the weakness of the counterculture, its critics seem to me largely correct.

Yet there is a deep plausibility, as well, in the theory that the youthful opposition is in historical terms a revolutionary movement. In particular, the "revolutionary" theorists accurately capture the growing feeling of frustration and the increasing sense of the exhaustion of the old order that obsess growing numbers of the educated young in industrialized nations. Furthermore, they correctly recognize the irony in the fact that the most prosperous and educated societies in world history have generated the most massive youthful opposition in world history. And in seeking to explain this unexpected opposition, the revolutionary theory understands well its relationship to the "systemic" failings of corporate liberalism—its failure to include large minorities in the general prosperity, its exploitative or destructive relationship to the developing nations, its use of advanced technology to manipulate the citizens in whose interest it allegedly governs, its neglect of basic human needs, values, and aspirations in a social calculus that sees men and women as merely "inputs" or "outputs" in complex organizations.

The strengths of each theory, however, are largely negative: in essence, each is at its best in pointing to the flaws of the culture or the social system defended by the other. But judged for its positive contribution, each theory tends to have parallel weaknesses: each disregards the facts at odds with its own central thesis. In order to do this, each operates at a different level of analysis: the counterrevolutionary theory at the level of social institutions, the revolutionary theory at the level of culture. As a consequence, each theory neglects precisely what the other theory correctly stresses.

The counterrevolutionary theory of the new opposition starts from an analysis of social institutions, modes of production, and the formal organization of human roles and relationships. Despite its emphasis upon the psychopathology of the new rebels, it is fundamentally a sociological theory of institutional changes and technological transformations. It stresses the importance of applied science, the growth of new educational institutions, and the power of the new elite that dominates the "knowledge industry." In defining the future, it emphasizes the further development of rational-bureaucratic institutions and the revolutionary impact of new electronic technology upon social organization, communication, and knowledge. But it tends to forget consciousness and culture, treating ideas, symbols, values, ideologies, aspirations, fantasies, and dreams largely as reflections of technological, economic, and social forces.

Theorists who argue that the new opposition is historically revolutionary operate at a quite different level of analysis. For them, the two key concepts are culture and consciousness. What matters most is feelings, aspirations, outlooks, ideologies, and world views. Charles Reich's recent analysis of three kinds of consciousness is explicit in asserting that institutions are secondary and in the last analysis unimportant. Most other revolutionary theorists also start from an analysis of a "new consciousness" to argue that the decisive revolution is a cultural revolution. How men view the world, how they organize their experience symbolically, what their values are—these are seen as historically determining. Institutional changes are said to follow changes in human aspirations and consciousness.

Daniel Bell has written of the disjuncture of social structure and culture in modern society. We need not accept his entire analysis to agree that this disjuncture is reflected in theories about youthful dissent. For on closer examination, they turn out to be talking about either social structure *or* culture, but rarely about both. The key weakness of the counterrevolutionary theory is its neglect of consciousness and culture, its assumption that social-structural, technological, and material factors will be decisive in determining the future. The parallel weakness of the revolutionary view of youthful dissent is its disregard of the way organized systems of production, technology, education, communication, and "social control" influence, shape, and may yet co-opt or destroy the youthful opposition. In fact, then, these two theories are not as contradictory as they seem: in many ways, they are simply talking about two different aspects of the modern world.

A second limitation of both theories is their assumption that the trends they define are historically inevitable. In this respect, both theories are eschatological as well as explanatory. The postindustrial, or technetronic, view assumes the future inevitability of a postindustrial, technetronic, technocratic society. Given this assumption, it follows logically that anyone who opposes the technetronic society is historically counterrevolutionary. Brzezinski, for example, writes in *Between Two Ages:*

> The Luddites were threatened by economic obsolescence and reacted against it. Today the militant leaders of the [student] reaction, as well as their ideologues, frequently come from those branches of learning which are more sensitive to the threat of social irrelevance. Their political activism is thus only a reaction to the more basic fear that the times are against them,

that a new world is emerging without either their assistance or their leadership.

Brzezinski's claim that the youth revolt constitutes a counterrevolutionary force clearly rests upon the assumption that the technetronic society is inevitable.

Exactly the same assumption of historical inevitability is made by supporters of the counterculture. Reich is very explicit about this in *The Greening of America:*

> [The revolution] will originate with the individual and with culture, and it will change the political structure only as its final act. It will not require violence to succeed, and it cannot be successfully resisted by violence. It is now spreading with amazing rapidity. . . . It is both necessary and inevitable, and in time it will include not only youth, but all people in America.

Given Reich's assumption that history is on the side of the counterculture, it follows automatically that those who oppose it are actually counterrevolutionary.

But this claim that the future is in fact predetermined by blind historical forces is open to major question. In retrospect, most previous claims about the historical inevitability of this or that trend have turned out to have been mere expressions of the wishes of those who made these claims. It makes equal or better sense to believe that "history" is on the side neither of the technetronic revolution nor of the counterculture. In fact, we may deny that history is on anyone's side, arguing that history is simply made by human beings, acting individually and in concert, influenced by the institutions in which they live *and* by their consciousness and culture.

If we reject the assumption of historical inevitability, both the counterrevolutionary and the revolutionary theories must be understood in part as efforts to justify a set of special interests by attributing historical inevitability to them, and perhaps ultimately as exercises in the use of prophecy to convince others of the truth of the prophecy and thereby to make the prophecy self-fulfilling. Andrew Greeley has compared Charles Reich with the ancient Hebrew prophets. The similarities are vivid. Although the more academic prose of Brzezinski, Feuer, or Bettelheim does not lend itself so readily to comparisons with the Old Testament, the same prophetic tendencies are there as well. But in either case, the claim that God or His modern-day equivalents—history, technology, and culture—are on our side is best understood as a claim that men make to rally support and persist despite adversity.

What both theories fail to comprehend is the extent to which the emergence of a new youthful opposition requires us to embark upon a critical re-examination of concepts of man, society, and their interrelationship that we have heretofore taken largely for granted. This inability to come to grips with the theoretical challenge posed by the new opposition is seen clearly in each theory's attitude toward education. Neoliberals who view student dissent as largely counterrevolutionary are committed to a view of education as socialization. Given this view, it follows that a postindustrial society characterized by prolonged higher education should be a society where youthful dissent is rare. The eruption of wide-scale disaffection among the most educated products of the most industrialized societies thus requires neoliberal theories to posit wide-scale "deviant socialization," or else to argue that higher education is failing to "do its job." In fact, however, the extensive evidence concerning the backgrounds of young dissenters provides little support for the "deviant socialization" interpretation of the new opposition. And paradoxically, those institutions of higher education that liberals have traditionally seen as doing the "best job" seem to be the breeding grounds for the greatest disaffection.

Those who view youthful disaffection as a revolutionary phenomenon are faced with the same dilemma. They tend to see higher education as a way of "integrating" or "co-opting" youth into the existing society. It therefore comes as a surprise that higher education seems to promote disaffection and to be closely related to the emergence of a youthful counterculture. But those who view the youth movement as revolutionary have so far failed to offer any adequate explanation of why many young men and women in so many nations have escaped the net of socialization.

The fact that theorists of neither persuasion can explain the contemporary correlation between higher education and dissent indicates the need for a critical analysis of our prevailing assumptions concerning human malleability, social equilibrium, and socialization. To undertake this re-examination will be the task of many years; it will necessarily be the work of a generation, not of an individual, but it is impressive that, for all of the talk today about "radical thought" and the "New Left," the basic assumptions of liberalism have been subjected to so little fundamental criticism.

What follows is not an attempt to provide this critical reanalysis, or even to outline it. Rather, it is an agenda, or more precisely, some items on an agenda which, if accomplished, might move us toward a better understanding of the meaning of the new opposition and of contemporary society. This agenda is presented tentatively, and largely as an indication of the theoretical problems that have been opened up by a decade of dissent. Since it is easier to point out the flaws in the views of others than to propose unflawed alternatives to them, even these items for an agenda are bound to be anticlimactic. But not to run the risks of at least suggesting an agenda would be even worse.

In brief, the work I believe needs to be done falls into three broad categories. First, there must be a critical reanalysis and reformulation of the theoretical assumptions with which we attempt to understand man and society. Second, we must begin to come to terms with the characteristics of modern society and modern man in their own right, and not in terms of strained analogies to the past. Third, a revised theoretical framework and a better understanding of contemporary man in society should help define a new political agenda.

Plasticity, Equilibrium, and Socialization

The first assumption to be reanalyzed critically is the assumption of virtually limitless human malleability and influenceability. Without denying that men can adapt to most surroundings, that they often conform to the pressures of their peers, or that they internalize social norms and cultural concepts, we need to rediscover and emphasize those elements in "human nature" that make men less than totally plastic.

I believe that the most fruitful line of inquiry will involve an intensive study of the sequences and stages of human development, and especially of those developmental processes that remain more or less constant regardless of historical era or social context. We need to return to Freud's concept of human development as not simply a smooth process of internalizing societal expectations, but rather as the arduous work of mastering internal conflict, without which psychological growth could not occur. Equally relevant is the developmental psychology of Jean Piaget, who insists that the child's growth proceeds through psychologically necessary stages and sequences that cannot be short-circuited. In the developmental process as defined by both Freud and Piaget, the imprint of the social environment is assimilated and interpreted through the steadily changing internal structures of personality, which has its own laws and imperatives.

To trace the full implications of a developmental view of personality for a theory of man and society would be the topic of a lengthy work. Here it should suffice to note that a developmental approach clearly contradicts the almost exclusively environmental view of psychological change that has dominated liberal thought. Critically interpreted, the work of Freud and Piaget may help us understand man not merely as an adjusting and adapting animal, but as a creature whose growth has both important societal prerequisites and a dynamic of its own. We can then think of man as possessing a "human nature" that can be "violated" by social expectations; we may then be better able to see man as possessing innate potentials for autonomy and integration that may at times lead him into conflict with his society.

We will also need to explore in detail the ways in which these developmental potentials may be actualized or frustrated by any given social or historical context. Recent studies that demonstrate the existence of developmental potentials that are not actualized in most men and women under contemporary conditions point to sociohistorical influences upon adult personality of a kind that have not heretofore been studied. I have elsewhere argued that one important factor in the emergence of a new opposition is the unfolding, on a mass scale, of developmental potentials that in the past were actualized, if at all, only in a tiny minority of men and women.

A related task should involve a critical scrutiny of the large body of studies of attitude change, group pressures, and interpersonal influence. We will need to distinguish, for example, more sharply than we have done so far between attitudes and belief systems on the one hand and the cognitive frameworks or developmental levels within which any given attitude or belief is held. William James long ago contrasted the once-born and the twice-born: the once-born are those who unreflectively and "innocently" accept the convictions of their childhoods; the twice-born are those who may adhere to exactly the same convictions, but who do so in a different way after a protracted period of doubt, criticism, and examination of these beliefs. Viewed as attitudes, the beliefs of the once-born and the twice-born may be identical: but the mind-set, cognitive framework, or developmental level of the once- and twice-born are extremely different. In other words, we need to examine not only the beliefs men hold, but the *way* they hold them—the complexity, richness, and structure of their views of the world. Politically and socially, it may be more important that members of a given subculture possess a relativistic view of truth than that they are conservatives or liberals.

Finally, the role of conflict in human development needs to be re-examined. Liberal psychology has tended to minimize the catalytic importance of conflict in growth: conflict was seen as neurotic, undesirable, and productive of regression. But there is much current evidence that individuals who attain high levels of complexity in feeling, thinking, and judging do *so as a result of* conflict, not in its absence. Students of cognitive development, like observers of personality development, find that disequilibrium, tension, and imbalance tend to produce growth. If this is true, then the absence of psychological conflict or tension may be as pathological as the overabundance of conflict, and the liberal view of the ideal man as smoothly socialized and conflict-free may need to be discarded.

To add further items to this agenda for psychology would take us to still more technical topics. The point is that, in ways we have not yet understood, our theories of human nature, our psychological research, and our methodologies have all been influenced by the largely unstated assumptions of human plasticity and smooth accommodation to pressures of the social environment. We need not deny that men are in some ways plastic and influenceable in order to consider anew everything in man that makes him unmalleable, uninfluenceable, and resistant to socialization.

Turning to broader theories of society, a comparable critical re-examination of basic assumptions seems in order. Above all, the utility of the equilibrium model of society must be examined. Increasingly, critical soci-

ologists have begun to suggest that a "conflict" model of society and of social change may be more suited to the facts of contemporary history than a
theory of societal balance. Just as we should appreciate the catalytic role
of conflict in human development, so the critical importance of conflict in
social change must be acknowledged. Both human and social development,
I believe, are best viewed as dialectic processes, involving force, counterforce, and potential resolution; thesis, antithesis, and potential synthesis. At
a societal level, such a view would require us to start from change, struggle, revolution, and transformation as the basic and "natural" state of affairs rather than viewing them as unfortunate exceptions that require
special explanation.

This view of society would put social change in the first chapter, not
in the last chapter as one of the unexplained problems of our theory. It
would see conflict between individuals, groups, and historical forces as a
necessary and vital component of historical change, not as a result of a
"failure" of the "mechanisms of social control." It would also entail that
any given "resolution" of conflicting historical forces should in turn generate new antithetical forces which will oppose that resolution, thus continuing the dialectic of change. A sociology based on the theory of conflict
would especially attempt to understand the processes by which new conflicts are generated out of apparent equilibrium, rather than focusing solely
upon how equilibrium is maintained.

Such a view of society obviously moves us away from liberalism and
toward Marxism. But Marxism, too, must be examined critically. Just as we
today should reject the nineteenth-century biology and physics upon which
Freud based his psychological determinism and many of his specific views
of personality, so we need not continue to accept the nineteenth-century
economism and millenialism of Marxist thought. Marx's view that the critical historical conflict was class conflict, although it reflected the facts of the
mid-nineteenth century, may less clearly reflect the realities of the late
twentieth century. And the nineteenth-century optimism which led Marx to
believe that historical conflict would ultimately be progressively resolved,
like his millenial view of the classless state as the end of historical conflict,
seems today unwarranted. Finally, we must question whether the historical
dialectic in fact "stopped" at the end point defined by Marx, or whether it
continues today in ways that Marx could not have foreseen.

However we reinterpret Marx, one corollary of a dialectic view of social change is that the historical significance of a group, institution, social
force, or ideology will inevitably change as historical conditions change. A
group that is progressive during one historical era may become reactionary
at a later period. Marx emphasized that during its struggle against feudal-
ism, the *bourgeoisie* was a progressive force, although during the nineteenth century, the triumphant *bourgeoisie* had become reactionary in its
opposition of the demands of the revolutionary working class. Following

the logic of a dialectic analysis would lead us to expect that the once-revolutionary proletariat might in its turn become defensive and opposed to progressive social change. And especially as the rate of historical change accelerates, the transformation of social groups from progressive to reactionary, from revolutionary to counterrevolutionary, may well occur during the lifetime of their members.

If we re-examine critically both the concept of malleable man and the concept of stable society, then we must also re-examine the concept of socialization as the key process whereby the individual is joined to society. We need not deny that socialization occurs in order to point to other processes of equal or greater importance that connect the individual and society in more complex ways. For example, as Erik Erikson has noted, every society must accommodate itself to the developmental needs of the growing child. By attending more carefully to the in-born developmental schedules and potentials of the child, adolescent, youth, and adult, we may better understand the constraints upon society's capacity to "integrate" individuals of any given age. Just as it is not possible for the seven-year-old to comprehend hypothetico-deductive reasoning, so it may not be possible for the highly educated, relativistic youth to accept his society's norms and precepts without criticism. Instead of emphasizing only how society molds the individual to meet social needs, we must also consider how human needs and developmental processes set outer limits on what societies can reasonably expect of their members.

If we abandon the notion of society as a stable and homogeneous entity, then the process whereby individuals and their societies interrelate becomes vastly more complex. For if every society contains within it important internal conflicts, then growing children are exposed not to a stable, self-consistent set of social expectations and cultural values, but to social and cultural contradictions. Intrapsychic conflicts and social contradictions will thus be mutually related, although never in a simple one-to-one fashion. Furthermore, in times of rapid historical change, the societal conflicts to which one generation is exposed will differ from those of the previous generation; partly for this reason, individuals of different historical generations will typically differ from each other in basic personality.

The full agenda for the re-examination of our understanding of the relationship between men and societies will be lengthy. But as we examine our theoretical assumptions, it will not suffice simply to reject out of hand what I have termed "liberal" views. The goal must be more ambitious: it must be to analyze these views critically, preserving what is valid in them while complementing them with new understanding of the inherent logic of human development, of the central role of conflict in social change, and of the forces in man that militate against acquiescent acceptance of the existing social order.

Contradictions Within the Knowledge Sector

The second, related theoretical task is to understand in detail the special characteristics of modern personality and modern society. Even if a critical analysis of the basic assumptions of liberal thought were completed, the substance of a more adequate account of what is unique about our own era would still be lacking. Here, once again, I can only indicate the general lines of thought that seem most likely to be worth pursuing.

If we start from a dialectical view of historical change, but admit that Marx's juxtaposition of a revolutionary proletariat and a reactionary *bourgeoisie* did not necessarily mark the last stage in the dialectic, then we must entertain seriously the possibility that the conflicts about which Marx wrote have been largely resolved and that new conflicts have today begun to emerge. I believe it is useful and accurate to consider the corporate liberal state as embodying to a large extent the synthesis of the class conflicts that preoccupied Marx. In this respect, liberal theorists were correct in arguing that earlier conflicts between capitalist entrepreneurs and exploited workers had been softened and essentially reconciled by the growth of powerful bureaucratic trade unions able to negotiate with large but publicly regulated corporations. The "welfare state" indeed mitigated many of the most vicious exploitations of unrestrained nineteenth-century capitalism. The "liberal consensus" of the mid-twentieth century tolerated a wide spectrum of political opinion and many forms of deviant behavior. Furthermore, if "ideology" is narrowly defined to mean Stalinism, fascism, and Nazism, then it was largely accurate to say that the age of ideology was dead.

In the period before and after the Second World War, then, the dominant class conflicts of the nineteenth and early twentieth centuries were increasingly resolved, reconciled, or synthesized in the liberal-democratic-capitalist or socialist states in Western Europe, America, and, after the war, Japan. These new industrial states proved themselves immensely productive economically and immensely inventive technologically. Older problems of mass poverty increasingly disappeared, while the proportion of workers involved in primary and secondary production dwindled to a decreasing minority. First in America, and then increasingly in Western Europe and Japan, the middle class grew to be the largest class, the working class became increasingly prosperous, and both classes became more and more committed to the preservation of the existing society. Especially during the years of the Cold War, a domestic equilibrium was reached in the liberal democracies, and this equilibrium provided the empirical ground upon which liberal social thought grew and by which it seemed confirmed. To be sure, like all historical syntheses, this one was far from complete: large minorities were excluded from the general prosperity; problems of poverty amidst affluence continued; subtle forms of imperialism replaced the earlier forms, and so on. Yet all things considered, the decades from 1945 to 1965 were remarkable for the absence of basic social conflict in all of the highly industrialized non-Communist nations.

The ascendency of the corporate liberal state, however, did not mark an end to social conflict or to the dialectic of history. The successes of the emergent technological society were purchased at an enormous moral and ecological price. Fulfilling the promises of liberalism was far from complete, and it became apparent that the liberal program itself would not suffice to fulfill them. Increases in national productivity were not enough to include in the mainstream of affluence those whose poverty was "structural" rather than merely economic. Racism persisted in America despite a century's public commitment to end it. Effective political power remained in the hands of a small minority of the population. It is therefore incorrect to say that the traditional economic, social, and political conflicts of industrial societies were totally "solved." It is more accurate to say that for the first time in history the day could be foreseen when with the techniques at hand they *might* be solved, but that liberal social thought and liberal reformism proved largely ineffective in solving them.

The inability of liberalism to complete its own agenda was one of the new contradictions that became apparent only with the advent of the corporate liberal society. The second contradiction was in some ways more profound, and even more directly related to the emergence of a youthful opposition. The liberal democratic states in America, Western Europe, and Japan provided a large proportion of the people with material goods, social security, cultural opportunities, and relative political freedom, all of which had been the goals of previous generations. There thus arose a new generation that took for granted the accomplishments of corporate liberalism, expressing neither gratitude nor admiration for these achievements. To this new generation, what were instead important were first of all the inabilities of a liberal society to fulfill its own promises; and second, the surfacing of a set of cultural and psychological goals that had previously been deferred in the liberal society. These newly surfaced aspirations had to do above all with the quality of life, the possibilities for self-expression, full human development, self-actualization, the expansion of consciousness, and the pursuit of empathy, sentience, and experience.

I have elsewhere tried to outline in more detail some of the emergent aspirations of the new youthful opposition. Here it should be enough to reiterate that the roots of this new opposition lie precisely in the successes of liberalism—e.g., its success in extending to most of the population the material and social benefits it had promised, but its inability to complete the process or to define goals beyond abundance. To the new generation, and specifically to the most affluent, educated, and secure members of this generation, the historical successes of the corporate liberal state were less important than its moral, ecological, psychological, and cultural failures.

To understand the new conflicts in corporate liberal society, I believe we must above all examine the role of the "knowledge sector." For the liberal-democratic and industrialized nations are increasingly dominated neither by capitalists nor by workers, but by a vast new "intelligentsia" of educated professionals who exert unprecedented influence on both public policy and private practice. In some ways their contemporary role is analogous to the traditional role of intellectuals, artists, and Bohemians in earlier historical eras. But because of their increasing numbers and influence, they occupy an altogether different place in technological societies. What they share is that the enterprises in which they are engaged depend upon extensions, manipulations, or applications of knowledge and ideas. The knowledge sector thus includes not only universities, scientific laboratories, research institutes, and the world of creative artists, but a much broader set of enterprises including corporate research and development, the communications industry, data analysis and data processing, the major higher professions, advertising, merchandising, administrative science, personnel management, entertainment, systems analysis, and so on. So defined, the knowledge sector is clearly that sector of contemporary industrialized societies that has grown most rapidly in size and power.

Neo-Marxist theorists have tended to see this knowledge sector as a "new working class" or "technical intelligentsia"—merely the handmaiden of the capitalist managers and politicians assumed to exercise real power. Theorists of the postindustrial state, in contrast, have emphasized the dominance of the knowledge sector in advanced societies, viewing academics as the key professionals and universities as the key institutions of the postindustrial society. Still others, operating in a more traditional liberal framework, have seen the knowledge sector as one of many "interest groups" competing in the process of defining social and political policy.

But in the end, none of these characterizations seems quite adequate to define the unique role of the knowledge sector in the technological societies. Only by remote analogy can workers in this sector be considered a true "working class," for only rarely are they the direct or indirect victims of capitalist exploitation. On the face of it, the argument of Bell, Brzezinski, and others that the knowledge sector constitutes the dominant sector of technological societies seems closer to the truth. But this view in turn tends to exaggerate the power of the academic profession and the indispensability of such institutions as universities to technological society. It is also tempting to accept the liberal analysis of the knowledge sector as merely one of many interest groups; but this view, too, fails to acknowledge the very special powers that today accrue to those who possess knowledge and the visible tokens of its possession: higher degrees, recognition in the knowledge community, access to the mass media, and so on.

Rather than define the knowledge sector as a new working class, as a ruling group, or as another interest group, we would do better to start by assuming that its relationship to the rest of society cannot be adequately

understood in historical analogies. To try to define the relationship between the knowledge sector and the rest of society in terms of capitalist-
worker analogies is like attempting to define the capitalist-worker relationship as a kind of lord-vassal relationship. Often exploited yet more often
manipulating, immensely influential yet vastly vulnerable, an interest
group but one that possesses unprecedented power, the role of the knowledge sector in modern society must be defined as unprecedented, new, and
sui generis. Indeed, one of the major theoretical tasks ahead is the careful
definition and explication of the relationship between this new sector and
the remainder of society.

Spokesmen for the knowledge sector have tended to define this sector
as relatively value-free and "objective" in its approach to human and social
problems. The plausibility of this view rests upon the propensity of the
knowledge sector to invoke "scientific" analyses of problems, to define rationality in quantitative terms, and to attempt to exclude "irrational" feelings or "sentimental" moral considerations from decision making. The main
agents of the knowledge sector have usually presented themselves as neutral, cool, and technical servants of others, as less concerned with ultimate
moral ends than with efficiency, accuracy, rationality, and the levelheaded
consideration of the costs and benefits of alternative courses of action. One
of the chief characteristics of the knowledge sector, even as it has moved
toward increasing influence, has been to publicly proclaim its "neutrality"
—its indifference to the major moral, psychological, and political questions
of the day.

Yet in the last decade, it has become clear that the "value-free" self-
definition of the knowledge sector masks an important ideology, an ideology increasingly recognized and challenged by the new opposition. This
ideology can be termed "technism," that is, a set of pseudo-scientific assumptions about the nature and resolution of human and social problems.
Most highly articulated in various forms of systems analysis, technism insists that the highest rationality involves measurement and consigns the in-
commensurable (feelings, values, "intangibles") to a lesser order of rationality and reality. Military policies are therefore judged in terms of
quantitative indices like body counts, kilotonnage, sorties flown, mega-
deaths, planes lost, or enemy dead per dollar. Education is seen as a complex form of human "processing," with freshmen as "inputs," graduates as
"outputs," dropouts as "wastage," and efficiency measured in terms of
"Ph.D. production" or "lifetime income increments." Technism further assumes that innovation is desirable, that growth is imperative, that whatever is technically possible should be done, and that large quantities are
preferable to small ones. Drawing heavily upon the mystique of science,
technism adds to true science a series of further assumptions that qualify it
as an ideology, albeit one that prefers not to recognize itself or be recognized as such.

Paradoxically, however, it is from within the knowledge sector that today there also emerges the most astringent critique of technism. Institutions of higher education, once predicted to become the central institutions of postindustrial society, have indeed become the prime exemplars of a technist approach to problems of government, business, and social planning; but they have also become the prime generators of the antitechnist, romantic, expressive, moralistic, anarchic humanism of the new opposition. Rejecting technism, this opposition stresses all those factors in human life and social experience that do not fit the technist equations. If "value-free," objective technism is the dominant voice of the dominant knowledge sector, then expressive, subjective anarchism is the subversive voice. Theodore Roszak's eulogy of the counterculture is illustrative, for Roszak abhors above all what he calls "objective consciousness"—the technist consciousness of the scientist or program analyst. The new opposition can thus be seen as the ideological reflection of an emergent contradiction *within* the knowledge sector, as the new antithesis to the knowledge sector's technism, as embodying a counteremphasis upon people, upon "creative disorder," upon the nonquantifiable, the subjective, and the qualitative. Increasingly, this contradiction between objective technism and subjective anarchism defines the key ideological polarity of our time.

The intimate relationship between the knowledge sector and the new opposition is also apparent when we examine the social origins of the members of the opposition. For the core of the counterculture consists not of the children of the working class or of the lower middle class, but of the children of the knowledge sector. I have elsewhere insisted that the new opposition is not monolithic, and that we must distinguish its "political" from its "cultural" wing. Available evidence suggests that members of the political wing tend to be recruited disproportionately from among the children of professors, social workers, ministers, scientists, lawyers, and artists. These young men and women are the most concerned with institutional, social, and political change, and are also most likely to express solidarity with the basic values of their parents. Recruits to the cultural, expressive, aesthetic, or "hippie" wing of the counterculture, in contrast, tend to be drawn to a much greater degree from the families of media executives, entertainers, advertising men, merchandisers, scientific administrators, and personnel managers. These young men and women are more concerned with the expansion of consciousness, the development of alternative life styles, and the pursuit of communal ways of living. As a rule, they reject not only the conventional values and institutions of American society, but the values and life styles of their parents. The parents of the "politicals" are thus the more established members of the knowledge sector, while the parents of the "culturals" are the "newly arrived," whose membership in the knowledge sector is more tenuous and ambivalent. If we accept the analogy between knowledge in technological society and capital in industrial society, the parents of the political wing of the opposition are more often the holders of "old money," while the parents of the cultural wing are more often *"nouveaux riches."*

A variety of factors within the knowledge sector clearly co-operate to generate its own opposition. Among these, for example, are the ambiva lences of the parents of youthful dissenters toward the very knowledge sector in which they are employed. But no factor is of greater importance than the impact of higher education upon its recruits. Higher education bears a paradoxical relationship to the knowledge sector. On the one hand, higher education is essential for the maintenance and growth of the knowledge sector; but on the other hand, higher education provides many of the catalysts that push students to develop a critical consciousness which leads them to become part of the youthful opposition, and thus to oppose the dominant ideology of the knowledge sector.

To explore this paradox fully should again be the topic of a lengthy essay. Here I can only emphasize the obvious fact that technological societies require extremely high levels of knowledge and education of their members. "Knowledge societies" like our own must expose millions of young people to ideas, and in such a way as to encourage a critical analysis of these ideas. For only up to a point can higher education in a technological society be narrowly technical. By definition technical education attempts to teach the student a given body of knowledge, along with methods for applying that knowledge to the solution of problems. But when, as today, existing bodies of knowledge change rapidly, and when existing techniques for applying knowledge to the solution of problems become quickly obsolete, then a system of higher education that remains exclusively technical teaches obsolescence. To avoid this, higher education must encourage students to examine ideas critically, to take multiple points of view in looking at a particular problem, and to become familiar with contrasting ways of looking at the world. Higher education must therefore attempt to produce in students a "critical" approach to a particular area or subject matter.

But once a student has acquired the ability to approach one subject critically, it is hard to prevent him from applying the same critical orientation to other areas of life and society. Given the discovery that there are many distinct perspectives on "truth" in natural science, engineering, or literature, the student is likely to become a relativist in moral and ideological matters as well. Taught to challenge traditional beliefs in a narrow academic arena, at least some students will move quickly to challenge traditional moral codes in society. What can be thought of as a "critical consciousness"—a mind-set disposed to question, examine, probe, and challenge—tends to generalize from the area where it was first learned to other areas, and finally to all of life. The result is, increasingly, an across-the-board relativization of knowledge, a pervasive individualization of morality.

Precisely because a technological society cannot rely exclusively upon a narrowly technical system of higher education, it must foster a high degree of critical consciousness among its most educated products, and this critical consciousness is readily turned against the dominant assumptions and practices of the technological society. In a way not often acknowledged by educators but increasingly sensed by the general public, higher education today is "subversive" in that it is helping to create youths who challenge many of the basic assumptions of their society. Prolonged mass higher education is a major factor in "producing" millions of young dissenters from the social order that creates them.

This argument indicates that higher education is a key process whereby the contradictions of technological society are being generated. To be sure, higher education also has a socializing function, as pointed out by liberal theories, and for many of those who are exposed to it, socialization remains its primary result. Especially when higher education remains narrowly technical, and when students by previous inclination or present experience reject alternative views of the world and accept conventional definitions of morality, then education performs the function currently assigned it by most liberals and radicals, namely, the function of integrating the individual into society. But increasingly, higher education conspires with the mass media and the juxtaposition of cultures within modern societies to create millions of young men and women who are unwilling to accept the existing social order uncritically.

These notes on contemporary society are obviously incomplete, sketchy, and doubtless often wrong. They should indicate, however, my conviction that in analyzing contemporary technological societies, we do well to start from one of the central points emphasized by the "counterrevolutionary" theorists, namely the ascendancy of the knowledgee sector. But an analysis of the meaning of this sector, I believe, leads not to the conclusion that it will inevitably triumph, but rather to the realization that the knowledge sector is riven through with basic contradictions, and that it is generating its own critics on a mass scale.

A New Politics

The connection between social theory and political action is exceedingly complex. No matter how refined, precise, and detailed a theory, it does not necessarily or automatically lead to a political agenda. Yet on the other hand, political action in the absence of social theory tends to be random, haphazard, trial-and-error, and empirical in the worst sense. Such is the case with much of what today passes as "radical politics": lacking any grounding in critical social theory, it tends to consist in *ad hoc* reactions of moral indignation, to lack any long-range direction, to fritter away the best energies of its members in internecine battles, or to adopt programs inspired by a pop-Marxist analysis of guerrilla warfare in some far-off ex-colonial nation.

The alternative is to try to think seriously about the basic issues and forces in contemporary industrialized societies. The arguments outlined above indicate my basic agreement with the counterrevolutionary theorists of youth that we are in a period of transition "between two ages," in Brzezinski's phrase, and that this transition is likely to be prolonged and difficult. This analysis also suggests, however, that the emergence of a new opposition is a sign of the surfacing of new contradictions within the dominant knowledge sector of technological society, and specifically, that youthful dissent is the expression of an historically revolutionary trend.

Several general political implications follow from this line of reasoning. For one, it follows that visions of immediate social or political revolution are based on a flawed social and historical analysis. The processes of sociohistorical change in which we are living are long-term, secular processes, which will take at least a generation to work themselves out. Those who have a serious interest in effecting meaningful social change must therefore be prepared to devote decades, and even a lifetime, to this enterprise; those whose energies flag after a week, a month, or a year will be of little help.

If we view the youthful opposition as reflecting emerging contradictions within the dominant knowledge sector of technological societies, then we would be wrong to ally ourselves politically with either the "value-free" technism that I have defined as thesis in this conflict, or with the subjective anarchism that I have defined as the antithesis. In the long run, what will be called for will be a synthesis of technism with anarchism, of "scientific objectivity" with the romantic expressiveness of the counterculture. It would therefore be a political mistake to embrace unreservedly the future of either the systems analyst or of the tribal communard. Instead we should work toward a future that could bring together the enormous power placed in man's hands by his technology and the vision of human liberation proclaimed by the counterculture. A politics that aligns itself with either the thesis or the antithesis will be a politics that settles for too little.

Another corollary of the views outlined here concerns the need to support a particular kind of higher education. Those who bitterly oppose the new opposition are already eager to limit higher education to technical education, eliminating or de-emphasizing its critical component. This strategy, if successful, could well reduce the numbers of those who possess that critical consciousness which seems vital for membership in the new opposition. It is therefore important for all who sympathize with the opposition to seek to extend higher education that is truly critical. The current radical attack upon higher education is, I think, misguided when it fails to discriminate between technical and critical education. Higher education in the broad sense not only has been but should continue to be the nursery for the new opposition. And the possibility that the new opposition might eventually generate enough political power to create major social changes depends in large part on the continuing creation, through education, of an ever-larger minority (and eventually even a majority) who share the basic orientations of that opposition. This process will take, at the very least, a generation. But it will not occur at all unless higher education as critical education is nurtured.

It also follows from these comments that those who today argue that the working class in the highly industrialized nations retains its revolutionary potential are incorrect. If we insist that the dialectic of social change did not cease with Marx's death, then it makes theoretical sense that groups like the working class, which once were revolutionary, might have become largely counterrevolutionary. Empirical evidence supports this proposition: the new "revolutionary class" appears to be a subsector of the knowledge sector, while the working class constitutes a conservative and at times a reactionary force. No political program today can or should neglect the real interests of the dwindling and often still exploited working class. But political programs based on the assumption that the working class in the industrialized nations can be exhorted to assume its "true" revolutionary role are built upon an historical mirage.

The proposition that social forces that begin as progressive generally end as reactionary obviously applies to the youthful opposition itself. As the youthful opposition ceases to be youthful, it must constantly guard against further evolution into a reactionary force. Already we can envision how this could occur: the collectivism of the counterculture could readily become an insistence upon the abrogation of individual rights; the tribalism of consciousness III could well portend a society of coercive group membership; the counterculture's opposition to technism could degenerate into a mindless hatred of reason, science, intellect, reflection, and accuracy. Today the youthful opposition is so weak politically that none of these dangers seems socially or politically important. But should the opposition gain in strength, its own reactionary potentials might well unfold.

In essence, then, a politics consistent with this agenda must be one that rejects both the "value-free" technism of corporate liberalism and the subjective anarchism of the counterculture, attempting instead the painful and slow work of creating a synthesis of the institutions of technological society with the culture of oppositional youth. That synthesis must ultimately entail the creation of a culture where the concept of liberation is not merely a facile slogan, but a commitment to the hard work of creating institutions within which genuine human relatedness may be attained. That synthesis must attempt to combine new-culture participation with old-culture competence, consciousness III enthusiasm with consciousness II professionalism—and all of this in ways that have hardly begun to be imagined, much less tried. It must involve an effort to turn modern technology around so that it facilitates man's liberation instead of encouraging his manipulation, so that it makes wars less possible rather than more likely, so that it helps men understand each other rather than oppose one another.

It is easy to call for a synthesis in general terms; it will be difficult to achieve it in practice. Nor do I believe that such a political synthesis is inevitable or even highly probable. We are indeed at an historical juncture, a turning point, a cultural and institutional crisis. And the youth revolt, the counterculture, the new opposition—these define one pole, one catalyst, one ingredient in that crisis. But history is not necessarily on the side of progress, synthesis, or the good. What happens in the next decades will depend not upon blind institutional and cultural forces, but upon the intelligence, good will, and hard work of countless individual men and women. It is possible today to begin to imagine a society far better than any society men have known—a society where technology serves man, where abundance makes possible higher levels of human development, where men and women attain new freedom not only from hunger, injustice, and tyranny, but from the inner coercions of greed, power-lust, and envy. The political agenda should be to move toward these goals, and to do so even in the absence of certainty that history is on our side.

SUGGESTED READING

In addition to Keniston's *The Uncommitted* ° (1965) and *Young Radicals* ° (1968), see a collection of his essays written in the 1960's, *Youth and Dissent* (1971), from which the preceding essay is taken. For defenses of the counterculture, see Philip Slater's *The Pursuit of Loneliness* ° (1970); Charles Reich's *The Greening of America* ° (1970); Theodore Roszak's *The Making of a Counter Culture* ° (1969); and Abbie Hoffman's *Woodstock Nation: A Talk-Rock Album* ° (1969). Work critical of youth culture includes Lewis Feuer's *The Conflict of Generations: The Character and Significance of Student Movements* (1969); Raymond Aron's *The Elusive Revolution: Anatomy of a Student Revolt* (1969); and Alvin Toffler's *Future Shock* (1970). Other critics of students in the 1960's are George F. Kennan, in *Democracy and the Student Left* ° (1968), which also contains replies to Kennan; and John W. Aldridge, in *In the Country of the Young* (1970).

On the development of the New Left see *The New Left: A Documentary History,* ° edited by Massimo Teodori (1969); *The New Student Left: An Anthology,* ° edited by Mitchell Cohen and Dennis Hale (1967); *The New Left,* edited by Priscilla Long (1969); Paul Jacobs and Saul Landau's *The New Radicals: A Report with Documents* ° (1966), Phillip Abbott Luce's *The New Left* ° (1966);

Jack Newfield's *A Prophetic Minority* ° (1966); and Howard Zinn's *SNCC: The New Abolitionists* ° (1964–65).

For accounts of protest on individual campuses, see Hal Draper's *Berkeley: The Student Revolt* ° (1965); *The Berkeley Student Revolt,*° edited by Seymour M. Lipset and S. S. Wolin (1965); *Revolution at Berkeley,*° edited by Michael Miller and Susan Gilmore (1965); Jerry L. Avorn, *et al., Up Against the Ivy Wall: A History of the Columbia Crisis* ° (1968); Lawrence E. Eichel, *et al., The Harvard Strike* ° (1970); and James M. Michener's *Kent State* ° (1971).

On student unrest in general, see a volume by the Editors of the *Atlantic, The Troubled Campus* (1966); *Beyond Berkeley: A Source Book in Student Values*, edited by Christopher G. Katope and Paul G. Zolbrod (1966); the entire June 1966 issue of *Comparative Education Review*; and David Mallery's *Ferment on the Campus* (1966). Among articles worth consulting are Donald R. Brown's "Student Stress and the Institutional Environment," *Journal of Social Issues*, XXIII (1967); Richard E. Flacks's "The Liberated Generation: An Exploration of the Roots of Student Protest," *Journal of Social Issues* XXIII (1967); and D. Westley and R. Braungart's "Class and Politics in the Family Backgrounds of Student Political Activists," *American Sociological Review*, XXXI (1966).

Jerome H. Skolnick, director of a task force for the National Commission on the Causes and Prevention of Violence, submitted a report entitled *The Politics of Protest* (1969), of which the part on student protest is useful. See also the *Report of the President's Commission on Campus Unrest* ° (1971).

MARLENE DIXON

Why Women's Liberation

INTRODUCTION

Amid the growing challenges to authority and social roles in the late 1960's, American women began to understand that they were oppressed, and to organize to free themselves from these restraints. Thus, the women's liberation movement—which was actually many movements with varying and even competing analyses and programs—was created. The movement can be loosely traced to a few sources in the 1960's. For many women the major initial intellectual influence was Betty Friedan's *The Feminine Mystique* (1963), a best-selling analysis of the unhappiness of middle-class housewives who found that their self-contained world of home, husband, and children did not yield the promised fulfillment. The book's white, middle-class perspective, its orientation toward college women and professional careers, and its emphasis on advertising and women's magazines as the sources of the "mystique," implied that women could find achievement and fulfillment in their lives without any structural changes in American society. The diagnosis did not cut very deeply, and the prescription did not seem costly.

Other women joined the movement as a result of their experiences in the civil rights movement, Students for a Democratic Society, and radical organizations on campus. These women, mostly students, realized that they were being relegated to inferior roles in organizations that they had joined in order to advance human dignity and equality. Too often the women were secretaries, the men leaders. The men argued doctrine while the women made coffee. In this pattern of dominance and subordination there was enough male sexual exploitation (legends linger of sexual conquests by some of the radical men and of the women who bragged they "made it" with leaders) to dramatize the problems. These women came to recognize their oppression, to express naked resentment, and to articulate perceptive objections. Just as blacks in the civil rights movement had told whites a few years before that the problems of race relations were caused by white racism, women began to conclude that their major problems were caused by "male chauvinism."

For working women the processes of discrimination and oppression also became more visible and often unacceptable. They realized that they were barred from many careers and often pushed into duller, lower-paying jobs. On the average, women earned about half of what men earned, and even when allowances are made for education and experience, the pattern of discrimination still prevails. In 1968, for example, full-time white men workers received an average income of $8,000, while white women received only $4,700. Nonwhite men earned an average of $5,600, but nonwhite women earned only $3,675 (Bureau of the Census, *Consumer Income,* P-60, No. 66 [Dec. 23, 1969]). Put bluntly, white women tended to earn less than black men, and black women were the primary victims of both racial and sexual prejudice.

In the following essay, Marlene Dixon, a radical sociologist now at McGill University, sketches the background of the women's liberation movement and offers a brief analysis of the sources of women's oppression—"male supremacy, marriage, and the structure of wage labor." She concludes that radical social change is necessary for substantial improvement in the position of women, and that socialism is a minimum requirement.

Such analyses, while meeting increasing favor, have also been criticized by liberals, blacks, and radicals. Many liberal Americans of both sexes contend that equality is possible within the present economic and political system. For them, the oppression is not inextricably linked to capitalism, and therefore liberation is compatible with the economic system. Some radicals and more blacks, however, challenge Professor Dixon's analysis from another direction. They question one of her fundamental assumptions: "The intrinsic radicalism of the struggle for women's liberation necessarily links women with all other oppressed groups." For some of these critics, black liberation requires that race, not sex, shape the issues and strategies, and women's liberation, by defining an antagonism between black men and women, threatens racial solidarity. To some white radicals, the issues of economic exploitation remain significant, but they are unwilling to view women as an exploited class. For these radicals, a primary emphasis on feminism is a luxury that only middle-class whites can afford.

Moving beyond these criticisms, there are other issues that have begun to command the attention of some women and fewer men: What relationships, attitudes, and behavior represent full equality and liberation? Is marriage compatible with liberation? Is sexual exploitation inevitable and does full liberation mean greater isolation of the sexes? Does the liberation of women also require the liberation of men? Must the role of the male be redefined to liberate men *and* women? These are among the basic problems that some radical groups are seeking to answer.

*T*he 1960's has been a decade of liberation; women have been swept up by that ferment along with blacks, Latins, American Indians and poor whites—the whole soft underbelly of this society. As each oppressed group in turn discovered the nature of its oppression in American society, so women have discovered that they too thirst for free and fully human lives. The result has been the growth of a new women's movement, whose base encompasses poor black and poor white women on relief, working women exploited in the labor force, middle class women incarcerated in the split level dream house, college girls awakening to the fact that sexiness is not the crowning achievement in life, and movement women who have discovered that in a freedom movement they themselves are not free. In less than four years women have created a variety of organizations, from the nationally-based middle class National Organization of Women (NOW) to local radical and radical feminist groups in every major city in North America. The new movement includes caucuses within nearly every New Left group and within most professional associations in the social sciences. Ranging in politics from reform to revolution, it has produced critiques of almost every segment of American society and constructed an ideology that rejects every hallowed cultural assumption about the nature and role of women.

As is typical of a young movement, much of its growth has been underground. The papers and manifestos written and circulated would surely comprise two very large volumes if published, but this literature is almost unknown outside of women's liberation. Nevertheless, where even a year ago organizing was slow and painful, with small cells of six or ten women, high turnover, and an uphill struggle against fear and resistance, in 1969 all that has changed. Groups are growing up everywhere with women eager to hear a hard line, to articulate and express their own rage and bitterness. Moving about the country, I have found an electric atmosphere of excitement and responsiveness. Everywhere there are doubts, stirrings, a desire to listen, to find out what it's all about. The extent to which groups have become politically radical is astounding. A year ago the movement stressed male chauvinism and psychological oppression; now the emphasis is on understanding the economic and social roots of women's oppression, and the analyses range from social democracy to Marxism. But the most striking change of all in the last year has been the loss of fear. Women are no longer afraid that their rebellion will threaten their very identity as women. They are not frightened by their own militancy, but liberated by it. Women's Liberation is an idea whose time has come.

The old women's movement burned itself out in the frantic decade of the 1920's. After a hundred years of struggle, women won a battle, only to lose the campaign: the vote was obtained, but the new millennium did not arrive. Women got the vote and achieved a measure of legal emancipation, but the real social and cultural barriers to full equality for women remained untouched.

For over 30 years the movement remained buried in its own ashes. Women were born and grew to maturity virtually ignorant of their own history of rebellion, aware only of a caricature of blue stockings and suffragettes. Even as increasing numbers of women were being driven into the labor force by the brutal conditions of the 1930's and by the massive drain of men into the military in the 1940's, the old ideal remained: a woman's place was in the home and behind her man. As the war ended and men returned to resume their jobs in the factories and offices, women were forced back to the kitchen and nursery with a vengeance. This story has been repeated after each war and the reason is clear: women form a flexible, cheap labor pool which is essential to a capitalist system. When labor is scarce, they are forced onto the labor market. When labor is plentiful, they are forced out. Women and blacks have provided a reserve army of unemployed workers, benefiting capitalists and the stable male white working class alike. Yet the system imposes untold suffering on the victims, blacks and women, through low wages and chronic unemployment.

With the end of the war the average age at marriage declined, the average size of families went up, and the suburban migration began in earnest. The political conservatism of the '50s was echoed in a social conservatism which stressed a Victorian ideal of the woman's life: a full womb and selfless devotion to husband and children.

As the bleak decade played itself out, however, three important social developments emerged which were to make a rebirth of the women's struggle inevitable. First, women came to make up more than a third of the labor force, the number of working women being twice the prewar figure. Yet the marked increase in female employment did nothing to better the position of women, who were more occupationally disadvantaged in the 1960's than they had been 25 years earlier. Rather than moving equally into all sectors of the occupational structure, they were being forced into the low paying service, clerical and semi-skilled categories. In 1940, women had held 45 per cent of all professional and technical positions; in 1967, they held only 37 per cent. The proportion of women in service jobs meanwhile rose from 50 to 55 per cent.

Second, the intoxicating wine of marriage and suburban life was turning sour; a generation of women woke up to find their children grown and a life (roughly 30 more productive years) of housework and bridge parties stretching out before them like a wasteland. For many younger women, the empty drudgery they saw in the suburban life was a sobering contradiction to adolescent dreams of romantic love and the fulfilling role of woman as wife and mother.

Third, a growing civil rights movement was sweeping thousands of young men and women into a moral crusade—a crusade which harsh political experience was to transmute into the New Left. The American Dream was riven and tattered in Mississippi and finally napalmed in Viet-Nam. Young Americans were drawn not to Levittown, but to Berkeley, the Haight-Ashbury and the East Village. Traditional political ideologies and cultural myths, sexual mores and sex roles with them, began to disintegrate in an explosion of rebellion and protest.

The three major groups which make up the new women's movement —working women, middle class married women and students—bring very different kinds of interests and objectives to women's liberation. Working women are most concerned with the economic issues of guaranteed employment, fair wages, job discrimination and child care. Their most immediate oppression is rooted in industrial capitalism and felt directly through the vicissitudes of an exploitative labor market.

Middle class women, oppressed by the psychological mutilation and injustice of institutionalized segregation, discrimination and imposed inferiority, are most sensitive to the dehumanizing consequences of severely limited lives. Usually well educated and capable, these women are rebelling against being forced to trivialize their lives, to live vicariously through husbands and children.

Students, as unmarried middle class girls, have been most sensitized to the sexual exploitation of women. They have experienced the frustration of one-way relationships in which the girl is forced into a "wife" and companion role with none of the supposed benefits of marriage. Young women have increasingly rebelled not only against passivity and dependency in their relationships but also against the notion that they must function as sexual objects, being defined in purely sexual rather than human terms, and being forced to package and sell themselves as commodities on the sex market.

Each group represents an independent aspect of the total institutionalized oppression of women. Their differences are those of emphasis and immediate interest rather than of fundamental goals. All women suffer from economic exploitation, from psychological deprivation, and from exploitative sexuality. Within women's liberation there is a growing understanding that the common oppression of women provides the basis for uniting across class and race lines to form a powerful and radical movement.

Racism and Male Supremacy

Clearly, for the liberation of women to become a reality it is necessary to destroy the ideology of male supremacy which asserts the biological and social inferiority of women in order to justify massive institutionalized oppression. Yet we all know that many women are as loud in their disavowal of this oppression as are the men who chant the litany of "a woman's place is in the home and behind her man." In fact, women are as trapped in their false consciousness as were the mass of blacks 20 years ago, and for much the same reason.

As blacks were defined and limited socially by their color, so women are defined and limited by their sex. While blacks, it was argued, were preordained by God or nature, or both, to be hewers of wood and drawers of water, so women are destined to bear and rear children, and to sustain their husbands with obedience and compassion. The Sky-God tramples through the heavens and the Earth Mother-Goddess is always flat on her back with her legs spread, putting out for one and all.

Indeed, the phenomenon of male chauvinism can only be understood when it is perceived as a form of racism, based on stereotypes drawn from a deep belief in the biological inferiority of women. The so-called "black analogy" is no analogy at all; it is the same social process that is at work, a process which both justifies and helps perpetuate the exploitation of one group of human beings by another.

The very stereotypes that express the society's belief in the biological inferiority of women recall the images used to justify the oppression of blacks. The nature of women, like that of slaves, is depicted as dependent, incapable of reasoned thought, childlike in its simplicity and warmth, martyred in the role of mother, and mystical in the role of sexual partner. In its benevolent form, the inferior position of women results in paternalism; in its malevolent form, a domestic tyranny which can be unbelievably brutal.

It has taken over 50 years to discredit the scientific and social "proof" which once gave legitimacy to the myths of black racial inferiority. Today most people can see that the theory of the genetic inferiority of blacks is absurd. Yet few are shocked by the fact that scientists are still busy "proving" the biological inferiority of women.

In recent years, in which blacks have led the struggle for liberation, the emphasis on racism has focused only upon racism against blacks. The fact that "racism" has been practiced against many groups other than blacks has been pushed into the background. Indeed, a less forceful but more accurate term for the phenomenon would be "social Darwinism." It was the opinion of the social Darwinists that in the natural course of things the "fit" succeed (i.e., oppress) and the "unfit" (i.e., the biologically inferior) sink to the bottom. According to this view, the very fact of a group's oppression proves its inferiority and the inevitable correctness of its low position. In this way each successive immigrant group coming to America was decked out in the garments of "racial" or biological inferiority until the group was sufficiently assimilated, whereupon Anglo-Saxon venom would turn on a new group filling up the space at the bottom. Now two groups remain, neither of which has been assimilated according to the classic American pattern: the "visibles"—blacks and women. It is equally true for both: "it won't wear off."

Yet the greatest obstacle facing those who would organize women remains women's belief in their own inferiority. Just as all subject populations are controlled by their acceptance of the rightness of their own status, so women remain subject because they believe in the rightness of their own oppression. This dilemma is not a fortuitous one, for the entire society is geared to socialize women to believe in and adopt as immutable necessity their traditional and inferior role. From earliest training to the grave, women are constrained and propagandized. Spend an evening at the movies or watching television, and you will see a grotesque figure called woman presented in a hundred variations upon the themes of "children, church, kitchen" or "the chick sex-pot."

For those who believe in the "rights of mankind," the "dignity of man," consider that to make a woman a person, a human being in her own right, you would have to change her sex: imagine Stokely Carmichael "prone and silent"; imagine Mark Rudd as a Laugh-In girl; picture Rennie Davis as Miss America. Such contradictions as these show how pervasive and deep-rooted is the cultural contempt for women, how difficult it is to imagine a woman as a serious human being, or conversely, how empty and degrading is the image of woman that floods the culture.

Countless studies have shown that black acceptance of white stereotypes leads to mutilated identity, to alienation, to rage and self-hatred.
Human beings cannot bear in their own hearts the contradictions of those
who hold them in contempt. The ideology of male supremacy and its effect
upon women merits as serious study as has been given to the effects of
prejudice upon Jews, blacks, and immigrant groups.

It is customary to shame those who would draw the parallel between
women and blacks by a great show of concern and chest beating over the
suffering of black people. Yet this response itself reveals a refined combination of white middle class guilt and male chauvinism, for it overlooks several essential facts. For example, the most oppressed group within the feminine population is made up of black women, many of whom take a dim
view of the black male intellectual's adoption of white male attitudes of
sexual superiority (an irony too cruel to require comment). Neither are
those who make this pious objection to the racial parallel addressing themselves very adequately to the millions of white working class women living
at the poverty level, who are not likely to be moved by this middle class
guilt-ridden one-upmanship while having to deal with the boss, the factory,
or the welfare worker day after day. They are already dangerously resent-
ful of the gains made by blacks, and much of their "racist backlash" stems
from the fact that they have been forgotten in the push for social change.
Emphasis on the real mechanisms of oppression—on the commonality of
the process—is essential lest groups such as these, which should work in
alliance, become divided against one another.

White middle class males already struggling with the acknowledgment of their own racism do not relish an added burden of recognition:
that to white guilt must soon be added "male." It is therefore understandable that they should refuse to see the harshness of the lives of most women
—to honestly face the facts of massive institutionalized discrimination
against women. Witness the performance to date: "Take her down off the
platform and give her a good fuck," "Petty Bourgeois Revisionist Running
Dogs," or in the classic words of a Berkeley male "leader," "Let them eat
cock."

Among whites, women remain the most oppressed—and the most
unorganized—group. Although they constitute a potential mass base for
the radical movement, in terms of movement priorities they are ignored;
indeed they might as well be invisible. Far from being an accident, this
omission is a direct outgrowth of the solid male supremist beliefs of white
radical and left-liberal men. Even now, faced with both fact and agitation,
leftist men find the idea of placing any serious priority upon women so out-
rageous, such a degrading notion, that they respond with a virulence far
out of proportion to the modest requests of movement women. This only
shows that women must stop wasting their time worrying about the chauvinism of men in the movement and focus instead on their real priority: organizing women.

Marriage: Genesis of Women's Rebellion

The institution of marriage is the chief vehicle for the perpetuation of the oppression of women; it is through the role of wife that the subjugation of women is maintained. In a very real way the role of wife has been the genesis of women's rebellion throughout history.

Looking at marriage from a detached point of view one may well ask why anyone gets married, much less women. One answer lies in the economics of women's position, for women are so occupationally limited that drudgery in the home is considered to be infinitely superior to drudgery in the factory. Secondly, women themselves have no independent social status. Indeed, there is no clearer index of the social worth of a woman in this society than the fact that she has none in her own right. A woman is first defined by the man to whom she is attached, but more particularly by the man she marries, and secondly by the children she bears and rears—hence the anxiety over sexual attractiveness, the frantic scramble for boyfriends and husbands. Having obtained and married a man the race is then on to have children, in order that their attractiveness and accomplishments may add more social worth. In a woman, not having children is seen as an incapacity somewhat akin to impotence in a man.

Beneath all of the pressures of the sexual marketplace and the marital status game, however, there is a far more sinister organization of economic exploitation and psychological mutilation. The housewife role, usually defined in terms of the biological duty of a woman to reproduce and her "innate" suitability for a nurturant and companionship role, is actually crucial to industrial capitalism in an advanced state of technological development. In fact, the housewife (some 44 million women of all classes, ethnic groups and races) provides, unpaid, absolutely essential services and labor. In turn, her assumption of all household duties makes it possible for the man to spend the majority of his time at the workplace.

It is important to understand the social and economic exploitation of the married woman, since the real productivity of her labor is denied by the commonly held assumption that she is dependent on her husband, exchanging her keep for emotional and nurturant services. Margaret Benston, a radical women's liberation leader, points out:

> In sheer quantity, household labor, including child care, constitutes a huge amount of socially necessary production. Nevertheless, in a society based on commodity production, it is not usually considered even as "real work" since it is outside of trade and the marketplace. This assignment of household work as the function of a special category "women" means that this group *does* stand in a different relationship to production. . . . The material basis for the inferior status of women is to be found in just this definition of women. In a society in which money determines value, women are a group who work outside the money economy. Their work is not worth

money, is therefore valueless, is therefore not even real work. And women themselves, who do this valueless work, can hardly be expected to be worth as much as men, who work for money.

Women are essential to the economy not only as free labor, but also as consumers. The American system of capitalism depends for its survival on the consumption of vast amounts of socially wasteful goods, and a prime target for the unloading of this waste is the housewife. She is the purchasing agent for the family, but beyond that she is eager to buy because her own identity depends on her accomplishments as a consumer and her ability to satisfy the wants of her husband and children. This is not, of course, to say that she has any power in the economy. Although she spends the wealth, she does not own or control it—it simply passes through her hands.

In addition to their role as housewives and consumers, increasing numbers of women are taking outside employment. These women leave the home to join an exploited labor force, only to return at night to assume the double burden of housework on top of wage work—that is, they are forced to work at two full-time jobs. No man is required or expected to take on such a burden. The result: two workers from one household in the labor force with no cutback in essential female functions—three for the price of two, quite a bargain.

Frederick Engels, now widely read in women's liberation, argues that, regardless of her status in the larger society, within the context of the family the woman's relationship to the man is one of proletariat to bourgeoisie. One consequence of this class division in the family is to weaken the capacity of men and women oppressed by the society to struggle together against it.

In all classes and groups, the institution of marriage functions to a greater or lesser degree to oppress women; the unity of women of different classes hinges upon our understanding of that common oppression. The 19th century women's movement refused to deal with marriage and sexuality, and chose instead to fight for the vote and elevate the feminine mystique to a political ideology. That decision retarded the movement for decades. But 1969 is not 1889. For one thing, there now exist alternatives to marriage. The most original and creative politics of the women's movement has come from a direct confrontation with the issue of marriage and sexuality. The cultural revolution—experimentation with life-styles, communal living, collective child-rearing—have all come from the rebellion against dehumanized sexual relationships, against the notion of women as sexual commodities, against the constriction and spiritual strangulation inherent in the role of a wife.

Lessons have been learned from the failures of the earlier movement as well. The feminine mystique is no longer mistaken for politics, nor gaining the vote for winning human rights. Women are now all together at the bottom of the work world, and the basis exists for a common focus of struggle for all women in American society. It remains for the movement to understand this, to avoid the mistakes of the past, to respond creatively to the possibilities of the present.

Women's oppression, although rooted in the institution of marriage, does not stop at the kitchen or the bedroom door. Indeed, the economic exploitation of women in the workplace is the most commonly recognized aspect of the oppression of women.

Most women who enter the labor force do not work for "pin money" or "self-fulfillment." Sixty-two per cent of all women working in 1967 were doing so out of economic need (i.e., were either alone or with husbands earning less than $5000 a year). In 1963, 36 per cent of American families had an income of less than $5000 a year. Women from these families work because they must; they contribute 35 to 40 percent of the family's total income when working full-time, and 15 to 20 per cent when working part-time.

Despite their need, however, women have always represented the most exploited sector of the industrial labor force. Child and female labor were introduced during the early stages of industrial capitalism, at a time when most men were gainfully employed in crafts. As industrialization developed and craft jobs were eliminated, men entered the industrial labor force, driving women and children into the lowest categories of work and pay. Indeed, the position of women and children industrial workers was so pitiful, and their wages so small, that the craft unions refused to organize them. Even when women organized themselves and engaged in militant strikes and labor agitation—from the shoemakers of Lynn, Massachusetts, to the International Ladies' Garment Workers and their great strike of 1909—male unionists continued to ignore their needs. As a result of this male supremacy in the unions, women remain essentially unorganized, despite the fact that they are becoming an ever larger part of the labor force.

The trend is clearly toward increasing numbers of women entering the work force: women represented 55 per cent of the growth of the total labor force in 1962, and the number of working women rose from 16.9 million in 1957 to 24 million in 1962. There is every indication that the number of women in the labor force will continue to grow as rapidly in the future.

Job discrimination against women exists in all sectors of work, even in occupations which are predominantly made up of women. This discrimination is reinforced in the field of education, where women are being short-changed at a time when the job market demands higher educational levels. In 1962, for example, while women constituted 53 per cent of the graduating high school class, only 42 per cent of the entering college class were women. Only one in three people who received a B.A. or M.A. in that year was a woman, and only one in ten who received a Ph. D. was a woman. These figures represent a decline in educational achievement for women since the 1930's, when women received two out of five of the B.A. and M.A. degrees given, and one out of seven of the Ph.D.s. While there has been a dramatic increase in the number of people, including women, who go to college, women have not kept pace with men in terms of educational achievement. Furthermore, women have lost ground in professional employment. In 1960 only 22 per cent of the faculty and other professional staff at colleges and universities were women—down from 28 per cent in 1949, 27 per cent in 1930, 26 per cent in 1920. 1960 does beat 1919 with only 20 per cent—"you've come a long way, baby"—right back to where you started! In other professional categories: 10 per cent of all scientists are women, 7 per cent of all physicians, 3 per cent of all lawyers, and 1 per cent of all engineers.

Even when women do obtain an education, in many cases it does them little good. Women, whatever their educational level, are concentrated in the lower paying occupations. The figures in Chart A tell a story that most women know and few men will admit: most women are forced to work at clerical jobs, for which they are paid, on the average, $1600 less per year than men doing the same work. Working class women in the service and operative (semi-skilled) categories, making up 30 per cent of working women, are paid $1900 less per year on the average than are men. Of all working women, only 13 per cent are professionals (including low-

CHART A
Comparative Statistics For Men and Women
in the Labor Force, 1960

OCCUPATION	PERCENTAGE OF WORKING WOMEN IN EACH OCCUPATIONAL CATEGORY	INCOME OF YEAR-ROUND FULL-TIME WORKERS		NUMBERS OF WORKERS IN MILLIONS	
		WOMEN	MEN	WOMEN	MEN
Professional	13%	$4358	$7115	3	5
Managers, Officials and Proprietors	5	3514	7241	1	5
Clerical	31	3586	5247	7	3
Operatives	15	2970	4977	4	9
Sales	7	2389	5842	2	3
Service	15	2340	4089	3	3
Private Household	10	1156	—	2	—

Sources: U.S. Department of Commerce, Bureau of the Census: "Current Population Reports," P-60, No. 37, and U.S. Department of Labor, Bureau of Labor Statistics and U.S. Department of Commerce, Bureau of the Census.

pay and low-status work such as teaching, nursing and social work), and they earn $2600 less per year than do professional men. Household workers, the lowest category of all, are predominantly women (over 2 million) and predominantly black and third world, earning for their labor barely over $1000 per year.

Not only are women forced onto the lowest rungs of the occupational ladder, they are in the lowest income levels as well. The most constant and bitter injustice experienced by all women is the income differential. While women might passively accept low status jobs, limited opportunities for advancement, and discrimination in the factory, office and university, they choke finally on the daily fact that the male worker next to them earns more, and usually does less. In 1965 the median wage or salary income of year-round full-time women workers was only 60 per cent of that of men, a 4 per cent loss since 1955. Twenty-nine per cent of working women earned less than $3000 a year as compared with 11 per cent of the men; 43 per cent of the women earned from $3000 to $5000 a year as compared with 19 per cent of the men; and 9 per cent of the women earned $7000 or more as compared with 43 per cent of the men.

What most people do not know is that in certain respects, women suffer more than do non-white men, and that black and third world women suffer most of all.

CHART B
Median Annual Wages For Men and Women
by Race, 1960

WORKERS	MEDIAN ANNUAL WAGE
Males, White	$5137
Males, Non-White	$3075
Females, White	$2537
Females, Non-White	$1276

Source: U.S. Department of Commerce, Bureau of the Census. Also see: President's Commission on the Status of Women, 1963.

Women, regardless of race, are more disadvantaged than are men, including non-white men. White women earn $2600 less than white men and $1500 less than non-white men. The brunt of the inequality is carried by 2.5 million non-white women, 94 per cent of whom are black. They earn $3800 less than white men, $1900 less than non-white men, and $1200 less than white women.

There is no more bitter paradox in the racism of this country than that the white man, articulating the male supremacy of the white male middle class, should provide the rationale for the oppression of black women by black men. Black women constitute the largest minority in the

United States, and they are the most disadvantaged group in the labor force. The further oppression of black women will not liberate black men, for black women were never the oppressors of their men—that is a myth of the liberal white man. The oppression of black men comes from institution-alized racism and economic exploitation: from the world of the white man. Consider the following facts and figures.

The percentage of black working women has always been proportion-ately greater than that of white women. In 1900, 41 per cent of black women were employed, as compared to 17 per cent for white women. In 1963, the proportion of black women employed was still a fourth greater than that of whites. In 1960, 44 per cent of black married women with chil-dren under six years were in the labor force, in contrast to 29 per cent for white women. While job competition requires ever higher levels of educa-tion, the bulk of illiterate women are black. On the whole, black women—who often have the greatest need for employment—are the most discrimi-nated against in terms of opportunity. Forced by an oppressive and racist society to carry unbelievably heavy economic and social burdens, black women stand at the bottom of that society, doubly marked by the caste signs of color and sex.

The rise of new agitation for the occupational equality of women also coincided with the re-entry of the "lost generation"—the housewives of the 1950's—into the job market. Women from middle class backgrounds, faced with an "empty nest" (children grown or in school) and a widowed or di-vorced rate of one-fourth to one-third of all marriages, returned to the workplace in large numbers. But once there they discovered that women, middle class or otherwise, are the last hired, the lowest paid, the least often promoted, and the first fired. Furthermore, women are more likely to suffer job discrimination on the basis of age, so the widowed and divorced suffer particularly, even though their economic need to work is often ur-gent. Age discrimination also means that the option of work after child-rearing is limited. Even highly qualified older women find themselves forced into low-paid, unskilled or semi-skilled work—if they are lucky enough to find a job in the first place.

The realities of the work world for most middle class women—that they become members of the working class, like it or not—are understand-ably distant to many young men and women in college who have never had to work, and who tend to think of the industrial "proletariat" as a rev-olutionary force, to the exclusion of "bourgeois" working women. Their image of the "pampered middle class woman" is factually incorrect and po-litically naive. It is middle class women forced into working class life who are often the first to become conscious of the contradiction between the "American Dream" and their daily experience.

Faced with discrimination on the job—after being forced into the lower levels of the occupational structure—millions of women are inescapably presented with the fundamental contradictions in their unequal treatment and their massive exploitation. The rapid growth of women's liberation as a movement is related in part to the exploitation of working women in all occupational categories.

Male supremacy, marriage, and the structure of wage labor—each of these aspects of women's oppression has been crucial to the resurgence of the women's struggle. It must be abundantly clear that radical social change must occur before there can be significant improvement in the social position of women. Some form of socialism is a minimum requirement, considering the changes that must come in the institutions of marriage and the family alone. The intrinsic radicalism of the struggle for women's liberation necessarily links women with all other oppressed groups.

The heart of the movement, as in all freedom movements, rests in women's knowledge, whether articulated or still only an illness without a name, that they are not inferior—not chicks, nor bunnies, nor quail, nor cows, nor bitches, nor ass, nor meat. Women hear the litany of their own dehumanization each day. Yet all the same, women know that male supremacy is a lie. They know they are not animals or sexual objects or commodities. They know their lives are mutilated, because they see within themselves a promise of creativity and personal integration. Feeling the contradiction between the essentially creative and self-actualizing human being within her, and the cruel and degrading less-than-human role she is compelled to play, a woman begins to perceive the falseness of what her society has forced her to be. And once she perceives this, she knows that she must fight.

Women must learn the meaning of rage, the violence that liberates the human spirit. The rhetoric of invective is an equally essential stage, for in discovering and venting their rage against the enemy—and the enemy in everyday life is men—women also experience the justice of their own violence. They learn the first lessons in their own latent strength. Women must learn to know themselves as revolutionaries. They must become hard and strong in their determination, while retaining their humanity and tenderness.

There is a rage that impels women into a total commitment to women's liberation. That ferocity stems from a denial of mutilation; it is a cry for life, a cry for the liberation of the spirit. Roxanne Dunbar, surely one of the most impressive women in the movement, conveys the feelings of many:

> We are damaged—we women, we oppressed, we disinherited. There are very few who are not damaged, and they rule. . . . The oppressed trust those who rule more than they trust themselves, because self-contempt emerges from powerlessness. Anyway, few oppressed people believe that life

could be much different. . . . We are damaged and we have the right to
hate and have contempt and to kill and to scream. But for what? . . . Do
we want the oppressor to admit he is wrong, to withdraw his misuse of us?
He is only too happy to admit guilt—then do nothing but try to absorb and
exorcize the new thought. . . . That does not make up for what I have lost,
what I never had, and what all those others who are worse off than I never
had. . . . Nothing will compensate for the irreparable harm it has done to
my sisters. . . . How could we possibly settle for anything remotely less,
even take a crumb in the meantime less, than total annihilation of a system
which systematically destroys half its people. . . .

SUGGESTED READING

An important, path-breaking, and often forgotten volume analyzing
women in history and in modern society is Simone de Beauvoir's *The
Second Sex* ° (1953). Kate Millet's *Sexual Politics* ° (1970) offers
more in the title than it delivers in fact because the volume is deeply
concerned with the treatment of women in literature and often
coerces subtle analyses into ill-fitting molds of the author's making. A
broader, more thoughtful, volume that also notes the narrow treatment of women in literature is Leslie Fiedler's *Love and Death in the
American Novel* ° (1960). Germaine Greer's *The Female Eunuch*
(1971) is a powerful, intentionally impressionistic analysis of modern
women.

A special issue of *Daedalus*, later printed as *The Woman in
America,* ° edited by Robert Lifton (1964) contains a number of useful articles, including Alice Rossi's "Equality Between the Sexes: An
Immodest Proposal." Among the valuable collections are *The Sister-
hood Is Powerful,*° edited by Robin Morgan (1970), perhaps the best
introduction to woman's liberation; *Voices From Women's Liberation,* ° edited by Leslie B. Tanner (1970); and *Masculine/Femi-
nine,* ° edited by Betty and Theodore Roszak (1969), which has an
annoying habit of heavily abridging some of the materials.

Among the journals and newspapers of the new movement are
*Women: A Journal of Liberation; Off Our Backs; Up From Under;
No More Fun and Games; It Ain't Me Babe; Mother Lode; NOW
Acts;* and *Washington Newsletter for Women.*

Midge Decter, in "The Liberated Woman," *Commentary*, XLI
(Oct. 1970) presents an *ad hominem* critique of the movement. In
"The Prisoner of Sex," *Harper's*, CCXLII (Mar. 1971), an essay which
later appeared as a book, Norman Mailer tried to raise some basic issues about sexual relations and identity, but marred his analysis with
petty attacks on Kate Millett and a self-indulgence that led many critics to view his effort, unfairly, as simply male machismo.

JOHN KENNETH GALBRAITH

The New Industrial State: The Role of the State

INTRODUCTION

For decades American radicals have decried the political and economic power of the major corporations and their alliance with or control of the state. Marxist and non-Marxist radicals alike have denied that political power is broadly distributed. They have often emphasized the easy movement from corporate leadership to federal positions and argued that the occupants of these high offices represent only one class and set of interests.

Traditionally liberals have assailed this analysis, charging its proponents with gross oversimplification, ideological distortion —even blindness. While they too have worried about industrial concentration and the power of large corporations, they usually have viewed the central state as an independent force—a likely restraint on private power. By the early 1950's, however, even liberals came to extol the benefits of large-scale corporate enterprise and were little concerned about restricting its power.

Among those undisturbed by oligopoly was Harvard economist John Kenneth Galbraith. In *American Capitalism: The Theory of Countervailing Power* (1952; revised, 1956) he acknowledged economic concentration but he identified a self-regulating mechanism (countervailing power) that restrains powerful corporations and protects consumers. Even though much of the economy was dominated by oligopolies, which normally avoid price competiton, Galbraith found that the struggle between large buyers and large sellers (in noninflationary periods) would restrain

FROM John Kenneth Galbraith, "The New Industrial State: The Role of the State," *The Listener*, LXXVI (December 8, 1966), pp. 841–43, 853. Reprinted by permission of the author.

the power of both. United States Steel, for example, cannot economically coerce General Motors because the automobile company may always turn to another steel producer. On the basis of this sanguine theory, he concluded that the government should use its antitrust powers sparingly. Galbraith also viewed labor unions as countervailing powers: they represent and protect the interests of workers, thus providing a counterweight to corporate powers.

Professional economists have pointed out many defects in Galbraith's theory: it relied unwarrantedly on competition at the retail level, neglected the control that vertical integration has bestowed on major corporations (consider, for example, the power of automobile producers over dealers), disregarded interlocking directorates, and failed to explain adequately the steady or rising administered prices during recent recessions. Even Galbraith acknowledged that countervailing power will not operate effectively in demand inflation, when there is little incentive for buyers to resist the demands of sellers (of materials or labor), since additional costs can be passed on to the consumer. Despite these criticisms, the theory of countervailing power in the economy won wide popularity in the 1950's, supporting as it did the pluralists' description of American society—that political power was broadly distributed, that interest groups competed for limited benefits and comfortably participated in the healthy American consensus.

Another volume by Galbraith, *The Affluent Society,* New York (1958), expresses the thinking of liberal intellectuals of the late 1950's and early 1960's. Like David Riesman and other pluralists, Galbraith assumed that America was a middle-class society and that the problems of the business cycle and poverty had been largely solved. (He acknowledged that there were some "pockets" of poverty, Appalachia for example, and some "case" poverty such as the aged and infirm.) Lamenting the unwarranted emphasis on production for its own sake, he urged in the book a shift in spending from the private to the public sector. To improve the quality of American life (devalued, as he saw it, by advertising and symbolized by the tail fins then popular on Cadillacs) he recommended greater public expenditures on education, health, and recreation. Though Galbraith's volume largely avoided the problem of power, it seemed implicitly to embrace pluralism.

Yet, in *The Industrial State* (presented in part first as the Reith lectures in 1966 on the BBC and then published in 1967), which stands in relation to *The Affluent Society* "as a house to a window," Galbraith presents a theory of modern capitalism that is close to the radical analysis. Departing from his earlier pluralism, he argues that the five hundred or so largest corporations share personnel and common values with the state and possess dominant political and economic power. Subscribing to the

Berle-Means thesis of the divorce of management from ownership and emphasizing the corporation's dependence on planning
and technology, he concludes that power in the modern corporation is diffused among a large group of managers and experts.
This "Technostructure" does not aim to maximize profits but to
advance its "social goals" and its own security through corporate
expansion, technological development, and control of its own
capital and consumer markets. For control of the larger economic environment, the corporations call on the government to
provide a necessary level of aggregate demand and support
for expensive technology. (Labor, he finds, acquiesces generally
in this system and provides added stability at the price of demands for higher wages.) The overall result is policies formulated
and implemented by an expanded ruling group—the corporate
"Technostructure" and state managers.

In some ways Galbraith's analysis is not far from recent
Marxist interpretations, but he usually stops short of Marxist conclusions. He acknowledges, for example, that the interests and
ideology of large corporations dominate foreign policy and admits that corporations depend on expanding markets. But he believes that the state does not have to find such markets abroad,
that it can and will create them at home by expanding consumer
demand. Like the Marxists, he also admits that defense spending
has been an important source of postwar prosperity, but he is
convinced that these expenditures can be transferred to such
projects as road construction or the space program provided that
these projects expand technological knowledge as well as aggregate demand. Unlike many Marxists, he assumes that the modern
industrial system must be directed by an elite, and he hopes that
a new elite (the educational and scientific estate) will use technology and economic power to achieve the goals he outlined in
The Affluent Society—intellectual and esthetic development and
social welfare. The improved society of Galbraith's vision, managed by a large liberal elite, is the same society that the New
Left finds a nightmare.

Galbraith's treatment of the "Technostructure" is troubling.
His definition is loose and his analysis fails to acknowledge the
operation of power within a stratified corporate hierarchy in
which thousands of employees may contribute expertise but a very
restricted group makes the important decisions. On these
grounds alone, one might question Galbraith's belief that individuals serve a corporation in order to bring its "social goals" into
line with their own. Even within the "Technostructure," some of
Galbraith's critics argue, effective power is narrowly concentrated. Its holders define the goals and behavior of the corporation, and usually the limits of behavior and publicly expressed
values by the corporation's representatives.

Galbraith's analysis of the economic and corporate system
seems flawed in other respects also. Recent studies have ques-

tioned whether the separation of management and ownership is very great; they conclude that corporations are still interested in maximization of profit and adopt strategies and values to achieve this preeminent "social goal." In addition, as such critics note, long-run profit maximization does not necessarily differ in practice from the quest for growth and security. Professional economists have also questioned whether mature corporations have established the control over the market that Galbraith attributes to them. His theory of the "revised sequence"—that the corporation through advertising frees itself from responding to the consumer's desires and instead creates predictable wants for its product —is too simple.

Despite these criticisms, Galbraith's statements represent an important interpretation of modern American capitalism. As an occasional economic adviser to John F. Kennedy during his pre-Presidential years, as ambassador to India during the early Kennedy administration, and as the chairman of the Americans for Democratic Action, Galbraith has commanded a wide audience, and his insights, while often fragmentary and exaggerated, are not unrepresentative of contemporary liberal views of the modern American political economy.

I have undertaken to show in these lectures that the modern industrial society, or that part of it which is composed of the large corporations, is in major essentials a planned economy. By that I mean that production decisions are taken not in response to consumer demand as expressed in the market; rather they are taken by producers. These decisions are reflected in the prices that are set in the markets and in the further steps that are taken to insure that people will buy what is produced and sold at those prices. The ultimate influence is authority.

The role of such planning authority is also manifested in the prices that are set for the things that business enterprises buy. It is reflected in the further steps that insure that the requisite materials and components for production will be forthcoming at these prices; and it is manifested in the decisions to withhold earnings for reinvestment and thus for the expansion of the firms and ultimately the economy.

I am not arguing that market influences are entirely excluded from effect on these decisions. Economics, as it exists rather than as it is sometimes taught, has very few pure cases. It is a cocktail, a compote. But the notion that the consumer is the sovereign influence in the economy—that all decision begins with him—is a pure case that will not do. Or it will serve only for those who wish to believe in fairy tales. The important decisions in the modern economy are made by producing organizations in the service of their own goals. And, in one way or another, public behaviour is accommodated to these decisions. Thus, the planning.

In the non-socialist economy, the modern large corporation is the basic planning unit. For some planning tasks it is exceedingly competent. I have just now mentioned the more important. The large corporation can effectively fix minimum prices. It can manage consumer wants. In conjunction with other corporations, it can control prices of production requirements and arrange supplies at these prices. And it can extract from revenues the savings it needs for growth and expansion. But some things it cannot do. Though the modern corporation can set and maintain minimum prices, it cannot set maximum prices and wages. It cannot, in other words, prevent wages from forcing up prices and prices from forcing up wages in the familiar inflation spiral. And while it can manage the demand for individual products, it cannot control total demands—it cannot insure that total purchasing power in the economy will be equal, or approximately equal, to the supply of goods that can be produced by the current working force.

There are two other planning tasks that the large corporation cannot perform. It cannot supply the specialized manpower that modern technology, and organization and planning, require. It can train but it cannot educate. And it cannot absorb the risks and costs that are associated with very advanced forms of scientific and technical development—with the development of atomic power or supersonic air transport or anti-missile defences or weapons systems or other such requirements of modern civilized living.

I come now to a conclusion of some importance. The shortcomings of the large corporation, as a planning instrument, define the role of the modern state in economic policy. Wherever the private corporation cannot do the job, the state comes in and performs the required function. Wherever the private firm can do the job—as in setting minimum prices or managing consumer demand—the state is required to remain out. The private firm cannot fix maximum prices, so we have the state setting what in the United States we call wage and price guideposts and what here in Britain is called a pay and wage freeze. The private firm cannot regulate aggregate demand so the state comes in to manipulate taxes, public spending, and bank lending— to implement what we call modern Keynesian policy. The private firm cannot supply specialized manpower so we have a great expansion in publicly supported education. Private firms cannot afford to underwrite the Concord or what we call the SST. So governments—British, French, or American— come in to underwrite that job.

Our attitudes on the proper role of the state are firmly fixed by what private firms can or cannot do. A private corporation is perfectly capable of setting minimum prices for cigarettes; of persuading people to buy a new and totally implausible detergent; or of developing a new and more drastic kind of laxative. This being so, this planning is naturally held to be sacred to private enterprise.

The planning functions of the state are less sacred as public tasks. Most of them are assumed to serve some special function. Or they have an improvised or *ad hoc* aspect. They are not yet seen as part of an overall structure of planning that dovetails with private planning. Thus, ceilings on wages and prices are perpetual emergency actions; Keynesian regulation of aggregate demand is thought to have been occasioned by the particular imperatives of full employment and growth; the expansion of education is regarded as the result of a new enlightenment following the second world war; the underwriting of especially expensive technology is a pragmatic response to the urgent social need for faster travel, emigration to the moon, bigger explosions, and, of course, competition with the Soviet Union.

So to regard matters is to fail to see the nature of modern planning. It is also to assume that it is purely an accident that the state comes in to perform the planning tasks that are beyond private reach. There are many reasons for trying so to avert our eyes. Economists have a deeply vested interest in the market. It is our intellectual stock-in-trade. In the United States, where faith in free enterprise is deep, it is painful for us to concede that we have graduated into a directed or planned economy. And in Britain it is equally repugnant to socialists to realize that planning, which was supposed to originate with the state, has come into existence very largely under private auspices. Perhaps, with so many people finding the truth so unpleasant, it would contribute to general contentment were it just suppressed. But this is not practical. You cannot depend on people to leave an unpleasant truth alone. The planning functions of the state are not *ad hoc* or separate developments. They are a closely articulated set of functions which supplement and fill the gaps in the planning of the modern large firm. Together these provide a comprehensive planning apparatus. It decides what people should have and then arranges that they will get it and that they will want it. Not the least of its achievements is in leaving them with the impression that the controlling decisions are theirs.

I would like now to examine in slightly more detail these planning functions of the modern state.

On the fixing of maximum wages and prices, the guideposts or wage and price freeze, I have only a word or two to add. It stands very much in relation to modern economic policy as does prostitution to the theory of business management. Both are widely recognized to exist and to serve a function. But no one wants to admit of their permanent need. They are not aspects of the good society. And certainly no one wishes to study them in order to see how they could be made more efficient, or more serviceable to the general public. It would be well were we to recognize that wage and price fixing, at least, is indispensable in the planned economy. The next step would be to learn how this wage and price fixing could be made more effective and more equitable. Even the universities might, in time, desert the fictions of the free market for the modern reality of regulation and control. That, however, may be optimistic. Thorstein Veblen once observed: "It has generally held true that the accredited learned class and the seminaries of the higher learning have looked askance at all innovation."

The Keynesian regulation of aggregate demand also requires only a word. It is a thoroughly well-established feature of modern industrial planning, although economists have pictured it *not* as a necessary aspect of planning but as a way of improving the market economy. The need for it follows in fact directly from modern industrial planning. As we have seen, corporations decide authoritatively what they will reserve from earnings for reinvestment and expansion. This planned corporate withholding is overwhelmingly important as a source of savings in the non-Soviet countries, as planned withholding by the state is the overwhelmingly important source of savings in the socialist economies. But in the non-Soviet economies there is no mechanism which insures that the amounts so withheld for investment will be matched in the economy as a whole by what is invested. That is to say there is no mechanism outside the state. So there must be direct action by the state to equate the two. And this the state does, primarily by manipulating spending and taxation. The need to equate the planned savings and the planned investment of the large corporations is not of course the only reason for such action. Saving and investment elsewhere in the economy must also be matched. But corporate savings and investment are by far the largest and most important in the total.

The successful regulation of demand requires that the quantitative role of the state in the modern economy be relatively large. Demand is regulated by increasing or decreasing the expenditures of the state or decreasing or increasing the taxes the state collects. Only when the state is large and its revenues substantial will these changes be large enough to serve. One effective way of insuring the requisite size is to have the state underwrite modern technology, which is admirably expensive. Such is the case with modern weaponry, space exploration, even highway and airport design. Technology . . . is a prime instrument in destroying the effectiveness of the market. But it does help make possible the planning that replaces the market.

The next function of the state is to provide the specialized and trained manpower which the industrial system cannot supply to itself. This has led in our time to a very great expansion in education, and especially in higher education, and this has been true in all of the advanced countries. In 1900 there were 24,000 teachers in colleges and universities in the United States; in 1920 there were 49,000; by 1970, three years hence, there will be 480,000. This is rarely pictured as an aspect of modern economic development; it is the vanity of educators like myself that we have the initiating power in this new enlightenment. But it is significant that when industry required for its purposes millions of unlettered proletarians, that is what the educational system supplied. As industry has come to need engineers, sales executives, copywriters, computer programmers, personnel managers, information retrieval specialists, product planners, and executive panjandrums, that is what the educational system has come to provide. I might say that anyone who listens to lectures should on occasion ask for some proof that is related to his common experience. And all who lecture should welcome this test. It arrests the mandarinism which is the principal occupational hazard of lecturers.

For proof of the point I have just made on specialized manpower you have only to turn to your Sunday, or even your daily, newspaper. Here you will find that every kind of esoteric and arcane specialism is being sought. Electronic engineers, senior systems programmers, instrument engineers, minerals dressing engineers, work study engineers, lady assistant training officers, and technically oriented personnel for an Embodiment Selling Team are my culling from a single London newspaper.

Once the ability to obtain capital was decisive for the firm that was seeking to expand. Now it is the supply of such manpower. Once in the industrially advanced world the community—or the nation—that wanted more industry gave first thought to its capital supply, and how to reassure the bankers. Now it gives first thought to its educational system: how to obtain the required specialists.

Nor can we be altogether happy about education that is so motivated. There is danger that it will be excessively vocational. We shall have a race of men who are strong on telemetry and space communications but who cannot read anything but a blueprint or write anything but a computer programme. When we realize that our new concern for education is the result not of a new enlightenment but a response to the needs of industrial planning, we shall begin to worry, I think, a good deal about the future of liberal and humane education. In the end college and university rectors, presidents and vice-chancellors may even make speeches about it, believing, as so many of these excellent men do, that a thoughtful speech is an effective substitute for serious action.

Much the most interesting of the planning functions of the state is the underwriting of expensive technology. Few changes in economic life have ever proceeded with such explosive rapidity. Few have so undermined conventional concepts of public and private enterprise. This activity includes . . . the direct financing of research and development; this is something on which the United States Government in 1962 spent an estimated $10.6 billions. This was more than its total dollar outlays for the United States Government for all purposes, military or civilian, before the second world war.

But this activity also involves the provision of a guaranteed market for a large number of highly technical products from aircraft to missiles to electronic gear to space vehicles. Nearly all of this expenditure—some 80–85 per cent.—goes to the large corporation, which is to say that it is in the planned sector of the American economy with which these lectures are concerned.[1] This activity brings the modern large corporation into the most intimate association with the state; in the case of public agencies such as the United States Atomic Energy Commission or the United States Air Force, it

---

[1] About 100 corporations and their subsidiaries accounted for 73.4 per cent of total Federal procurement in 1964. (H. L. Nieburg, *In The Name of Science.* Chicago Quadrangle Press, 1966, p. 192.)

is no longer easy to say where the public sector ends and the private sector begins. The private sector becomes, in effect, an extended arm of the public bureaucracy. I might add that no one flaunts the banner of private enterprise so aggressively as the firm that does 75 per cent. of its business with the government and yearns to have more.

In the past, it has been argued by good Keynesians that there is nothing very special about a particular kind of government business. Replying to standard Marxian charges that capitalism depends excessively on armaments, Keynesians have pointed out that spending for housing, concert halls and theatres, for more automobiles to drive into central London and for more highways to allow more automobiles to drive into central London, and for more radios to amuse people while they are sitting in the resulting traffic jams, and for other of the attributes of modern gracious living would serve just as well as spending on armaments. But this is not so certain. It is not that the Marxians are right; it is one of the rules of discourse that this must never be conceded. It is rather that the simple Keynesian view is incomplete.

The expenditures I have just mentioned for concert halls and highways would not serve to underwrite technology as do present expenditures of the state. And this underwriting is a function . . . that is beyond the reach of private planning. Replacement of military spending, with its emphasis on underwriting advanced technology, would have to be therefore by other equally technical outlays if it was to serve the same purpose. Otherwise, technology would have to be curtailed to that level where corporate planning units could underwrite it on their own. And this curtailment under present circumstances would be very, very drastic.

I find myself, in consequence of this analysis, a considerable supporter of the space race. It is not that I think that exploring the Moon, Mars, or even Saturn—which has always seemed to me the most original of the lot—is of high social urgency. And pleasant as it would be to select the passengers for the first flights, especially if they promise to be one-way, I imagine that President Johnson will want to do this himself. But the space race allows an extensive underwriting of advanced technology. And it does this in a field of activity where spending is large and where, in contrast with weapons and weapons systems, competition with the Soviets is comparatively safe and comparatively benign. So the turning of technological knowledge to this particular competition does not seem to me to be something we can entirely regret.

We see the modern corporation, in the technological aspects of its activities, moving into a very close association with the state. The state is the principal customer for such technology and the underwriter of major risk. In the planning of tasks and missions, the mapping of development work and the execution of contracts, there is nowadays a daily and intimate association between the bureaucracy and the large so-called private firm. But one thing, you will say, keeps them apart. You will say the state after all is in pursuit of broad national goals, whatever these may be. And the private firm is there to make money—in the more solemn language of economics it is there to maximise profits. This difference in goals, you will say, will always sufficiently differentiate the state from private enterprise.

But here again we find that the reality supplies that indispensable thread of consistency. For power, as we have seen, has passed from the owners of the corporation to the managers, and to the scientists and technicians. They now exercise full and autonomous power and, not surprisingly, they exercise it in their own interest. And this interest differs from that of the owners. For the managers and technicians security of return is more important than the level of total earnings. It is only when earnings fail that the power of the managers is threatened. And growth is more important to the managers than maximum earnings. That is because those in charge do not get the profits—or anyhow not much of them. But they—the scientists and technicians—do get the promotions, enlarged opportunities, higher salaries and prestige which go with growth of the firm. I might say here that for clarifying these matters I have been greatly indebted to the brilliant Cambridge economist Robin Marris, who has written very lucidly and very wisely on this question.

So here, following this line of thought, we encounter a remarkable fact. For economic security and growth as we reflect on it are also prime goals of the modern state. Nothing has been more emphasized in modern economic policy than the prevention of depression or recession. It is something that politicians promise automatically and without any perceptible thought. And no test of social achievement is so completely and totally accepted as the rate of economic growth. It is the common measure of accomplishment of all the economic systems. Transcending political faith, religion, occupation, or all except eccentric philosophical persuasion, the value of economic growth is something on which Americans, Russians, Englishmen, Frenchmen, Germans, Italians, and Yugoslavs all agree. I gather that not even the modern Irish dissent.

So there is in fact no conflict between essential goals and the goals of the leaders in the modern firms. On the contrary, there is a large symmetry. Both seek security. Both value growth. We have seen that, as an aspect of its planning, the modern industrial enterprise accommodates the behavior and beliefs of the individual consumer to its needs. It is reasonable to assume that it has also accommodated our social objectives and associated beliefs to what it needs. In any case, we may assume that there has been an interaction between state and firm which has brought the two to a unity of view.

A very sombre thought will occur to many of you here. We have seen that the state is necessary for underwriting the technology of modern industrial enterprise. Much of this it does within the framework of its military expenditure. In the consumer's goods economy, the wants and beliefs of the consumer, including his conviction that happiness is associated with the consumption of goods, these are all accommodated, in greater or less measure, to what producers need and want to produce. Is this true also of the state? Does it respond in its military procurement to what the supplying firms need to sell, and the technology that they wish to have underwritten? Are images of foreign policy in the planned industrial communities—in the United States, the Soviet Union, great industrial countries of western Europe—shaped by industrial need? Do we have an image of conflict because that serves techno-logical and therewith planning need?

We cannot exclude that possibility; on the contrary, it is most plausible. We should also recall that it is a conclusion that was reached rather more intuitively by President Eisenhower while he was President of the United States. In President Eisenhower's now famous valedictory he warned of the influence of the "conjunction of an immense military establishment and a large arms industry." Our image is of a foreign policy which prescribes what will be required in responding armaments. This again will do for those for whom the mind is an instrument for evading reality. All others will see the possibility here of a two-way flow of influence. The image of the foreign pol-icy affects the demand of the state on industry. But the needs of economic planning may affect the view of the state on foreign policy. And there can be few matters where it will be safer to be guided by reality. It will also be ob-served that I am not confining my argument here to any particular planned economy, west or east. We had better, at least in the beginning, worry lest it might be true of all.

SUGGESTED READING

Kenneth Boulding in *Book Week* (July 16, 1967) presents a thought-ful critical review of Galbraith's *The New Industrial State* (1967). George C. Allen's "Economic Fact and Fantasy: A Rejoinder to Gal-braith's Reith Lectures" (Institute of Economic Affairs, 1967, Occa-sional Paper 14) also challenges Galbraith's theory of market control. Robert Solow's review, "The New Industrial State: Son of Affluence," *Public Interest*, No. 9 (Fall 1967), led to a further discussion in that issue and in *Public Interest*, No. 11 (Spring 1968), with Robin Morris' "Galbraith, Solow, and the Truth about Corporations," which sup-ported Galbraith, thereby provoking a rejoinder from Solow in the same issue. The most penetrating Marxist criticism of Galbraith's the-sis is Ralph Milliband's "Professor Galbraith and American Capital-ism," in John Saville and Ralph Milliband, eds., *The Socialist Regis-ter, 1968* (1968); Milliband contends, among other points, that Galbraith's definition of the "Technostructure" is so broad that he ac-tually argues (contrary to our introductory remarks and most critics) that power is widely diffused and practically democratic.

The Berle-Means thesis on the separation of management and ownership—on which Galbraith rests much of his analysis—has been criticized by Gabriel Kolko in *Wealth and Power in America* ° (1962); Don Villarejo in "Stock Ownership and Control of Corpora-tions," *New University Thought*, II (Autumn 1961) and (Winter 1962); and Robert Fitch and Mary Oppenheimer in "Who Rules the

Corporations?," *Socialist Revolution*, I (July–Aug. through Nov.–Dec. 1970). Fitch and Oppenheimer, after pointing to the two ways in which the Berle-Means thesis has been interpreted in terms of the role of directors of the board, argue that finance capital still prevails, with banks holding much of the corporate stock and having substantial representation on the boards of directors and control of (or influence over) major corporations. The Fitch-Oppenheimer analysis provoked a substantial critique by James O'Connor in *Socialist Revolution*, II (Jan.–Feb. 1971), with a rejoinder by Fitch.

Arnold Rose's *The Power Structure* ° (1967) is a defense of pluralist theories. C. Wright Mills, in *The Power Elite* ° (1956), attributes power to those in the "command positions"—the leaders of industry, the military, and the executive branch of government. G. William Domhoff and Hoyt B. Ballard, editors of *C. Wright Mills and the Power Elite* ° (1968), provide a collection of essays on Mills's theory and book, including Mills's reply to his critics and a challenging, temperate review by Talcott Parson, "The Distribution of Power in American Society," *World Politics*, X (Oct. 1957).

Paul Baran and Paul Sweezy's *Monopoly Capital: The American Economic and Social Order* ° (1966) is a radical analysis by two leading Marxist scholars. Their arguments on "surplus value" have been assailed by liberal scholars, while some radicals have faulted them for assuming that the Berle-Means analysis of the separation of management and ownership is correct. Their contentions about power are anticipated briefly in Sweezy's "The American Ruling Class," *Monthly Review*, III (May and June 1951).

G. William Domhoff's *Who Rules America?* ° (1967) assaults pluralist conclusions about power and tries to wed elite and class theories. His analysis has been faulted on several grounds. His criteria for class membership are arbitrary and he generalizes rather loosely from social origins of some key office holders to upper-class control of institutions. His *The Higher Circles: The Governing Class in America* ° (1970) extends his analysis, discusses the upper class as a social class, examines some liberal reform within the framework of corporate liberalism, and looks at the power elite and foreign policy.

Political Power: A Reader in Theory and Research,° edited by Roderick Bell *et al.* (1969); *Apolitical Politics: A Critique of Behavioralism*,° edited by Charles McCoy and John Playford (1967); and *Power in Postwar America*,° edited by Richard Gillam (1971), are the best collections, along with Domhoff and Ballard on Mills, available on power in America. The Gillam volume also offers a fine critical bibliography on much of the literature available up to early 1970. *Up Against the American Myth*,° edited by Tom Christoffel *et al.* (1970), offers radical (and sometimes left-liberal) critiques of corporate capitalism and the society that its editors believe its shapes. Assar Lindbeck's *The Political Economy of the New Left: An Outsider's View* ° (1971) is overrated, but he does note usefully the enthusiasm of some on the left to reject both the market and a bureaucracy, which is the alternative source for allocating resources.